Readings in Social
and Political Philosophy

READINGS
in Social
and Political
Philosophy

SECOND EDITION

edited by

ROBERT M. STEWART

New York • *Oxford*
OXFORD UNIVERSITY PRESS
1996

Oxford University Press

Oxford   New York
Athens   Auckland   Bangkok   Bombay
Calcutta   Cape Town   Dar es Salaam   Delhi
Florence   Hong Kong   Istanbul   Karachi
Kuala Lumpur   Madras   Madrid   Melbourne
Mexico City   Nairobi   Paris   Singapore
Taipei   Tokyo   Toronto

and associated companies in
Berlin   Ibadan

Library of Congress Cataloging-in-Publication Data
Readings in social and political philosophy / edited by Robert M.
Stewart.—2nd ed.
    p.   cm.
  Includes bibliographical references.
  ISBN 0-19-509518-9
    1. Liberty.   2. Equality.   3. Justice.   4. Allegiance.
5. Representative government and representation.   I. Stewart,
Robert Michael.
JC571.R435   1996
320'.01'1—dc20   95-16120

9 8 7 6 5 4 3 2 1

Printed in the United States of America
on acid-free paper

ACKNOWLEDGMENTS

I wish to thank the friends and colleagues who advised and encouraged me in the preparation of the first edition of this volume, particularly Susan Levin, Alfred Louch, John Rawls, and Lynn Thomas, as well as Anthony Graybosch for his valuable suggestions about additions to this revised edition. I am indebted to my friend and former teacher Anthony Woozley for permission to include his fine translation of Plato's *Crito*.

I also want to express my gratitude to Cynthia Read and Angela Blackburn, formerly philosophy editors for Oxford University Press in the United States, and to their successor, Robert Miller, for their support in this project. Editorial assistant Grace Suh and associate editor Paul Schlotthauer were very helpful and patient with my questions and oversights. Finally, I want to thank Dan Barnett, Judy Collins, and Tania Strishak for their expert help in preparing the manuscript.

Chico, California   R. M. S.
May 1995

CONTENTS

III   Justice and Equality

IV   Democracy and Representation

INTRODUCTION

Western social and political philosophy, since its beginnings in the writings of Plato and Aristotle, has been concerned primarily with a set of basic questions about the nature of authority and political obligation, the idea of liberty and its proper limitations, conceptions of the just and good society, and the best form of government. These problems naturally arise when the perceived interests of individuals, groups, and institutions come into conflict, particularly in times of general social change and political instability, as people become increasingly aware of new possibilities. The legitimacy of power is questioned, as is the basis of supposedly binding relationships between particular persons and governments. Individuals, groups, or nations demand more freedom, a recognition of rights, greater justice in the distribution of goods, or a larger share in political decision making. Very abstract questions about social relationships and values come immediately to the forefront of debate: What is freedom? How do we determine what rights people have? Is there a standard of justice that transcends the civil laws of actual states? Is popular government possible, or even desirable? Of what kind, and under what conditions?

Philosophers traditionally have attempted systematic answers to these and related questions. Indeed, until the development of political science as a separate discipline, political philosophers sought to explain social phenomena and political behavior, often in an historical context, as well as to clarify problematic concepts, evaluate existing institutions, and argue for social ideals. The evolution of empirical social science, together with the more limited conception of the scope of philosophy now prevalent, has led philosophers interested in social and political problems to focus mainly on conceptual and normative issues. In fact, until the early 1970s, there was relatively little interest among contemporary English-speaking philosophers in substantive questions of social and political relations. The resurgence of this interest is a welcome development, whatever its explanation. Real-world concerns, changing conceptions of philosophical method and its relation to practice, and the publication of several important large-scale works, such as John Rawls's *A Theory of Justice* and Robert Nozick's *Anarchy, State, and Utopia,* are certainly part of the reason. A growing interest among Anglo-American philosophers in Continental thought is also evident. While most analytically trained philosophers have worked within the liberal tradition (very broadly understood), significant research is being done by those sympathetic to Marxism, phenomenology, and Critical Theory.

What is important to see, however, is that contemporary political and social philosophers are, for the most part, concerned with many of the same questions that occupied the ancient Greeks and the early modern philosophers. It is, of course, true that there are significant differences between many of the concepts employed, for example, by Plato and by Hobbes. But both were concerned with the rational justification of certain political institutions, the problem of reconciling individual welfare with social constraints and the common good, and the understanding of human behavior in social contexts. Questions about freedom, justice, and democracy are interpreted differently by the great philosophers; yet there is enough of a conceptual overlap that it is fair to say that the history of political philosophy reveals a continuing debate over many of the same general issues.

For the social contract theorists of the early modern period—Hobbes, Locke, Rousseau, and others—the problem of political obligation was fundamental. They aimed to give a general account of why individuals are obligated to obey the laws of certain governments, at least under some conditions. If we assume at the outset, as they did, that human beings have a natural right to liberty, then it is most unclear how such an obligation could arise. Is it grounded in morality, in rationality, in the common good? Exactly how does it come about that I must obey my government under any conditions, even when it is generally just and beneficent? Anarchists, obviously, deny that there is any moral obligation or rational case for allegiance. If it could be shown, however, that all rational persons consent, or would agree, to submit to the laws of certain governments, under specifiable conditions, then the anarchist will have been refuted without denying his assumption of a basic right to liberty. The selections in the first part of this book address these issues from different perspectives.

Most of us believe that freedom of the individual is a basic value, if not in some sense a natural, right. But what do we mean by words such as "liberty," "force," and "coercion"? Or, to put it somewhat differently, what kinds of things constitute restrictions upon or denials of freedom? Does liberty involve not being hindered from doing whatever we want to do? Whatever we might wish to do? Or only what it would be, in some sense, rational for us to do? Certainly, it is necessary to have some restraints on freedom. People disagree, however, about what restrictions should be placed on individual liberty, even when they mean the same thing by the term. This suggests that some value certain kinds of freedom—specific liberties—more than others do. Philosophers such as John Stuart Mill have tried to give an account of what makes freedom valuable, under what conditions, and for whom; an adequate theory of this type can serve as a basis for rational and principled restraint when liberty conflicts with other basic values. The second part of this book includes readings that deal with these conceptual and normative questions.

Justice is sometimes said to be the primary virtue of social institutions. Most philosophers would agree that it is, at least, one of the most significant respects in which legal and political arrangements, as well as economic systems and social hierarchies, may be evaluated. We tend to think, moreover, that there is some kind of connection between justice and equality. Yet the precise relationship between these concepts is a matter of sharp dispute. This is especially obvious when we debate questions of distributive justice—who is entitled to what share of the benefits of social cooperation, and who must bear what burdens. Libertarians such as Nozick follow classical liberals (particularly Locke) in defending a right to private property based on conceptions of legitimate acquisition and voluntary transfer. Egalitarians— of whom Rousseau, Rawls, and Ronald Dworkin are representative—emphasize the arbitrariness and deprivation that appear to be a necessary part of such a system of "natural liberty." They argue for more equal distributions of wealth and opportunity through political means, based on conceptions of the equal worth of human beings. In the third part of this collection the central problems of distributive justice are taken up by a diverse group of authors whose work has been influential.

Many of us believe that democratic forms of government are most conducive to promoting justice and liberty and the easiest to justify to those who question their authority. But what makes a government truly democratic? It is impossible to have direct votes of all citizens on most political decisions, outside of the smallest units of political organization. Can we remedy this by electing representatives? Is it possible for someone else, against whom I might have voted, to represent my interests? What is representation? If we can arrive at an adequate conception of representative democracy, we must still show that it is the most desirable form of government, at least for certain societies. What intrinsic or extrinsic features of democratic procedures and institutions make democratic governments most desirable? The final part of this volume includes selections dealing with these fundamental questions.

I
POLITICAL OBLIGATION AND CONSENT

The first important discussion of political obligation in Western thought is to be found in Plato's *Crito*. Socrates, condemned to death by the Athenian democracy, must decide whether to take an opportunity to escape arranged for him by friends. He knows that he is innocent but believes that it is never right to return a wrong with another wrong. In an imaginary dialogue with the Laws, Socrates confronts several arguments for the position that it would be an act of injustice for him to escape. The first involves a paternal conception of the state, according to which citizens are in the position of children, owing their existence and upbringing to their father, the Laws; violence against the state is akin to, but greater than, a sin against one's parents, whom one must either persuade or obey. Of more interest to modern thought, however, are the other two central arguments: that acts of disobedience would destroy the Laws and the state, without which the good life is impossible, and that Socrates, having freely chosen to remain in Athens upon attaining adulthood, agreed "in deed if not in word" to obey its laws—an agreement without exceptions for what might be faulty decisions by its courts. The former can be interpreted as a broadly utilitarian argument, while the latter is a clear statement of the view that the obligation to obey one's government rests on individual consent.

Locke, in the second of his *Two Treatises of Government*, accords consent a central place in his argument for limited political obligation. By nature, men are equally free, apart from the moral constraints of natural law, which require us to preserve ourselves and others. Since the right to punish violators of the law of nature belongs to everyone as well, Locke is concerned to show how government might legitimately acquire a monopoly to perform that function. In the state of nature, people will tend to be partial to their own interests and overly zealous in matters of punishment, but reason will lead them to agree to form a political community as the proper remedy. Unlike Hobbes, however, Locke distinguishes clearly between the state of nature and the state of war, and insists that absolute monarchy is worse than life outside civil society; hence, it cannot be within the terms of the original contract. Political power, defined as the right to make and enforce laws for the preservation of property (rights) and the defense of the commonwealth, is thus the result of a voluntary transfer of individual rights. Exercise of unlimited power by a government is thus not, strictly speaking, use of political power at all. The government that civil society creates will be characterized by a separation of powers and its policies determined by majority rule. A monarchy or legislative body that seriously abuses its trust may be justly overthrown. Thus Locke attempts to explain the origin, extent, and end of civil government in broad outline. To account for the duty of allegiance that individuals have with respect to particular governments and the obligation of resident aliens to obey the law, he invokes a distinction between express and tacit consent, arguing that the latter may be given through the acceptance of an inheritance or even the mere use of the roads or being within the boundaries of a particular commonwealth.

Hume's essay "Of the Original Contract" calls into question the theoretical usefulness of the contractarian model. Conservative theories of divine right, he points out, would seem to have the defect of justifying all government to the degree that they justify any. The liberal contract theory, on the other hand, is at best true only as an explanation of the origins of society; no one knows of any actual promise to establish government—indeed, most states rest on usurpation or conquest. Hume distinguishes two kinds of moral duties—those instinctive or natural and those conventional or social. The former class of duties includes those related to love of children, gratitude, and pity, while the latter arise from a sense of what is necessary for society and the general welfare, for example, justice, fidelity (promise keeping), and allegiance (obedience to the magistrate). There is no reason, Hume argues, to found the duty of allegiance on that of fidelity, because both are based on social utility. What else could ground the obligation to keep a promise? Utility thus directly provides a justification for allegiance, and the contract argument is seen to be unnecessary as well as unsound.

Hanna Pitkin distinguishes four different questions that political theorists who address the general problem of political obligation often confuse: (1) that of the limits of obligation (when is one obligated to obey, and when not?), (2) that of the locus of sovereignty (whom is one obligated to obey?), (3) that of the difference between legitimate authority and mere coercion (is there any real difference?), and (4) that of the justification of obligation (why is one obligated to obey even a legitimate authority?). Plato and Locke, she maintains, begin with arguments about actual consent in their attempts to deal with these questions; yet they are driven in the final analysis to what she terms a "nature of government" justification. In the *Crito,* Socrates says that we are obligated to keep our agreements if they are right, which seems to mean more than that they are voluntary and informed. Socrates believed that he was right to consent to the laws of Athens because they were generally good ones. Pitkin argues that Locke also ultimately rested his case on considerations of the nature of government, since tacit consent by itself is no guard against a tyranny that permits free emigration. Locke would insist that men in the state of nature agree to form a commonwealth in order to best preserve their rights; a tyranny, as we noted earlier, would violate the original agreement, and therefore those born into one would presumably not need to consider consenting. In the second part of her essay "Obligation and Consent," reprinted here, Pitkin applies the nature of government theory to some important cases and examines its relations to traditional consent theory in the light of recent developments in analytic philosophy.

A. John Simmons provides a critical assessment of another argument that is—if not itself a version of consent theory—closely related to the standard contractarian argument. The principle of fair play, as expressed in some early articles of H. L. A. Hart and John Rawls, concerns schemes of social cooperation that are just and mutually beneficial, yet can only succeed if there is general support, everyone (or most everyone) doing his or her part, which involves some sacrifice of one kind or another. A further feature of this sort of arrangement is that individuals have an incentive to become "free riders"—when most others do their part, one can still benefit from the scheme without doing one's own. In this kind of situation, one might argue, someone who has voluntarily accepted the benefits of the scheme is bound by considerations of fairness to do his share. Simmons examines this view in detail and discusses its relevance to questions of political obligation.

Crito

PLATO

The scene is Socrates' cell in the Athens prison on a morning in 399 B.C., where he is awaiting the carrying out of the death sentence that the court had pronounced on him a few weeks earlier, after convicting him of the offences of religious heresy and of corrupting the young. The time is shortly before dawn: Socrates is still asleep, and his old friend Crito is sitting beside the bed. He has come to visit Socrates unusually early, bearing the news that he is likely to be required to drink the fatal hemlock the following day. Crito wants to persuade him to agree to his friends arranging for him to escape from prison before it is too late. The conversation that follows is between the two men after Socrates has woken up.

SOCRATES: Why have you come at this hour, Crito? Or, isn't it still early?

CRITO: It certainly is.

SOCRATES: About what time is it?

CRITO: It is early light, just before dawn.

SOCRATES: I am surprised that the prison guard answered you.

CRITO: He is used to me now, Socrates, because I come and go here so often—partly too, he has had some favours from me.

SOCRATES: Have you just arrived, or have you been here for some time?

CRITO: For quite some time.

SOCRATES: Then why didn't you wake me immediately, instead of sitting silently beside me?

CRITO: Heavens no, Socrates. I wouldn't have chosen to be in such a sleepless and distressed state as I am—and yet I have been wondering at you, as I observed how peacefully you sleep; and I purposely didn't wake you, so that you could continue as peacefully as possible. Often indeed throughout my life have I counted you happy for your temperament, but most of all now in your present plight, for the easy and gentle way you bear it.

SOCRATES: Well indeed, Crito, it would be inappropriate for a man as old as myself to show distress if the time has now come when he must die.

CRITO: And yet other people of your age, Socrates, are caught in similar plights, but their age doesn't spare them from being angry at the fate which has come on them.

SOCRATES: That's true. But now why have you come so early?

CRITO: Bearing bad news, Socrates, not for you, as it seems, but for myself and for all those close to you bad news and heavy news, which I think that I would find it the heaviest to bear.

SOCRATES: What news is this? Has the vessel arrived from Delos, the one whose arrival marks the time when I must die?[1]

Plato, *Crito*, translated by A. D. Woozley, from *Law and Obedience: The Arguments of Plato's Crito*. London: Duckworth, 1979. Reprinted with permission of the translator.

CRITO: It hasn't arrived yet, but I think it will get here today from what is reported by some people who have come from Sunium and left it there. It is clear, then, from their news that it will get here today, and it will have to be tomorrow that you end your life.

SOCRATES: Well, with the gods' help, Crito, if this is their pleasure, let it be so. But yet I don't think the boat will come today.

CRITO: How do you tell that?

SOCRATES: I'll tell you. It is the day after the one when the boat arrives, I believe, that I have to die.

CRITO: Well, that's certainly what those who are in charge of these things say.

SOCRATES: Then I do not think the boat will arrive during the day which is coming on us, but on the next day. And I tell that from a dream I had a little while ago during the night. And you're likely to have been timely in not waking me.

CRITO: What then was the dream?

SOCRATES: I thought a woman approached me, who was beautiful and comely, wearing white clothes, and she addressed me and said: 'Socrates, On the third day thou art to come to the rich land of Phthia.'[2]

CRITO: That was a strange dream, Socrates.

SOCRATES: And yet a perfectly clear one, as it seems to me, Crito.

CRITO: Only too clear, very likely. But, my dear Socrates, even now listen to me and let yourself be saved. As for myself, if you die, it will be not one disaster only: apart from being bereft of an intimate friend, such a one as I shall never find again, I shall also appear to many people, who don't know you and me well, as one who was able to save you, if I had been willing to spend what it would cost, but neglected to do so. And yet what could be a more shameful reputation than that—to be thought to value money more than friends? For most people will not believe that it was you yourself who were not prepared to get away from here, although we were eager to do it.

SOCRATES: But why should we, my good Crito, care so much about popular opinion? For the most enlightened people, who are more worth considering, will believe that things have been done in just the way they have been done.

CRITO: But surely you see, Socrates, that one has to pay attention to popular opinion. Your present predicament makes it clear enough that the people are capable of performing, not the smallest of ills, but just about the greatest, if one is discredited among them.

SOCRATES: Crito, would that the people were able to perform the greatest ills, so that they were also capable of performing the greatest goods—that would be splendid. But, as it is, they can do neither: they cannot make a man wise, and they cannot make him foolish, but they act quite haphazardly.

CRITO: Well, let that be so. But tell me this, Socrates. You're not, I hope, concerned for me and the rest of your friends, lest, if you do escape from this place, common informers will make trouble for us for having snatched you out of here, and that we shall be required either to lose all our property or to pay heavy fines, or even to suffer something further in addition? If you do have some such fear, please forget it; for we have the right to run this risk in rescuing you, indeed an even greater risk, if need be. But be advised by me, and do as I say.

SOCRATES: Yes, I am concerned about those things, Crito, and many others too.

CRITO: Then don't be afraid of it—and in any case the sum isn't great for which some people are willing to rescue you and get you away from here. Then don't you see how cheap these informers are, and that it wouldn't need much money to fix them? You already have at your disposal my money—which will be enough, in my opinion; and furthermore, just supposing that out of some anxiety for me you think you shouldn't spend my money, there are these visitors to Athens who are prepared to spend theirs. One of them has actually provided sufficient funds for this very purpose, Simmias from Thebes, while Cebes is ready to do it, and many others too. So, as I say, don't from fear on that account hesitate to save yourself, and don't let what you said in court make difficulties for you—I mean that, if you were to go away, you wouldn't know what to do with yourself.[3] For, in general, there are many places where they will welcome you if you go there; and, in particular, if you want to go to Thessaly, I have people there who have been guests of mine, who will esteem you very highly and will provide you with security, so that nobody in Thessaly will cause you any trouble.

What is more, Socrates, I don't think that what you are trying to do is right, throwing your life away when saving it is possible; and you are striving to have the very thing happen to you for which your enemies would strive, and indeed did strive when they were wanting to destroy you. In addition I, at any rate, think you are betraying your sons, whom you would go away and abandon, when you could bring them up and educate them—as far as you're concerned, they will fare in whatever way they happen to fare; but in fact, very probably, they will happen to fare in that kind of way which does usually befall orphans after the loss of their parents. For either one shouldn't have children, or one should share and go through with the trouble of raising and educating them—while you seem to me to be choosing the easiest way out. But, whatever a man of virtue and courage would choose that is what one should choose, at least if one claims to have cared for virtue all one's life. For I am ashamed, both on your account and for us your close friends, that the whole affair concerning you should seem to have been managed with a lack of courage on our part: there was the way your case came into court, when it was possible for it not to have gone into court at all, there was the way the actual course of the trial went, and lastly there is this, the crowning absurdity, that through a faint-heartedness and failure of courage of ours you appear to have got away from us— we didn't save you and you didn't save yourself, when it was perfectly possible and manageable if we had been the slightest help at all. So realise, Socrates, that at the same time as the bad outcome there is the disgrace for you and us. But consider—although it's

no longer the time for considering, the time for that is past: there is only one thing to consider. Everything must be carried out in the course of the coming night; but, if we delay, we cannot do it, and the possibility is no longer there. All ways round, Socrates, be persuaded by me, and do as I say.

SOCRATES: My dear Crito, your concern for me would count for a lot if there were some truth behind it; otherwise, the greater it is, the harder it is to handle. So, we have to consider whether we must do what you recommend or not—given that this is not now for the first time the case, but that it has always been my way not to follow the call of anything else in me rather than that of reason—that is, whatever seemed to me best on reflection. Certainly the considerations which I used to declare previously I cannot reject now, when this misfortune has fallen on me; they seem to me to be very much what they were, and I respect and honour the same ones as before. If we have no better ones to proclaim in the present situation, be sure that I certainly shall not agree with you, not even if the power of public opinion were to scare us like children even more than already, by visiting us with imprisonment and death and confiscation of wealth. How then are we most temperately to consider the matter? Perhaps, if we take up the argument which you give about the opinions of others. Was it always well said or not that one should pay attention to some opinions, but not to others? Or was it fine to say it before the requirement that I die arose, but now it has become clear that it was said ill and for the sake of argument, and that it was really childish nonsense? I am eager to pursue this enquiry with you, Crito, in order to see whether the principle seems any different to me, given my present position, or whether it is the same, and whether we should say goodbye to it or should obey it. In my opinion something of this kind was always asserted by those who thought they had something to say, something, that is, like what I said just now, that of the opinions which men hold some should be taken seriously, and others not. In heaven's name,

Crito, doesn't this seem to you to be well said? I ask you because you are not likely, as far as human prospects go, to die tomorrow, and the present calamity would not distort your judgment. Now consider—does it not seem to you to be justifiably enough said that one should not respect every opinion that men express, but only some and not others—and again not every man's opinions, but only those of some and not of others? What do you say? Isn't that a fair claim?

CRITO: Yes, it is.

SOCRATES: Then the good opinions one should respect, the bad ones not?

CRITO. Yes.

SOCRATES: And are good opinions those of wise people, bad ones those of foolish people?

CRITO: How else?

SOCRATES: Well then, how well said was the following? When a man is in physical training and practising at it, does he pay attention to favourable and unfavourable comments and opinions from everybody, or just to those of that one individual who happens to be his physician or his trainer?

CRITO: To the latter only.

SOCRATES: Then he should fear the criticisms and welcome the praise just of that one man, and not of the many others.

CRITO: Obviously.

SOCRATES: This then is the way he must practise and train and eat and drink, whatever way seems right to the one man, the one with knowledge and expertise, rather than in the ways that seem right to all the others.

CRITO: That's so.

SOCRATES: Well then. If he doesn't obey the one man, and shows no respect for his opinion and his praise, but listens to what is said by the many who have no expert knowledge, will he not come to some harm?

CRITO: How can he avoid it?

SOCRATES: What is the harm, and where does it aim—at what part of the disobedient person?

CRITO: Obviously at his body; for that is what is being ruined.

SOCRATES: You're right. Then are the rest of things like that, Crito—to save us going through them all individually? Especially concerning the just and the unjust, fine and shameful, good and bad, about which we are deliberating—should we follow the opinion of the many and fear that? Or should we go by the opinion of the one man, if there is such a man with expert knowledge, before whom we should feel shame and fear more than before all the others taken together? If we don't follow him, we shall destroy and mutilate that part of us which is improved by right conduct and ruined by ill conduct. Isn't that so?

CRITO: I certainly think so, Socrates.

SOCRATES: Well then, if we take that part of us which is improved by healthy living and corrupted by unhealthy living, and if we ruin it by not adhering to the opinion of those who really know, is life worth living for us with that part corrupted? And that part of us is our body. Isn't that so?

CRITO: Yes.

SOCRATES: Then is our life worth living with a body that is in bad condition and corrupted?

CRITO: No way.

SOCRATES: But is our life worth living with that part of us corrupted, where what is *morally wrong* mutilates, and what is *right* benefits? Or do we think to be less important than the body that part of us, whatever it is in us, with which right and wrong are concerned?

CRITO: Certainly not.

SOCRATES: Instead it is more valuable?

CRITO: Yes, much.

SOCRATES: In that case, good sir, we should not at all take into account here what most people will say about us, but only what the man says who knows about right and wrong—I mean the one man and the real truth. So, in the first place, you are not making a correct proposal here, when you propose that we must take into account popular opinion about the right, the fine and the good and their opposites. 'And yet,' somebody might say, 'the people do have the capability of putting us to death.'

CRITO: Indeed, that's clear—for it would be said, Socrates. You're right.

SOCRATES: But, dear friend, this line of argument which we have just been through seems to me to be still just as it was before. And this in turn is what you must examine to see if it still holds good for us or not, namely that it is not living but living well that is to be most highly prized.

CRITO: But it does hold.

SOCRATES: And the proposition that living well is identical with living honourably and justly—does that hold or not?

CRITO: Yes, it does.

SOCRATES: Then, following on what we have agreed, this has to be examined—whether it is right for me to try to get away from here without being released by the city, or whether it is not right. And if it seems right, then let us try; but, if it does not, we are to drop it. As for the considerations which you mention about the spending of money and about reputation and about the upbringing of children, I'm afraid those are really the notions of those many people who, without any understanding, would lightly kill a man and indeed bring him back to life again, if they were able to. But we, on the other hand, since the argument thus persuades us, should consider nothing else at all save what we just now mentioned, namely whether we shall be acting rightly in laying out money and giving thanks to those who will get me out of here—by 'we' I mean rescuers and rescued alike—or whether we shall really be acting wrongly in doing all those things. And, if it appears that we would be doing what was wrong, then surely we must not take into account as against doing wrong either our having to die if we stay here and do nothing, or our having to suffer anything else.

CRITO: I think that what you *say* is good, Socrates—but do look at what we are to *do*.

SOCRATES: Let us examine it together, good friend, and, if you have any counterargument to my argument, produce it and I shall do what you say. Otherwise, stop right now, dear man, saying the same thing over and over, that I must get away from here against the city's will; I attach much importance to acting in this matter having per-

suaded you, rather than against your will. Now consider the basic principle of our enquiry, to see if for you it is satisfactorily stated, and try to reply to my questions in what you think to be the best way.

CRITO: I'll certainly try.

SOCRATES: Do we say that on no account are we to act unjustly if we can help it? Or that in some cases one is to act unjustly, in others not? Is it the case that there is no way in which doing what is unjust is either good or honourable, as we have many times agreed in the past? Or have all those things that we used to agree on been discarded in these last few days? Have you and I at our age, Crito, been all this time earnestly conversing with each other and failing to notice that we are no different from children? Or isn't it above all the case that things are as we used to maintain before—that, whether the public says so or not, and whether we have to bear a fate that is harder even than our present, or whether we get an easier fate, acting unjustly is utterly bad and shameful for the man who does it? Is that what we say or not?

CRITO: It is what we say.

SOCRATES: In no circumstances then must one act unjustly.

CRITO: No, indeed.

SOCRATES: Then a man who has been unjustly treated must not act unjustly in return, as most people think—for in *no* circumstances must one act unjustly.

CRITO: Apparently he should not.

SOCRATES: Well, what about this? Must one treat people badly, Crito, or not?

CRITO: Certainly not, Socrates.

SOCRATES: Well. For a man who has been treated badly to give back bad treatment in return—is that, as most people say, just, or is it unjust?

CRITO: It is not just at all.

SOCRATES: For perhaps treating men badly does not differ at all from treating them unjustly.

CRITO: That's true.

SOCRATES: Then one must neither return unjust treatment to any men nor treat them badly, no matter what treatment one gets from them. And look out, Crito, that in conceding these points you do not agree to something which is in fact contrary to your view; for I know that only a few people do or will hold this view. So, between those who hold such a view and those who do not there is no common ground of argument, but they necessarily look down on each other when they see their respective standpoints. Therefore, do you too consider very thoroughly whether you share my view with me, and whether we are to make that the starting point of our deliberations, namely that it is never the part of an upright man either to act unjustly or to return unjust treatment for unjust treatment received, or, if he is being badly treated, to defend himself by retaliating with bad treatment—or whether you dissociate yourself from, and do not share, the principle from which I started. For I myself have believed this for a long time, and still do; but, if you have formed some other opinion, say so and instruct me. However, if you hold to our old view, then listen to the next point.

CRITO: But I do hold to it and agree with it: speak on.

SOCRATES: Well, here's the next point, or rather question. Must a man do whatever he has agreed to do, provided that what he has agreed to do is right, or is he to act deceitfully?

CRITO: He must do it.

SOCRATES: Now observe what follows. If we go away from here without persuading the city to let us go, do we treat some badly, and those at that whom least of all we should treat badly—or not? Do we stand by our agreements (if they are right) or not?

CRITO: I have no answer to your question, Socrates; for I don't understand it.

SOCRATES: But look at it this way. Suppose, as we are about to run away from here (or whatever else it should be called) the laws and state of Athens were to confront us and say:

'Tell us, Socrates, what is it that you have in mind to do? Do you intend to do anything else by this exploit to which you are putting your hand than to destroy both ourselves the laws and the entire city—at least as far as you can? Or do you think it is possible for that city to exist and not to be overthrown in which the decisions of courts do not prevail, but by the actions of individuals are set aside and made ineffective?'

What shall we say, Crito, in answer to those questions and others of that kind? For there is a lot that one could say, especially if one were a public speaker, in support of this law which was being destroyed, the one that declares that court decisions, once reached, are binding. Or shall we say to them: 'Yes, that is what I intend, for the city wronged us and gave the wrong verdict at the trial'? Shall we say that—or what?

CRITO: Emphatically that, Socrates.

SOCRATES: Then what if the laws replied: 'Socrates, was that what was agreed between ourselves and you, or was it that you would abide by the judgments of the city's courts?'

Then, if we showed suprise at their saying that, perhaps they would go on: 'Socrates, do not be surprised at what we say, but answer us—since it is your own practice to use question and answer. Come now, what charge do you have against us and Athens that you are trying to destroy us? First, did we not beget you, and was it not through us that your father married your mother and produced you? Explain then, do you have some complaint against the marriage laws among us, that we are not as we should be?'

'I have no complaint,' I should say.

'Well, is it the laws concerning the upbringing of children, together with the education which you received? Or didn't the laws ordained for that area prescribe well, when they ordered your father to provide you with a cultural and physical education?'

'They prescribed well,' I should say.

'Well. Now, since you were born, brought up and educated, could you deny, first, that you were our offspring and servant—both yourself and your forefathers? And, if that is so, then do you think that justice is on all fours for you and for us, and do you think that whatever we try to do to you it is just for you to do back to us? Or is it that, on the one hand, as regards justice you were not on equal terms with your father, or with your master (if you happened to have one), so as to give back to them what treatment you received from them—it would amount to your not talking back when you were criticised, and not hitting back when you were struck, and not behaving in any other similar manner? But, on the other hand, in relation to your native land and its laws, will that be allowable to you, so that, if we try to destroy you, believing that to be just, then you too will attempt to the best of your ability to destroy in return us your laws and your country, and will you say that in doing that you are doing what is just, you the man who really cultivates virtue? Or are you so clever that it has escaped your notice that your country is more to be prized and revered, and is more sacred than your mother, your father and all the rest of your forebears, and is held in greater esteem both among gods and among men (those who have understanding); and that you must pay honour to, and be more submissive, even servile, to your country when it is angry than to your father; and that you must either persuade it or do what it commands, and that you must undergo without fuss anything it orders you to undergo, whether it is a beating or imprisonment, or whether it lead you out to war, to be wounded or to die; that that is what you have to do, and that is how justice is, and that you must not give ground or withdraw or leave your post, but in war and lawcourts alike, and everywhere else too you must do whatever your city and country orders, or else persuade it in accordance with where justice really is; and that to use violence against either mother or father is impious, and that far less even than against them is it to be used against your country?'

What shall we reply to that, Crito? That what the laws are saying is true, or not?

CRITO: It seems true to me.

SOCRATES: 'Consider next, Socrates,' perhaps the laws would say, 'whether we are correct in asserting this, that you are not trying to treat us justly in what you are trying to do. For we, having begotten, nurtured and educated you, and having given to you, as to all the rest of the citizens, your share of all the fine things that we could, declare, by the fact of granting the privilege to any Athenian who wishes it, when he comes of age and sees how things are in the city, and sees us the laws, that anybody who is not satisfied with us is permitted to take what belongs to him and to emigrate to wherever he pleases. And not one of us laws stands in the way or forbids it if one of you wishes to go to a colony, in the event that we and Athens do not satisfy him, or if he wishes to go and remove himself elsewhere—we do not stop him going wherever he wishes, keeping what he owns. But whoever of you stays behind, seeing the way in which we decide our cases in court and the other ways in which we manage our city, we say that he has thereby, by his act of staying, agreed with us that he will do what we demand of him; and we say that the man who does not obey wrongs us in three ways: that he does not obey us his parents, that he does not obey us who brought him up, and that, having agreed to obey us, he neither does so nor persuades us, if there is anything which we are not doing right; although we propose rather than harshly demand that he do what he is told to do, although we allow him one of two choices, either to persuade us or to do as we say, he does neither. Now we say that you too, Socrates, will be subject to these charges, if you do what you have in mind; and in your case this applies not less than to other Athenians, but more than to almost anyone.'

Then, if I were to say, 'Now, why?', perhaps they would attack me quite justifiably by saying that, as a matter of fact, I have given this agreement to them more emphatically than almost any other Athenian. For they would say:

'Socrates, we have strong proof that you are satisfied with us and the state. For, if you were not more than usually satisfied, you would never have remained in residence here more than is usual for other Athenians: you never left the city for a festival, except on one occasion for the Isthmus, you never went anywhere else except on military service, you never went abroad as other people do; nor did you have any desire to acquaint yourself with another city or with other laws, but we and our city were enough for you. So strongly did you choose us and agree that you would fulfil the role of a citizen under us; apart from everything else you fathered children here, showing that the city pleased you. Then again, at the time of the actual trial you could, if you had wanted, have put forward banishment as the sentence which you thought would be appropriate, and what you are now trying to do against the city's will you could then have done with it. But you at that time prided yourself on not complaining if you had to die, you chose, so you said, death in preference to exile. Yet now you are neither ashamed of those protestations, nor do you show regard for us the laws, as you try to destroy us; you are behaving just as the meanest kind of slave would, trying to run away contrary to the compacts and agreements by which you covenanted with us to conduct yourself as a citizen of Athens.

'First, then, give your answer to this question of ours, whether we are right in maintaining that you have, not by what you have said but by what you have done, agreed to live under us as a citizen? Or is that not the truth?'

What are we to reply to that, Crito? Can we do anything but agree with them?

CRITO: We have to agree, Socrates.

SOCRATES: 'Then are you doing anything else,' they would say, 'but violating the compacts and agreements made with us, agreements which you entered into victimised neither by coercion nor by misrepresentation; nor were you forced to make up your mind in a hurry, but you had seventy years, in which it was possible for you to move away if we were not satisfactory to you, or if the agreements seemed to you to be unjust. But you chose neither Sparta nor Crete, which you assert on every occasion to be states with good laws,[4] nor any other city in Greece or abroad—indeed you were away from the city less even than the lame, the blind and the rest

of the physically handicapped. It is quite clear that you above all other Athenians were pleased with your city and with us, its laws—for who would be pleased with a city without laws? And now indeed do you stand by your agreements? You do, if you are persuaded by us, Socrates; and you will not become a figure of ridicule for leaving the city.

'For consider now, if you commit these transgressions and do something wrong in any of these ways, what good will you do either to yourself or to those close to you? As far as the latter are concerned, it is fairly clear that they will risk being prosecuted themselves and being deprived of their citizenship or their property. While, as for yourself, if you go to one of the nearby cities, to Thebes or to Megara—for they both have good systems of law—you will be arriving there, Socrates, as an enemy of the state, and everybody who cares for their cities will look at you with suspicion as a destroyer of laws, and you will reinforce the jury's opinion, so that they will be convinced that they gave the correct verdict; for anybody who is a destroyer of laws would certainly be believed to be a destroyer of youth and of witless men. Will you then avoid cities with good laws, and men of the most decent kind? And, if you do that, will life be worth living for you? Or will you try to associate with those men and be shameless enough to converse with them—what will you say to them, Socrates? Will it be what you say here, that virtue and justice are the most valuable things men have, together with the usages and institutions of law? And do you not think that ''the Socrates business'' will appear discreditable? You certainly should. Maybe you will keep away from these parts, and end up instead in Thessaly among Crito's friends. For there there is extreme disorder and lack of moral discipline; and perhaps they would take pleasure in hearing your funny story—how you escaped from prison by putting on some disguise, by wearing a jerkin or some other such outfit as runaways use, and altering your appearance. And will nobody remark that, as an old man with very likely only a short time left to live, you had the presumption to want so much to hang on to life, while violating the most important laws? Perhaps not, if you do not trouble anybody; otherwise you will hear many remarks, Socrates, that will be unworthy of you. You will live by insinuating yourself into everybody's favour and behaving like a servant to them— what will you be doing but eating well in Thessaly, as though you had travelled there just for food and drink? As for that talk about justice and the rest of virtue, where, tell us, will that be? But is it that you want to live for the sake of your sons, to bring them up and educate them? Will you do that by taking them to Thessaly, making foreigners of them, so that they can enjoy that too? Or, instead of that, will they be better brought up and educated if they are brought up here, with you still alive but not with them—for your friends will take care of them? Is it really the case that, if you go away to Thessaly, they will take care of them, but that, if you go away to the next world, they will not? Surely, if there is anything to be got from those who call themselves your friends, you must suppose that they will help in that way.

'Now, Socrates, in obedience to us who reared you, do not make either children or life or anything else to be of more account that what is just, in order that when you reach the other world you may have all that to present in your defence before the rulers there. For, if you behave in the way you propose, it does not seem that it will be better for you here, or more just in relation to men or heaven, nor for any of your friends either; and it will not be the better for you when you arrive there. But, as things now stand, you will leave here, if you do, wronged not by us the laws but by men; on the other hand, if you depart having so shamefully returned injustice for injustice and bad treatment for bad treatment, violating, that is, your own agreements and compacts made with us, and behaving badly towards those whom least of all you should treat in such a way (we mean yourself, your friends, your country and our-

selves), then we shall be angry with you while you live, and our brethren the laws in the other place will not receive you kindly there, knowing full well that you have tried, for your part, to destroy us. Do not let Crito persuade you to follow his advice rather than ours.'

That, Crito my dear friend, be assured is what I believe I hear them saying, just as the celebrants of the Corybantic rites believe they hear the sound of the pipes; and the echo of their arguments reverberates in my mind, and makes me unable to hear anything else. But understand that, as to what I now believe, if you have anything to say against it, you will be wasting your time. Nevertheless, if you think you will achieve anything more, have your say.

CRITO: There is nothing, Socrates, that I can say.

SOCRATES: Well, let it be, Crito, and let us do things this way, since this is the way in which God is leading us.

Notes

1. In Athens the execution of a death sentence usually followed within a day of its pronouncement. But it happened that the opening of Socrates' trial coincided with the beginning of a religious mission to Delos, and that, as no executions were allowed to take place until the mission was completed with the boat's return to Athens, there was in his case a delay of several weeks between the passing of the sentence and his death.
2. This line is almost a quotation from Homer. *Il.* ix. 363. Phthia was the home of Achilles.
3. 'I know quite well that wherever I go the young will listen to me talking, as they do here. If I keep them away from me, they would banish me (persuading their elders to do it); alternatively, if I do not keep them away, then their fathers and family would banish me for the sake of those same young people.' (*Apol.* 37d)
4. It is interesting, if historically correct, that Socrates admired those two states for their legal systems. Plato in his final work, the *Laws,* written some forty or more years later, took the same pair of states as his starting point; from criticism of the defects of their legal systems he developed a legal code for his own Utopia.

From *Second Treatise of Civil Government*

JOHN LOCKE

II. Of the State of Nature

4. To understand political power aright, and derive it from its original, we must consider, what state all men are naturally in, and that is, a state of perfect freedom to order their actions, and dispose of their possessions and persons, as they think fit, within the bounds of the law of nature, without asking leave, or depending upon the will of any other man.

A state also of equality, wherein all the power and jurisdiction is reciprocal, no one having more than another; there being nothing more evident, than that creatures of the same species and rank, promiscuously born to all the same advantages of nature, and the use of the same faculties, should also be equal one amongst another without subordination or sub-jection, unless the lord and master of them all should, by any manifest declaration of his will, set one above another, and confer on him, by an evident and clear appointment, an un-doubted right to dominion and sovereignty.

5. This equality of men by nature, the ju-dicious Hooker looks upon as so evident in it-self, and beyond all question, that he makes it the foundation of that obligation to mutual love amongst men, on which he builds the duties they owe one another, and from whence he de-rives the great maxims of justice and charity. His words are:

The like natural inducement hath brought men to know that it is no less their duty, to love others than themselves; for seeing those things which are equal, must needs all have one measure; if I cannot but wish to receive good, even as much at every man's hands, as any man can wish unto his own soul, how should I look to have any part of my desire herein satisfied, unless myself be careful to satisfy the like desire, which is undoubtedly in other men. We all being of one and the same nature; to have any thing offered them repugnant to this desire, must needs in all respects grieve them as much as me; so that if I do harm, I must look to suffer, there being no reason that others should shew greater measure of love to me, than they have by me shewed unto them; my desire therefore to be loved of my equals in nature, as much as possible may be, imposeth upon me a natural duty of bearing to themward fully the like affection; from which relation of equality between ourselves and them that are as ourselves, what sev-eral rules and canons natural reason hath drawn, for direction of life, no man is ignorant. *Eccl. Pol.,* bk. i.

6. But though this be a state of liberty, yet it is not a state of licence: though man in that state have an uncontrollable liberty to dispose of his person or possessions, yet he has not liberty to destroy himself, or so much as any creature in his possession, but where some no-bler use than its bare preservation calls for it. The state of nature has a law of nature to gov-ern it, which obliges every one, and reason,

John Locke, from *Second Treatise of Civil Government*, reprinted from *Social Contract*, ed. Sir Ernest Barker, by permission of Oxford University Press. Copyright Oxford University Press, 1960.

which is that law, teaches all mankind, who will but consult it, that being all equal and independent, no one ought to harm another in his life, health, liberty, or possessions: for men being all the workmanship of one omnipotent, and infinitely wise maker; all the servants of one sovereign master, sent into the world by his order, and about his business; they are his property, whose workmanship they are, made to last during his, not one another's pleasure: and being furnished with like faculties, sharing all in one community of nature, there cannot be supposed any such subordination among us, that may authorize us to destroy one another, as if we were made for one another's uses, as the inferior ranks of creatures are for ours. Every one, as he is bound to preserve himself, and not to quit his station wilfully, so by the like reason, when his own preservation comes not in competition, ought he as much as he can to preserve the rest of mankind, and not unless it be to do justice on an offender, take away, or impair the life, or what tends to the preservation of the life, the liberty, health, limb or goods of another.

7. And that all men may be restrained from invading others' rights, and from doing hurt to one another, and the law of nature be observed, which willeth the peace and preservation of all mankind, the execution of the law of nature is, in that state, put into every man's hands, whereby every one has a right to punish the transgressors of that law to such a degree, as may hinder its violation. For the law of nature would, as all other laws that concern men in this world, be in vain, if there were nobody that in the state of nature had a power to execute that law, and thereby preserve the innocent and restrain offenders. And if any one in the state of nature may punish another for any evil he has done, every one may do so: for in that state of perfect equality where naturally there is no superiority or jurisdiction of one over another, what any may do in prosecution of that law, every one must needs have a right to do.

8. And thus, in the state of nature, one man comes by a power over another; but yet no absolute or arbitrary power, to use a criminal, when he has got him in his hands, according to the passionate heats, or boundless extravagancy of his own will; but only to retribute to him, so far as calm reason and conscience dictates, what is proportionate to his transgression, which is so much as may serve for reparation and restraint: for these two are the only reasons why one man may lawfully do harm to another, which is that we call punishment. In transgressing the law of nature, the offender declares himself to live by another rule than that of reason and common equity, which is that measure God has set to the actions of men for their mutual security, and so he becomes dangerous to mankind, the tie, which is to secure them from injury and violence, being slighted and broken by him, which being a trespass against the whole species, and the peace and safety of it, provided for by the law of nature, every man upon this score, by the right he hath to preserve mankind in general, may restrain, or where it is necessary, destroy things noxious to them, and so may bring such evil on any one, who hath transgressed that law, as may make him repent the doing of it, and thereby deter him, and, by his example others, from doing the like mischief. And in this case, and upon this ground, every man hath a right to punish the offender, and be executioner of the law of nature.

9. I doubt not but this will seem a very strange doctrine to some men; but before they condemn it, I desire them to resolve me, by what right any prince or state can put to death, or punish an alien, for any crime he commits in their country. 'Tis certain their laws, by virtue of any sanction they receive from the promulgated will of the legislative, reach not a stranger: they speak not to him, nor, if they did, is he bound to hearken to them. The legislative authority, by which they are in force over the subjects of that commonwealth, hath no power over him. Those who have the supreme power of making laws in England, France or Holland, are to an Indian, but like the rest of the world, men without authority: and therefore, if by the law of nature every man hath not a power to punish offences against it, as he soberly judges the case to require, I see not how the magistrate of any community can punish an alien of another country;

since, in reference to him, they can have no more power than what every man naturally may have over another.

10. Besides the crime which consists in violating the law, and varying from the right rule of reason, whereby a man so far becomes degenerate, and declares himself to quit the principles of human nature and to be a noxious creature, there is commonly injury done, and some person or other, some other man receives damage by his transgression; in which case he who hath received any damage, has, besides the right of punishment common to him with other men, a particular right to seek reparation from him that has done it: and any other person, who finds it just, may also join with him that is injured, and assist him in recovering from the offender so much as may make satisfaction for the harm he has suffered.

11. From these two distinct rights, the one of punishing the crime for restraint, and preventing the like offence, which right of punishing is in everybody; the other of taking reparation, which belongs only to the injured party, comes it to pass that the magistrate, who by being magistrate hath the common right of punishing put into his hands, can often, where the public good demands not the execution of the law, remit the punishment of criminal offences by his own authority, but yet cannot remit the satisfaction due to any private man for the damage he has received. That, he who has suffered the damage has a right to demand in his own name, and he alone can remit: the damnified person has this power of appropriating to himself the goods or service of the offender, by right of self-preservation, as every man has a power to punish the crime, to prevent its being committed again, by the right he has of preserving all mankind, and doing all reasonable things he can in order to that end: and thus it is, that every man, in the state of nature, has a power to kill a murderer, both to deter others from doing the like injury, which no reparation can compensate, by the example of the punishment that attends it from every body, and also to secure men from the attempts of a criminal, who having renounced reason, the common rule and measure God hath given to mankind, hath, by the unjust violence and slaughter he hath committed upon one, declared war against all mankind, and therefore may be destroyed as a lion or a tiger, one of those wild savage beasts, with whom men can have no society nor security: and upon this is grounded that great law of nature, *Whoso sheddeth man's blood, by man shall his blood be shed*. And Cain was so fully convinced, that every one had a right to destroy such a criminal, that after the murder of his brother, he cries out, *Every one that findeth me shall slay me;* so plain was it writ in the hearts of all mankind.

12. By the same reason may a man in the state of nature punish the lesser breaches of that law. It will perhaps be demanded, with death? I answer, each transgression may be punished to that degree, and with so much severity, as will suffice to make it an ill bargain to the offender, give him cause to repent, and terrify others from doing the like. Every offence, that can be committed in the state of nature, may in the state of nature be also punished equally, and as far forth as it may, in a commonwealth: for though it would be besides my present purpose, to enter here into the particulars of the law of nature, or its measures of punishment; yet, it is certain there is such a law, and that too as intelligible and plain to a rational creature, and a studier of that law, as the positive laws of commonwealths: nay, possibly plainer; as much as reason is easier to be understood, than the fancies and intricate contrivances of men, following contrary and hidden interests put into words; for so truly are a great part of the municipal laws of countries, which are only so far right, as they are founded on the law of nature, by which they are to be regulated and interpreted.

13. To this strange doctrine, *viz.* That in the state of nature every one has the executive power of the law of nature, I doubt not but it will be objected, that it is unreasonable for men to be judges in their own cases, that self-love will make men partial to themselves and their friends: and on the other side, ill-nature, passion and revenge will carry them too far in punishing others; and hence nothing but confusion and disorder will follow; and that therefore God hath certainly appointed govern-

ment to restrain the partiality and violence of men. I easily grant that civil government is the proper remedy for the inconveniences of the state of nature, which must certainly be great where men may be judges in their own case, since 'tis easy to be imagined, that he who was so unjust as to do his brother an injury, will scarce be so just as to condemn himself for it; but I shall desire those who make this objection, to remember, that absolute monarchs are but men; and if government is to be the remedy of those evils, which necessarily follow from men's being judges in their own cases, and the state of nature is therefore not to be endured, I desire to know what kind of government that is, and how much better it is than the state of nature, where one man commanding a multitude, has the liberty to be judge in his own case, and may do to all his subjects whatever he pleases, without the least question or control of those who execute his pleasure? and in whatsoever he doth, whether led by reason, mistake or passion, must be submitted to? which men in the state of nature are not bound to do one to another. And if he that judges, judges amiss in his own, or any other case, he is answerable for it to the rest of mankind.

14. 'Tis often asked as a mighty objection, where are, or ever were there any men in such a state of nature? To which it may suffice as an answer at present, that since all princes and rulers of *independent* governments all through the world, are in a state of nature, 'tis plain the world never was, nor never will be, without numbers of men in that state. I have named all governors of *independent* communities, whether they are, or are not, in league with others: for 'tis not every compact that puts an end to the state of nature between men, but only this one of agreeing together mutually to enter into one community, and make one body politic; other promises, and compacts, men may make one with another, and yet still be in the state of nature. The promises and bargains for truck, etc. between the two men in the desert island, mentioned by Garcilasso de la Vega, in his history of Peru; or between a Swiss and an Indian, in the woods of America, are binding to them, though they are perfectly in a state of nature, in reference to one another: for truth

and keeping of faith belongs to men as men, and not as members of society.

15. To those that say, there were never any men in the state of nature, I will not only oppose the authority of the judicious Hooker, *Eccl. Pol.* bk. i. *sect.* 10, where he says, "the laws which have been hitherto mentioned, *i.e.,* the laws of nature, do bind men absolutely, even as they are men, although they have never any settled fellowship, never any solemn agreement amongst themselves what to do, or not to do: but forasmuch as we are not by ourselves sufficient to furnish ourselves with competent store of things, needful for such a life as our nature doth desire, a life fit for the dignity of man; therefore to supply those defects and imperfections which are in us, as living singly and solely by ourselves, we are naturally induced to seek communion and fellowship with others: this was the cause of men uniting themselves at first in politic societies." But I moreover affirm, that all men are naturally in that state, and remain so, till by their own consents they make themselves members of some politic society; and I doubt not in the sequel of this discourse, to make it very clear.

III. Of the State of War

16. The state of war is a state of enmity and destruction: and therefore declaring by word or action, not a passionate and hasty, but sedate, settled design upon another man's life, puts him in a state of war with him against whom he has declared such an intention, and so has exposed his life to the other's power to be taken away by him, or any one that joins with him in his defense, and espouses his quarrel, it being reasonable and just I should have a right to destroy that which threatens me with destruction; for by the fundamental law of nature, man being to be preserved, as much as possible, when all cannot be preserved, the safety of the innocent is to be preferred; and one may destroy a man who makes war upon him, or has discovered an enmity to his being, for the same reason that he may kill a wolf or a lion, because such men are not under the ties of the common law of reason, have no other rule but that of force and violence, and so may be

treated as beasts of prey, those dangerous and noxious creatures that will be sure to destroy him whenever he falls into their power.

17. And hence it is that he who attempts to get another man into his absolute power does thereby put himself into a state of war with him; it being to be understood as a declaration of a design upon his life. For I have reason to conclude that he who would get me into his power without my consent would use me as he pleased when he had got me there, and destroy me too when he had a fancy to it; for nobody can desire to have me in his absolute power unless it be to compel me by force to that which is against the right of my freedom—*i.e.,* make me a slave. To be free from such force is the only security of my preservation, and reason bids me look on him as an enemy to my preservation who would take away that freedom which is the fence to it; so that he who makes an attempt to enslave me thereby puts himself into a state of war with me. He that in the state of nature would take away the freedom that belongs to any one in that state must necessarily be supposed to have a design to take away everything else, that freedom being the foundation of all the rest; as he that in the state of society or commonwealth must be supposed to design to take away from them everything else, and so be looked on as in a state of war.

18. This makes it lawful for a man to kill a thief who has not in the least hurt him, nor declared any design upon his life, any farther than by the use of force, so to get him in his power as to take away his money, or what he pleases, from him; because using force, where he has no right to get me into his power, let his pretence be what it will, I have no reason to suppose that he who would take away my liberty would not, when he had me in his power, take away everything else. And therefore it is lawful for me to treat him as one who has put himself into a state of war with me—*i.e.,* kill him if I can; for to that hazard does he justly expose himself whoever introduces a state of war, and is aggressor in it.

19. And here we have the plain difference between the state of nature and the state of war, which however some men have confounded,

are as far distant as a state of peace, goodwill, mutual assistance, and preservation; and a state of enmity, malice, violence and mutual destruction are one from another. Men living together according to reason without a common superior on earth, with authority to judge between them, are properly in the state of nature. But force, or a declared design of force upon the person of another, where there is no common superior on earth to appeal to for relief, is the state of war; and 'tis the want of such an appeal gives a man the right of war even against an aggressor, though he be in society and a fellow-subject. Thus, a thief whom I cannot harm, but by appeal to the law, for having stolen all that I am worth, I may kill when he sets on me to rob me but of my horse or coat, because the law, which was made for my preservation, where it cannot interpose to secure my life from present force, which if lost is capable of no reparation, permits me my own defence and the right of war, a liberty to kill the aggressor, because the aggressor allows not time to appeal to our common judge, nor the decision of the law, for remedy in a case where the mischief may be irreparable. Want of a common judge with authority puts all men in a state of nature; force without right upon a man's person makes a state of war both where there is, and is not, a common judge.

20. But when the actual force is over, the state of war ceases between those that are in society and are equally on both sides subjected to the fair determination of the law; because then there lies open the remedy of appeal for the past injury, and to prevent future harm; but where no such appeal is, as in the state of nature, for want of positive laws, and judges with authority to appeal to, the state of war, once begun, continues with a right to the innocent party to destroy the other whenever he can, until the aggressor offers peace, and desires reconciliation on such terms as may repair any wrongs he has already done, and secure the innocent for the future; nay, where an appeal to the law and constituted judges lies open, but the remedy is denied by a manifest perverting of justice, and a barefaced wresting of the laws to protect or indemnify the violence or injuries of some men or party of men, there it is hard

to imagine any thing but a state of war: for wherever violence is used, and injury done, though by hands appointed to administer justice, it is still violence and injury, however coloured with the name, pretences, or forms of law, the end whereof being to protect and redress the innocent, by an unbiassed application of it, to all who are under it; wherever that is not *bona fide* done, war is made upon the sufferers, who having no appeal on earth to right them, they are left to the only remedy in such cases, an appeal to Heaven.

21. To avoid this state of war (wherein there is no appeal but to Heaven, and wherein every the least difference is apt to end, where there is no authority to decide between the contenders) is one great reason of men's putting themselves into society, and quitting the state of nature. For where there is an authority, a power on earth from which relief can be had by appeal, there the continuance of the state of war is excluded, and the controversy is decided by that power. Had there been any such court, any superior jurisdiction on earth, to determine the right between Jephtha and the Ammonites, they had never come to a state of war, but we see he was forced to appeal to Heaven. *The Lord the judge* (says he) *be judge this day between the Children of Israel, and the Children of Ammon, Judges* xi. 27, and then prosecuting and relying on his appeal, he leads out his army to battle. And therefore in such controversies, where the question is put, *who shall be judge?* it cannot be meant, who shall decide the controversy; every one knows what Jephtha here tells us, that *the Lord the judge shall judge*. Where there is no judge on earth, the appeal lies to God in heaven. That question then cannot mean, Who shall judge whether another hath put himself in a state of war with me, and whether I may, as Jephtha did, appeal to Heaven in it? Of that I myself can only be judge in my own conscience, as I will answer it at the one great day, to the supreme Judge of all men.

IV. Of Slavery

22. The natural liberty of man is to be free from any superior power on earth, and not to be under the will or legislative authority of man, but to have only the law of nature for his rule. The liberty of man in society is to be under no other legislative power but that established by consent in the commonwealth, nor under the dominion of any will, or restraint of any law, but what the legislative shall enact according to the trust put in it. Freedom, then, is not what Sir Robert Filmer tells us, *O.A.* 55. *A liberty for every one to do what he lists, to live as he pleases, and not to be tied by any laws;* but freedom of men under government is to have a standing rule to live by, common to every one of that society, and made by the legislative power erected in it. A liberty to follow my own will in all things where the rule prescribes not, not to be subject to the inconstant, uncertain, unknown, arbitrary will of another man, as freedom of nature is to be under no other restraint but the law of nature.

23. This freedom from absolute, arbitrary power is so necessary to, and closely joined with, a man's preservation, that he cannot part with it but by what forfeits his preservation and life together. For a man, not having the power of his own life, cannot, by compact or his own consent, enslave himself to any one, nor put himself under the absolute, arbitrary power of another to take away his life when he pleases. Nobody can give more power than he has himself; and he that cannot take away his own life cannot give another power over it. Indeed, having by his fault forfeited his own life by some act that deserves death, he to whom he has forfeited it may, when he has him in his power, delay to take it, and make use of him to his own service; and he does him no injury by it. For, whenever he finds the hardship of his slavery outweigh the value of his life, 'tis in his power, by resisting the will of his master, to draw on himself the death he desires.

24. This is the perfect condition of slavery, which is nothing else but the state of war continued between a lawful conqueror and a captive. For, if once compact enter between them, and make an agreement for a limited power on the one side, and obedience on the other, the state of war and slavery ceases as long as the compact endures; for, as has been said, no man can by agreement pass over to another that

which he hath not in himself, a power over his own life.

I confess, we find among the Jews, as well as other nations, that men did sell themselves; but 'tis plain this was only to drudgery, not to slavery; for it is evident the person sold was not under an absolute, arbitrary, despotical power. For the master could not have power to kill him at any time, whom at a certain time he was obliged to let go free out of his service; and the master of such a servant was so far from having an arbitrary power over his life that he could not at pleasure so much as maim him, but the loss of an eye or tooth set him free, Exod. xxi.

V. Of Property

25. Whether we consider natural reason, which tells us that men, being once born, have a right to their preservation, and consequently to meat and drink and such other things as Nature affords for their subsistence, or *revelation,* which gives us an account of those grants God made of the world to Adam, and to Noah and his sons, 'tis very clear that God, as King David says, *Psalm* cxv. 16, *has given the earth to the children of men,* given it to mankind in common. But, this being supposed, it seems to some a very great difficulty how any one should ever come to have a property in anything, I will not content myself to answer, that, if it be difficult to make out *property* upon a supposition that God gave the world to Adam and his posterity in common, it is impossible that any man but one universal monarch should have any *property* upon a supposition that God gave the world to Adam and his heirs in succession, exclusive of all the rest of his posterity; but I shall endeavour to shew how men might come to have a property in several parts of that which God gave to mankind in common, and that without any express compact of all the commoners.

26. God, who hath given the world to men in common, hath also given them reason to make use of it to the best advantage of life and convenience. The earth and all that is therein is given to men for the support and comfort of their being. And though all the fruits it naturally produces, and beasts it feeds, belong to mankind in common, as they are produced by the spontaneous hand of nature, and no body has originally a private dominion exclusive of the rest of mankind in any of them, as they are thus in their natural state, yet being given for the use of men, there must of necessity be a means to appropriate them some way or other before they can be of any use, or at all beneficial, to any particular man. The fruit or venison which nourishes the wild Indian, who knows no enclosure, and is still a tenant in common, must be his, and so his—*i.e.,* a part of him, that another can no longer have any right to it before it can do him any good for the support of his life.

27. Though the earth and all inferior creatures be common to all men, yet every man has a *property* in his own *person*. This nobody has any right to but himself. The *labour* of his body and the *work* of his hands, we may say, are properly his. Whatsoever, then, he removes out of the state that nature hath provided and left it in, he hath mixed his labour with it, and joined to it something that is his own, and thereby makes it his property. It being by him removed from the common state nature placed it in, it hath by this labour something annexed to it that excludes the common right of other men. For this labour being the unquestionable property of the labourer, no man but he can have a right to what that is once joined to, at least where there is enough, and as good left in common for others.

28. He that is nourished by the acorns he picked up under an oak, or the apples he gathered from the trees in the wood, has certainly appropriated them to himself. Nobody can deny but the nourishment is his. I ask, then, when did they begin to be his? when he digested? or when he ate? or when he boiled? or when he brought them home? or when he picked them up? And 'tis plain, if the first gathering made them not his, nothing else could. That labour put a distinction between them and common. That added something to them more than Nature, the common mother of all, had done, and so they became his private right. And will any one say he had no right to those acorns or apples he thus appropriated be-

cause he had not the consent of all mankind to make them his? Was it a robbery thus to assume to himself what belonged to all in common? If such a consent as that was necessary, man had starved, notwithstanding the plenty God had given him. We see in commons, which remain so by compact, that 'tis the taking any part of what is common, and removing it out of the state Nature leaves it in, which begins the property, without which the common is of no use. And the taking of this or that part does not depend on the express consent of all the commoners. Thus, the grass my horse has bit, the turfs my servant has cut, and the ore I have digged in any place, where I have a right to them in common with others, become my property without the assignation or consent of any body. The labour that was mine, removing them out of that common state they were in, hath fixed my property in them.

29. By making an explicit consent of every commoner necessary to any one's appropriating to himself any part of what is given in common, children or servants could not cut the meat which their father or master had provided for them in common without assigning to every one his peculiar part. Though the water running in the fountain be every one's, yet who can doubt but that in the pitcher is his only who drew it out? His labour hath taken it out of the hands of Nature where it was common, and belonged equally to all her children, and hath thereby appropriated it to himself.

30. Thus this law of reason makes the deer that Indian's who hath killed it; 'tis allowed to be his goods who hath bestowed his labour upon it, though, before, it was the common right of every one. And amongst those who are counted the civilized part of mankind, who have made and multiplied positive laws to determine property, this original law of nature for the beginning of property, in what was before common, still takes place, and by virtue thereof, what fish any one catches in the ocean, that great and still remaining common of mankind; or what ambergris any one takes up here is by the labour that removes it out of that common state nature left it in, made his property who takes that pains about it. And even amongst us, the hare that any one is hunting is

thought his who pursues her during the chase. For being a beast that is still looked upon as common, and no man's private possession, whoever has employed so much labour about any of that kind as to find and pursue her has thereby removed her from the state of nature wherein she was common, and hath begun a property.

31. It will perhaps be objected to this, that if gathering the acorns or other fruits of the earth, etc., makes a right to them, then any one may engross as much as he will. To which I answer, Not so. The same law of nature that does by this means give us property, does also bound that property too. *God has given us all things richly,* I Tim. vi. 12. Is the voice of reason confirmed by inspiration? But how far has he given it us, *to enjoy?* As much as any one can make use of to any advantage of life before it spoils, so much he may by his labour fix a property in. Whatever is beyond this is more than his share, and belongs to others. Nothing was made by God for man to spoil or destroy. And thus considering the plenty of natural provisions there was a long time in the world, and the few spenders, and to how small a part of that provision the industry of one man could extend itself and engross it to the prejudice of others, especially keeping within the bonds set by reason of what might serve for his use, there could be then little room for quarrels or contentions about property so established.

32. But the chief matter of property being now not the fruits of the earth and the beasts that subsist on it, but the earth itself, as that which takes in and carries with it all the rest, I think it is plain that property in that too is acquired as the former. As much land as a man tills, plants, improves, cultivates, and can use the product of, so much is his property. He by his labour does, as it were, enclose it from the common. Nor will it invalidate his right to say, Every body else has an equal title to it, and therefore he cannot appropriate, he cannot enclose, without the consent of all his fellow-commoners, all mankind. God, when he gave the world in common to all mankind, commanded man also to labour, and the penury of his condition required it of him. God and his reason commanded him to subdue the earth—

i.e., improve it for the benefit of life and therein lay out something upon it that was his own, his labour. He that in obedience to this command of God, subdued, tilled, and sowed any part of it, thereby annexed to it something that was his property, which another had no title to, nor could without injury take from him.

33. Nor was this appropriation of any parcel of land, by improving it, any prejudice to any other man, since there was still enough and as good left, and more than the yet unprovided could use. So that, in effect, there was never the less left for others because of his enclosure for himself. For he that leaves as much as another can make use of does as good as take nothing at all. No body could think himself injured by the drinking of another man, though he took a good draught, who had a whole river of the same water left him to quench his thirst. And the case of land and water, where there is enough of both, is perfectly the same.

34. God gave the world to men in common, but since he gave it them for their benefit and the greatest conveniences of life they were capable to draw from it, it cannot be supposed he meant it should always remain common and uncultivated. He gave it to the use of the industrious and rational (and labour was to be his title to it); not to the fancy or covetousness of the quarrelsome and contentious. He that had as good left for his improvement as was already taken up needed not complain, ought not to meddle with what was already improved by another's labour; if he did 'tis plain he desired the benefit of another's pains, which he had no right to, and not the ground which God has given him, in common with others, to labour on, and whereof there was as good left as that already possessed, and more than he knew what to do with, or his industry could reach to.

35. 'Tis true, in land that is common in England or any other country, where there are plenty of people under government who have money and commerce, no one can enclose or appropriate any part without the consent of all his fellow-commoners; because this is left common by compact, i.e., by the law of the land, which is not to be violated. And, though it be common in respect of some men, it is not so to all mankind, but is the joint property of this country, or this parish. Besides, the remainder, after such enclosure, would not be as good to the rest of the commoners as the whole was, when they could all make use of the whole; whereas in the beginning and first peopling of the great common of the world it was quite otherwise. The law man was under was rather for appropriating. God commanded, and his wants forced him to labour. That was his property, which could not be taken from him wherever he had fixed it. And hence subduing or cultivating the earth and having dominion, we see, are joined together. The one gave title to the other. So that God, by commanding to subdue, gave authority so far to appropriate. And the condition of human life, which requires labour and materials to work on, necessarily introduces private possessions.

36. The measure of property nature has well set by the extent of men's labour and the conveniency of life. No man's labour could subdue or appropriate all, nor could his enjoyment consume more than a small part; so that it was impossible for any man, this way, to entrench upon the right of another or acquire to himself a property to the prejudice of his neighbour, who would still have room for as good and as large a possession (after the other had taken out his) as before it was appropriated. Which measure did confine every man's possession to a very moderate proportion, and such as he might appropriate to himself without injury to any body in the first ages of the world, when men were more in danger to be lost, by wandering from their company, in the then vast wilderness of the earth, than to be straitened for want of room to plant in. And the same measure may be allowed still, without prejudice to any body, as full as the world seems. For, supposing a man or family, in the state they were at first, peopling of the world by the children of Adam or Noah; let him plant in some inland vacant places of America, we shall find that the possessions he could make himself, upon the measures we have given, would not be very large, nor, even to this day, prejudice the rest of mankind or give them reason to complain or think themselves injured by this man's encroachment, though the race of men have now spread themselves to all corners of

the world, and do infinitely exceed the small number which was at the beginning. Nay, the extent of ground is of so little value without labour that I have heard it affirmed in Spain itself a man may be permitted to plough, sow, and reap, without being disturbed, upon land he has no other title to, but only his making use of it. But, on the contrary, the inhabitants think themselves beholden to him who, by his industry on neglected, and consequently waste land, has increased the stock of corn, which they wanted. But be this as it will, which I lay no stress on, this I dare boldly affirm, that the same rule of propriety (viz.), that every man should have as much as he could make use of, would hold still in the world, without straitening any body, since there is land enough in the world to suffice double the inhabitants, had not the invention of money, and the tacit agreement of men to put a value on it, introduced (by consent) larger possessions and a right to them; which, how it has done, I shall by and by shew more at large.

37. This is certain, that in the beginning, before the desire of having more than man needed had altered the intrinsic value of things, which depends only on their usefulness to the life of man, or had agreed that a little piece of yellow metal, which would keep without wasting or decay, should be worth a great piece of flesh or a whole heap of corn, though men had a right to appropriate by their labour, each one to himself, as much of the things of nature as he could use, yet this could not be much, nor to the prejudice of others, where the same plenty was still left, to those who would use the same industry.

Before the appropriation of land, he who gathered as much of the wild fruit, killed, caught, or tamed as many of the beasts as he could—he that so employed his pains about any of the spontaneous products of nature as any way to alter them from the state nature put them in, by placing any of his labour on them, did thereby acquire a propriety in them; but if they perished in his possession without their due use—if the fruits rotted or the venison putrified before he could spend it, he offended against the common law of nature, and was liable to be punished: he invaded his neigh-

bour's share for he had no right farther than his use called for any of them, and they might serve to afford him conveniences of life.

38. The same measures governed the possession of land, too. Whatsoever he tilled and reaped, laid up and made use of before it spoiled, that was his peculiar right; whatsoever he enclosed, and could feed and make use of, the cattle and product was also his. But if either the grass of his enclosure rotted on the ground, or the fruit of his planting perished without gathering and laying up, this part of the earth, notwithstanding his enclosure, was still to be looked on as waste, and might be the possession of any other. Thus, at the beginning, Cain might take as much ground as he could till and make it his own land, and yet leave enough to Abel's sheep to feed on: a few acres would serve for both their possessions. But as families increased and industry enlarged their stocks, their possessions enlarged with the need of them; but yet it was commonly without any fixed property in the ground they made use of till they incorporated, settled themselves together, and built cities, and then, by consent, they came in time to set out the bounds of their distinct territories and agree on limits between them and their neighbours, and by laws within themselves settled the properties of those of the same society. For we see that in that part of the world which was first inhabited, and therefore like to be best peopled, even as low down as Abraham's time, they wandered with their flocks and their herds, which was their substance, freely up and down—and this Abraham did in a country where he was a stranger. Whence it is plain that, at least, a great part of the land lay in common, that the inhabitants valued it not, nor claimed property in any more than they made us of; but when there was not room enough in the same place for their herds to feed together, they, by consent, as Abraham and Lot did, Gen. xiii. 5, separated and enlarged their pasture where it best liked them. And for the same reason, Esau went from his father and his brother, and planted in Mount Seir, Gen. xxxvi. 6.

39. And thus, without supposing any private dominion and property in Adam over all the world, exclusive of all other men, which can

no way be proved, nor any one's property be made out from it, but supposing the world, given as it was to the children of men in common, we see how labour could make men distinct titles to several parcels of it for their private uses, wherein there could be no doubt of right, no room for quarrel.

40. Nor is it so strange as perhaps before consideration, it may appear, that the property of labour should be able to overbalance the community of land, for 'tis labour indeed that puts the differences of value on every thing; and let any one consider what the difference is between an acre of land planted with tobacco or sugar, sown with wheat or barley, and an acre of the same land lying in common without any husbandry upon it, and he will find that the improvement of labour makes the far greater part of the value. I think it will be but a very modest computation to say, that of the products of the earth useful to the life of man, nine-tenths are the effects of labour: nay, if we will rightly estimate things as they come to our use, and cast up the several expenses about them, what in them is purely owing to nature and what to labour, we shall find that in most of them ninety-nine hundredths are wholly to be put on the account of labour.

41. There cannot be a clearer demonstration of any thing than several nations of the Americans are of this, who are rich in land and poor in all the comforts of life; whom nature, having furnished as liberally as any other people with the materials of plenty, i.e., a fruitful soil, apt to produce in abundance what might serve for food, raiment, and delight; yet, for want of improving it by labour, have not one hundredth part of the conveniences we enjoy. And a king of a large and fruitful territory there feeds, lodges, and is clad worse than a day labourer in England.

42. To make this a little clearer, let us but trace some of the ordinary provisions of life, through their several progresses, before they come to our use, and see how much they receive of their value from humane industry. Bread, wine, and cloth are things of daily use and great plenty; yet notwithstanding acorns, water, and leaves, or skins must be our bread, drink and clothing, did not labour furnish us with these more useful commodities. For whatever bread is more worth than acorns, wine than water, and cloth or silk than leaves, skins or moss, that is wholly owing to labour and industry. The one of these being the food and raiment which unassisted nature furnishes us with; the other provisions which our industry and pains prepare for us, which how much they exceed the other in value, when any one hath computed, he will then see how much labour makes the far greater part of the value of things we enjoy in this world; and the ground which produces the materials is scarce to be reckoned in as any, or at most, but a very small part of it; so little, that even amongst us, land that is left wholly to nature, that hath no improvement of pasturage, tillage, or planting, is called, as indeed it is, waste; and we shall find the benefit of it amount to little more than nothing.

43. An acre of land that bears here twenty bushels of wheat, and another in America, which, with the same husbandry, would do the like, are, without doubt, of the same natural, intrinsic value. But yet the benefit mankind receives from one in a year is worth five pounds, and the other possibly not worth a penny; if all the profit an Indian received from it were to be valued and sold here, at least I may truly say, not one thousandth. 'Tis labour, then, which puts the greatest part of value upon land, without which it would scarcely be worth any thing; 'tis to that we owe the greatest part of all its useful products; for all that the straw, bran, bread, of that acre of wheat, is more worth than the product of an acre of as good land which lies waste is all the effect of labour. For 'tis not barely the ploughman's pains, the reaper's and thresher's toil, and the baker's sweat, is to be counted into the bread we eat; the labour of those who broke the oxen, who digged and wrought the iron and stones, who felled and framed the timber employed about the plough, mill, oven, or any other utensils, which are a vast number, requisite to this corn, from its sowing to its being made bread, must all be charged on the account of labour, and received as an effect of that: nature and the earth furnished only the almost worthless materials as in themselves. 'Twould be a strange catalogue of things that industry provided and

made use of about every loaf of bread before it came to our use if we could trace them;
iron, wood, leather, bark, timber, stone, bricks,
coals, lime, cloth, dyeing-drugs, pitch, tar,
masts, ropes, and all the materials made use of
in the ship that brought any of the commodities
made us of by any of the workman, to any part
of the work, all which 'twould be almost impossible, at least too long, to reckon up.

44. From all which it is evident, that though
the things of nature are given in common, man
(by being master of himself, and proprietor of
his own person, and the actions or labour of it)
had still in himself the great foundation of
property; and that which made up the great part
of what he applied to the support or comfort
of his being, when invention and arts had improved the conveniences of life, was perfectly his own, and did not belong in common to
others.

45. Thus labour, in the beginning, gave a
right of property, wherever any one was
pleased to employ it, upon what was common,
which remained a long while, the far greater
part, and is yet more than mankind makes use
of. Men at first, for the most part, contented
themselves with what unassisted nature offered
to their necessities; and though afterwards, in
some parts of the world, where the increase of
people and stock, with the use of money, had
made land scarce, and so of some value, the
several communities settled the bounds of their
distinct territories, and, by laws, within themselves, regulated the properties of the private
men of their society, and so, by compact and
agreement, settled the property which labour
and industry began; and the leagues that have
been made between several states and kingdoms, either expressly or tacitly disowning all
claim and right to the land in the other's possession, have, by common consent, given up
their pretences to their natural common right,
which originally they had to those countries;
and so have, by positive agreement, settled a
property amongst themselves, in distinct parts
of the world; yet there are still great tracts of
ground to be found, which the inhabitants
thereof, not having joined with the rest of mankind in the consent of the use of their common
money, lie waste, and are more than the people

who dwell on it, do, or can make use of, and
so still lie in common; though this can scarce
happen amongst that part of mankind that have
consented to the use of money.

46. The greatest part of things really useful
to the life of man, and such as the necessity of
subsisting made the first commoners of the
world look after, as it doth the Americans
now, are generally things of short duration,
such as, if they are not consumed by use, will
decay and perish of themselves. Gold, silver,
and diamonds are things that fancy or agreement hath put the value on, more than real use
and the necessary support of life. Now of
those good things which nature hath provided
in common, every one had a right (as hath
been said) to as much as he could use, and
had a property in all that he could effect with
his labour; all that his industry could extend
to, to alter from the state nature had put it in,
was his. He that gathered a hundred bushels
of acorns or apples had thereby a property in
them, they were his goods as soon as gathered. He was only to look that he used them
before they spoiled, else he took more than
his share, and robbed others. And, indeed, it
was a foolish thing, as well as dishonest, to
hoard up more than he could make use of. If
he gave away a part to any body else, so that
it perished not uselessly in his possession,
these he also made use of. And if he also bar-
tered away plums that would have rotted in a
week, for nuts that would last good for his
eating a whole year, he did no injury; he
wasted not the common stock; destroyed no
part of the portion of goods that belonged to
others, so long as nothing perished uselessly
in his hands. Again, if he would give his nuts
for a piece of metal, pleased with its colour,
or exchange his sheep for shells, or wool for a
sparkling pebble or a diamond, and keep those
by him all his life, he invaded not the right of
others; he might heap up as much of these durable things as he pleased; the exceeding of
the bound of his just property not lying in the
largeness of his possession, but the perishing
of anything uselessly in it.

47. And thus came in the use of money,
some lasting thing that men might keep without spoiling, and that, by mutual consent, men

would take in exchange for the truly useful but perishable supports of life.

48. And as different degrees of industry were apt to give men possessions in different proportions, so this invention of money gave them the opportunity to continue and enlarge them. For supposing an island, separate from all possible commerce with the rest of the world, wherein there were but a hundred families, but there were sheep, horses, and cows, with other useful animals, wholesome fruits, and land enough for corn for a hundred thousand times as many, but nothing in the island, either because of its commonness or perishableness, fit to supply the place of money. What reason could any one have there to enlarge his possessions beyond the use of his family, and a plentiful supply to its consumption, either in what their own industry produced, or they could barter for like perishable, useful commodities with others? Where there is not something both lasting and scarce, and so valuable to be hoarded up, there men will not be apt to enlarge their possessions of land, were it never so rich, never so free for them to take. For I ask, what would a man value ten thousand or an hundred thousand acres of excellent land, ready cultivated and well stocked, too, with cattle, in the middle of the inland parts of America, where he had no hopes of commerce with other parts of the world, to draw money to him by the sale of the product? It would not be worth the enclosing, and we should see him give up again to the wild common of Nature whatever was more than would supply the conveniences of life, to be had there for him and his family.

49. Thus, in the beginning, all the world was America, and more so than that is now; for no such thing as money was any where known. Find out something that hath the use and value of money amongst his neighbours, you shall see the same man will begin presently to enlarge his possessions.

50. But since gold and silver, being little useful to the life of man, in proportion to food, raiment, and carriage, has its value only from the consent of men, whereof labour yet makes in great part the measure, it is plain that the consent of men have agreed to a dispropor-

tionate and unequal possession of the earth, I mean out of the bounds of society and compact; for in governments the laws regulate it; they having, by consent, found out and agreed in a way how a man may rightfully, and without injury, possess more than he himself can make use of by receiving gold and silver, which may continue long in a man's possession without decaying for the overplus, and agreeing those metals should have a value.

51. And thus, I think, it is very easy to conceive, without any difficulty, how labour could at first begin a title of property in the common things of nature, and how the spending it upon our uses bounded it; so that there could then be no reason of quarrelling about title, nor any doubt about the largeness of possession it gave. Right and conveniency went together. For as a man had a right to all he could employ his labour upon, so he had no temptation to labour for more than he could make use of. This left no room for controversy about the title, nor for encroachment on the right of others. What portion a man carved to himself was easily seen; and it was useless as well as dishonest to carve himself too much, or take more than he needed.[. . .]

VI. Of Paternal Power

57. The law that was to govern Adam was the same that was to govern all his posterity, the law of reason. But his offspring having another way of entrance into the world, different from him, by a natural birth, that produced them ignorant, and without the use of reason, they were not presently under that law. For no body can be under a law that is not promulgated to him; and this law being promulgated or made known by reason only, he that is not come to the use of his reason cannot be said to be under this law; and Adam's children being not presently as soon as born under this law of reason, were not presently free. For law, in its true notion, is not so much the limitation as the direction of a free and intelligent agent to his proper interest, and prescribes no farther than is for the general good of those under the law. Could they be happier without it, the law, as a useless thing, would of itself vanish; and that

ill deserves the name of confinement which hedges us in only from bogs and precipices. So that however it may be mistaken, the end of law is not to abolish or restrain, but to preserve and enlarge freedom; for in all the states of created beings capable of laws, where there is no law there is no freedom; for liberty is to be free from restraint and violence from others, which cannot be where there is no law; and is not, as we are told, *a liberty for every man to do what he lists.* (For who could be free, when every other man's humour might domineer over him?) But a liberty to dispose and order freely as he lists his person, actions, possessions, and his whole property within the allowance of those laws under which he is, and therein not to be subject to the arbitrary will of another, but freely follow his own.

58. The power, then, that parents have over their children arises from that duty which is incumbent on them, to take care of their offspring during the imperfect state of childhood. To inform the mind, and govern the actions of their yet ignorant nonage, till reason shall take its place and ease them of that trouble, is what the children want, and the parents are bound to. For God having given man an understanding to direct his actions, has allowed him a freedom of will and liberty of acting, as properly belonging thereunto, within the bounds of that law he is under. But whilst he is in an estate wherein he has no understanding of his own to direct his will, he is not to have any will of his own to follow. He that understands for him must will for him too; he must prescribe to his will, and regulate his actions, but when he comes to the estate that made his father a freeman, the son is a freeman too.

59. This holds in all the laws a man is under, whether natural or civil. Is a man under the law of nature? What made him free of that law? what gave him a free disposing of his property, according to his own will, within the compass of that law? I answer, a state of maturity wherein he might be supposed capable to know that law, that so he might keep his actions within the bounds of it. When he has acquired that state, he is presumed to know how far that law is to be his guide, and how far he may make use of his freedom, and so

comes to have it; till then, some body else must guide him, who is presumed to know how far the law allows a liberty. If such a state of reason, such an age of discretion made him free, the same shall make his son free too. Is a man under the law of England? What made him free of that law? That is, to have the liberty to dispose of his actions and possessions, according to his own will, within the permission of that law? A capacity of knowing that law. Which is supposed, by that law, at the age of twenty-one, and in some cases sooner. If this made the father free, it shall make the son free too. Till then, we see the law allows the son to have no will, but he is to be guided by the will of his father or guardian, who is to understand for him And if the father die, and fail to substitute a deputy in this trust, if he hath not provided a tutor to govern his son during his minority, during his want of understanding, the law takes care to do it: some other must govern him and be a will to him till he hath attained to a state of freedom, and his understanding be fit to take the government of his will. But after that the father and son are equally free, as much as tutor and pupil after nonage, equally subjects of the same law together, without any dominion left in the father over the life, liberty, or estate of his son, whether they be only in the state and under the law of nature, or under the positive laws of an established government.

60. But if through defects that may happen out of the ordinary course of nature, anyone comes not to such a degree of reason wherein he might be supposed capable of knowing the law, and so living within the rules of it, he is never capable of being a free man, he is never let loose to the disposure of his own will, because he knows no bounds to it, has not understanding, its proper guide; but is continued under the tuition and government of others all the time his own understanding is incapable of that charge. And so lunatics and idiots are never set free from the government of their parents: *Children who are not as yet come unto those years whereat they may have; and innocents, which are excluded by a natural defect from ever having;* Thirdly, *Madmen, which, for the present, cannot possibly have the use of right reason to guide themselves,*

have, for their guide, the reason that guideth other men which are tutors over them, to seek and procure their good for them, says Hooker, *Eccl. Pol.,* bk. i, sect. 7. All which seems no more than that duty which God and nature has laid on man, as well as other creatures, to preserve their offspring till they can be able to shift for themselves, and will scarce amount to an instance or proof of parents' regal authority.

61. Thus we are born free as we are born rational; not that we have actually the exercise of either: age that brings one, brings with it the other too. And thus we see how natural freedom and subjection to parents may consist together, and are both founded on the same principle. A child is free by his father's title, by his father's understanding, which is to govern him till he hath it of his own. The freedom of a man at years of discretion, and the subjection of a child to his parents, whilst yet short of that age, are so consistent and so distinguishable, that the most blinded contenders for monarchy, *by right of fatherhood,* cannot miss this *difference,* the most obstinate cannot but allow their consistency. For were their doctrine all true, were the right heir of Adam now known, and, by that title, settled a monarch in his throne, invested with all the absolute unlimited power Sir Robert Filmer talks of, if he should die as soon as his heir was born, must not the child, notwithstanding he were never so free, never so much sovereign, be in subjection to his mother and nurse, to tutors and governors, till age and education brought him reason and ability to govern himself and others? The necessities of his life, the health of his body, and the information of his mind would require him to be directed by the will of others and not his own; and yet will anyone think that this restraint and subjection were inconsistent with, or spoiled him of, that liberty or sovereignty he had a right to, or gave away his empire to those who had the government of his nonage? This government over him only prepared him the better and sooner for it. If any body should ask me when my son is of age to be free, I shall answer, just when his monarch is of age to govern. *But at what time,* says the judicious Hooker, *Eccl. Pol.,* bk. i, sect. 6, *a man may be said to have attained so far forth the use of reason as sufficeth to make him capable of those laws whereby he is then bound to guide his actions; this is a great deal more easy for sense to discern than for anyone, by skill and learning, to determine.*

62. Commonwealths themselves take notice of, and allow that there is a time when men are to begin to act like free men, and therefore, till that time, require not oaths of fealty or allegiance, or other public owning of, or submission to, the government of their countries.

63. The freedom then of man and liberty of acting according to his own will, is grounded on his having reason, which is able to instruct him in that law he is to govern himself by, and make him known how far he is left to the freedom of his own will. To turn him loose to an unrestrained liberty, before he has reason to guide him, is not the allowing him the privilege of his nature to be free, but to thrust him out amongst brutes, and abandon him to a state as wretched and as much beneath that of a man as theirs. This is that which puts the authority into the parents' hands to govern the minority of their children. God hath made it their business to employ this care on their offspring, and hath placed in them suitable inclinations of tenderness and concern to temper this power, to apply it as his wisdom designed it, to the children's good as long as they should need to be under it.[. . .]

VII. Of Political or Civil Society

87. Man being born, as has been proved, with a title to perfect freedom and an uncontrolled enjoyment of all the rights and privileges of the law of nature, equally with any other man, or number of men in the world, hath by nature a power not only to preserve his property, that is, his life, liberty, and estate, against the injuries and attempts of other men, but to judge of and punish the breaches of that law in others, as he is persuaded the offence deserves, even with death itself, in crimes where the heinousness of the fact, in his opinion, requires it. But because no political society can be, nor subsist, without having in itself the power to preserve the property, and in order thereunto punish the offences of all those of that society:

there, and there only, is political society, where every one of the members hath quitted this natural power, resigned it up into the hands of the community in all cases that exclude him not from appealing for protection to the law established by it. And thus all private judgement of every particular member being excluded, the community comes to be umpire, by settled standing rules; indifferent, and the same to all parties: And by men having authority from the community for the execution of those rules, decides all the differences that may happen between any members of that society concerning any matter of right, and punishes those offences which any member hath committed against the society with such penalties as the law has established; whereby it is easy to discern who are, and who are not, in political society together. Those who are united into one body, and have a common established law and judicature to appeal to, with authority to decide controversies between them and punish offenders, are in civil society one with another; but those who have no such common appeal, I mean on earth, are still in the state of nature, each being, where there is no other, judge for himself and executioner; which is, as I have before showed it, the perfect state of nature.

88. And thus the commonwealth comes by a power to set down what punishment shall belong to the several transgressions they think worthy of it, committed amongst the members of that society (which is the power of making laws) as well as it has the power to punish any injury done unto any of its members by anyone that is not of it (which is the power of war and peace); and all this for the preservation of property of all the members of that society, as far as is possible. But though every man entered into society has quitted his power to punish offences against the law of nature in prosecution of his own private judgement, yet with the judgement of offences which he has given up to the legislative in all cases where he can appeal to the magistrate, he has given up a right to the commonwealth to employ his force for the execution of the judgements of the commonwealth whenever he shall be called to it, which, indeed, are his own judgements, they being made by himself or his representa-

tive. And herein we have the original of the legislative and executive power of civil society, which is to judge by standing laws how far offences are to be punished when committed within the commonwealth; and also by occasional judgements founded on the present circumstances of the fact, how far injuries from without are to be vindicated, and in both these to employ all the force of all the members when there shall be need.

89. Wherever therefore any number of men are so united into one society as to quit everyone his executive power of the law of nature, and to resign it to the public, there and there only is a political or civil society. And this is done wherever any number of men, in the state of nature, enter into society to make one people, one body politic under one supreme government: or else when anyone joins himself to and incorporates with any government already made. For hereby he authorizes the society, or which is all one, the legislative thereof, to make laws for him as the public good of the society shall require, to the execution whereof his own assistance (as to his own decrees) is due. And this puts men out of a state of nature into that of a commonwealth, by setting up a judge on earth with authority to determine all the controversies and redress the injuries that may happen to any member of the commonwealth; which judge is the legislative or magistrates appointed by it. And wherever there are any number of men, however associated, that have no such decisive power to appeal to, there they are still in the state of nature.

90. And hence it is evident that absolute monarchy, which by some men is counted for the only government in the world, is indeed inconsistent with civil society, and so can be no form of civil government at all. For the end of civil society being to avoid and remedy those inconveniences of the state of nature which necessarily follow from every man's being judge in his own case, by setting up a known authority, to which every one of that society may appeal upon any injury received, or controversy that may arise, and which everyone of the society ought to obey[1] wherever any persons are who have not such an authority to appeal to, for the decision of any

difference between them there, those persons are still in the state of nature. And so is every absolute prince in respect of those who are under his *dominion.*

91. For he being supposed to have all, both legislative and executive, power in himself alone, there is no judge to be found, no appeal lies open to anyone, who may fairly and indifferently, and with authority decide, and from whence relief and redress may be expected of any injury or inconveniency that may be suffered from him, or by his order. So that such a man, however entitled, Czar, or Grand Signior, or how you please, is as much in the state of nature, with all under his dominion, as he is with the rest of mankind. For wherever any two men are, who have no standing rule and common judge to appeal to on earth, for the determination of controversies of right betwixt them, there they are still in the state of nature, and under all the inconveniencies of it, with only this woeful difference to the subject, or rather slave of an absolute prince,[2] That whereas, in the ordinary state of nature, he has a liberty to judge of his right, and according to the best of his power, to maintain it; but whenever his property is invaded by the will and order of his monarch, he has not only no appeal, as those in society ought to have, but, as if he were degraded from the common state of rational creatures, is denied a liberty to judge of, or defend his right, and so is exposed to all the misery and inconveniences that a man can fear from one, who being in the unrestrained state of nature, is yet corrupted with flattery and armed with power.[. . .]

VIII. Of the Beginning of Political Societies

95. Men being, as has been said, by nature all free, equal, and independent, no one can be put out of his estate and subjected to the political power of another without his own consent, which is done by agreeing with other men, to join and unite into a community for their comfortable, safe, and peaceable living, one amongst another, in a secure enjoyment of their properties, and a greater security against any that are not of it. This any number of men

may do, because it injures not the freedom of the rest; they are left, as they were, in the liberty of the state of nature. When any number of men have so consented to make one community or government, they are thereby presently incorporated, and make one body politic, wherein the majority have a right to act and conclude the rest.

96. For, when any number of men have, by the consent of every individual, made a community, they have thereby made that community one body, with a power to act as one body, which is only by the will and determination of the majority. For that which acts as community, being only the consent of the individuals of it, and it being one body, must move one way, it is necessary the body should move that way whither the greater force carries it, which is the consent of the majority, or else it is impossible it should act or continue one body, one community, which the consent of every individual that united into it agreed that it should; and so everyone is bound by that consent to be concluded by the majority. And therefore we see that in assemblies empowered to act by positive laws where no number is set by that positive law which empowers them, the act of the majority passes for the act of the whole, and of course determines as having, by the law of nature and reason, the power of the whole.

97. And thus every man, by consenting with others to make one body politic under one government, puts himself under an obligation to everyone of that society to submit to the determination of the majority, and to be concluded by it; or else this original compact, whereby he with others incorporates into one society, would signify nothing, and be no compact if he be left free and under no other ties than he was in before in the state of nature. For what appearance would there be of any compact? What new engagement if he were no farther tied by any decrees of the society than he himself thought fit and did actually consent to? This would be still as great a liberty as he himself had before his compact, or anyone else in the state of nature hath, who may submit himself and consent to any acts of it if he thinks fit.

98. For if the consent of the majority shall not in reason be received as the act of the whole, and conclude every individual, nothing but the consent of every individual can make any thing to be the act of the whole, which, considering the infirmities of health and avocations of business, which in a number though much less than that of a commonwealth, will necessarily keep many away from the public assembly; and the variety of opinions and contrariety of interests which unavoidably happen in all collections of men, 'tis next impossible ever to be had. And, therefore, if coming into society be upon such terms, it will be only like Cato's coming into the theatre, *tantum ut exiret*. Such a constitution as this would make the mighty *Leviathan* of a shorter duration than the feeblest creatures, and not let it outlast the day it was born in, which cannot be supposed till we can think that rational creatures should desire and constitute societies only to be dissolved. For where the majority cannot conclude the rest, there they cannot act as one body, and consequently will be immediately dissolved again.

99. Whosoever therefore out of a state of nature unite into a community, must be understood to give up all the power necessary to the ends for which they unite into society to the majority of the community, unless they expressly agreed in any number greater than the majority. And this is done by barely agreeing to unite into one political society, which is all the compact that is, or needs be, between the individuals that enter into or make up a commonwealth. And thus, that which begins and actually constitutes any political society is nothing but the consent of any number of freemen capable of a majority, to unite and incorporate into such a society. And this is that, and that only, which did or could give beginning to any lawful government in the world.[. . .]

119. Every man being, as has been showed, naturally free, and nothing being able to put him into subjection to any earthly power, but only his own consent, it is to be considered what shall be understood to be a sufficient declaration of a man's consent to make him subject to the laws of any government. There is a common distinction of an express and a tacit

consent, which will concern our present case. No body doubts but an express consent of any man, entering into any society, makes him a perfect member of that society, a subject of that government. The difficulty is, what ought to be looked upon as a tacit consent, and how far it binds, i.e., how far anyone shall be looked on to have consented, and thereby submitted to any government, where he has made no expressions of it at all. And to this I say, that every man that hath any possession of enjoyment of any part of the dominions of any government doth thereby give his tacit consent, and is as far forth obliged to obedience to the laws of that government, during such enjoyment, as any one under it, whether this his possession be of land to him and his heirs for ever, or a lodging only for a week; or whether it be barely travelling freely on the highway; and, in effect, it reaches as far as the very being of anyone within the territories of that government.

120. To understand this the better, it is fit to consider that every man when he at first incorporates himself into any commonwealth, he, by his uniting himself thereunto, annexes also, and submits to the community those possessions which he has, or shall acquire, that do not already belong to any other government. For it would be a direct contradiction for anyone to enter into society with others for the securing and regulating of property, and yet to suppose his land, whose property is to be regulated by the laws of the society, should be exempt from the jurisdiction of that government to which he himself, the proprietor of the land, is subject. By the same act, therefore, whereby anyone unites his person, which was before free, to any commonwealth, by the same he unites his possessions, which were before free, to it also; and they become, both of them, person and possession, subject to the government and dominion of that commonwealth as long as it hath a being. Whoever therefore, from thenceforth, by inheritance, purchase, permission, or otherwise enjoys any part of the land so annexed to, and under the government of that commonwealth, must take it with the condition it is under; that is, of submitting to the government of the commonwealth, under

whose jurisdiction it is, as far forth as any subject of it.

121. But since the government has a direct jurisdiction only over the land and reaches the possessor of it (before he has actually incorporated himself in the society) only as he dwells upon and enjoys that, the obligation anyone is under by virtue of such enjoyment to submit to the government begins and ends with the enjoyment; so that whenever the owner, who has given nothing but such a tacit consent to the government, will, by donation, sale or otherwise, quit the said possession, he is at liberty to go and incorporate himself into any other commonwealth, or agree with others to begin a new one *in vacuis locis,* in any part of the world they can find free and unpossessed; whereas he that has once, by actual agreement and any express declaration, given his consent to be of any commonweal, is perpetually and indispensably obliged to be, and remain unalterably a subject to it, and can never be again in the liberty of the state of nature, unless by any calamity the government he was under comes to be dissolved; or else by some public act cuts him off from being any longer a member of it.

122. But submitting to the laws of any country, living quietly, and enjoying privileges and protection under them, makes not a man a member of that society; this is only a local protection and homage due to and from all those who, not being in a state of war, come within the territories belonging to any government, to all parts whereof the force of its law extends. But this no more makes a man a member of that society, a perpetual subject of that commonwealth, than it would make a man a subject to another in whose family he found it convenient to abide for some time, though, whilst he continued in it, he were obliged to comply with the laws and submit to the government he found there. And thus we see that foreigners, by living all their lives under another government, and enjoying the privileges and protection of it, though they are bound, even in conscience, to submit to its administration as far forth as any denizen, yet do not thereby come to be subjects or members of that commonwealth. Nothing can make any man so

but his actually entering into it by positive engagement and express promise and compact. This is that which I think, concerning the beginning of political societies, and that consent which makes anyone a member of any commonwealth.

IX. Of the Ends of Political Society and Government

123. If man in the state of nature be so free as has been said; if he be absolute lord of his own person and possessions; equal to the greatest and subject to no body, why will he part with his freedom? Why will he give up this empire, and subject himself to the dominion and control of any other power? To which 'tis obvious to answer, that though in the state of nature he hath such a right, yet the enjoyment of it is very uncertain and constantly exposed to the invasion of others; for all being kings as much as he, every man his equal, and the greater part no strict observers of equity and justice, the enjoyment of the property he has in this state is very unsafe, very unsecure. This makes him willing to quit this condition which, however free, is full of fears and continual dangers; and 'tis not without reason that he seeks out and is willing to join in society with others who are already united, or have a mind to unite for the mutual preservation of their lives, liberties, and estates, which I call by the general name, property.

124. The great and chief end therefore, of men's uniting into commonwealths, and putting themselves under government, is the preservation of their property; to which in the state of nature there are many things wanting.

First, There wants an established, settled, known law, received and allowed by common consent to be the standard of right and wrong, and the common measure to decide all controversies between them. For though the law of nature be plain and intelligible to all rational creatures, yet men, being biased by their interest, as well as ignorant for want of study of it, are not apt to allow of it as a law binding to them in the application of it to their particular cases.

125. *Secondly,* In the state of nature there

wants a known and indifferent judge, with authority to determine all differences according to the established law. For everyone in that state being both judge and executioner of the law of nature, men being partial to themselves, passion and revenge is very apt to carry them too far, and with too much heat in their own cases, as well as negligence and unconcernedness, make them too remiss in other men's.

126. *Thirdly,* In the state of nature there often wants power to back and support the sentence when right, and to give it due execution. They who by any injustice offended, will seldom fail where they are able by force to make good their injustice. Such resistance many times makes the punishment dangerous, and frequently destructive to those who attempt it.

127. Thus mankind, notwithstanding all the privileges of the state of nature, being but in an ill condition while they remain in it, are quickly driven into society. Hence it comes to pass, that we seldom find any number of men live any time together in this state. The inconveniences that they are therein exposed to by the irregular and uncertain exercise of the power every man has of punishing the transgressions of others, make them take sanctuary under the established laws of government, and therein seek the preservation of their property. 'Tis this makes them so willingly give up every one his single power of punishing to be exercised by such alone as shall be appointed to it amongst them, and by such rules as the community, or those authorized by them to that purpose, shall agree on. And in this we have the original right and rise of both the legislative and executive power as well as of the governments and societies themselves.

128. For in the state of nature to omit the liberty he has of innocent delights, a man has two powers.

The first is to do whatsoever he thinks fit for the preservation of himself and other within the permission of the law of nature; by which law, common to them all, he and all the rest of mankind are one community, make up one society distinct from all other creatures and were it not for the corruption and viciousness of degenerate men, there would be no need of any other, no necessity that men should separate from this great and natural community, and associate into less combinations.

The other power a man has in the state of nature is the power to punish the crimes committed against that law. Both these he gives up when he joins in a private, if I may so call it, or particular political society, and incorporates into any commonwealth separate from the rest of mankind.

129. The first power, *viz.* of doing whatsoever he thought fit for the preservation of himself and the rest of mankind, he gives up to be regulated by laws made by the society, so far forth as the preservation of himself and the rest of that society shall require; which laws of the society in many things confine the liberty he had by the law of nature.

130. *Secondly,* the power of punishing he wholly gives up, and engages his natural force (which he might before employ in the execution of the law of nature, by his own single authority, as he thought fit) to assist the executive power of the society as the law thereof shall require. For being now in a new state, wherein he is to enjoy many conveniences from the labour, assistance, and society of others in the same community, as well as protection from its whole strength, he is to part also with as much of his natural liberty, in providing for himself, as the good, prosperity, and safety of the society shall require, which is not only necessary but just, since the other members of the society do the like.

131. But though men when they enter into society give up the equality, liberty, and executive power they had in the state of nature into the hands of the society, to be so far disposed of by the legislative as the good of the society shall require, yet it being only with an intention in everyone the better to preserve himself, his liberty and property (for no rational creature can be supposed to change his condition with an intention to be worse), the power of the society or legislative constituted by them can never be supposed to extend farther than the common good, but is obliged to secure everyone's property by providing against those three defects above-mentioned that made the state of nature so unsafe and uneasy. And so, whoever has the legislative or

supreme power of any commonwealth, is bound to govern by established standing laws, promulgated and known to the people, and not by extemporary decrees, by indifferent and upright judges, who are to decide controversies by those laws; and to employ the force of the community at home only in the execution of such laws, or abroad to prevent or redress foreign injuries and secure the community from inroads and invasion. And all this to be directed to no other end but the peace, safety, and public good of the people.[. . .]

XI. Of the Extent of the Legislative Power

134. The great end of men's entering into society being the enjoyment of their properties in peace and safety, and the great instrument and means of that being the laws established in that society, the first and fundamental positive law of all commonwealths is the establishing of the legislative power; as the first and fundamental natural law, which is to govern even the legislative itself, is the preservation of the society, and (as far as will consist with the public good) of every person in it. This legislative is not only the supreme power of the commonwealth, but sacred and unalterable in the hands where the community have once placed it; nor can any edict of anybody else, in what form soever conceived, or by what power soever backed, have the force and obligation of a law which has not its sanction from that legislative which the public has chosen and appointed; for without this the law could not have that which is absolutely necessary to its being a law, the consent of the society, over whom nobody can have a power to make laws[3] but by their own consent and by authority received from them; and therefore all the obedience, which by the most solemn ties anyone can be obliged to pay, ultimately terminates in this supreme power, and is directed by those laws which it enacts. Nor can any oaths to any foreign power whatsoever, or any domestic subordinate power, discharge any member of the society from his obedience to the legislative, acting pursuant to their trust, nor oblige him to any obedience contrary to the laws so enacted or farther than

they do allow, it being ridiculous to imagine one can be tied ultimately to obey any power in the society which is not the supreme.

135. Though the legislative, whether placed in one or more, whether it be always in being or only by intervals, though it be the supreme power in every commonwealth, yet:

First, It is not, nor can possibly be, absolutely arbitrary over the lives and fortunes of the people. For it being but the joint power of every member of the society given up to that person or assembly which is legislator, it can be no more than those persons had in a state of nature before they entered into society, and gave it up to the community. For nobody can transfer to another more power than he has in himself, and nobody has an absolute arbitrary power over himself, or over any other, to destroy his own life, or take away the life or property of another. A man, as has been proved, cannot subject himself to the arbitrary power of another; and having, in the state of nature, no arbitrary power over the life, liberty, or possession of another, but only so much as the law of nature gave him for the preservation of himself and the rest of mankind, this is all he doth, or can give up to the commonwealth, and by it to the legislative power, so that the legislative can have no more than this. Their power in the utmost bounds of it is limited to the public good of the society.[4] It is a power that hath no other end but preservation, and therefore can never have a right to destroy, enslave, or designedly to impoverish the subjects; the obligations of the law of nature cease not in society, but only in many cases are drawn closer, and have, by human laws, known penalties annexed to them to enforce their observation. Thus the law of nature stands as an eternal rule to all men, legislators as well as others. The rules that they make for other men's actions must, as well as their own and other men's actions, be conformable to the law of nature, i.e. to the will of God, of which that is a declaration, and the fundamental law of nature being the preservation of mankind, no human sanction can be good or valid against it.

136. *Secondly,* The legislative or supreme authority cannot assume to itself a power to

rule by extemporary arbitrary decrees, but is bound to dispense justice and decide the rights of the subject by promulgated standing laws,[5] and known authorized judges. For the law of nature being unwritten, and so nowhere to be found but in the minds of men, they who, through passion or interest, shall miscite or misapply it, cannot so easily be convinced of their mistake where there is no established judge; and so it serves not as it ought, to determine the rights and fence the properties of those that live under it, especially where everyone is judge, interpreter, and executioner of it too, and that in his own case; and he that has right on his side, having ordinarily but his own single strength, hath not force enough to defend himself from injuries or to punish delinquents. To avoid these inconveniencies which disorder men's properties in the state of nature, men unite into societies that they may have the united strength of the whole society to secure and defend their properties, and may have standing rules to bound it by which everyone may know what is his. To this end it is that men give up all their natural power to the society they enter into, and the community put the legislative power into such hands as they think fit, with this trust, that they shall be governed by declared laws, or else their peace, quiet, and property will still be at the same uncertainty as it was in the state of Nature.

137. Absolute arbitrary power, or governing without settled standing laws, can neither of them consist with the ends of society and government, which men would not quit the freedom of the state of nature for, and tie themselves up under, were it not to preserve their lives, liberties, and fortunes, and by stated rules of right and property to secure their peace and quiet. It cannot be supposed that they should intend, had they a power so to do, to give to any one or more an absolute arbitrary power over their persons and estates, and put a force into the magistrate's hand to execute his unlimited will arbitrarily upon them; this were to put themselves into a worse condition than the state of nature, wherein they had a liberty to defend their right against the injuries of others, and were upon equal terms of force to maintain it, whether invaded by a single man or many

in combination. Whereas by supposing they have given up themselves to the absolute arbitrary power and will of a legislator, they have disarmed themselves, and armed him to make a prey of them when he pleases; he being in a much worse condition that is exposed to the arbitrary power of one man who has the command of a hundred thousand than he that is exposed to the arbitrary power of a hundred thousand single men, nobody being secure, that his will who has such a command is better than that of other men, though his force be a hundred thousand times stronger. And, therefore, whatever form the commonwealth is under, the ruling power ought to govern by declared and received laws, and not by extemporary dictates and undetermined resolutions, for then mankind will be in a far worse condition than in the state of nature if they shall have armed one or a few men with the joint power of a multitude, to force them to obey at pleasure the exorbitant and unlimited decrees of their sudden thoughts, or unrestrained, and till that moment, unknown wills, without having any measure set down which may guide and justify their actions. For all the power the government has, being only for the good of the society, as it ought not to be arbitrary and at pleasure, so it ought to be exercised by established and promulgated laws, that both the people may know their duty, and be safe and secure within the limits of the law, and the rulers, too, kept within their due bounds, and not to be tempted by the power they have in their hands to employ it to purposes, and by such measures as they would not have known, and own not willingly.

138. *Thirdly,* The supreme power cannot take from any man any part of his property without his own consent. For the preservation of property being the end of government, and that for which men enter into society, it necessarily supposed and requires that the people should have property, without which they must be supposed to lose that by entering into society which was the end for which they entered into it; too gross an absurdity for any man to own. Men therefore in society having property, they have such a right to the goods, which by the law of the community are theirs, that no-

body hath a right to their substance, or any part of it, from them without their own consent; without this they have no property at all. For I have truly no property in that which another can by right take from me when he pleases against my consent. Hence it is a mistake to think that the supreme or legislative power of any commonwealth can do what it will, and dispose of the estates of the subject arbitrarily, or take any part of them at pleasure. This is not much to be feared in governments where the legislative consists wholly or in part in assemblies which are variable, whose members upon the dissolution of the assembly are subjects under the common laws of their country, equally with the rest. But in governments where the legislative is in one lasting assembly, always in being, or in one man as in absolute monarchies, there is danger still, that they will think themselves to have a distinct interest from the rest of the community, and so will be apt to increase their own riches and power by taking what they think fit from the people. For a man's property is not at all secure, though there be good and equitable laws to set the bounds of it between him and his fellow-subjects, if he who commands those subjects have power to take from any private man what part he pleases of his property, and use and dispose of it as he thinks good.

139. But government, into whatsoever hands it is put, being as I have before showed, entrusted with this condition, and for this end, that men might have and secure their properties, the prince or senate, however it may have power to make laws for the regulating of property between the subjects one amongst another, yet can never have a power to take to themselves the whole, or any part of the subjects' property, without their own consent; for this would be in effect to leave them no property at all. And to let us see that even absolute power, where it is necessary, is not arbitrary by being absolute, but is still limited by that reason, and confined to those ends which required it in some cases to be absolute, we need look no farther than the common practice of martial discipline. For the preservation of the army, and in it of the whole commonwealth, requires an absolute obedience to the command

of every superior officer, and it is justly death to disobey or dispute the most dangerous or unreasonable of them; but yet we see that neither the sergeant that could command a soldier to march up to the mouth of a cannon, or stand in a breach where he is almost sure to perish, can command that soldier to give him one penny of his money; nor the general that can condemn him to death for deserting his post, or not obeying the most desperate orders, cannot yet with all his absolute power of life and death dispose of one farthing of that soldier's estate, or seize one jot of his goods; whom yet he can command anything, and hang for the least disobedience. Because such a blind obedience is necessary to that end for which the commander has his power, *viz.* the preservation of the rest, but the disposing of his goods has nothing to do with it.

140. 'Tis true, governments cannot be supported without great charge, and 'tis fit everyone who enjoys his share of the protection should pay out of his estate his proportion for the maintenance of it. But still it must be with his own consent, i.e. the consent of the majority, giving it either by themselves or their representatives chosen by them; for if anyone shall claim a power to lay and levy taxes on the people by his own authority, and without such consent of the people, he thereby invades the fundamental law of property, and subverts the end of government. For what property have I in that which another may be right take when he pleases himself?

141. *Fourthly,* The legislative cannot transfer the power of making laws to any other hands, for it being but a delegated power from the people, they who have it cannot pass it over to others. The people alone can appoint the form of the commonwealth, which is by constituting the legislative, and appointing in whose hands that shall be. And when the people have said, We will submit, and be governed by laws made by such men, and in such forms, nobody else can say other men shall make laws for them; nor can they be bound by any laws but such as are enacted by those whom they have chosen and authorized to make laws for them. The power of the legislative being derived from the people by a positive voluntary

grant and institution, can be no other than what that positive grant conveyed, which being only to make laws, and not to make legislators, the legislative can have no power to transfer their authority of making laws, and place it in other hands.

142. These are the bounds which the trust that is put in them by the society and the law of God and nature have set to the legislative power of every commonwealth, in all forms of government.

First, They are to govern by promulgated established laws, not to be varied in particular cases, but to have one rule for rich and poor, for the favourite at Court, and the countryman at plough.

Secondly, These laws also ought to be designed for no other end ultimately but the good of the people.

Thirdly, They must not raise taxes on the property of the people without the consent of the people given by themselves or their deputies. And this properly concerns only such governments where the legislative is always in being, or at least where the people have not reserved any part of the legislative to deputies, to be from time to time chosen by themselves.

Fourthly, The legislative neither must nor can transfer the power of making laws to anybody else, or place it anywhere but where the people have.[. . .]

XIX. Of the Dissolution of Government

211. He that will with any clearness speak of the dissolution of government, ought in the first place to distinguish between the dissolution of the society and the dissolution of the government. That which makes the community, and brings men out of the loose state of nature into one politic society, is the agreement which every one has with the rest to incorporate and act as one body, and so be one distinct commonwealth. The usual, and almost only way whereby this union is dissolved, is the inroad of foreign force making a conquest upon them. For in that case (not being able to maintain and support themselves as one entire and independent body) the union belonging to that body which consisted therein, must necessarily cease, and so every one return to the state he was in before, with a liberty to shift for himself and provide for his own safety, as he thinks fit, in some other society. Whenever the society is dissolved, 'tis certain the government of that society cannot remain. Thus conquerors' swords often cut up governments by the roots, and mangle societies to pieces, separating the subdued or scattered multitude from the protection of and dependence on that society which ought to have preserved them from violence. The world is too well instructed in, and too forward to allow of this way of dissolving of governments, to need any more to be said of it; and there wants not much argument to prove that where the society is dissolved, the government cannot remain; that being as impossible as for the frame of an house to subsist when the materials of it are scattered and dissipated by a whirlwind, or jumbled into a confused heap by an earthquake.

212. Besides this overturning from without, governments are dissolved from within,

First, When the legislative is altered, civil society being a state of peace amongst those who are of it, from whom the state of war is excluded by the umpirage which they have provided in their legislative for the ending all differences that may arise amongst any of them. 'Tis in their legislative that the members of a commonwealth are united and combined together into one coherent living body. This is the soul that gives form, life, and unity to the commonwealth. From hence the several members have their mutual influence, sympathy, and connexion. And therefore when the legislative is broken, or dissolved, dissolution and death follows. For the essence and union of the society consisting in having one will, the legislative, when once established by the majority has the declaring and, as it were, keeping of that will. The constitution of the legislative is the first and fundamental act of society, whereby provision is made for the continuation of their union under the direction of persons and bonds of laws, made by persons authorized thereunto, by the consent and appointment of the people, without which no one man, or number of men, amongst them can have authority of making laws that shall be binding to the rest. When any one, or more, shall take upon them to make laws whom the people have not appointed so to do, they make laws without authority, which the people are not therefore bound to obey; by which means they come again to be out of subjection, and may constitute to themselves a new legislative, as they think best, being in full liberty to resist the force of those who, without authority, would impose any thing upon them. Every one is at the disposure of his own will, when those who had, by the delegation of the society, the declaring of the public will, are excluded from it, and others usurp the place who have no such authority or delegation.[. . .]

221. There is therefore Secondly another way whereby governments are dissolved, and that is, when the legislative, or the prince, either of them act contrary to their trust.

First, The legislative acts against the trust reposed in them when they endeavour to invade the property of the subject, and to make themselves, or any part of the community, masters or arbitrary disposers of the lives, liberties, or fortunes of the people.

222. The reason why men enter into society is the preservation of their property; and the end why they choose and authorize a legislative is that there may be laws made, and rules set, as guards and fences to the properties of all the members of the society, to limit the power and moderate the dominion of every part and member of the society. For since it can never be supposed to be the will of the society that the legislative should have a power to destroy that which every one designs to secure by entering into society, and for which the people submitted themselves to legislators of their own making: whenever the legislators endeavour to take away and destroy the property of the people, or to reduce them to slavery under arbitrary power, they put themselves into a state of war with the people, who are thereupon absolved from any farther obedience, and are left to the common refuge which God hath provided for all men against force and violence. Whensoever therefore the legislative shall transgress this fundamental rule of society, and either by ambition, fear, folly, or corruption,

endeavour to grasp themselves, or put into the hands of any other, an absolute power over the lives, liberties, and estates of the people, by this breach of trust they forfeit the power the people had put into their hands for quite contrary ends, and it devolves to the people; who have a right to resume their original liberty, and by the establishment of a new legislative (such as they shall think fit), provide for their own safety and security, which is the end for which they are in society. What I have said here concerning the legislative in general holds true also concerning the supreme executor, who having a double trust put in him, both to have a part in the legislative and the supreme execution of the law, acts against both, when he goes about to set up his own arbitrary will as the law of the society. He acts also contrary to his trust when he employs the force, treasure, and offices of the society to corrupt the representatives and gain them to his purposes, when he openly pre-engages the electors, and prescribes, to their choice, such whom he has, by solicitations, threats, promises, or otherwise, won to his designs, and employs them to bring in such who have promised beforehand what to vote and what to enact. Thus to regulate candidates and electors, and new model the ways of election, what is it but to cut up the government by the roots, and poison the very fountain of public security? For the people having reserved to themselves the choice of their representatives as the fence to their properties, could do it for no other end but that they might always be freely chosen, and so chosen, freely act and advise as the necessity of the commonwealth and the public good should, upon examination and mature debate, be judged to require. This, those who give their votes before they hear the debate, and have weighed the reasons on all sides, are not capable of doing. To prepare such an assembly as this, and endeavour to set up the declared abettors of his own will, for the true representatives of the people, and the law-makers of the society, is certainly as great a breach of trust, and as perfect a declaration of a design to subvert the government, as is possible to be met with. To which, if one shall add rewards and punishments visibly employed to the same end, and all the arts of perverted law made use of to take off and destroy all that stand in the way of such a design, and will not comply and consent to betray the liberties of their country, 'twill be past doubt what is doing. What power they ought to have in the society who thus employ it contrary to the trust went along with it in its first institution, is easy to determine; and one cannot but see that he who has once attempted any such thing as this cannot any longer be trusted.

223. To this, perhaps, it will be said, that the people being ignorant and always discontented, to lay the foundation of government in the unsteady opinion and uncertain humour of the people, is to expose it to certain ruin; and no government will be able long to subsist if the people may set up a new legislative whenever they take offence at the old one. To this I answer, quite the contrary. People are not so easily got out of their old forms as some are apt to suggest. They are hardly to be prevailed with to amend the acknowledged faults in the frame they have been accustomed to. And if there be any original defects, or adventitious ones introduced by time or corruption, 'tis not an easy thing to get them changed, even when all the world sees there is an opportunity for it. This slowness and aversion in the people to quit their old constitutions has in the many revolutions (that) have been seen in this kingdom, in this and former ages, still kept us to, or after some interval of fruitless attempts, still brought us back again to our old legislative of king, lords and commons; and whatever provocations have made the crown be taken from some of our princes' heads, they never carried the people so far as to place it in another line.

224. But 'twill be said, this hypothesis lays a ferment for frequent rebellion. To which I answer:

First, No more than any other hypothesis. For when the people are made miserable, and find themselves exposed to the ill usage of arbitrary power; cry up their governors as much as you will for sons of *Jupiter,* let them be sacred and divine, descended or authorized from Heaven; give them out for whom or what you please, the same will happen. The people generally ill treated, and contrary to right, will

be ready upon any occasion to ease themselves of a burden that sits heavy upon them. They will wish and seek for the opportunity, which in the change, weakness, and accidents of humane affairs, seldom delays long to offer it self. He must have lived but a little while in the world, who has not seen examples of this in his time; and he must have read very little who cannot produce examples of it in all sorts of governments in the world.

225. Secondly, I answer, such revolutions happen not upon every little mismanagement in public affairs. Great mistakes in the ruling part, many wrong and inconvenient laws, and all the slips of human frailty will be borne by the people without mutiny or murmur. But if a long train of abuses, prevarications, and artifices, all tending the same way, make the design visible to the people, and they cannot but feel what they lie under, and see whither they are going, 'tis not to be wondered that they should then rouse themselves, and endeavour to put the rule into such hands which may secure to them the ends for which government was at first erected, and without which, ancient names and specious forms are so far from being better, that they are much worse than the state of nature or pure anarchy; the inconveniences being all as great and as near, but the remedy farther off and more difficult.

226. Thirdly, I answer, That this power in the people of providing for their safety anew by a new legislative when their legislators have acted contrary to their trust by invading their property, is the best fence against rebellion, and the probablest means to hinder it. For rebellion being an opposition, not to persons, but authority, which is founded only in the constitutions and laws of the government; those, whoever they be, who by force break through, and by force justify their violation of them, are truly and properly rebels. For when men, by entering into society and civil government, have excluded force, and introduced laws for the preservation of property, peace, and unity amongst themselves; those who set up force again in opposition to the laws, do *rebellare*— that is, bring back again the state of war, and are properly rebels, which they who are in power, by the pretence they have to authority,

the temptation of force they have in their hands, and the flattery of those about them being likeliest to do, the properest way to prevent the evil is to shew them the danger and injustice of it who are under the greatest temptation to run into it.[. . .]

Notes

1. "The public power of all society is above every soul contained in the same society, and the principal use of that power is to give laws unto all that are under it, which laws in such cases we must obey, unless there be reason showed which may necessarily enforce that the law of reason or of God doth enjoin the contrary." Hooker *Eccl. Pol.,* bk. 1, sec. 16.

2. "To take away all such mutual grievances, injuries, and wrongs—i.e., *such as attend men in the state of nature,* there was no way but only by growing into composition and agreement amongst themselves by ordaining some kind of government public, and by yielding themselves subject thereunto, that unto whom they granted authority to rule and govern, by them the peace, tranquility, and happy estate of the rest might be procured. Men always knew that where force and injury were offered, they might be defenders of themselves. They knew that, however men may seek their own commodity, yet if this were done with injury unto others, it was not to be suffered, but by all men and all good means to be withstood. Finally, they knew that no man might, in reason, take upon him to determine his own right, and according to his own determination proceed in maintenance thereof, in as much as every man is towards himself, and them whom he greatly affects, partial; and therefore that strifes and troubles would be endless, except they gave their common consent, all to be ordered by some whom they should agree upon, without which consent there would be no reason that one man should take upon him to be lord or judge over another." Hooker *Eccl. Pol.,* bk. 1, sec. 10.

3. "The lawful power of making laws to command whole politic societies of men, belonging so properly unto the same entire societies, that for any prince or potentate, of what kind soever upon earth, to exercise the same of himself, and not by express com-

mission immediately and personally received from God, or else by authority derived at the first from their consent, upon whose persons they impose laws, it is no better than mere tyranny. Laws they are not, therefore, which public approbation hath not made so." Hooker *Eccl. Pol.,* bk. 1, sec. 10.

"Of this point, therefore, we are to note that such men naturally have no full and perfect power to command whole politic multitudes of men, therefore utterly without our consent we could in such sort be at no man's commandment living. And to be commanded, we do consent when that society, whereof we be a part, hath at any time before consented, without revoking the same after by the like universal agreement. . . . Laws therefore human, of what kind soever, are available by consent." Ibid.

4. "Two foundations there are which bear up public societies; the one a natural inclination whereby all men desire sociable life and fellowship; the other an order, expressly or secretly agreed upon, touching the manner of their union in living together. The latter is that which we call the law of a commonweal, the very soul of a politic body, the parts whereof are by law animated, held together, and set on work in such actions as the common good requireth. Laws politic, ordained for external order and regiment amongst men, are never framed as they should be, unless presuming the will of man to be inwardly obstinate, rebellious, and averse from all obedience to the sacred laws of his nature; in a word, unless presuming man to be in regard of his depraved mind little better than a wild beast, they do accordingly provide notwithstanding, so to frame his outward actions, that they be no hindrance unto the common good, for which societies are instituted. Unless they do this they are not perfect." Hooker *Eccl. Pol.,* bk. 1, sec. 10.

5. "Human laws are measures in respect of men whose actions they must direct, howbeit such measures they are as have also their higher rules to be measured by, which rules are two—the law of God and the law of Nature; so that laws human must be made according to the general laws of Nature, and without contradiction to any positive law of Scripture, otherwise they are ill made." Hooker *Eccl. Pol.,* bk. 3, sec. 9.

"To constrain men to anything inconvenient doth seem unreasonable." Hooker *Eccl. Pol.,* bk. 1, sec. 10.

Of the Original Contract

DAVID HUME

As no party, in the present age, can well support itself without a philosophical or speculative system of principles annexed to its political or practical one, we accordingly find, that each of the factions into which this nation is divided has reared up a fabric of the former kind, in order to protect and cover that scheme of actions which it pursues. The people being commonly very rude builders, especially in this speculative way, and more especially still when actuated by party-zeal, it is natural to imagine that their workmanship must be a little unshapely, and discover evident marks of that violence and hurry in which it was raised. The one party, by tracing up government to the Deity, endeavoured to render it so sacred and inviolate, that it must be little less than sacrilege, however tyrannical it may become, to touch or invade it in the smallest article. The other party, by founding government altogether on the consent of the people, suppose that there is a kind of *original contract,* by which the subjects have tacitly reserved the power of resisting their sovereign, whenever they find themselves aggrieved by that authority, with which they have, for certain purposes, voluntarily intrusted him. These are the speculative principles of the two parties, and these, too, are the practical consequences deduced from them.

I shall venture to affirm, *That both these systems of speculative principles are just; though not in the sense intended by the parties:* and, *That both the schemes of practical consequences are prudent; though not in the extremes to which each party, in opposition to the other, has commonly endeavoured to carry them.*

That the Deity is the ultimate author of all government, will never be denied by any, who admit a general providence, and allow, that all events in the universe are conducted by an uniform plan, and directed to wise purposes. As it is impossible for the human race to subsist, at least in any comfortable or secure state, without the protection of government, this institution must certainly have been intended by that beneficent Being, who means the good of all his creatures: and as it has universally, in fact, taken place, in all countries, and all ages, we may conclude, with still greater certainty, that it was intended by that omniscient Being who can never be deceived by any event or operation. But since he gave rise to it, not by any particular or miraculous interposition, but by his concealed and universal efficacy, a sovereign cannot, properly speaking, be called his vicegerent in any other sense than every power or force, being derived from him, may be said to act by his commission. Whatever actually happens is comprehended in the general plan or intention of Providence; nor has the greatest and most lawful prince any more reason, upon that account, to plead a peculiar sacredness or inviolable authority, than an inferior magistrate, or even an usurper, or even a robber and a pirate. The same Divine Superintendent, who, for wise purposes, invested a Titus or a Trajan with authority, did also, for purposes no doubt equally wise, though unknown, bestow power on a Borgia or an Angria. The same causes, which gave rise to the sovereign power in every state, established likewise every petty jurisdiction in it, and every limited authority. A constable, therefore, no less than a king, acts by a divine commission, and possesses an indefeasible right.

When we consider how nearly equal all men are in their bodily force, and even in their mental powers and faculties, till cultivated by education, we must necessarily allow, that nothing but their own consent could, at first, associate them together, and subject them to any authority. The people, if we trace government to its first origin in the woods and deserts, are the source of all power and jurisdiction, and voluntarily, for the sake of peace and order, abandoned their native liberty, and received laws from their equal and companion. The conditions upon which they were willing to submit, were either expressed, or were so clear and obvious, that it might well be esteemed superfluous to express them. If this, then, be meant by the *original contract,* it cannot be denied, that all government is, at first, founded on a contract, and that the most ancient rude combinations of mankind were formed chiefly by that principle. In vain are we asked in what records this charter of our liberties is registered. It was not written on parchment, nor yet on leaves or barks of trees. It preceded the use of writing, and all the other civilized arts of life. But we trace it plainly in the nature of man, and in the equality, or something approaching equality, which we find in all the individuals of that species. The force, which now prevails, and which is founded on fleets and armies, is plainly political, and derived from authority, the effect of established government. A man's natural force consists only in the vigour of his limbs, and the firmness of his courage; which could never subject multitudes to the command of one. Nothing but

their own consent, and their sense of the advantages resulting from peace and order, could have had that influence.

Yet even this consent was long very imperfect, and could not be the basis of a regular administration. The chieftain, who had probably acquired his influence during the continuance of war, ruled more by persuasion than command; and till he could employ force to reduce the refractory and disobedient, the society could scarcely be said to have attained a state of civil government. No compact or agreement, it is evident, was expressly formed for general submission; an idea far beyond the comprehension of savages: each exertion of authority in the chieftain must have been particular, and called forth by the present exigencies of the case: the sensible utility, resulting from his interposition, made these exertions become daily more frequent; and their frequency gradually produced an habitual, and, if you please to call it so, a voluntary, and therefore precarious, acquiescence in the people.

But philosophers, who have embraced a party (if that be not a contradiction in terms), are not contented with these concessions. They assert, not only that government in its earliest infancy arose from consent, or rather the voluntary acquiescence of the people; but also that, even at present, when it has attained its full maturity, it rests on no other foundation. They affirm, that all men are still born equal, and owe allegiance to no prince or government, unless bound by the obligation and sanction of a *promise.* And as no man, without some equivalent, would forego the advantages of his native liberty, and subject himself to the will of another, this promise is always understood to be conditional, and imposes on him no obligation, unless he meet with justice and protection from his sovereign. These advantages the sovereign promises him in return; and if he fail in the execution, he has broken, on his part, the articles of engagement, and has thereby freed his subject from all obligations to allegiance. Such, according to these philosophers, is the foundation of authority in every government, and such the right of resistance possessed by every subject.

But would these reasoners look abroad into the world, they would meet with nothing that, in the least, corresponds to their ideas, or can warrant so refined and philosophical a system. On the contrary, we find every where princes who claim their subjects as their property, and assert their independent right of sovereignty, from conquest or succession. We find also every where subjects who acknowledge this right in their prince, and suppose themselves born under obligations of obedience to a certain sovereign, as much as under the ties of reverence and duty to certain parents. These connexions are always conceived to be equally independent of our consent, in Persia and China; in France and Spain; and even in Holland and England, wherever the doctrines above-mentioned have not been carefully inculcated. Obedience or subjection becomes so familiar, that most men never make any inquiry about its origin or cause, more than about the principle of gravity, resistance, or the most universal laws of nature. Or if curiosity ever move them; as soon as they learn that they themselves and their ancestors have, for several ages, or from time immemorial, been subject to such a form of government or such a family, they immediately acquiesce, and acknowledge their obligation to allegiance. Were you to preach, in most parts of the world, that political connexions are founded altogether on voluntary consent or mutual promise, the magistrate would soon imprison you as seditious for loosening the ties of obedience; if your friends did not before shut you up as delirious, for advancing such absurdities. It is strange that an act of the mind, which every individual is supposed to have formed, and after he came to the use of reason too, otherwise it could have no authority; that this act, I say, should be so much unknown to all of them, that over the face of the whole earth, there scarcely remain any traces or memory of it.

But the contract, on which government is founded, is said to be the *original contract;* and consequently may be supposed too old to fall under the knowledge of the present generation. If the agreement, by which savage men first associated and conjoined their force, be

here meant, this is acknowledged to be real; but being so ancient, and being obliterated by a thousand changes of government and princes, it cannot now be supposed to retain any authority. If we would say any thing to the purpose, we must assert that every particular government which is lawful, and which imposes any duty of allegiance on the subject, was, at first, founded on consent and a voluntary compact. But, besides that this supposes the consent of the fathers to bind the children, even to the most remote generations (which republican writers will never allow), besides this, I say, it is not justified by history or experience in any age or country of the world.

Almost all the governments which exist at present, or of which there remains any record in story, have been founded originally, either on usurpation or conquest, or both, without any pretence of a fair consent or voluntary subjection of the people. When an artful and bold man is placed at the head of an army or faction, it is often easy for him, by employing, sometimes violence, sometimes false pretences, to establish his dominion over a people a hundred times more numerous than his partisans. He allows no such open communication, that his enemies can know, with certainty, their number or force. He gives them no leisure to assemble together in a body to oppose him. Even all those who are the instruments of his usurpation may wish his fall; but their ignorance of each other's intention keeps them in awe, and is the sole cause of his security. By such arts as these many governments have been established; and this is all the *original contract* which they have to boast of.

The face of the earth is continually changing, by the increase of small kingdoms into great empires, by the dissolution of great empires into smaller kingdoms, by the planting of colonies, by the migration of tribes. Is there any thing discoverable in all these events but force and violence? Where is the mutual agreement or voluntary association so much talked of?

Even the smoothest way by which a nation may receive a foreign master, by marriage or a will, is not extremely honourable for the people; but supposes them to be disposed of, like a dowry or a legacy, according to the pleasure or interest of their rulers.

But where no force interposes, and election takes place; what is this election so highly vaunted? It is either the combination of a few great men, who decide for the whole, and will allow of no opposition; or it is the fury of a multitude, that follow a seditious ringleader, who is not known, perhaps, to a dozen among them, and who owes his advancement merely to his own impudence, or to the momentary caprice of his fellows.

Are these disorderly elections, which are rare too, of such mighty authority as to be the only lawful foundation of all government and allegiance?

In reality, there is not a more terrible event that a total dissolution of government, which gives liberty to the multitude, and makes the determination or choice of a new establishment depend upon a number, which nearly approaches to that of the body of people: for it never comes entirely to the whole body of them. Every wise man then wishes to see, at the head of a powerful and obedient army, a general who may speedily seize the prize, and give to the people a master which they are so unfit to choose for themselves. So little correspondent is fact and reality to those philosophical notions.

Let not the establishment at the *Revolution* deceive us, or make us so much in love with a philosophical origin to government, as to imagine all others monstrous and irregular. Even that event was far from corresponding to these refined ideas. It was only the succession, and that only in the regal part of the government, which was then changed: and it was only the majority of seven hundred, who determined that change for near ten millions. I doubt not, indeed, but the bulk of those ten millions acquiesced willingly in the determination: but was the matter left, in the least, to their choice? Was it not justly supposed to be, from that moment, decided, and every man punished, who refused to submit to the new sovereign? How otherwise could the matter have ever been brought to any issue or conclusion?

The republic of Athens was, I believe, the most extensive democracy that we read of in history: yet if we make the requisite allowances for the women, the slaves, and the strangers, we shall find, that that establishment was not at first made, nor any law ever voted, by a tenth part of those who were bound to pay obedience to it; not to mention the islands and foreign dominions, which the Athenians claimed as theirs by right of conquest. And as it is well known that popular assemblies in that city were always full of license and disorder, not withstanding the institutions and laws by which they were checked; how much more disorderly must they prove, where they form not the established constitution, but meet tumultuously on the dissolution of the ancient government, in order to give rise to a new one? How chimerical must it be to talk of a choice in such circumstances?

The Achæans enjoyed the freest and most perfect democracy of all antiquity; yet they employed force to oblige some cities to enter into their league, as we learn from Polybius.

Harry the IVth and Harry the VIIth of England, had really no title to the throne but a parliamentary election; yet they never would acknowledge it, lest they should thereby weaken their authority. Strange, if the only real foundation of all authority be consent and promise?

It is in vain to say, that all governments are, or should be, at first, founded on popular consent, as much as the necessity of human affairs will admit. This favours entirely my pretension. I maintain, that human affairs will never admit of this consent, seldom of the appearance of it; but that conquest or usurpation, that is, in plain terms, force, by dissolving the ancient governments, is the origin of almost all the new ones which were ever established in the world. And that in the few cases where consent may seem to have taken place, it was commonly so irregular, so confined, or so much intermixed either with fraud or violence, that it cannot have any great authority.

My intention here is not to exclude the consent of the people from being one just foundation of government where it has place. It is surely the best and most sacred of any. I only pretend, that it has very seldom had place in any degree, and never almost in its full extent; and that, therefore, some other foundation of government must also be admitted.

Were all men possessed of so inflexible a regard to justice, that, of themselves, they would totally abstain from the properties of others; they had for ever remained in a state of absolute liberty, without subjection to any magistrate or political society: but this is a state of perfection, of which human nature is justly deemed incapable. Again, were all men possessed of so perfect an understanding as always to know their own interests, no form of government had ever been submitted to but what was established on consent, and was fully canvassed by every member of the society: but this state of perfection is likewise much superior to human nature. Reason, history, and experience shew us, that all political societies have had an origin much less accurate and regular; and were one to choose a period of time when the people's consent was the least regarded in public transactions, it would be precisely on the establishment of a new government. In a settled constitution their inclinations are often consulted; but during the fury of revolutions, conquests, and public convulsions, military force or political craft usually decides the controversy.

When a new government is established, by whatever means, the people are commonly dissatisfied with it, and pay obedience more from fear and necessity, than from any idea of allegiance or of moral obligation. The prince is watchful and jealous, and must carefully guard against every beginning or appearance or insurrection. Time, by degrees, removes all these difficulties, and accustoms the nation to regard, as their lawful or native princes, that family which at first they considered as usurpers or foreign conquerors. In order to found this opinion, they have no recourse to any notion of voluntary consent or promise, which, they know, never was, in this case, either expected or demanded. The original establishment was formed by violence, and submitted to from necessity. The subsequent administration is also supported by power, and acquiesced in by the people, not as a matter of choice, but of obligation. They imagine not that their consent gives their prince a title: but they willingly consent, because they think, that, from long possession, he has acquired a title, independent of their choice or inclination.

Should it be said, that, by living under the dominion of a prince which one might leave, every individual has given a *tacit* consent to his authority, and promised him obedience; it may be answered, that such an implied consent can only have place where a man imagines that the matter depends on his choice. But where he thinks (as all mankind do who are born under established governments) that, by his birth, he owes allegiance to a certain prince or certain form of government; it would be absurd to infer a consent or choice, which he expressly, in this case, renounces and disclaims.

Can we seriously say, that a poor peasant or artisan has a free choice to leave his country, when he knows no foreign language or manners, and lives, from day to day, by the small wages which he acquires? We may as well assert that a man, by remaining in a vessel, freely consents to the dominion of the master; though he was carried on board while asleep, and must leap into the ocean and perish, the moment he leaves her.

What if the prince forbid his subjects to quit his dominions; as in Tiberius's time, it was regarded as a crime in a Roman knight that he had attempted to fly to the Parthians, in order to escape the tyranny of that emperor?[1] Or as the ancient Muscovites prohibited all travelling under pain of death? And did a prince observe, that many of his subjects were seized with the frenzy of migrating to foreign countries, he would, doubtless, with great reason and justice, restrain them, in order to prevent the depopulation of his own kingdom. Would he forfeit the allegiance of all his subjects by so wise and reasonable a law? Yet the freedom of their choice is surely, in that case, ravished from them.

A company of men, who should leave their native country, in order to people some uninhabited region, might dream of recovering their native freedom; but would soon find, that their prince still laid claim to them, and called them his subjects, even in their new settlement. And in this he would but act conformably to the common ideas of mankind.

The truest *tacit* consent of this kind that is ever observed, is when a foreigner settles in any country, and is beforehand acquainted with the prince, and government, and laws, to which he must submit: yet is his allegiance, though more voluntary, much less expected or depended on, than that of a natural born subject. On the contrary, his native prince still asserts a claim to him. And if he punish not the renegade, when he seizes him in war with his new prince's commission; this clemency is not founded on the municipal law, which in all countries condemns the prisoner; but on the consent of princes, who have agreed to this indulgence, in order to prevent reprisals.

Did one generation of men go off the stage at once, and another succeed, as is the case with silkworms and butterflies, the new race, if they had sense enough to choose their government, which surely is never the case with men, might voluntarily, and by general consent, establish their own form of civil polity, without any regard to the laws or precedents which prevailed among their ancestors. But as human society is in perpetual flux, one man every hour going out of the world, another coming into it, it is necessary, in order to preserve stability in government, that the new brood should conform themselves to the established constitution, and nearly follow the path which their fathers, treading in the footsteps of theirs, had marked out to them. Some innovations must necessarily have place in every human institution; and it is happy where the enlightened genius of the age give these a direction to the side of reason, liberty, and justice: but violent innovations no individual is entitled to make: they are even dangerous to be attempted by the legislature: more ill than good is ever to be expected from them: and if history affords examples to the contrary, they are not to be drawn into precedent, and are only to be regarded as proofs, that the science of politics affords few rules, which will not admit of some exception, and which may not sometimes be controlled by fortune and accident. The violent innovations in the reign of

Henry VIII proceeded from an imperious monarch, seconded by the appearance of legislative authority: those in the reign of Charles I were derived from faction and fanaticism; and both of them have proved happy in the issue. But even the former were long the source of many disorders, and still more dangers; and if the measures of allegiance were to be taken from the latter, a total anarchy must have place in human society, and a final period at once be put to every government.

Suppose that an usurper, after having banished his lawful prince and royal family, should establish his dominion for ten or a dozen years in any country, and should preserve so exact a discipline in his troops, and so regular a disposition in his garrisons that no insurrection had ever been raised, or even murmur heard against his administration: can it be asserted that the people, who in their hearts abhor his treason, have tacitly consented to his authority, and promised him allegiance, merely because, from necessity, they live under his dominion? Suppose again their native prince restored, by means of an army, which he levies in foreign countries: they receive him with joy and exultation, and shew plainly with what reluctance they had submitted to any other yoke. I may now ask, upon what foundation the prince's title stands? Not on popular consent surely: for though the people willingly acquiesce in his authority, they never imagine that their consent made him sovereign. They consent; because they apprehend him to be already by birth, their lawful sovereign. And as to that tacit consent, which may now be inferred from their living under his dominion, this is no more than what they formerly gave to the tyrant and usurper.

When we assert, that all lawful government arises from the consent of the people, we certainly do them a great deal more honour than they deserve, or even expect and desire from us. After the Roman dominions became too unwieldy for the republic to govern them, the people over the whole known world were extremely grateful to Augustus for that authority which, by violence, he had established over them; and they shewed an equal disposition to submit to the successor whom he left them by his last will and testament. It was afterwards their misfortune, that there never was, in one family, any long regular succession; but that their line of princes was continually broken, either by private assassinations or public rebellions. The *prætorian* bands, on the failure of every family, set up one emperor; the legions in the East a second; those in Germany, perhaps a third; and the sword alone could decide the controversy. The condition of the people in that mighty monarchy was to be lamented, not because the choice of the emperor was never left to them, for that was impracticable, but because they never fell under any succession of masters who might regularly follow each other. As to the violence, and wars, and bloodshed, occasioned by every new settlement, these were not blameable, because they were inevitable.

The house of Lancaster ruled in this island about sixty years; yet the partisans of the white rose seemed daily to multiply in England. The present establishment has taken place during a still longer period. Have all views of right in another family been utterly extinguished, even though scarce any man now alive had arrived at the years of discretion when it was expelled, or could have consented to its dominion, or have promised it allegiance?—a sufficient indication, surely, of the general sentiment of mankind on this head. For we blame not the partisans of the abdicated family merely on account of the long time during which they have preserved their imaginary loyalty. We blame them for adhering to a family which we affirm has been justly expelled, and which, from the moment the new settlement took place, had forfeited all title to authority.

But would we have a more regular, at least a more philosophical, refutation of this principle of an original contract, or popular consent, perhaps the following observations may suffice.

All *moral* duties may be divided into two kinds. The *first* are those to which men are impelled by a natural instinct or immediate propensity which operates on them, independent of all ideas of obligation, and of all views either to public or private utility. Of this nature are love of children, gratitude to benefactors,

pity to the unfortunate. When we reflect on the advantage which results to society from such humane instincts, we pay them the just tribute of moral approbation and esteem: but the person actuated by them feels their power and influence antecedent to any such reflection.

The *second* kind of moral duties are such as are not supported by any original instinct of nature, but are performed entirely from a sense of obligation, when we consider the necessities of human society, and the impossibility of supporting it, if these duties were neglected. It is thus *justice,* or a regard to the property of others, *fidelity,* or the observance of promises, become obligatory, and acquire an authority over mankind. For as it is evident that every man loves himself better than any other person, he is naturally impelled to extend his acquisitions as much as possible; and nothing can restrain him in this propensity but reflection and experience, by which he learns the pernicious effects of that license, and the total dissolution of society which must ensue from it. His original inclination, therefore, or instinct, is here checked and restrained by a subsequent judgment or observation.

The case is precisely the same with the political or civil duty of *allegiance* as with the natural duties of justice and fidelity. Our primary instincts lead us either to indulge ourselves in unlimited freedom, or to seek dominion over others; and it is reflection only which engages us to sacrifice such strong passions to the interest of peace and public order. A small degree of experience and observation suffices to teach us, that society cannot possibly be maintained without the authority of magistrates, and that this authority must soon fall into contempt where exact obedience is not paid to it. The observation of these general and obvious interests is the source of all allegiance, and of that moral obligation which we attribute to it.

What necessity, therefore, is there to found the duty of *allegiance* or obedience to magistrates on that of *fidelity* or a regard to promises, and to suppose, that it is the consent of each individual which subjects him to government, when it appears that both allegiance and fidelity stand precisely on the same foundation, and are both submitted to by mankind, on account of the apparent interests and necessities of human society? We are bound to obey our sovereign, it is said, because we have given a tacit promise to that purpose. But why are we bound to observe our promise? It must here be asserted, that the commerce and intercourse of mankind, which are of such mighty advantage, can have no security where men pay no regard to their engagements. In like manner, may it be said that men could not live at all in society, at least in a civilized society, without laws, and magistrates, and judges, to prevent the encroachments of the strong upon the weak, of the violent upon the just and equitable. The obligation to allegiance being of like force and authority with the obligation to fidelity, we gain nothing by resolving the one into the other. The general interests or necessities of society are sufficient to establish both.

If the reason be asked of that obedience, which we are bound to pay to government, I readily answer, *Because society could not otherwise subsist;* and this answer is clear and intelligible to all mankind. Your answer is, *Because we should keep our word.* But besides, that no body, till trained in a philosophical system, can either comprehend or relish this answer; besides this, I say, you find yourself embarassed when it is asked, *Why we are bound to keep our word?* Nor can you give any answer but what would, immediately, without any circuit, have accounted for our obligation to allegiance.

But *to whom is allegiance due? And who is our lawful sovereign?* This question is often the most difficult of any, and liable to infinite discussions. When people are so happy that they can answer, *Our present sovereign, who inherits, in a direct line, from ancestors that have governed us for many ages,* this answer admits of no reply, even though historians, in tracing up to the remotest antiquity the origin of that royal family, may find, as commonly happens, that its first authority was derived from usurpation and violence. It is confessed that private justice, or the abstinence from the properties of others, is a most cardinal virtue. Yet reason tells us that there is no property in durable objects, such as lands or houses, when

carefully examined in passing from hand to hand, but must, in some period, have been founded on fraud and injustice. The necessities of human society, neither in private nor public life, will allow of such an accurate inquiry; and there is no virtue or moral duty but what may, with facility, be refined away, if we indulge a false philosophy in sifting and scrutinizing it, by every captious rule of logic, in every light or position in which it may be placed.

The questions with regard to private property have filled infinite volumes of law and philosophy, if in both we add the commentators to the original text; and in the end, we may safely pronounce, that many of the rules there established are uncertain, ambiguous, and arbitrary. The like opinion may be formed with regard to the succession and rights of princes, and forms of government. Several cases no doubt occur, especially in the infancy of any constitution, which admit of no determination from the laws of justice and equity; and our historian Rapin pretends, that the controversy between Edward the Third and Philip de Valois was of this nature, and could be decided only by an appeal to heaven, that is, by war and violence.

Who shall tell me, whether Germanicus or Drusus ought to have succeeded to Tiberius, had he died while they were both alive, without naming any of them for his successor? Ought the right of adoption to be received as equivalent to that of blood, in a nation where it had the same effect in private families, and had already, in two instances, taken place in the public? Ought Germanicus to be esteemed the elder son, because he was born before Drusus; or the younger, because he was adopted after the birth of his brother? Ought the right of the elder to be regarded in a nation, where he had no advantage in the succession of private families? Ought the Roman empire at that time to be deemed hereditary, because of two examples; or ought it, even so early, to be regarded as belonging to the stronger, or to the present possessor, as being founded on so recent an usurpation?

Commodus mounted the throne after a pretty long succession of excellent emperors, who had acquired their title, not by birth, or public election, but by the fictitious rite of adoption. That bloody debauchee being murdered by a conspiracy, suddenly formed between his wench and her gallant, who happened at that time to be *Prætorian Præfect;* these immediately deliberated about choosing a master to human kind, to speak in the style of those ages; and they cast their eyes on Pertinax. Before the tyrant's death was known, the *Præfect* went secretly to that senator, who, on the appearance of the soldiers, imagined that his execution had been ordered by Commodus. He was immediately saluted emperor by the office and his attendants, cheerfully proclaimed by the populace, unwillingly submitted to by the guards, formally recognized by the senate, and passively received by the provinces and armies of the empire.

The discontent of the *Prætorian* bands broke out in a sudden sedition, which occasioned the murder of that excellent prince; and the world being now without a master, and without government, the guards thought proper to set the empire formally to sale. Julian, the purchaser, was proclaimed by the soldiers, recognized by the senate, and submitted to by the people; and must also have been submitted to by the provinces, had not the envy of the legions begotten opposition and resistance. Pescennius Niger in Syria elected himself emperor, gained the tumultuary consent of his army, and was attended with the secret good-will of the senate and people of Rome. Albinus in Britain found an equal right to set up his claim; but Severus, who governed Pannonia, prevailed in the end above both of them. That able politician and warrior, finding his own birth and dignity too much inferior to the imperial crown, professed, at first, an intention only of revenging the death of Pertinax. He marched as general into Italy, defeated Julian, and, without our being able to fix any precise commencement even of the soldiers' consent, he was from necessity acknowledged emperor by the senate and people, and fully established in his violent authority, by subduing Niger and Albinus.

Inter hæc Gordianus Cæsar (says Capitolinus, speaking of another period) *sublatus a militibus.* Imperator *est appellatus, quia non erat alius in præsenti.* It is to be remarked, that Gordian was a boy of fourteen years of age.

Frequent instances of a like nature occur in the history of the emperors; in that of Alexander's successors; and of many other countries: nor can any thing be more unhappy than a despotic government of this kind; where the succession is disjointed and irregular, and must be determined, on every vacancy, by force or election. In a free government, the matter is often unavoidable, and is also much less dangerous. The interests of liberty may there frequently lead the people, in their own defence, to alter the succession of the crown. And the constitution, being compounded of parts, may still maintain a sufficient stability, by resting on the aristocratical or democratical members, though the monarchical be altered, from time to time, in order to accommodate it to the former.

In an absolute government, when there is no legal prince who has a title to the throne, it may safely be determined to belong to the first occupant. Instances of this kind are but too frequent, especially in the eastern monarchies. When any race of princes expires, the will or destination of the last sovereign will be regarded as a title. Thus the edict of Louis the XIVth, who called the bastard princes to the succession in case of the failure of all the legitimate princes, would, in such an event, have some authority.[2] Thus the will of Charles the Second disposed of the whole Spanish monarchy. The cession of the ancient proprietor, especially when joined to conquest, is likewise deemed a good title. The general obligation, which binds us to government, is the interest and necessities of society; and this obligation is very strong. The determination of it to this or that particular prince, or form of government, is frequently more uncertain and dubious. Present possession has considerable authority in these cases, and greater than in private property; because of the disorders which attend all revolutions and changes of government.

We shall only observe, before we conclude, that though an appeal to general opinion may justly, in the speculative sciences of metaphysics, natural philosophy, or astronomy, be deemed unfair and inconclusive, yet in all questions with regard to morals, as well as criticism, there is really no other standard, by which any controversy can ever be decided. And nothing is a clearer proof, that a theory of this kind is erroneous, than to find, that it leads to paradoxes repugnant to the common sentiments of mankind, and to the practice and opinion of all nations and all ages. The doctrine, which founds all lawful government on an *original contract,* or consent of the people, is plainly of this kind; nor has the most noted of its partisans, in prosecution of it, scrupled to affirm, *that absolute monarchy is inconsistent with civil society, and so can be no form of civil government at all;*[3] and *that the supreme power in a state cannot take from any man, by taxes and impositions, any part of his property, without his own consent or that of his representatives.*[4] What authority any moral reasoning can have, which leads into opinions so wide of the general practice of mankind, in every place but this single kingdom, it is easy to determine.

The only passage I meet with in antiquity, where the obligation of obedience to government is ascribed to a promise, is in Plato's *Crito;* where Socrates refuses to escape from prison, because he had tacitly promised to obey the laws. Thus he builds a *Tory* consequence of passive obedience on a *Whig* foundation of the original contract.

New discoveries are not to be expected in these matters. If scarce any man, till very lately, ever imagined that government was founded on compact, it is certain that it cannot, in general, have any such foundation.

The crime of rebellion among the ancients was commonly expressed by the terms νεωτερίζειν, *novas res moliri.*

Notes

1. Tacitus *Ann.,* bk. 6, cap. 14.
2. It is remarkable, that in the remonstrance of the Duke of Bourbon and the legitimate princes, against this destination of Louis the XIVth, the doctrine of the *original contract* is insisted on, even in that absolute government. The French nation, say they, choosing Hugh Capet and his posterity to rule over them and their posterity, where the former line fails, there is a tacit right reserved to choose a new royal family; and this right is invaded by calling the bastard princes to the throne, without the consent of the nation. But the Comte de Boulainvilliers, who wrote in defence of the bastard princes, ridicules this notion of an original contract, especially when applied to Hugh Capet; who mounted the throne, says he, by the same arts which have ever been employed by all conquerors and usurpers. He got his title, indeed, recognized by the states after he had put himself in possession: but is this a choice or contract? The Comte de Boulainvilliers, we may observe, was a noted republican; but being a man of learning, and very conversant in history, he knew that the people were almost never consulted in these revolutions and new establishments, and that time alone bestowed right and authority on what was commonly at first founded on force and violence. See *État de la France,* vol. 3.
3. Locke, Second Treatise of Civil Government, chap. 7, sec. 90.
4. Ibid., chap. 11, secs 138–140.

Obligation and Consent, II

HANNA F. PITKIN

A reexamination of even the most venerable traditional problems of political theory can
sometimes yield surprisingly new and relevant
results.[1] The problem of political obligation, for
example, and its most popular "solution," based
on consent, turn out on reexamination to be
rather different from what we have come to assume about them. The problem of political obligation resolves itself into at least four mutually
related but partially independent questions:

1. The limits of obligation ("*When* are you
   obligated to obey, and when not?")
2. The locus of sovereignty ("*Whom* are you
   obligated to obey?")
3. The difference between legitimate authority
   and mere coercion ("Is there *really* any difference; are you ever *really* obligated?")
4. The justification of obligation ("*Why* are
   you ever obligated to obey even a legitimate
   authority?")

And the consent theory of obligation, as
exemplified in Locke's *Second Treatise* and
Joseph Tussman's *Obligation and the Body
Politic,* turns out to yield a new formulation—
perhaps a new interpretation of consent theory,
perhaps an alternative to it—that might be labelled either the doctrine of the "nature of the
government" or the doctrine of "hypothetical
consent."[2]

It teaches that your obligation depends not
on any actual act of consenting, past or present,
by yourself or your fellow-citizens, but on the
character of the government. If it is a good,
just government doing what a government
should, then you must obey it; if it is a tyrannical, unjust government trying to do what no
government may, then you have no such obligation. Or to put it another way, your obligation depends not on whether you have
consented but on whether the government is
such that you *ought* to consent to it, whether
its actions are in accord with the authority a
hypothetical group of rational men in a hypothetical state of nature would have (had) to
give to any government they were founding.
Having shown how this formulation emerges
from Locke's and Tussman's ideas, I want now
to defend it as a valid response to what troubles
us about political obligation, and as a response
more consonant than most with the moral realities of human decisions about obedience and
resistance. At the same time the discussion
should also demonstrate how many different or
even conflicting things that one might want to
call "consent" continue to be relevant—a fact
which may help to explain the tenacity of
traditional consent theory in the face of its
manifest difficulties. Such a defense and demonstration, with a detailed attention to such decisions, are difficult; the discussion from here

Hanna F. Pitkin, "Obligation and Consent, II," from *American Political Science Review*, 60 (1966): 39–52. Reprinted by permission of the author and publisher.

on will be more speculative, and will raise more questions than it answers.

1. The Theory Applied

Our new doctrine seems most obviously satisfactory as a response to question three, concerning the difference between legitimate authority and mere coercion. For it teaches that legitimate authority is precisely that which *ought* to be obeyed, to which one ought to consent, which deserves obedience and consent, to which rational men considering all relevant facts and issues would consent, to which consent can be justified. Anything or anyone else who tries to command us is then merely coercing, and is not entitled to our obedience. This answer to the question is essentially what Wittgenstein calls a "point of grammar"; it reminds us of the way concepts like "authority," "legitimacy," "law" are related in our language (and therefore in our world) to concepts like "consent" and "obedience."[3] To call something a legitimate authority is normally to imply that it ought to be obeyed. You cannot, without further rather elaborate explanation, maintain simultaneously *both* that this government has legitimate authority over you *and* that you have no obligation to obey it. Thus if you say that you consent to it (recognize it as an authority), that statement itself is normally a recognition of the obligation to obey, at least at the moment it is uttered. Part of what "authority" means is that those subject to it are obligated to obey. As an answer to question three, then, this doctrine tells us (something about) what legitimate authority *is* by reminding us of something about what "legitimate authority" *means*. But of course that is not yet to provide criteria for telling apart the two species—legitimate authority and mere coercion—when you encounter them in reality.

Thus, insofar as our *real* need is for a practical way of deciding whether to obey or resist this government right now, or which of two rival authorities to follow, our new theory seems less adequate. Its response to our question three does not seem immediately helpful with questions one and two; and surely those are of the most concern to real people confronted with decisions about action. It just does not seem very helpful to tell a man considering resistance to authority: you must obey if the government is such that you ought to obey. But neither is traditional consent theory very helpful to this man; indeed, one of its weaknesses has always been this matter of detailed application. Perhaps it is even a mistake to assume that a theory of political obligation is supposed to tell a man directly what to do in particular cases.[4]

One might argue, however, that such a theory should at least tell him what sorts of considerations are relevant to his decision, direct his attention and tell him where to look.[5] And in that regard, I suggest that traditional consent theory is defective, for it directs such a man's attention to the wrong place. It teaches him to look at himself (for his own consent) or at people around him (for theirs), rather than at the merits of the government. Where it demands obedience, consent theory does so on the grounds that he or the majority have consented; where it justifies resistance, it does so on the grounds that consent was never given or has been exceeded. Thus the man who must choose is directed to the question: have I (we) consented to this? The new doctrine formulated in this essay seems at least to have the virtue of pointing such a man in the right direction. For it tells him: look to the nature of the government—its characteristics, structure, activities, functioning. This is not much of a guide, but it is a beginning much more usefully related to what men need to think about when they make such choices.

Let us consider seriously what sorts of things people really think about when they confront a genuine decision about obedience and resistance, and what sorts of things they ought to think about. But anyone who undertakes to do that is immediately overwhelmed by the complexity and multiplicity of what seems relevant, and by the many different imaginable cases. We need to consider a list of specific cases at least as diverse as these:

Socrates, as presented in the *Crito* and the *Apology*.
An ordinary criminal.

An American student engaging in civil disobedience.

A Mississippi Negro who decides to join a revolutionary group.

A South African Negro who decides to join a revolutionary group.

A minor official in Nazi Germany, who continues to carry out his functions.

Even a brief review of such cases teaches at least this much: the occasions for contemplating and possibly engaging in disobedience are extremely varied; and a great many kinds of non-obedience are available, from flight through crime to attempted revolution.[6] Some forms of non-obedience are violent, others not; some are personal and others organized; some are isolated actions and others a systematic program of action; some are directed against a particular law or decree and others against an entire system of government. To a person confronted with a real decision about resistance or obedience, it makes an enormous difference what kind of action is contemplated. Circumstances that may justify escape or isolated refusal to obey a particular law may not suffice to justify revolution; indeed, some forms of resistance (like civil disobedience) may even be provided for within a political system.

Next, we may notice that all of our examples are, or could reasonably be, people in conflict. Socrates may never have been in doubt as to what he would do, but his friends certainly disagreed with him at first; and he cast his own argument in the form of a confrontation between the desire "to play truant" and the admonitions of the laws. All of our examples (with the exception of the criminal?) might have good, serious reasons for resistance. None of them ought to feel entirely free to pursue those reasons without first weighing them against something else—his prima facie obligation to obey. One might say: all these men ought to feel a certain tie to their governments, their societies, in the sense in which Socrates feels such a tie, but some of them might nevertheless be justified in disobeying or resisting. That he does not sufficiently feel such a tie, that he has no (good) reason, no justification for disobedience, is precisely what makes the case of an "ordinary" criminal different from

the rest. This is at least in accord with the formula offered by our new theory: normally law, authority, government are to be obeyed and resistance requires justification. You are not morally free to resist as a matter of whim.

The real person confronted by a problematic situation about obedience needs to know that, but he obviously needs to know much more. He needs to know much more specifically when resistance is justified and what might count as a justification. Does he learn this by thinking about his own past consent or that of his fellow-citizens, as traditional consent theory would suggest? Or does he learn it by assessing the nature and quality of the government?

Our cases of potential disobedience show an interesting division in this respect. Three of them—the student and the two Negroes—seem quite unlikely to think much about their own past consent—when and whether they consented, how often and how seriously, expressly or tacitly, and so on. What they are likely to think about is the "outrageous" conduct and "oppressive, unjust" structure of the government, and of the possible consequences of resistance. The criminal (since we have defined him as "ordinary") is not likely to think about either obligations to obey or justifications for his action. The Nazi might well cite his consent to the Fuehrer, his oath of office, pledges of absolute obedience, and so on, as a justification for continued obedience despite "certain unpleasant government measures that perhaps ought not to have been taken." And Socrates is passionately aware of his ties to the Athenian laws, the gratitude he owes them for past favors, the power of his past consent to them.

Thus both Socrates and the Nazi do seem to look to past consent rather than to the nature of the government. But the significance of this fact has yet to be assessed; for on closer examination, each of their cases reveals an important weakness in traditional consent theory. From the case of the Nazi we can learn that even express consent may not be enough; and from that of Socrates, the difficulties of applying past consent as a guide to action.

It might be tempting to say that of our six cases, only Socrates is truly moral, for only he thinks about his obligations and commitments to the laws. But the example of the Nazi saves us from this simplistic response, by showing that sometimes past promises and oaths are not enough to determine present obligations. Sometimes a man who cites even an express oath to obedience, is being not admirable but hypocritical, refusing to recognize where his real duty lies. We would not want to say that past oaths and promises count for nothing, that they can be ignored at will. We all feel the power of the argument that you ought to be consistent, that it isn't fair to pick up your marbles and go home just because it's your turn to lose under the rules you have accepted so far. But that is partly because such a partisan assessment of the rules is likely to be biased. If you can in fact show that the rules are really unfair, then any time is a good time to change them. Again, normally rules and authorities are to be obeyed; when occasions for questioning this obligation arise, what is ultimately needed is an assessment of the rules or authorities. Mere reference to your "going along with them" in the past is not enough.

No doubt if a man had no political obligation he could acquire one by a promise or contract. But that by no means proves that political obligation can be acquired *only* by promise or contract; it may be that a quite independent political obligation is sometimes reinforced by an oath to obey, at other times (partly) countered by a promise to resist. A personal past commitment to obey need not settle the matter.

Indeed, the case of the Nazi calls attention to something traditional consent theory seems to have overlooked: the duty to resist. There are times in human history when men are not merely free(d) from an obligation to obey, but positively obligated to oppose the powers that be. The authors of the Declaration of Independence recognized this, despite their heavy reliance on Locke; for they saw resistance to tyranny not merely as man's right but as his duty. Locke, and traditional consent theory in general, make no provisition for such a duty, nor can it be easily accommodated within their framework. There is provision in Locke's system for majority resistance to a tyrannical government, and a duty to follow such a majority. But *individual* resistance has a highly ambiguous status at best, and is certainly *not* a duty.[7]

For if political obligation arises from contract, the violation or overstepping of this contract leaves each individual free to do as he likes with regard to the tyranny. True, the individual is still then bound by natural law; but natural law does not command the punishment of offenders, it only permits it. And amending the Lockeian system on this score would obviously require fundamental changes in its individualistic presuppositions.

Similarly, traditional consent theory teaches that at times of civil war or successful revolution, when an old authority structure collapses, each individual is free to place his consent anew wherever he wishes and thinks best for himself. If he thinks fit to follow a highway robber then, he is free to do so. But when we contemplate real cases, would we not rather want to maintain that even in chaos there is responsibility, that even then the individual has some obligation to think of others as well as himself, the welfare of society or mankind as well as his own?

It seems that insufficient attention has been given to the failure of traditional consent theory to provide for any obligation to resist; or any obligation to choose responsibly when new authorities must be chosen. Indeed, divine right, prescription and utilitarianism can accommodate such obligations far more easily than a contract theory can. As for the "nature of the government" or "hypothetical consent" doctrine developed in this essay, it too would presumably require amendment on this score. An enlarged version might hold: your obligation is to obey what deserves obedience and consent, and to resist what deserves resistance and rejection (leaving the important possibility that many persons or agencies deserve neither obedience nor resistance). But it is not obvious to me whether the obligation to resist tyranny should be construed as a part of political obligation at all, or as an occasional alternative to it. The question seems related to that of whether revolution is a special part of political life or a breakdown of the political.

II. The Case of Socrates

Though the Nazi may continue to obey on the grounds that he has sworn to do so, we may find that he thereby fails to perform his true obligations. Why, then, does Socrates' position equally founded on past personal consent strike us as so exemplary and moral? I would suggest that the distinguishing thing about Socrates' situation is this: he can find no fault with the Athenian laws, nor even with the Athenian way of administering them. Only his own particular conviction and sentence are (almost fortuitously) unjust. And his dialogue with the laws is essentially a way of expressing or establishing this fact. Socrates' past consent is not so much compelling in its own right, as it is a way of expressing and reinforcing his present judgment that there is nothing basically wrong with the system, no justification for resistance. What amazes us about him is not this judgment, nor the refusal to accept a single case of injustice as a justification for disobedience. These are relatively ordinary positions to take. What amazes us about him is that he construes disobedience so widely, to include even flight; and that he is willing to perform his obligation down to the minutest detail, even at the cost of his life.[8]

The suggestion is, then, that Socrates' focus on his past acceptance of the laws and his gratitude to them is in fact an evaluation of the Athenian government (or the expression of such an evaluation). We need to recall that this same moral Socrates refused to carry out an "authoritative" order given him in the time of the Thirty Tyrants, because it was unjust, and would apparently have refused to carry out injustice voted by a democratic majority as well.[9] In those earlier situations, one may suppose, what Socrates thought about was the injustice of what he had been ordered to do, and of those who issued the order, not his own (tacit?) consent to them.

To this line of argument a traditional consent theorist might respond: Socrates looks to his own past consent in order to find and determine its limits, in order to see whether this new governmental action does not exceed what he had consented to. But if we take that seriously as a model of what the moral man must do when he contemplates resistance, we set him an extremely difficult task. How is Socrates to know *to what* he has consented, particularly if

his consent has been tacit? Surely it is not enough to say that he has consented only to those precise things the government did in the past, so that any new or unprecedented action is automatically ultra vires. But if not that, then to what does one give tacit consent? Is it to the particular people then in authority, or to the authority of the office they hold, or to the laws that define and limit that office, or to the body that makes those laws, or to the Constitution that lays down rules and procedures for the making of laws, or to the principles behind that Constitution, or to the fellow-members of the society, or even to all mankind? In particular cases, these various foci of loyalty may come into conflict; then knowing that one has consented to them all at a time when they were in agreement is no help for deciding what to do.

In short, though two of our examples do look to their own past consent in deciding what to do, one of them thereby fails to perform his true obligation, and the other seems to be using the language of consent to express a favorable assessment of the government. Furthermore, we have noted at least two disadvantages of personal consent as a criterion: the difficulty of knowing *to what* you have consented (especially if consent was tacit), and the fact that even an express oath to obey may sometimes be outweighed by an obligation to resist.

Besides an individual's personal consent, traditional consent theory offers as an alternative criterion the "consent of the governed," the consent of all, or a majority of one's fellow-citizens. Of such consent, too, we would have to say that it cannot simply be dismissed as irrelevant. Even our Negro in Mississippi or South Africa might think about how widely shared his grievances are. But again, the consent or dissent of the majority cannot by itself be decisive for defining your obligation. Majorities are sometimes wrong, and have been known to do evil. Resistance might be justified in Athens under the Thirty Tyrants or in Nazi Germany despite the majority.

But majority consent does enter the argument at another level, in a way quite different from the relevance of personal consent. Majority consent may be relevant as a *way* of assessing, as *evidence about* the nature of the government, given that the nature of the government bears on political obligation. In fact, a variety of considerations each of which we might want to call "consent of the governed" can be used in the process of evaluating a government. They may come into conflict with each other, and their relative weight and importance will be a matter of one's political values, of what kind of government he thinks desirable or even tolerable.

It is useful to distinguish here between the "procedural" criteria yielded by the consent of the governed for assessing a government, and the "substantive" ones. Procedural criteria are those which concern the institutional structure and political functioning of the government, the way in which it makes decisions and takes actions. To assess its nature, we want to know about the way a government functions in relation in the governed—whether it is responsive to them or forces its policies on them. Thus we look for machinery for the expression of popular desires; we look for the degree of popular participation in or control over decisions, for channels for the redress of grievances, for access to power. At the same time we look also for signs of repression, of propaganda, of coercion. We look, of course, not merely at the institutions defined on paper, but at their actual functioning in the largest social sense. Denial of suffrage to Negroes in South Africa is very different from denial of suffrage to women in Switzerland (and theorists would do well to think about why this is so). But roughly speaking, a government is likely to seem to us deserving if it is open to the governed, reprehensible if it rules them against their will. This general criterion may well be expressed by some formula like "the consent of the governed"; but that formula must not be taken too simply, and that criterion must not be regarded as our only one.

Besides this vague cluster of procedural criteria, we have in addition substantive ones. We may look also at the substance of what the government does—whether it pursues good, benevolent, justifiable policies. A government that systematically harms its subjects, whether out of misguided good intentions or simply for the selfish gain of the rulers, is to that extent illegitimate—even if the subjects do not know it, even if they "consent" to being abused. But even here "the consent of the governed" is *relevant* as important evidence, for one of the main ways we estimate whether people are being well treated is by whether they seem to like what they get. Only we may sometimes need to consider other evidence as well; the consent or dissent of the governed need not be decisive as to the goodness or justness of a government's policies.

It is the relationship between at least these two kinds of criteria that is likely to determine our assessment of a government, whether it deserves support or opposition. Thus we may all agree that a government pursuing very bad policies and forcing them on its subjects, so that it is obviously doing great harm to them and other countries, and doing so despite their attempts at protest and without their consent—such a government clearly is the occasion for resistance. Conversely, if we find a government that truly has the consent of its subjects although they have wide sources of information and true opportunities to dissent and criticize, and if that government pursues only the most praiseworthy policies, then few of us would urge revolution or resistance to it. The problematic cases are, of course, the ones in between, where procedure and substance are partly good, partly bad, and you need to make evaluations and decisions. Here it begins to be a matter of your metapolitics—how you think of men and societies, what positions you are willing to take and defend, and take responsibility for.

Suppose, for example, that a government is procedurally open, with genuine channels for controlling policy from below, but it engages in vicious policies. Then, one might want to say, the citizen is not free to engage in revolution; he has channels available and it is his duty to use them, to change the policy. But what if he tries to do so, and fails because the majority continues to approve of the wickedness? What if he is a member of a permanent minority group, being systematically abused and exploited by an eager, consenting majority? Then the seemingly open channels of consent are not truly open to him. Might there not come a point when violent minority resistance of some sort is justified?

Or suppose that a government is benevolent, so no one can criticize its actions, but in procedure it is simply autocratic and dictatorial. Is revolution justified against a benevolent dictatorship? This might be the case, for example, if men need political participation in order to be really well, in order to reach their full human potential. Then bad procedure would itself become a substantive grievance.

The theoretical complications possible here are legion, but at least this much seems clear: evaluating a government in order to decide whether it deserves obedience or resistance, requires attention both to the way it works and to what it does. In both cases something like consent is relevant; it may be a formula for expressing some rather complex requirements concerning opportunities for dissent and participation, or it may be evidence of good policies. Thus even if we adhere to the doctrine of hypothetical consent or the nature of government, majority consent may still be relevant in a subordinate capacity for assessing a government, for working out more detailed answers to our questions one and two about consent, the specific practical "when" and "whom" of obedience. But here "the consent of the governed" is not one simple thing, decisive for obligation; rather, it is relevant in a number of different, potentially conflicting ways.

And all of these ways put together differ, in turn, not merely from personal consent, but also from the doctrine of hypothetical consent developed in this essay.[10] That legitimate authority is such that one ought to consent to it, is a precept built into English grammar, into the meanings of these terms. That a legitimate government is one which has the consent of (a majority of) the governed—is procedurally responsive to them or looks after their interests, or both—is one particular position about what kind of government is desirable for men. More accurately, it is a cluster of positions, depending on the relative weight given to procedural and substantive criteria. Though these positions are very widely shared today, and though they were shared by almost all traditional con-

sent theorists, they are not the only conceivable positions on this subject. Someone might undertake to argue, for example, that a government is legitimate only to the extent that it fosters high culture, or to the extent that it promotes the evolution of a master race. That would be to reject majority consent as any sort of criterion for assessing a government. But the doctrine of hypothetical consent holds even for someone taking such an unorthodox position; even for him, a legitimate government would be the one that deserves consent, to which everyone ought to consent. Both the philosophical weakness and the historical persistence and strength of traditional consent theory rest in its failure to distinguish these very different arguments.

Finally, even if we succeed in evaluating a government, that does not seem fully to settle how we must behave toward it. One final, important consideration seems relevant: the action taken must be appropriate. To the diversity of ways in which one can obey or support, resist or overthrow a government, there correspond a diversity of conditions when the various actions may be appropriate or justified. The fact that some action is justified, that some abuse has taken place, does not mean that just any action will do. A man mistreated by his superior may kick his dog. We can understand, and perhaps even sympathize, but surely the action is not justified. Not just any violation of law will qualify as civil disobedience or attempted revolution. This observation is presumably related to the traditional assertion of consent theorists, that it is necessary to "exhaust the remedies" available, to suffer "a long train of abuses" before violent resistance is justified. Where other actions are appropriate, revolution may not be called for.

Thus it begins to seem that a decision about obedience and resistance ought to be measured not merely against the character of the government, but against all the relevant social circumstances—what alternatives one can envision, and what consequences resistance is likely to have. Revolution would not seem justified, for example, if one had no hope of its being followed by an improvement in conditions. If it would simply substitute one tyranny for another, or if it would annihilate the human race through the resulting violence, then it does not seem justified.[11]

But a doctrine that casts its net so wide, making all social circumstances at least potentially relevant, that sees both an obligation to obey and an obligation to resist, and that stresses so much the individual burden of decision, seems very close to the social utilitarianism examined in the first half of this essay. It seems to say, with the social utilitarian, you are obligated to obey when that is best on the whole for society (all of mankind?), and obligated to resist when *that* is best on the whole. But that formula, and social utilitarianism, seem to neglect again the obligatory nature of law and authority in normal circumstances, the prima facie obligation to obey. Being subject to law, government, authority means precisely an obligation (normally) to do what *they* say is best, rather than judge the welfare of society for yourself and act on your private judgment. Yet there are times when you must resist in the name of something very like the welfare of society. Whether these two positions are compatible remains somehow problematic; but before we can make a final stab at the matter, we must finish applying our new doctrine to our four questions about political obligation.

III. Justifying Political Obligation

We come now to question four, the matter of justification: "why are you ever obligated to obey even legitimate authority?" Here again our "nature of the government" doctrine does not at first seem a very useful answer. For it can only say: because of the nature of the government, because the government is such that you ought to obey it and consent to it, because a rational man would do so. But that answer is not likely to still the question. For someone genuinely puzzled about obligation in this (philosophical) way is likely to persist: "how does that 'ought' bind me, *why* must I do what a rational man would do, what if I don't *want* to be rational?"

But the reader may have noticed by now that all of the theories and versions of theories we have considered are subject to this same diffi-

culty to some extent. Some seem better designed to cope with it than others; yet we can always push the question further back: why must I do what God commands, why must I do what history teaches, why must I do what is best for me personally, why must I do what I have promised? Even traditional consent theory is liable to this difficulty; and it is remarkable that despite Hume's early criticism, we continue to believe in consent theory while ignoring this problem. For Hume had already told the consent theorist:

> You find yourself embarrassed when it is asked, *Why we are bound to keep our word?* Nor can you give any answer but what would, immediately, without any circuit, have accounted for our obligation to allegiance.[12]

The obligation to keep one's word is no more "natural" and self-evident and indubitable than political obligation itself; though either may sometimes reinforce the other, neither can give the other absolute justification. The two obligations are essentially separate and equal in status.[13] Why, then, does the traditional consent theorist, so doubtful about the validity of political obligation, take the obligation of keeping contracts as obvious? Why, if he imagines a state of nature, is it always stripped of political authority but inveitably equipped with a natural law that dictates the keeping of one's word? Hume uses these questions as a rhetorical device to attack consent theory, but they can also be taken seriously as a way of learning something more about the consent theorist.

For a theorist does not choose his beliefs and his doubts. The traditional consent theorist simply finds himself in doubt about (the justification of, or limits of, or validity of) political obligation; it just seems obvious to him that there is a problem about it. And he simply is not in doubt about promises or contracts; it just seems obvious to him that they oblige.

At one level one can argue that both the consent theorist's doubt and his assumption spring from the peculiar picture of man and society he seems to hold. If your picture of man in the abstract is of a man fully grown, complete with his own private needs, interests, feelings, desires, beliefs and values, and if you therefore never think about how he grew up and became the particular person he became, then he may well seem to you an ineluctably *separate* unit, his ties to other individuals may seem mysterious or illusory and will require explanation. Given man as such a separate, self-contained unit, it does indeed seem strange that he might have obligations not of his own choosing, perhaps even without being aware of them, or even against his will. Furthermore, self-assumed obligations may then strike you as a way of overcoming this separateness. For it is easy to confuse the fact that promises and contracts are self-assumed, with the idea that the *obligation to keep* them is self-assumed as well. That is, the person who makes a promise seems to recognize and commit himself to the institution of promises; the person who makes a contract seems to acknowledge thereby the binding character of contracts, so that a later refusal to accept them as binding strikes one as a kind of self-contradiction. But of course this is a confusion. The making of particular promises or contracts presupposes the social institution of promising or contracts, and the obligation to keep promises cannot itself be founded on a promise.

In truth, there is something profoundly wrong with the consent theorist's picture of man. Every free, separate, adult, consenting individual was first shaped and molded by his parents and (as we say) society. It is only as a result of their influence that he becomes the particular person he does become, with his particular interests, values, desires, language and obligations. The only thing truly separate about us is our bodies; our selves are manifestly social. But surely even the consent theorist knows this, so the problem becomes why he nevertheless holds, or is held captive by, a different and peculiar picture. Could that picture be not so much the cause as the by-product of his philosophical doubt?

After all, consent theorists are not the only ones troubled about political obligation. Political theorists of other persuasions have also been led, or have led themselves sometimes to ask "why are you ever obligated to obey even legitimate authority?" But if none of the the-ories of political obligation is able to deal adequately with that question, it must be quite peculiar, not nearly as straightforward as it looks. Perhaps it is a question that cannot be fully answered in the ordinary way. But what sort of question is that; and if it cannot be answered, how should it be treated? Tussman rejects it as a symptom of "moral disorder"; I would suggest instead that it is a symptom of philosophical disorder, the product of a philosophical paradox. If so, it will not disappear—the theorist will not stop being bothered by it—unless we can show how and why it arises, why anyone should so much as suppose that political obligation in general needs (or can have) a general justification. But that would require a discussion of the nature of philosophical puzzlement far beyond the scope of this essay.

What can be done here is something much more limited and less effective. Having suggested that the status of political obligation and of the obligation to keep promises is essentially the same—that neither is more "natural" than or can serve as an absolute justification for the other—we can approach our question four about political obligation by first pursuing a parallel question about promises. For in the area of promises some extremely useful work has been done in philosophy in recent years—work which can be applied to the problem of political obligation.[14]

Philosophers have sometimes asked a question like our question four about promises: "why are you (ever) obligated to keep (any of) your promises (whatsoever); why do promises oblige?" This question, too, can be answered in terms of divine commandment or utilitarian consequences, social or individual; and here, too, the answers are less than satisfactory. "God commands you to keep your word" is no answer to the nonbeliever, nor to someone heretical enough to demand proof of God's will. The utilitarian response tends to dissolve the obligation altogether, so that your duty is always to do what produces the best results, quite apart from whether you have made any promises on the subject. And, of course, a consent argument is out of the question here ("you have promised to keep your promises?").

What has been suggested by philosophers is this: "promise" is not just a word. Promising is a social practice, something we *do,* something children have to learn *how* to do. It has rules, penalties, roles and moves almost in the way that games have them. Children do not learn what a promise is by having one pointed out to them; they learn gradually about what it means to "make a promise," "keep (or break) a promise," "be unable to promise but certainly intend to try," "have said something which, in the circumstances, amounted to a promise," and so on. Promising is not just producing certain sounds ("I promise"), for a phonograph might make those sounds, or a man rehearsing a play, or a philosopher explaining the practice, yet none of these would actually be promising. Promising, rather, is taking on an obligation. That is, "to promise" does not mean "to make certain sounds," but rather "to take on an obligation."

Now, of course, we do not always do what we have promised. Sometimes we act contrary to our obligations, and sometimes we are wholly or partly excused from performing what we had promised. If for example, keeping a promise would frustrate the purpose for which it was made, or would lead to great evil, or has become impossible, we may be excused from performing. So about any particular promise we have made it may sometimes be relevant to ask: am I still obligated to perform or not? That is, normally, in principle promises oblige; a promise is a certain kind of obligation. But sometimes, under certain circumstances, there is reason to question or withdraw or cancel that obligation in a particular case. In such circumstances we weigh the alternatives, the possible consequences of performance and failure to perform. But our obligations, including that of the promise, continue to be among the factors that must be weighed in the decision. The obligation of a promise does not simply disappear when there is occasion to question it; it only is sometimes outweighed.

But philosophers are sometimes led to wonder *categorically,* about *all* promises: do they oblige; what are the reasons pro and con; why am I ever obligated to keep any promise? And here, of course, there are no *particular* circumstances to weigh in the balance; the question is abstract and hypothetical. What sort of answer is possible to this question? First, that this is what a promise *is,* what "promise" means. A promise is a self-assumed obligation. If you *assume* an obligation and have not yet performed it, nor been excused from it, then you *have* an obligation; in much the same way as someone who puts on a coat, has a coat on.[15] To ask why promises oblige is to ask why (self-assumed) obligations oblige. And to the question why obligations oblige the only possible answer would seem to be that this is what the words mean.

Beyond this one can only paraphrase Wittgenstein: there are a hundred reasons; there is no reason. There is no absolute, deductive answer to the question "why does any promise ever oblige?" beyond calling attention to the meaning of the words. There is no absolute, indubitable principle from which the obligation can be deduced. It is, to be sure, related to any number of other principles, obligations and values; but the relationship is more like a network (or patchwork) than like a hierarchical pyramid. It is simply a mistake to suppose that there might be such an absolute principle, such a deductive proof. We have no right to expect one. (Why, then, does the philosopher expect one; why can we ourselves be led to share his expectation when we are in a "philosophical mood"?)

John Rawls has pointed out that utilitarianism will not do as a criterion for the keeping of particular promises—as a standard for *when* promises oblige.[16] To say "keep your promises only when that maximizes pleasure and minimizes pain" is to miss precisely the *obligatory* nature of a promise; having once promised you are not free to decide what to do merely on utilitarian grounds. But, Rawls says, utilitarian considerations *are* relevant at a different level of argument, for assessing the social practice of promising. For we can ask "must we (should we) have an institution like promising and promise-keeping at all?" And here utilitarian reasons seem relevant; we may try to justify the social practice by its useful consequences.

Stanley Cavell has argued that this implies a degree of freedom of choice on our parts which we do not in fact have.[17] To evaluate the practice of promising pro and con, we would have to envision alternatives. And how shall we envision a society which knows no obligation to keep one's word? (For it is not, of course, the particular English locution "I promise" that is being assessed, but the practice of assuming obligations and holding people to their word.) We seem to have no choice about the pros and cons of such an institution. It is not socially useful; it is indispensable to the very concept of society and human life.

But even if we could and did evaluate as Rawls suggests, and "decide" that the institution of promising is on balance socially useful, even this would not provide an absolute justification for the keeping of particular promises. For what are we to answer the man who says: "granted that we must have the practice of promising, and granted promising means taking on an obligation; still, why am *I* obliged to keep my promise? Why can't *I* be an exception?" To him we can only say, that is how obligation and promises work. Of course you *can* refuse to keep your promise, but then you are failing to perform an obligation.

Now the same line of reasoning can be applied to the question "why does even a legitimate government, a valid law, a genuine authority ever obligate me to obey?" As with promises, and as our new doctrine about political obligation suggests, we may say that this is what "legitimate government," "valid law," "genuine authority" *mean*. It is part of the concept, the meaning of "authority" that those subject to it are required to obey, that it has a right to command. It is part of the concept, the meaning of "law," that those to whom it is applicable are obligated to obey it. As with promises, so with authority, government and law: there is a prima facie obligation involved in each, and normally you must perform it. Normally a man is not free to decide on utilitarian grounds whether or not he will do a certain thing, if that thing happens to be against the law or required by law; he is not free to make a decision on his own the way he would be free where the law is silent. The ex-

istence of the law on this subject normally constitutes an obligation, just as having promised normally constitutes an obligation, so that one is not free to decide what to do just as if no promise had been made. (This is not, of course, to say that everything claiming to be law is law, that everyone claiming to have authority has it, that every statement alleged to be a promise is in fact one. It says only: *if* something is a promise, law, obligation, *then* normally it obliges.) This kind of response to question four is obviously almost the same as the one our doctrine of hypothetical consent yielded to question three: government and authority are concepts grammatically related to obligation and obedience. A legitimate government is one that you ought to obey and ought to consent to because that is what the words mean. But as before, this answer is likely to seem purely formal, and empty. It will not satisfy someone genuinely puzzled about the justification of political obligation.

But as with promises, all that one can say beyond calling attention to the meanings of the words, is that no absolute, deductive justification exists or is necessary. There are no absolute first principles from which this obligation could be derived. It is related to all kinds of other obligations in all kinds of ways, to be sure, but the relationship is not hierarchical and deductive. In particular, as we have seen, the obligatory nature of promises is no more or no less absolute and indubitable than the obligation to obey laws. Again, following Rawls' suggestion, one might attempt a utilitarian assessment of such institutions or practices as law, government and authority. And here, I suppose, there may be somewhat more room for discussion than with promises. For it is not at all obvious that government and law are indispensable to human social life. But can we conceive society without any such thing as authority? One function of the idea of the state of nature in classical consent theories does seem to be a kind of indirect demonstration of the utilitarian advantages of having governments and laws. If such things did not exist, Locke seems to argue, we would have to invent them.[18]

But as with promises, even a recognition of

the necessity or utilitarian advantages of such things as authority, law and government is no absolute answer to the man who is questioning his particular obligation to obey, who wants to be an exception. There is no such absolute answer, and can be none. Nothing we say is absolutely beyond question. Again, you *can* disobey but in the absence of excuses or justifications you violate an obligation when you do so.

The parallel between promises and authority as obligations is not perfect. For one thing, promises are explicitly taken on oneself; political obligation (I have argued) need not be. Furthermore, promises are normally made to particular persons, whereas political obligation is sometimes confounded by our question two, by the problem of rival authorities. We have noted the difficulty of determining to whom or what consent is given: particular officials, their positions, the laws, the Constitution, the people of the society. This means, among other things, that political obligation is open to a kind of challenge not normally relevant to promises. We saw that, following Rawls, both promises and political obligation can be challenged at two very different levels: sometimes we may claim to be excused from performing in a particular case (for instance because of conflicting obligations or overwhelming difficulties). And sometimes we may want to challenge and assess the whole institution with the obligations it defines. But in addition, political obligation can be challenged also on a third level. Sometimes we may refuse to obey neither because our particular case is exceptional, nor because we question such obligation categorically, but because the one who is claiming authority over us does not in fact have it. We may resist a government that has become tyrannical not as a special, personal exception, and not because we are against government, but because *this* government no longer deserves obedience. Such a challenge is made on principle, *in accord* (as it were) with the "rules" of political obligation.

But the differences between promises and political obligation do not affect the point to be made here. That point concerns our question four, the search for a justification for having to

obey (or having to keep a promise); and it is essentially twofold. First, we have said, "authority," "law," and "government" are grammatically, conceptually related to obligation, as is "promise." And beyond this, the quest for some "higher," absolute, deductive justification is misguided. Insofar, then, as the grammatical point does not seem to still the question, does not get at what someone philosophically puzzled wants to ask, what is needed is not a better justification, but an account of why the philosopher is driven to ask the question in the first place.

IV. The Duality of Obligation

As Locke suggests in his preface, the consent theorist's purpose is a dual one. He wants both to show that men are sometimes justified in making revolutions, and to show that men are normally bound to obey governments and laws. And this is, indeed, what must be shown, since both these things are in fact true. The fact is that on one hand men are in some sense above or outside the institutions of their society, its laws, its government. They can measure and judge these institutions. Though they have not themselves made them they can change them; and sometimes even violent change may be justified. On the other hand, men are also part of and subject to their society, bound by its norms and authorities. Not every attempt at revolution is justified.

To say that men are both superior to their government and subject to it is to express a paradox. Because it seems so paradoxical, the traditional social contract theorists saw it instead as a temporal sequence: *first* men were free and could make a commonwealth, *then* they became bound by it (within the limits of a contract). We have seen some of the difficulties that result. Finding an accurate and unparadoxical way to express this paradoxical truth seems to me the most interesting problem connected with political obligation, but it is important to notice that this problem is not confined to political obligation. We are both superior to and subject to *all* our obligations, and *that* is what requires an accounting. Discussing it will reveal one final, rather subtle way in which obligation both is and is not a matter of consent—but all obligation, not just the obligation to obey.

We are familiar enough from ethics with the view of a number of philosophers (notably Kant) that an action is not fully moral unless the actor knows what he is doing and does it for the right reasons. An action done for selfish motives but accidentally producing some charitable result is not (really, fully) a charitable action. A moral action is one taken *because* it is right, on principle. On analogy we might want to say that a man cannot (really, fully) obey an order unless he recognizes that it is an order that the man issuing it has authority over him. He cannot (really, fully) obey a law or a government unless he recognizes it as valid law or legitimate government; only then will what he does (really, fully) *be* obeying. If I "order" a leaf to fall from a tree, and the leaf immediately does so, it is not obeying my order; if I silently and secretly "order" my neighbor to mow his lawn and he does so, he is not (really, fully) obeying my order. Even if he hears and understands what I am saying, he is not (really, fully) obeying me unless he recognizes what I say as an order, considers me as having authority to order him about, and mows the lawn *because* of my order.

Consequently, the capacity for this kind of awareness and intention is a precondition for being fully obligated. This is why leaves cannot be obligated (except in storybooks, where they are anthropomorphized), and children cannot fully do so. It may be right to punish or reward a child, but the child is not yet fully a moral agent capable of recognizing and therefore of having obligations.

It is not difficult to regard this kind of awareness and intention as a form of consenting to one's obligation. If (really, fully) obeying an order presupposes the recognition of it as an order and of the man who issues it as having authority, then surely that recognition resembles a kind of (perhaps tacit) consent to his authority. And then it becomes easy to take a final further step, and say you are not (really, fully) obligated unless you recognize, acknowledge, accept, acquiesce in, consent to that obligation. Such a line of reasoning un-

doubtedly has heightened the appeal of consent theory for a number of writers, and it clearly is the main basis for Tussman's stress on consent. He chooses agreement rather than force or habit as the nature of political association precisely because,

"I have a duty to . . ." seems to follow from "I have agreed to" in a way that it does not follow from "I am forced to" or "I am in the habit of." This is sometimes expressed as the view that obligations are, or even must be voluntarily assumed.[19]

But even if one accepts these transitions and concludes that obligation in the full moral sense always requires consent, it by no means follows that obligation consists *only* of this inner awareness and intent. For that would imply that anyone failing or refusing to consent for any reason whatsoever is thereby excused from the obligation in question, does not have that obligation, cannot meaningfully be blamed or criticized for failing to perform it.[20] But no major ethical theorist, least of all Kant, would be willing to accept that consequence, any more than Tussman is willing to let the morally unaware clods in society disobey laws whenever they please.

It is necessary to recognize that obligation has not one, but two fundamental aspects—the inner, "awareness" aspect stressed by Tussman, and an outer aspect having to do with the way others see what we do, how it looks objectively. These two aspects of obligation may be seen as corresponding to two familiar strains in ethical theory: the teleological, concerned with the consequences of action, and the deontological, concerned with its motives.[21] The former deals primarily in the outer, shared world of facts and events, and takes as fundamental the concept of the *good:* the latter deals primarily in the inner, personal world of thoughts and feelings, and takes as fundamental the concept of *right.* I would suggest, following Cavell, that both are a necessary part of any valid account of morality and obligation, that neither can be ignored outright in assessing action.

Those moral philosophers who have stressed the deontological side of moral appraisal have been concerned particularly with the matter of giving praise: a person does not deserve full credit for an act of charity, of courage, of obedience, unless his intentions were charitable, courageous, obedient. He should not get full credit for an action that merely looks charitable "from the outside," if his own perception of what he was doing was quite otherwise. To a lesser extent this is also true of blame: you are responsible for the damage you do, no matter how good your intentions were, but good intentions may be a *partial* excuse. Those philosophers who have stressed the teleological orientation of moral appraisal have been more concerned with blame or responsibility, but most particularly with duty. Your duty is not merely to intend good behavior, but to behave well; the performance and its results are what define your duty.

But in a way this dichotomization—deontology for praise, teleology for duty—misses the point. For the real difficulty is in determining *what* action has been performed, what actually was done. It is naming the action (correctly) that is the problem: was it, should we call it, an act of charity, an act of obedience, considering what took place, considering his intentions? Having put it that way, one wants to say that the two modes of assessment are always both relevant, but not equally relevant to all actions. To the assessment of certain actions, inner intention is much more relevant; to the assessment of others, outer events will seem decisive. Lying is more a matter of inner intent, deceiving more a matter of outward results. Moreover it may be that, in a broader sense, whole categories of action vary in this respect. It may be, for example, that inner awareness is categorically more relevant in face-to-face, personal relationships than in public, political conduct. We do care more about motive and intention in assessing personal relationships and actions—love, anger and forgiveness—than in assessing political actions in the public realm.

If this is so, it deserves more attention than it has received from political theorists. No doubt it has something to do with the fact that in personal morality there is no umpire, no arbiter or judge; it is of the essence of morality that we confront each other directly. In the political, public realm, on the other hand, the normal situation is one where official "interpreters" are supplied by the society to tell the individual what the law or Constitution says, whether he has or has not committed grand larceny. But what happens at times of resistance or revolution is precisely that these normal official interpreters are themselves called into question. We are both bound by, and yet sometimes free to challenge or change all our obligations; but political obligation has an additional complexity, in that its *content* seems to be a subordination to the judgment of others.[22]

But if normally law and authority oblige and resistance requires justification, and if normally judgment is to some extent subordinated to that of the authorities, and if revolutionary situations are precisely the ones that are not normal in these respects, then the crucial question seems to be: *who is to say?*[23] Who is to say what times are normal and what times are not, when resistance is justified or even obligatory? If we say "each individual must decide for himself," we seem to deny the normally binding character of law and authority. If we say "society" or "the majority" or "the duly constituted authorities decide," then we seem to deny the right to resist, since it may be the majority or the authorities themselves that need to be challenged. Yet these seem to be the only two alternatives.

The matter is very difficult, though the question seems so simple. This essay will only briefly indicate a direction in which a solution might be sought. What needs to be said seems to be this: the decision both is and is not up to each individual. Each individual does and must ultimately decide for himself and is responsible for his decision; but he may make a wrong decision and thereby fail to perform his obligations. But then who is to say someone has made a wrong decision? Anyone can say, but not everyone who cares to say will judge correctly; he may be right or wrong. And who decides that?

Each person decides for himself what to say and do; yet people sometimes speak and act in ways that are cowardly or cruel, thoughtless or irresponsible. And it is not merely up to the actor to assess his own action in this respect. Other people who want or need to assess the action may also do so; each of them will make a decision for which he bears responsibility, yet none of these decisions is absolutely definitive. The judge trying a would-be rebel makes a decision; the foreign onlooker asked to give money for a revolutionary cause makes a decision; the historian examining the record in a later generation makes a decision.[24] Each of us who talks or thinks or acts with regard to the situation assesses it, and no theory or God or Party can get us off that hook.

But that does not mean that all judgments are arbitrary or merely a matter of personal preference or whim. Some decisions are made arbitrarily or whimsically or selfishly or foolishly; others are made on principle, rationally, responsibly. These are ways or modes of deciding; none of them characterizes decision as such. And an individual's decision does not become rational, responsible or right merely because he thinks it is, merely because he urgently wants it to be. What is ultimately needed here is a better understanding of the role played in our language and our lives by assessments like "he was right," "he made a bad decision," "he betrayed the cause," and the like.

Who is to say? I want to answer, each person who cares to, will say—not merely the one who acts, not merely his associates, not merely those in authority over him, not merely the detached historian or observer. No one has the last word because there is no last word. But in order to make that clear, one would have to say a great deal more about how language functions, and why we are so persistently inclined to suppose that there must be a last word.

Notes

1. This and part of the following paragraph are intended to summarize the argument of "Obligation and Consent—I," *American Political Science Review* 59 (December 1965): 990–999.
2. John Locke, *Second Treatise of Civil Government,* 1764 [reprinted in part in this volume]; Joseph Tussman, *Obligation and the Body Politic* (New York: Oxford, 1960).
3. Ludwig Wittgenstein, *Philosophical Investigations* (New York: Macmillan, 1953). See also Stanley Louis Cavell, "The Claim to Rationality." Ph. D. dissertation, Harvard University, 1961, esp. chap. 1.
4. See, for example, Margaret Macdonald, "The Language of Political Theory," in ed. A. Flew *Logic and Language: First Series* (Oxford: Basil Blackwell, 1960), pp. 167–186.
5. This suggestion is advanced, against Miss Macdonald's argument, in S. I. Benn and R. S. Peters, *Social Principles and the Democratic State* (London: George Allen & Unwin, 1959), pp. 299–301.
6. Something like this point is suggested by Tussman, *Obligation,* p. 43.
7. Locke, *Second Treatise,* pars. 121, 149, 168, 203–204, 208–209, 211–212, 220, 232, 240–243.
8. Plato *Crito* [50]: "are you not going by an act of yours to overturn us—the laws, and the whole state, as far as in you lies?" trans. B. Jowett (New York: Random House, 1937)
9. Plato *Apology* 32.
10. For the latter distinction, compare Benn and Peters, *Social Principles,* pp. 329–331.
11. One difficulty of this discussion is that it seems to make human decisions look excessively rational. Are any abstract principles of this kind really relevant to what real people think about when they must decide? Is a man on the point of rebellion or revolution not much more likely to be moved by strong emotion—by an overwhelming anger or sense of outrage?

But I would like to suggest that the human capacity for outrage is, as it were, the emotional correlate to rational moral principles. It is our inner, helpless response to a violation of principles of right and wrong, as we sense them, perhaps quite inarticulately. Outrage (unlike mere anger) is an emotion of principle. I take it that this is what Albert Camus means when he insists that "the act of rebellion is not, essentially, an egoistic act," even though it can, "of course" have "egoistic motives." *The Rebel* (New York: Vintage, 1956), p. 16. The rebel, the man who acts from a sense of outrage, says not merely "I don't want to put up with this," but "No man ought to have to put up with this." And by feeling "no man ought . . ." he acts, in a sense, on principle. Compare Tussman, *Obligation,* pp. 78–79.

Of course a man's feeling that his situation is outrageous is one thing; whether the situation is in fact outrageous is another. A three-year-old may feel outraged at not being allowed to drink the detergent. We may sympathize with his feelings, but cannot condone the resulting violence. Not every feeling of outrage is a valid assessment of the world; but then, not every rational judgment that the limits of contractual obligation have been exceeded is valid either. No doubt rational judgments are more likely to be right; that is one advantage of rationality.

12. David Hume, "Of the Original Contract" [reprinted in this volume] in *The Social Contract,* ed. Sir Ernest Barker (New York: Oxford, 1960), p. 161.

13. This assertion is not about the relative claims that the two obligations—political obedience and promise-keeping—have on us, where they come into conflict. It seems obvious to me that no single, binding principle could be found to govern such a question. There are occasions when a vitally important promise is clearly a more important obligation than obedience to some minor law; on the other hand, the keeping of a minor promise is no excuse whatsoever for treason. But the assertion that the two obligations are separate and equal is not meant to bear on this question. It is meant only to say: there is no reason to suppose that promising is more "natural" or basic than obeying authority, and hence no reason to derive the latter from the former.

14. See particularly J. L. Austin, *Philosophical Papers* (Oxford: Clarendon, 1961), chaps. 3, 6, 10; John Rawls, "Two Concepts of Rules," *Philosophical Review* 64 (January 1955): 3–32; and S. L. Cavell, "Must We Mean What We Say?" in *Ordinary Language,* ed. V. C. Chappell (Englewood Cliffs, N.J.: Prentice-Hall, 1964), esp. pp. 94–101.

15. Compare Cavell, "Must We Mean What We Say?", pp. 96, 99.

16. "Two Concepts of Rules," part 2.

17. "The Claim to Rationality," chap. 8.

18. It is significant, in this respect, that consent theorists so often speak of contracts or covenants, rather than simple promises or oaths. For of course the idea of a contract or covenant implies that you get something in return for the obligation you take on, and in a way at least suggest the informal additional ties of gratitude. But there are other differences as well, a contract being more formal and usually more explicit than a promise.

19. *Obligation,* p. 8.

20. Benn and Peters, *Social Principles,* p. 322.

21. This and the next three paragraphs lean heavily on Cavell, "The Claim to Rationality," p. 323 and all of part 2.

22. Compare Tussman, *Obligation,* pp. 86–95. It is tempting to construe the problem in relation to Hannah Arendt's discussion of action: *The Human Condition* (1958), Part 5. The human situation is precarious, and human action fallible in unpredictable ways. Both privately as individuals, and collectively as a society, we try to some extent to overcome this uncertainty, this fallibility. We make commitments, tie ourselves down for the future. As individuals, for example, we make promises. As a society, for example, we try to act and plan beyond the lifetimes of individuals, through the education of our children, or through the establishment of laws and institutions. As we reduce the uncertainty of private future action by telling others what we will do so that they can count on it, so we reduce the uncertainty of public future action by telling others and ourselves what we will do and how, so that we can all count on it. Yet in both private and collective action, uncertainty remains and things go wrong. We do not always live up to our commitments, and promised actions do not always accomplish their intended purpose. Institutions do not always function as intended either; they produce quite different goals, pursue other principles than those they were supposed to embody. Thus sometimes we need to review, replace or reject commitments we have made; sometimes it must be right for us to do so.

    And where do human beings get the standards by which on such occasions they assess their government and find it wanting? Well, surely from the very society which they criticize with these standards. That this is possible—that we learn both the existing rules and criteria for assessing rules *together,* and yet can use the latter on occasion to criticize the former—may well be the most important single fact about social life.

23. Compare Tussman, *Obligation,* pp. 44–46.

24. Thus not only citizens, but also bystanders and commentators may need to decide about a government. Their problems are not the same, to be sure. The citizen must decide whether to obey or resist; the bystander never had an obligation to obey, so he at most must decide whether or whom to assist; the commentator only makes a judgment. Therefore the evaluation of governments as to their legitimacy, their entitlement-to-be-obeyed-by-their-subjects, is a topic that ranges beyond problems of political obligation.

The Principle of
Fair Play

A. JOHN SIMMONS

I

The traditional consent theory account of political obligation can be understood as advancing two basic claims. (1) All or most citizens,
at least within reasonably just political communities, have political obligations (that is,
moral obligations or duties to obey the law and
support the political institutions of their countries of residence). (2) All political obligations
are grounded in personal consent (express or
tacit). Today most political philosophers (and
non-philosophers, I suspect) are still prepared
to accept (1). But (2) has been widely rejected
largely because it entails, in conjunction with
(1), that all or most of us have undertaken political obligations by *deliberate consensual
acts*. And this seems not even approximately
true. If it is not true, then (1) requires a defense
employing a more complex account of special
rights and obligations than the one offered by
consent theory.

One popular way of defending (1) relies on
what has been called "the principle of fair
play" (or "the principle of fairness").[1] Advocates of this principle argue that promises
and deliberate consent are not the only possible
grounds of special rights and obligations; the
acceptance of benefits within certain sorts of
cooperative schemes, they maintain, is by itself

sufficient to generate such rights and obligations. It is these arguments I want to examine.
I begin with a brief discussion of the principle
of fair play as it has appeared in recent philosophical literature. From there I proceed to a
more general evaluation of the principle (in
Sections II and IV) and of the theory of political obligation which uses it (in Sections III
and V).

The first concise formulation of the principle
of fair play was provided by H. L. A. Hart:

> A third important source of special rights and ob-
> ligations which we recognize in many spheres of life
> is what may be termed mutuality of restrictions, and
> I think political obligation is intelligible only if we
> see what precisely this is and how it differs from the
> other right-creating transactions (consent, promis-
> ing) to which philosophers have assimilated it.

Hart's explanation of the "special transaction"
he has in mind runs as follows:

> When a number of persons conduct any joint en-
> terprise according to rules and thus restrict their lib-
> erty, those who have submitted to these restrictions
> when required have a right to a similar submission
> from those who have benefited by their submission.
> The rules may provide that officials should have au-
> thority to enforce obedience ... but the moral obli-
> gation to obey the rules in such circumstances is due

to the cooperating members of the society, and they have the correlative moral right to obedience.[2]

While Hart does not refer to this source of special rights and obligations in terms of fairness or fair play, he does note later that "in the case of mutual restrictions we are in fact saying that this claim to interfere with another's freedom is justified because it is fair."[3] We can understand him, then, to be claiming that, in the situation described, a beneficiary has an obligation to "do his fair share" by submitting to the rules when they require it; others who have cooperated before have a right to this fair distribution of the burdens of submission.

Hart's brief account of the principle of fair play, of course, leaves many important questions unanswered. What, for instance, are we to count as an "enterprise"? Are only participants in the enterprise obligated to do their part, or do obligations fall on all who benefit from the enterprise? Why is a set of rules necessary? Clearly a fuller treatment of the principle is essential for our purposes, and John Rawls provides one in his 1964 essay, "Legal Obligation and the Duty of Fair Play."[4] There Rawls builds on Hart's account to give both a more complete account of the principle of fair play and an extensive discussion of its application to constitutional democracies. His central presentation of the principle echoes Hart's:

The principle of fair play may be defined as follows. Suppose there is a mutually beneficial and just scheme of social cooperation, and that the advantages it yields can only be obtained if everyone, or nearly everyone, cooperates. Suppose further that cooperation requires a certain sacrifice from each person, or at least involves a certain restriction of his liberty. Suppose finally that the benefits produced by cooperation are, up to a certain point, free: that is, the scheme of cooperation is unstable in the sense that if any one person knows that all (or nearly all) of the others will continue to do their part, he will still be able to share a gain from the scheme even if he does not do his part. Under these conditions a person who has accepted the benefits of the scheme is bound by a duty of fair play to do his part and not to take advantage of the free benefits by not cooperating.[5]

The context within which obligations (or duties—Rawls is not very concerned here with the distinction between them) of fair play can arise, as described by Rawls, can be seen to exhibit three important features, parallel to those we can discern in Hart's account.

(1) There must be an active scheme of social cooperation. This does not really advance us much beyond Hart's "enterprise," but I think that both writers clearly intended that the principle cover a broad range of schemes, programs, and enterprises differing in size and in significance. Thus, both a tenant organization's program to improve conditions in an apartment building and an entire political community's cooperative efforts to preserve social order seem to qualify as "enterprises" or "schemes of social cooperation" of the appropriate sort. Rawls does set two explicit conditions, however, which help us limit the class of "schemes" he has in mind. First, they must be "mutually beneficial." This condition is, I think, implicit in Hart's account as well; indeed, the principle would be obviously objectionable in its absence. Second, the schemes must be just. This condition is nowhere alluded to by Hart, and I will consider it carefully in Section II.

(2) Cooperation under the scheme involves at least a restriction of one's liberty. Rawls does not mention here, as Hart does, that this restriction must be in accord with a system of rules which govern the scheme by determining the requirements of cooperation (although his later "institutional" language does follow Hart's requirement). Frankly, I can see no good reason to insist that the enterprise be governed by rules. Mightn't an enterprise be of the right sort which, say, assigned burdens fairly but not in accord with any preestablished rules? Cannot doing one's part be obligatory under considerations of fair play even if "one's part" is not specified by the rules?

(3) The benefits yielded by the scheme may be received in at least some cases by someone who does not cooperate when his turn comes; here Rawls again makes explicit a condition which Hart clearly has in mind (since "free riding" is a problem only when this conditions

obtains). But Rawls adds to this the condition that the benefits in question can be obtained only if nearly all of the participants cooperate. I confess that I again do not see the necessity of this condition. Would it be any less unfair to take the benefits of the cooperative sacrifices of others if those benefits could still be obtained when one-third or one-half of the participants neglected their responsibilities towards the scheme? Would this make that neglect justifiable? Surely not. A scheme which requires uniform cooperation when only 50 percent cooperation is needed may perhaps be an inefficient scheme; but it is not clear that this would make considerations of fair play inapplicable. Consider a community scheme to preserve water pressure. This scheme prohibits watering lawns in the evening, when in fact if half of the members watered their lawns there would be no lowering of water pressure. Surely this is an inefficient plan, compared to alternatives. But once the plan was instituted, would a member be any more justified in watering his lawn in the evening than if only a few people's so doing would lower the water pressure? I think it is clear that he would not be. Certainly free-riding is more dangerous to the scheme's successful provision of benefits when Rawls' requirement obtains; it may then be even more objectionable in those cases. But this additional objectionable element seems to have nothing to do with considerations of *fair play*.[6]

Rawls' account seems to conform to either the letter or the spirit of Hart's account fairly consistently. One significant addition Rawls makes, however, is to move beyond Hart's simple requirement that an individual must benefit from the scheme in order to become bound. Rawls specifies that the obligation depends on "our having accepted and our intention to continue accepting the benefits of a just scheme of cooperation. . . ."[7] We have, then, a move from mere benefaction in Hart's case, to a positive *acceptance* of benefits in Rawls' account. (The "intention to continue accepting benefits" seems quite beside the point here, and Rawls drops that clause in later versions; I shall ignore it.) While the distinction between benefiting and accepting benefits is usually not

easy to draw in actual cases, that there is such a distinction, and that it is of great significance to moral questions, is undeniable. Suppose that I am kidnapped by a mad doctor and dragged to his laboratory, where he forces on me an injection of an experimental drug. When I discover that as a result of the injection my intelligence and strength have greatly increased, it is undeniable that I have benefited from the injection; but it would be a simple abuse of language to say that I had "accepted" the benefits which I received. It seems clear, then, that we can distinguish, at least in some cases, between mere receipt and positive acceptance of benefits. And it seems equally clear that this distinction may play a crucial role in determining whether or what obligations arise from my having benefited from another's actions.

To have accepted a benefit in the right sense, I must have wanted that benefit when I received it or must have made some effort to get the benefit or, at least, must not have actively attempted to avoid getting it. I will try to be more precise about this distinction later; here I want only to suggest that Rawls apparently does not see mere benefaction as sufficient to generate an obligation of fair play. He stresses instead the necessity that the benefits be voluntarily accepted by the beneficiary.

II

I want now to return to consider briefly another of Rawls' conditions for the generation of obligations of fair play. The condition states that only when the scheme or institution in question is just can any obligations of fair play (relative to that scheme) arise. This claim is part of a more general thesis that we can never be bound to support or comply with unjust arrangements. Although Rawls never advances this general thesis in so many words, it follows from his (unacceptable) claim that *all* obligations are accounted for by the principle of fair play, conjoined with the absence of any natural duties which could account for such a bond.[8]

Rawls' requirement that the scheme of cooperation be just is put forward quite casually in the essay we have been considering; and although he calls it an "essential condition," as far as I can see he offers no defense of this claim. Even in the more recent statement of this requirement in *A Theory of Justice,* we are given little in the way of justification. While he suggests that the condition is necessary to guarantee the requisite "background conditions" for obligation, he elaborates on this point only by suggesting a (strained) analogy with the case of promise-making: "extorted promises are void ab initio."[9] I have argued elsewhere that this observation is quite irrelevant.[10] It is a failure in terms of voluntariness that renders extorted promises non-binding, and the injustice of an institution need not affect the voluntariness of either consent to its rules or acceptance of benefits from it. Rawls' only argument for his "justice condition," then, seems to be a non sequitur.

As Rawls supplies us with no real argument for the justice condition, let us try to construct some for him. Two sorts of arguments suggest themselves as defenses of this condition; the first concerns the purpose of the scheme or the ends it promotes, while the second more directly concerns distribution within the scheme. Our first argument would run as follows: we cannot have obligations to do the morally impermissible, or to support schemes whose purposes are immoral or which promote immoral ends. Since unjust schemes fall within this category, we cannot have an obligation to cooperate within unjust schemes. Now there are a number of difficulties with this as a defense of Rawls' justice condition. One obvious problem is this: why does Rawls only disqualify *unjust* schemes, rather than all schemes which promote or aim at *immoral* ends? Why does Rawls not include the more general prohibition?

The reason is, I think, that while these immoral ends of the scheme provide us with a reason for working against it, the justice condition is meant to be tied to the principle in a more intimate fashion. But what is this fashion? Thus far, nothing we have said about fair play seems to have anything to do with the moral status of the scheme's purposes. The intuitive force of the principle of fair play seems to be preserved even for criminal conspiracies, for example. The special rights and obligations which arise under the principle are thought to

do so because of the special relationships which exist between the cooperating participants; a fair share of the burdens is thought to be owed by a benefiting participant simply because others have sacrificed to allow him to benefit within a cooperative scheme. No reference is made here to the morally acceptable status of the scheme. Simple intuitions about fair play, then, do not seem to provide a reason for disqualifying unjust cooperative schemes. Rather, they suggest that obligations of fair play can, at least sometimes, arise within such schemes.

But perhaps another sort of support can be given to Rawls' condition. This second argument concerns distribution within the scheme, and it certainly has the Rawlsian flavor. We suggest first that, in effect, the justice condition amends the principle to read that a person is bound to do his fair share in supporting a cooperative scheme only if he has been allocated a fair share of the benefits of the scheme. Previously, the principle of fair play required only that the individual have accepted benefits from the scheme in order to be bound, where now it requires that he have accepted benefits *and* have been allocated at least a fair share of benefits. The role of the justice condition now appears to be important, to be an intimate feature of our intuitions about fair play. For if a scheme is just, each participant will be allocated a fair share of the benefits of cooperation; thus, anyone who benefits at all from the scheme has the opportunity to benefit to the extent of a fair share (although he may *accept* less than this). We are guaranteed that the principle of fair play will only apply to individuals who have been fairly treated. Our feeling that a person ought not to have a share equally in supporting a scheme that treats him unfairly is given voice in this condition. The justice condition, then, on this argument, serves the purpose of assuring that a man is bound to do his fair share only if he is allocated a fair share of benefits (and accepts some of them).

I think that this is an important feature of our intuitions about fair play, and it also seems a natural way of reading Rawls. In fact, this may be the argument that Rawls is suggesting when, in elaborating on the principle, he notes that if the scheme is just, "each person receives a fair share when all (himself included) do their part."[11] (Rawls' observation is, strictly speaking, false; the justice of a scheme does not guarantee that each person either receives or accepts a fair share.) But if this *is* the argument Rawls intends for his justice condition, there are serious difficulties for it to overcome. The motivation for including the requirement is (on this reading) to guarantee that an individual not become bound to carry a fair share of the burdens of a cooperative scheme if he has been allocated less than a fair share of its benefits; it is unfair to demand full cooperation from one to whom full benefits are denied. But if *this* is our reason for including the justice condition, we have surely included too much. Why should we think that the whole scheme must be just for this sort of intuition to be given play? Rawls' justice condition requires that *everyone* be allocated a fair share of benefits if *anyone* is to be bound by an obligation of fair play. But the reasons we have given for including this condition seem only to require that for a particular individual to be bound, *he* must be allocated a fair share. This says nothing about the allocation of benefits in general, or about what benefits *others* are allocated. If some individuals within an unjust scheme are allocated less than a fair share of benefits, then our reasons would support the view that *they* are not bound to carry a fair share of the burdens. But nothing said yet about feelings of fair play seems to exempt from obligation those individuals to whom a fair share of benefits is in fact allocated within an *unjust* scheme. So again the point of Rawls' justice condition comes into doubt.

These arguments may prompt us to think more about the notion of a "fair share" of the burdens of cooperation. For if we understand by this phrase a share of the total burden proportionate to the share of the total benefits allocated to the individual, then we may have no problem in accepting that anyone who accepts *any* benefits from a cooperative scheme is bound to do his "fair share." Our belief that only an individual who is allocated a fair share of the benefits is bound to cooperate may be false. For it seems eminently fair to hold that

each is bound to cooperate to the extent that he is allowed to benefit from a cooperative scheme; thus, those who are allocated the largest shares of benefits owe the largest share of burdens. But even one who is allocated a very small share of the benefits is bound to carry a small share of the burdens (provided he accepts the benefits).

Now it is clear that these intuitions cannot be given full play in the case of schemes whose burdens cannot be unequally distributed. But there may seem to be other difficulties involved in the interpretation of the fair-play principle sketched above. First, it seems to entail that the better-off are bound to support unjust schemes which favor them, and the more discriminatory the scheme, the more strongly they must support it. And second, it seems to entail that those who are allocated tiny, unfair shares of the benefits are still bound to cooperate with the unjust scheme which mistreats them. These may again seem to be good reasons to limit the principle's application to just schemes. I think this appearance is misleading. For, first, the principle under discussion does not entail that the better-off must support unjust schemes which favor them. While it does specify that they are obligated to repay by cooperation the sacrifices made in their behalf by the other members, the injustice of the scheme is a strong reason for opposing it, which gains in strength with the degree of injustice. Thus, there are moral considerations which may override the obligations of fair play (depending, of course, on the degree of the injustice of the scheme, among other things). And if we think of the burdens as sacrifices to be made, it seems only fair that the unjustly favored should be heavily burdened. As for the apparent result that the unjustly treated are still bound to support the scheme (even if to a lesser degree) which discriminates against them, this result can also be seen to be mistaken. For if we remember that benefits must be *accepted* in order for an individual to be bound under the principle, the unfairly treated have the option of refusing to accept benefits, hence sparing themselves the obligation to support a scheme which treats them unfairly (and they have, as well, the duty to oppose such unjust schemes, regardless of what obligations they are under). The idea, then, is that only if they willingly accept the benefits of the scheme are participants bound to bear the burdens of cooperation, and only then in proportion to the benefits allocated to them.

I am not sure just how much of the Hart-Rawls conception of the principle of fair play this analysis captures. But the considerations raised above seem to me to be good reasons for rejecting Rawls' "justice condition." While we can, of course, agree with Rawls that intolerably unjust schemes ought not to be furthered (and, in fact, ought to be opposed), there is no logical difficulty, at least, in holding that we may sometimes have obligations of fair play to cooperate within unjust schemes. And the arguments suggest that there may be no non-logical difficulties either.

III

I want to pause here to comment briefly on the theory of political obligation which uses the principle of fair play, and specifically on the changes which this account introduces into our conception of political obligation. There are, of course, important continuities between this "fair-play account" and the traditional consent theory account mentioned earlier. While one approach locates the ground of obligation in the acceptance of benefits and the other in consensual acts, both are "obligation-centered" accounts and, as such, both stress the essential voluntariness of the generation of the obligation.[12] But defenders of the fair-play account of political obligation wish to stress as well its significant departures from consent theory; the fair-play account requires a cooperative scheme as the context within which obligations arise, and obviates the need for *deliberate undertakings* of obligation. How these changes might be thought to constitute improvements over the consent theory account seems fairly clear.

First, the fair-play account involves viewing political communities in a different way than consent theory; specifically, they are viewed as "communities" in a fairly strict sense. We are to understand political communities as being

fundamentally, or at least in part, cooperative enterprises on a very large scale. Citizens thus are thought to stand in a cooperate relationship to their fellows, rather than in an adversary relationship with the government. And this former view may seem to some more realistic than the latter.

But clearly the major advantage which the fair-play account of political obligation is thought by its advocates to have is that of providing a *general* account of our political bonds. No deliberate undertaking is necessary to become obligated under the principle of fair play. One can become bound without trying to and without knowing that one is performing an act which generates an obligation. Since mere acceptance of benefits within the right context generates the obligation, one who accepts benefits within the right context can become bound unknowingly. This is an important difference from consent theory's account, which stressed the necessity of a deliberate undertaking. Thus, while one can neither consent nor accept benefits (in the right sense) unintentionally, one can accept benefits without being aware of the moral consequences of so doing (while being unaware of the moral consequences of consenting defeats the claim that consent was given). The significance of this difference, of course, lies in the possibility of giving a *general* account of political obligation in the two cases. For consent theory's failure to give a general account stemmed from the lack of citizens in modern states who had voluntarily undertaken political obligations in the sense required. At least initially, however, it seems much more plausible to suggest that most or all of us have accepted benefits, as is required under the principle of fair play. Thus, the possibility of giving a general account using this principle seems to be vastly increased over one which uses a principle of consent. This would *not* be the case, however, if accepting benefits in the right sense required having an understanding of the moral consequences of such acceptance. For certainly most citizens who receive the benefits of government do not have such an understanding.

Exactly what "accepting the benefits of government'' amounts to, of course, is not yet entirely clear. Neither is the identity of the ''cooperative scheme'' embodied in political communities. These points will be discussed as we continue. My aim here has been simply to mention what might seem to be advantages of the fair-play account; whether or not these ''advantages'' are genuine remains to be seen. But regardless of the advantages this account may have over the consent-theory account, it surely falls short on one score. Consent is a *clear* ground of obligation. If we are agreed on anything concerning moral requirements, it is that promising and consenting generate them. In specifying a different ground of obligation, the account using the principle of fair play draws away from the paradigm of acts that generate obligations. And to those who are strongly wedded to this paradigm of consent, such as Robert Nozick, the principle of fair play may seem a sham.

IV

In Chapter 5 of *Anarchy, State, and Utopia,* Nozick argues against accepting the principle of fair play as a valid moral principle, not just in political settings, but in any settings whatsoever. He begins by describing a cooperative scheme of the sort he thinks Hart and Rawls have in mind, and then suggests that benefaction within that scheme may *not* bind one to do one's part:

> Suppose some of the people in your neighborhood (there are 364 other adults) have found a public address system and decide to institute a system of public entertainment. They post a list of names, one for each day, yours among them. On his assigned day (one can easily switch days) a person is to run the public address system, play records over it, give news bulletins, tell amusing stories he has heard, and so on. After 138 days on which each person has done his part, your day arrives. Are you obligated to take your turn? You *have* benefited from it, occasionally opening your window to listen, enjoying some music or chuckling at someone's funny story. The other people *have* put themselves out. But must you answer the call when it is your turn to do so? As it stands, surely not. Though you benefit from

the arrangement, you may know all along that 364 days of entertainment supplied by others will not be worth your giving up *one* day. You would rather not have any of it and not give up a day than have it all and spend one of your days at it. Given these preferences, how can it be that you are required to participate when your scheduled times comes?[13]

On the basis of this example and others, Nozick concludes that we are never bound to cooperate in such contexts (unless we have given our consent to be constrained by the rules of the cooperative scheme).

Now, to be fair, Nozick does not simply pick the weakest form of the principle of fair play and then reject it for its inadequacy in hard cases; he has, in fact, a suggestion for improving the principle in response to the cases he describes. Having noticed, I suppose, that the case described above favors his conclusions largely because of the negligible value of the benefits received, Nozick suggests that ''at the very least one wants to build into the principle of fairness the condition that the benefits to a person from the actions of others are greater than the cost to him of doing his share'' (Nozick, p. 94). There is certainly something right about this; something like this must be built into the idea of a useful cooperative scheme. On the other hand, we can imagine a defender of the principle saying ''if you weren't prepared to do your part you ought not to have taken *any* benefits from the scheme, no matter how insignificant.'' Nozick, of course, has more to say on this point, and so do I.

Even if we do modify the principle with this condition, however, Nozick has other arguments against it. ''The benefits might only barely be worth the cost to you of doing your share, yet others might benefit from *this* institution much more than you do; they all treasure listening to the public broadcasts. As the person least benefited by the practice, are you obligated to do an equal amount for it?'' (Nozick, p. 94). The understood answer is no, but we might agree with this answer without agreeing that it tells against the principle. For if we understand that ''doing one's part'' or ''doing one's fair share'' is not necessarily ''doing an equal part,'' but rather ''doing a part proportionate to the part of the benefits received,'' then the one who benefits least from a co-operative scheme will *not* be bound to share equally in the burdens of cooperation. I argued for this interpretation in Section II, and if we accept it, Nozick's PA system example may no longer seem so troublesome. For we might be willing to admit that the individual in question, because he benefited so little, was bound to cooperate but not to the same extent as others who benefit more from the scheme. Would being obligated to do one's part in the PA scheme seem quite so objectionable if one's part was only, say, an hour's worth of broadcasting, as opposed to that of the PA enthusiasts, whose parts were one and a half days of broadcasting? There are, perhaps, not clear answers to these questions.

But surely the defender of the principle of fair play will have more fundamental objections to Nozick's case than these. In the first place, the individual in Nozick's PA example does not seem to be a *participant* in the scheme in the sense that Hart and Rawls may have in mind. While he does live in the neighborhood within which the scheme operates, and he does benefit from it, he is still very much of an "innocent bystander." The PA system scheme has been built up around him in such a way that he could not escape its influence. And, of course, the whole force of Nozick's example lies in our feeling that others ought not to be able to *force* any scheme they like upon us, with the attendant obligations. The PA case would be precisely such a case of "forced" obligation. So naturally we may find Nozick's criticism of the principle of fair play convincing, if we believe the principle to entail that we *do* have obligations under the PA scheme.

But it seems clear that Hart and Rawls did not mean for the principle to apply to such cases of "innocent bystanders" (though admittedly neither emphasizes the point). Nozick's case seems to rest on a reading of the principle which runs contrary to the spirit of their remarks, a reading according to which the principle binds everyone who benefits from a cooperation scheme, regardless of their relations to it. And Nozick is surely right that a

moral principle which had those results *would* be an outrageous one. People who have no significant relationship at all with some cooperative scheme may receive incidental benefits from its operation. Thus, imagine yourself a member of some scheme which benefits you immensely by increasing your income. Your friends and relatives may benefit incidentally from the scheme as well if, say, you now become prone to send them expensive presents. But the suggestion that their benefiting in this way obligates them to do their part in the scheme is absurd.

Hart and Rawls can most fairly be read as holding that only beneficiaries who are also participants (in some significant sense) are bound under the principle of fair play. And on this reading, of course, Nozick's PA system example does not seem to be a case to which the principle applies; the individual in question is not a participant in the scheme, having had nothing to do with its institution, and having done nothing to lead anyone to believe that he wished to become involved in the scheme. The example, then, cannot serve as a counterexample to Hart's principle. In fact, all of Nozick's examples in his criticisms of Hart are examples in which an "outsider" has some benefit thrust on him by some cooperative scheme to which he is in no way tied (see Nozick's "street-sweeping," "lawn-mowing," and "book-thrusting" examples, pp. 94–95). But if I am right, these examples do not tell against the principle of fair play, since the benefits accruing to "outsiders" are not thought by Hart and Rawls to bind under that principle.

The problem of specifying who are "outsiders," and consequently whose benefits will count, is a serious one, especially in the political applications of the principle. And it seems that the problem may provide ammunition for a serious counterattack by someone such as Nozick against the principle of fair play. We have maintained, remember, that only "participants" or "insiders" in the cooperative scheme are candidates for being obligated under the principle to do their share in cooperating. Those "outsiders" who benefit from the scheme's operation are not bound under the principle of fair play. But how exactly do we differentiate between these outsiders and the insiders? What relationship must hold between an individual and a cooperative scheme for him to be said to be a participant in some significant sense?

This is a hard question to answer, but we have already considered some cases where an individual is *not* a participant in the right sense. Thus, merely being a member of some group, other members of which institute a scheme, is not enough to make one a participant or an "insider." Although Nozick's man is a "member" of an identifiable group, namely his neighborhood, this "membership" does not suffice to make him a participant in any scheme his neighbors dream up. Normally, we would want to say that for an individual to be a real participant in a cooperative scheme, he must have either (1) pledged his support or tacitly agreed to be governed by the scheme's rules, or (2) played some active role in the scheme after its institution. It is not enough to be associated with the "schemers" in some vague way to make one an "insider" or a participant; one must go out and do things to become a participant and to potentially be bound under the principle of fair play.

Now we can imagine an opponent of the principle accepting these remarks concerning whose benefiting will count, and accepting our criticism of Nozick's PA system counterexample, and still responding to our discussion by posing the following dilemma. We are agreed, the Nozickian begins, that "outsiders" fall outside the scope of Hart's principle; not just anyone who benefits from a cooperative scheme will be bound to do his share in it. And we are agreed that mere membership in some group, other members of which conduct some cooperative scheme, is insufficient to make one an "insider." And we are agreed that one becomes an "insider" by the means described above, perhaps among others. But the problem is this. In becoming an "insider" one must do something which involves either an express or a tacit undertaking to do one's part in the scheme. So if the principle of fair play can bind only "insiders" in a cooperative scheme,

it will bind only those individuals who have *already* become bound to do their part in the scheme in becoming "insiders." The principle is superfluous; it collapses into a principle of consent. All and only those individuals who have actually undertaken to do their part in the scheme are bound by the principle of fair play to do their part in the scheme. Benefiting under the scheme is quite irrelevant, for benefiting only counts under the principle for "insiders." But "insiders" are already bound to the scheme, whether they benefit from it or not.

This argument, if it is acceptable, counts heavily against the principle of fair play. For that principle was supposed to show us how individuals could become bound to some cooperative enterprise *without* actually giving their consent to it. But if the principle can only plausibly be thought to bind those who have already consented to going along with the enterprise, the principle's usefulness becomes highly doubtful. We can explain whatever obligations participants in the enterprise are thought to have simply in terms of a principle of consent, quite independent of considerations of fair play.

But is this sort of argument acceptable? Is it true that I cannot become a participant in the right sense without giving at least tacit consent to the scheme? Surely many participants in cooperative schemes have given their consent, either express or tacit, and are bound to their schemes regardless of what else they do to bind themselves. But these are not the individuals with whom Hart and Rawls are primarily concerned. With all our discussion of "participation," we are overlooking a feature of the principle of fair play which Rawls saw as essential to the generation of the obligation. The principle of fair play does not specify that all participants in cooperative schemes are bound to do their part, or even that all participants who benefit from the schemes are so bound. It states rather that those who *accept* the benefits of a cooperative scheme are bound to cooperate. This distinction between accepting benefits and merely receiving benefits has been lost somewhere in the shuffle. It is a distinction which is *completely* overlooked in Nozick's discussion of the principle of fair play. But it seems to me that this distinction is crucial in settling the problem of how to distinguish participants (or "insiders") from "outsiders."

For Rawls and Hart, the principle of fair play accounts for the obligations of those whose active role in the scheme consists of accepting the benefits of its workings. One becomes a participant in the scheme precisely by accepting the benefits it offers; the other ways in which one can become a participant are not important to considerations of fair play. And individuals who have merely *received* benefits from the scheme have the same status relative to it as those who have been unaffected by the scheme; they are not in any way bound to do their part in the scheme unless they have independently undertaken to do so. If, as I've suggested, the acceptance of benefits constitutes the sort of "participation" in a scheme with which Rawls and Hart are concerned, we can understand why neither Rawls nor Hart specifically limits the application of the principle to *participants* in the scheme. This limitation has already been accomplished by making obligation conditional on the acceptance of benefits. This means, of course, that the principle cannot be read as the outrageous one which requires anyone at all who benefits from the scheme to do his part in it.

But understanding the principle in this way also helps us see why the Nozickian line of argument we have considered cannot succeed. The Nozickian tried to persuade us that an individual could not become a participant, or an "insider," without doing something which amounted to giving his consent to do his part in the scheme. But it seems clear that a man *can* accept benefits from a scheme and be a participant in that sense without giving his consent to the scheme. And further, such acceptance of benefits *does* seem to obligate him to do his part. Let me support and clarify this claim with an example.

Imagine that in Nozick's neighborhood the need for public entertainment is not the only matter of concern. There is also a problem with the neighborhood's water supply; the water pumped through their pipes has developed an unpleasant taste and an odd yellow tinge. A neighborhood meeting is called, at which a ma-

jority votes to dig a public well near the center of the neighborhood, to be paid for and maintained by the members of the neighborhood. Some of the members clearly give their consent to the proposed scheme. Others, who vote against the proposal, do not. Jones, in particular, announces angrily that he wants to have nothing to do with the scheme and that he will certainly not pledge his support. Nothing, he claims, could make him consent to such a ridiculous enterprise. But in spite of his opposition, the well is dug, paid for, and maintained by the other members of the neighborhood. Jones, as expected, contributes nothing to this effort.

Now the benefits of clear, fresh water are available to the neighborhood, and Jones begins to be envious of his neighbors, who go to the well daily. So he goes to the well every night and, knowing that the water will never be missed, takes some home with him for the next day. It seems clear to me that Jones is a perfect example of a "free rider." And it also seems clear that, having accepted benefits from the scheme (indeed, he has gone out of his way to obtain them), he has an obligation to do his part within it. But he certainly does not seem to have *consented* to the scheme. We have, then, a case in which an individual has an obligation to do his part within a cooperative scheme which is *not* accounted for by a principle of consent. We would, I think, account for that obligation precisely in terms of fair play. Jones has made himself a participant in the scheme by accepting its benefits, although he has refused to give his consent. So the Nozickian argument does not succeed.

I have tried to show, then, that the principle of fair play does not collapse into a principle of consent. While many participants in cooperative schemes will be bound to do their parts because they have consented to do so, many others will be bound because they have accepted benefits from the scheme. The obligations of the latter will fall under the principle of fair play. We should not think, because of the peculiarity of Jones' position in our example, that only the obligations of free-riders like Jones will be accounted for by the principle. For it is possible to *go along* with a cooperative scheme (as Jones does not) without consenting to it, becoming bound through one's acceptance of benefits. In fact, I think that *most* participants in cooperative schemes do nothing which can be thought to constitute consent. It is not necessary to refuse to give one's consent, as Jones does, in order not to give it. Consent is not given to a scheme by any behavior short of express dissent. Most participants in cooperative schemes simply go along with the schemes, taking their benefits and carrying their burdens. But if they do not expressly undertake to support the schemes, and if their behavior does not constitute a response to a clear choice situation, I do not think that we can ascribe consent to them. Certainly by going along with a scheme, we lead others to *expect* certain future performances from us; but this does not show that we have *undertaken* to perform according to expectations. Thus, the obligations which participants in cooperative schemes have (relative to those schemes) will not normally be grounded in consent.

The reading of the principle which I have given obviously places a very heavy load on the notion of "acceptance," a notion to which we have as yet given no clear meaning (and Rawls and Hart certainly give us no help on this count). It is not, as suggested in Section I, at all easy to distinguish in practice between benefits that have been accepted and those that have only been received, although some cases seem clearly to fall on the "merely received" side. Thus, benefits we have actively resisted getting, and those which we have gotten unknowingly or in ways over which we have had no control at all, seem clearly *not* to be benefits we have accepted. To have accepted a benefit, I think, we would want to say that an individual must either (1) have tried to get (and succeeded in getting) the benefit, or (2) have taken the benefit willingly and knowingly.

Consider now Nozick's example of the program that involves "thrusting books" into unsuspecting people's houses. Clearly the benefits in question are merely received, not accepted. "One cannot," Nozick writes, "whatever one's purposes, just act so as to give people benefits and then demand (or

seize) payment. Nor can a group of persons do this" (p. 95). I am suggesting that, on the contrary, the principle of fair play does *not* involve justifying this sort of behavior; people are only bound under the principle when they have accepted benefits.

Nozick's first-line example, the PA scheme, however, is slightly more difficult. For here the benefits received are not forced upon you, as in the "book-thrusting" case, or gotten in some other way which is outside your control. Rather, the benefits are what I will call "open"; while they can be avoided, they cannot be avoided without considerable inconvenience. Thus, while I can avoid the (questionable) benefits the PA system provides by remaining indoors with the windows closed, this is a considerable inconvenience. The benefits are "open" in the sense that I cannot avoid receiving them, even if I want to, without altering my life style (economists often have such benefits in mind in speaking of "public goods"). Many benefits yielded by cooperative schemes (in fact most benefits, I should think) are "open" in this way. A neighborhood organization's program to improve the neighborhood's appearance yields benefits which are "open." And the benefits of government are mostly of this sort. The benefits of the rule of law, protection by the armed forces, pollution control, and so on can be avoided only by emigration.

We can contrast these cases of "open" benefits with benefits that are only "readily available." If instead of a PA system, Nozick's group had decided to rent a building in the middle of town in which live entertainment was continuously available to neighborhood members, the benefits of the scheme would only be "readily available." A good example of the distinction under consideration would be the distinction between two sorts of police protection, one sort being an "open" benefit, the other being only "readily available." Thus, the benefits which I receive from the continuous efforts of police officers to patrol the streets, capture criminals, and eliminate potential threats to my safety, are benefits which are "open." They can be avoided only by leaving the area which the police force protects. But I may also request *special* protection by the police, if I fear for my life, say, or if I need my house to be watched while I'm away. These benefits are "readily available." Benefits which are "readily available" can be easily avoided without inconvenience.

Now I think that clear cases of the acceptance of benefits, as opposed to receipt, will be easy to find where benefits which are only "readily available" are concerned. Getting these benefits will involve going out of one's way, making some sort of effort to get the benefit, and hence there will generally be no question that the benefit was accepted in the sense we have described. The principle of fair play seems most clearly to apply in cases such as these. These will be cases where our actions may obviously fall short of constituting *consent* to do our part in the scheme in question, but where our acceptance of benefits binds us to do our part because of considerations of fair play. When we accept benefits in such cases, it may be necessary that we be aware that the benefits in question *are* the fruits of a cooperative scheme, in order for us to be willing to ascribe any obligations of fair play; but it will *not* be necessary that some express or tacit act of consent have been performed.

The examples of "open" benefits are, of course, harder to handle. Nozick's comments seem quite reasonable with respect to them. For surely it is very implausible to suggest that if we are unwilling to do our part, we must alter our life styles in order to avoid enjoying these benefits. As Nozick suggests, there is surely no reason why, when the street-sweeping scheme comes to your town, you must "imagine dirt as you traverse the street, so as not to benefit as a free rider" (p. 94). Nozick's comments here do not, however, strike against the principle of fair play in any obvious way. For as I have interpreted it, the principle does not apply to cases of mere receipt of benefits from cooperative schemes; and the cases where the benefits are "open" in this way seem to be cases of mere receipt of benefits. Certainly it would be peculiar if a man, who by simply going about his business in a normal fashion benefited unavoidably from some cooperative scheme, were told that

he had voluntarily accepted benefits which generated for him a special obligation to do his part.

This problem of "acceptance" and "open benefits" is a serious one, and there are real difficulties involved in solving it. It may look, for instance, as if I am saying that a genuine acceptance of open benefits is impossible. But I would not want to be pushed so far. It seems to me that it is possible to accept a benefit which is (in one sense) unavoidable; but it is not at all the *normal* case that those who receive open benefits from a scheme have also accepted those benefits. In the case of benefits which are only "readily available," receipt of the benefits is generally *also* acceptance. But this is not so in the case of open benefits. I suggested earlier that accepting a benefit involved either (1) trying to get (and succeeding in getting) the benefit, or (2) taking the benefit willingly and knowingly. Getting benefits which are "readily available" normally involves (1) trying to get the benefit. It is not clear, however, how one would go about *trying* to get an open benefit which is not distributed by request, but is rather received by everyone involved, whether they want it or not. If open benefits can be accepted, it would seem that method (2) of accepting benefits is the way in which this is normally accomplished. We can take the open benefits which we receive willingly and knowingly. But doing so involves a number of restrictions on our attitudes toward and beliefs about the open benefits we receive. We cannot, for instance, regard the benefits as having been forced upon us against our will, or think that the benefits are not worth the price we must pay for them. And taking the benefits "knowingly" seems to involve an understanding of the status of those benefits relative to the party providing them. Thus, in the case of open benefits provided by a cooperative scheme, we must understand that the benefits *are* provided by the cooperative scheme in order to accept them.

The necessity of satisfying such conditions, however, seems to significantly reduce the number of individuals who receive open benefits, who can be taken to have *accepted* those benefits. And it will by no means be a standard case in which all beneficiaries of a cooperative scheme's workings have accepted the benefits they receive.

I recognize, of course, that problems concerning "acceptance" remain. But even if they did not, my reading of the principle of fair play, as binding only those who have accepted benefits, would still face difficulties. The fact remains that we *do* criticize persons as "free-riders" (in terms of fair play) for not doing their part, even when they have *not* accepted benefits from a cooperative scheme. We often criticize them merely because they *receive* benefits without doing their part in the cooperative scheme. Let us go back to Nozick's neighborhood and imagine another, more realistic cooperative scheme in operation, this one designed to beautify the neighborhood by assigning to each resident a specific task involving landscaping or yard work. Home owners are required to care for their yards and to do some work on community property on weekends. There are also a number of apartments in the neighborhood, but because the apartment grounds are cared for by the landlords, apartment dwellers are expected only to help on community property (they are expected to help because even tenants are granted full community membership and privileges; and it is reasoned that all residents have an equal interest in the neighborhood's appearance, at least during the time they remain). Two of these apartment dwellers, Oscar and Willie, refuse to do their part in the scheme. Oscar refuses because he hates neatly trimmed yards, preferring crabgrass, long weeds, and scraggly bushes. The residents do not feel so bad about Oscar (although they try to force him out of the neighborhood), since he does not seem to be benefiting from their efforts without putting out. He hates what they are doing to the neighborhood. Willie, however, is another case altogether. He values a neat neighborhood as much as the others; but he values his spare time more than the others. While he enjoys a beautiful neighborhood, the part he is expected to play in the cooperative scheme involves too much of his time. He makes it clear that he would prefer to have an ugly neighborhood to joining such a scheme.

So while the others labor to produce an al-most spotless neighborhood, Willie enjoys the benefits resulting from their efforts while doing nothing to help. And it seems to me that Willie is *just* the sort of person who would be accused by the neighborhood council of "free-riding," of unfairly benefiting from the cooperative efforts of others; for he receives exactly the same benefits as the others while contributing nothing. Yet Willie has not accepted the benefits in question, for he thinks that the price being demanded is too high. He would prefer doing without the benefits to having the benefits and the burdens.

So it looks as if the way in which we have filled out the principle of fair play is not entirely in accord with some common feelings about matters of fair play; for these common feelings do not seem to require acceptance of benefits within the scheme, as our version of the principle does. It is against these "ordinary feelings about fair play" (and not against the "filled-out" principle we have been describing), I think, that Nozick's arguments, and the "Nozickian" arguments suggested, strike most sharply.

But Willie's position is *not* substantially different from that of the salesman, Sam, whose sole territory is the neighborhood in question. Sam works eight hours every day in the neighborhood, enjoying its beauty, while Willie (away at work all day) may eke out his forty weekly hours of enjoyment if he stays home on weekends. Thus, Sam and Willie receive substantially the same benefits. Neither Sam nor Willie has done anything at all to ally himself with the cooperative scheme, and neither has "accepted" the fruits of that scheme. Willie is a "member" of the community only because the council voted to award "membership" to tenants, and he has made no commitments. To make the parallel complete, we can even suppose that Sam, beloved by all the residents, is named by the council an "honorary member." But if the neighborhood council accused Sam, the salesman, of "free-riding" and demanded that *he* work on community property, their position would be laughable. Why, though, should Willie, who is like Sam in all important respects, be any *more* vulnerable to such accusations and demands?

The answer is that he is *not* any more vulnerable; if ordinary feelings about obligations of fair play insist that he *is* more vulnerable, those feelings are mistaken. But in fairness to Nozick, the way that Hart and Rawls phrase their account of the principle of fair play *does* sometimes look as if it expresses those (mistaken) feelings about fair play. As Rawls states it,

> The main idea is that when a number of persons engage in a mutually advantageous cooperative venture according to rules, and thus restrict their liberty in ways necessary to yield advantages for all, those who have submitted to these restrictions have a right to a similar acquiescence on the part of those who have benefited from their submission. We are not to gain from the cooperative labors of others without doing our fair share.[14]

This certainly looks like a condemnation of Willie's actions. Of course, the way in which Rawls fills out this idea, in terms of accepting benefits and taking advantage of the scheme, points in quite a different direction; for on the "filled-out" principle, Willie is not bound to cooperate, and neither is the salesman.

It looks, then, as if we have a choice to make between a general principle (which binds all beneficiaries of a scheme) which is *very* implausible, and a more limited principle which is more plausible. I say that we have a choice to make simply because it seems clear that the limited principle is much more limited than either Hart or Rawls realized. For if my previous suggestions were correct, participants in cooperative schemes which produce "open" benefits will not always have a right to cooperation on the part of those who benefit from their labors. And this does not look like a result that either Hart or Rawls would be prepared to accept. Perhaps it is, after all, just the result Nozick wished to argue for.

V

When we move to political communities the "schemes of social cooperation" with which we will be concerned will naturally be schemes on a rather grand scale. We may, with Rawls, think that the maintenance of the legal order should be "construed as a system of social cooperation," or perhaps we will want to identify all the workings of that set of political institutions governing "political society" generally as the operation of "the most complex example" of a cooperative scheme (as Hart seems to).[15] The details of the interpretation which we accept are not particularly important here. We must simply imagine a cooperative scheme large enough that "doing our part" will involve all of the things normally thought of as the requirements of political obligation; and regardless of how we characterize this scheme in its particulars, the difficulties involved in an account of political obligation using the principle of fair play will be common to all particular versions.[16]

To begin, we face an immediate problem of "membership," of distinguishing the "insiders" from the "outsiders." Ideally, of course, the account wants all and only the citizens of the state in question to be the "insiders" relative to the cooperative scheme in operation in the state. The "all" in "all and only" can be sacrificed here, since an account which applies only to some members of a political community is not obviously objectionable; but the "only" in "all and only" must not be compromised. For obvious reasons, we cannot accept an account of political obligation which binds non-citizens to do their part in the cooperative political enterprises of a foreign country.

But most "insiders" or citizens, even in constitutional democracies, seem to be very much in the same sort of position as Nozick's man. They are not obviously tied to the grand cooperative scheme of political life any more than Nozick's man is tied to his PA scheme. We are, after all, born into political communities; and being "dropped into" a cooperative scheme does not seem significantly different from having a scheme "built up around you."

I tried to suggest earlier, of course, that the right way to distinguish the "insiders" relative to some scheme was through the notion of the "acceptance" of benefits from that scheme. While it is clear that at least most citizens in most states *receive* benefits from the workings of their legal and political institutions, how plausible is it to say that they have voluntarily *accepted* those benefits? Not, I think, very plausible. The benefits in question have been mentioned before: the rule of law, protection by armed forces, pollution control, maintenance of highway systems, avenues of political participation, and so on. But these benefits are what we have called "open" benefits. It is precisely in cases of such "open" benefits that it is least plausible to suggest that benefits are being *accepted* by most beneficiaries. It will, of course, be difficult to be certain about the acceptance of benefits in actual cases; but on any natural understanding of the notion of "acceptance," our having accepted open benefits involves our having had certain attitudes toward and beliefs about the benefits we have received (as noted in Section IV). Among other things, we must regard the benefits as flowing from a cooperative scheme rather than seeing them as "free" for the taking. And we must, for instance, think that the benefits we receive are worth the price we must pay for them, so that we would take the benefits if we had a choice between taking them (with the burdens involved) or leaving them. These kinds of beliefs and attitudes are necessary if the benefaction is to be plausibly regarded as constituting voluntary participation in the cooperative scheme.

But surely most of us do not have these requisite attitudes toward or beliefs about the benefits of government. At least many citizens barely notice (and seem disinclined to think about) the benefits they receive. And many more, faced with high taxes, with military service which may involve fighting in foreign "police actions," or with unreasonably restrictive laws governing private pleasures, believe that the benefits received from governments are not worth the price they are forced to pay. While such beliefs may be false, they seem nonetheless incompatible with the "acceptance" of the open benefits of government. Further, it must be admitted that, even in democratic political communities, these benefits are commonly regarded as purchased (with taxes) from a central authority, rather than as accepted from the cooperative efforts of our fellow citizens. We may feel, for instance, that if debts are owed at all, they are owed not to those around us, but to our government. Again, these attitudes seem inconsistent with the suggestion that the open benefits are accepted, in the strict sense of "acceptance." Most citizens will, I think, fall into one of these two classes: those who have not "accepted" because they have not taken the benefits (with accompanying burdens) willingly, and those who have not "accepted" because they do not regard the benefits of government as the products of a cooperative scheme. But if most citizens cannot be thought to have voluntarily accepted the benefits of government from the political cooperative scheme, then the fair-play account of political obligation will not be suitably general in its application, even within democratic states. And if we try to make the account more general by removing the limitations set by our strict notion of "acceptance," we open the floodgates and turn the principle of fair play into the "outrageous" principle discussed earlier. We seem forced by such observations to conclude that citizens generally in no actual states will be bound under the principle of fair play.

These suggestions raise serious doubts about the Hart-Rawls contention that at least some organized political societies can be thought of as ongoing cooperative schemes on a very large scale. While such a claim may be initially attractive, does it really seem reasonable to think of any actual political communities on the model of the kinds of neighborhood cooperative schemes we have discussed in this chapter? This seems to me quite unrealistic. We must remember that where there is no consciousness of cooperation, no common plan or purpose, no cooperative scheme exists. I do not think that many of us can honestly say that we regard our political lives as a process of working together and making necessary sacrifices for the purpose of improving the common lot. The centrality and apparent independence of governments does not make it natural to think of political life in this way.

Perhaps, then, we ought not to think of modern political communities as essentially or in part large-scale cooperative ventures. No doubt there is a sense in which society in general (and political society in particular) can be understood as a "cooperative venture," even though no consciousness of cooperation or common purpose is to be found. Social man is thought of as governed by public systems of rules designed to regulate his activities in ways which increase the benefits accruing to all. Perhaps it is this rather loose sense of "cooperative scheme" which Hart and Rawls have in mind when they imagine political communities as cooperative schemes.[17] But we should remember that whatever intuitive plausibility the principle of fair play has, derives from our regarding it as an acceptable moral principle for cooperative schemes in the *strict* sense. Clearly the considerations which lead us to accept the principle of fair play as determining our obligations in the context of a neighborhood organization's cooperative programs may in no way be mirrored in the context of "cooperative schemes" understood in the loose sense mentioned above. So that while talk of cooperative schemes on the level of political communities may not be obviously objectionable, such cooperative schemes will not be among those to which we should be inclined to apply the principle of fair play.

These brief remarks all point toward the conclusion that at very best the principle of fair play can hope to account for the political obligations of only a very few citizens in a very few actual states, it is more likely, however, that it accounts for no such obligations at all. While we have seen that the principle does not "collapse" into a principle of consent, we have also seen that in an account of political obligation, the principle has very little to recommend it, either as a supplement to, or a replacement for, principles of fidelity and consent. In particular, the main advantage which the fair-play account was thought to have over consent theory's account, namely, an advantage in *generality*, turns out to be no advantage at all.

Acknowledgment

This paper is an abbreviated and revised version of material from Chapter 5 of *Moral Principles and Political Obligations* (Princeton University Press, 1979). I would like to thank David Lyons and the Editors for helpful suggestions about earlier drafts of the paper.

Notes

1. These are John Rawls' two names for the principle, from "Legal Obligation and the Duty of Fair Play," *Law and Philosophy,* ed. S. Hook (New York: New York University Press, 1964) and *A Theory of Justice* (Cambridge: Harvard University Press, 1971). The same principle was alluded to by C. D. Broad in "On the Function of False Hypotheses in Ethics," *International Journal of Ethics* 26 (April 1916), and developed by H. L. A. Hart (see later in text).

2. "Are There Any Natural Rights?" *Philosophical Review* 64 (April 1955): 185.

3. Ibid., pp. 190–191.

4. See note 1 above. The versions of the principle which Rawls presents elsewhere do not differ substantially from this 1964 version, however, contrary to his claims in this version he does argue in *A Theory of Justice* that this principle cannot be used to account for political obligations.

5. "Legal Obligation and the Duty of Fair Play," pp. 9–10.

6. This argument also seems to me to provide an effective response to a recent attack on the principle of fair play made by M. B. E. Smith, in "Is There a Prima Facie Obligation to Obey the Law?" *Yale Law Journal* 82 (1973). Smith argues that failing to cooperate in a scheme after receiving benefits is only unfair if by this failure we deny someone else benefits within the scheme. But my example is precisely a case in which the failure to cooperate may not deny anyone else benefits within the scheme. And still it seems clear that failure to cooperate is unfair, for the individual's failure to do his part *takes advantage* of the others, who act in good faith. Whether or not my cooperation is necessary for benefiting other members, it is not fair for me, as a participant in the scheme, to decide not to do my part when the others do theirs. For these reasons, Smith's argument is unpersuasive.

7. "Legal Obligation and the Duty of Fair Play," p. 10.

8. *A Theory of Justice,* p. 112.

9. Ibid., p. 343.

10. A. John Simmons, "Tacit Consent and Political Obligation," *Philosophy & Public Affairs* 5 (Spring 1976): 277–278.

11. *A Theory of Justice,* p. 112.

12. By "obligation-centered" I mean simply that according to the account most or all of the people who are bound by political bonds are bound by *obligations* (that is, moral requirements originating in some voluntary performance). "Obligation-centered" accounts are to be opposed, of course, to "duty-centered" accounts.

13. Robert Nozick, *Anarchy, State, and Utopia* (New York: Basic Books, 1974), p. 93. Citations of Nozick in the text refer to this work.

14. *A Theory of Justice,* p. 112.
15. Rawls, "Legal Obligation and the Duty of Fair Play," p. 17; Hart, "Are There Any Natural Rights?" pp. 185–186.
16. One limitation is obvious from the start. Only reasonably democratic political communities will be candidates for a fair-play account of political obligation; for only where we can see the political workings of the society as a voluntary cooperative venture will the principle apply.
17. See Rawls, *A Theory of Justice,* for example, pp. 4, 84.

SUGGESTED FURTHER READING

Allen, R. E. *Socrates and Legal Obligation*. Minneapolis. University of Minnesota Press, 1980.

Ashcraft, Richard. *Locke's* Two Treatises of Government. London: Allen and Unwin, 1987.

Bedau, Hugo, ed. *Civil Disobedience*. New York: Pegasus, 1969.

Bennett, John. "A Note on Locke's Theory of Tacit Consent." *Philosophical Review* 88 (1979): 224–234.

Bookman, J. T. "Plato on Political Obligation." *Western Political Quarterly* 25 (1972): 260–267.

Boucher, Daniel, and Paul Kelly, eds. *The Social Contract from Hobbes to Rawls*. London: Routledge, 1994.

Carter, April. *Authority and Democracy*. London: Routledge & Kegan Paul, 1979.

Crittenden, Jack. *Beyond Individualism: Reconstituting the Liberal Self*. New York: Oxford, 1992.

De Lue, Steven M. *Political Obligation in a Liberal State*. Albany, N.Y.: SUNY Press, 1989.

Dunn, J. M. "Consent in the Political Theory of John Locke." Reprinted in *Life, Liberty and Property,* ed. G. Schochet. Belmont: Wadsworth, 1971.

———. *The Political Thought of John Locke*. Cambridge: University Press, 1969.

Farrell, D. M. "Coercion, Consent, and the Justification of Political Power: A New Look at Locke's Consent Claim." *Archiv Fur Rechts-Und Sozialphilosophie* 65 (1979): 521–543.

Flathman, R. E. *Political Obligation*. New York: Atherton, 1972.

———. *The Practice of Political Authority*. Chicago: University of Chicago Press, 1980.

Gough, J. W. *John Locke's Political Philosophy*. 2nd ed. Oxford: Clarendon, 1956.

———. *The Social Contract*. Oxford: Clarendon, 1936.

Green, Leslie. *The Authority of the State*. Oxford: Clarendon Press, 1988.

Green, T. H. *Lectures on the Principles of Political Obligation and Other Writings,* edited by Paul Harris and John Morrow. Cambridge: University Press, 1986.

Harris, Paul, ed. *On Political Obligation*. London: Routledge, 1989.

Hart, H. L. A. "Legal and Moral Obligation." In *Essays in Moral Philosophy,* edited by A. I. Melden. Seattle: University of Washington Press, 1958.

Horton, John. *Political Obligation*. London: Macmillan, 1992.

Kendall, W. *John Locke and the Doctrine of Majority-Rule*. Urbana: University of Illinois Press, 1965.

Klosko, George. "Political Obligation and Gratitude." *Philosophy and Public Affairs* 18 (1989): 352–358.

———. "Political Obligation and the Natural Duties of Justice," *Philosophy and Public Affairs* 23 (1994): 225–250.

Kraut, Richard. *Socrates and the State*. Princeton: Princeton University Press, 1984.

MacPherson, C. B. *The Political Theory of Possessive Individualism.* New York: Oxford University Press, 1962.

McPherson, Thomas. *Political Obligation.* London: Routledge & Kegan Paul, 1967.

Medina, Vincente. *Social Contract Theories: Political Obligation or Anarchy?* Savage, Md.: Rowman and Littlefield, 1990.

Nozick, Robert. *Anarchy, State, and Utopia.* New York: Basic Books, 1974.

Partridge, P. H. *Consent and Consensus.* London: Praeger, 1971.

Pateman, Carole. "Political Obligation and Conceptual Analysis." In *Philosophy, Politics, and Society,* 5th series, edited by P. Laslett and J. Fishkin. New Haven: Yale University Press, 1979.

———. *The Problem of Political Obligation: A Critique of Liberal Theory.* New York: John Wiley and Sons, 1979.

Pennock, J. Roland, and J. W. Chapman, eds. *Nomos XII: Political and Legal Obligation.* New York: Atherton, 1970.

———. *Nomos XXIX: Authority Revisited.* New York: New York University Press, 1987.

Pitkin, Hanna F. "Obligation and Consent." *American Political Science Review* 59 (1965): 990–999; 60 (1966): 39–52.

Plamenatz, John. *Consent, Freedom, and Political Obligation.* 2nd ed. Oxford: Clarendon, 1968.

Raphael, D. D. *Problems of Political Philosophy.* New York: Praeger, 1967.

Rawls, John. "Legal Obligation and the Duty of Fair Play." In *Law and Philosophy,* edited by Sidney Hook. New York: New York University Press, 1964.

———. *A Theory of Justice.* Cambridge, Mass.: Harvard University Press, 1971.

Rosen, Frederick. "Obligation and Friendship in Plato's *Crito*." *Political Theory* 1 (1973): 307–316.

Simmons, A. John. "Inalienable Rights and Locke's *Treatises.*" *Philosophy and Public Affairs* 12 (1983): 175–204.

———. *The Lockean Theory of Rights.* Princeton: Princeton University Press, 1992.

———. *Moral Principles and Political Obligations.* Princeton: Princeton University Press, 1979.

———. *On the Edge of Anarchy: Locke, Consent, and the Limits of Society.* Princeton: Princeton University Press, 1993.

Singer, Peter. *Democracy and Disobedience.* New York: Oxford University Press, 1974.

Steinberg, Jules. *Locke, Rousseau, and the Idea of Consent.* Westport, Conn.: Greenwood, 1978.

Tussman, Joseph. *Obligation and the Body Politic.* Oxford: University Press, 1960.

Von Leyden, W. *Hobbes and Locke: The Politics of Freedom and Obligation.* New York: St. Martin's Press, 1982.

Waldman, Theodore. "A Note on John Locke's Concept of Consent." *Ethics* 68 (1957): 45–50.

Waldron, Jeremy. "Special Ties and Natural Duties." *Philosophy and Public Affairs* 22 (1993): 3–30.

Walker, A. D. M. "Obligations of Gratitude and Political Obligation." *Philosophy and Public Affairs* 18 (1989): 359–364.

———. "Political Obligation and the Argument from Gratitude." *Philosophy and Public Affairs* 17 (1988): 191–211.

Walzer, Michael. *Obligations: Essays on Disobedience, War, and Citizenship.* New York: Simon and Schuster, 1971.

Wasserstrom, Richard A. "The Obligation to Obey the Law." *UCLA Law Review* 10 (1963): 780–807.

Wolff, R. P. *In Defense of Anarchism.* New York: Harper and Row, 1970.

Woozley, A. D. *Law and Obedience: The Arguments of Plato's* Crito. London: Duckworth, 1979.

II

FREEDOM AND
COERCION

Among the central concepts of social and political thought, freedom or liberty is perhaps the most vague and ambiguous, yet also one of the most prized and contested. Theories of political obligation, justice, and democracy typically include or presuppose a conception of freedom, and even egalitarians, whose ideal arguably conflicts with liberty, often attempt to interpret freedom as essentially related to the kind of equality they favor. Disputes over conceptions of liberty—their relations to notions of constraint and coercion, opportunity and ability, rationality and self-determination, rights and value—obviously cannot be resolved by appeal to ordinary usage. While one conception might be more consistent with common ways of speaking than others, which can work in its behalf, political thinkers are usually motivated in their acceptance of a particular definition by considerations of theoretical usefulness (clarity, precision, ability to draw important distinctions), which in turn depends partly on the basic values and political ideals of the philosopher in question. Substantive issues about what makes freedom valuable and the conditions under which it may justifiably be limited are not separable from conceptual questions.

Hobbes's theoretical concerns led him to adopt a negative conception of liberty—a particularly uncompromising account—as the absence of external obstacles or impediments to movement, interpreted in quite strict physical terms. He distinguishes between lack of ability and unfreedom by means of the location of the impediment; thus, an invalid lacks the power to walk, not the freedom, since limitation is in his constitution, not outside him. Following what he believes to be ordinary usage, Hobbes defines a free man as someone not hindered from doing what he is willing and able to do. But he also contends that a man who acts out of fear of the law is nevertheless acting freely, a conclusion sharply at odds with common thought, which regards laws backed by sanctions as genuine hindrances. Indeed, Hobbes describes civil laws as "artificial chains," arguing that they are preferable still to the state of nature and that the authority to make and enforce them was freely given in the original covenant. He distinguishes corporal liberty from the liberty of subjects, which concerns those spheres of action not covered by the laws or dictates of the sovereign. In any case, while Hobbes's idea of freedom might not be entirely clear, it is plainly motivated by his aims of giving a scientific account of political phenomena and justifying absolute authority.

Isaiah Berlin's "Two Concepts of Liberty" outlines the history of negative and positive conceptions, their philosophical presuppositions, and their implications for political practice. Negative liberty, as already suggested, is a matter of the absence of certain kinds of interference, such as deliberate and coercive pressures, with the pursuit of one's desires. Positive liberty, in Berlin's sense, involves being motivated by purposes that are rationally self-determined, as opposed to being inspired by one's irrational passions, false consciousness, or the external manipulations of others. Berlin proposes that negative freedom is characteristically involved in answers to the question "What is the area within which the person or group is or should be left to do or be what he is able, without interference by others?" Positive freedom, in contrast, usually relates to the question "What or who is the source of control or interference that can determine someone to do or be X rather than Y?" Underlying positive conceptions, Berlin maintains, is a dualistic theory of the person, in which higher reason ("our true selves") is distinguished from our lower passions; self-mastery enables us to control our lower selves, which is true liberty. Freedom is logically related to notions of autonomy and authenticity in positive theories, whose proponents argue that true freedom is not liberty to act from irrationality or ignorance or to do what is wrong. The danger Berlin sees in positive conceptions is that the values they imply are not the only or most important ones; moreover, totalitarian ideologies and paternalistic legislators invoke them in attempting to justify coercion by portraying it as its opposite. Liberals recognize that freedom is one of many social values, including justice, equality, democracy, welfare, and culture, and that it often has to be restricted for the sake of those values as well as its own. But Berlin insists that freedom should not be sacrificed without a full awareness of what is being given up. Liberty understood as an absence of obstacles, resulting from alterable human practices, to possible choices and actions—negative liberty—is thus to be preferred. Arguing against Berlin in the selection that follows, Charles Taylor contends that positive conceptions need not presuppose dubious theories of the self; nor are they at odds with the ideals of modern liberalism, insofar as both place considerable significance on self-realization. Positive theories are more adequate than negative accounts of liberty in a number of respects, most importantly, in asserting that we cannot avoid the assessment of motives in our judgments about freedom and unfreedom. What forms of society are most conducive to the promotion of positive liberty, Taylor adds, remains an open question.

Self-realization is indeed central to Mill's utilitarian liberalism. His classic essay *On Liberty* is an articulate defense of the principle that the only justification for interference, whether by legal force or "the moral coercion of public opinion," with the liberty of individuals, is self-protection. Normal and mature persons cannot, in a civilized society, rightly be compelled to do or refrain from something for their own good; harm to others must be established. The proper scope of basic liberty, Mill believes, includes conscience, thought, and feeling (which cannot be practically separated from its public expression), tastes, pursuits, and choice of life plan, and association with others, so long as it is voluntary, informed, and without harmful intent. Mill's "simple principle," which states a necessary rather than a sufficient condition for coercion, applies only when persons are capable of improvement by free and equal exchange of ideas. His defense of the liberty of thought and discussion is central: if a repressed opinion is true, one will be denied the opportunity of gaining knowledge, whereas if it is false, public discussion will strengthen belief in the opposing truth and clarify its grounds further. When the prevailing opinion and the repressed belief each contain part of the truth, full freedom of expression enables the entire truth to be known. Mill is especially concerned with the tendency of modern democracies to impose a tyranny of public opinion, suppressing the individuality that is essential to the improvement of the person and the advancement of society. Conceiving of utility as "grounded on the permanent interests of man as a progressive being," Mill holds that a liberal social order can be justified on utilitarian grounds, without appeal to doctrines of natural rights. In the final part of his essay Mill applies his doctrine to a range of controversial cases.

Willmoore Kendall criticizes Mill's basic assumptions from a traditionalist conservative standpoint. He argues that Mill has "a false conception of the nature of society"—it is not "a debating club devoted above all to the pursuit of truth"—as well as a false view of human beings, one that implies that speech cannot hurt. Were it implemented, Mill's radical doctrine would in the end produce intolerance and the breakdown of order, Kendall asserts. A defensible position is more moderate and accepts some basic rules, ensuring that fundamental values not themselves open to question are protected. Thomas Scanlon defends a liberal interpretation of freedom of expression in his essay, arguing that many things besides opinions, such as desires, attitudes, emotions, and fantasies, can be expressed and should be protected by the law. The right to express ourselves freely is important, he maintains, both because we have an interest in communicating to others what we think or feel and because we have an interest in others' thoughts and feelings. David Lyons considers possible interpretations of Mill's main principle in the light of his own applications to particular cases. He suggests a consistent rendering of Mill's statements that reveals his position to be more acceptable than often believed. Ronald Dworkin challenges the assumption that there is a right to liberty, even "basic" or "important" freedom. Instead, he proposes recognition of a right to equal consideration and respect, to be broken down into a right to equal treatment and a right to treatment as an equal, the latter having priority. Utilitarianism, Dworkin concludes, must be restricted in a particular way to guarantee egalitarian results.

Of the Liberty of Subjects

THOMAS HOBBES

Liberty, or freedom, signifies properly the absence of opposition—by opposition I mean external impediments of motion—and may be applied no less to irrational and inanimate creatures than to rational. For whatsoever is so tied or environed as it cannot move but within a certain space, which space is determined by the opposition of some external body, we say it has not liberty to go farther. And so of all living creatures while they are imprisoned or restrained with walls or chains, and of the water while it is kept by banks or vessels that otherwise would spread itself into a larger space, we use to say that they are not at liberty to move in such manner as without those external impediments they would. But when the impediment of motion is in the constitution of the thing itself, we use not to say it wants the liberty but the power to move—as when a stone lies still or a man is fastened to his bed by sickness.

And according to this proper and generally received meaning of the word, a FREEMAN *is he that in those things which by his strength and wit he is able to do is not hindered to do what he has a will to.* But when the words *free* and *liberty* are applied to anything but *bodies,* they are abused, for that which is not subject to motion is not subject to impediment; and therefore, when it is said, for example, the way is free, no liberty of the way is signified but of those that walk in it without stop. And when we say a gift is free, there is not meant any liberty of the gift but of the giver, that was not bound by any law or covenant to give it. So when we *speak freely,* it is not the liberty of voice or pronunciation but of the man, whom no law has obliged to speak otherwise than he did. Lastly, from the use of the word *free will,* no liberty can be inferred of the will, desire, or inclination but the liberty of the man, which consists in this: that he finds no stop in doing what he has the will, desire, or inclination to do.

Fear and liberty are consistent, as when a man throws his goods into the sea for *fear* the ship should sink, he does it nevertheless very willingly, and may refuse to do it if he will: it is therefore the action of one that was *free;* so a man sometimes pays his debt only for *fear* of imprisonment, which, because nobody hindered him from detaining, was the action of a man at *liberty.* And generally all actions which men do in commonwealths for *fear* of the law are actions which the doers had *liberty* to omit.

Liberty and *necessity* are consistent, as in the water that has not only *liberty* but a *necessity* of descending by the channel; so likewise in the actions which men voluntarily do, which, because they proceed from their will, proceed from *liberty,* and yet—because every act of man's will and every desire and inclination

Thomas Hobbes, "Of the Liberty of Subjects," from Book II, Chapter 21 of *Leviathan.* Reprinted with revisions of spelling and punctuation by permission of Oxford University Press. Copyright Oxford University Press, 1960.

proceeds from some cause, and that from another cause, in a continual chain whose first link is in the hand of God, the first of all causes—proceed from *necessity*. So that to him that could see the connection of those causes the *necessity* of all men's voluntary actions would appear manifest. And therefore God, that sees and disposes all things, sees also that the *liberty* of man in doing what he will is accompanied with the *necessity* of doing that which God will, and no more nor less. For though men may do many things which God does not command, nor is therefore author of them, yet they can have no passion nor appetite to anything of which appetite God's will is not the cause. And did not his will assure the *necessity* of man's will, and consequently of all that on man's will depends, the *liberty* of men would be a contradiction and impediment to the omnipotence and *liberty* of God. And this shall suffice, as to the matter in hand, of that natural *liberty* which only is properly called *liberty*.

But as men, for the attaining of peace and conservation of themselves thereby, have made an artificial man, which we call a commonwealth, so also have they made artificial chains, called *civil laws,* which they themselves by mutual covenants, have fastened at one end to the lips of that man or assembly to whom they have given the sovereign power, and at the other end to their own ears. These bonds, in their own nature but weak, may nevertheless be made to hold by the danger, though not by the difficulty, of breaking them.

In relation to these bonds only it is that I am to speak now of the *liberty of subjects.* For seeing there is no commonwealth in the world wherein there be rules enough set down for the regulating of all the actions and words of men, as being a thing impossible, it follows necessarily that in all kinds of actions by the laws pretermitted men have the liberty of doing what their own reasons shall suggest for the most profitable to themselves. For if we take liberty in the proper sense for corporal liberty—that is to say, freedom from chains and prison—it were very absurd for men to clamor as they do for the liberty they so manifestly enjoy. Again, if we take liberty for an exemption from laws, it is no less absurd for men to demand as they do that liberty by which all other men may be masters of their lives. And yet, as absurd as it is, this is it they demand, not knowing that the laws are of no power to protect them without a sword in the hands of a man or men to cause those laws to be put in execution. The liberty of a subject lies, therefore, only in those things which, in regulating their actions, the sovereign has pretermitted: such as is the liberty to buy and sell and otherwise contract with one another; to choose their own abode, their own diet, their own trade of life, and institute their children as they themselves think fit; and the like.[. . .]

Two Concepts
of Liberty

ISAIAH BERLIN

I

To coerce a man is to deprive him of freedom—freedom from what? Almost every moralist in human history has praised freedom.
Like happiness and goodness, like nature and
reality, the meaning of this term is so porous
that there is little interpretation that it seems
able to resist. I do not propose to discuss either
the history or the more than two hundred
senses of this protean word recorded by historians of ideas. I propose to examine no more
than two of these senses—but those central
ones, with a great deal of human history behind
them, and, I dare say, still to come. The first
of these political senses of freedom or liberty
(I shall use both words to mean the same),
which (following much precedent) I shall call
the 'negative' sense, is involved in the answer
to the question 'What is the area within which
the subject—a person or group of persons—is
or should be left to do or be what he is able
to do or be, without interference by other persons?' The second, which I shall call the positive sense, is involved in the answer to the
question 'What, or who, is the source of control or interference, that can determine
someone to do, or be, one thing rather than
another?' The two questions are clearly different, even though the answers to them may
overlap.

The Notion of 'Negative' Freedom

I am normally said to be free to the degree to
which no human being interferes with my activity. Political liberty in this sense is simply
the area within which a man can act unob-
structed by others. If I am prevented by other
persons from doing what I could otherwise do,
I am to that degree unfree; and if this area is
contracted by other men beyond a certain minimum, I can be described as being coerced, or,
it may be, enslaved. Coercion is not, however,
a term that covers every form of inability. If I
say that I am unable to jump more than 10 feet
in the air, or cannot read because I am blind,
or cannot understand the darker pages of Hegel, it would be eccentric to say that I am to
that degree enslaved or coerced. Coercion implies the deliberate interference of other human
beings within the area in which I could otherwise act. You lack political liberty or freedom
only if you are prevented from attaining a goal
by human beings.[1] Mere incapacity to attain a
goal is not lack of political freedom.[2] This is
brought out by the use of such modern expressions as 'economic freedom' and its coun-
terpart, 'economic slavery'. It is argued, very
plausibly, that if a man is too poor to afford
something on which there is no legal ban—a
loaf of bread, a journey round the world, recourse to the law courts—he is as little free to

Isaiah Berlin, "Two Concepts of Liberty," from the revised version of his Inaugural Lecture, "Two Concepts of
Liberty." Reprinted from *Four Essays on Liberty* by Sir Isaiah Berlin (1969) by permission of Oxford University
Press. Copyright Oxford University Press, 1969.

have it as he would be if it were forbidden him by law. If my poverty were a kind of disease, which prevented me from buying bread or paying for the journey round the world, or getting my case heard, as lameness prevents me from running, this inability would not naturally be described as a lack of freedom, least of all political freedom. It is only because I believe that my inability to get a given thing is due to the fact that other human beings have made arrangements whereby I am, whereas others are not, prevented from having enough money with which to pay for it, that I think myself a victim of coercion or slavery. In other words, this use of the term depends on a particular social and economic theory about the causes of my poverty or weakness. If my lack of material means is due to my lack of mental or physical capacity, then I begin to speak of being deprived of freedom (and not simply of poverty) only if I accept the theory.[3] If, in addition, I believe that I am being kept in want by a specific arrangement which I consider unjust or unfair, I speak of economic slavery or oppression. "The nature of things does not madden us, only ill will does," said Rousseau. The criterion of oppression is the part that I believe to be played by other human beings, directly or indirectly, with or without the intention of doing so, in frustrating my wishes. By being free in this sense I mean not being interfered with by others. The wider the area of non-interference the wider my freedom.

This is what the classical English political philosophers meant when they used this word.[4] They disagreed about how wide the area could or should be. They supposed that it could not, as things were, be unlimited, because if it were, it would entail a state in which all men could boundlessly interfere with all other men; and this kind of 'natural' freedom would lead to social chaos in which men's minimum needs would not be satisfied; or else the liberties of the weak would be suppressed by the strong. Because they perceived that human purposes and activities do not automatically harmonize with one another; and, because (whatever their official doctrines) they put high value on other goals, such as justice, or happiness, or culture, or security, or varying degrees of equality, they were prepared to curtail freedom in the interests of other values and, indeed, of freedom itself. For, without this, it was impossible to create the kind of association that they thought desirable. Consequently, it is assumed by these thinkers that the area of men's free action must be limited by law. But equally it is assumed, especially by such libertarians as Locke and Mill in England, and Constant and Tocqueville in France, that there ought to exist a certain minimum area of personal freedom which must on no account be violated; for if it is overstepped, the individual will find himself in an area too narrow for even that minimum development of his natural faculties which alone makes it possible to pursue, and even to conceive, the various ends which men hold good or right or sacred. It follows that a frontier must be drawn between the area of private life and that of public authority. Where it is to be drawn is a matter of argument, indeed of haggling. Men are largely interdependent, and no man's activity is so completely private as never to obstruct the lives of others in any way. 'Freedom for the pike is death for the minnows'; the liberty of some must depend on the restraint of others.[5] Still, a practical compromise has to be found.

Philosophers with an optimistic view of human nature, and a belief in the possibility of harmonizing human interests, such as Locke or Adam Smith and, in some moods, Mill, believed that social harmony and progress were compatible with reserving a large area for private life over which neither the state nor any other authority must be allowed to trespass. Hobbes, and those who agreed with him, especially conservative or reactionary thinkers, argued that if men were to be prevented from destroying one another, and making social life a jungle or a wilderness, greater safeguards must be instituted to keep them in their places, and wished correspondingly to increase the area of centralized control, and decrease that of the individual. But both sides agreed that some portion of human existence must remain independent of the sphere of social control. To invade that preserve, however small, would be despotism. The most eloquent of all defenders of freedom and privacy, Benjamin Constant, who had not forgotten the Jacobin dictatorship, declared that at the very least the liberty of religion, opinion, expression, property, must be guaranteed against arbitrary invasion. Jefferson, Burke, Paine, Mill, complied different catalogues of individual liberties, but the argument for keeping authority at bay is always substantially the same. We must preserve a minimum area of personal freedom if we are not to "degrade or deny our nature." We cannot remain absolutely free, and must give up some of our liberty to preserve the rest. But total self-surrender is self-defeating. What then must the minimum be? That which a man cannot give up without offending against the essence of his human nature. What is this essence? What are the standards which it entails? This has been, and perhaps always will be, a matter of infinite debate. But whatever the principle in terms of which the area of non-interference is to be drawn, whether it is that of natural law or natural rights, or of utility or the pronouncements of a categorical imperative, or the sanctity of the social contract, or any other concept with which men have sought to clarify and justify their convictions, liberty in this sense means liberty *from;* absence of interference beyond the shifting, but always recognizable, frontier. "The only freedom which deserves the name is that of pursuing our own good in our own way," said the most celebrated of its champions. If this is so, is compulsion ever justified? Mill had no doubt that it was. Since justice demands that all individuals be entitled to a minimum of freedom, all other individuals were of necessity to be restrained, if need be by force, from depriving anyone of it. Indeed, the whole function of law was the prevention of just such collisions: the state was reduced to what Lassalle contemptuously described as the functions of a nightwatchman or traffic policeman.

What made the protection of individual liberty so sacred to Mill? In his famous essay he declares that unless men are left to live as they wish "in the path which merely concerns themselves," civilization cannot advance; the truth will not, for lack of a free market in ideas, come to light; there will be no scope for spon-

taneity, originality, genius, for mental energy, for moral courage. Society will be crushed by the weight of "collective mediocrity." Whatever is rich and diversified will be crushed by the weight of custom, by men's constant tendency to conformity, which breeds only "withered capacities," "pinched and hidebound," "cramped and warped" human beings. "Pagan self-assertion is as worthy as Christian self-denial." "All the errors which a man is likely to commit against advice and warning are far outweighed by the evil of allowing others to constrain him to what they deem is good." The defence of liberty consists in the 'negative' goal of warding off interference. To threaten a man with persecution unless he submits to a life in which he exercises no choices of his goals; to block before him every door but one, no matter how noble the prospect upon which it opens, or how benevolent the motives of those who arrange this, is to sin against the truth that he is a man, a being with a life of his own to live. This is liberty as it has been conceived by liberals in the modern world from the days of Erasmus (some would say of Occam) to our own. Every plea for civil liberties and individual rights, every protest against exploitation and humiliation, against the encroachment of public authority, or the mass hypnosis of custom or organized propaganda, springs from this individualistic, and much disputed, conception of man.

Three facts about this position may be noted. In the first place Mill confuses two distinct notions. One is that all coercion is, in so far as it frustrates human desires, bad as such, although it may have to be applied to prevent other, greater evils; while non-interference, which is the opposite of coercion, is good as such, although it is not the only good. This is the negative conception of liberty in its classical form. The other is that men should seek to discover the truth or to develop a certain type of character of which Mill approved—fearless, original, imaginative, independent, non-conforming to the point of eccentricity, and so on—and that truth can be found, and such character can be bred, only in conditions of freedom. Both these are liberal views, but they are not identical, and the connexion between them is, at best, empirical. No one would argue that truth or freedom of self-expression could flourish where dogma crushes all thought. But the evidence of history tends to show (as, indeed, was argued by James Stephen in his formidable attack on Mill in his *Liberty, Equality, Fraternity*) that integrity, love of truth and fiery individualism grow at least as often in severely disciplined communities, among, for example, the puritan Calvinists of Scotland or New England, or under military discipline, as in more tolerant or indifferent societies; and if this is so accepted, Mill's argument for liberty as a necessary condition for the growth of human genius falls to the ground. If his two goals proved incompatible, Mill would be faced with a cruel dilemma, quite apart from the further difficulties created by the inconsistency of his doctrines with strict utilitarianism, even in his own humane version of it.[6]

In the second place, the doctrine is comparatively modern. There seems to be scarcely any discussion of individual liberty as a conscious political ideal (as opposed to its actual existence) in the ancient world. Condorcet has already remarked that the notion of individual rights is absent from the legal conceptions of the Romans and Greeks; this seems to hold equally of the Jewish, Chinese, and all other ancient civilizations that have since come to light.[7] The domination of this ideal has been the exception rather than the rule, even in the recent history of the West. Nor has liberty in this sense often formed a rallying cry for the great masses of mankind. The desire not to be impinged upon, to be left to oneself, has been a mark of high civilization both on the part of individuals and communities. The sense of privacy itself, of the area of personal relationships as something sacred in its own right, derives from a conception of freedom which, for all its religious roots, is scarcely older, in its developed state, than the Renaissance or the Reformation.[8] Yet its decline would mark the death of a civilization, of an entire moral outlook.

The third characteristic of this notion of liberty is of greater importance. It is that liberty in this sense is not incompatible with some kinds of autocracy, or at any rate with the absence of self-government. Liberty in this sense is principally concerned with the area of control, not with its source. Just as a democracy may, in fact, deprive the individual citizen of a great many liberties which he might have in some other form of society, so it is perfectly conceivable that a liberal-minded despot would allow his subjects a large measure of personal freedom. The despot who leaves his subjects a wide area of liberty may be unjust, or encourage the wildest inequalities, care little for order, or virtue, or knowledge; but provided he does not curb their liberty, or at least curbs it less than many other régimes, he meets with Mill's specification.[9] Freedom in this sense is not, at any rate logically, connected with democracy or self-government. Self-government may, on the whole, provide a better guarantee of the preservation of civil liberties than other régimes, and has been defended as such by libertarians. But there is no necessary connexion between individual liberty and democratic rule. The answer to the question 'Who governs me?' is logically distinct from the question 'How far does government interfere with me?' It is in this difference that the great contrast between the concepts of negative and positive liberty, in the end, consists.[10] For the 'positive' sense of liberty comes to light if we try to answer the question, not 'What am I free to do or be?', but 'By whom am I ruled?' or 'Who is to say what I am, and what I am not, to be or do?' The connexion between democracy and individual liberty is a good deal more tenuous than it seemed to many advocates of both. The desire to be governed by myself, or at any rate to participate in the process by which my life is to be controlled, may be as deep a wish as that of a free area for action, and perhaps historically older. But it is not a desire for the same thing. So different is it, indeed, as to have led in the end to the great clash of ideologies that dominates our world. For it is this—the 'positive' conception of liberty: not freedom from, but freedom to—which the adherents of the 'negative' notion represent as being, at times, no better than a specious disguise for brutal tyranny.

II

The Notion of 'Positive' Freedom

The 'positive' sense of the word 'liberty' derives from the wish on the part of the individual to be his own master. I wish my life and decisions to depend on myself, not on external forces of whatever kind. I wish to be the instrument of my own, not of other men's, acts of will. I wish to be a subject, not an object; to be moved by reasons, by conscious purposes which are my own, not by causes which affect me, as it were, from outside. I wish to be somebody, not nobody; a doer—deciding, not being decided for, self-directed and not acted upon by external nature or by other men as if I were a thing, or an animal, or a slave incapable of playing a human role, that is, of conceiving goals and policies of my own and realizing them. This is at least part of what I mean when I say that I am rational, and that it is my reason that distinguishes me as a human being from the rest of the world. I wish, above all, to be conscious of myself as a thinking, willing, active being, bearing responsibility for his choices and able to explain them by reference to his own ideas and purposes. I feel free to the degree that I believe this to be true, and enslaved to the degree that I am made to realize that it is not.

The freedom which consists in being one's own master, and the freedom which consists in not being prevented from choosing as I do by other men, may, on the face of it, seem concepts at no great logical distance from each other—no more than negative and positive ways of saying the same thing. Yet the "positive" and "negative" notions of freedom historically developed in divergent directions not always by logically reputable steps, until, in the end, they came into direct conflict with each other.

One way of making this clear is in terms of the independent momentum which the, initially perhaps quite harmless, metaphor of self-mastery acquired. "I am my own master"; "I am slave to no man"; but may I not (as, for instance, T. H. Green is always saying) be a slave to nature? Or to my own "unbridled"

passions? Are these not so many species of the identical genus "slave"—some political or legal, others moral or spiritual? Have not men had the experience of liberating themselves from spiritual slavery, or slavery to nature, and do they not in the course of it become aware, on the one hand, of a self which dominates, and, on the other, of something in them which is brought to heel? The dominant self is then variously identified with reason, with my "higher nature", with the self which calculates and aims at what will satisfy it in the long run, with my "real", or "ideal", or "autonomous" self, or with myself "at its best"; which is then contrasted with irrational impulse, uncontrolled desires, my "lower" nature, the pursuit of immediate pleasures, my "empirical" or "heteronomous" self, swept by every gust of desire and passion, needing to be rigidly disciplined if it is ever to rise to the full height of its "real" nature. Presently the two selves may be represented as divided by an even larger gap: the real self may be conceived as something wider than the individual (as the term is normally understood), as a social "whole" of which the individual is an element or aspect: a tribe, a race, a church, a state, the great society of the living and the dead and the yet unborn. This entity is then identified as being the "true" self which, by imposing its collective, or "organic", single will upon its recalcitrant "members", achieves its own, and, therefore, their, "higher" freedom. The perils of using organic metaphors to justify the coercion of some men by others in order to raise them to a "higher" level of freedom have often been pointed out. But what gives such plausibility as it has to this kind of language is that we recognize that it is possible, and at times justifiable, to coerce men in the name of some goal (let us say, justice or public health) which they would, if they were more enlightened, themselves pursue, but do not, because they are blind or ignorant or corrupt. This renders it easy for me to conceive of myself as coercing others for their own sake, in their, not my, interest. I am then claiming that I know what they truly need better than they know it themselves. What, at most, this entails is that they would not resist me if they were rational, and as wise as I, and understood their interests as I do. But I may go on to claim a good deal more than this. I may declare that they are actually aiming at what in their benighted state they consciously resist, because there exists within them an occult entity—their latent rational will, or their "true" purpose—and that this entity, although it is belied by all that they overtly feel and do and say, is their "real" self, of which the poor empirical self in space and time may know nothing or little; and that this inner spirit is the only self that deserves to have its wishes taken into account.[11] Once I take this view, I am in a position to ignore the actual wishes of men or societies, to bully, oppress, torture them in the name, and on behalf, of their "real" selves, in the secure knowledge that whatever is the true goal of man (happiness, fulfilment of duty, wisdom, a just society, self-fulfilment) must be identical with his freedom—the free choice of his "true", albeit submerged and inarticulate, self.

This paradox has been often exposed. It is one thing to say that I know what is good for X, while he himself does not; and even to ignore his wishes for its—and his—sake; and a very different one to say that he has *eo ipso* chosen it, not indeed consciously, not as he seems in everyday life, but in his role as a rational self which his empirical self may not know—the "real" self which discerns the good, and cannot help choosing it once it is revealed. This monstrous impersonation, which consists in equating what X would choose if he were something he is not, or at least not yet, with what X actually seeks and chooses, is at the heart of all political theories of self-realization. It is one thing to say that I may be coerced for my own good which I am too blind to see: this may, on occasion, be for my benefit; indeed it may enlarge the scope of my liberty; it is another to say that if it is my good, then I am not being coerced, for I have willed it, whether I know this or not, and am free—or "truly" free—even while my poor earthly body and foolish mind bitterly reject it, and struggle against those who seek however benevolently to impose it, with the greatest desperation.

This magical transformation, or sleight of hand (for which William James so justly mocked the Hegelians), can no doubt be perpetrated just as easily with the "negative" concept of freedom, where the self that should not be interfered with is no longer the individual with his actual wishes and needs as they are normally conceived, but the "real" man within, identified with the pursuit of some ideal purpose not dreamed of by his empirical self. And, as in the case of the "positively" free self, this entity may be inflated into some superpersonal entity—a state, a class, a nation, or the march of history itself, regarded as a more "real" subject of attributes than the empirical self. But the "positive" conception of freedom as self-mastery, with its suggestion of a man divided against himself, has in fact, and as a matter of the history of doctrines and of practice, lent itself more easily to this splitting of personality into two: the transcendent, dominant controller, and the empirical bundle of desires and passions to be disciplined and brought to heel. This demonstrates (if demonstration of so obvious a truth is needed) that the conception of freedom directly derives from the view that is taken of what constitutes a self, a person, a man. Enough manipulation with the definition of man, and freedom can be made to mean whatever the manipulator wishes. Recent history has made it only too clear that the issue is not merely academic.[. . .]

Notes

1. I do not, of course, mean to imply the truth of the converse.
2. Helvétius made this point very clearly: 'The free man is the man who is not in irons, nor imprisoned in a gaol, nor terrorized like a slave by the fear of punishment . . . it is not lack of freedom not to fly like an eagle or swim like a whale.'
3. The Marxist conception of social laws is, of course, the best-known version of this theory, but it forms a large element in some Christian and utilitarian, and all socialist, doctrines.
4. 'A free man', said Hobbes, 'is he that . . . is not hindered to do what he hath the will to do.' Law is always a 'fetter', even if it protects you from being bound in chains that are heavier than those of the law, say, arbitrary despotism or chaos. Bentham says much the same.
5. 'Freedom for an Oxford don', others have been

known to add, 'is a very different thing from freedom for an Egyptian peasant.'

This proposition derives its force from something that is both true and important, but the phrase itself remains a piece of political claptrap. It is true that to offer political rights, or safeguards against intervention by the state, to men who are half-naked, illiterate, underfed, and diseased is to mock their condition; they need medical help or education before they can understand, or make use of, an increase in their freedom. What is freedom to those who cannot make use of it? Without adequate conditions of freedom what is the value of freedom? First things come first: there are situations, as a nineteenth-century Russian radical writer declared, in which boots are superior to the works of Shakespeare; individual freedom is not everyone's primary need. For freedom is not the mere absence of frustration of whatever kind; this would inflate the meaning of the word until it meant too much or too little. The Egyptian peasant needs clothes or medicine before, and more than, personal liberty, but the minimum freedom that he needs today, and the greater degree of freedom that he may need tomorrow, is not some species of freedom peculiar to him, but identical with that of professors, artists, and millionaires.

What troubles the consciences of Western liberals is not, I think, the belief that the freedom that men seek differs according to their social or economic conditions, but that the minority who possess it have gained it by exploiting or, at least, averting their gaze from the vast majority who do not. They believe, with good reason, that if individual liberty is an ultimate end for human beings, none should be deprived of it by others; least of all that some should enjoy it at the expense of others. Equality of liberty; not to treat others as I should not wish them to treat me; repayment of my debt to those who alone have made possible my liberty or prosperity or enlightenment; justice, in its simplest and most universal sense—these are the foundations of liberal morality. Liberty is not the only goal of men. I can, like the Russian critic Belinsky, say that if others are to be deprived of it—if my brothers are to remain in poverty, squalor, and chains—then I do not want it for myself, I reject it with both hands and infinitely prefer to share their fate. But nothing is gained by a confusion of terms. To avoid glaring inequality or widespread misery I am ready to sacrifice some, or all, of my freedom: I may do so willingly and freely: but it is freedom that I am giving up for the sake of justice or equality or the love of my fellow men. I should be guilt-stricken, and rightly so, if I were not, in some circumstances, ready to make this sacrifice. But a sacrifice is not an increase in what is being sacrificed, namely freedom, however great the moral need or the compensation for it. Everything is what it is: liberty is liberty, not equality or fairness or justice or culture or human happiness or a quiet

conscience. If the liberty of myself or my class or nation depends on the misery of a number of other human beings, the system which promotes this is unjust and immoral. But if I curtail or lose my freedom, in order to lessen the shame of such inequality, and do not thereby materially increase the individual liberty of others, an absolute loss of liberty occurs. This may be compensated for by a gain in justice or in happiness or in peace, but the loss remains, and it is a confusion of values to say that although my 'liberal', individual freedom may go by the board, some other kind of freedom—'social' or 'economic'—is increased. Yet it remains true that the freedom of some must at times be curtailed to secure the freedom of others. Upon what principle should this be done? If freedom is a sacred, untouchable value, there can be no such principle. One or other of these conflicting principles must at any rate in practice yield: not always for reasons which can be clearly stated, let alone generalized into rules or universal maxims.

6. This is but another illustration of the natural tendency of all but a very few thinkers to believe that all the things they hold good must be intimately connected, or at least compatible, with one another. The history of thought, like the history of nations, is strewn with examples of inconsistent, or at least disparate, elements artificially yoked together in a despotic system, or held together by the danger of some common enemy. In due course the danger passes, and conflicts between the allies arise, which often disrupt the system, sometimes to the great benefit of mankind.

7. See the valuable discussion of this in Michel Villey, *Leçons d'Histoire de la Philosophie du Droit*, who traces the embryo of the notion of subjective rights to Occam.

8. Christian (and Jewish or Moslem) belief in the absolute authority of divine or natural laws, or in the equality of all men in the sight of God, is very different from belief in freedom to live as one prefers.

9. Indeed, it is arguable that in the Prussia of Frederick the Great or in the Austria of Josef II, men of imagination, originality, and creative genius, and, indeed, minorities of all kinds, were less persecuted and felt the pressure, both of institutions and custom, less heavy upon them than in many an earlier or later democracy.

10. 'Negative liberty' is something the extent of which, in a given case, it is difficult to estimate. It might, prima facie, seem to depend simply on the power to choose between at any rate two alternatives. Nevertheless, not all choices are equally free, or free at all. If in a totalitarian state I betray my friend under threat of torture, perhaps even if I act from fear of losing my job, I can reasonably say that I did not act freely. Nevertheless, I did, of course, make a choice, and could, at any rate in theory, have chosen to be killed or tortured or imprisoned. The mere existence of alternatives is not,

therefore, enough to make my action free (although it may be voluntary) in the normal sense of the word. The extent of my freedom seems to depend on (*a*) how many possibilities are open to me (although the method of counting these can never be more than impressionistic. Possibilities of action are not discrete entities like apples, which can be exhaustively enumerated); (*b*) how easy or difficult each of these possibilities is to actualize; (*c*) how important in my plan of life, given my character and circumstances, these possibilities are when compared with each other; (*d*) how far they are closed and opened by deliberate human acts; (*e*) what value not merely the agent, but the general sentiment of the society in which he lives, puts on the various possibilities. All these magnitudes must be 'integrated', and a conclusion, necessarily never precise, or indisputable, drawn from this process. It may well be that there are many incommensurable degrees of freedom, and that they cannot be drawn up on a single scale of magnitude, however conceived. Moreover, in the case of societies, we are faced by such (logically absurd) questions as 'Would arrangement X increase the liberty of Mr. A more than it would that of Messrs. B, C, and D between them, added together?' The same difficul-

ties arise in applying utilitarian criteria. Nevertheless, provided we do not demand precise measurement, we can give valid reasons for saying that the average subject of the King of Sweden is, on the whole, a good deal freer today than the average citizen of the Republic of Rumania. Total patterns of life must be compared directly as wholes, although the method by which we make the comparison, and the truth of the conclusions, are difficult or impossible to demonstrate. But the vagueness of the concepts, and the multiplicity of the criteria involved, is an attribute of the subject-matter itself, not of our imperfect methods of measurement, or incapacity for precise thought.

11. 'The ideal of true freedom is the maximum of power for all the members of human society alive to make the best of themselves', said T. H. Green in 1881. Apart from the confusion of freedom with equality, this entails that if a man chose some immediate pleasure—which (in whose view?) would not enable him to make the best of himself (what self?) what he is exercising is not 'true' freedom: and, if deprived of it, he would not lose anything that mattered. Green was a genuine liberal: but many a tyrant could use this formula to justify his worst oppression.

What's Wrong
with Negative Liberty

CHARLES TAYLOR

This is an attempt to resolve one of the issues that separate 'positive' and 'negative' theories of freedom, as these have been distinguished in Isaiah Berlin's seminal essay, "Two Concepts of Liberty."[1] Although one can discuss almost endlessly the detailed formulation of the distinction, I believe it is undeniable that there are two such families of conceptions of political freedom abroad in our civilisation.

Thus there clearly are theories, widely canvassed in liberal society, which want to define freedom exclusively in terms of the independence of the individual from interference by others, be these governments, corporations or private persons; and equally clearly these theories are challenged by those who believe that freedom resides at least in part in collective control over the common life. We unproblematically recognise theories descended from Rousseau and Marx as fitting in this category.

There is quite a gamut of views in each category. And this is worth bearing in mind, because it is too easy in the course of polemic to fix on the extreme, almost caricatural variants of each family. When people attack positive theories of freedom, they generally have some Left totalitarian theory in mind, according to which freedom resides exclusively in exercising collective control over one's destiny in a classless society, the kind of theory which underlies, for instance, official Communism. This

view, in its caricaturally extreme form, refuses to recognise the freedoms guaranteed in other societies as genuine. The destruction of "bourgeois freedoms" is no real loss of freedom, and coercion can be justified in the name of freedom if it is needed to bring into existence the classless society in which alone men are properly free. Men can, in short, be forced to be free.

Even as applied to official Communism, this portrait is a little extreme, although it undoubtedly expresses the inner logic of this kind of theory. But it is an absurd caricature if applied to the whole family of positive conceptions. This includes all those views of modern political life which owe something to the ancient republican tradition, according to which men's ruling themselves is seen as an activity valuable in itself, and not only for instrumental reasons. It includes in its scope thinkers like Tocqueville, and even arguably the J. S. Mill of *On Representative Government*. It has no necessary connection with the view that freedom consists *purely and simply* in the collective control over the common life, or that there is no freedom worth the name outside a context of collective control. And it does not therefore generate necessarily a doctrine that men can be forced to be free.

On the other side, there is a corresponding caricatural version of negative freedom which

Charles Taylor, "What's Wrong with Negative Liberty," reprinted from *The Idea of Liberty,* ed. Alan Ryan (Oxford University Press, 1979), by permission of the author. Copyright Charles Taylor, 1979.

tends to come to the fore. This is the tough-minded version, going back to Hobbes, or in another way to Bentham, which sees freedom simply as the absence of external physical or legal obstacles. This view will have no truck with other less immediately obvious obstacles to freedom, for instance, lack of awareness, or false consciousness, or repression, or other inner factors of this kind. It holds firmly to the view that to speak of such inner factors as relevant to the issue about freedom, to speak for instance of someone's being less free because of false consciousness, is to abuse words. The only clear meaning which can be given to freedom is that of the absence of external obstacles.

I call this view caricatural as a representative portrait of the negative view, because it rules out of court one of the most powerful motives behind the modern defence of freedom as individual independence, viz., the post-Romantic idea that each person's form of self-realisation is original to him/her, and can therefore only be worked out independently. This is one of the reasons for the defence of individual liberty by among others J. S. Mill (this time in his *On Liberty*). But if we think of freedom as including something like the freedom of self-fulfilment, or self-realisation according to our own pattern, then we plainly have something which can fail for inner reasons as well as because of external obstacles. We can fail to achieve our own self-realisation through inner fears, or false consciousness, as well as because of external coercion. Thus the modern notion of negative freedom which gives weight to the securing of each person's right to realise him/herself in his/her own way cannot make do with the Hobbes-Bentham notion of freedom. The moral psychology of these authors is too simple, or perhaps we should say too crude, for its purposes.

Now there is a strange asymmetry here. The extreme caricatural views tend to come to the fore in the polemic, as I mentioned above. But whereas the extreme "forced-to-be-free" view is one which the opponents of positive liberty try to pin on them, as one would expect in the heat of argument, the proponents of negative liberty themselves often seem anxious to es-

pouse their extreme, Hobbesian view. Thus even Isaiah Berlin, in his eloquent exposition of the two concepts of liberty, seems to quote Bentham[2] approvingly and Hobbes[3] as well. Why is this?

To see this we have to examine more closely what is at stake between the two views. The negative theories, as we saw, want to define freedom in terms of individual independence from others; the positive also want to identify freedom with collective self-government. But behind this lie some deeper differences of doctrines.

Isaiah Berlin points out that negative theories are concerned with the area in which the subject should be left without interference, whereas the positive doctrines are concerned with who or what controls. I should like to put the point behind this in a slightly different way. Doctrines of positive freedom are concerned with a view of freedom which involves essentially the exercising of control over one's life. On this view, one is free only to the extent that one has effectively determined oneself and the shape of one's life. The concept of freedom here is an exercise-concept.

By contrast, negative theories can rely simply on an opportunity-concept, where being free is a matter of what we can do, of what it is open to us to do, whether or not we do anything to exercise these options. This certainly is the case of the crude, original Hobbesian concept. Freedom consists just in there being no obstacle. It is a sufficient condition of one's being free that nothing stand in the way.

But we have to say that negative theories *can* rely on an opportunity-concept, rather than that they necessarily do so rely, for we have to allow for that part of the gamut of negative theories mentioned above which incorporates some notion of self-realisation. Plainly this kind of view can't rely simply on an opportunity-concept. We can't say that someone is free, on a self-realisation view, if he is totally unrealised, if for instance he is totally unaware of his potential, if fulfilling it has never even arisen as a question for him, or if he is paralysed by the fear of breaking with some norm which he has internalised but which does not authentically reflect him. Within this conceptual scheme, some degree of exercise is necessary for a man to be thought free. Or if we want to think of the internal bars to freedom as obstacles on all fours with the external ones, then being in a position to exercise freedom, having the opportunity, involves removing the internal barriers; and this is not possible without having to some extent realised myself. So that with the freedom of self-realisation, having the opportunity to be free requires that I already be exercising freedom. A pure opportunity-concept is impossible here.

But if negative theories can be grounded on either an opportunity- or an exercise-concept, the same is not true of positive theories. The view that freedom involves at least partially collective self-rule is essentially grounded on an exercise-concept. For this view (at least partly) identifies freedom with self-direction, i.e., the actual exercise of directing control over one's life.

But this already gives us a hint towards illuminating the above paradox, that while the extreme variant of positive freedom is usually pinned on its protagonists by their opponents, negative theorists seem prone to embrace the crudest versions of their theory themselves. For if an opportunity-concept is incombinable with a positive theory, but either it or its alternative can suit a negative theory, then one way of ruling out positive theories in principle is by firmly espousing an opportunity-concept. One cuts off the positive theories by the root, as it were, even though one may also pay a price in the atrophy of a wide range of negative theories as well. At least by taking one's stand firmly on the crude side of the negative range, where only opportunity concepts are recognised, one leaves no place for a positive theory to grow.

Taking one's stand here has the advantage that one is holding the line around a very simple and basic issue of principle, and one where the negative view seems to have some backing in common sense. The basic intuition here is that freedom is a matter of being able to do something or other, of not having obstacles in one's way, rather than being a capacity that we have to realise. It naturally seems more prudent to fight the Totalitarian Menace at this last-

ditch position, digging in behind the natural frontier of this simple issue, rather than engaging the enemy on the open terrain of exercise-concepts, where one will have to fight to discriminate the good from the bad among such concepts; fight, for instance, for a view of individual self-realisation against various notions of collective self-realisation, of a nation, or a class. It seems easier and safer to cut all the nonsense off at the start by declaring all self-realisation views to be metaphysical hogwash. Freedom should just be tough-mindedly defined as the absence of external obstacles.

Of course, there are independent reasons for wanting to define freedom tough-mindedly. In particular there is the immense influence of the anti-metaphysical, materialist, natural-science-oriented temper of thought in our civilisation. Something of this spirit at its inception induced Hobbes to take the line that he did, and the same spirit goes marching on today. Indeed, it is because of the prevalence of the spirit that the line is so easy to defend, forensically speaking, in our society.

Nevertheless, I think that one of the strongest motives for defending the crude Hobbes-Bentham concept, that freedom is the absence of external obstacles, physical or legal, is the strategic one above. For most of those who take this line thereby abandon many of their own intuitions, sharing as they do with the rest of us in a post-Romantic civilisation which puts great value on self-realisation, and values freedom largely because of this. It is fear of the Totalitarian Menace, I would argue, which has led them to abandon this terrain to the enemy.

I want to argue that this not only robs their eventual forensic victory of much of its value, since they become incapable of defending liberalism in the form we in fact value it, but I want to make the stronger claim that this Maginot Line mentality actually ensures defeat, as is often the case with Maginot Line mentalities. The Hobbes-Bentham view, I want to argue, is indefensible as a view of freedom.

To see this, let's examine the line more closely, and the temptation to stand on it. The advantage of the view that freedom is the absence of external obstacles is its simplicity.

It allows us to say that freedom is being able to do what you want, where what you want is unproblematically understood as what the agent can identify as his desires. By contrast an exercise-concept of freedom requires that we discriminate among motivations. If we are free in the exercise of certain capacities, then we are not free, or less free, when these capacities are in some way unfulfilled or blocked. But the obstacles can be internal as well as external. And this must be so, for the capacities relevant to freedom must involve some self-awareness, self-understanding, moral discrimination and self-control, otherwise their exercise couldn't amount to freedom in the sense of self-direction; and this being so, we can fail to be free because these internal conditions are not realised. But where this happens, where, for example, we are quite self-deceived, or utterly fail to discriminate properly the ends we seek, or have lost self-control, we can quite easily be doing what we want in the sense of what we can identify as our wants, without being free; indeed, we can be further entrenching our unfreedom.

Once one adopts a self-realisation view, or indeed, any exercise-concept of freedom, then being able to do what one wants can no longer be accepted as a sufficient condition of being free. For this view puts certain conditions on one's motivation. You are not free if you are motivated, through fear, inauthentically internalised standards, or false consciousness, to thwart your self-realisation. This is sometimes put by saying that for a self-realisation view, you have to be able to do what you really want, or to follow your real will, or to fulfil the desires of your own true self. But these formulas, particularly the last, may mislead, by making us think that exercise-concepts of freedom are tied to some particular metaphysic, in particular that of a higher and lower self. We shall see below that this is far from being the case, and that there is a much wider range of bases for discriminating authentic and inauthentic desires.

In any case, the point for our discussion here is that for an exercise-concept of freedom, being free can't just be a question of doing what you want in the unproblematic sense. It must

also be that what you want doesn't run against the grain of your basic purposes, or your self-realisation. Or to put the issue in another way, which converges on the same point, the subject himself can't be the final authority on the question whether he is free; for he cannot be the final authority on the question whether his desires are authentic, whether they do or do not frustrate his purposes.

To put the issue in this second way is to make more palpable the temptation for defenders of the negative view to hold their Maginot Line. For once we admit that the agent himself is not the final authority on his own freedom, do we not open the way to totalitarian manipulation? Do we not legitimate others, supposedly wiser about his purposes than himself, redirecting his feet on the right path, perhaps even by force, and all this in the name of freedom?

The answer is that of course we don't. Not by this concession alone. For there may also be good reasons for holding that others are not likely to be in a better position to understand his real purposes. This indeed plausibly follows from the post-Romantic view above that each person has his/her own original form of realisation. Some others, who know us intimately, and who surpass us in wisdom, are undoubtedly in a position to advise us, but no official body can possess a doctrine or a technique whereby they could know how to put us on the rails, because such a doctrine or technique cannot in principle exist if human beings really differ in their self-realisation.

Or again, we may hold a self-realisation view of freedom, and hence believe that there are certain conditions on my motivation necessary to my being free, but also believe that there are other necessary conditions which rule out my being forcibly led towards some definition of my self-realisation by external authority. Indeed, in these last two paragraphs I have given a portrait of what I think is a very widely held view in liberal society, a view which values self-realisation, and accepts that it can fail for internal reasons, but which believes that no valid guidance can be provided in principle by social authority, because of human diversity and originality, and holds that the attempt to impose such guidance will destroy other necessary conditions of freedom.

It is however true that totalitarian theories of positive freedom do build on a conception which involves discriminating between motivations. Indeed, one can represent the path from the negative to the positive conceptions of freedom as consisting of two steps: the first moves us from a notion of freedom as doing what one wants to a notion which discriminates motivations and equates freedom with doing what we really want, or obeying our real will, or truly directing our lives. The second step introduces some doctrine purporting to show that we cannot do what we really want, or follow our real will, outside of a society of a certain canonical form, incorporating true self-government. It follows that we can only be free in such a society, and that being free *is* governing ourselves collectively according to this canonical form.

We might see an example of this second step in Rousseau's view that only a social contract society in which all give themselves totally to the whole preserves us from other-dependence and ensures that we obey only ourselves; or in Marx's doctrine of man as a species-being who realises his potential in a mode of social production, and who must thus take control of this mode collectively.

Faced with this two-step process, it seems safer and easier to stop it at the first step, to insist firmly that freedom is just a matter of the absence of external obstacles, that it therefore involves no discrimination of motivation and permits in principle no second-guessing of the subject by any one else. This is the essence of the Maginot Line strategy. It is very tempting. But I want to claim that it is wrong. I want to argue that we cannot defend a view of freedom which doesn't involve at least some qualitative discrimination as to motive, i.e., which doesn't put some restrictions on motivation among the necessary conditions of freedom, and hence which could rule out second-guessing in principle.

There are some considerations one can put forward straight off to show that the pure Hobbesian concept won't work, that there are some discriminations among motivations which are essential to the concept of freedom as we use it. Even where we think of freedom as the absence of external obstacles, it is not the absence of such obstacles *simpliciter.* For we make discriminations between obstacles as representing more or less serious infringements of freedom. And we do this, because we deploy the concept against a background understanding that certain goals and activities are more significant than others.

Thus we could say that my freedom is restricted if the local authority puts up a new traffic light at an intersection close to my home; so that were previously I could cross as I liked, consistently with avoiding collision with other cars, now I have to wait until the light is green. In a philosophical argument, we might call this a restriction of freedom, but not in a serious political debate. The reason is that it is too trivial, the activity and purposes inhibited here are not really significant. It is not just a matter of our having made a trade-off, and considered that a small loss of liberty was worth fewer traffic accidents, or less danger for the children; we are reluctant to speak here of a loss of liberty at all; what we feel we are trading off is convenience against safety.

By contrast a law which forbids me from worshipping according to the form I believe in is a serious blow to liberty; even a law which tried to restrict this to certain times (as the traffic light restricts my crossing of the intersection to certain times) would be seen as a serious restriction. Why this difference between the two cases? Because we have a background understanding, too obvious to spell out, of some activities and goals as highly significant for human beings and others as less so. One's religious belief is recognised, even by atheists, as supremely important, because it is that by which the believer defines himself as a moral being. By contrast my rhythm of movement through the city traffic is trivial. We don't want to speak of these two in the same breath. We don't even readily admit that liberty is at stake in the traffic light case. For *de minimis non curat libertas.*

But this recourse to significance takes us beyond a Hobbesian scheme. Freedom is no longer just the absence of external obstacle *tout court,* but the absence of external obstacle to significant action, to what is important to man. There are discriminations to be made; some restrictions are more serious than others, some are utterly trivial. About many, there is of course controversy. But what the judgement turns on is some sense of what is significant for human life. Restricting the expression of people's religious and ethical convictions is more significant than restricting their movement around uninhabited parts of the country; and both are more significant than the trivia of traffic control.

But the Hobbesian scheme has no place for the notion of significance. It will allow only for purely quantitative judgements. On the toughest-minded version of his conception, where Hobbes seems to be about to define liberty in terms of the absence of physical obstacles, one is presented with the vertiginous prospect of human freedom being measurable in the same way as the degrees of freedom of some physical object, say a lever. Later we see that this won't do, because we have to take account of legal obstacles to my action. But in any case, such a quantitative conception of freedom is a non-starter.

Consider the following diabolical defence of Albania as a free country. We recognise that religion has been abolished in Albania, whereas it hasn't been in Britain. But on the other hand there are probably far fewer traffic lights per head in Tirana than in London. (I haven't checked for myself, but this is a very plausible assumption.) Suppose an apologist for Albanian Socialism were nevertheless to claim that this country was freer than Britain, because the number of acts restricted was far smaller. After all, only a minority of Londoners practise some religion in public places, but all have to negotiate their way through traffic. Those who do practise a religion generally do so on one day of the week, while they are held up at traffic lights every day. In sheer quantitative terms, the number of acts restricted by traffic lights must be greater than that restricted by a ban on public religious practice. So if Britain is considered a free society, why not Albania?

So the application even of our negative no-tion of freedom requires a background conception of what is significant, according to which some restrictions are seen to be without relevance for freedom altogether, and others are judged as being of greater and lesser importance. So some discrimination among motivations seems essential to our concept of freedom. A minute's reflection shows why this must be so. Freedom is important to us because we are purposive beings. But then there must be distinctions in the significance of different kinds of freedom based on the distinction in the significance of different purposes.

But of course, this still doesn't involve the kind of discrimination mentioned above, the kind which would allow us to say that someone who was doing what he wanted (in the unproblematic sense) wasn't really free, the kind of discrimination which allows us to put conditions on people's motivations necessary to their being free, and hence to second-guess them. All we have shown is that we make discriminations between more or less significant freedoms, based on discriminations among the purposes people have.

This creates some embarrassment for the crude negative theory, but it can cope with it by simply adding a recognition that we make judgements of significance. Its central claim that freedom just is the absence of external obstacles seems untouched, as also its view of freedom as an opportunity-concept. It is just that we now have to admit that not all opportunities are equal.

But there is more trouble in store for the crude view when we examine further what these qualitative discriminations are based on. What lies behind our judging certain purposes/feelings as more significant than others? One might think that there was room here again for another quantitative theory; that the more significant purposes are those we want more. But this account is either vacuous or false.

It is true but vacuous if we take wanting more just to mean being more significant. It is false as soon as we try to give wanting more an independent criterion, such as, for instance, the urgency or force of a desire, or the prevalence of one desire over another, because it is a matter of the most banal experience that the purposes we know to be more significant are not always those which we desire with the greatest urgency to encompass, nor the ones that actually always win out in cases of conflict of desires.

When we reflect on this kind of significance, we come up against what I have called elsewhere the fact of strong evaluation, the fact that we human subjects are not only subjects of first-order desires, but of second-order desires, desires about desires. We experience our desires and purposes as qualitatively discriminated, as higher or lower, noble or base, integrated or fragmented, significant or trivial, good and bad. This means that we experience some of our desires and goals as intrinsically more significant than others: some passing comfort is less important than the fulfilment of our lifetime vocation, our *amour propre* less important than a love relationship; while we experience some others as bad, not just comparatively, but absolutely: we desire not to be moved by spite, or some childish desire to impress at all costs. And these judgements of significance are quite independent of the strength of the respective desires: the craving for comfort may be overwhelming at this moment, we may be obsessed with our *amour propre,* but the judgement of significance stands.

But then the question arises whether this fact of strong evaluation doesn't have other consequences for our notion of freedom, than just that it permits us to rank freedoms in importance. Is freedom not at stake when we find ourselves carried away by a less significant goal to override a high significant one? Or when we are led to act out of a motive we consider bad or despicable?

The answer is that we sometimes do speak in this way. Suppose I have some irrational fear, which is preventing me from doing something I very much want to do. Say the fear of public speaking is preventing me from taking up a career that I should find very fulfilling, and that I should be quite good at, if I could just get over this "hang-up." It is clear that we experience this fear as an obstacle, and that we feel we are less than we would be if we could overcome it.

Or again, consider the case where I am very

attached to comfort. To go on short rations, and to miss my creature comforts for a time, makes me very depressed. I find myself making a big thing of this. Because of this reaction I can't do certain things that I should like very much to do, such as going on an expedition over the Andes, or a canoe trip in the Yukon. Once again, it is quite understandable if I experience this attachment as an obstacle, and feel that I should be freer without it.

Or I could find that my spiteful feelings and reactions which I almost can't inhibit are undermining a relationship which is terribly important to me. At times, I feel as though I am almost assisting as a helpless witness at my own destructive behaviour, as I lash out again with my unbridled tongue at her. I long to be able not to feel this spite. As long as I feel it, even control is not an option, because it just builds up inside until it either bursts out, or else the feeling somehow communicates itself, and queers things between us. I long to be free of this feeling.

These are quite understandable cases, where we can speak of freedom or its absence without strain. What I have called strong evaluation is essentially involved here. For these are not just cases of conflict, even cases of painful conflict. If the conflict is between two desires with which I have no trouble identifying, there can be no talk of lesser freedom, no matter how painful or fateful. Thus if what is breaking up my relationship is my finding fulfilment in a job which, say, takes me away from home a lot, I have indeed a terrible conflict, but I would have no temptation to speak of myself as less free.

Even seeing a great difference in the significance of the two terms doesn't seem to be a sufficient condition of my wanting to speak of freedom and its absence. Thus my marriage may be breaking up because I like going to the pub and playing cards on Saturday nights with the boys. I may feel quite unequivocally that my marriage is much more important than the release and comradeship of the Saturday night bash. But nevertheless I wouldn't want to talk of my being freer if I could slough off this desire.

The difference seems to be that in this case,

unlike the ones above, I still identify with the less important desire, I still see it as expressive of myself, so that I couldn't lose it without altering who I am, losing something of my personality. Whereas my irrational fear, my being quite distressed by discomfort, my spite—these are all things which I can easily see myself losing without any loss whatsoever to what I am. This is why I can see them as obstacles to my purposes, and hence to my freedom, even though they are in a sense unquestionably desires and feelings of mine.

Before exploring further what's involved in this, let's go back and keep score. It would seem that these cases make a bigger breach in the crude negative theory. For they seem to be cases in which the obstacles to freedom are internal; and if this is so, then freedom can't simply be interpreted as the absence of *external* obstacles; and the fact that I'm doing what I want, in the sense of following my strongest desire, isn't sufficient to establish that I'm free. On the contrary, we have to make discriminations among motivations, and accept that acting out of some motivations, for example irrational fear or spite, or this too great need for comfort, is not freedom, is even a negation of freedom.

But although the crude negative theory can't be sustained in the face of these examples, perhaps something which springs from the same concerns can be reconstructed. For although we have to admit that there are internal, motivational, necessary conditions for freedom, we can perhaps still avoid any legitimation of what I called above the second-guessing of the subject. If our negative theory allows for strong evaluation, allows that some goals are really important to us, and that other desires are seen as not fully ours, then can it not retain the thesis that freedom is being able to do what I want, that is, what I can identify myself as wanting, where this means not just what I identify as my strongest desire, but what I identify as my true, authentic desire or purpose? The subject would still be the final arbiter of his being free/unfree, as indeed he is clearly capable of discerning this in the examples above, where I relied precisely on the subject's own experience of constraint, of motives with

which he can't identify. We should have sloughed off the untenable Hobbesian reductive-materialist metaphysics, according to which only external obstacles count, as though action were just movement, and there could be no internal, motivational obstacles to our deeper purposes. But we would be retaining the basic concern of the negative theory, that the subject is still the final authority as to what his freedom consists in, and cannot be second-guessed by external authority. Freedom would be modified to read: the absence of internal or external obstacle to what I truly or authentically want. But we would still be holding the Maginot Line. Or would we?

I think not, in fact. I think that this hybrid or middle position is untenable, where we are willing to admit that we can speak of what we truly want, as against what we most strongly desire, and of some desires as obstacles to our freedom, while we still will not allow for second-guessing. For to rule this out in principle is to rule out in principle that the subject can ever be wrong about what he truly wants. And how can he never, in principle, be wrong, unless there is nothing to be right or wrong about in this matter?

That in fact is the thesis our negative theorist will have to defend. And it is a plausible one for the same intellectual (reductive-empiricist) tradition from which the crude negative theory springs. On this view, our feelings are brute facts about us; that is, it is a fact about us that we are affected in such and such a way, but our feelings can't themselves be understood as involving some perception or sense of what they relate to, and hence as potentially veridical or illusory, authentic or inauthentic. On this scheme, the fact that a certain desire represented one of our fundamental purposes, and another a mere force with which we cannot identify, would concern merely the brute quality of the affect in both cases. It would be a matter of the raw feel of these two desires that this was their respective status.

In such circumstances, the subject's own classification would be incorrigible. There is no such thing as an imperceptible raw feel. If the subject failed to experience a certain desire as fundamental, and if what we meant by "fundamental'' applied to desire was that the felt experience of it has a certain quality, then the desire couldn't be fundamental. We can see this if we look at those feelings which we can agree are brute in this sense: for instance, the stab of pain I feel when the dentist jabs into my tooth, or the crawling unease when someone runs his fingernail along the blackboard. There can be no question of misperception here. If I fail to ''perceive'' the pain, I am not in pain. Might it not be so with our fundamental desires, and those which we repudiate?

The answer is clearly no. For first of all, many of our feelings and desires, including the relevant ones for these kinds of conflicts, are not brute. By contrast with pain and the fingernail-on-blackboard sensation, shame and fear, for instance, are emotions which involve our experiencing the situation as bearing a certain import for us, as being dangerous or shameful. This is why shame and fear can be inappropriate, or even irrational, where pain and a frisson cannot. Thus we can be in error in feeling shame or fear. We can even be consciously aware of the unfounded nature of our feelings, and this is when we castigate them as irrational.

Thus the notion that we can understand all our feelings and desires as brute, in the above sense, is not on. But more, the idea that we could discriminate our fundamental desires, or those which we want to repudiate, by the quality of brute affect is grotesque. When I am convinced that some career, or an expedition in the Andes, or a love relationship, is of fundamental importance to me (to recur to the above examples), it cannot be just because of the throbs, élans or tremors I feel; I must also have some sense that these are of great significance for me, meet important, long-lasting needs, represent a fulfilment of something central to me, will bring me closer to what I really am, or something of the sort. The whole notion of our identity, whereby we recognise that some goals, desires, allegiances are central to what we are, while others are not or are less so, can make sense only against a background of desires and feelings which are not brute, but what

I shall call import-attributing, to invent a term of art for the occasion.

Thus we have to see our emotional life as made up largely of import-attributing desires and feelings, that is, desires and feelings which we can experience mistakenly. And not only can we be mistaken in this, we clearly must accept, in cases like the above where we want to repudiate certain desires, that we are mistaken.

For let us consider the distinction mentioned above between conflicts where we feel fettered by one desire, and those where we do not, where, for instance, in the example mentioned above, a man is torn between his career and his marriage. What made the difference was that in the case of genuine conflict both desires are the agent's, whereas in the cases where he feels fettered by one, this desire is one he wants to repudiate.

But what is it to feel that a desire is not truly mine? Presumably, I feel that I should be better off without it, that I don't lose anything in getting rid of it, I remain quite complete without it. What could lie behind this sense?

Well, one could imagine feeling this about a brute desire. I may feel this about my addiction to smoking, for instance—wish I could get rid of it, experience it as a fetter, and believe that I should be well rid of it. But addictions are a special case; we understand them to be unnatural, externally-induced desires. We couldn't say in general that we are ready to envisage losing our brute desires without a sense of diminution. On the contrary, to lose my desire for, and hence delectation in, oysters, mushroom pizza, or Peking duck would be a terrible deprivation. I should fight against such a change with all the strength at my disposal.

So being brute is not what makes desires repudiable. And besides, in the above examples the repudiated desires aren't brute. In the first case, I am chained by unreasoning fear, an import-attributing emotion, in which the fact of being mistaken is already recognised when I identify the fear as irrational or unreasoning. Spite, too, which moves me in the third case, is an import-attributing emotion. To feel spite is to see oneself and the target of one's resentment in a certain light; it is to feel in some way wounded, or damaged, by his success or good fortune, and the more hurt the more he is fortunate. To overcome feelings of spite, as against just holding them in, is to come to see self and other in a different light, in particular, to set aside self-pity, and the sense of being personally wounded by what the other does and is.

(I should also like to claim that the obstacle in the third example, the too great attachment to comfort, while not itself import-attributing, is also bound up with the way we see things. The problem is here not just that we dislike discomfort, but that we are too easily depressed by it; and this is something which we overcome only by sensing a different order of priorities, whereby small discomforts matter less. But if this is thought too dubious, we can concentrate on the other two examples.)

Now how can we feel that an import-attributing desire is not truly ours? We can do this only if we see it as mistaken, that is, the import or the good it supposedly gives us a sense of is not a genuine import or good. The irrational fear is a fetter, because it is irrational; spite is a fetter because it is rooted in a self-absorption which distorts our perspective on everything, and the pleasures of venting it preclude any genuine satisfaction. Losing these desires we lose nothing, because their loss deprives us of no genuine good or pleasure or satisfaction. In this they are quite different from my love of oysters, mushroom pizza, and Peking duck.

It would appear from this that to see our desires as brute gives us no clue as to why some of them are repudiable. On the contrary it is precisely their not being brute which can explain this. It is because they are import-attributing desires which are mistaken that we can feel that we would lose nothing in sloughing them off. Everything which is truly important to us would be safeguarded. If they were just brute desires, we couldn't feel this unequivocally, as we certainly do not when it comes to the pleasures of the palate. True, we also feel that our desire to smoke is repudiable,

but there is a special explanation here, which is not available in the case of spite.

Thus we can experience some desires as fetters, because we can experience them as not ours. And we can experience them as not ours because we see them as incorporating a quite erroneous appreciation of our situation and of what matters to us. We can see this again if we contrast the case of spite with that of another emotion which partly overlaps, and which is highly considered in some societies, the desire for revenge. In certain traditional societies this is far from being considered a despicable emotion. On the contrary, it is a duty of honour on a male relative to avenge a man's death. We might imagine that this too might give rise to conflict. It might conflict with the attempts of a new regime to bring some order to the land. The government would have to stop people taking vengeance, in the name of peace.

But short of a conversion to a new ethical outlook, this would be seen as a trade-off, the sacrifice of one legitimate goal for the sake of another. And it would seem monstrous were one to propose reconditioning people so that they no longer felt the desire to avenge their kin. This would be to unman them.[4]

Why do we feel so different about spite (and for that matter also revenge)? Because the desire for revenge for an ancient Icelander was his sense of a real obligation incumbent on him, something it would be dishonourable to repudiate; while for us, spite is the child of a distorted perspective on things.

We cannot therefore understand our desires and emotions as all brute, and in particular we cannot make sense of our discrimination of some desires as more important and fundamental, or of our repudiation of others, unless we understand our feelings to be import-attributing. This is essential to there being what we have called strong evaluation. Consequently the halfway position which admits strong evaluation, admits that our desires may frustrate our deeper purposes, admits therefore that there may be inner obstacles to freedom, and yet will not admit that the subject may be wrong or mistaken about these purposes—this position doesn't seem tenable. For the only way to make the subject's assessment incorrigible in principle would be to claim that there was nothing to be right or wrong about here; and that could only be so if experiencing a given feeling were a matter of the qualities of brute feeling. But this it cannot be if we are to make sense of the whole background of strong evaluation, more significant goals, and aims that we repudiate. This whole scheme requires that we understand the emotions concerned as import-attributing, as, indeed, it is clear that we must do on other grounds as well.

But once we admit that our feelings are import-attributing, then we admit the possibility of error, or false appreciation. And indeed, we have to admit a kind of false appreciation which the agent himself detects in order to make sense of the cases where we experience our own desires as fetters. How can we exclude in principle that there may be other false appreciations which the agent does not detect? That he may be profoundly in error, that is, have a very distorted sense of his fundamental purposes? Who can say that such people can't exist? All cases are, of course, controversial; but I should nominate Charles Manson and Andreas Baader for this category, among others. I pick them out as people with a strong sense of some purposes and goals as incomparably more fundamental than others, or at least with a propensity to act the having such a sense so as to take in even themselves a good part of the time, but whose sense of fundamental purpose was shot through with confusion and error. And once we recognise such extreme cases, how avoid admitting that many of the rest of mankind can suffer to a lesser degree from the same disabilities?

What has this got to do with freedom? Well, to resume what we have seen: our attributions of freedom make sense against a background sense of more and less significant purposes, for the question of freedom/unfreedom is bound up with the frustration/fulfilment of our purposes. Further, our significant purposes can be frustrated by our own desires, and where these are sufficiently based on misappreciation, we consider them as not really ours, and experience them as fetters. A man's freedom can

therefore be hemmed in by internal, motivational obstacles, as well as external ones. A man who is driven by spite to jeopardise his most important relationships, in spite of himself, as it were, or who is prevented by unreasoning fear from taking up the career he truly wants, is not really made more free if one lifts the external obstacles to his venting his spite or acting on his fear. Or at best he is liberated into a very impoverished freedom.

If through linguistic/ideological purism one wants to stick to the crude definition, and insist that men are equally freed from whom the same external obstacles are lifted, regardless of their motivational state, then one will just have to introduce some other term to mark the distinction, and say that one man is capable of taking proper advantage of his freedom, and the other (the one in the grip of spite, or fear) is not. This is because in the meaningful sense of "free," that for which we value it, in the sense of being able to act on one's important purposes, the internally fettered man is not free. If we choose to give "free" a special (Hobbesian) sense which avoids this issue, we'll just have to introduce another term to deal with it.

Moreover since we have already seen that we are always making judgements of degrees of freedom, based on the significance of the activities or purposes which are left unfettered, how can we deny that the man, externally free but still stymied by his repudiated desires, is less free than one who has no such inner obstacles?

But if this is so, then can we not say of the man with a highly distorted view of his fundamental purpose, the Manson or Baader of my discussion above, that he may not be significantly freer when we lift even the internal barriers to his doing what is in line with this purpose, or at best may be liberated into a very impoverished freedom? Should a Manson overcome his last remaining compunction against sending his minions to kill on caprice, so that he could act unchecked, would we consider him freer, as we should undoubtedly consider the man who had done away with spite or unreasoning fear? Hardly, and certainly not to the same degree. For what he sees as his purpose here partakes so much of the nature of spite and unreasoning fear in the other cases, that is, it is an aspiration largely shaped by confusion, illusion and distorted perspective.

Once we see that we make distinctions of degree and significance in freedoms depending on the significance of the purpose fettered/enabled, how can we deny that it makes a difference to the degree of freedom not only whether one of my basic purposes is frustrated by my own desires but also whether I have grievously misidentified this purpose? The only way to avoid this would be to hold that there is no such thing as getting it wrong, that your basic purpose is just what you feel it to be. But there is such a thing as getting it wrong, as we have seen, and the very distinctions of significance depend on this fact.

But if this is so, then the crude negative view of freedom, the Hobbesian definition, is untenable. Freedom can't just be the absence of external obstacles, for there may also be internal ones. And nor may the internal obstacles be just confined to those that the subject identifies as such, so that he is the final arbiter; for he may be profoundly mistaken about his purposes and about what he wants to repudiate. And if so, he is less capable of freedom in the meaningful sense of the word. Hence we cannot maintain the incorrigibility of the subject's judgements about his freedom, or rule out second-guessing, as we put it above. And at the same time, we are forced to abandon the pure opportunity-concept of freedom.

For freedom now involves my being able to recognise adequately my more important purposes, and my being able to overcome or at least neutralise my motivational fetters, as well as my way being free of external obstacles. But clearly the first condition (and, I would argue, also the second) require me to have become something, to have achieved a certain condition of self-clairvoyance and self-understanding. I must be actually exercising self-understanding in order to be truly or fully free. I can no longer understand freedom just as an opportunity-concept.

In all these formulations of the issue—opportunity- versus exercise-concept; whether freedom requires that we discriminate among motivations; whether it allows of second-guessing the subject—the extreme negative view shows up as wrong. The idea of holding the Maginot Line before this Hobbesian concept is misguided not only because it involves abandoning some of the most inspiring terrain of liberalism, which is concerned with individual self-realisation, but also because the line turns out to be untenable. The first step from the Hobbesian definition to a positive notion, to a view of freedom as the ability to fulfil my purposes, and as being greater the more significant the purposes, is one we cannot help taking. Whether we must also take the second step, to a view of freedom which sees it as realisable or fully realisable only within a certain form of society; and whether in taking a step of this kind one is necessarily committed to justifying the excesses of totalitarian oppression in the name of liberty; these are questions which must now be addressed. What is certain is that they cannot simply be evaded by a philistine definition of freedom which relegates them by fiat to the limbo of metaphysical pseudo-questions. This is altogether too quick a way with them.

Notes

1. [Reprinted in this volume.] From *Four Essays on Liberty* (New York: Oxford University Press, 1969).
2. Ibid., p. 148, note 1.
3. Ibid., p. 164.
4. Compare the unease we feel at the reconditioning of the hero of Anthony Burgess's *A Clockwork Orange*.

From "On Liberty"

JOHN STUART MILL

Chapter 1. Introductory

[. . .] The object of this Essay is to assert one very simple principle, as entitled to govern absolutely the dealings of society with the individual in the way of compulsion and control, whether the means used be physical force in the form of legal penalties or the moral coercion of public opinion. That principle is, that the sole end for which mankind are warranted, individually or collectively, in interfering with the liberty of action of any of their number, is self-protection. That the only purpose for which power can be rightfully exercised over any member of a civilized community, against his will, is to prevent harm to others. His own good, either physical or moral, is not a sufficient warrant. He cannot rightfully be compelled to do or forbear because it will be better for him to do so, because it will make him happier, because, in the opinions of others, to do so would be wise, or even right. There are good reasons for remonstrating with him, or reasoning with him, or persuading him, or entreating him, but not for compelling him, or visiting him with any evil, in case he do otherwise. To justify that, the conduct from which it is desired to deter him must be calculated to produce evil to some one else. The only part of the conduct of any one, for which he is amenable to society, is that which concerns others.

In the part which merely concerns himself, his independence is, of right, absolute. Over himself, over his own body and mind, the individual is sovereign.

It is, perhaps, hardly necessary to say that this doctrine is meant to apply only to human beings in the maturity of their faculties. We are not speaking of children, or of young persons below the age which the law may fix as that of manhood or womanhood. Those who are still in a state to require being taken care of by others, must be protected against their own actions as well as against external injury. For the same reason, we may leave out of consideration those backward states of society in which the race itself may be considered as in its nonage. The early difficulties in the way of spontaneous progress are so great, that there is seldom any choice of means for overcoming them; and a ruler full of the spirit of improvement is warranted in the use of any expedients that will attain an end, perhaps otherwise unattainable. Despotism is a legitimate mode of government in dealing with barbarians, provided the end be their improvement, and the means justified by actually effecting that end. Liberty, as a principle, has no application to any state of things anterior to the time when mankind have become capable of being improved by free and equal discussion. Until then there is nothing for them but implicit obedience to an Akbar or a Charlemagne, if they are so fortunate as to find one. But as soon as mankind have attained the capacity of being guided to their own improvement by conviction or persuasion (a period long since reached in all nations with whom we need here concern ourselves), compulsion, either in the direct form or in that of pains and penalties for non-compliance, is no longer admissible as a means to their own good, and justifiable only for the security of others.

It is proper to state that I forgo any advantage which could be derived to my argument from the idea of abstract right, as a thing independent of utility. I regard utility as the ultimate appeal on all ethical questions; but it must be utility in the largest sense, grounded on the permanent interests of man as a progressive being. Those interests, I contend, authorize the subjection of individual spontaneity to external control, only in respect to those actions of each, which concern the interest of other people. If any one does an act hurtful to others, there is a prima facie case for punishing him, by law, or, where legal penalties are not safely applicable, by general disapprobation. There are also many positive acts for the benefit of others, which he may rightfully be compelled to perform; such as, to give evidence in a court of justice; to bear his fair share in the common defence, or in any other joint work necessary to the interest of the society of which he enjoys the protection; and to perform certain acts of individual beneficence, such as saving a fellow creature's life, or interposing to protect the defenceless against ill-usage, things which whenever it is obviously a man's duty to do, he may rightfully be made responsible to society for not doing. A person may cause evil to others not only by his actions but by his inaction, and in either case he is justly accountable to them for the injury. The latter case, it is true, requires a much more cautious exercise of compulsion than the former. To make any one answerable for doing evil to others, is the rule; to make him answerable for not preventing evil, is comparatively speaking, the exception. Yet there are many cases clear enough and grave enough to justify that exception. In all things which regard the external

relations of the individual, he is *de jure* amenable to those whose interests are concerned, and if need be, to society as their protector. There are often good reasons for not holding him to the responsibility; but these reasons must arise from the special expediencies of the case: either because it is a kind of case in which he is on the whole likely to act better, when left to his own discretion, than when controlled in any way in which society have it in their power to control him, or because the attempt to exercise control would produce other evils, greater than those which it would prevent. When such reasons as these preclude the enforcement of responsibility, the conscience of the agent himself should step into the vacant judgement-seat, and protect those interests of others which have no external protection; judging himself all the more rigidly, because the case does not admit of his being made accountable to the judgement of his fellow-creatures.

But there is a sphere of action in which society, as distinguished from the individual, has, if any, only an indirect interest; comprehending all that portion of a person's life and conduct which affects only himself, or, if it also affects others, only with their free, voluntary, and undeceived consent and participation. When I say only himself, I mean directly, and in the first instance: for whatever affects himself, may affect others *through* himself; and the objection which may be grounded on this contingency, will receive consideration in the sequel. This, then, is the appropriate region of human liberty. It comprises, first, the inward domain of consciousness, demanding liberty of conscience, in the most comprehensive sense; liberty of thought and feeling; absolute freedom of opinion and sentiment on all subjects, practical or speculative, scientific, moral, or theological. The liberty of expressing and publishing opinions may seem to fall under a different principle, since it belongs to that part of the conduct of an individual which concerns other people; but, being almost of as much importance as the liberty of thought itself, and resting in great part on the same reasons, is practically inseparable from it. Secondly, the principle requires liberty of tastes and pursuits; of framing the plan of our life to suit our own character; of doing as we like, subject to such consequences as may follow; without impediment from our fellow-creatures, so long as what we do does not harm them, even though they should think our conduct foolish, perverse, or wrong. Thirdly, from this liberty of each individual, follows the liberty, within the same limits, of combination among individuals; freedom to unite, for any purpose not involving harm to others: the persons combining being supposed to be of full age and not forced or deceived.

No society in which these liberties are not, on the whole, respected, is free, whatever may be its form of government; and none is completely free in which they do not exist absolute and unqualified. The only freedom which deserves the name, is that of pursuing our own good in our own way, so long as we do not attempt to deprive others of theirs, or impede their efforts to obtain it. Each is the proper guardian of his own health, whether bodily, or mental and spiritual. Mankind are greater gainers by suffering each other to live as seems good to themselves, than by compelling each to live as seems good to the rest.[. . .]

It will be convenient for the argument, if instead of at once entering upon the general thesis, we confine ourselves in the first instance to a single branch of it, on which the principle here stated is, if not fully, yet to a certain point, recognized by the current opinions. This one branch is the Liberty of Thought: from which it is impossible to separate the cognate liberty of speaking and of writing. Although these liberties, to some considerable amount, form part of the political morality of all countries which profess religious toleration and free institutions, the grounds, both philosophical and practical, on which they rest, are perhaps not so familiar to the general mind, nor so thoroughly appreciated by many even of the leaders of opinion, as might have been expected. Those grounds, when rightly understood, are of much wider application than to only one division of the subject, and a thorough consideration of this part of the question will be found the best introduction to the remainder. Those to whom nothing which I am about to say will be new, may therefore, I hope, excuse

me, if on a subject which for now three centuries has been so often discussed, I venture on one discussion more.

Chapter 2. Of the Liberty of Thought and Discussion

The time, it is to be hoped, is gone by when any defence would be necessary of the "liberty of the press" as one of the securities against corrupt or tyrannical government. No argument, we may suppose, can now be needed, against permitting a legislature or an executive, not identified in interest with the people, to prescribe opinions to them, and determine what doctrines or what arguments they shall be allowed to hear. This aspect of the question, besides, has been so often and so triumphantly enforced by preceding writers, that it needs not be specially insisted on in this place. Though the law of England, on the subject of the press, is as servile to this day as it was in the time of the Tudors, there is little danger of its being actually put in force against political discussion, except during some temporary panic, when fear of insurrection drives ministers and judges from their propriety;[1] and, speaking generally, it is not, in constitutional countries, to be apprehended, that the government, whether completely responsible to the people or not, will often attempt to control the expression of opinion, except when in doing so it makes itself the organ of the general intolerance of the public. Let us suppose, therefore, that the government is entirely at one with the public, and never thinks of exerting any power of coercion unless in agreement with what it conceives to be their voice. But I deny the right of the people to exercise such coercion, either by themselves or by their government. The power itself is illegitimate. The best government has no more title to it than the worst. It is as noxious, or more noxious, when exerted in accordance with public opinion, than when in opposition to it. If all mankind minus one, were of one opinion, and only one person were of the contrary opinion, mankind would be no more justified in silencing that one person, than he, if he had the power, would be justified in silencing mankind. Were an opinion a personal possession of no value except to the owner; if to be obstructed in the enjoyment of it were simply a private injury, it would make some difference whether the injury was inflicted only on a few persons or on many. But the peculiar evil of silencing the expression of an opinion is, that it is robbing the human race; posterity as well as the existing generation; those who dissent from the opinion, still more than those who hold it. If the opinion is right, they are deprived of the opportunity of exchanging error for truth: if wrong, they lose, what is almost as great a benefit, the clearer perception and livelier impression of truth, produced by its collision with error.

It is necessary to consider separately these two hypotheses, each of which has a distinct branch of the argument corresponding to it. We can never be sure that the opinion we are endeavouring to stifle is a false opinion; and if we were sure, stifling it would be an evil still.

First: the opinion which it is attempted to suppress by authority may possibly be true. Those who desire to suppress it, of course deny its truth; but they are not infallible. They have no authority to decide the question for all mankind, and exclude every other person from the means of judging. To refuse a hearing to an opinion, because they are sure that it is false, is to assume that *their* certainty is the same thing as *absolute* certainty. All silencing of discussion is an assumption of infallibility. Its condemnation may be allowed to rest on this common argument, not the worse for being common.

Unfortunately for the good sense of mankind, the fact of their fallibility is far from carrying the weight in their practical judgement, which is always allowed to it in theory; for while every one well knows himself to be fallible, few think it necessary to take any precautions against their own fallibility, or admit the supposition that any opinion, of which they feel very certain, may be one of the examples of the error to which they acknowledge themselves to be liable.[. . .] Yet it is as evident in itself, as any amount of argument can make it, that ages are no more infallible than individuals; every age having held many opinions which subsequent ages have deemed not only false but absurd; and it is as certain that many opinions, now general, will be rejected by future ages, as it is that many, once general, are rejected by the present.

The objection likely to be made to this argument, would probably take some form as the following. There is no greater assumption of infallibility in forbidding the propagation of error, than in any other thing which is done by public authority on its own judgement and responsibility. Judgement is given to men that they may use it. Because it may be used erroneously, are men to be told they ought not to use it at all? To prohibit what they think pernicious, is not claiming exemption from error, but fulfilling the duty incumbent on them, although fallible, of acting on their conscientious conviction. If we were never to act on our opinions, because those opinions may be wrong, we should leave all our interests uncared for, and all our duties unperformed. An objection which applies to all conduct, can be no valid objection to any conduct in particular. It is the duty of governments, and of individuals, to form the truest opinions they can; to form them carefully, and never impose them upon others unless they are quite sure of being right. But when they are sure (such reasoners may say), it is not conscientiousness but cowardice to shrink from acting on their opinions, and allow doctrines which they honestly think dangerous to the welfare of mankind, either in this life or in another, to be scattered abroad without restraint, because other people, in less enlightened times, have persecuted opinions now believed to be true. Let us take care, it may be said, not to make the same mistake: but governments and nations have made mistakes in other things, which are not denied to be fit subjects for the exercise of authority: they have laid on bad taxes, made unjust wars. Ought we therefore to lay on no taxes, and, under whatever provocation, make no wars? Men, and governments, must act to the best of their ability. There is no such thing as absolute certainty, but there is assurance sufficient for the purposes of human life. We may, and must, assume our opinion to be true for the guidance of our own conduct: and it is assuming no more when we forbid bad men to pervert society by the propagation of opinions which we regard as false and pernicious.

I answer, that it is assuming very much more. There is the greatest difference between presuming an opinion to be true, because, with every opportunity for contesting it, it has not been refuted, and assuming its truth for the purpose of not permitting its refutation. Complete liberty of contradicting and disproving our opinion, is the very condition which justifies us in assuming its truth for purposes of action; and on no other terms can a being with human faculties have any rational assurance of being right.[. . .]

Strange it is, that men should admit the validity of the arguments for free discussion, but object to their being "pushed to an extreme"; not seeing that unless the reasons are good for an extreme case, they are not good for any case. Strange that they should imagine that they are not assuming infallibility, when they acknowledge that there should be free discussion on all subjects which can possibly be *doubtful,* but think that some particular principle or doctrine should be forbidden to be questioned because it is *so certain,* that is, because *they are certain* that it is certain. To call any proposition certain, while there is any one who would deny its certainty if permitted, but who is not permitted, is to assume that we ourselves, and those who agree with us, are the judges of certainty and judges without hearing the other side.[. . .]

In order more fully to illustrate the mischief of denying a hearing to opinions because we, in our own judgement, have condemned them, it will be desirable to fix down the discussion to a concrete case; and I choose, by preference, the cases which are least favorable to me—in which the argument against freedom of opinion, both on the score of truth and on that of utility, is considered the strongest. Let the opinions impugned be the belief in a God and in a future state, or any of the commonly received doctrines of morality. To fight the battle on such ground, gives a great advantage to an unfair antagonist; since he will be sure to say (and many who have no desire to be unfair will say it internally), Are these the doctrines which you do not deem sufficiently certain to be

taken under the protection of law? Is the belief in a God one of the opinions, to feel sure of which, you hold to be assuming infallibility? But I must be permitted to observe, that it is not the feeling sure of a doctrine (be it what it may) which I call an assumption of infallibility. It is the undertaking to decide that question *for others,* without allowing them to hear what can be said on the contrary side. And I denounce and reprobate this pretension not the less, if put forth on the side of my most solemn convictions. However positive any one's persuasion may be, not only of the falsity, but of the pernicious consequences—not only of the pernicious consequences, but (to adopt expressions which I altogether condemn) the immorality and impiety of an opinion; yet if, in pursuance of that private judgement, though backed by the public judgement of his country or his contemporaries, he prevents the opinion from being heard in its defence, he assumes infallibility. And so far from the assumption being less objectionable or less dangerous because the opinion is called immoral or impious, this is the case of all others in which it is most fatal. These are exactly the occasions on which the men of one generation commit those dreadful mistakes, which excite the astonishment and horror of posterity. It is among such that we find the instances memorable in history, when the arm of the law has been employed to root out the best men and the noblest doctrines; with deplorable success as to the men, though some of the doctrines have survived to be (as if in mockery) invoked, in defence of similar conduct towards those who dissent from *them,* or from their received interpretation.

Mankind can hardly be too often reminded, that there was once a man named Socrates, between whom and the legal authorities and public opinion of his time, there took place a memorable collision. Born in an age and country abounding in individual greatness, this man has been handed down to us by those who best knew both him and the age, as the most virtuous man in it; while *we* know him as the head and prototype of all subsequent teachers of virtue, the source equally of the lofty inspiration of Plato and the judicious utilitarianism of Aristotle, "i maëstri di color che sanno," the two head-springs of ethical as of all other philosophy. This acknowledged master of all the eminent thinkers who have since lived—whose fame, still growing after more than two thousand years, all but outweighs the whole remainder of the names which make his native city illustrious—was put to death by his countrymen, after a judicial conviction, for impiety and immorality. Impiety, in denying the gods recognized by the State; indeed his accuser asserted (see the ''Apologia'') that he believed in no gods at all. Immorality, in being, by his doctrines and instructions, a ''corruptor of youth.'' Of these charges the tribunal, there is every ground for believing, honestly found him guilty, and condemned the man who probably of all then born had deserved best of mankind, to be put to death as a criminal.

To pass from this to the only other instance of judicial iniquity, the mention of which, after the condemnation of Socrates, would not be an anti-climax: the event which took place on Calvary rather more than eighteen hundred years ago. The man who left on the memory of those who witnessed his life and conversation, such an impression of his moral grandeur, that eighteen subsequent centuries have done homage to him as the Almighty in person, was ignominiously put to death, as what? As a blasphemer. Men did not merely mistake their benefactor; they mistook him for the exact contrary of what he was, and treated him as that prodigy of impiety, which they themselves are now held to be, for their treatment of him. The feelings with which mankind now regard these lamentable transactions, especially the later of the two, render them extremely unjust in their judgement of the unhappy actors. These were, to all appearance, not bad men—not worse than men commonly are, but rather the contrary; men who possessed in a full, or somewhat more than a full measure, the religious, moral, and patriotic feelings of their time and people: the very kind of men who, in all times, our own included, have every chance of passing through life blameless and respected. The high-priest who rent his garments when the words were pronounced, which, according to all the ideas of his country, constituted the blackest guilt, was in all probability quite as

sincere in his horror and indignation, as the generality of respectable and pious men now are in the religious and moral sentiments they profess; and most of those who now shudder at his conduct, if they had lived in his time, and had been born Jews, would have acted precisely as he did. Orthodox Christians who are tempted to think that those who stoned to death the first martyrs must have been worse men than they themselves are, ought to remember that one of those persecutors was Saint Paul.[. . .]

. . . But it is not the minds of heretics that are deteriorated most, by the ban placed on all inquiry which does not end in the orthodox conclusions. The greatest harm done is to those who are not heretics, and whose whole mental development is cramped, and their reason cowed, by the fear of heresy. Who can compute what the world loses in the multitude of promising intellects combined with timid characters, who dare not follow out any bold, vigorous, independent train of thought, lest it should land them in something which would admit of being considered irreligious or immoral? Among them we may occasionally see some man of deep conscientiousness, and subtile and refined understanding, who spends a life in sophisticating with an intellect which cannot silence, and exhausts the resources of ingenuity in attempting to reconcile the promptings of his conscience and reason with orthodoxy, which yet he does not, perhaps, to the end succeed in doing. No one can be a great thinker who does not recognize, that as a thinker it is his first duty to follow his intellect to whatever conclusions it may lead. Truth gains more even by the errors of one who, with due study and preparation, thinks for himself, than by the true opinions of those who only hold them because they do not suffer themselves to think. Not that it is solely, or chiefly, to form great thinkers, that freedom of thinking is required. On the contrary, it is as much, and even more indispensable, to enable average human beings to attain the mental stature which they are capable of. There have been, and may again be, great individual thinkers, in a general atmosphere of mental slavery. But there never has been, nor ever will be, in that atmosphere, an intellectually active people. Where any people has made a temporary approach to such a character, it has been because the dread of heterodox speculation was for a time suspended. Where there is a tacit convention that principles are not to be disputed; where the discussion of the greatest questions which can occupy humanity is considered to be closed, we cannot hope to find that generally high scale of mental activity which has made some periods of history so remarkable. Never when controversy avoided the subjects which are large and important enough to kindle enthusiasm, was the mind of a people stirred up from its foundations, and the impulse given which raised even persons of the most ordinary intellect to something of the dignity of thinking beings.[. . .]

Let us now pass to the second division of the argument, and dismissing the supposition that any of the received opinions may be false, let us assume them to be true, and examine into the worth of the manner in which they are likely to be held, when their truth is not freely and openly canvassed. However unwillingly a person who has a strong opinion may admit the possibility that his opinion may be false, he ought to be moved by the consideration that however true it may be, if it is not fully, frequently, and fearlessly discussed, it will be held as a dead dogma, not a living truth.

There is a class of persons (happily not quite so numerous as formerly) who think it enough if a person assents undoubtingly to what they think true, though he has no knowledge whatever of the grounds of the opinion, and could not make a tenable defence of it against the most superficial objections. Such persons, if they can once get their creed taught from authority, naturally think that no good, and some harm, comes of its being allowed to be questioned. Where their influence prevails, they make it nearly impossible for the received opinion to be rejected wisely and considerately, though it may still be rejected rashly and ignorantly; for to shut out discussion entirely is seldom possible, and when it once gets in, beliefs not grounded on conviction are apt to give way before the slightest semblance of an argument. Waiving, however, this possibility—

assuming that the true opinion abides in the mind, but abides as a prejudice, a belief independent of, and proof against argument—this is not the way in which truth ought to be held by a rational being. This is not knowing the truth. Truth, thus held, is but one superstition the more, accidentally clinging to the words which enunciate a truth.

If the intellect and judgement of mankind ought to be cultivated, a thing which Protestants at least do not deny, on what can these faculties be more appropriately exercised by any one, than on the things which concern him so much that it is considered necessary for him to hold opinions on them? If the cultivation of the understanding consists in one thing more than in another, it is surely in learning the grounds of one's own opinions. Whatever people believe, on subjects on which it is of the first importance to believe rightly, they ought to be able to defend against at least the common objections. But, some one may say, "Let them be *taught* the grounds of their opinions. It does not follow that opinions must be merely parroted because they are never heard controverted. Persons who learn geometry do not simply commit the theorems to memory, but understand and learn likewise the demonstrations; and it would be absurd to say that they remain ignorant of the grounds of geometrical truths, because they never hear any one deny, and attempt to disprove them." Undoubtedly: and such teaching suffices on a subject like mathematics, where there is nothing at all to be said on the wrong side of the question. The peculiarity of the evidence of mathematical truths is, that all the argument is on one side. There are no objections, and no answers to objections. But on every subject on which difference of opinion is possible, the truth depends on a balance to be struck between two sets of conflicting reasons. Even in natural philosophy, there is always some other explanation possible of the same facts: some geocentric theory instead of heliocentric, some phlogiston instead of oxygen; and it has to be shown why that other theory cannot be the true one: and until this is shown, and until we know it is shown, we do not understand the grounds of our opinion. But when we turn to subjects infinitely more complicated, to morals, religion, politics, social relations, and the business of life, three-fourths of the arguments for every disputed opinion consist in dispelling the appearances which favor some opinion different from it. The greatest orator, save one, of antiquity, has left it on record that he always studied his adversary's case with as great, if not with still greater, intensity then even his own. What Cicero practised as the means of forensic success, requires to be imitated by all who study any subject in order to arrive at the truth. He who knows only his own side of the case, knows little of that. His reasons may be good, and no one may have been able to refute them. But if he is equally unable to refute the reasons on the opposite side; if he does not so much as know what they are, he has no ground for preferring either opinion. The rational position for him would be suspension of judgement, and unless he contents himself with that, he is either led by authority, or adopts, like the generality of the world, the side to which he feels most inclination. Nor is it enough that he should hear the arguments of adversaries from his own teachers, presented as they state them, and accompanied by what they offer as refutations. That is not the way to do justice to the arguments, or bring them into real contact with his own mind. He must be able to hear them from persons who actually believe them; who defend them in earnest, and do their very utmost for them. He must know them in their most plausible and persuasive form; he must feel the whole force of the difficulty which the true view of the subject has to encounter and dispose of; else he will never really possess himself of the portion of truth which meets and removes that difficulty. Ninety-nine in a hundred of what are called educated men are in this condition; even of those who can argue fluently for their opinions. Their conclusion may be true, but it might be false for anything they know: they have never thrown themselves into the mental position of those who think differently from them, and considered what such persons may have to say; and consequently they do not, in any proper sense of the word, know the doctrine which they themselves profess. They do not know those parts of it which

explain and justify the remainder; the considerations which show that a fact which seemingly conflicts with another is reconcilable with it, or that, of two apparently strong reasons, one and not the other ought to be preferred. All that part of the truth which turns the scale, and decides the judgement of a completely informed mind, they are strangers to; nor is it ever really known, but to those who have attended equally and impartially to both sides, and endeavored to see the reasons of both in the strongest light. So essential is this discipline to a real understanding of moral and human subjects, that if opponents of all important truths do not exist, it is indispensable to imagine them, and supply them with the strongest arguments which the most skilful devil's advocate can conjure up.

To abate the force of these considerations, an enemy of free discussion may be supposed to say, that there is no necessity for mankind in general to know and understand all that can be said against or for their opinions by philosophers and theologians. That it is not needful for common men to be able to expose all the misstatements or fallacies of an ingenious opponent. That it is enough if there is always somebody capable of answering them, so that nothing likely to mislead uninstructed persons remains unrefuted. That simple minds, having been taught the obvious grounds of the truths inculcated on them, may trust to authority for the rest, and being aware that they have neither knowledge nor talent to resolve every difficulty which can be raised, may repose in the assurance that all those which have been raised have been or can be answered, by those who are specially trained to the task.

Conceding to this view of the subject the utmost that can be claimed for it by those most easily satisfied with the amount of understanding of truth which ought to accompany the belief of it; even so, the argument for free discussion is no way weakened. For even this doctrine acknowledges that mankind ought to have a rational assurance that all objections have been satisfactorily answered; and how are they to be answered if that which requires to be answered is not spoken? or how can the answer be known to be satisfactory, if the objectors have no opportunity of showing that it is unsatisfactory? If not the public, at least the philosophers and theologians who are to resolve the difficulties, must make themselves familiar with those difficulties in their most puzzling form; and this cannot be accomplished unless they are freely stated, and placed in the most advantageous light which they admit of.[. . .]

If, however, the mischievous operation of the absence of free discussion, when the received opinions are true, were confined to leaving men ignorant of the grounds of those opinions, it might be thought that this, if an intellectual, is no moral evil, and does not affect the worth of the opinions, regarded in their influence on the character. The fact, however, is, that not only the grounds of the opinion are forgotten in the absence of discussion, but too often the meaning of the opinion itself. The words which convey it, cease to suggest ideas, or suggest only a small portion of those they were originally employed to communicate. Instead of a vivid conception and a living belief, there remain only a few phrases retained by rote; or, if any part, the shell and husk only of the meaning is retained, the finer essence being lost. The great chapter in human history which this fact occupies and fills, cannot be too earnestly studied and meditated on.

It is illustrated in the experience of almost all ethical doctrines and religious creeds. They are full of meaning and vitality to those who originate them, and to the direct disciples of the originators. Their meaning continues to be felt in undiminished strength, and is perhaps brought out into even fuller consciousness, so long as the struggle lasts to give the doctrine or creed an ascendency over other creeds. At least it either prevails, and becomes the general opinion, or its progress stops; it keeps possession of the ground it has gained, but ceases to spread further. When either of these results has become apparent, controversy on the subject flags, and gradually dies away. The doctrine has taken its place, if not as a received opinion, as one of the admitted sects or divisions of opinion: those who hold it have generally inherited, not adopted it; and conversion from one of these doctrines to another, being now

an exceptional fact, occupies little place in the thoughts of their professors. Instead of being, as at first, constantly on the alert either to defend themselves against the world, or to bring the world over to them, they have subsided into acquiescence, and neither listen, when they can help it, to arguments against their creed, nor trouble dissentients (if there be such) with arguments in its favor. From this time may usually be dated the decline in the living power of the doctrine.[. . .]

But what! (it may be asked) Is the absence of unanimity an indispensable condition of true knowledge? Is it necessary that some part of mankind should persist in error, to enable any to realize the truth? Does a belief cease to be real and vital as soon as it is generally received—and is a proposition never thoroughly understood and felt unless some doubt of it remains? As soon as mankind have unanimously accepted a truth, does the truth perish within them? The highest aim and best result of improved intelligence, it has hitherto been thought, is to unite mankind more and more in the acknowledgment of all important truths: and does the intelligence only last as long as it has not achieved its object? Do the fruits of conquest perish by the very completeness of the victory?

I affirm no such thing. As mankind improve, the number of doctrines which are no longer disputed or doubted will be constantly on the increase: and the well-being of mankind may almost be measured by the number and gravity of the truths which have reached the point of being uncontested. The cessation, on one question after another, of serious controversy, is one of the necessary incidents of the consolidation of opinion; a consolidation as salutary in the case of true opinions, as it is dangerous and noxious when the opinions are erroneous. But though this gradual narrowing of the bounds of diversity of opinion is necessary in both senses of the term, being at once inevitable and indispensable, we are not therefore obliged to conclude that all its consequences must be beneficial. The loss of so important an aid to the intelligent and living apprehension of a truth, as is afforded by the necessity of explaining it to, or defending it against, opponents, though most sufficient to outweigh, is no trifling drawback from, the benefit of its universal recognition. Where this advantage can no longer be had, I confess I should like to see the teachers of mankind endeavoring to provide a substitute for it; some contrivance for making the difficulties of the question as present to the learner's consciousness, as if they were pressed upon him by a dissentient champion, eager for his conversion.[. . .]

It still remains to speak of one of the principal causes which make diversity of opinion advantageous, and will continue to do so until mankind shall have entered a stage of intellectual advancement which at present seems at an incalculable distance. We have hitherto considered only two possibilities: that the received opinion may be false, and some other opinion, consequently, true; or that, the received opinion being true, a conflict with the opposite error is essential to a clear apprehension and deep feeling of its truth. But there is a commoner case than either of these; when the conflicting doctrines, instead of being one true and the other false, share the truth between them; and the nonconforming opinion is needed to supply the remainder of the truth, of which the received doctrine embodies only a part. Popular opinions, on subjects not palpable to sense, are often true, but seldom or never the whole truth. They are a part of the truth; sometimes a greater, sometimes a smaller part, but exaggerated, distorted, and disjoined from the truths by which they ought to be accompanied and limited. Heretical opinions, on the other hand, are generally some of these suppressed and neglected truths, bursting the bonds which kept them down, and either seeking reconciliation with the truth contained in the common opinion, or fronting it as enemies and setting themselves up, with similar exclusiveness, as the whole truth. The latter case is hitherto the most frequent, as in the human mind, one-sidedness has always been the rule, and many-sidedness an exception. Hence, even in revolutions of opinion, one part of the truth usually sets while another rises. Even progress, which ought to superadd, for the most part only substitutes one partial and incomplete truth for another; improvement consisting chiefly in this, that the new fragment of truth is more wanted, more adapted to the needs of the time, than that which it displaces. Such being the partial character of prevailing opinions, even when resting on a true foundation; every opinion which embodies somewhat of the portion of truth which the common opinion omits, ought to be considered precious, with whatever amount of error and confusion that truth may be blended.[. . .]

We have now recognized the necessity to the mental well-being of mankind (on which all their other well-being depends) of freedom of opinion, and freedom of the expression of opinion, on four distinct grounds; which we will now briefly recapitulate.

First, if any opinion is compelled to silence, that opinion may, for aught we can certainly know, be true. To deny this is to assume our own infallibility.

Secondly, though the silenced opinion be an error, it may, and very commonly does, contain a portion of truth; and since the general or prevailing opinion on any subject is rarely or never the whole truth, it is only by the collision of adverse opinions that the remainder of the truth has any chance of being supplied.

Thirdly, even if the received opinion be not only true, but the whole truth; unless it is suffered to be, and actually is, vigorously and earnestly contested, it will, by most of those who receive it, be held in the manner of a prejudice, with little comprehension or feeling of its rational grounds. And not only this, but, fourthly, the meaning of the doctrine itself will be in danger of being lost, or enfeebled, and deprived of its vital effect on the character and conduct: the dogma becoming a mere formal profession, inefficacious for good, but cumbering the ground, and preventing the growth of any real and heartfelt conviction from reason or personal experience.[. . .]

Chapter 3. Of Individuality, As One of the Elements of Well-Being

Such being the reasons which make it imperative that human beings should be free to form opinions, and to express their opinions without reserve; and such the baneful consequences to the intellectual, and through that to the moral nature of man, unless this liberty is either conceded, or asserted in spite of prohibition; let us next examine whether the same reasons do not require that men should be free to act upon their opinions—to carry these out in their lives, without hindrance, either physical or moral, from their fellow men, so long as it is at their own risk and peril. This last proviso is of course indispensable. No one pretends that actions should be as free as opinions. On the contrary, even opinions lose their immunity, when the circumstances in which they are expressed are such as to constitute their expression a positive instigation to some mischievous act. An opinion that corn-dealers are starvers of the poor, or that private property is robbery, ought to be unmolested when simply circulated through the press, but may justly incur punishment when delivered orally to an excited mob assembled before the house of a corn-dealer, or when handed about among the same mob in the form of a placard. Acts, of whatever kind, which, without justifiable cause, do harm to others, may be, and in the more important cases absolutely require to be, controlled by the unfavourable sentiments, and, when needful, by the active interference of mankind. The liberty of the individual must be thus far limited; he must not make himself a nuisance to other people. But if he refrains from molesting others in what concerns them, and merely acts according to his own inclination and judgement in things which concern himself, the same reasons which show that opinion should be free, prove also that he should be allowed, without molestation, to carry his opinions into practice at his own cost. That mankind are not infallible; that their truths, for the most part, are only half-truths; that unity of opinion, unless resulting from the fullest and freest comparison of opposite opinions, is not desirable, and diversity not an evil, but a good, until mankind are much more capable than at present of recognizing all sides of the truth, are principles applicable to men's modes of action, not less than to their opinions. As it is useful that while mankind are imperfect there should be different experiments of living; that free scope should be given to varieties of character, short

of injury to others; and that the worth of different modes of life should be proved practically, when any one thinks fit to try them. It is desirable, in short, that in things which do not primarily concern others, individuality should assert itself. Where, not the person's own character, but the traditions or customs of other people are the rule of conduct, there is wanting one of the principal ingredients of human happiness, and quite the chief ingredient of individual and social progress.

In maintaining this principle, the greatest difficulty to be encountered does not lie in the appreciation of means towards an acknowledged end, but in the indifference of persons in general to the end itself. If it were felt that the free development of individuality is one of the leading essentials of well-being; that it is not only a co-ordinate element with all that is designated by the terms civilization, instruction, education, culture, but is itself a necessary part and condition of all those things; there would be no danger that liberty should be undervalued, and the adjustment of the boundaries between it and social control would present no extraordinary difficulty. But the evil is, that individual spontaneity is hardly recognized by the common modes of thinking, as having any intrinsic worth, or deserving any regard on its own account. The majority, being satisfied with the ways of mankind as they now are (for it is they who make them what they are), cannot comprehend why those ways should not be good enough for everybody; and what is more, spontaneity forms no part of the ideal of the majority of moral and social reformers, but is rather looked on with jealousy, as a troublesome and perhaps rebellious obstruction to the general acceptance of what these reformers, in their own judgement, think would be best for mankind. Few persons, out of Germany, even comprehend the meaning of the doctrine which Wilhelm von Humboldt, so eminent both as a savant and as a politician, made the text of a treatise—that "the end of man, or that which is prescribed by the eternal or immutable dictates of reason, and not suggested by vague and transient desires, is the highest and most harmonious development of his powers to a complete and consistent whole''; that, therefore, the object ''towards which every human being must ceaselessly direct his efforts, and on which especially those who design to influence their fellow men must ever keep their eyes, is the individuality of power and development''; that for this there are two requisites, ''freedom, and variety of situations''; and that from the union of these arise ''individual vigour and manifold diversity,'' which combine themselves in ''originality.''[2]

Little, however, as people are accustomed to a doctrine like that of von Humboldt, and surprising as it may be to them to find so high a value attached to individuality, the question, one must nevertheless think, can only be one of degree. No one's idea of excellence in conduct is that people should do absolutely nothing but copy one another. No one would assert that people ought not to put into their mode of life, and into the conduct of their concerns, any impress whatever of their own judgement, or of their own individual character. On the other hand, it would be absurd to pretend that people ought to live as if nothing whatever had been known in the world before they came into it; as if experience had as yet done nothing towards showing that one mode of existence, or of conduct, is preferable to another. Nobody denies that people should be so taught and trained in youth, as to know and benefit by the ascertained results of human experience. But it is the privilege and proper condition of a human being, arrived at the maturity of his faculties, to use and interpret experience in his own way. It is for him to find out what part of recorded experience is properly applicable to his own circumstances and character. The traditions and customs of other people are, to a certain extent, evidence of what their experience has taught *them;* presumptive evidence, and as such, have a claim to his deference: but, in the first place, their experience may be too narrow; or they may not have interpreted it rightly. Secondly, their interpretation of experience may be correct, but unsuitable to him. Customs are made for customary circumstances, and customary characters; and his circumstances or his character may be uncustomary. Thirdly, though the customs be both

good as customs, and suitable to him, yet to conform to custom, merely *as* custom, does not educate or develop in him any of the qualities which are the distinctive endowment of a human being. The human faculties of perception, judgement, discriminative feeling, mental activity, and even moral preference, are exercised only in making a choice. He who does anything because it is the custom, makes no choice. He gains no practice either in discerning or in desiring what is best. The mental and moral, like the muscular powers, are improved only by being used. The faculties are called into no exercise by doing a thing merely because others do it, no more than by believing a thing only because others believe it. If the grounds of an opinion are not conclusive to the person's own reason, his reason cannot be strengthened, but is likely to be weakened, by his adopting it: and if the inducements to an act are not such as are consentaneous to his own feelings and character (where affection, or the rights of others, are not concerned) it is so much done towards rendering his feelings and character inert and torpid, instead of active and energetic.

He who lets the world, or his own portion of it, choose his plan of life for him, has no need of any other faculty than the ape-like one of imitation. He who chooses his plan for himself, employs all his faculties. He must use observation to see, reasoning and judgement to foresee, activity to gather materials for decision, discrimination to decide, and when he has decided, firmness and self-control to hold to his deliberate decision. And these qualities he requires and exercises exactly in proportion as the part of his conduct which he determines according to his own judgement and feelings is a large one. It is possible that he might be guided in some good path, and kept out of harm's way, without any of these things. But what will be his comparative worth as a human being? It really is of importance, not only what men do, but also what manner of men they are that do it. Among the works of man, which human life is rightly employed in perfecting and beautifying, the first in importance surely is man himself. Supposing it were possible to get houses built, corn grown, battles fought, causes tried, and even churches erected and prayers said, by machinery—by automatons in human form—it would be a considerable loss to exchange for these automatons even the men and women who at present inhabit the more civilized parts of the world, and who assuredly are but starved specimens of what nature can and will produce. Human nature is not a machine to be built after a model, and set to do exactly the work prescribed for it, but a tree, which requires to grow and develop itself on all sides, according to the tendency of the inward forces which make it a living thing.[. . .]

It is not by wearing down into uniformity all that is individual in themselves, but by cultivating it and calling it forth, within the limits imposed by the rights and interests of others, that human beings become a noble and beautiful object of contemplation; and as the works partake the character of those who do them, by the same process human life also becomes rich, diversified, and animating, furnishing more abundant aliment to high thoughts and elevating feelings, and strengthening the tie which binds every individual to the race, by making the race infinitely better worth belonging to. In proportion to the development of his individuality, each person becomes more valuable to himself, and is therefore capable of being more valuable to others. There is a greater fullness of life about his own existence, and when there is more life in the units there is more in the mass which is composed of them. As much compression as is necessary to prevent the stronger specimens of human nature from encroaching on the rights of others, cannot be dispensed with; but for this there is ample compensation even in the point of view of human development. The means of development which the individual loses by being prevented from gratifying his inclinations to the injury of others, are chiefly obtained at the expense of the development of other people. And even to himself there is a full equivalent in the better development of the social part of his nature, rendered possible by the restraint put upon the selfish part. To be held to rigid rules of justice for the sake of others, develops the feelings and capacities which have the good of others

for their object. But to be restrained in things not affecting their good, by their mere displeasure, develops nothing valuable, except such force of character as may unfold itself in resisting the restraint. If acquiesced in, it dulls and blunts the whole nature. To give any fair play to the nature of each, it is essential that different persons should be allowed to lead different lives. In proportion as this latitude has been exercised in any age, has that age been noteworthy to posterity. Even despotism does not produce its worst effects, so long as individuality exists under it; and whatever crushes individuality is despotism, by whatever name it may be called, and whether it professes to be enforcing the will of God or the injunctions of men.

Having said that individuality is the same thing with development, and that it is only the cultivation of individuality which produces, or can produce, well-developed human beings, I might here close the argument: for what more or better can be said of any condition of human affairs, than that it brings human beings themselves nearer to the best thing they can be? or what worse can be said of any obstruction to good, than that it prevents this? Doubtless, however, these considerations will not suffice to convince those who most need convincing; and it is necessary further to show, that these developed human beings are of some use to the undeveloped—to point out to those who do not desire liberty, and would not avail themselves of it, that they may be in some intelligible manner rewarded for allowing other people to make use of it without hindrance.

In the first place, then, I would suggest that they might possibly learn something from them. It will not be denied by anybody, that originality is a valuable element in human affairs. There is always need of persons not only to discover new truths, and point out when what were once truths are true no longer, but also to commence new practices, and set the example of more enlightened conduct, and better taste and sense in human life. This cannot well be gainsaid by anybody who does not believe that the world has already attained perfection in all its ways and practices. It is true that this benefit is not capable of being rendered by everybody alike: there are but few persons, in comparison with the whole of mankind, whose experiments, if adopted by others, would be likely to be any improvement on established practice. But these few are the salt of the earth; without them, human life would become a stagnant pool. Not only is it they who introduce good things which did not before exist; it is they who keep the life in those which already existed. If there were nothing new to be done, would human intellect cease to be necessary? Would it be a reason why those who do the old things should forget why they are done, and do them like cattle, not like human beings? There is only too great a tendency in the best beliefs and practices to degenerate into the mechanical; and unless there were a succession of persons whose ever-recurring originality prevents the grounds of those beliefs and practices from becoming merely traditional, such dead matter would not resist the smallest shock from anything really alive, and there would be no reason why civilization should not die out, as in the Byzantine Empire. Persons of genius, it is true, are, and are always likely to be, a small minority; but in order to have them, it is necessary to preserve the soil in which they grow. Genius can only breathe freely in an *atmosphere* of freedom. Persons of genius are, *ex vi termini, more* individual than any other people—less capable, consequently, of fitting themselves, without hurtful compression, into any of the small number of moulds which society provides in order to save its members the trouble of forming their own character. If from timidity they consent to be forced into one of these moulds, and to let all that part of themselves which cannot expand under the pressure remain unexpanded, society will be little the better for their genius. If they are of a strong character, and break their fetters, they become a mark for the society which has not succeeded in reducing them to commonplace, to point at with solemn warning as ''wild,'' ''erratic,'' and the like; such as if one should complain of the Niagara river for not flowing smoothly between its banks like a Dutch canal.

I insist thus emphatically on the importance of genius, and the necessity of allowing it to unfold itself freely both in thought and in practice, being well aware that no one will deny the position in theory, but knowing also that almost every one, in reality, is totally indifferent to it. People think genius a fine thing if it enables a man to write an exciting poem, or paint a picture. But in its true sense, that of originality in thought and action, though no one says that it is not a thing to be admired, nearly all, at heart, think that they can do very well without it. Unhappily this is too natural to be wondered at. Originality is the one thing which unoriginal minds cannot feel the use of. They cannot see what it is to do for them: how should they? If they could see what it would do for them, it would not be originality. The first service which originality has to render them, is that of opening their eyes: which being once fully done, they would have a chance of being themselves original. Meanwhile, recollecting that nothing was ever yet done which some one was not the first to do, and that all good things which exist are the fruits of originality, let them be modest enough to believe that there is something still left for it to accomplish, and assure themselves that they are more in need of originality, the less they are conscious of the want.

In sober truth, whatever homage may be professed, or even paid, to real or supposed mental superiority, the general tendency of things throughout the world is to render mediocrity the ascendant power among mankind. In ancient history, in the middle ages, and in a diminishing degree through the long transition from feudality to the present time, the individual was a power in himself; and if he had either great talents or a high social position, he was a considerable power. At present individuals are lost in the crowd. In politics it is almost a triviality to say that public opinion now rules the world. The only power deserving the name is that of masses, and of governments while they make themselves the organ of the tendencies and instincts of masses. This is as true in the moral and social relations of private life as in public transactions. Those whose opinions go by the name of public opinion, are not always the same sort of public: in America they are the whole white population; in England, chiefly the middle class. But they are always a mass, that is to say, collective mediocrity. And what is a still greater novelty, the mass do not now take their opinions from dignitaries in Church or State, from ostensible leaders, or from books. Their thinking is done for them by men much like themselves, addressing them or speaking in their name, on the spur of the moment, through the newspapers. I am not complaining of all this. I do not assert that anything better is compatible, as a general rule, with the present low state of the human mind. But that does not hinder the government of mediocrity from being mediocre government. No government by a democracy or a numerous aristocracy, either in its political acts or in the opinions, qualities, and tone of mind which it fosters, ever did or could rise above mediocrity, except in so far as the sovereign Many have let themselves by guided (which in their best times they always have done) by the counsels and influence of a more highly gifted and instructed One or Few. The initiation of all wise or noble things, comes and must come from individuals; generally at first from some one individual. The honour and glory of the average man is that he is capable of following that initiative; that he can respond internally to wise and noble things, and be led to them with his eyes open. I am not countenancing the sort of "hero-worship" which applauds the strong man of genius for forcibly seizing on the government of the world and making it do his bidding in spite of itself. All he can claim is, freedom to point out the way. The power of compelling others into it, is not only inconsistent with the freedom and development of all the rest, but corrupting to the strong man himself. It does seem, however, that when the opinions of masses of merely average men are everywhere become or becoming the dominant power, the counterpoise and corrective to that tendency would be, the more and more pronounced individuality of those who stand on the higher eminences of thought. It is in these circumstances most especially, that exceptional individuals, instead of being deterred, should be encouraged in acting differently from the mass. In other times there was no advantage in their doing so, unless they acted not only dif-

ferently, but better. In this age, the mere example of nonconformity, the mere refusal to bend the knee to custom, is itself a service. Precisely because the tyranny of opinion is such as to make eccentricity a reproach, it is desirable, in order to break through that tyranny, that people should be eccentric. Eccentricity has always abounded when and where strength of character has abounded; and the amount of eccentricity in a society has generally been proportional to the amount of genius, mental vigour, and moral courage which it contained. That so few now dare to be eccentric, marks the chief danger of the time.

I have said that it is important to give the freest scope possible to uncustomary things, in order that it may in time appear which of these are fit to be converted into customs. But independence of action, and disregard of custom, are not solely deserving of encouragement for the chance they afford that better modes of action, and customs more worthy of general adoption, may be struck out; not is it only persons of decided mental superiority who have a just claim to carry on their lives in their own way. There is no reason that all human existence should be constructed on some one or some small number of patterns. If a person possesses any tolerable amount of common sense and experience, his own mode of laying out his existence is the best, not because it is the best in itself, but because it is his own mode. Human beings are not like sheep; and even sheep are not undistinguishably alike. A man cannot get a coat or a pair of boots to fit him, unless they are either made to his measure, or he has a whole warehouseful to choose from: and is it easier to fit him with a life than with a coat, or are human beings more like one another in their whole physical and spiritual conformation than in the shape of their feet? If it were only that people have diversities of taste, that is reason enough for not attempting to shape them all after one model. But different persons also require different conditions for their spiritual development; and can no more exist healthily in the same moral, than all the variety of plants can in the same physical, atmosphere and climate. The same things which are helps to one person towards the cultivation of his higher nature, are hindrances to another. The same mode of life is a healthy excitement to one, keeping all his faculties of action and enjoyment in their best order, while to another it is a distracting burthen, which suspends or crushes all internal life. Such are the differences among human beings in their sources of pleasure, their susceptibilities of pain, and the operation on them of different physical and moral agencies, that unless there is a corresponding diversity in their modes of life, they neither obtain their fair share of happiness, nor grow up to the mental, moral, and aesthetic stature of which their nature is capable. Why then should tolerance, as far as the public sentiment is concerned, extend only to tastes and modes of life which extort acquiescence by the multitude of their adherents?[. . .]

Chapter 4. Of the Limits to the Authority of the State over the Individual

What, then, is the rightful limit to the sovereignty of the individual over himself? Where does the authority of society begin? How much of human life should be assigned to individuality, and how much to society?

Each will receive its proper share, if each has that which more particularly concerns it. To individuality should belong the part of life in which it is chiefly the individual that is interested; to society, the part which chiefly interests society.

Though society is not founded on a contract, and though no good purpose is answered by inventing a contract in order to deduce social obligations from it, every one who receives the protection of society owes a return for the benefit, and the fact of living in society renders it indispensable that each should be bound to observe a certain line of conduct towards the rest. This conduct consists, first, in not injuring the interests of one another; or rather certain interests, which, either by express legal provision or by tacit understanding, ought to be considered as rights; and secondly, in each person's bearing his share (to be fixed on some equitable principle) of the labors and sacrifices incurred for defending the society or its members

from injury and molestation. These conditions society is justified in enforcing, at all costs to those who endeavor to withhold fulfilment. Nor is this all that society may do. The acts of an individual may be hurtful to others, or wanting in due consideration for their welfare, without going the length of violating any of their constituted rights. The offender may then be justly punished by opinion, though not by law. As soon as any part of a person's conduct affects prejudicially the interests of others, society has jurisdiction over it, and the question whether the general welfare will or will not be promoted by interfering with it, becomes open to discussion. But there is no room for entertaining any such question when a person's conduct affects the interests of no persons besides himself, or needs not affect them unless they like (all the persons concerned being of full age, and the ordinary amount of understanding). In all such cases there should be perfect freedom, legal and social, to do the action and stand the consequences.

It would be a great misunderstanding of this doctrine, to suppose that it is one of selfish indifference, which pretends that human beings have no business with each other's conduct in life, and that they should not concern themselves about the well-doing or well-being of one another, unless their own interest is involved. Instead of any diminution, there is need of a great increase of disinterested exertion to promote the good of others. But disinterested benevolence can find other instruments to persuade people to their good, than whips and scourges, either of the literal or the metaphorical sort. I am the last person to undervalue the self-regarding virtues; they are only second in importance, if even second, to the social. It is equally the business of education to cultivate both. But even education works by conviction and persuasion as well as by compulsion, and it is by the former only that, when the period of education is past, the self-regarding virtues should be inculcated. Human beings owe to each other help to distinguish the better from the worse, and encouragement to choose the former and avoid the latter. They should be forever stimulating each other to increased exercise of their higher faculties, and increased direction of their feelings and aims towards wise instead of foolish, elevating instead of degrading, objects and contemplations. But neither one person, nor any number of persons, is warranted in saying to another human creature of ripe years, that he shall not do with his life for his own benefit what he chooses to do with it. He is the person most interested in his own well-being: the interest which any other person, except in cases of strong personal attachment, can have in it, is trifling, compared with that which he himself has; the interest which society has in him individually (except as to his conduct to others) is fractional, and altogether indirect: while, with respect to his own feelings and circumstances, the most ordinary man or woman has means of knowledge immeasurably surpassing those that can be possessed by anyone else. The interference of society to overrule his judgement and purposes in what only regards himself, must be grounded on general presumptions; which may be altogether wrong, and even if right, are as likely as not to be misapplied to individual cases, by persons no better acquainted with the circumstances of such cases than those are who look at them merely from without. In this department, therefore, of human affairs, Individuality has its proper field of action. In the conduct of human beings towards one another, it is necessary that general rules should for the most part be observed, in order that people may know what they have to expect; but in each person's own concerns, his individual spontaneity is entitled to free exercise. Considerations to aid his judgement, exhortations to strengthen his will, may be offered to him, even obtruded on him, by others; but he, himself, is the final judge. All errors which he is likely to commit against advice and warning, are far outweighed by the evil of allowing others to constrain him to what they deem his good.[. . .]

What I contend for is, that the inconveniences which are strictly inseparable from the unfavorable judgement of others, are the only ones to which a person should ever be subjected for that portion of his conduct and character which concerns his own good, but which does not affect the interests of others in their

relations with him. Acts injurious to others require a totally different treatment. Encroachment on their rights; infliction on them of any loss or damage not justified by his own rights; falsehood or duplicity in dealing with them; unfair or ungenerous use of advantages over them; even selfish abstinence from defending them against injury—these are fit objects of moral reprobation, and, in grave cases, of moral retribution and punishment. And not only these acts, but the dispositions which lead to them, are properly immoral, and fit subjects of disapprobation which may rise to abhorrence. Cruelty of disposition; malice and ill-nature; that most anti-social and odious of all passions, envy; dissimulation and insincerity; irascibility on insufficient cause, and resentment disproportioned to the provocation; the love of domineering over others; the desire to engross more than one's share of advantages (the Πλεονεξία of the Greeks); the pride which derives gratification from the abasement of others; the egotism which thinks self and its concerns more important than everything else, and decides all doubtful questions in his own favor—these are moral vices, and constitute a bad and odious moral character: unlike the self-regarding faults previously mentioned, which are not properly immoralities, and to whatever pitch they may be carried, do not constitute wickedness. They may be proofs of any amount of folly, or want of personal dignity and self-respect; but they are only a subject of moral reprobation when they involve a breach of duty to others, for whose sake the individual is bound to have care for himself. What are called duties to ourselves are not socially obligatory, unless circumstances render them at the same time duties to others. The term duty to oneself, when it means anything more than prudence, means self-respect or self-development; and for none of these is any one accountable to his fellow-creatures, because for none of them is it for the good of mankind that he be held accountable to them.[. . .]

The distinction here pointed out between the part of a person's life which concerns only himself, and that which concerns others, many persons will refuse to admit. How (it may be asked) can any part of the conduct of a member of society be a matter of indifference to the other members? No person is an entirely isolated being; it is impossible for a person to do anything seriously or permanently hurtful to himself, without mischief reaching at least to his near connections, and often far beyond them. If he injures his property, he does harm to those who directly or indirectly derived support from it, and usually diminishes, by a greater or less amount, the general resources of the community. If he deteriorates his bodily or mental faculties, he not only brings evil upon all who depended on him for any portion of their happiness, but disqualifies himself for rendering the services which he owes to his fellow-creatures generally; perhaps becomes a burden on their affection or benevolence; and if such conduct were very frequent, hardly any offence that is committed would detract more from the general sum of good. Finally, if by his vices or follies a person does no direct harm to others, he is nevertheless (it may be said) injurious by his example; and ought to be compelled to control himself, for the sake of those whom the sight or knowledge of his conduct might corrupt or mislead.

And even (it will be added) if the consequences of misconduct could be confined to the vicious or thoughtless individual, ought society to abandon to their own guidance those who are manifestly unfit for it? If protection against themselves is confessedly due to children and persons under age, is not society equally bound to afford it to persons of mature years who are equally incapable of self-government? If gambling, or drunkenness, or incontinence, or idleness, or uncleanliness, are as injurious to happiness, and as great a hindrance to improvement, as many or most of the acts prohibited by law, why (it may be asked) should not law, so far as is consistent with practicability and social convenience, endeavor to repress these also? And as a supplement to the unavoidable imperfections of law, ought not opinion at least to organize a powerful police against these vices, and visit rigidly with social penalties those who are known to practice them? There is no question here (it may be said) about restricting individuality, or impeding the trial of new and original experiments in living. The only thing it is sought to prevent are things which have been tried and condemned from the beginning of the world until now; things which experience has shown not to be useful or suitable to any person's individuality. There must be some length of time and amount of experience, after which a moral or prudential truth may be regarded as established: and it is merely desired to prevent generation after generation from falling over the same precipice which has been fatal to their predecessors.

I fully admit that the mischief which a person does to himself, may seriously affect, both through their sympathies and their interests, those nearly connected with him, and in a minor degree, society at large. When, by conduct of this sort, a person is led to violate a distinct and assignable obligation to any other person or persons, the case is taken out of the self-regarding class, and becomes amenable to moral disapprobation in the proper sense of the term. If, for example, a man, through intemperance or extravagance, becomes unable to pay his debts, or, having undertaken the moral responsibility of a family, becomes from the same cause incapable of supporting or educating them, he is deservedly reprobated, and might be justly punished; but it is for the breach of duty to his family or creditors, not for the extravagance. If the resources which ought to have been devoted to them, had been diverted from them for the most prudent investment, the moral culpability would have been the same. George Barnwell murdered his uncle to get money for his mistress, but if he had done it to set himself up in business, he would equally have been hanged. Again, in the frequent case of a man who causes grief to his family by addiction to bad habits, he deserves reproach for his unkindness or ingratitude; but so he may for cultivating habits not in themselves vicious, if they are painful to those with whom he passes his life, or who from personal ties are dependent on him for their comfort. Whoever fails in the consideration generally due to the interests and feelings of others, not being compelled by some more imperative duty, or justified by allowable self-preference, is a subject of moral disapprobation for that failure, but not for the cause of it, nor for the errors, merely personal to himself, which may have remotely led to it. In like manner, when a person disables himself, by conduct purely self-regarding, from the performance of some definite duty incumbent on him to the public, he is guilty of a social offence. No person ought to be punished simply for being drunk; but a soldier or a policeman should be punished for being drunk on duty. Whenever, in short, there is a definite damage, or a definite risk of damage, either to an individual or to the public, the case is taken out of the province of liberty, and placed in that of morality or law.

But with regard to the merely contingent, or, as it may be called, constructive injury which a person causes to society, by conduct which neither violates any specific duty to the public, nor occasions perceptible hurt to any assignable individual except himself; the inconvenience is one which society can afford to bear, for the sake of the greater good of human freedom. If grown persons are to be punished for not taking proper care of themselves, I would rather it were for their own sake, than under pretence of preventing them from impairing their capacity of rendering to society benefits which society does not pretend it has a right to exact. But I cannot consent to argue the point as if society had no means of bringing its weaker members up to its ordinary standard of rational conduct, except waiting till they do something irrational, and then punishing them, legally or morally, for it. Society has had absolute power over them during all the early portion of their existence: it has had the whole period of childhood and nonage in which to try whether it could make them capable of rational conduct in life. The existing generation is master both of the training and the entire circumstances of the generation to come; it cannot indeed make them perfectly wise and good, because it is itself so lamentably deficient in goodness and wisdom; and its best efforts are not always, in individual cases, its most successful ones; but it is perfectly well able to make the rising generation, as a whole, as good as, and a little better than, itself. If society lets any considerable number of its members grow up mere children, incapable of being acted on

by rational consideration of distant motives, society has itself to blame for the consequences.[. . .]

But the strongest of all the arguments against the interference of the public with purely personal conduct, is that when it does interfere, the odds are that it interferes wrongly, and in the wrong place. On questions of social morality, or duty to others, the opinion of the public, that is, of an overruling majority, though often wrong, is likely to be still oftener right; because on such questions they are only required to judge of their own interests; of the manner in which some mode of conduct, if allowed to be practised, would affect themselves. But the opinion of a similar majority, imposed as a law on the minority, on questions of self-regarding conduct, is quite as likely to be wrong as right; for in these cases public opinion means, at the best, some people's opinion of what is good or bad for other people; while very often it does not even mean that; the public, with the most perfect indifference, passing over the pleasure or convenience of those whose conduct they censure, and considering only their own preference. There are many who consider as an injury to themselves any conduct which they have a distaste for, and resent it as an outrage to their feelings; as a religious bigot, when charged with disregarding the religious feelings of others, has been known to retort that they disregard his feelings, by persisting in their abominable worship or creed. But there is no parity between the feeling of a person for his own opinion, and the feeling of another who is offended at his holding it; no more than between the desire of a thief to take a purse, and the desire of the right owner to keep it. And a person's taste is as much his own peculiar concern as his opinion or his purse. It is easy for any one to imagine an ideal public, which leaves the freedom and choice of individuals in all uncertain matters undisturbed, and only requires them to abstain from modes of conduct which universal experience has condemned. But where has there been seen a public which set any such limit to its censorship? or when does the public trouble itself about universal experience? In its interferences with personal conduct it is seldom thinking of anything but the enormity of acting or feeling differently from itself; and this standard of judgement, thinly disguised, is held up to mankind as the dictate of religion and philosophy, by nine tenths of all moralists and speculative writers. These teach that things are right because they are right; because we feel them to be so. They tell us to search in our own minds and hearts for laws of conduct binding on ourselves and on all others. What can the poor public do but apply these instructions, and make their own personal feelings of good and evil, if they are tolerably unanimous in them, obligatory on all the world?[. . .]

Chapter 5. Applications

The principles asserted in these pages must be more generally admitted as the basis for discussion of details, before a consistent application of them to all the various departments of government and morals can be attempted with any prospect of advantage. The few observations I propose to make on questions of detail, are designed to illustrate the principles, rather than to follow them out to their consequences. I offer, not so much applications, as specimens of application; which may serve to bring into greater clearness the meaning and limits of the two maxims which together form the entire doctrine of this Essay, and to assist the judgement in holding the balance between them, in the cases where it appears doubtful which of them is applicable to the case.

The maxims are, first, that the individual is not accountable to society for his actions, in so far as these concern the interests of no person but himself. Advice, instruction, persuasion, and avoidance by other people if thought necessary by them for their own good, are the only measures by which society can justifiably express its dislike or disapprobation of his conduct. Secondly, that for such actions as are prejudicial to the interests of others, the individual is accountable, and may be subjected either to social or to legal punishment, if society is of opinion that the one or the other is requisite for its protection.

In the first place, it must by no means be supposed, because damage, or probability of damage, to the interests of others, can alone justify the interference of society, that therefore it always does justify such interference. In many cases, an individual, in pursuing a legitimate object, necessarily and therefore legitimately causes pain or loss to others, or intercepts a good which they had a reasonable hope of obtaining. Such oppositions of interest between individuals often arise from bad social institutions, but are unavoidable while those institutions last; and some would be unavoidable under any institutions. Whoever succeeds in an overcrowded profession, or in a competitive examination; whoever is preferred to another in any contest for an object which both desire, reaps benefit from the loss of others, from their wasted exertion and their disappointment. But it is, by common admission, better for the general interest of mankind, that persons should pursue their objects undeterred by this sort of consequences. In other words, society admits no right, either legal or moral, in the disappointed competitors, to immunity from this kind of suffering; and feels called on to interfere, only when means of success have been employed which it is contrary to the general interest to permit—namely, fraud or treachery, and force.

Again, trade is a social act. Whoever undertakes to sell any description of goods to the public, does what affects the interest of other persons, and of society in general; and thus his conduct, in principle, comes within the jurisdiction of society: accordingly, it was once held to be the duty of governments, in all cases which were considered of importance, to fix prices, and regulate the processes of manufacture. But it is now recognized, though not till after a long struggle, that both the cheapness and the good quality of commodities are most effectually provided for by leaving the producers and sellers perfectly free, under the sole check of equal freedom to the buyers for supplying themselves elsewhere. This is the so-called doctrine of Free Trade, which rests on grounds different from, though equally solid with, the principle of individual liberty asserted in this Essay. Restrictions on trade, or on production for purposes of trade, are indeed restraints; and all restraint, *quâ* restraint, is an evil: but the restraints in question affect only that part of conduct which society is competent to restrain, and are wrong solely because they do not really produce the results which it is desired to produce by them. As the principle of individual liberty is not involved in the doctrine of Free Trade, so neither is it in most of the questions which arise respecting the limits of that doctrine; as for example, what amount of public control is admissible for the prevention of fraud by adulteration; how far sanitary precautions, or arrangements to protect workpeople employed in dangerous occupations, should be enforced on employers. Such questions involve considerations of liberty, only in so far as leaving people to themselves is always better, *caeteris paribus,* than controlling them: but that they may be legitimately controlled for these ends, is in principle undeniable. On the other hand, there are questions relating to interference with trade, which are essentially questions of liberty; such as the Maine Law, already touched upon; the prohibition of the importation of opium into China; the restriction of the sale of poisons; all cases, in short, where the object of the interference is to make it impossible or difficult to obtain a particular commodity. These interferences are objectionable, not as infringements on the liberty of the producer or seller, but on that of the buyer.

One of these examples, that of the sale of poisons, opens a new question; the proper limits of what may be called the functions of police; how far liberty may legitimately be invaded for the prevention of crime, or of accident. It is one of the undisputed functions of government to take precautions against crime before it has been committed, as well as to detect and punish it afterwards. The preventive function of government, however, is far more liable to be abused, to the prejudice of liberty, than the punitory function; for there is hardly any part of the legitimate freedom of action of a human being which would not admit of being represented, and fairly too, as increasing the facilities for some form or other of delinquency. Nevertheless, if a public authority, or even a private person, sees any one evidently preparing to commit a crime, they are not bound to look on inactive until the crime is committed, but may interfere to prevent it. If poisons were never bought or used for any purpose except the commission of murder, it would be right to prohibit their manufacture and sale. They may, however, be wanted not only for innocent but for useful purposes, and restrictions cannot be imposed in the one case without operating in the other. Again, it is a proper office of public authority to guard against accidents. If either a public officer or any one else saw a person attempting to cross a bridge which had been ascertained to be unsafe, and there were no time to warn him of his danger, they might seize him and turn him back, without any real infringement of his liberty; for liberty consists in doing what one desires, and he does not desire to fall into the river. Nevertheless, when there is not a certainty, but only a danger of mischief, no one but the person himself can judge of the sufficiency of the motive which may prompt him to incur the risk: in this case, therefore (unless he is a child, or delirious, or in some state of excitement or absorption incompatible with the full use of the reflecting faculty), he ought, I conceive, to be only warned of the danger; not forcibly prevented from exposing himself to it. Similar considerations, applied to such a question as the sale of poisons, may enable us to decide which among the possible modes of regulation are or are not contrary to principle. Such a precaution, for example, as that of labelling the drug with some word expressive of its dangerous character, may be enforced without violation of liberty: the buyer cannot wish not to know that the thing he possesses has poisonous qualities. But to require in all cases the certificate of a medical practitioner, would make it sometimes impossible, always expensive, to obtain the article for legitimate uses. The only mode apparent to me, in which difficulties may be thrown in the way of crime committed through this means, without any infringement, worth taking into account, upon the liberty of those who desire the poisonous substance for other purposes, consists in providing what, in the apt language of Bentham, is called 'preappointed evidence'. This provision is familiar to every one in the case of contracts. It is usual and right that the law, when a contract is entered into, should require as the condition of its enforcing performance, that certain formalities should be observed, such as signatures, attestation of witnesses, and the like, in order that in case of subsequent dispute, there may be evidence to prove that the contract was really entered into, and that there was nothing in the circumstances to render it legally invalid: the effect being, to throw great obstacles in the way of fictitious contracts, or contracts made in circumstances which, if known, would destroy their validity. Precautions of a similar nature might be enforced in the sale of articles adapted to be instruments of crime. The seller, for example, might be required to enter in a register the exact time of the transaction, the name and address of the buyer, the precise quality and quantity sold; to ask the purpose for which it was wanted, and record the answer he received. When there was no medical prescription, the presence of some third person might be required, to bring home the fact to the purchaser, in case there should afterwards be reason to believe that the article had been applied to criminal purposes. Such regulations would in general be no material impediment to obtaining the article, but a very considerable one to making an improper use of it without detection.

The right inherent in society, to ward off crimes against itself by antecedent precautions, suggests the obvious limitations to the maxim, that purely self-regarding misconduct cannot properly be meddled with in the way of prevention or punishment. Drunkenness, for example, in ordinary cases, is not a fit subject for legislative interference; but I should deem it perfectly legitimate that a person, who had once been convicted of any act of violence to others under the influence of drink, should be placed under a special legal restriction, personal to himself; that if he were afterwards found drunk, he should be liable to a penalty, and that if when in that state he committed another offence, the punishment to which he would be liable for that other offence should be increased in severity. The making himself drunk, in a person whom drunkenness excites to do harm to others, is a crime against others.

So, again, idleness, except in a person receiving support from the public, or except when it constitutes a breach of contract, cannot without tyranny be made a subject of legal punishment; but if, either from idleness or from any other avoidable cause, a man fails to perform his legal duties to others, as for instance to support his children, it is no tyranny to force him to fulfil that obligation, by compulsory labour, if no other means are available.

Again, there are many acts which, being directly injurious only to the agents themselves, ought not to be legally interdicted, but which, if done publicly, are a violation of good manners, and coming thus within the category of offences against others, may rightfully be prohibited. Of this kind are offences against decency; on which it is unnecessary to dwell, the rather as they are only connected indirectly with our subject, the objection to publicity being equally strong in the case of many actions not in themselves condemnable, nor supposed to be so.

There is another question to which an answer must be found, consistent with the principles which have been laid down. In cases of personal conduct supposed to be blameable, but which respect for liberty precludes society from preventing or punishing, because the evil directly resulting falls wholly on the agent; what the agent is free to do, ought other persons to be equally free to counsel or instigate? This question is not free from difficulty. The case of a person who solicits another to do an act, is not strictly a case of self-regarding conduct. To give advice or offer inducements to any one, is a social act, and may, therefore, like actions in general which affect others, be supposed amenable to social control. But a little reflection corrects the first impression, by showing that if the case is not strictly within the definition of individual liberty, yet the reasons on which the principle of individual liberty is grounded, are applicable to it. If people must be allowed, in whatever concerns only themselves, to act as seems best to themselves at their own peril, they must equally be free to consult with one another about what is fit to be so done; to exchange opinions, and give and receive suggestions. Whatever it is permitted to do, it must be permitted to advise to do. The question is doubtful, only when the instigator derives a personal benefit from his advice; when he makes it his occupation, for subsistence or pecuniary gain, to promote what society and the State consider to be an evil. Then, indeed, a new element of complication is introduced; namely, the existence of classes of persons with an interest opposed to what is considered as the public weal, and whose mode of living is grounded on the counteraction of it. Ought this to be interfered with, or not? Fornication, for example, must be tolerated, and so must gambling; but should a person be free to be a pimp, or to keep a gambling-house? The case is one of those which lie on the exact boundary line between two principles, and it is not at once apparent to which of the two it properly belongs. There are arguments on both sides. On the side of toleration it may be said, that the fact of following anything as an occupation, and living or profiting by the practice of it, cannot make that criminal which would otherwise be admissible; that the act should either be consistently permitted or consistently prohibited; that if the principles which we have hitherto defended are true, society has no business, *as* society, to decide anything to be wrong which concerns only the individual; that it cannot go beyond dissuasion, and that one person should be as free to persuade, as another to dissuade. In opposition to this it may be contended, that although the public, or the State, are not warranted in authoritatively deciding, for purposes of repression or punishment, that such or such conduct affecting only the interests of the individual is good or bad, they are fully justified in assuming, if they regard it as bad, that its being so or not is at least a disputable question: That, this being supposed, they cannot be acting wrongly in endeavouring to exclude the influence of solicitations which are not disinterested, of instigators who cannot possibly be impartial—who have a direct personal interest on one side, and that side the one which the State believes to be wrong, and who confessedly promote it for personal objects only. There can surely, it may be urged, be nothing lost, no sacrifice of good, by so ordering matters that persons shall make

their election, either wisely or foolishly, on their own prompting, as free as possible from the arts of persons who stimulate their inclinations for interested purposes of their own. Thus (it may be said) though the statutes respecting unlawful games are utterly indefensible—though all persons should be free to gamble in their own or each other's houses, or in any place of meeting established by their own subscriptions, and open only to the members and their visitors—yet public gambling-houses should not be permitted. It is true that the prohibition is never effectual, and that, whatever amount of tyrannical power may be given to the police, gambling-houses can always be maintained under other pretences; but they may be compelled to conduct their operations with a certain degree of secrecy and mystery, so that nobody knows anything about them but those who seek them; and more than this, society ought not to aim at. There is considerable force in these arguments. I will not venture to decide whether they are sufficient to justify the moral anomaly of punishing the accessory, when the principal is (and must be) allowed to go free; of fining or imprisoning the procurer, but not the fornicator, the gambling-house keeper, but not the gambler. Still less ought the common operations of buying and selling to be interfered with on analogous grounds. Almost every article which is bought and sold may be used in excess, and the sellers have a pecuniary interest in encouraging that excess; but no argument can be founded on this, in favour, for instance, of the Maine Law; because the class of dealers in strong drinks, though interested in their abuse, are indispensably required for the sake of their legitimate use. The interest, however, of these dealers in promoting intemperance is a real evil, and justifies the State in imposing restrictions and requiring guarantees which, but for that justification, would be infringements of legitimate liberty.

A further question is, whether the State, while it permits, should nevertheless indirectly discourage conduct which it deems contrary to the best interests of the agent; whether, for example, it should take measures to render the means of drunkenness more costly, or add to the difficulty of procuring them by limiting the number of the places of sale. On this as on most other practical questions, many distinctions require to be made. To tax stimulants for the sole purpose of making them more difficult to be obtained, is a measure differing only in degree from their entire prohibition; and would be justifiable only if that were justifiable. Every increase of cost is a prohibition, to those whose means do not come up to the augmented price; and to those who do, it is a penalty laid on them for gratifying a particular taste. Their choice of pleasures, and their mode of expending their income, after satisfying their legal and moral obligations to the State and to individuals, are their own concern, and must rest with their own judgement. These considerations may seem at first sight to condemn the selection of stimulants as special subjects of taxation for purposes of revenue. But it must be remembered that taxation for fiscal purposes is absolutely inevitable; that in most countries it is necessary that a considerable part of that taxation should be indirect; that the State, therefore, cannot help imposing penalties, which to some persons may be prohibitory, on the use of some articles of consumption. It is hence the duty of the State to consider, in the imposition of taxes, what commodities the consumers can best spare; and *a fortiori,* to select in preference those of which it deems the use, beyond a very moderate quantity, to be positively injurious. Taxation, therefore, of stimulants, up to the point which produces the largest amount of revenue (supposing that the State needs all the revenue which it yields) is not only admissible, but to be approved of.

The question of making the sale of these commodities a more or less exclusive privilege, must be answered differently, according to the purposes to which the restriction is intended to be subservient. All places of public resort require the restraint of a police, and places of this kind peculiarly, because offences against society are especially apt to originate there. It is, therefore, fit to confine the power of selling these commodities (at least for consumption on the spot) to persons of known or vouched-for respectability of conduct; to make such regulations respecting hours of opening and closing as may be requisite for public surveillance, and to withdraw the license if breaches of the peace repeatedly take place through the connivance or incapacity of the keeper of the house, or if it becomes a rendezvous for concocting and preparing offences against the law. Any further restriction I do not conceive to be, in principle, justifiable. The limitation in number, for instance, of beer and spirit houses, for the express purpose of rendering them more difficult of access, and diminishing the occasions of temptation, not only exposes all to an inconvenience because there are some by whom the facility would be abused, but is suited only to a state of society in which the labouring classes are avowedly treated as children or savages, and placed under an education of restraint, to fit them for future admission to the privileges of freedom. This is not the principle on which the labouring classes are professedly governed in any free country; and no person who sets due value on freedom will give his adhesion to their being so governed, unless after all efforts have been exhausted to educate them for freedom and govern them as freemen, and it has been definitively proved that they can only be governed as children. The bare statement of the alternative shows the absurdity of supposing that such efforts have been made in any case which needs be considered here. It is only because the institutions of this country are a mass of inconsistencies, that things find admittance into our practice which belong to the system of despotic, or what is called paternal, government, while the general freedom of our institutions precludes the exercise of the amount of control necessary to render the restraint of any real efficacy as a moral education.

It was pointed out in an early part of this Essay, that the liberty of the individual, in things wherein the individual is alone concerned, implies a corresponding liberty in any number of individuals to regulate by mutual agreement such things as regard them jointly, and regard no persons but themselves. This question presents no difficulty, so long as the will of all the persons implicated remains unaltered; but since that will may change, it is often necessary, even in things in which they alone are concerned, that they should enter into engagements with one another; and when they do, it is fit, as a general rule, that those engagements should be kept. Yet, in the laws, probably, of every country, this general rule has some exceptions. Not only persons are not held to engagements which violate the rights of third parties, but it is sometimes considered a sufficient reason for releasing them from an engagement, that it is injurious to themselves. In this and most other civilized countries, for example, an engagement by which a person should sell himself, or allow himself to be sold, as a slave, would be null and void; neither enforced by law nor by opinion. The ground for thus limiting his power of voluntarily disposing of his own lot in life, is apparent, and is very clearly seen in this extreme case. The reason for not interfering, unless for the sake of others, with a person's voluntary acts, is consideration for his liberty. His voluntary choice is evidence that what he so chooses is desirable, or at the least endurable, to him, and his good is on the whole best provided for by allowing him to take his own means of pursuing it. But by selling himself for a slave, he abdicates his liberty; he forgoes any future use of it beyond that single act. He therefore defeats, in his own case, the very purpose which is the justification of allowing him to dispose of himself. He is no longer free; but is thenceforth in a position which has no longer the presumption in its favour, that would be afforded by his voluntarily remaining in it. The principle of freedom cannot require that he should be free not to be free. It is not freedom, to be allowed to alienate his freedom. These reasons, the force of which is so conspicuous in this peculiar case, are evidently of far wider application; yet a limit is everywhere set to them by the necessities of life, which continually require, not indeed that we should resign our freedom, but that we should consent to this and the other limitation of it. The principle, however, which demands uncontrolled freedom of action in all that concerns only the agents themselves, requires that those who have become bound to one another, in things which concern no third party, should be able to release one another from the engagement: and

even without such voluntary release, there are perhaps no contracts or engagements, except those that relate to money or money's worth, of which one can venture to say that there ought to be no liberty whatever of retractation. Baron Wilhelm von Humboldt, in the excellent essay from which I have already quoted, states it as his conviction, that engagements which involve personal relations or services, should never be legally binding beyond a limited duration of time; and that the most important of these engagements, marriage, having the peculiarity that its objects are frustrated unless the feelings of both the parties are in harmony with it, should require nothing more than the declared will of either party to dissolve it. This subject is too important, and too complicated, to be discussed in a parenthesis, and I touch on it only so far as is necessary for purposes of illustration. If the conciseness and generality of Baron Humboldt's dissertation had not obliged him in this instance to content himself with enunciating his conclusion without discussing the premises, he would doubtless have recognized that the question cannot be decided on grounds so simple as those to which he confines himself. When a person, either by express promise or by conduct, has encouraged another to rely upon his continuing to act in a certain way—to build expectations and calculations, and stake any part of his plan of life upon that supposition—a new series of moral obligations arises on his part towards that person, which may possibly be overruled, but cannot be ignored. And again, if the relation between two contracting parties has been followed by consequences to others; if it has placed third parties in any peculiar position, or, as in the case of marriage, has even called third parties into existence, obligations arise on the part of both the contracting parties towards those third persons, the fulfilment of which, or at all events the mode of fulfilment, must be greatly affected by the continuance or disruption of the relation between the original parties to the contract. It does not follow, nor can I admit, that these obligations extend to requiring the fulfilment of the contract at all costs to the happiness of the reluctant party; but they are a necessary element in the question; and even if, as Von Humboldt maintains, they ought to make no difference in the *legal* freedom of the parties to release themselves from the engagement (and I also hold that they ought not to make *much* difference), they necessarily make a great difference in the *moral* freedom. A person is bound to take all these circumstances into account, before resolving on a step which may affect such important interests of others; and if he does not allow proper weight to those interests, he is morally responsible for the wrong. I have made these obvious remarks for the better illustration of the general principle of liberty, and not because they are at all needed on the particular question, which, on the contrary, is usually discussed as if the interest of children was everything, and that of grown persons nothing.

I have already observed that, owing to the absence of any recognized general principles, liberty is often granted where it should be withheld, as well as withheld where it should be granted; and one of the cases in which, in the modern European world, the sentiment of liberty is the strongest, is a case where, in my view, it is altogether misplaced. A person should be free to do as he likes in his own concerns; but he ought not to be free to do as he likes in acting for another, under the pretext that the affairs of the other are his own affairs. The State, while it respects the liberty of each in what specially regards himself, is bound to maintain a vigilant control over his exercise of any power which it allows him to possess over others. This obligation is almost entirely disregarded in the case of the family relations, a case, in its direct influence on human happiness, more important than all others taken together. The almost despotic power of husbands over wives needs not be enlarged upon here, because nothing more is needed for the complete removal of the evil, than that wives should have the same rights, and should receive the protection of law in the same manner, as all other persons; and because, on this subject, the defenders of established injustice do not avail themselves of the plea of liberty, but stand forth openly as the champions of power. It is in the case of children, that misapplied notions of liberty are a real obstacle to the fulfilment by the State of its duties. One would almost think that a man's children were supposed to be literally, and not metaphorically, a part of himself, so jealous is opinion of the smallest interference of law with his absolute and exclusive control over them; more jealous than of almost any interference with his own freedom of action: so much less do the generality of mankind value liberty than power. Consider, for example, the case of education. Is it not almost a self-evident axiom, that the State should require and compel the education, up to a certain standard, of every human being who is born its citizen? Yet who is there that is not afraid to recognize and assert this truth? Hardly any one indeed will deny that it is one of the most sacred duties of the parents (or, as law and usage now stand, the father), after summoning a human being into the world, to give to that being an education fitting him to perform his part well in life towards others and towards himself. But while this is unanimously declared to be the father's duty, scarcely anybody, in this country, will bear to hear of obliging him to perform it. Instead of his being required to make any exertion or sacrifice for securing education to the child, it is left to his choice to accept it or not when it is provided gratis! It still remains unrecognized, that to bring a child into existence without a fair prospect of being able, not only to provide food for its body, but instruction and training for its mind, is a moral crime, both against the unfortunate offspring and against society; and that if the parent does not fulfil this obligation, the State ought to see it fulfilled, at the charge, as far as possible, of the parent.

Were the duty of enforcing universal education once admitted, there would be an end to the difficulties about what the State should teach, and how it should teach, which now convert the subject into a mere battle-field for sects and parties, causing the time and labour which should have been spent in educating, to be wasted in quarrelling about education. If the government would make up its mind to *require* for every child a good education, it might save itself the trouble of *providing* one. It might leave to parents to obtain the education where and how they pleased, and content itself with helping to pay the school fees of the poorer classes of children, and defraying the entire school expenses of those who have no one else to pay for them. The objections which are urged with reason against State education, do not apply to the enforcement of education by the State, but to the State's taking upon itself to direct that education: which is a totally different thing. That the whole or any large part of the education of the people should be in State hands, I go as far as any one in deprecating. All that has been said of the importance of individuality of character, and diversity in opinions and modes of conduct, involves, as of the same unspeakable importance, diversity of education. A general State education is a mere contrivance for moulding people to be exactly like one another: and as the mould in which it casts them is that which pleases the predominant power in the government, whether this be a monarch, a priesthood, an aristocracy, or the majority of the existing generation in proportion as it is efficient and successful, it establishes a despotism over the mind, leading by natural tendency to one over the body. An education established and controlled by the State should only exist, if it exist at all, as one among many competing experiments, carried on for the purpose of example and stimulus, to keep the others up to a certain standard of excellence. Unless, indeed, when society in general is in so backward a state that it could not or would not provide for itself any proper institutions of education, unless the government undertook the task: then, indeed, the government may, as the less of two great evils, take upon itself the business of schools and universities, as it may that of joint-stock companies, when private enterprise, in a shape fitted for undertaking great works of industry, does not exist in the country. But in general, if the country contains a sufficient number of persons qualified to provide education under government auspices, the same persons would be able and willing to give an equally good education on the voluntary principle, under the assurance of remuneration afforded by a law rendering education compulsory, combined with State aid to those unable to defray the expense.

The instrument for enforcing the law could be no other than public examinations, extending to all children, and beginning at an early age. An age might be fixed at which every child must be examined, to ascertain if he (or she) is able to read. If a child proves unable, the father, unless he has some sufficient ground of excuse, might be subjected to a moderate fine, to be worked out, if necessary, by his labour, and the child might be put to school at his expense. Once in every year the examination should be renewed, with a gradually extending range of subjects, so as to make the universal acquisition, and what is more, retention, of a certain minimum of general knowledge, virtually compulsory. Beyond that minimum, there should be voluntary examinations on all subjects, at which all who come up to a certain standard of proficiency might claim a certificate. To prevent the State from exercising, through these arrangements, an improper influence over opinion, the knowledge required for passing an examination (beyond the merely instrumental parts of knowledge, such as languages and their use) should, even in the higher classes of examinations, be confined to facts and positive science exclusively. The examinations on religion, politics, or other disputed topics, should not turn on the truth or falsehood of opinions, but on the matter of fact that such and such an opinion is held, on such grounds, by such authors, or schools, or churches. Under this system, the rising generation would be no worse off in regard to all disputed truths, than they are at present; they would be brought up either churchmen or dissenters as they now are, the State merely taking care that they should be instructed churchmen, or instructed dissenters. There would be nothing to hinder them from being taught religion, if their parents chose, at the same schools where they were taught other things. All attempts by the State to bias the conclusions of its citizens on disputed subjects, are evil; but it may very properly offer to ascertain and certify that a person possesses the knowledge, requisite to make his conclusions, on any given subject, worth attending to. A student of philosophy would be the better for being able to stand an examination both in Locke and in Kant, whichever of the two he takes up with, or even if with neither: and there is no reasonable objection to examining an atheist in the evidences of Christianity, provided he is not required to profess a belief in them. The examinations, however, in the higher branches of knowledge should, I conceive, be entirely voluntary. It would be giving too dangerous a power to governments, were they allowed to exclude any one from professions, even from the profession of teacher, for alleged deficiency of qualifications: and I think, with Wilhelm von Humboldt, that degrees, or other public certificates of scientific or professional acquirements, should be given to all who present themselves for examination, and stand the test; but that such certificates should confer no advantage over competitors, other than the weight which may be attached to their testimony by public opinion.

It is not in the matter of education only, that misplaced notions of liberty prevent moral obligations on the part of parents from being recognized, and legal obligations from being imposed, where there are the strongest grounds for the former always, and in many cases for the latter also. The fact itself, of causing the existence of a human being, is one of the most responsible actions in the range of human life. To undertake this responsibility—to bestow a life which may be either a curse or a blessing—unless the being on whom it is to be bestowed will have at least the ordinary chances of a desirable existence, is a crime against that being. And in a country either over-peopled, or threatened with being so, to produce children, beyond a very small number, with the effect of reducing the reward of labour by their competition, is a serious offence against all who live by the remuneration of their labour. The laws which, in many countries on the Continent, forbid marriage unless the parties can show that they have the means of supporting a family, do not exceed the legitimate powers of the State: and whether such laws be expedient or not (a question mainly dependent on local circumstances and feelings), they are not objectionable as violations of liberty. Such laws are interferences of the State to prohibit a mischievous act—an act injurious to others, which ought to be a subject of reprobation, and social stigma, even when it is not deemed expedient to superadd legal punishment. Yet the current ideas of liberty, which bend so easily to real infringements of the freedom of the individual in things which concern only himself, would repel the attempt to put any restraint upon his inclinations when the consequence of their indulgence is a life or lives of wretchedness and depravity to the offspring, with manifold evils to those sufficiently within reach to be in any way affected by their actions. When we compare the strange respect of mankind for liberty, with their strange want of respect for it, we might imagine that a man had an indispensable right to do harm to others, and no right at all to please himself without giving pain to any one.

I have reserved for the last place a large class of questions respecting the limits of government interference, which, though closely connected with the subject of this Essay, do not, in strictness, belong to it. These are cases in which the reasons against interference do not turn upon the principle of liberty: the question is not about restraining the actions of individuals, but about helping them: it is asked whether the government should do, or cause to be done, something for their benefit, instead of leaving it to be done by themselves, individually, or in voluntary combination.

The objections to government interference, when it is not such as to involve infringement of liberty, may be of three kinds.

The first is, when the thing to be done is likely to be better done by individuals than by the government. Speaking generally, there is no one so fit to conduct any business, or to determine how or by whom it shall be conducted, as those who are personally interested in it. This principle condemns the interferences, once so common, of the legislature, or the officers of government, with the ordinary processes of industry. But this part of the subject has been sufficiently enlarged upon by political economists, and is not particularly related to the principles of this Essay.

The second objection is more nearly allied to our subject. In many cases, though individuals may not do the particular thing so well, on the average, as the officers of government, it is nevertheless desirable that it should be done by them, rather than by the government, as a means to their own mental education—a mode of strengthening their active faculties, exercising their judgement, and giving them a familiar knowledge of the subjects with which they are thus left to deal. This is a principal, though not the sole, recommendation of jury trial (in cases not political); of free and popular local and municipal institutions; of the conduct of industrial and philanthropic enterprises by voluntary associations. These are not questions of liberty, and are connected with that subject only by remote tendencies; but they are questions of development. It belongs to a different occasion from the present to dwell on these things as parts of national education; as being, in truth, the peculiar training of a citizen, the practical part of the political education of a free people, taking them out of the narrow circle of personal and family selfishness, and accustoming them to the comprehension of joint interests, the management of joint concerns— habituating them to act from public or semi-public motives, and guide their conduct by aims which unite instead of isolating them from one another. Without these habits and powers, a free constitution can neither be worked nor preserved; as is exemplified by the too-often transitory nature of political freedom in countries where it does not rest upon a sufficient basis of local liberties. The management of purely local business by the localities, and of the great enterprises of industry by the union of those who voluntarily supply the pecuniary means, is further recommended by all the advantages which have been set forth in this Essay as belonging to individuality of development, and diversity of modes of action. Government operations tend to be everywhere alike. With individuals and voluntary associations, on the contrary, there are varied experiments, and endless diversity of experience. What the State can usefully do, is to make itself a central depository, and active circulator and diffuser, of the experience resulting from many trials. Its business is to enable each experimentalist to benefit by the experiments of others; instead of tolerating no experiments but its own.

The third, and most cogent reason for restricting the interference of government, is the great evil of adding unnecessarily to its power. Every function super-added to those already exercised by the government, causes its influence over hopes and fears to be more widely diffused, and converts, more and more, the active and ambitious part of the public into hangers-on of the government, or of some party which aims at becoming the government. If the roads, the railways, the banks, the insurance offices, the great joint-stock companies, the universities, and the public charities, were all of them branches of the government; if, in addition, the municipal corporations and local boards, with all that now devolves on them, became departments of the central administration; if the employés of all these different enterprises were appointed and paid by the government, and looked to the government for every rise in life; not all the freedom of the press and popular constitution of the legislature would make this or any other country free otherwise than in name. And the evil would be greater, the more efficiently and scientifically the administrative machinery was constructed—the more skilful the arrangements for obtaining the best qualified hands and heads with which to work it. In England it has of late been proposed that all the members of the civil service of government should be selected by competitive examination, to obtain for those employments the most intelligent and instructed persons procurable; and much has been said and written for and against this proposal. One of the arguments most insisted on by its opponents, is that the occupation of a permanent official servant of the State does not hold out sufficient prospects of emolument and importance to attract the highest talents, which will always be able to find a more inviting career in the professions, or in the service of companies and other public bodies. One would not have been surprised if this argument had been used by the friends of the proposition, as an answer to its principal difficulty. Coming from the opponents it is strange enough. What is urged as an objection is the safety-valve of the proposed system. If indeed all the high talent of the country *could* be drawn into the service of the government, a proposal tending to bring about that result might well inspire uneasiness. If every part of the business of society which required organized concert, or large and comprehensive views, were in the hands of the government, and if government offices were universally filled by the ablest men, all the enlarged culture and practised intelligence in the country, except the purely speculative, would be concentrated in a numerous bureaucracy, to whom alone the rest of the community would look for all things: the multitude for direction and dictation in all they had to do; the able and aspiring for personal advancement. To be admitted into the ranks of this bureaucracy, and when admitted, to rise therein, would be the sole objects of ambition. Under this régime, not only is the outside public ill-qualified, for want of practical experience, to criticize or check the mode of operation of the bureaucracy, but even if the accidents of despotic or the natural working of popular institutions occasionally raise to the summit a ruler or rulers of reforming inclinations, no reform can be effected which is contrary to the interest of the bureaucracy. Such is the melancholy condition of the Russian empire, as shown in the accounts of those who have had sufficient opportunity of observation. The Czar himself is powerless against the bureaucratic body; he can send any one of them to Siberia, but he cannot govern without them, or against their will. On every decree of his they have a tacit veto, by merely refraining from carrying it into effect. In countries of more advanced civilization and of a more insurrectionary spirit, the public, accustomed to expect everything to be done for them by the State, or at least to do nothing for themselves without asking from the State not only leave to do it, but even how it is to be done, naturally hold the State responsible for all evil which befalls them, and when the evil exceeds their amount of patience, they rise against the government and make what is called a revolution; whereupon somebody else, with or without legitimate authority from the nation, vaults into the seat, issues his orders to the bureaucracy, and everything goes on much as it did before; the bureaucracy being unchanged, and nobody else being capable of taking their place.

A very different spectacle is exhibited among a people accustomed to transact their own business. In France, a large part of the people having been engaged in military service, many of whom have held at least the rank of non-commissioned officers, there are in every popular insurrection several persons competent to take the lead, and improvise some tolerable plan of action. What the French are in military affairs, the Americans are in every kind of civil business; let them be left without a government, every body of Americans is able to improvise one, and to carry on that or any other public business with a sufficient amount of intelligence, order, and decision. This is what every free people ought to be: and a people capable of this is certain to be free; it will never let itself be enslaved by any man or body of men because these are able to seize and pull the reins of the central administration. No bureaucracy can hope to make such a people as this do or undergo anything that they do not like. But where everything is done through the bureaucracy, nothing to which the bureaucracy is really adverse can be done at all. The constitution of such countries is an organization of the experience and practical ability of the nation, into a disciplined body for the purpose of governing the rest; and the more perfect that organization is in itself, the more successful in drawing to itself and educating for itself the persons of greatest capacity from all ranks of the community, the more complete is the bondage of all, the members of the bureaucracy included. For the governors are as much the slaves of their organization and discipline, as the governed are of the governors. A Chinese mandarin is as much the tool and creature of a despotism as the humblest cultivator. An individual Jesuit is to the utmost degree of abasement the slave of his order, though the order itself exists for the collective power and importance of its members.

It is not, also, to be forgotten, that the absorption of all the principal ability of the country into the governing body is fatal, sooner or later, to the mental activity and progressiveness of the body itself. Banded together as they are—working a system which, like all systems, necessarily proceeds in a great measure by fixed rules—the official body are under the constant temptation of sinking into indolent routine, or, if they now and then desert that mill-horse round, of rushing into some half-examined crudity which has struck the fancy of some leading member of the corps: and the sole check to these closely allied, though seemingly opposite, tendencies, the only stimulus which can keep the ability of the body itself up to a high standard, is liability to the watchful criticism of equal ability outside the body. It is indispensable, therefore, that the means should exist, independently of the government, of forming such ability, and furnishing it with the opportunities and experience necessary for a correct judgement of great practical affairs. If we would possess permanently a skilful and efficient body of functionaries—above all, a body able to originate and willing to adopt improvements; if we would not have our bureaucracy degenerate into a pedantocracy, this body must not engross all the occupations which form and cultivate the faculties required for the government of mankind.

To determine the point at which evils, so formidable to human freedom and advancement, begin, or rather at which they begin to predominate over the benefits attending the collective application of the force of society, under its recognized chiefs, for the removal of the obstacles which stand in the way of its well-being; to secure as much of the advantages of centralized power and intelligence, as can be had without turning into governmental channels too great a proportion of the general activity—is one of the most difficult and complicated questions in the art of government. It is, in a great measure, a question of detail, in which many and various considerations must be kept in view, and no absolute rule can be laid down. But I believe that the practical principle in which safety resides, the ideal to be kept in view, the standard by which to test all arrangements intended for overcoming the difficulty, may be conveyed in these words: the greatest dissemination of power consistent with efficiency; but the greatest possible centralization of information, and diffusion of it from the centre. Thus, in municipal administration, there would be, as in the New England States, a very minute division among separate officers, chosen by the localities, of all business which

is not better left to the persons directly interested; but besides this, there would be, in each department of local affairs, a central superintendence, forming a branch of the general government. The organ of this superintendence would concentrate, as in a focus, the variety of information and experience derived from the conduct of that branch of public business in all the localities, from everything analogous which is done in foreign countries, and from the general principles of political science. This central organ should have a right to know all that is done, and its special duty should be that of making the knowledge acquired in one place available for others. Emancipated from the petty prejudices and narrow views of a locality by its elevated position and comprehensive sphere of observation, its advice would naturally carry much authority; but its actual power, as a permanent institution, should, I conceive, be limited to compelling the local officers to obey the laws laid down for their guidance. In all things not provided for by general rules, those officers should be left to their own judgement, under responsibility to their constituents. For the violation of rules, they should be responsible to law, and the rules themselves should be laid down by the legislature; the central administrative authority only watching over their execution, and if they were not properly carried into effect, appealing, according to the nature of the case, to the tribunals to enforce the law, or to the constituencies to dismiss the functionaries who had not executed it according to its spirit. Such, in its general conception, is the central superintendence which the Poor Law Board is intended to exercise over the administrators of the Poor Rate throughout the country. Whatever powers the Board exercises beyond this limit, were right and necessary in that peculiar case, for the cure of rooted habits of maladministration in matters deeply affecting not the localities merely, but the whole community; since no locality has a moral right to make itself by mismanagement a nest of pauperism, necessarily overflowing into other localities, and impairing the moral and physical condition of the whole labouring community. The powers of administrative coercion and subordinate legislation possessed by the Poor Law Board (but which, owing to the state of opinion on the subject, are very scantily exercised by them), though perfectly justifiable in a case of first-rate national interest, would be wholly out of place in the superintendence of interests purely local. But a central organ of information and instruction for all the localities, would be equally valuable in all departments of administration. A government cannot have too much of the kind of activity which does not impede, but aids and stimulates, individual exertion and development. The mischief begins when, instead of calling forth the activity and powers of individuals and bodies, it substitutes its own activity for theirs; when, instead of informing, advising, and, upon occasion, denouncing, it makes them work in fetters, or bids them stand aside and does their work instead of them. The worth of a State, in the long run, is the worth of the individuals composing it; and a State which postpones the interests of *their* mental expansion and elevation, to a little more of administrative skill, or of that semblance of it which

practice gives, in the details of business; a State which dwarfs its men, in order that they may be more docile instruments in its hands even for beneficial purposes—will find that with small men no great thing can really be accomplished; and that the perfection of machinery to which it has sacrificed everything, will in the end avail it nothing, for want of the vital power which, in order that the machine might work more smoothly, it has preferred to banish.

Notes

1. These words had scarcely been written, when, as if to give them an emphatic contradiction, occurred the Government Press Prosecutions of 1858. That ill-judged interference with the liberty of public discussion has not, however, induced me to alter a single word in the text, nor has it at all weakened my conviction that, moments of panic excepted, the era of pains and penalties for political discussion has, in our own country, passed away.
2. *The Sphere and Duties of Government,* from the German of Baron Wilhelm von Humboldt, pp. 11–13.

The "Open Society" and Its Fallacies

WILLMOORE KENDALL

A little over 100 years ago John Stuart Mill wrote in his essay *On Liberty* that "... there ought to exist the fullest liberty of professing and discussing, as a matter of ethical conviction, any doctrine, however immoral it may be considered."[1] The sentence from which this is taken is not *obiter:* Chapter Two of his book is devoted to arguments, putatively philosophical in character, which if they were sound would warrant precisely such a conclusion;[2] we have therefore every reason to assume that Mill meant by the sentence just what it says. The topic of Chapter Two is the entire "communications" process in civilized society ("advanced" society, as Mill puts it),[3] and the question he raises is whether there should be limitations on that process.[4] He treats that problem as the central problem of all civilized societies, the one to which all other problems are subordinate, because of the consequences, good or ill, that a society must bring upon itself according as it adopts this or that solution to it. And he has supreme confidence in the rightness of the solution he offers. Presumably to avoid all possible misunderstanding, he provides several alternative statements of it, each of which makes his intention abundantly clear, namely, that society must be so organized as to make that solution its supreme law. "Fullest," that is, absolute freedom of thought and speech, he asserts by clear implication[5] in the entire argument of the chapter, is not to be one of several competing goods society is to foster, one that on occasion might reasonably be sacrificed, in part at least, to the preservation of other goods; i.e., he refuses to recognize any competing good in the name of which it can be limited. The silencing of dissenters on behalf of a received doctrine, of an accepted idea—this is an alternative statement—is *never* justified:[6] it can only do hurt, unwarranted hurt, alike to the person silenced, to the individual or group that silences, to the doctrine or idea on behalf of which the silencing is done, and to the society in the name of which the silencers silence.[7] The quotation I started with is, then, merely the strongest, the most intransigent, of several formulations of a general prescription he makes for advanced societies. We shall do well to examine it, phrase-by-phrase, before proceeding:

"There ought to exist"—*ought,* so that the prescription is put forward on ethical grounds—"the fullest liberty"—a liberty, i.e., that no one (individual, group, government, even society as a whole) is entitled to interfere with—"of professing and discussing"—that is, of publicly propagating—"as a matter of ethical conviction"—which, however, as any reader can quickly satisfy himself by reexamining Chapter II, is not intended to exclude other types of conviction, "intellectual" conviction for example—"any doctrine"—and "doctrine" is not intended to exclude, either,

Willmoore Kendall, "The 'Open Society' and Its Fallacies," from *American Political Science Review,* 54 (1960): 972–979. Reprinted by permission of the publisher.

since he uses the term synonymously with "idea" and "opinion"—"however immoral it may be considered"—where "immoral" also is used merely to cover what Mill considers the extreme case, the case in which, he supposes, people are least likely to refrain from silencing; and he would be equally willing, as the context shows, to write "however wrong," that is, "however incorrect," "however dangerous," "however foolish," or even "however harmful," and where "it may be considered" is recognizably short-hand for "it may be considered by anyone whomsoever."

It is fashionable, these days, in part because of a fairly recent book by the scientist-philosopher K. R. Popper,[8] to call the kind of society Mill had in mind an "open society"—by at least implied contrast with a "closed" society, that is, an "hermetically sealed" society, in which Mill's grand principle is, by definition, *not* observed. And we are told, variously, by writers whom we may call (because they so call themselves) Liberals, that we have an open society and ought to protect it against the machinations of those who would like to close it; or that we have a closed society and ought, heeding Mill's arguments, to turn it forthwith into an open society; or that democracy, freedom, progress—any or all of them —must stand or fall, according as we maintain or inaugurate or return to an open society; or that all who are opposed to the idea of the open society are authoritarians, enemies of human freedom, totalitarians. We are told all this, however, at least in its application to civilized societies in general (as opposed to the United States in particular),[9] on grounds that have not varied perceptibly since Mill set them down in the *Essay*. We are still dealing, then, with Mill's issue; and we shall think more clearly about it, I believe, if we keep it stated as much as possible in his terms—for no subsequent pleader for the open society has possessed his clarity or vigor of mind—as follows: Ought there to exist in organized society—the United States, e.g.—that "fullest liberty of professing and discussing" that Mill argues for? On what theoretical grounds can that liberty be defended? Is openness of the kind Mill's society would possess one of the characteristics of the

good society? Before attempting to deal with these questions, let me pause to clarify certain aspects of his position.

I

First, Mill must not be understood as saying, over-all, something *more* extravagant than he is actually saying. He is fully aware of the necessity for laws against libel and slander, and does not deem them inconsistent with his doctrine.[10] He is aware, also, of organized society's need to protect its younger members against certain forms of expression;[11] which is to say that his "fullest liberty of professing and discussing" is to obtain only among adults. Laws prohibiting, e.g, the circulation of obscene literature amongst school-children, or, e.g., utterance calculated to undermine the morals (however the society chooses to define morals) of a minor, are presumably not proscribed. Nor does the doctrine outlaw sanctions against incitement to crime[12]—provided, one must hasten to add, nothing political is involved (Mill would permit punishment for incitement to, e.g., tyrannicide, only if it could be shown to have resulted in an overt act).[13] And, finally—a topic about which, as it seems to me, there is much confusion amongst commentators on Mill—he would permit the police to disperse a mob where a riot is clearly imminent, even if its shoutings did bear upon some political, social, or economic issue; but not, he makes abundantly clear, on grounds of any official exception to the doctrinal tendency of the shoutings. The individuals concerned would be free to resume their agitation the following morning.[14]

This is an important point because the passage in question, dealing with the mob at the corn-merchant's house, has given Mill an undeserved reputation for having been an adherent of the clear-and-present-danger doctrine as we know it today. We may perhaps clear it up best as follows. The situations covered by the clear-and-present-danger doctrine, as applied, e.g., to the Communist "threat," and by parallel doctrines in contemporary political theory,[15] are those in which Mill was *most* concerned to maintain absolute liberty of discussion—those situations, namely, in which the ideas being expressed have a tendency dangerous to the established political, social, or economic order. We must not, then, suppose his society to be one in which anarchists, or defenders of polygamy, for example, could be silenced because of the likelihood of their picking up supporters and, finally, winning the day; since for Mill the likelihood of their picking up supporters is merely a further reason for letting them speak. *All* utterance with a bearing on public policy—political, social or economic—is to be permitted, no matter what some members of society, even the majority, even all the members save some lonely dissenter,[16] may happen to think of it. Mill must, then, also not be understood as saying something *less* extravagant than he is actually saying.

Second, what is at issue for Mill is not merely unlimited freedom of speech (as just defined) but, as he makes abundantly clear, unlimited freedom of thought as well, *and* a way of life appropriate to their maintenance. To put it otherwise: when we elevate freedom of thought and speech to the position of society's highest good, it ceases to be merely freedom of thought and speech, and becomes—with respect to a great many important matters—the society's ultimate standard of *order*.

Mill did not dwell upon the inescapable implications of this aspect of his position; it has been left to his epigones, especially in the United States, to think the position out. The open society, they tell us repeatedly, *must* see to it that all doctrines start out equal in the market-place of ideas; for society to assign an advantaged position to these doctrines rather than those would be tantamount to suppressing those; society can, therefore, have no orthodoxy, no public truth, no standard, upon whose validity it is entitled to insist; outside its private homes, its churches, and perhaps its non-public schools, it therefore cannot indoctrinate; *all* questions are for it open questions, and must, publicly, be treated as open. If it has public schools and universities, it will be told (and with unexceptionable logic), these also must treat all questions as open—otherwise what happens to the freedom of thought and so, ul-timately, the freedom of speech of the student who might have thought differently had his teachers not treated some questions as closed? Even if in their hearts and souls all the members of the open society believe in a particular religion, or a particular church, each must nevertheless be careful in his public capacity to treat all religions and churches as equal, to treat dissent, when and as it occurs, as the peer of dogma, to treat the voodoo missionary from Cuba as on an equal plane with an Archbishop of his own church.[17] The open society's first duty (so its custodians will remind it, and if not those at home then those abroad)[18] is to freedom; and that means that it is *not* free to give public status to its beliefs, its standards, and its loyalties. Mill's disciples are completely faithful to the spirit of his thought when they insist that if we mean business about freedom, that is how it is going to have to be. The open society confers "freedom" upon its members; but it does so at the cost of its own freedom as a society.

Third, Mill denies the existence—that is to say, at any particular place and moment—not only of a public truth,[19] but of any truth whatever unless it be the truth of the denial itself. (Let us not press this last too far, however, lest it seem a mere "debater's" point; it is of course, the Achilles' heel of all skepticisms.) Reduced to its simplest terms, the argument of the *Essay* runs as follows: whenever and wherever men disagree about a teaching, a doctrine, an opinion, an idea, we have no way of knowing which party is correct; the man (or group) who moves to silence a teaching on the ground that it is incorrect attributes to himself a kind of knowledge (Mill says an "infallibility") that no one is ever entitled to claim short of (if then) the very case where the question is sure not to arise—that is, where there is unanimity, and so no temptation to silence to begin with. When, therefore, Mill's followers demand the elevation of skepticism to the status of a national religion, and the remaking of society in that image, they are not reading into his position something that is not there—for all that Mill himself, as I have intimated, preserves a discreet silence on the detailed institutional consequences of his position. They are, rather, only making specific applications of notions that, for Mill, are the point of departure for the entire discussion.

The *basic* position, in fine, is not that society must have no public truth, no orthodoxy, no preferred doctrines, *because* it must have freedom of speech; but that it must not have them *for the same reason* that it must have freedom of speech, namely: because, in any given situation, no supposed truth has any proper claim to special treatment, and this in turn because it may turn out to be incorrect—nay, *will* turn out to be at least partially incorrect, since each competing idea is at most a partial truth. Nor is that all: Mill's freedom of speech doctrine is not merely derivative from a preliminary assault upon truth itself;[20] it is *inseparable from* that assault and cannot, I contend, be defended on any other ground. It is incompatible with religious, or any other, belief.

Fourth, Mill is not saying that no man must be silenced because every man has a "right" to freedom of speech. Consistent skeptic that he is, he warns us—and from an early moment—that he disclaims any advantage that might accrue to his argument from an appeal to abstract right; he is going to justify his position in terms of "utility," in terms of "the permanent interest of a man [sic] as a progressive being,"[21] whatever that may mean; and he sticks scrupulously to at least the first half of the promise throughout the *Essay*. This raises interesting questions as to (a) what Mill could have meant—whether indeed he means anything at all that people committed to the idea of abstract right might find intelligible—by such words as "ethical," "immoral," etc.; as to (b) the pains Mill takes, throughout his main argument, to reduce the question, "Should some types of expression be prohibited in civilized society because the ideas they express are wicked?" to the question, "Should some types of expression be prohibited because they are intellectually incorrect?"; and as to (c) the kind of moral fervor his followers have poured into the propagation of his views. Everything reduces itself for Mill to intellectual argument, where you either win or draw or lose by the sheer appeal to reason—which, for Mill, excludes *ex hypothesi* any appeal to revelation or

authority, for that would merely precipitate an endless discussion as to the status, from the standpoint of reason, of revelation and authority.

The notion of a "right" to freedom of speech, a capacity on the part of every man to say what he pleases that society must respect, because he is *entitled* to it—of a right that men have to live in the kind of society that Mill projects—is a later development. It occurs in different countries for different reasons and under different auspices; but to the extent that it is intended seriously it represents a complete break with Mill. Those who appeal to such a notion therefore have in his own shrewd example a warning that they must not attempt to do so on his grounds;[22] and much current confusion about the open society would be avoided if they would but take the warning to heart. In short, if we are going to speak of a *right* to freedom of speech, a *right* to live in an open society, we are going to have to justify it with arguments of a different character from Mill's, and so move the discussion onto a plane entirely different from Mill's. We are, above all, going to have to subordinate what we have to say to certain rules of discourse from which Mill, by his own fiat, is happily free. For any such right is inconceivable save as one component of a system or complex of rights, that mutually limit and determine one another and are meaningless save as they are deemed subject to the general proposition that we are not entitled to the exercise of *any* right unless we discharge the duties correlative to that right. Once we begin to argue from premises of that sort we shall begin to talk sense, not nonsense, about freedom of speech and the open society. And the essence of the sense, I hasten to add, will be found to lie in the fact that we are no longer driving the roots of our doctrine into the soil of skepticism, because (as I have suggested already) once we speak of a right[23] we have already ceased to be skeptics. And nothing is more certain than that we shall come out with something quite different from Popper's conception of the open society.

Fifth, Mill was fully aware (as his disciples seem not to be) both of the novelty and of the revolutionary character of his proposal for a society organized around the notion of freedom of speech. Just as he deliberately cuts himself off from any appeal to the notion of abstract right, so does he cut himself off from any appeal to tradition. Not only had no one ever before taught his doctrine concerning freedom of speech. No one had ever taught a doctrine even remotely like his. No one, indeed, had ever discussed such a doctrine even as a matter of speculative fancy.[24] Hardly less than Machiavelli, and more than Hobbes, Mill is in full rebellion against both religion and philosophy, and so in full rebellion also against the traditional society that embodies them.[25] Hardly less than Machiavelli, he conceives himself a "new prince in a new state,"[26] obliged to destroy what has preceded him so that he may create what he feels stirring within him.[27] Hardly less than Machiavelli, again, he is a teacher of *evil:* all truths that have preceded his are (as we have noted in passing above) at most partial truths, and enjoy even that status only because Mill confers it upon them.[28] To reverse a famous phrase, Mill thinks of himself as standing not upon the shoulders of giants but of pygmies. He appeals to no earlier teacher,[29] identifies himself with nothing out of the past; and his doctrine of freedom of speech is, as I have intimated already, the unavoidable logical consequence of the denials from which his thought moves. Not, however, because it is in fact to be the public policy of the society he will found, not because it is to govern his followers' actions with respect to the freedom of thought of others, but because it is the perfect weapon—perfect because of its alleged connection with the quest for truth—to turn upon the traditional society that he must overthrow. For he who would destroy a society must first destroy the public truth it conceives itself as embodying; and Mill's doctrine of freedom of speech, to the extent that it gets itself accepted publicly, does precisely that. I do not, I repeat, believe it can be separated from the evil teaching that underlies it; and nothing could be more astonishing than the incidence of persons amongst us who because of their religious commitments must repudiate the evil teaching, yet continue to embrace the doctrine.

Sixth, Mill's most daring *démarche* in the *Essay* (and Popper's in the *Open Society and Its Enemies*) is that of confronting the reader with a series of false dilemmas: unlimited freedom of speech or all-out thought-control; the open society or the closed society; etc. I say "false" for two reasons: first, because unlimited freedom of speech and the open society are not real alternatives at all, as I hope shortly to show. And second, because the dilemmas as posed conceal the real choices available to us, which are always choices as to how-open-how-closed our society is to be, and thus not choices between two possibilities but choices among an infinite range of possibilities. Mill would have us choose between never silencing and declaring ourselves infallible, as Popper would have us believe that a society cannot be a little bit closed, any more than a woman can be a little bit pregnant. All our knowledge of politics bids us not to fall into that trap. Nobody wants all-out thought-control or the closed society; and nobody has any business pretending that somebody else wants them. For the real question is, how open can a society be and still remain open at all? Or, to put it differently, is there any surer prescription for arriving, willy nilly, in spite of ourselves, at the closed society, than is involved in current pleas for the open society?

II

That brings me to the central business of this article, which I may put as follows. Let us adjourn objections to open society doctrines on the ground that they are rooted in demonstrably evil teachings. Let us also suppose, *arguendo,* that we have organized a society in accordance with Mill's prescriptions, and for Mill's reasons. Have we then cause to suppose, as Mill thinks, that we shall end up forwarding the interests of truth? In other words, Mill offers us not only an exhortation but a prediction, and we wish merely to know what would in fact happen if we did what he tells us to do. My contention will be that, once the question is put in that way,[30] we run up against some insuperable objections to his prescriptions in and of themselves—objections, moreover, that remain equally valid even if one starts out, unlike Mill, from a supposed "right," whether natural or constitutional, to freedom of speech. I shall argue the objections in a logical order such that if each in turn were overcome the remaining ones would still stand.

Mill's proposals have as one of their tacit premises a false conception of the nature of society, and are, therefore, unrealistic on their face. They assume that society is, so to speak, a *debating club* devoted above all to the pursuit of truth, and capable therefore of subordinating itself—and all other considerations, goods, and goals—to that pursuit. Otherwise, the proposals would go no further than to urge upon society the common-sense view that the pursuit of truth is *one* of the goods it ought to cherish (even perhaps that one which it is most likely, in the press of other matters, to fail to make sufficient provision for); that it will neglect this good only at its own peril (a point that could easily be demonstrated); and that, accordingly, it should give hard and careful thought to what kind of provision it can make for it without disrupting unduly the pursuit of other goods. But we know only too well that society is *not* a debating club—all our experience of society drives the point home—and that, even if it were one, like the UN General Assembly, say, the chances of its adopting the pursuit of truth as its supreme good are negligible. Societies, alike by definition and by the teaching of history, cherish a whole series of goods among others, their own self-preservation, the *living* of the truth they believe themselves to embody already, and the communication of that truth (pretty much intact, moreover) to future generations, their religion, etc.—which they are not only likely to value as much as or more than the pursuit of truth, but *ought* to value as much as or more than the pursuit of truth, because these are *preconditions* of the pursuit of truth.

To put it a little differently, the proposals misconceive the strategic problem, over against organized society, of those individuals who *do* value the pursuit of truth above all other things. That strategic problem we may state as follows: *fortunate* that society that has even a small handful—a "select minority," in Ortega y Gasset's phrase—of persons who value the

pursuit of truth in the way in which Mill imagines a society valuing it. *Fortunate* that select minority in such a society, if it can prevail upon the society, to provide it with the leisure and resources with which to engage in the pursuit of truth; or, failing that, at least not to stand in the way of its pursuit of truth. And *wise* that society whose decision-makers see deeply enough into things to provide that select minority—even in the context of guarantees against its abusing its privileges—the leisure and the resources it needs for the pursuit of truth. To ask more than that of society, to ask that it give that select minority freedom to treat publicly all questions as open questions, as open not only for itself in the course of its discharge of its own peculiar function but for everybody, is Utopian in the worst sense of the word; and so, certain to defeat the very purpose the asking is intended to serve. By asking for all, even assuming that all to be desirable, we imperil our chances of getting that little we might have got had we asked only for that little.

If we nevertheless waive that objection, we confront another, namely, that the proposals have as a further tacit premise a false conception of human beings, and how they act in organized society. Concretely, Mill not only assumes that speech (the professing and discussing of any doctrine, however immoral) is incapable of doing hurt in society. (He has to assume this, since he calls for non-interference with speech, while the overriding principle of the *Essay* is that society is always entitled to interfere in order to prevent hurt, whether to itself or to its individual members.) This is disturbing enough: Socrates, we recall, taught otherwise, namely, that he who teaches my neighbor evil does *me* hurt. But Mill also assumes (else again his proposal is romantic) that people can be persuaded either to *be* indifferent toward the possible tendency of what their neighbors are saying, or at least to *act* as if they were indifferent. We know nothing about people, I suggest, that warrants our regarding such an assumption, once it is brought out into the open, as valid. Thus his proposals, like all political proposals that call implicitly for the refashioning of human nature, can be enforced only through some large-scale institutional co-ercion. And I believe it to be this consideration, above all, that explains the failure of Mill's followers, to date, to persuade any organized society to adopt his proposals. We have no ex-perience of unlimited freedom of speech as Mill defines it, of the open society as Popper defines it, unless, after a fashion and for a brief moment in Weimar Germany—an experience no organized society will be eager to repeat.

Let us now turn to still another objection. I contend that such a society will become *intol-erant,* one in which the pursuit of truth can only come to a halt. Whatever the private con-victions of the society's individual members concerning what Plato teaches us to call the important things (that is, the things with which truth is primarily concerned), the society itself is now, by definition, dedicated to a national religion of skepticism, to the suspension of judgment as *the* exercise of judgment *par ex-cellence.* It can, to be sure, tolerate all expres-sion of opinion that is predicated upon its own view of truth; but what is it to do with the man who steps forward to urge an opinion, to con-duct an inquiry, *not* predicated on that view? What is it to do with the man who, with every syllable of faith he utters, challenges the very foundations of skeptical society? What can it say to him except, "Sir, you cannot enter into our discussions, because you and we have no common premises from which discussion be-tween us can be initiated?" What can it do, in a word, but silence him, and look on helplessly as within its own bosom the opinions about the important things descend into an ever greater conforming dullness? Nor—unlike traditional society, which did *not* regard all questions as open questions—need it hesitate to silence him. The proposition that all opinions are equally—and hence infinitely—valuable, said to be the unavoidable inference from the prop-osition that all opinions are equal, is only one—and perhaps the less likely—of two possible inferences, the other being: all opin-ions are equally—and hence infinitely—*with-out* value, so what difference does it make if one, particularly one not our own, gets sup-pressed?[31] This we may fairly call the central paradox of the theory of freedom of speech. In

order to practice tolerance on behalf of the pur-suit of truth, you have first to value and believe in not merely the pursuit of truth but Truth itself, with all its accumulated riches to date. The all-questions-are-open-questions society cannot do that; it cannot, therefore, practice tolerance towards those who disagree with it. It must persecute—and so, on its very own showing, arrest the pursuit of truth.

I next contend that such a society as Mill prescribed will descend ineluctably into ever-deepening *differences of opinion,* into progres-sive breakdown of those common premises upon which alone a society can conduct its af-fairs by discussion, and so into the abandon-ment of the discussion process and the arbitrament of public questions by violence and civil war. This is the phenomenon—we may call it the dispersal of opinion—to which Rousseau, our greatest modern theorist of the problem, recurred again and again in his writ-ings.[32] The all-questions-are-open-questions society cannot endeavor to arrest it, by giving preferred status to certain opinions and, at the margin, mobilizing itself internally for their de-fense; for by definition it places a *premium* upon dispersion by inviting irresponsible spec-ulation and irresponsible utterance. As time passes, moreover, the extremes of opinion will—as they did in Weimar—grow further and further apart, so that (for the reason noted above) their bearers can less and less tolerate even the thought of one another, still less one another's presence in society. And again the ultimate loser is the pursuit of truth.

Still another tacit premise of the proposals is the extraordinary notion that the discussion process, which correctly understood does in-deed forward the pursuit of truth, and does in-deed call for *free* discussion, is one and the same thing with Mill's unlimited freedom of speech. They rest, in consequence, upon a false conception of the discussion process. What they will produce is not truth but rather only deafening noise and demoralizing confusion. For the essence of Mill's freedom of speech is the divorce of the right to speak from the duties correlative to the right; the right to speak is a right to speak *ad nauseam,* and with impunity. It is shot through and through with the egalitarian overtones of the French Revolution, which are as different from the measured aristocratic overtones of the pursuit of truth by discussion, as understood by the tradition Mill was attacking, as philosophy is different from phosphorus.

Of the latter point we may sufficiently satisfy ourselves, it seems to me, by recalling how the discussion process works in those situations in which men who are products of the tradition organize themselves for a serious venture in the pursuit of truth—as they do in, say, a branch of scholarship, an academic *discipline,* and the community of truth-seekers corresponding to it.[33]

Such men demonstrably proceed on some such principles as these: (a) The pursuit of truth is indeed forwarded by the exchange of opinions and ideas among many; helpful suggestions do indeed emerge sometimes from surprising quarters; but one does not leap from these facts to the conclusion that helpful suggestions may come from just anybody. (b) The man or woman who wishes to exercise the right to be heard has a logically and temporally prior obligation to *prepare* himself for participation in the exchange, and to prepare himself in the manner defined by the community. Moreover (c), from the moment he begins to participate in the exchange, he must make manifest, by his behavior, his sense of the duty to act as if the other participants had something to teach him—the duty, in a word, to see to it that the exchange goes forward in an atmosphere of courtesy and mutual self-respect. Next (d), the entrant must so behave as to show that he understands that scholarly investigation did not begin with his appearance on the scene, that there is a strong presumption that prior investigators have not labored entirely in vain, and that the community is the custodian of—let us not sidestep the *mot juste*—an *orthodoxy,* no part of which it is going to set lightly to one side. (e) That orthodoxy must be understood as concerning first and foremost the frame of reference within which the exchange of ideas and opinions is to go forward. That frame of reference is, to be sure, subject to change, but this is a matter of meeting the arguments that led originally to its adoption, and

meeting them in recognition that the ultimate decision, as to whether or not to change it, lies with the community. (f) The entrant, insofar as he wishes to challenge the orthodoxy, must expect barriers to be placed in his way, and must not be astonished if he is punished, at least in the short term, by what are fashionably called "deprivations"; he must, indeed, recognize that the barriers and the deprivations are a necessary part of the organized procedure by which truth is pursued. (g) Access to the channels of communication that represent the community's central ritual (the learned journals, that is to say) is something that the entrant wins by performing the obligation to produce a craftsmanlike piece of work. (h) The ultimate fate of the entrant who disagrees with the orthodoxy but cannot persuade the community to accept his point of view is, quite simply, isolation within or banishment from the community.

No suggestion is made that this is a complete statement of the rules as we see them operating about us in the scholarly disciplines, or that the particular forms of words employed are the happiest, or most accurate, that could be found. They do, however, seem to me to suggest the broad outlines of the paradigm of the free discussion process as it goes forward in an academic community, and to drive home its differences from the freedom of speech process as Mill defines it. Nor, I think, could anything be more obvious than the answer to the question, which of the two is the more likely to forward the pursuit of truth? But this is not all. *The* point about Mill's model is that by giving equal privileges to those who are in fact opposed to or ignorant of the discussion process, it constitutes a major onslaught against Truth. The two paradigms are not only different, but incompatible.

It would not be easy, of course, to transfer the rules of the discussion process set forth here to the public forum of a society; nor is there any point in denying that the transfer would involve our openly conceding to society far greater powers, particularly as regards silencing the ill-mannered, the ignorant, the irrelevant, than it would ever enjoy under Mill's prescription. Here, however, two things must be kept in mind. First (however reluctant we may be to admit it), that society always has, and constantly exercises, the power to silence. And second, that no society is likely, within the foreseeable future, to remake itself in the image of either of the two paradigms. The question, always, is that of which of the two we accept as the ideal toward which we try to move. That is the real issue at stake between the proponents and opponents of the "open society."

Notes

1. *On Liberty and Considerations on Representative Government,* ed. R. B. McCallum (Oxford, 1946), p. 14 fn. [Reprinted in this volume.]

2. That is approximately how Mill himself puts it: the words preceding what I have quoted are, "If the arguments of the present chapter are of any validity, . . ." The chapter is entitled "Of the Liberty of Thought and Discussion."

3. Cf. ibid., p. 9: ". . . we may leave out of consideration those backward states of society in which the race itself may be considered as in its nonage." The distinction seems to turn variously (ibid.) on whether "mankind have become capable of being improved by free and equal discussion" and whether they "have attained the capacity of being guided to their own improvement by conviction or persuasion." On the latter point he adds, perhaps a little optimistically: ". . . a period long since reached in all nations with whom we need here concern ourselves." Cf. ibid. p. 59, where he refers, astonishingly, to "the present low state of the human mind," that being the point he needs to establish the thesis there in question.

4. Who should be permitted, in the fashionable jargon of the "communications" literature, "to say what, and to whom."

5. Those who regard "absolute" as too strong a term to be deemed a synonym of "fullest" may wish to be reminded of the following passage (ibid., p. 11): ". . . the appropriate region of human liberty . . . comprises . . . liberty of conscience in the most comprehensive sense: liberty of thought and feeling; *absolute* freedom of opinion and sentiment on all subjects, practical or speculative, scientific, moral, or theological. [And the] liberty of expressing and publishing opinions . . . is practically inseparable from [liberty of thought] . . ." (italics added). And cf. ibid.: "No society . . . is completely free in which [these liberties] . . . do not exist *absolute and unqualified*" (italics added).

6. Cf. ibid., p. 14: ". . . I deny the right of the people to exercise such coercion, either by themselves or their government. The power itself is illegitimate. The best government has no more title to it than

the worst." The statement could hardly be more sweeping.

7. Not to speak of "mankind." Cf. ibid., pp. 14–15: ". . . the peculiar evil of silencing the expression of an opinion is, that it is robbing the human race: . . . those who dissent from the opinion, still more than those who hold it."

8. K. R. Popper, *The Open Society and Its Enemies* (London, 1945), 2 vols. The term "open society" is of course much older (Bergson uses a distinction between "open" and "closed" society in *Les deux sources de la morale et de la religion,* though for a quite different purpose). Popper wedded the term "open society" to Mill's ideas, and the term "closed society" to those of his bêtes noires, Plato especially.

9. The exception is necessary, because the American arguments are often based on the meaning of the Constitution of the United States, the First Amendment especially.

10. Cf. *On Liberty,* p. 73: "Whenever, in short, there is a definite damage, or a definite risk of [definite?] damage, either to an individual or to the public, the case is taken out of the province of liberty, and placed in that of morality and law."

11. Cf. ibid., p. 72: ". . . protection against themselves is confessedly due to children and persons under age. . . ."

12. Cf. ibid., p. 49: ". . . even opinions lose their immunity when the circumstances in which they are expressed are such as to constitute their expression a positive instigation to some mischievous act." To this writer's mind a curious concession, which Mill ought *not* to have made. Once it is made, a society wishing to silence this or that form of persuasive utterance has only to declare the behavior it is calculated to produce a crime, and it may silence— with Mill's blessing.

13. Cf. ibid., p. 14 fn.

14. Cf. ibid., p. 49.

15. E.g., the doctrine that enemies of liberty must not be permitted to take advantage of "civil liberties" in order to undermine and destroy them; or the doctrine that a free society is entitled to interfere with free expression in order to perpetuate its own existence. Mill would certainly not have countenanced either doctrine.

16. Cf. ibid., p. 14: "If all mankind were of one opinion, and only one person were of the contrary opinion, mankind would be no more justified in silencing that one person, than he, if he had the power, would be justified in silencing all mankind."

17. Who, after all, is to say which is right?

18. As witness the sermons addressed by the New York press to the Trujillo regime.

19. Except, we must remind ourselves, the public truth that there is no public truth.

20. Ibid., passim.

21. Ibid., p. 9.

22. We must distinguish here between a "natural" or

"ethical" "right" to freedom of expression and a mere constitutional right. The case for the latter could of course be rested upon Mill's grounds, insofar as they are valid.

23. Again, we must except the merely constitutional right.

24. Plato, of course, contemplates a freedom of speech *situation* in bk. 9 of the *Republic;* but merely to show that it can result only in disaster.

25. Cf. Leo Strauss, *Thoughts on Machiavelli* (Glencoe, 1958), chap. 4, passim.

26. Cf. ibid., p. 9.

27. Cf. ibid., chap. 2, passim.

28. Cf. *On Liberty,* pp. 42–46.

29. That he had broken sharply with his father and with Bentham is, I take it, a commonplace.

30. I.e., as a problem for "empirical" political theory.

31. Cf. Bertrand de Jouvenel, *On Sovereignty* (Chicago: 1957), p. 288: "One of the strangest intellectual illusions of the nineteenth century was the idea that toleration could be ensured by moral relativism. . . . The relativist tells us that the man professing opinion A ought to respect opinion B, because his own opinion A has no more intrinsic value than B. But in that case B has no more than A. Attempts to impose either would be attempts to impose what had no intrinsic value; but also suppression of either would be suppression of what had no intrinsic value. And in that case there is no

crime . . . in the suppression of contrary opinions." On equality of opinions in Mill, see note 16 above. On the progress in Mill from "equally valuable" to "equally and infinitely valuable," cf. *On Liberty,* p. 46: ". . . truth has no chance but in proportion as every side of it, every opinion which embodies any fraction of the truth, not only finds advocates, but is so advocated as to be listened to." And the presumption, he insists, is that every opinion *does* contain some fraction of the truth: ". . . it is always probable that dissentients have something worth hearing . . . and that truth would lose something by their silence" (p. 42).

32. See *Social Contract,* 4, 1, as also *The Discourse on the Sciences and Arts,* passim, and Rousseau's famous letter of 1767 to the Marquis of Mirabeau. Cf. de Jouvenel, *On Sovereignty,* p. 286: "The whole of [Rousseau's] . . . large stock of political wisdom consists in contrasting the dispersion of feelings in a people morally disintegrated by the progress of the 'sciences and arts,' with the natural unity of a people in which dissociation has not occurred." As de Jouvenel notes (p. 287), Rousseau, though himself a Protestant, deplored the introduction of Protestantism into France, and on these grounds.

33. A similar point might be developed over the difference between Mill's freedom of speech and the free discussion of the traditional American town-meeting.

Freedom of Expression and Categories of Expression

THOMAS M. SCANLON, JR.

Freedom of expression, as a philosophical problem, is an instance of a more general problem about the nature and status of rights. Rights purport to place limits on what individuals or the state may do, and the sacrifices they entail are in some cases significant. Thus, for example, freedom of expression becomes controversial when expression appears to threaten important individual interests, in a case like the Skokie affair, or to threaten some important national interest such as the ability to raise an army. The general problem is, if rights place limits on what can be done even for good reasons, what is the justification for these limits?

A second philosophical problem is how we decide what these limits are. Rights appear to be something we can reason about, and this reasoning process does not appear to be merely a calculation of consequences. In many cases, we seem to decide whether a given policy infringes freedom of expression simply by consulting our conception of what this right entails. And while there are areas of controversy, there is a wide range of cases in which we all seem to arrive at the same answer. But I doubt that any of us could write out a brief, non-circular definition of freedom of expression whose mechanical application to these clear cases would yield the answers on which we all agree. In what, then, does our agreement consist?

My aim in this paper is to present an account of freedom of expression that provides at least a few answers to these general questions. I will also address a more specific question about freedom of expression itself. What importance should a theory of freedom of expression assign to categories of expression such as political speech, commercial speech, libel and pornography? These categories appear to play an important role in informal thought about the subject. It seems central to the controversy about the *Skokie* case, for example, that the proposed ordinance threatened the ability of unpopular *political* groups to hold demonstrations.[1] I doubt whether the residents of Skokie would have been asked to pay such a high price to let some other kind of expression proceed. To take a different example, laws against false or deceptive advertising and the ban on cigarette advertising on television suggest that we are willing to accept legal regulation of the form and content of commercial advertising that we would not countenance if it were applied to other forms of expression. Why should this be so?

While I do not accept all of these judgements, I find it hard to resist the idea that different categories of expression should to some degree be treated differently in a theory of freedom of expression. On the other hand some ideas of freedom of expression seem to apply

Thomas M. Scanlon, "Freedom of Expression and Categories of Expression," from the *University of Pittsburgh Law Review*, 40 (1979): 519–550. Reprinted with permission of the author and publisher.

across the board, regardless of category: intervention by government to stop the publication of what it regards as a false or misleading view seems contrary to freedom of expression whether the view concerns politics, religion, sex, health, or the relative desirability of two kinds of automobile.

So the question is, to what extent are there general principles of freedom of expression, and to what extent is freedom of expression category-dependent? To the degree that the latter is true, how are the relevant categories defined?

I will begin by considering the individual interests that are the basis of our special concern with expression. In section three I will consider how several theories of freedom of expression have been based on certain of these interests, and I will sketch an answer to the first two questions raised above. Finally, in sections four and five, I will discuss the place of categories of expression within the framework I have proposed and apply this to the particular categories of political speech, commercial speech, and pornography.

Interests

What are the interests with which freedom of expression is concerned? It will be useful to separate these roughly into those interests we have in being able to speak, those interests we have in being exposed to what others have to say, and those interests we have as bystanders who are affected by expression in other ways. Since, however, I want to make it clear that "expression" as I am using it is not limited to speech, I will refer to these three groups of interests as the interests of participants, the interests of audiences, and the interests of bystanders.

Participant Interests

The actions to which freedom of expression applies are actions that aim to bring something to the attention of a wide audience. This intended audience need not be the widest possible audience ("the public at large"), but it must be more than one or two people. Private

conversations are not, in general, a matter of freedom of expression, not because they are unimportant to us but because their protection is not the aim of this particular doctrine. (It is a matter, instead, of privacy or of personal liberty of some other sort.) But private conversations might be viewed differently if circumstances were different. For example, if telephone trees (or whispering networks) were an important way of spreading the word because we lacked newspapers and there was no way for us to gather to hear speeches, then legal restrictions on personal conversations could infringe freedom of expression as well as being destructive of personal liberty in a more general sense. What this shows, I think, is that freedom of expression is to be understood primarily in terms of the interests it aims to protect and only secondarily in terms of the class of actions whose protection is, under a given set of circumstances, an adequate way to safeguard these interests.

The most general participant interest is, then, an interest in being able to call something to the attention of a wide audience. This ability can serve a wide variety of more specific purposes. A speaker may be interested in increasing his reputation or in decreasing someone else's, in increasing the sales of his product, in promoting a way of life, in urging a change in government, or simply in amusing people or shocking them. From a social point of view, these interests are not all equally important, and the price that a society is required to pay in order to allow acts of expression of a particular kind to flourish will sometimes be a function of the value of expression of that kind.

This is one reason why it would be a mistake to look for a distinction between pure speech (or expression), which is protected by freedom of expression, and expression that is part of some larger course of action, which is not so protected. It is true that some acts of expression seem not to qualify for First Amendment protection because of the larger courses of action of which they are a part (assault, incitement). But what distinguishes these from other acts of expression is not just that they are part of larger courses of action (which is true of almost all acts of expression), but rather the character of the particular courses of action of which they form a part. Their exclusion from First Amendment protection should be seen as a special case of the more general phenomenon just mentioned: the protection to which an act of expression is entitled is in part a function of the value of the larger purposes it serves.

This cannot mean, of course, that the protection due a given act of expression depends on the actual value of the particular purposes at which it aims. It would be clearly antithetical to freedom of expression, for example, to accord greater protection to exponents of true religious doctrines than to exponents of false and misleading ones. Despite the fact that the objectives at which these two groups aim are of very different value, their acts of expression are (other things being equal) accorded equal status. This is so because the "further interest" that is at stake in the two cases is in fact the same, namely the interest we all have in being able to follow and promote our religious beliefs whatever they may be.

Here, then, is one way in which categories of expression arise. We are unwilling to bear the social costs of granting to just any expressive purpose the opportunities for expression that we would demand for those purposes to which we, personally, attach greatest importance. At the most concrete level, however, there is no agreement about the values to be attached to allowing particular acts of expression to go forward. It is just this lack of consensus, and the consequent unacceptability of allowing governments to regulate acts of expression on the basis of their perceived merits, that makes freedom of expression an important issue. In order to formulate a workable doctrine of freedom of expression, therefore, we look for something approaching a consensus on the relative importance of interests more abstractly conceived—the interest in religious expression, the interest in political expression, etc. Even this more abstract consensus is only approximate,[2] however, and never completely stable. As people's values change, or as a society becomes more diverse, consensus erodes. When this happens, either the ranking of interests must change or the categories of interests must be redefined, generally in a more abstract

manner.[3] Recent shifts in attitudes toward religion have provoked changes of both these kinds. As religion (or, as it is more natural to say here, one's religion) has come to be seen more as a matter of private concern on a par with other private interests, it has become harder to justify assigning religious concerns the pre-eminent value they have traditionally received. In order to make contemporary sense of this traditional assignment of values, on the other hand, there has been a tendency to redefine "religion" more abstractly as "a person's ultimate values and deepest convictions about the nature of life," thereby preserving some plausibility for the claim that we can all agree on the importance of religion in one's life even though we may have different beliefs.

The categories of participant interests I have been discussing are naturally identified with familiar categories of expression: political speech, commercial speech, etc. But we should not be too quick to make this identification. The type of protection that a given kind of expression requires is not determined by participant values alone. It also depends on such factors as the costs and benefits to nonparticipants and the reliability of available forms of regulation. Not surprisingly, these other factors also play a role in how categories of expression are defined. As will later become apparent, the lack of clarity concerning these categories results in part from the difficulty of seeing how these different elements are combined in their definition.[4]

Audience Interests

The interests of audiences are no less varied than those of participants: interests in being amused, informed on political topics, made aware of the pros and cons of alternatives available in the market, and so on. These audience interests conflict with those of participants in an important way. While participants sometimes aim only at communicating with people who are already interested in what they have to present, in a wide range of important cases their aims are broader: they want to gain the attention of people who would not otherwise consider their message. What audiences generally want, on the other hand, is to have expression available to them should they want to attend to it. Expression that grabs one's attention whether one likes it or not is generally thought of as a cost. But it should not be thought of only as a cost, even from the audience's point of view. As Mill rightly emphasized,[5] there is significant benefit in being exposed to ideas and attitudes different from one's own, though this exposure may be unwelcome. If we had complete control over the expression we are exposed to, the chances are high that we would use this power to our detriment. The important and difficult question however, is, when unwanted exposure to expression is a good thing from the audience's point of view.

This question is relatively easy to answer if we think of it as a problem of balancing temporary costs of annoyances, shock, or distraction against the more lasting benefits of a broadened outlook or deepened understanding. But it becomes more complicated if we take into account the possibility of more lasting costs such as being misled, having one's sensibilities dulled and cheapened, or acquiring foolish desires. This balancing task is simplified in the way we often think about expression by a further assumption about the audience's control. We are inclined to think that what would be ideal from the audience's point of view would be always to have the choice whether or not to be exposed to expression. Similarly, we have a tendency to assume that, having been exposed, an audience is always free to decide how to react: what belief to form or what attitude to adopt. This freedom to decide enables the audience to protect itself against unwanted long-range effects of expression. If we saw ourselves as helplessly absorbing as a belief every proposition we heard expressed, then our views of freedom of expression would be quite different from what they are. Certainly we are not like that. Nonetheless, the control we exercise over what to believe and what attitudes to adopt is in several respects an incomplete protection against unwarranted effects of expression.

To begin with, our decisions about what to believe are often mistaken, even in the best of circumstances. More generally, the likelihood of our not being mistaken, and hence the reliability of our critical rationality as a defense mechanism, varies widely from case to case depending on our emotional state, the degree of background information we possess, and the amount of time and energy we have to assess what we hear. As these things vary, so too does the value of being exposed to expression and the value of being able to avoid it. Commonly recognized cases of diminished rationality such as childhood, panic, and mental illness are just extreme instances of this common variation.

Quite apart from the danger of mistakenly believing what we hear, there is the further problem that a decision to disbelieve a messages does not erase all the effects it may have on us. Even if I dismiss what is said or shown to me as foolish and exaggerated, I am slightly different for having seen or heard it. This difference can be trivial but it can also be significant and have a significant effect on my later decisions. For example, being shown powerful photographs of the horrors of war, no matter what my initial reaction to them may be, can have the effect of heightening (or ultimately of dulling) my sense of the human suffering involved, and this may later affect my opinions about foreign policy in ways I am hardly aware of.

Expression influencing us in this way is a good thing, from the point of view of our interests as audiences, if it affects our future decisions and attitudes by making us aware of good reasons for them, so long as it does not interfere with our ability to weigh these reasons against others. Expression is a bad thing if it influences us in ways that are unrelated to relevant reasons, or in ways that bypass our ability to consider these reasons. "Subliminal advertising" is a good example of this. What is bad about it is not just that it is "subliminal," *i.e.* that we are influenced by it without being aware of that influence. This, I think, happens all the time and is, in many cases, unobjectionable. What is objectionable about subliminal advertising, if it works, is that it causes us to act—to buy popcorn, say, or to read Dostoevsky—by making us think we have a good reason for so acting, even though we probably have no such reason. Suddenly finding myself with the thought that popcorn would taste good or that *Crime and Punishment* would be just the thing is often good grounds for acting in the relevant way. But such a thought is no reason for action if it is produced in me by messages flickered on the screen rather than by facts about my present state that indeed make this a good moment to go out for popcorn or to lie down with a heavy book.

I have assumed here that subliminal advertising works by leading us to form a false belief: we acquire a positive feeling toward popcorn which we then take, mistakenly, to be a sign that we would particularly enjoy some popcorn. One can easily imagine, however, that the effect is deeper.[6] Suppose that what the advertising does is to change us so that we both have a genuine desire for popcorn and will in fact enjoy it. One can still raise the question whether being affected in this way is a good thing for us, but an answer to it cannot rely on the claim that we are made to think that we have a reason to buy popcorn when in fact we do not. For in this case we will have as good a reason to buy popcorn as we ever do: we want some and will enjoy it if we get it. Advertising of this kind will be a bad thing from the audience's point of view if one is worse off for having acquired such a desire, perhaps because it leads one to eat unhealthily, or because it distracts one from other pursuits, or for some other reason.

It is particularly galling to think of such effects being produced in us by another agent whose aim is to have us benefit him through actions we would not otherwise choose. But the existence of a conscious manipulator is not essential to the objections I have presented. It is a bad thing to acquire certain desires or to be influenced by false reasons, and these things are bad whether or not they are brought about by other agents. But while the existence of a conscious manipulator is not essential to this basic objection, it can be relevant in two further ways. What we should want in general is to have our beliefs and desires produced by processes that are reliable—processes whose effectiveness depends on the grounds for the

beliefs and on the goodness of the desires it produces. We prefer to be aware of how we are being affected partly because this critical awareness increases the reliability of the process; although, as I have said, this safeguard is commonly overrated. Particularly where effects on us escape our notice, the existence of an agent controlling these effects can decrease the reliability of the process: the effects produced will be those serving this agent's purposes, and there may be no reason to think that what serves his purposes will be good from our point of view. (Indeed, the reverse is suggested by the fact that he chooses surreptitious means.) So the existence of a controlling agent can be relevant because of its implications for the reliability of the process. Beyond the question of reliability, however, we may simply prefer to have the choice of whether or not to acquire a given desire; we may prefer this even where there is no certainty as to which desire it is better to have. This provides a further reason for objecting to effects produced in us by others (although this reason seems to hold as well against effects produced by inanimate causes).

The central audience interest in expression, then, is the interest in having a good environment for the formation of one's beliefs and desires. From the point of view of this interest, freedom of expression is only one factor among many. It is important to be able to hear what others wish to tell us, but this is not obviously more important than having affirmative rights of access to important information or to basic education. Perhaps freedom of expression is thought to differ in being purely negative: it consists merely in not being denied something and is therefore more easily justified as a right than are freedom of information or the right to education, which require others to provide something for us. But this distinction does not withstand a careful scrutiny. To begin with, freedom of expression adequately understood requires affirmative protection for expression, not just the absence of interference. Moreover, even nonintervention involves costs, such as the annoyance and disruption that expression may cause. On the other side, restrictions on freedom of information include not only failures to provide information but also attempts to conceal what would otherwise become public. When a government makes such an attempt for the purpose of stopping the spread of undesirable political opinions, this contravenes the same audience interests as an attempt to restrict publication, and the two seem to be objectionable on the same grounds. The fact that there is in the one case no "participant" whose right to speak is violated, but only a fact that remains undiscovered, seems not to matter.

Bystander Interests

I have mentioned that both participants and audiences can sometimes benefit from restrictions on expression as well as from the lack thereof. But the most familiar arguments for restricting expression appeal to the interests of bystanders. I will mention these only briefly. First are interests in avoiding the undesirable side effects of acts of expression themselves: traffic jams, the noise of crowds, the litter from leafletting. Second, and more important, are interests in the effect expression has on its audience. A bystander's interests may be affected simply by the fact that the audience has acquired new beliefs if, for example, they are beliefs about the moral character of the bystander. More commonly, bystanders are affected when expression promotes changes in the audience's subsequent behavior.

Regulation of expression to protect any of these bystander interests can conflict with the interests of audiences and participants. But regulation aimed at protecting bystanders against harms of the first type frequently strikes us as less threatening than that aimed at protecting bystanders against harmful changes in audience belief and behavior. This is true in part because the types of regulation supported by the two objectives are different. Protecting bystanders against harmful side effects of acts of expression calls for regulation only of the time, place, and manner of expression, and in many cases such regulation merely inconveniences audiences and participants. It *need* not threaten central interests in expression. Regulation to protect interests of the second kind, however,

must, if it is successful, prevent effective communication of an idea. It is thus in direct conflict with the interests of participants and, at least potentially, of audiences as well. But this contrast is significant only to the degree that there are some forms of effective expression through which participant and audience interests can be satisfied without occasioning bystander harms of the first type: where there is no surplus of effective means of expression, regulation of time, place, and manner can be just as dangerous as restrictions on content.

Theories

Although "freedom of expression" seems to refer to a right of participants not to be prevented from expressing themselves, theoretical defenses of freedom of expression have been concerned chiefly with the interests of audiences and, to a lesser extent, those of bystanders. This is true, for example, of Mill's famous defense in *On Liberty*,[7] which argues that a policy of non-interference with expression is preferable to a policy of censorship on two grounds: first, it is more likely to promote the spread of true beliefs and, second, it contributes to the well-being of society by fostering the development of better (more independent and inquiring) individuals. A similar emphasis on audience values is evident in Alexander Meiklejohn's theory.[8] He argues that First Amendment freedom of speech derives from the right of citizens of a democracy to be informed in order that they can discharge their political responsibilities as citizens.

This emphasis can be explained, I think, by the fact that theories of freedom of expression are constructed to respond to what are seen as the most threatening arguments for restricting expression. These arguments have generally proceeded by calling attention to the harms that unrestricted expression may bring to audiences and bystanders: the harm, for example, of being misled, or that of being made less secure because one's neighbors have been misled or provoked into disaffection and unrest. The conclusion drawn is that government, which has the right and even the duty to protect its citizens against such harms, may and should do so by preventing the expression in question. Responding to this argument, theories of freedom of expression have tended to argue either that the interests in question are not best protected by restricting expression (Mill) or that "protecting" citizens in this way is illegitimate on other grounds (Meiklejohn).

The dialectical objective of Mill's argument helps to explain why, although he professes to be arguing as a utilitarian, he concentrates on just two goods, true belief and individual growth, and never explicitly considers how these are to be balanced off against other goods that would have to be taken into account in a full utilitarian argument.

The surprising narrowness of Meiklejohn's theory can be similarly explained. Meiklejohn was reacting against the idea that a "clear and present danger" could justify a government in acting to protect its citizens by curbing the expression of threatening political ideas. This seemed to him to violate the rights of those it claimed to protect. Accordingly, he sought to explain the "absolute" character of the First Amendment by basing it in a right to be informed and to make up one's own mind. But is there such a right? Meiklejohn saw the basis for one in the deliberative role of citizens in a democratic political order. But a right so founded does not apply to all forms of expression. Debates over artistic merit, the best style of personal life, or the promotion of goods in the marketplace may have their importance, but Meiklejohn saw these forms of expression as pursuits on a par with many others, unable to claim any distinct right to immunity from regulation. He was thus led to concede that these activities, in the main, fall outside the area of fundamental First Amendment protection or, rather, that they qualify for it only insofar as their general importance makes them relevant to political decisions.

This narrowness is an unsatisfactory feature of what is in many ways an interesting and appealing theory. Moreover, given this emphasis on political rights as the basis of First Amendment protection of speech, it is particularly surprising that Meiklejohn's theory should take audience values—the right of citizens to be informed—as the only fundamental ones. For prominent among the political rights of democratic citizens is the right to participate in the political process—in particular, the right to argue for one's own interests and point of view and to attempt to persuade one's fellow citizens. Such rights of participation do not entirely derive from the need of one's fellow citizens to be informed; the right to press one's case and to try to persuade others of its validity would not evaporate if it could be assumed that others were already perfectly informed on the questions at issue. Perhaps Meiklejohn would respond by saying that what is at stake is not a matter of being informed in the narrow sense of possessing all the relevant information. Democratic citizens also need to have the arguments for alternative policies forcefully presented in a way that makes their strengths and weaknesses more apparent, stimulates critical deliberation, and is conducive to the best decision. Surely, it might be asked, when political participation reaches the point where it becomes irrelevant to or even detracts from the possibility of good political decisions, what is the argument in its favor? I will return to this question of the relation between participant and non-participant interests in section five.[9]

Several years ago I put forward a theory of freedom of expression[10] that was very much influenced by Meiklejohn's views. Like him, I wanted to state a principle of freedom of expression which had a kind of absoluteness or at least a partial immunity from balancing against other concerns. But I wanted my theory to be broader than Meiklejohn's. I wanted it to cover more than just political speech, and I thought it should give independent significance to participant and audience interests. The basis of my theory was a single, audience-related principle applying to all categories of expression.

The Millian Principle:
There are certain harms which, although they would not occur but for certain acts of expression, nonetheless cannot be taken as part of a justification for legal restrictions on these acts. These harms are: (a) harms to certain individuals which consist in their coming to have false beliefs as a result of those acts

of expression; (b) harmful consequences of acts performed as a result of those acts of expression, where the connection between the acts of expression and the subsequent harmful acts consists merely in the fact that the act of expression led the agents to believe (or increased their tendency to believe) these acts to be worth performing.[11]

I undertook to defend this principle by showing it to be a consequence of a particular idea about the limits of legitimate political authority: namely, that the legitimate powers of government are limited to those that can be defended on grounds compatible with the autonomy of its citizens—compatible, that is, with the idea that each citizen is sovereign in deciding what to believe and in weighing reasons for action.[12] This can be seen as a generalized version of Meiklejohn's idea of the political responsibility of democratic citizens.

The Millian Principle was intended to rule out the arguments for censorship to which Mill and Meiklejohn were responding. It did this by ruling that the harmful consequences to which these arguments appeal cannot count as potential justifications for legal restriction of expression. But there are other ways to arrive at policies that would strike us as incompatible with freedom of expression. One such way would be to restrict expression excessively, simply on the ground that it is a nuisance or has other undesirable consequences of a kind that the Millian Principle does allow to be weighed. So the second component in a theory of the type I described counters "excessive" restriction of this type by specifying that participant and audience interests in expression are to receive high values when they are balanced against competing goods. (As I have indicated, these values vary from one type of expression to another.) But freedom of expression does not only require that there should be "enough" expression. The two further components of the theory require that the goods of expression (for both participants and audiences) should be distributed in ways that are in accord both with the general requirements of distributive justice and with whatever particular rights there may be, such as rights to

political participation, that support claims for access to means of expression.

This theory identifies the Millian Principle as the only principle concerned specifically with *expression* (as opposed to a general principle of justice) that applies with the same force to all categories of expression. If correct, then, it would answer one of the questions with which I began.[13] But is it correct? I now think that it is not.[14]

To begin with, the Millian Principle has what seems to be implausible consequences in some cases. For example, it is hard to see how laws against deceptive advertising or restrictions such as the ban on cigarette advertising on television could be squared with this principle. There are, of course, ways in which these objections might be answered. Perhaps the policies in question are simply violations of freedom of expression. If, on the other hand, they are acceptable this is because they are examples of justified paternalism, and my original theory did allow for the Millian Principle to be set aside in such cases.[15] But the theory provided for this exception only in cases of severely diminished rationality, because it took the view that any policy justified on grounds violating the Millian Principle would constitute paternalism of a particularly strong form.[16] The advertising cases seem to be clear counterexamples to this latter claim. More generally, clause (a) of the Millian Principle, taken as a limitation that can be set aside only in cases where our rational capacities are severely diminished, constitutes a rejection of paternalism that is too strong and too sweeping to be plausible. An acceptable doctrine of justified paternalism must take into account such factors as the value attached to being able to make one's own decisions, as well as the costs of so doing and the risks of empowering the government to make them on one's behalf. As the advertising examples show, these factors vary from case to case even where no general loss of rational capacities has occurred.

But the problems of the Millian Principle are not limited to cases of justified paternalism. The principle is appealing because it protects important audience interests—interests in deciding for one's self what to believe and what reasons to act on. As I have remarked earlier, these interests depend not only on freedom of expression, but also on other forms of access to information, education, and so on. Consideration of these other measures shows that there are in general limits to the sacrifices we are willing to make to enhance our decision-making capacity. Additional information is sometimes not worth the cost of getting it. The Millian Principle allows some of the costs of free expression to be weighed against its benefits, but holds that two important classes of costs must be ignored. Why should we be willing to bear unlimited costs to allow expression to flourish provided that the costs are of these particular kinds? Here it should be borne in mind that the Millian Principle is a restriction on the authority of legitimate governments. Now it may well be that, as I would argue, there is *some* restriction of this kind on the costs that governments may take as grounds for restricting expression, and that this is so because such a restriction is a safeguard that is more than worth the costs involved. But an argument for this conclusion, if it is to avoid the charge of arbitrariness and provide a convincing account of the exact form that the restriction takes, must itself be based on a full consideration of all the relevant costs.

What these objections mainly point to, then, is a basic flaw in the argument I offered to justify the Millian Principle. There are many ways in which the appealing, but notoriously vague and slippery notion of individual autonomy can be invoked in political argument. One way is to take autonomy, understood as the actual ability to exercise independent rational judgment, as a good to be promoted. Referring to "autonomy" in this sense is a vague, somewhat grandiloquent and perhaps misleading way of referring to some of the most important audience interests described in section two. The intuitive arguments I have offered in the present section appeal to the value of autonomy in this sense. These audience interests were also taken into account in the second component of my earlier theory. My argument for the Millian Principle, on the other hand, employed the idea of autonomy in a different

way, namely as a constraint on justifications of authority. Such justifications, it was held, must be compatible with the thesis that citizens are equal, autonomous rational agents.[17]

The idea of such a constraint now seems to me mistaken. Its appeal derives entirely from the value of autonomy in the first sense, that is, from the importance of protecting central audience interests. To build these interests in at the outset as constraints on the process of justification gives theoretical form to the intuition that freedom of expression is based on considerations that cannot simply be outweighed by competing interests in the manner that "clear and present danger" or "pure balancing" theories of the First Amendment would allow. But to build these audience interests into the theory in this way has the effect of assigning them greater and more constant weight than we in fact give them. Moreover, it prevents us from even asking whether these interests might in some cases be better advanced if we could shield ourselves from some influences. In order to meet the objections raised to the Millian Principle, it is necessary to answer such questions, and, in general, to take account of the variations in audience interests under varying circumstances. But this is not possible within the framework of the argument I advanced.

Most of the consequences of the Millian Principle are ones that I would still endorse. In particular, I still think that it is legitimate for the government to promote our personal safety by restricting information about how to make your own nerve gas,[18] but not legitimate for it to promote our safety by stopping political agitation which could, if unchecked, lead to widespread social conflict. I do not think that my judgment in the latter case rests simply on the difficulty of predicting such consequences or on the idea that the bad consequences of allowing political controversy will in each such case be outweighed by the good. But I do not think that the difference between the two cases can be found in the distinction between restricting means and restricting reasons, as my original article suggested. The difference is rather that where political issues are involved governments are notoriously partisan and unreliable. Therefore, giving government the authority to make policy by balancing interests in such cases presents a serious threat to particularly important participant and audience interests. To the degree that the considerations of safety involved in the first case are clear and serious, and the participant and audience interests that might suffer from restriction are not significant, regulation could be acceptable.

In this way of looking at things, political speech stands out as a distinctively important category of expression. Meiklejohn's mistake, I think, was to suppose that the differences in degree between this category and others mark the boundaries of First Amendment theory. My mistake, on the other hand, was that in an effort to generalize Meiklejohn's theory beyond the category of political speech, I took what were in effect features particular to this category and presented them, under the heading of autonomy, as a priori constraints on justifications of legitimate authority.

In order to avoid such mistakes it is useful to distinguish several different levels of argument. At one extreme is what might be called the "level of policy," at which we might consider the overall desirability or undesirability of a particular action or policy, *e.g.,* an ordinance affecting expression. At the other extreme is what might be called the "foundational level." Argument at this level is concerned with identifying the ultimate sources of justification relevant to the subject at hand. In the case of expression, these are the relevant participant, audience, and bystander interests and the requirements of distributive justice applicable to their satisfaction. Intermediate between these levels is the "level of rights."[19] The question at this level is what limitations and requirements, if any, must be imposed on policy decisions if we are to avoid results that would be unacceptable with respect to the considerations that are defined at the fundamental level? To claim that something is a right, then, is to claim that some limit or requirement on policy decisions is *necessary* if unacceptable results are to be avoided, and that this particular limit or requirement is a *feasible* one, that is, that its acceptance provides adequate protection against such results and does so at

tolerable cost to other interests. Thus, for example, to claim that a particular restriction on searches and seizures is part of a right of privacy would be to claim that it is a feasible form of necessary protection for our important and legitimate interests in being free from unwanted observation and intrusion. What rights there are in a given social setting at a given time depends on which judgments of necessity and feasibility are true at that place and time.[20] This will depend on the nature of the main threats to the interests in question, on the presence or absence of factors tending to promote unequal distribution of the means to their satisfaction, and particularly on the characteristics of the agents (private individuals or governments) who make the relevant policy decisions: what power do they have, and how are they likely to use this power in the absence of constraints?

Most of us believe that freedom of expression is a right. That is, we believe that limits on the power of governments to regulate expression are necessary to protect our central interests as audiences and participants, and we believe that such limits are not incompatible with a healthy society and a stable political order. Hundreds of years of political history support these beliefs. There is less agreement as to exactly how this right is to be understood—what limits and requirements on decision making authority are necessary and feasible as ways of protecting central participant and audience interests and insuring the required equity in the access to means of expression. This is less than surprising, particularly given the fact that the answer to this question changes, sometimes rapidly, as conditions change. Some threats are constant—for example the tendency of governments to block the expression of critical views—and these correspond to points of general agreement in the definition of the right. But as new threats arise—from, for example, changes in the form or ownership of dominant means of communication—it may be unclear, and a matter subject to reasonable disagreement, how best to refine the right in order to provide the relevant kinds of protection at a tolerable cost. This disagreement is partly empirical—a disagreement about what is likely to happen if certain powers are or are not granted to governments. It is also in part a disagreement at the foundational level over the nature and importance of audience and participant interests and, especially, over what constitutes a sufficiently equal distribution of the means to their satisfaction. The main role of a philosophic theory of freedom of expression, in addition to clarifying what it is we are arguing about, is to attempt to resolve these foundational issues.

What reasons are there for taking this view of rights in general and of freedom of expression in particular? One reason is that it can account for much of what we in fact believe about rights and can explain what we do in the process of defending and interpreting them. A second reason is that its account of the bases of rights appears to exhaust the relevant concerns: if a form of regulation of expression presents no threat to the interests I have enumerated, nor to the equitable distribution of the means to their satisfaction, what further ground might there be to reject it as violating freedom of expression? Beyond these two reasons, all I can do in defense of my view is to ask, what else? If rights are not instrumental in the way I have described, what are they and what are the reasons for taking them seriously?

Categories

Let me distinguish two ways in which arguments about freedom of expression may involve distinctions between categories of expression. First, not every participant or audience interest is capable of exerting the same upward pressure on the costs freedom of expression requires us to bear. Freedom of expression often requires that a particular form of expression—leafletting or demonstrations near public buildings—be allowed despite high bystander costs because important participant or audience interests would otherwise be inadequately or unequally served. Such arguments are clearly category-dependent: their force depends on the importance of the particular participant or audience interests in question. But, once it is concluded on the basis of such an argument that a given mode of ex-

pression must be permitted, there is the further question whether its use must be permitted for any form of expression or whether it may be restricted to those types of expression whose value was the basis for claiming that this mode of expression must be allowed. If the latter, then not only will categories of interests be assigned different weights in arguments about the content of the right of freedom of expression, but the application of this right to particular cases will also involve determining the category to which the acts in question belong. I will refer to these two forms of categorization as, respectively, categories of interests and categories of acts.

This distinction can be illustrated by considering the ways in which "political speech" can serve as a category. For the purposes of this discussion, I will assume that "political" is to be interpreted narrowly as meaning, roughly, "having to do with the electoral process and the activities of government." We can distinguish a category of interests in expression that are political in this sense, including both participant interests in taking part in the political process and audience (and bystander) interests in the spread of information and discussion about political topics. As a category of acts, on the other hand, "political speech" might be distinguished[21] either by participant intent— expression with a political purpose—or by content and effect—expression that concerns political issues or contributes to the understanding of political issues. These two definitions correspond, roughly, to the two sets of interests just mentioned. I will assume for the moment that the category of political speech is to be understood to include acts falling under either of these definitions.

While the political interests in expression are not uniquely important, the fact that they are inadequately or very unequally served constitutes a strong reason for enlarging or improving available modes of expression. Their particular importance as a source of upward pressure is something that rational argument about freedom of expression must recognize. Must "political speech" be recognized as a category of acts as well? That is, can the fact that an act of expression has the relevant political intent or content exempt it from regulation that would otherwise be compatible with freedom of expression?

Special standards for defamation applicable to expression concerning "public officials," "public figures," or "public issues"[22] indicate that something like "political speech" does function as a category of acts in the current legal understanding of freedom of expression. Reflection on the *Skokie* case may also suggest that "political speech" has a special place in our intuitive understanding of this right. It seems unlikely that expression so deeply offensive to bystanders would be deemed to be protected by freedom of expression if it did not have a political character—if, for example, its purpose had been merely to provide entertainment or to promote commerce. But I do not see how this interpretation of freedom of expression can be defended, at least unless "political" is understood in a very broad sense in which any important and controversial question counts as a "political issue." Expression that is political in the narrow sense is both important and in need of protection, but it is not unique in either respect. Furthermore, even if "political" is understood broadly, the idea that access to a mode of expression can be made to depend on official determination of the "political" nature of one's purposes or one's message does not sit comfortably with the basic ideas of freedom of expression.

This suggests a second, more plausible analysis of the *Skokie* case, one which relies more heavily on categories of interests and less on categories of acts. The judgment that the Nazi march is protected may reflect the view that no[23] ordinance giving local authorities the power to ban such a march could give adequate protection to central interests in political expression. This argument avoids any judgment as to whether the content and purposes of this particular march were "genuinely political." It relies instead on the judgment that such a march could not be effectively and reliably distinguished from political expression that it is essential to protect.

The distinction between categories of interests and categories of acts can be used to explain some of the ambivalence about categories

noted at the beginning of this article. Reference to categories of interests is both important and unavoidable in arguments about freedom of expression. Categories of acts may also be unavoidable—"expression" is itself such a category, and assault, for example, is distinguished from it on the basis of participant intent—but there are good reasons for being wary of categories of acts and for keeping their use to a minimum. Even where there is agreement on the relative importance of various interests in expression, the purposes and content of a given expressive act can be a matter of controversy and likely misinterpretation, particularly in those situations of intense conflict and mistrust in which freedom of expression is most important. (Well-known difficulties in the application of laws against incitement are a good illustration of this point.) Thus the belief that the fundamental principles of freedom of expression must transcend categories derives in part from the recognition that categories of acts rest on distinctions—of intent and content—that a partisan of freedom of expression will instinctively view with suspicion. Nonetheless, in interpreting freedom of expression, we are constantly drawn toward categories of acts as we search for ways of protecting central interests in expression while avoiding unacceptable costs. The current struggle to define the scope of special standards of defamation[24] is a good example of this process. Identifying the categories of acts that can actually be relied upon to give the protection we want is a matter of practical and strategic judgment, not of philosophical theory.

I have mentioned the possibility of official misapplication as one reason for avoiding categories of acts, but this is not the only problem. A second difficulty is the fact that it is extremely difficult to regulate one category of speech without restricting others as well. Here the recent campaign financing law is an instructive example.[25] The basic aim of restricting money spent during a campaign in order to increase the fairness of this particular competition is entirely compatible with freedom of expression. The problem is that in order to regulate spending effectively, it was deemed necessary to make campaign funds flow through a single committee for each candidate. In order to do this a low limit was placed on the amount any private person or group could spend on expression to influence the campaign. But since spending on expression to influence a campaign cannot be clearly separated from expression on political topics generally, the limit on private spending constituted an unacceptable restriction on expression. Limits on spending for "campaign speech" are in principle as compatible with freedom of expression as limits on the length of speeches in a town meeting: both are acceptable when they enhance the fairness of the proceedings. Unlike a town meeting, however, "campaign speech" is not easily separated from other expression on political topics, hence not easily regulated in a way that leaves this other expression unaffected.

In addition to the difficulty of regulating one category without affecting others, there is the further problem that the categories within which special regulation is held to be permissible may themselves suffer from dangerous overbreadth. I believe that this is true, for example, of the category of commercial speech. Presumably "commercial speech" is to be defined with reference to participant intent: expression by a participant in the market for the purpose of attracting buyers or sellers. It is not identical with advertising, which can serve a wide variety of expressive purposes, and it cannot be defined by its subject matter: *Consumer Reports* has the same subject matter as much commercial speech, but it is entitled to "full" First Amendment protection. Why, then, would anyone take commercial speech to be subject to restrictions that would not be acceptable if applied to other forms of expression? This view is widely held, or has been until recently,[26] and it appears to be supported by the acceptability of laws against false or deceptive advertising, the regulation of cigarette advertising and restriction on the form of classified advertisements of employment opportunities. One reason for this attitude may be that the participant and audience interests at stake in commercial speech—promoting one's business, learning what is available in the market—are not generally perceived as standing in

much danger from overrestriction. There is, we are inclined to think, plenty of opportunity for advertising, and we are in no danger of being deprived of needed information if advertising is restricted. In fact, the relevant audience interests are in much more danger from excessive exposure to advertising, and from false and deceptive advertising. In addition, laws against such advertising seem acceptable in a way that analogous laws against false or deceptive political or religious claims would not be, first because there are reasonably clear and objective criteria of truth in this area, and second, we regard the government as much less partisan in the competition between commercial firms than in the struggle between religious or political views.

Much of this is no doubt true, but it does not support the generalization that commercial speech as a category is subject to less stringent requirements of freedom of expression. The restrictions I have mentioned, where they seem justified, can be supported by arguments that are applicable in principle to other forms of expression (for example, by appeals to qualified paternalism, or to the advantages for audiences of protection against an excessive volume of expression). It is a mistake to think that these arguments are applicable only to commercial speech or that all commercial speech is especially vulnerable to them. In particular, if, as I believe, the assumption that governments are relatively neutral and trustworthy in this area is one reason for our complacent attitude toward regulation of commercial speech, this assumption should be made explicit and treated with care. There are many cases that clearly count as commercial speech in which our traditional suspicions of governmental regulation of expression are as fully justified as they are elsewhere. One such example might be an advertising battle between established energy companies and anti-establishment commercial enterprises promoting alternative energy sources.[27]

Pornography

In this final section I will consider the category of pornography. This example will illustrate both the problems of categories, just discussed, and some of the problems concerning participant and audience interests that were discussed in section two above.

The question to ask about pornography is, why restrict it? I will consider two answers. The first appeals to the interest people have in not being unwillingly exposed to offensive material. By offense, I do not mean a reaction grounded in disapproval but an immediate discomfort analogous to pain, fear, or acute embarrassment. I am willing to assume for purposes of argument that many people do have such a reaction to some sexual material, and that we should take seriously their interest in being protected against it. I also agree that what offends most people will differ from place to place depending on experience and custom. Therefore the appropriate standards of protection may also vary. But if this were the only reason for restricting pornography the problem would have an easy solution: restrict what can be displayed on the public streets or otherwise forced on an unwilling audience but place no restrictions whatever on what can be shown in theaters, printed in books, or sent through the mails in plain brown wrappers. The only further requirement is that the inconvenience occasioned by the need to separate the two groups should be fairly shared between them.

The idea that this solution should be acceptable to all concerned rests on specific assumptions about the interests involved. It is assumed that consumers of pornography desire private enjoyment, that sellers want to profit from selling to those who have this desire, and that other people want to avoid being forced to see or hear what they regard as offensive. Rarely will one find three sets of interests that are so easily made compatible. There are of course certain other interests which are left out of this account. Perhaps some people want to enjoy pornography in public; their pleasure depends on the knowledge that they are disturbing other people. Also, sellers may want to reach a larger audience in order to increase profits, so they would like to use more stimulating advertisements. Finally, those who wish to restrict pornography may be offended not only by the sight of it but even by the knowledge that some people are enjoying it out of their sight; they will be undisturbed only if it is stopped. But none of these interests has significant weight. There is, to be sure, a general problem of explaining what makes some interests important and others, like these, less significant; but this is not a problem peculiar to freedom of expression.

Unfortunately, offense is not the only reason to restrict pornography. The main reason, I think, is the belief that the availability, enjoyment, and even the legality of pornography will contribute to undesirable changes in our attitudes toward sex and in our sexual mores. We all care deeply about the character of the society in which we will live and raise our children. This interest cannot be simply dismissed as trivial or illegitimate. Nor can we dismiss as empirically implausible the belief that the evolution of sexual attitudes and mores is strongly influenced by the books and movies that are generally available and widely discussed, in the way that we can dismiss the belief that pornography leads to rape. Of course, expression is not the only thing that can influence society in these ways. This argument against pornography has essentially the same form as well-known arguments in favor of restricting non-standard sexual conduct.[28] If the interest to which these arguments appeal is, as I have conceded, a legitimate one, how can the arguments be answered?

I think that transactions "between consenting adults" can sometimes legitimately be restricted on the ground that, were such transactions to take place freely, social expectations would change, people's motives would be altered, and valued social practices would as a result become unstable and decline. I think, for example, that some commercial transactions might legitimately be restricted on such grounds. Thus Richard Titmuss,[29] opposing legalization of blood sales in Britain, claims that the availability of blood on a commercial basis weakens people's sense of interdependence and leads to a general decline in altruistic motivation. Assuming for the purposes of argument that this empirical claim is correct, I am inclined to think that there is no objection to admitting this as a reason for making the sale of blood illegal. To ban blood sales for this reason seems at first to be objectionable because it represents an attempt by the state to maintain a certain state of mind in the population. What is objectionable about many such attempts, which violate freedom of expression, is that they seek to prevent changes of mind by preventing people from considering and weighing possible reasons for changing their minds. Such interventions run contrary to important audience interests. As far as I can see, however, the presence of a market in blood does not put us in a better position to decide how altruistic we wish to be.

There are of course other objections to outlawing the sale of blood, objections based simply on the value of the opportunity that is foreclosed. Being deprived of the opportunity to sell one's blood does not seem to me much of a loss. In the case of proposed restrictions on deviant sexual conduct, however, the analogous costs to the individuals who would be restricted are severe—too severe to be justified by the considerations advanced on the other side. In fact, the argument for restriction seems virtually self-contradictory on this score. What is the legitimate interest that people have in the way their social mores evolve? It is in large part the legitimate interest they have in not being under pressure to conform to practices they find repugnant under pain of being thought odd and perhaps treated as an outcast. But just this interest is violated in an even more direct way by laws against homosexual conduct.

The case for restricting pornography might be answered in part by a similar argument, but there is also a further issue, more intrinsic to the question of freedom of expression. Once it is conceded that we all have legitimate and conflicting interests in the evolution of social attitudes and mores, the question arises how this conflict can fairly be resolved. In particular, is majority vote a fair solution? Can the majority be empowered to preserve attitudes they like by restricting expression that would promote change? The answer to this question is clearly no. One reason is that, as Meiklejohn would emphasize, the legitimacy of majoritarian political processes themselves depends

upon the assumption that the voters have free access to information and are free to attempt to persuade and convince each other. Another reason is that, unlike a decision where to build a road, this is an issue that need not be resolved by a clear decision at any one time. There is hence no justification for allowing a majority to squeeze out and silence a minority. A fair alternative procedure is available: a continuing process of "informal politics" in which the opposing groups attempt to alter or to preserve the social consensus through persuasion and example.

This response to the argument for restricting pornography has several consequences. First, since it rests upon viewing public interaction under conditions of freedom of expression as an informal political process that is preferable to majority voting as a way of deciding certain important questions, the response is convincing only if we can argue that the process is in fact fair. It will not be if, for example, access to the main means of expression, and hence the ability to have an influence on the course of public debate, are very unequally distributed in the society. Thus, equity in the satisfaction of participant interests, discussed above as one goal of freedom of expression, arises here in a new way as part of a defense of freedom of expression against majority control.

A second consequence of the argument is that time, place, and manner restrictions on obscene material, which at first seemed a satisfactory solution to the problem of offense, are no longer so obviously satisfactory. Their appeal as a solution rested on the supposition that, since the interests of consumers and sellers of pornography were either purely private or simply commercial, unwilling audiences were entitled to virtually complete protection, the only residual problem being the relatively trivial one of how to apportion fairly the inconvenience resulting from the need to shield the two groups from each other. But if what the partisans of pornography are entitled to (and what the restrictors are trying to deny them) is a fair opportunity to influence the sexual mores of the society, then it seems that they, like participants in political speech in the narrow sense,[30] are entitled to at least a certain degree of access even to unwilling audiences. I do not find this conclusion a particularly welcome one, but it seems to me difficult to avoid once the most important arguments against pornography are taken seriously. Let me conclude by considering several possible responses.

The argument I have presented starts from the high value to be assigned to the participant interest in being able to influence the evolution of attitudes and mores in one's society. But while some publishers of "obscene" materials have this kind of crusading intent, undoubtedly many others do not. Perhaps the proper conclusion of my argument is not that any attempt to publish and disseminate offensive sexual material is entitled to full First Amendment protection but, at most, that such protection can be claimed where the participant's intent is of the relevant "political" character. This would construe "pornography" as a category of acts in the sense defined above: sexually offensive expression in the public forum need not be allowed where the intent is merely that of the pornographer—who aims only to appeal to a prurient interest in sex—but must be allowed where the participant has a "serious" interest in changing society. To take "the obscene" as a category of acts subject to extraordinary regulation would involve, on this view, the same kind of overbreadth that is involved when "commercial speech" is seen as such a category. In each case features typical of at most some instances are taken to justify special treatment of the category as a whole.

As I indicated in [the preceding section] distinctions based on participant intent cannot be avoided altogether in the application of the right of freedom of expression, but they are nearly always suspect. This is particularly so in the present case; expression dealing with sex is particularly likely to be characterized, by those who disapprove of it, as frivolous, unserious, and of interest only to dirty minds. To allow expression in this area to be regulated on the basis of participant intent would be to set aside a normal caution without, as far as I can see, any ground for doing so.

The conclusion that unwilling audiences cannot be fully protected against offensive expression might be avoided in a second way. Even if the "political interest" in expression on sexual topics is an important interest, and even if it supports a right of access to unwilling audiences, there is a further question whether this interest requires the presentation of "offensive" material. Perhaps it would be enough to be entitled to present material that "deals with" the question of sexual mores in a sober and non-offensive manner. Perhaps Larry Flynt and Ralph Ginzburg should, on the one hand, be free to sell as much pornography as they wish for private consumption, and they should on the other hand be free to write newspaper editorials and books, make speeches, or go on television as much as they can to crusade for a sexually liberated society. But the latter activity, insofar as it presses itself on people's attention without warning, is subject to the requirement that it not involve offense.

On the other side, it can be claimed that this argument rests on an overly cognitive and rationalistic idea of how people's attitudes change. Earnest treatises on the virtues of a sexually liberated society can be reliably predicted to have no effect on prevailing attitudes toward sex. What is more likely to have such an effect is for people to discover that they find exciting and attractive portrayals of sex which they formerly thought offensive or, vice versa, that they find boring and offensive what they had expected to find exciting and liberating. How can partisans of sexual change be given a fair chance to make this happen except through a relaxation of restrictions on what can be publicly displayed? I do not assume that the factual claims behind this argument are correct. My question rather is, if they were correct what would follow? From the fact that frequent exposure to material previously thought offensive is a likely way to promote a change in people's attitudes, it does not follow that partisans of change are entitled to use this means. Proponents of a change in attitude are not entitled to use just *any* expressive means to effect their aim even if the given means is the only one that would actually have the effect they desire: audience interests must also be considered. It must be asked whether exposure to these means leads to changes in one's tastes and preferences through a process that is, like sub-liminal advertising, both outside of one's rational control and quite independent of the relevant grounds for preference, or whether, on the contrary, the exposure to such influences is in fact part of the best way to discover what one really has reason to prefer. I think that a crucial question regarding the regulation of pornography and other forms of allegedly corrupting activity lies here.

It is often extremely difficult to distinguish influences whose force is related to relevant grounds for the attitudes they produce from influences that are the work of irrelevant factors. Making this distinction requires, in many cases, a clearer understanding than we have both of the psychological processes through which our attitudes are altered and of the relevant grounds for holding the attitudes in question. The nature of these grounds, in particular, is often a matter of too much controversy to be relied upon in defining a right of freedom of expression. The power to restrict the presentation of "irrelevant influences" seems threatening because it is too easily extended to restrict any expression likely to mislead.

Subliminal advertising is in this respect an unusual case, from which it is hard to generalize. A law against subliminal advertising could be acceptable on First Amendment grounds because it could be framed as a prohibition simply of certain techniques—the use of hidden words or images—thus avoiding controversial distinctions between relevant and irrelevant influences. Where we are concerned with the apparent—as opposed to the hidden—content of expression, however, things become more controversial (even though it is true that what is clearly seen or heard may influence us, and be designed to do so, in ways that we are quite unaware of).

The case for protecting unwilling audiences against influence varies considerably from one kind of offensive expression to another, even within the class of what is generally called pornography. The separation between the way one's attitudes are affected by unwanted exposure to expression and the relevant grounds for forming such attitudes is clearest in the case of pornography involving violence or torture.

The reasons for being opposed to, and revolted by, these forms of behavior are quite independent of the question whether one might, after repeated exposure, come to find them exciting and attractive. This makes it plausible to consider such changes in attitude produced by unchosen exposure to scenes of violence as a kind of harm that an unwilling audience is entitled to protection against.[31] The question is whether this protection can be given without unacceptably restricting other persuasive activity involving scenes of violence, such as protests against war.

The argument for protection of unwilling audiences is much weaker where what is portrayed are mildly unconventional sexual attitudes or practices, not involving violence or domination. Here it is more plausible to say that discovering how one feels about such matters when accustomed to them is the best way of discovering what attitude towards them one has reason to hold. The lack of independent grounds for appraising these attitudes makes it harder to conceive of changes produced by expression as a kind of harm or corruption. Even here there are some independent grounds for appraisal, however.[32] Attitudes towards sex involve attitudes towards other people, and the reasons for or against holding *these* attitudes may be quite independent of one's reactions to portrayals of sex, which are, typically, highly impersonal. I believe that there are such grounds for regarding as undesirable changes in our attitudes towards sex produced by pornography, or for that matter by advertising, and for wanting to be able to avoid them. But, in addition to the problem of separability, just mentioned with regard to portrayals of violence, these grounds may be too close to the substantive issues in dispute to be an acceptable basis for the regulation of expression.

It seems, then, that an argument based on the need to protect unwilling audiences against being influenced could justify restriction of at most some forms of offensive expression. This leaves us with the residual question how much offense must be tolerated in order for persuasion and debate regarding sexual mores to go forward. Here the clearest arguments are by comparison with other categories of expression. The costs that audiences and bystanders are required to bear in order to provide for free political debate are generally quite high. These include very significant psychological costs, as the *Skokie* case indicates. Why should psychological costs of that particular kind occasioned by obscenity be treated differently (or given a particularly high value)? A low cost threshold would be understandable if the issues at stake were trivial ones, but by the would-be restrictors' own account this is not so. I do not find the prospect of increased exposure to offensive expression attractive, but it is difficult to construct a principled argument for restriction that is consistent with our policy towards other forms of expression and takes the most important arguments against pornography seriously.

Notes

*Versions of this paper were presented at the University of Minnesota and the University of California at Berkeley as well as at the Pittsburgh symposium. I am grateful to members of all these audiences for helpful comments. I have also benefited greatly from discussions of this topic with Marshall Cohen, Clark Glymour, and Derek Parfit.

1. Village of Skokie v. National Socialist Party of America, 69 Ill. 2d 605, 373 N.E. 2d 21 (1978).
2. How the existence of an approximate consensus, even though it is only approximate, can contribute to the legitimacy of the agreed-upon values as a basis for justification is a difficult problem which I cannot here discuss.
3. I have assumed here that categories of interests are disrupted by a decrease in consensus and an increase in diversity of views since this is the course of change we are most familiar with. I suppose that the reverse process—in which increasing consensus makes an abstract category seem pointlessly abstract and leads to its being redefined to include what was before only a special case—is at least possible. On the former, more familiar kind of transition, see E. Durkheim, "Individualism and the Intellectuals," in *Emile Durkheim on Morality and Society,* 43 edited by R. Bellah (1973). See also E. Durkheim, *Division of Labor in Society,* translated by G. Simpson (1933). Perhaps Marx's view of the transition to a socialist society includes an instance of the latter kind.
4. Here libel provides a good example. One reason for assigning it low status as a category of expressive acts is the low value attached to the participant interest in insulating people and damaging their reputations. This is something we sometimes want to do, but it gets low weight in our social calculus.

Another reason is the high value we attach to not having our reputations damaged. These are not unrelated, but they do not motivate concern with the same class of actions. Other relevant considerations include the interest we may have in performing or having others perform acts which incidentally damage reputations. A defensible definition of libel as a category of expressive acts will be some resultant of all these factors, not simply of the first or the second alone.

5. J. Mill, *On Liberty,* ch. 2, ed. C. Shields (1956).
6. Here I am indebted to the discussion following the presentation of this paper at Berkeley and to comments by members of my graduate seminar for the spring term 1979.
7. J. Mill, *On Liberty,*
8. A. Meiklejohn, *Political Freedom* (1960).
9. Ibid., pp. 32–34 *infra.*
10. Scanlon, *A Theory of Freedom of Expression, Philosophy & Public Affairs* 1, no. 204 (1972).
11. Ibid., p. 213.
12. Ibid., p. 215.
13. See p. 140 *supra.*
14. In what follows I am indebted to a number of criticisms, particularly to objections raised by Robert Amdur and by Gerald Dworkin.
15. Scanlon, *Theory,* p. 220.
16. Ibid., p. 221.
17. Ibid., p. 215.
18. Ibid., p. 211–13.
19. For a presentation of this view at greater length, see Scanlon, "Rights, Goals and Fairness," in *Public and Private Morality,* edited by S. Hampshire (1978).
20. Of course there may be multiple solutions to the problem; that is, different ways in which a right might be defined to give adequate protection to the interests in question. In such a case what there is a right to initially is *some* protection of the relevant kind. At this point the right is incompletely defined. Once one adequate form of protection becomes established as a constraint on policy making, the other alternatives are no longer *necessary* in the relevant sense. In this respect our rights are partly determined by convention.
21. Distinguished, that is, from other forms of protected expression. I am concerned here only with what marks speech as political. A full definition of "political speech" (i.e. permissible political expression) would, in order to exclude such things as bombings, take into account features other than those mentioned here. See note 4 *supra.*
22. See the line of cases following New York Times Co. v. Sullivan, 376 U.S. 254 (1964). See, e.g., Curtis Publishing Co. v. Butts, 388 U.S. 130 (1967); Gertz v. Robert Welch, Inc., 418 U.S. 323 (1974); Herbert v. Lando, 99 S.Ct. 1635 (1979); Hutchinson v. Proxmire, 99 S.Ct. 2675 (1979).
23. Of course an actual decision need only find a particular ordinance unconstitutional. I take it, however, that an intuitive judgment that an action is

protected by freedom of expression is broader than this and implies that *no* acceptable ordinance could restrict that action.

24. See cases cited note 22 *supra.*

25. Buckley v. Valeo, 424 U.S. 1 (1976). Federal Election Campaign Act of 1971, Pub. L. No. 92-225, 86 Stat. 3 (1972), as amended by Federal Election Campaign Act Amendments of 1974, Pub. L. No. 93-443, 88 Stat. 1263 (1974), as amended by Federal Election Campaign Act Amendments of 1976, Pub. L. No. 94-283, 90 Stat. 475 (1976).

26. See Bates v. State Bar of Arizona, 433 U.S. 350 (1977) *reh. denied* 434 U.S. 881 (1977); Virginia Pharmacy Bd. v. Virginia Consumer Council, 425 U.S. 748 (1976).

27. It might be claimed that insofar as this example has the character I mention it is an instance of political, not merely commercial, speech. Certainly it does have a political element. Nonetheless, the intentions of the participants (and the interests of audiences) may be thoroughly commercial. The political element of the controversy triggers First Amendment reactions because it raises the threat of partisan regulation, not because the interests at stake, on the part of either participants or audience, are political.

28. See Devlin, The Enforcement of Morals (1965).

29. R. Titmuss, *The Gift Relationship,* chs. 13–15 (1971). See also Singer, "Altruism and Commerce," *Philosophy & Public Affairs* 2, no. 312 (1973).

30. Perhaps Meiklejohn would defend "offensive" discussion of sexual topics in a similar fashion, construing it as a form of political speech. Several differences should be noted, however. First, my argument appeals to participant interests rather than to the audience interests Meiklejohn emphasizes. Second, the politics I am concerned with here is an informal process distinct from the formal democratic institutions he seems to have in mind. Par-

ticipation in this informal process is not important merely as a preliminary to making decisions in one's offical capacity as a citizen. But even if Meiklejohn would not construe the political role of citizens this narrowly, a further difference remains. Having an influence on the evolving mores of one's society is, in my view, only one important participant interest among many, and I would not make the validity of all First Amendment claims depend on their importance for our role in politics of either the formal or the informal sort. It is true, however, that those ideas controversial enough to be in greatest need of First Amendment protection are likely also to be the subject of politics in one or both of these senses. See note 27 *supra.*

31. Prohibiting the display of such scenes for willing audiences is a separate question. So is their presentation to children. Here and throughout this article I am concerned only with adults.

32. Here the moral status of attitudes and practices may become relevant. Moral considerations have been surprisingly absent from the main arguments for restricting pornography considered in this section: the notion of offense quite explicitly abstracts from moral appraisal, and the importance of being able to influence the future mores of one's society does not depend on the assumption that one's concern with these mores is based in morality. A person can have a serious and legitimate interest in preserving (or eliminating) certain customs even if these are matters of no *moral* significance. But morality is relevant to the argument for audience protection since, if sexual attitudes are a matter of morality, this indicates that they can be appraised on grounds that are independent of subjective reaction, thus providing a possible basis for claiming that a person who has come to have a certain attitude (and to be content with having it) has been made worse off.

Liberty and Harm to Others

DAVID LYONS

This paper is part of an extended program of research with two aims: to understand Mill's moral and political philosophy, and to develop a utilitarian doctrine in its most plausible or least vulnerable form, in order to identify what, if anything, may reasonably be said for or against utilitarianism as a general type of doctrine. These aims fit together because I have found when trying to interpret Mill that he suggests lines of development somewhat different and in some ways more promising than the usual versions of utilitarianism.

The Principle of Liberty is not a simple corollary of utilitarianism, and Mill argues for it. I am not concerned with his arguments for it, however, so much as I am with his applications of it, since they tell us how it is to be understood. The Principle of Liberty is like a Principle of Utility in that nonmoral conditions involving human welfare are given as justifying conduct. But the Principle of Liberty is narrower than a Principle of Utility, in at least two ways: it concerns harms to others, not welfare generally, and it concerns coercive intervention, not action generally.

Discussions of the Principle of Liberty often seem to get off on the wrong foot and to lack the scholarly charity that we usually confer on philosophical writing that is considered worth reading. I hope to rectify that sort of error here. I hope to show that the Principle of Liberty is

more acceptable than it might otherwise seem, though I do not pretend to offer an unqualified defense of it.

I. Mill's Principle

Mill's Principle of Liberty asserts

that the sole end for which mankind are warranted, individually or collectively, in interfering with the liberty of action of any of their number is self-protection. That the only purpose for which power can be rightfully exercised over any member of a civilized community, against his will, is to prevent harm to others. [I,9][1]

The prevention of harm to others is regarded by Mill as a good reason, and the only good reason, for "compulsion and control" of the individual, or, in other words, for the direction of behavior by threats, penalties, and force. [I,9]

In the course of his initial presentation of this principle, Mill offers some examples of interference it would allow. He begins with the obvious case: "If anyone does an act hurtful to others, there is a prima facie case for punishing him by law or, where legal penalties are not safely applicable, by general disapprobation." [I,11] Not all such conduct should be prohibited, since there can be overriding reasons against doing so. Sometimes, for example,

David Lyons, "Liberty and Harm to Others," from *Canadian Journal of Philosophy,* Suppl. Vol. V (1980). Copyright © 1980 by the Canadian Association for Publishing in Philosophy. Reprinted by permission of the author and publisher.

"the attempt to exercise control would produce other evils, greater than those which it would prevent." [I,11] This suggests that coercive regulations are required by Mill not just to prevent harm, but to do so efficiently or economically. In any case, conduct that is harmful to others is clearly subject to control under Mill's principle. And one must suppose that the same is true of conduct that threatens to cause harm—reckless driving, say, as well as bodily assault.

But Mill does not stop there. The passage continues with other examples of justified "compulsion and control." Mill says:

There are also many positive acts for the benefit of others which he may rightfully be compelled to perform, such as to give evidence in a court of justice, to bear his fair share in the common defense or in any other joint work necessary to the interest of the society of which he enjoys the protection, and to perform certain acts of individual beneficence, such as saving a fellow creature's life or interposing to protect the defenseless against ill-usage—things which whenever it is obviously a man's duty to do he may rightfully be made responsible to society for not doing. [I,11]

I shall refer to these examples by saying that, in Mill's view, one may legitimately be required (at least in certain circumstances) to co-operate in joint undertakings and to act as a good samaritan.

These examples are presented by Mill as coercive requirements that would be permitted by his principle. D. G. Brown has argued, however, that they clash with it instead; and, partly for this reason, he has suggested that the Principle of Liberty is untenable.[2] Brown believes

that we have duties to help other people which go beyond the avoidance of harming them; that the performance of such duties can legitimately be extracted from us, very commonly in our roles as citizens and taxpayers; and that such exactions are not permitted by Mill's main principle. (p. 158)[3]

Brown reasons in this way because he believes that Mill's Principle of Liberty does not allow interference unless the conduct that is interfered with can itself be considered harmful to other persons.[4] Such a principle would allow restrictions against bodily assault and reckless driving, for example, but it would not sanction either cooperation or good samaritan requirements.

Brown's interpretation of Mill is important because it forms part of a systematic study of Mill's doctrines, developed with reasonable charity. Brown furthermore avoids two errors that are commonly found in commentaries on Mill. He does not assume without question the textbook reading of Mill as an "act utilitarian," as one who holds that our sole or overriding moral obligation is to maximize utility. And he does not allow his interpretation of Mill's Principle of Liberty to get bogged down in discussions of Mill's distinction between "self-regarding" conduct (a term used by Mill) and "other-regarding" conduct (a term not even used by him). Brown proceeds, more usefully, to consider Mill's actual statement of the Principle as well as his substantive applications of it. I believe, however, that Brown is mistaken about Mill's view on several important points, and I shall here defend a different reading of the Principle of Liberty.

On the reading I propose, freedom may be limited only for the purpose of preventing harm to other persons, but the conduct that is interfered with need not itself be considered harmful or dangerous to others. Such a principle both conforms to Mill's definitive statement and accommodates his examples. The cooperation and good samaritan requirements that Mill refers to could not be justified on the ground that they prevent conduct that causes harm to others; but it can be argued that such regulations nevertheless work in other ways to prevent harm to others. This version of Mill's principle is one that he could readily endorse. It does justice to his own intentions and stays within the limits of his general position on morality and politics. Most importantly, it seems a more plausible principle than the one that Brown attributes to Mill, and one to be preferred by someone who accepts the idea that harm-prevention justifies "compulsion and control." But I shall stop short of claiming unequivocally that this principle is what Mill must have had in mind. The text suggests that Mill is, in fact, confused about some of the relevant differences between these versions of his Principle of Liberty and fails to face these issues squarely.

My argument proceeds as follows. In Section II I discuss the differences between Brown's version of the principle and mine and show how Mill's examples can be accommodated. In Section III I consider the problem of deciding which version best fits Mill's text. In Section IV I go beyond Brown's argument and deal with other difficulties for the reading I propose, including other reasons for thinking that Mill's own examples cannot be accommodated.

II. Harm-Prevention

Mill's principle, we have seen, allows interference with conduct that is itself harmful or dangerous to others, such as bodily assault and reckless driving. So much is certain. But harm to others can be prevented not just by interfering with acts that can be said to cause, or that threaten to cause, harm to other persons, and the other possibilities are extremely important.

Consider good samaritan requirements. When someone has been injured or is in danger, harm (or further harm) to him might be averted if another person comes to his aid. It makes no difference here what, if anything, can be said to cause the harm or danger. If the Principle of Liberty says flatly (as on my reading it does) that the prevention of harm to others justifies interfering with my liberty, then it might justify interfering with my liberty in this sort of case. I might be required to come to another's aid, in order to prevent harm to him, even if I may not be said to have caused the harm that he will suffer if I should fail to help him when I can. In such cases, it cannot be assumed that someone who fails to help prevent harm can be said to cause the harm. Suppose, for example, that I am in a position to save a drowning man. If I fail to do so, I will have failed to prevent harm to him. But it does not follow that my failure can be said to cause the harm. For, as Brown observes (p. 145), the drowning man may have tried to take his own life or may have been pushed by a third party, in which cases the harm done would not be attributable to me, even though I failed to in-

tervene. In sum, lives can be saved and injuries minimized—harm to others can be prevented—not only by interfering with, preventing, or otherwise suppressing harmful and dangerous conduct but also by requiring or otherwise eliciting helpful, harm-preventing conduct. This would seem to be the very point of one class of Mill's examples, in which we would be required "to perform certain acts of individual beneficence, such as saving a fellow creature's life or interposing to protect the defenseless against ill-usage."

Brown formulates Mill's Principle of Liberty as follows:

(L) The liberty of action of the individual ought prima facie to be interfered with if and only if his conduct is harmful to others. (p. 135)

In other words, there is only one good reason for interfering with a person's conduct, namely, that the conduct is harmful (or dangerous) to others. This may be called *harmful conduct-prevention principle*. It does not allow interference except with conduct that causes (or at least threatens) harms to others. It would not sanction good samaritan requirements.

Mill's definitive statement of his principle is not so restricted. It can be understood to say:

(L*) The prevention of harm to other persons is a good reason, and the only good reason, for restricting behavior.

This may be called a *general harm-prevention principle*. It would not exclude good samaritan requirements. Someone who believes that there may be circumstances in which one may justifiably be required to come to others' aid, even though one is not responsible for their difficulties, should prefer a general harm-prevention principle, like (L*), to a narrower harmful-conduct-prevention principle, like (L).

Another important class of cases is represented by cooperation requirements. Like good samaritan requirements, these would not normally be thought of as interfering with conduct that causes harm to others. But these are unlike good samaritan requirements, and thus warrant separate treatment, because they typically require acts that would not normally be credited, at least in the same direct way, with preventing harm. The prevention of harm to others here is more a function of the requirements themselves or of the patterns of behavior they create. Furthermore, in many such cases, each member of the community stands to benefit from the regulations—oneself as well as others, though only the benefits to others are relevant in justifying restrictions on one's conduct under the Principle of Liberty.

Consider Mill's example of being required to give testimony in court. How is harm prevented here? It is true that giving testimony in compliance with a subpoena can sometimes be credited with preventing harm to others, as when it secures for someone an acquittal against a criminal charge or a successful defense against a damage claim. But it is unlikely that Mill meant or we would want to limit a subpoena rule to just such cases. One would presumably wish it to apply (as it does now), for example, to prosecution witnesses in a criminal proceeding. Compliance with a general subpoena rule can just as readily have the opposite effect upon the individuals who are most directly involved—by securing a conviction, say, or ensuring a successful damage claim. The harm-prevention grounds for such a rule would not be like the case for good samaritan requirements.

If the requirement that one give testimony in court can be justified in harm-prevention terms, it is likely to be by reasoning of the following sort. Courts, though costly and burdensome, are needed to settle and prevent disputes and for an effective system of social regulations. Courts are needed to prevent evils that are worse than the evils they entail. (For simplicity, we should assume that the substantive rules to be enforced can themselves be justified in harm-prevention terms. Otherwise, a harm-prevention defense of court rules and operations would have to be qualified severely.) Various rules are required if courts are to operate effectively. One of these requires persons under certain circumstances to give testimony. It is needed as part of an institution that helps to prevent harm. It might thus be justified on the basis of harm-prevention, even though it cannot plausibly be treated as the prohibition of harmful or dangerous conduct. For the point

of such a rule is not to interfere with conduct that would independently be characterized as harmful or dangerous to others, but is rather to redirect behavior so as to help create a social practice that will help prevent harm.

In this sort of case, the harm to be prevented may well be "public," that is, presumably affecting all the members of a community, neighborhood, or class, at least in the form of danger or insecurity. This means that one may very well stand to benefit from the regulation of one's own behavior. Benefits to oneself are, of course, irrelevant to the justification of a rule under the Principle of Liberty. But, from the fact that the harm is public it follows not only that one stands to benefit but also that others benefit too, and this fact makes it possible to justify such regulations under that principle.

I do not wish to place great emphasis on the distinction between cooperation and good samaritan requirements. In the latter case, it is natural to think of one person's directly helping another by, say, removing him from danger or administering first aid, while in the former case one thinks of behavior within complex institutional settings or of coordination among a number of individuals, where one person's efforts could not possibly prevent the harm in question. But intermediate or mixed cases are clearly possible. For example, the coordinated efforts of a number of persons, perhaps within an institutional setting, may be needed to help a drowning, trapped, injured, or ill person. The contrast between cooperation and good samaritan requirements is useful here chiefly to suggest a variety of ways in which conduct may be regulated to prevent harm to other persons. It is not meant to suggest a sharp dichotomy or an exhaustive catalogue of cases.

It should also be emphasized that we are speaking here only of preventing harm and not of using coercion to promote benefits in general. One might object to the latter while accepting the former. Now, if one is concerned with preventing harm and believes that harm prevention may justify interference with an individual's freedom of action, then one should regard cooperation requirements as important cases. For they may well provide the *only* means of preventing or eliminating some significant harms, such as malnutrition and starvation, emotional disturbances, illness, and disease, vulnerability to attack, homelessness, and so on. In fact, it is difficult to think of major social problems that might be dealt with just by limiting conduct that causes or threatens to cause harm to others. A principle that excluded other ways of preventing or eliminating harm would restrict such efforts very seriously.

Before concluding this part of the discussion, we might consider some examples that Brown himself proposes. He says:

There can be no guarantee that joint works necessary to the interest of society will not include institutional care for the mentally defective, urban redevelopment, or foreign aid to countries whose economic conditions might otherwise lead to war. I cannot see how refusal to co-operate in such efforts toward alleviation of existing problems could be shown to constitute causing harm to others. (p. 146)

The last remark makes clear the context of these examples: Brown is claiming that what I am calling cooperation requirements cannot be reconciled to a harmful conduct prevention principle, that is, to Mill's Principle of Liberty on Brown's reading of it. I grant that point. But now the question arises whether they can be reconciled to a broader harm-prevention principle. The short answer to this question is, it all depends. It is plausible to suppose that foreign aid for the purpose of preventing war could be justified on grounds of harm-prevention; but other examples will depend more clearly on circumstances that are variable. To take one example: urban redevelopment, as I have seen it, in New York City and Boston, could not generally be so justified, since it is often used not to prevent or eliminate harms to others but to provide greater comforts and conveniences for relatively comfortable members of society while it actually undermines the conditions of those who are displaced and ignores their unmet basic needs.

I suggest, therefore, that the general harm-prevention version of the Principle of Liberty is more plausible than the narrower harmful conduct-prevention version. Furthermore, it appears that the former can, while the latter cannot, account for Mill's own examples.

III. Problems of Interpretation

Mill's definitive statement of his Principle of Liberty supports the general harm-prevention reading, since it predicates interference on the prevention of harm to others and does not require that it be limited to the prevention of conduct that causes harm. Mill's own examples seem to accord with a general harm-prevention principle, though they clash with the narrower harmful conduct prevention principle attributed to Mill. Can we then conclude that (L*) is closer than (L) to Mill's evident intentions? Mill does not permit us this luxury.

Brown thinks it clear that Mill means (L) and not (L*). He says, "Mill consistently writes and argues as if he had specified, not that interference with the conduct should prevent harm to others, but rather that the conduct itself should be harmful to others" (p. 135) One cannot deny that Mill's words sometimes imply this and thus support Brown's reading. My purpose in this section is to emphasize that the evidence is equivocal.

I have already offered reasons for the general harm-prevention reading of Mill's principle. Evidence on the other side includes a number of passages which suggest the narrower harmful conduct-prevention principle. For example, in the very paragraph in which Mill gives his definitive statement, he says that, to justify threats or penalties against a person, "the conduct from which it is desired to deter him must be calculated to produce evil to someone else." [I,9] Indeed, his use of the term "self-protection" in the general statement of the principle might be taken as suggesting the narrower reading.

But Brown's reasons for ascribing (L) rather than (L*) to Mill do not end with such evidence. They also turn upon the following line of argument. Immediately after Mill offers his cooperation and good samaritan examples, he says, "A person may cause evil to others not only by his actions but by his inaction, and in either case he is justly accountable to them for the injury." [I,11] This suggests that Mill illicitly regards those requirements as equivalent to prohibitions against conduct that causes harm to others: if one fails to comply with them, one causes harm, not by one's act, but by one's omission, or "inaction." Brown argues that Mill would have no reason to suggest such a thing—to conflate failing to prevent harm with causing harm (by inaction)—unless he wished to assure his readers that the examples do not clash with his principle, which then must be understood to allow interference only with conduct that causes harm to others.

Brown then suggests that Mill is obliged to do this because of his other doctrinal commitments. The one emphasized by Brown is Mill's endorsement of a Principle of Enforcing Morality, which can be understood as follows:

(M) The liberty of action of the individual ought prima facie to be interfered with if and only if his conduct is prima facie morally wrong. (p. 148)

Thus, when Mill accepts a specific duty, he is committed to its enforcement. But Mill's examples represent his acceptance of "duties to help people which go beyond the avoidance of harming them." (p. 158) The result is an uncomfortable predicament for Mill, which he resolves by misdescribing his examples, imagining that they fall within the limits of his Principle of Liberty. Brown concludes that "Mill has achieved consistency at the cost of truth." (p. 133)

The attribution of (L) to Mill thus forms part of a significant systematic interpretation of Mill's doctrines, a scholarly effort to which I cannot do justice here. I must confess I have strong reservations about Brown's claim that "Mill believes in the enforcement of morality," at least as a characterization of Mill's position in *Utilitarianism,* on which Brown relies.[5] But, in any case, Brown cannot defend his reading of Mill's principle by claiming that the Principle of Enforcing Morality accounts for either Mill's examples or the predicament in which, on Brown's interpretation, Mill finds himself; nor can he claim that "Mill has achieved consistency at the cost of truth." The Principle of Enforcing Morality does not tell us what our duties are; it simply commits one who holds it to the enforcement of whatever

duties we happen to have. It is therefore incapable of explaining why Mill believes that we have duties to cooperate in joint undertakings and to act as good samaritans. This is especially embarrassing for Brown's consistency claim. For, on Brown's reading, Mill is committed not just to (L) and (M), which can be understood as compatible,[6] but also to those troublesome examples. Mill's acceptance of the duties to cooperate and to be a good samaritan can be explained in either of two ways. It might rest on some further doctrine (beyond (L) and (M)) or else it might represent Mill's independent moral judgment, in which case it can be thought of as a doctrine in itself. Either way, it clashes, on Brown's account, with (L) and (M). For Mill is seen by Brown as committed (a) to certain "duties to help other people which go beyond the avoidance of harming them" and, (b) by virtue of the Principle of Enforcing Morality, to their enforcement, while (c) their enforcement is incompatible with his Principle of Liberty. On this reconstruction, Mill's position is untenable, and he cannot achieve consistency without a change of doctrine. He does not achieve consistency but merely papers over his embarrassment by misconstruing his own examples, thus sacrificing truth along with consistency. Furthermore, Brown's straightforward exposure of Mill's misdescriptions suggests that Mill exercises a considerable capacity for self-deception. These results are less generous to Mill than Brown may well intend. In any case, they should lead us to investigate alternative interpretations of Mill's doctrines.

On my account, no special explanation is required for Mill's cooperation and good samaritan examples, since they are accommodated by his Principle of Liberty. Mill faces no inconsistencies. And he endorses the most plausible principle of the type he is evidently defending.

So much for the larger questions raised by Brown's systematic reading. Let us return, now, to the most directly relevant text, Mill's own commentary on his examples. As we have seen, just after Mill presents his troublesome illustrations he observes, "A person may cause evil to others not only by his actions but also by his inaction, and in either case he is justly accountable to them for the injury.'' [I,11] But this is not the end of his commentary. Brown quotes the rest, but sees no further point in it. Here is how it continues:

The latter case, it is true, requires a much more cautious exercise of compulsion than the former. To make anyone answerable for *doing evil* to others is the rule; to make him answerable for *not preventing evil* is, comparatively speaking, the exception. Yet there are cases clear enough and grave enough to justify that exception. [I,11; emphasis added]

This passage shows that Mill acknowledges the very distinction that, on Brown's reading, he is supposed to neglect—between conduct that causes harm and conduct that fails to prevent harm to others. Furthermore, in employing the distinction as he does, Mill seems to be saying that he would allow interference not just to inhibit harmful conduct but also to elicit acts that prevent harm to others.

In other words, the evidence offered by this passage is equivocal. Mill's initial comment on causing evil by inaction suggests some confusion about the character of his own examples, as if he wishes to limit interference to conduct that causes harm to others. In the continuation of the passage, however, he explicitly extends interference to conduct that does not cause harm, but that fails to prevent harm, as his good samaritan examples require.

It should be observed that Mill's comments make no special allowance for cooperation requirements. From his silence on the matter, one might infer that Mill regards them as equivalent to good samaritan requirements—as if answering a subpoena were like saving a drowning person's life. That seems untenable. The failure to comply with cooperation requirements does not amount to such a simple failure to prevent harm to others. Indeed, it may have no effect at all upon harm-prevention.

Suppose that cooperation requirements are justified because they are instrumental in preventing public harms, such as social insecurity and polluted air. We can then assume that each person in the community has a stake in the effective operation of the rules and therefore in (roughly speaking) general compliance with

them, that is, compliance that is sufficiently widespread to make the joint undertaking as effective as it could be. But we cannot infer from this that any single act of noncompliance places some relevant interest of some other individual at a finite and nonnegligible risk; a single act of noncompliance cannot be assumed to undermine harm-prevention efforts. It might, but then again it might not; and it is at least conceivable that one should know when a single isolated act of noncompliance will have no such consequences. Suppose, for example, that certain substances are dangerous only when they reach a critical concentration in the atmosphere. A pollution control rule might prohibit any release of such substances into the atmosphere, or it might try to reduce the frequency of such acts or the amounts of chemicals released, on the understanding that concentrations of that substance in the atmosphere below the critical level are entirely innocuous. Suppose, however, that an efficiently economical pollution control rule prohibits any release of the substance into the atmosphere, simply because it would in fact be practically impossible to administer any less rigorous rule and the upshot would be failure. It might then be the case that some particular person on at least one occasion could know that this release of a small quantity of the chemical into the atmosphere will be an isolated act of noncompliance with the rule and that the harmful concentration will never be reached. His act of noncompliance might have no effect on harm-prevention efforts and thus could not be assimilated to the failure to save a drowning man.

It must be admitted, however, that such cases may in fact be rare or even nonexistent. And, when one is reasoning about such matters probabilistically, with an eye on large-scale social engineering, there is a natural temptation to assume that we are never in a position absolutely to rule out such effects of noncompliant acts. One might then conclude that the relevant interests of each member of the community are put to some finite nonnegligible risk by any violation of the rules. If there is an error here, it should not be exaggerated. One who reasons in this way need not suppose that a single act of noncompliance causes harm to others, or even that it straightforwardly fails to prevent harm. He need only suppose that there is always, in such a case, some risk that harm-prevention efforts will be adversely affected. One who reasons in this way might tend to assimilate cooperation requirements to good samaritan requirements. This might help to explain why Mill fails to give separate treatment to cooperation examples.

But all of this is highly speculative and we are left, in any case, with the impression that Mill fails to appreciate the complexity of his own commitments. There is clear evidence that he wishes to allow interference not only to inhibit conduct that causes harm to others but also to elicit harm-preventing conduct, broadly construed. At the same time, there is evidence that Mill tends to back off from this commitment or else does not fully recognize the theoretical decision that he faces.

IV. Benefits and Fairness

I have accepted Brown's claim that a harmful conduct-prevention principle cannot accomodate cooperation or good samaritan requirements. Brown would, I think, agree in turn with one of my claims, namely, that good samaritan requirements can plausibly be reconciled with a general harm-prevention principle. But he appears to reject the idea that such a principle could also accommodate cooperation requirements. He says that "the general prevention of harm would not stretch to cover a fair share of every joint work necessary to the interest of society." (p. 146) He gives no defense or explanation for this assertion. One can imagine, however, why cooperation requirements might be thought incompatible with a harm-prevention principle. One reason might be the notion that such requirements are in fact predicated on promoting benefits beyond mere harm-prevention. Another concerns Mill's references to "fair shares." I will deal with these in turn.

The distinction between increasing benefits generally and merely preventing or eliminating harms is taken for granted by Mill. He assumes that some benefits would go beyond harm-prevention and thus that their promotion could

not serve in the justification of enforced requirements. This point requires some further explanation.

It might be assumed that Mill, as a utilitarian, should be understood in effect as following today's fashion in such matters and count the satisfaction of an existing preference as a benefit and its frustration as a harm. Mill's talk of "pleasures" and "pains" might easily suggest this. But important features of his moral and political doctrines, especially those concerning justice and liberty, seem to imply the following sort of view. While it is easy to be mistaken about what constitutes a positive benefit to another person, harms are unproblematic. Harms thus concern interests that are readily appreciated; most if not all of these are, at bottom, common to all persons. They are not to be understood in terms of mere existing preferences but rather as conditions that must be satisfied if one is to live well as a human being; they include physical necessities, personal security, social freedom (from oppressive custom as well as others' interference), and a variety of experiences and opportunities for self-development. To the extent that one is denied or deprived of such conditions, one suffers what Mill counts as "harm."

The question that we face is whether Mill's cooperation examples concern requirements that could not be justified on the basis of preventing harms (on Mill's view or any other), but could only be justified on the ground that they would increase benefits beyond harm-prevention. Mill's words imply the contrary. None of his original examples suggest that cooperation requirements may be exacted in order to obtain positive benefits, and his restatement of them later in the essay *On Liberty* implies the opposite. He says that "the fact of living in society renders it indispensable that each should observe a certain line of conduct toward the rest," which includes "each person's bearing his share (to be fixed upon some equitable principle) of the labors and sacrifices incurred for defending the society or its members from injury and molestation." [IV, 3; cf. also IV, 7] This tells us that Mill has in mind preventing harms rather than increasing benefits.

It might be noted that Mill first introduces his examples by saying that "There are also many positive acts for the benefit of others which he may rightfully be compelled to perform," which could suggest that he means "acts for the positive benefit of others" and not just acts intended to prevent harm. But this cannot be Mill's real meaning. For under the heading "positive acts for the benefit of others" he includes not only cooperation but also good samaritan requirements, and these are clearly meant to prevent harm and not to promote further benefits. Mill's words are, after all, transparent: the examples he is introducing concern requirements and thus positive acts rather than prohibitions and omissions.

Let us turn, then, to Mill's talk about "fair shares." His official doctrine is that restrictions on liberty may be imposed only for the purpose of preventing harm to others. He acknowledges that other types of reason might argue against particular restrictions, but he is unclear what they might be. The only examples he provides are these: Coercive measures might not be required or might be counter-productive either because the individuals are likely to act better on their own or the intervention would produce as side effects more harm than it would prevent. [1, 11] These particular strictures can readily be understood, since Mill is evidently committed not only to harm-prevention but also to preserving liberty, interfering with it as little as possible.[7] So, while Mill allows the definite need for some coercive intervention, he wishes to minimize it, as well as to minimize the incidental harm that social intervention entails. None of this commits Mill to considering the fairness of an enforced requirement. Fairness presumably requires that the benefits of harm-prevention and the burdens of incidental harm and loss of liberty be distributed in a certain way, according to merit or desert and respecting individual rights. Fairness could conceivably object to some rules predicated upon harm-prevention, rules that Mill would otherwise be willing to accept. We can imagine, for example, that Mill would be prepared to endorse the least burdensome rule among a set of equally effective alternatives, that is, the one that prevents a given harm or

set of harms at a minimal loss of liberty and a minimal cost in incidental harms. At the same time, we can imagine that such a rule would be condemned by fairness on the ground that it does not distribute benefits and burdens equitably. Mill's references in his cooperation examples to considerations of fairness would seem, then, to commit him to rejecting such minimally burdensome but effective rules in favor of rules with greater social costs or more extensive limitations on liberty.

Such an abstract, theoretical possibility cannot be denied. But I think the potential problems here might easily be exaggerated. Compare the argument that utilitarianism is defective because it requires that benefits be maximized (and burdens minimized) and thus ignores considerations of justice, which concern their distribution. It is sometimes said, for example, that slavery, which involves the unjust exploitation of some for the sake of others' benefits, might be justified on utilitarian grounds, which shows that utilitarianism is defective. This is, I think, in many ways a highly questionable argument against utilitarianism. But my point just now is that some relevant features of this purely abstract argument against utilitarianism are not available in the cases we must consider with regard to fairness and harm-prevention. The Principle of Liberty permits some "tradeoffs," but it never sanctions the imposition of burdens on some for the sake of others' positive benefits. No benefits beyond harm-prevention can justify coercion under the Principle of Liberty. The trade-offs it allows are these: loss of liberty (plus some incidental harm by way of side effects or social costs of enforcement) in order to prevent or eliminate greater harm to others. Details of distribution aside, this is a morally respectable position.

The potential problems might be exaggerated in other ways too. An example will help to show this. Mill is concerned specifically with rules that impose requirements such as giving testimony in court or providing some form of public service. Let us take the familiar example of military service, which he suggests. Suppose a society must mobilize a military force in order to defend itself against unwarranted attack. Harm-prevention dictates that the mobilization be effective: it must be adequate to secure the community against attack. And it presumably wishes to minimize the harm and loss of liberty that may be required for that purpose. Fairness requires that the burdens be distributed in a certain way. It is worth noting that fairness does not argue, all by itself, for the basic restriction in such a case: it simply sets limits on the means used to achieve other legitimate purposes. It has no objection to minimizing harm and loss of liberty, other things being equal, and it would not require that burdens be imposed when they would not be at all effective in achieving the basic harm-prevention project. For simplicity's sake, let us make some assumptions that will not affect the main point of this example. Let us assume that the persons selected by fairness to shoulder the burdens of military service are capable of achieving the harm-prevention objective; that the only relevant burdens are military service; that these burdens fall equally heavily upon anyone who shoulders them; that the benefit is security from attack, which all stand to receive; and that all members of the community are equally capable of performing the required service. Now, fairness requires either that these burdens fall on some particular members of the community (because they owe such service to others, let us say, or the others have the right to be excused from service) or it does not. In either case, there are two possibilities: either the class picked out as eligible for military service contains just enough members for that purpose, so that all must serve, or it contains more than enough, so that some might be excused if loss of liberty and other social costs are to be minimized. If the eligible class contains just enough members for the purpose, then there is no conflict between fairness and harm-prevention, since fairness does not require any restrictions upon liberty that could not be justified on harm-prevention grounds alone. If the class contains more than enough members, then I assume that fairness would not object to minimizing burdens by excusing some in a fair (e.g., random) manner, such as a lottery. In this case, too, then, fairness would not conflict with harm-prevention.

I do not mean that there is no difference between the two criteria, that they must inevitably approve of just the same rules for harm-prevention. Clearly, we have been assuming, on the contrary, that harm-prevention can accept some assignments of burdens that are unfairly made. Suppose, for example, that only a portion of the community is required for military service. Fairness might require that those who have not served before, in such a situation, should be chosen first, while harm-prevention would, other things being equal, be indifferent to which members are chosen, so long as enough are mobilized and not too many. This is agreed. My point is, rather, that many arguments from fairness do not require extra burdens, beyond those that could be justified on harm-prevention grounds; they require only certain distributions of those burdens. Whenever burdens can be minimized without affecting harm-prevention efforts, fairness would approve so long as the results are achieved in accordance with some fair procedure. To this extent, arguments from fairness do not function as reasons for imposing restrictions. They accordingly appear compatible with Mill's Principle of Liberty, which only requires economical harm-prevention. And to this degree, at least, it seems reasonable to conclude that cooperation limited by fairness is compatible with the Principle of Liberty and thus that Mill's examples might present no difficulties for him.

If considerations of fairness are to present a more substantial threat either to Mill's principle or to his example, there must be cases in which they object, in effect, to minimizing burdens in the course of harm-prevention. For, if they do, then they might be regarded as functioning as independent reasons for coercive intervention, and therefore as conflicting with the Principle of Liberty.

I do not believe that Mill regards them in that way. He discusses justice in *Utilitarianism,* and he says there that "Justice is a name for certain classes of moral rules which concern the essentials of human well-being more nearly, and are therefore of more absolute obligation, than any other guidance of life."[8] Mill plainly believes that injustice and unfairness threaten the most vital of human interests, and that the protection of those interests is the rationale behind the corresponding principles. He thus regards considerations of justice and fairness as rooted in, not as independent of, harm-prevention. More important, Mill understands these principles as exerting independent weight in moral reasoning, relative to welfare arguments.

On the usual reading of Mill, he is understood to hold that we are always morally bound to promote the general welfare—that any other way of acting is fundamentally wrong. He acknowledges that we require guidance from some "secondary" rules, based on past experience concerning the most reliable ways of promoting welfare. Mill's appeal to considerations of fairness, then, would be understood as an appeal to a particular collection of rules of thumb, rules that specifically concern certain fundamental human interests, but which are to be followed because experience counsels adherence to them, as the best way of promoting welfare. On my reading of Mill, however, this is a caricature of his approach to morality and justice.[9]

Mill asserts, as a conceptual claim, that morality concerns moral rights and obligations. Moral principles lay down obligations; the principles of justice lay down obligations that correlate with others' personal rights. To be moral is to perform our obligations; to be just is to respect others' rights. To be just, then, one must reject rules that violate others' rights. Mill recognizes no general "obligation" to "maximize utility"; considerations of the general welfare do not enter directly into moral reasoning. Mill believes, of course, that welfare considerations provide the only sound basis for moral principles. But adherence to such principles is not equivalent or reducible to maximizing utility. The principles of justice are predicated on protecting the vital interests of human beings, such as personal security and freedom from others' intervention. They are based on large-scale, long-term arguments about those interests. These arguments yield principles, such as the Principle of Liberty itself, which lay down rights and obligations that must be respected (save when they are overridden by other moral rights or obligations). In

this respect, Mill may be said to "take rights seriously": for they exert independent weight in moral argument; mere welfare arguments cannot override them. Such rights are consequently capable of conflicting with, and overruling, arguments based on harm-prevention alone. Equally effective and economical restrictions could be distinguished by Mill on the basis of the principles of justice. If any rules predicated simply upon harm-prevention would violate moral rights, they must be rejected. Thus fairness could, in Mill's view, be rooted in harm-prevention and still serve, in effect, as an independent condition to be satisfied by morally acceptable restrictions.

Mill's Principle of Liberty must be understood accordingly. One of the reasons that Mill must recognize as vetoing a harm-prevention rule is that it violates moral rights. This reconciles Mill to the idea of accepting rules that impose more than the minimal burdens required for harm-prevention alone, if such rules should be entertained. But this qualification on the Principle of Liberty is itself predicated upon the protection of certain vital human interests, or in other words upon the prevention of harm to others.

Mill's view will not satisfy the critics of utilitarianism who maintain that justice and fairness are independent of utility. They may be right. I have only sketched the sort of view suggested by Mill and described how it might overcome some fundamental obstacles to a utilitarian account of justice. But the adequacy of such an account has no more been established than the contrary.

All of this is, however, beside the point, if we are primarily concerned with Mill's doctrine of liberty. His utilitarian account of justice, while relevant to an understanding of his cooperation examples and the Principle of Liberty itself, is not entailed by the Principle of Liberty. Thus, even if one believes that justice is independent of utility, one might wish to consider whether Mill is nonetheless on the right track about liberty and harm to others. For it is not obvious—though it seems often to be assumed—that considerations of justice and fairness, all by themselves, not only help to determine what conduct is right and wrong but also justify measures of coercion. One might question this. One who rejected Mill's account of justice might consistently accept his Principle of Liberty. One might find reason to agree that considerations of fairness alone never justify coercion, that only harm-prevention does.

Acknowledgment

Work on this paper was supported by a fellowship from the National Endowment for the Humanities, which I am happy to acknowledge. Earlier versions were read at the University of Calgary, Simon Fraser University, and the University of Washington, where I received many helpful comments. I am especially grateful to Jonathan Bennett, D. G. Brown, David Copp, Samuel Scheffler, and Barry Smith for criticisms.

Notes

1. All references in brackets are to chapters and paragraphs of John Stuart Mill, *On Liberty* [Reprinted in this volume] (first published 1859).

2. D. G. Brown, "Mill on Liberty and Morality," *Philosophical Review* 81 (1972): 133–158.

3. All page references within parentheses are to the article by Brown, ibid.

4. Or at least dangerous; cf. ibid., p. 135, n. 2.

5. The relevant passage is *Utilitarianism,* chap. 5, para. 14. For my interpretation, see "Mill's Theory of Morality," *Nous* 10 (1976): 101–120.

6. Since the Principle of Liberty purports to tell us the sole valid ground for coercive intervention, the Principle of Enforcing Morality must be understood to say, not that immorality is itself a justification for interference, but rather that there is some such justification whenever conduct is wrong. It is therefore somewhat misleading for Brown to say (p. 146) that "Mill believes in the enforcement of morality."

7. Cf. Brown, pp. 137–139.

8. *Utilitarianism,* chap. 5, par. 32.

9. I discuss this further in "Human Rights and the General Welfare," *Philosophy & Public Affairs* 6 (1977): 113–129, and also in "Mill's Theory of Justice," in *Values and Morals: Essays in Honor of William Frankena, Charles Stevenson, and Richard Brandt,* ed. A. I. Goldman and J. Kim (Dordrecht: Reidel, 1978), 1–20.

We Do Not Have a Right to Liberty

RONALD DWORKIN

Liberties, Not Liberty

Do we have a right to liberty?[1] Thomas Jefferson thought so, and since his day the right to liberty has received more play than his competing rights to life and the pursuit of happiness. Liberty gave its name to the most influential political movement of the last century, and many of those who now despise liberals do so on the ground that they are not sufficiently libertarian. Of course, almost everyone concedes that the right to liberty is not the only political right, and that therefore claims to freedom must be limited, for example, by restraints that protect the security or property of others. Nevertheless, the consensus in favor of some right to liberty is a vast one, though it is, as I shall argue in this essay, misguided.

The right to liberty is popular all over this political spectrum. The rhetoric of liberty fuels every radical movement from international wars of liberation to campaigns for sexual freedom and women's liberation. But liberty has been even more prominent in conservative service. Even the mild social reorganizations of the antitrust and unionization movements, and of the early New Deal, were opposed on the grounds that they infringed the right to liberty, and just now efforts to achieve some racial justice through techniques like the busing of black and white schoolchildren are bitterly opposed on that ground.

It has become common, indeed, to describe the great social issues of American politics, and in particular the racial issue, as presenting a conflict between the demands of liberty and those of equality. It may be, it is said, that the poor and the black and the uneducated and the unskilled have an abstract right to equality, but the prosperous and the whites and the educated and the able have a right to liberty as well, and any efforts at social reorganization in aid of the first set of rights must reckon with and respect the second. Everyone except the extremist recognizes, therefore, the need to compromise between equality and liberty. Every piece of important social legislation, from tax policy to integration plans, is shaped by the supposed tension between these two goals.

I have this supposed conflict between equality and liberty in mind when I ask whether we have a right to liberty, as Jefferson and everyone else have supposed. That is a crucial question. If freedom to choose one's schools, or employees, or neighborhood is simply something that we all want, like air conditioning or lobsters, then we are not entitled to hang on to these freedoms in the face of what we concede to be the rights of others to an equal share of respect and resources. But if we can say not simply that we want these freedoms,

Ronald Dworkin, "We Do Not Have a Right to Liberty," from *Liberty and the Rule of Law,* ed. R. Cunningham (College Station: Texas A & M University Press, 1979). Reprinted by permission of Liberty Fund, Inc., Indianapolis, Indiana.

but that we are ourselves entitled to them, then we have established at least a basis for demanding a compromise.

There is now a movement, for example, in favor of a proposed constitutional amendment that would guarantee every schoolchild the legal right to attend a "neighborhood school" and thus outlaw busing. The suggestion that neighborhood schools somehow rank with jury trials as constitutional values would seem silly but for the sense many Americans have that forcing schoolchildren into buses is somehow as much an interference with the fundamental right to liberty as segregated schooling was an insult to equality. But that seems to me absurd; indeed it seems to me absurd to suppose that men and women have any general right to liberty at all, at least as liberty has traditionally been conceived by its champions.

I have in mind the traditional definition of liberty as the absence of constraints placed by a government upon what a man might do if he wants to. Isaiah Berlin, in the most famous modern essay on liberty, put the matter this way: "The sense of freedom, in which I use this term, entails not simply the absence of frustration but the absence of obstacles to possible choices and activities—absence of obstructions on roads along which a man can decide to walk." This conception of liberty is doggedly neutral among the various activities a man might pursue, the various roads he might wish to walk. It diminishes a man's liberty when we prevent him from talking or making love as he wishes, but it also diminishes his liberty when we prevent him from murdering or defaming others. These latter constraints may be justifiable, but only because they are compromises necessary to protect the liberty or security of others, and not because they do not, in themselves, infringe the independent value of liberty. Bentham said that any law whatsoever is an "infraction" of liberty, and though some such infractions might be necessary, it is obscurantist to pretend that they are not infractions after all. In this neutral, all-embracing sense of liberty, liberty and equality are plainly in competition. Laws are needed to protect equality, and laws are inevitably compromises of liberty.

Liberals like Berlin are content with this neutral sense of liberty because it seems to encourage clear thinking. It allows us to identify just what is lost, though perhaps unavoidably, when men accept constraints on their actions for some other goal or value. It would be an intolerable muddle, in this view, to use the concept of liberty or freedom in such a way that we counted a loss of freedom only when men were prevented from doing something that we thought they ought to do. It would allow totalitarian governments to masquerade as liberal simply by arguing that they prevent men from doing only what is wrong. Worse, it would obscure the most distinctive point of the liberal tradition, which is that interfering with a man's free choice to do what he might want to do is in and of itself an insult to humanity, a wrong that may be justified but can never be wiped away by competing considerations. For a true liberal, any constraint upon freedom is something that a decent government must regret and keep to the minimum necessary to accommodate the other rights of its constituents.

In spite of this tradition, however, the neutral sense of liberty seems to me to have caused more confusion than it has cured, particularly when it is joined to the popular and inspiring idea that men have a right to liberty. For we can maintain the idea that men have a right to liberty as such, in the neutral sense of liberty, only by so watering down the idea of a right that the right to liberty is something hardly worth having at all.

The term *right* is used in politics and philosophy in many different senses, some of which I have tried to disentangle elsewhere.[2] In order sensibly to ask whether we have a right to liberty in the neutral sense, we must fix on some one meaning of *right*. It would not be difficult to find a sense of that term in which we could say with some confidence that men have a right to liberty. We might say, for example, that someone has a right to liberty if it is in his interest to have liberty, that is, if he either wants it or if it would be good for him to have it. In this sense, I would be prepared to concede that men have a right to liberty. But in this sense I would also have to concede that men have a right, at least generally, to vanilla ice cream. My concession about liberty, moreover, would have very little value in political debate. I should want to claim, for example, that men have a right to equality in a much stronger sense, that they do not simply want equality but that they are entitled to it, and I would therefore not recognize the claim that men want liberty as requiring any compromise in the efforts that I believe are necessary to give other men the equality to which they are entitled.

If the right to liberty is to play the role cut out for it in political debate, therefore, it must be a right in a much stronger sense. In the article just mentioned I defined a strong sense of right that seems to me to capture the claims men mean to make when they appeal to political and moral rights. I do not propose to repeat my analysis here, but only to summarize it in this way. A successful claim of right, in the strong sense I described, has this consequence. If someone has a right to something, then it is wrong for the government to deny it to him even though it would be in the general interest to do so. This sense of a right (which might be called the antiutilitarian concept of a right) seems to me very close to the sense of right principally used in political and legal writing and argument in recent years. It marks the distinctive concept of an individual right against the state which is the heart, for example, of constitutional theory in the United States.

I do not think that the right to liberty would come to very much, or have much power in political argument, if it relied on any sense of the right any weaker than that. If we settle on this concept of a right, however, then it seems plain that there exists no general right to liberty as such. I have no political right to drive up Lexington Avenue. If the government chooses to make Lexington Avenue one-way downtown, it is a sufficient justification that this would be in the general interest, and it would be ridiculous for me to argue that for some reason it would nevertheless be wrong. The vast bulk of the laws which diminish my liberty are justified on utilitarian grounds, as being in the general interest or for the general welfare; if, as Bentham supposes, each of these laws diminishes my liberty, they nevertheless

do not take away from me anything that I have a right to have. It will not do, in the one-way-street case, to say that although I have a right to drive up Lexington Avenue, nevertheless the government for special reasons is justified in overriding that right. That seems silly because the government needs no special justification—but only *a* justification—for this sort of legislation. So I can have a political right to liberty, such that every act of constraint diminishes or infringes that right, only in such a weak sense of right that the so-called right to liberty is not competitive with strong rights, like the right to equality, at all. In any strong sense of right, which would be competitive with the right to equality, there exists no general right to liberty at all.

It may now be said that I have misunderstood the claim that there is a right to liberty. It does not mean to argue, it will be said, that there is a right to all liberty, but simply to important or basic liberties. Every law is, as Bentham said, an infraction of liberty, but we have a right to be protected against only fundamental or serious infractions. If the constraint on liberty is serious or severe enough, then it is indeed true that the government is not entitled to impose that constraint simply because that would be in the general interest; the government is not entitled to constrain liberty of speech, for example, whenever it thinks that would improve the general welfare. So there is, after all, a general right to liberty as such, provided that that right is restricted to important liberties or serious deprivations. This qualification does not affect the political arguments I described earlier, it will be said, because the rights to liberty that stand in the way of full equality are rights to basic liberties like, for example, the right to attend a school of one's choice.

But this qualification raises an issue of great importance for liberal theory, which those who argue for a right to liberty do not face. What does it mean to say that the right to liberty is limited to basic liberties, or that it offers protection only against serious infractions of liberty? That claim might be spelled out in two different ways, with very different theoretical and practical consequences. Let us suppose two cases in which government constrains a man from doing what he might want to do: (1) the government prevents a man from speaking his mind on political issues; (2) the government prevents a man from driving his car up-town on Lexington Avenue. What is the connection between these two cases, and the difference between them, such that though they are both cases in which a man is constrained and deprived of liberty, his right to liberty is infringed only in the first, and not in the second?

On the first of the two theories we might consider, the citizen is deprived of the same commodity—namely, liberty—in both cases, but the difference is that in the first case the amount of that commodity taken away from him is, for some reason, either greater in amount or greater in its impact than in the second. But that seems bizarre. It is very difficult to think of liberty as a commodity. If we do try to give liberty some operational sense, such that we can measure the relative diminution of liberty occasioned by different sorts of laws or constraints, then the result is unlikely to match our intuitive sense of what are the basic liberties and what are not. Suppose, for example, we measure a diminution in liberty by calculating the extent of frustration that it induces. We shall then have to face the fact that laws against theft, and even traffic laws, impose constraints that are felt more keenly by most men than constraints on political speech would be. We might take a different tack, and measure the degree of loss of liberty by the impact that a particular constraint has on future choices. But we should then have to admit that the ordinary criminal code reduces choice for most men more than laws which forbid fringe political activity. So the first theory—that the difference between cases covered and those not covered by our supposed right to liberty is a matter of degree—must fail.

The second theory argues that the difference between the two cases has to do, not with the degree of liberty involved, but with the special character of the liberty involved in the case covered by the right. On this theory, the offense involved in a law that limits free speech is of a different character, and not just different

in degree, from a law that prevents a man from driving up Lexington Avenue. That sounds plausible, though as we shall see it is not easy to state what this difference in character comes to, or why it argues for a right in some cases though not in others. My present point, however, is that if the distinction between basic liberties and other liberties is defended in this way, then the notion of a general right to liberty as such has been entirely abandoned. If we have a right to basic liberties not because they are cases in which the commodity of liberty is somehow especially at stake, but because an assault on basic liberties injures us or demeans us in some way that goes beyond its impact on liberty, then what we have a right to is not liberty at all, but to the values or interests or standing that this particular constraint defeats.

This is not simply a question of terminology. If I am right then the right to liberty is a misconceived concept that does a disservice to political thought in at least two ways. First, the idea of a right to liberty creates a false sense of a necessary conflict between liberty and other values when social regulation, like the busing program, is proposed. Second, the idea of a fundamental right to liberty provides too easy an answer to the question of why we regard certain kinds of restraints, like the restraint on free speech or the exercise of religion, as especially unjust. The idea of a right to liberty allows us to say that these constraints are unjust because they have a special impact on liberty as such. Once we recognize that this answer is spurious, then we shall have to face the difficult question of what is indeed at stake in these cases.

I should like to turn at once to that question. If there is no general right to liberty, then why do citizens in a democracy have rights to any specific kind of liberty, like freedom of speech or religion or political activity? It is no answer to say that if individuals have these rights, then the community will be better off in the long run as a whole. This idea—that individual rights may lead to overall utility—may or may not be true, but it is irrelevant to the defense of rights as such, because when we say that someone has a right to speak his mind freely, in the relevant political sense, we mean that he is entitled to do so even if this would not be in the general interest. If we want to defend individual rights in the sense in which we claim them, then we must try to discover something beyond utility that argues for these rights.

I mentioned one possibility earlier. We might be able to make out a case that individuals suffer some special damage when the traditional rights are invaded. On this argument, there is something about the liberty to speak out on political issues such that, if that liberty is denied, the individual suffers a special kind of damage which makes it wrong to inflict that damage upon him even though the community as a whole would benefit. This line of argument will appeal to those who themselves would feel special deprivation at the loss of their political and civil liberties, but it is nevertheless a difficult argument to pursue for two reasons.

First, there are a great many men, and they are undoubtedly in the majority even in a democracy like the United States, who do not exercise the political liberties that they have and who would not count the loss of these liberties as especially grievous. Second, we lack a psychological theory which would justify and explain the theory that the loss of civil liberties, or any particular liberties, involves inevitable or even likely psychological damage. On the contrary, there is now a lively tradition in psychology, led by psychologists like Laing, who argue that a good deal of mental instability in modern societies may be traced to the demand for too much liberty rather than too little. In their account, the need to choose, which follows from liberty, is an unnecessary source of destructive tension. These theories are not necessarily persuasive, but until we can be confident that they are wrong, we cannot assume that psychology demonstrates the opposite, however appealing that might be on political grounds.

If we want to argue for a right to certain liberties, therefore, we must find another ground, and there is only one plausible alternative. We must argue on ground of political morality that it is wrong to deprive individuals of these liberties, for some reason, apart from direct psychological damage, in spite of the fact that the common interest would be served by doing so. I put the matter this vaguely because there is no reason to assume, in advance, that only one kind of reason would support that moral position. It might be that a just society would recognize a variety of individual rights, some grounded on very different sorts of moral considerations from others. In what remains of this essay I shall try to describe only one possible ground for rights. It does not follow that men and women in civil society have only the rights that the argument I shall make would support, but it does follow that they have at least these rights, and that is important enough.

What Rights Do We Have?

The central concept of my argument will be the concept not of liberty but of equality. I presume that we all accept the following postulates of political morality. Government must treat those whom it governs with concern, that is, as human beings who are capable of suffering and frustration, and with respect, that is, as human beings who are capable of forming and acting on intelligent conceptions of how their lives should be lived. Government must treat people not only with concern and respect, but with equal concern and respect. It must not distribute goods or opportunities unequally on the ground that some citizens are entitled to more because they are worthy of more concern. It must not constrain liberty on the ground that one man's conception of the good life of one group is nobler than, or superior to, another's. These postulates, taken together, state what might be called the liberal conception of equality, but it is a conception of equality, not of liberty, that they state.

The sovereign question of political theory, within a state supposed to be governed by the liberal conception of equality, is: What inequalities in goods, opportunities, and liberties are permitted in such a state, and why? The beginning of an answer lies in the following distinction. Citizens governed by the liberal conception of equality each have a right to equal concern and respect. But there are two different rights that might be comprehended by that abstract right. The first is the right to equal treatment, that is, to the same distribution of goods or opportunities that anyone else has or is given. The Supreme Court, in the Reapportionment cases, held that citizens have a right to equal treatment in the distribution of voting power; it held that one man must be given one vote in spite of the fact that a different distribution of votes might in fact work for the general benefit. The second is the right to treatment as an equal. This is the right, not to an equal distribution of some good or opportunity, but the right to equal concern and respect in the political decision about how these goods and opportunities are to be distributed. Suppose the question is raised whether an economic policy that allows unemployment to rise is in the general interest. Those who will be unemployed have a right that their prospective loss be taken into account in deciding whether the general interest is served by the policy. They may not simply be ignored in that calculation. But when their interest is taken into account it may nevertheless be outweighed by the interests of others who will gain from the policy, and in that case their right to equal concern and respect, so defined, would provide no objection. In the case of economic policy, therefore, we might wish to say that those who will be unemployed if inflation is reduced have a right to treatment as equals in the decision whether that policy would serve the general interest, but they have no right to equal treatment in the distribution of jobs that would prevent the policy even if it passed that test.

I propose that the right to treatment as an equal must be taken to be fundamental under the liberal conception of equality and that the more restrictive right to equal treatment holds only in those special circumstances in which, for some special reason, it follows from the more fundamental right, as perhaps it does in the special circumstance of the Reapportionment cases. I also propose that individual rights to distinct liberties must be recognized only when the fundamental right to treatment as an equal can be shown to require these rights. If this is correct, then the right to distinct liberties does not conflict with any supposed competing

right to equality, but, on the contrary, follows from a conception of equality conceded to be more fundamental.

I must now show, however, how the familiar rights to distinct liberties—those established, for example, in our Constitution—might be thought to be required by that fundamental conception of equality. I shall try to do this, for present purposes, only by providing a skeleton of the more elaborate argument that would have to be made to defend any particular liberty on this basis, and then show why it would be plausible to expect that the more familiar political and civil liberties would be supported by such an argument if it were in fact made.

A government that respects the liberal conception of equality may properly constrain liberty only on certain very limited types of justification. I shall adopt, for purposes of making this point, the following crude typology of political justifications. There are, first, arguments of principle, which support a particular constraint on liberty on the argument that the constraint is required to protect the distinct right of some individual who will be injured by the exercise of the liberty. There are, second, arguments of policy, which support constraints on the different ground that such constraints are required to reach some overall political goal, that is, to realize some state of affairs in which the community as a whole, and not just certain individuals, is better off by virtue of the constraint. Arguments of policy might be further subdivided in this way. Utilitarian arguments of policy argue that the community as a whole will be better off because (to put the point roughly) more of its citizens will have more of what they want overall, even though some of them will have less. Ideal arguments of policy, on the other hand, argue that the community will be better off, not because more of its members will have more of what they want, but because the community will be in some way closer to an ideal community, whether its members desire the improvement in question or not.

The liberal conception of equality sharply limits the extent to which ideal arguments of policy may be used to justify any constraint on liberty. Such arguments cannot be used if the ideal in question is itself controversial within the community. Constraints cannot be defended, for example, directly on the ground that they contribute to a culturally sophisticated community, whether the community wants the sophistication or not, because that argument would violate the canon of the liberal conception of equality that prohibits a government from relying on the claim that certain forms of life are inherently more valuable than others.

Utilitarian arguments of policy, however, would seem secure from that objection. They do not suppose that any form of life is inherently more valuable than any other, but instead base their claim that constraints on liberty are necessary to advance some collective goal of the community only on the fact that that goal happens to be desired more widely or more deeply than any other. Utilitarian arguments of policy, therefore, seem not to oppose but, on the contrary, to embody the fundamental right of equal concern and respect because they treat the wishes of each member of the community on a par with the wishes of any other, with no bonus or discount reflecting the view that that member is more or less worthy of concern than any other, or his views more or less worthy of respect than other views.

This appearance of egalitarianism has, I think, been the principal source of the great appeal that utilitarianism has had, as a general political philosophy, over the last century. In a recent article, however, I pointed out that the egalitarian character of a utilitarian argument is often an illusion.[3] I will not repeat, but only summarize, my argument here.

Utilitarian arguments fix on the fact that a particular constraint on liberty will make more people happier, or satisfy more of their preferences, depending upon whether psychological or preference utilitarianism is in play. But people's overall preference for one policy over another may be seen to include, on further analysis, preferences that are both personal, because they state a preference for the assignment of one set of goods or opportunities to him, and external because they state a preference for one assignment of goods or opportunities to others. But a utilitarian argument that assigns critical weight to the external preferences of members of the community will not be egalitarian in the sense under consideration. It will not respect the right of everyone to be treated with equal concern and respect.

Suppose, for example, that a number of individuals in the community hold racist rather than utilitarian political theories. They believe, not that each man is to count for one and no one for more than one in the distribution of goods, but, rather, that a black man is to count for less and a white man, therefore, to count for more than one. That is an external preference, but it is nevertheless a genuine preference for one policy over another, the satisfaction of which will bring pleasure. Nevertheless, if this preference or pleasure is given the normal weight in a utilitarian calculation, and blacks suffer accordingly, then their own assignment of goods and opportunities will depend, not simply on the competition among personal preferences that abstract statements of utilitarianism suggest, but precisely on the fact that they are thought less worthy of concern and respect than others are.

Suppose, to take a different case, that many members of that community disapprove on moral grounds of homosexuality, or contraception, or pornography, or expressions of adherence to the Communist Party. They prefer not only that they themselves not indulge in these activities but that no one else do so either, and they believe that a community that permits rather than prohibits these acts is inherently a worse community. These are external preferences, but, once again, they are no less genuine, nor less a source of pleasure when satisfied and displeasure when ignored, than purely personal preferences. Once again, however, if these external preferences are counted in a manner that justifies a constraint on liberty, then those constrained suffer, not simply because their personal preferences have lost in a competition for scarce resources with the personal preferences of others, but precisely because their conception of a proper or desirable form of life is despised by others.

These arguments justify the following important conclusion. If utilitarian arguments of policy are to be used to justify constraints either on distributional inequalities or on liberty, then care must be taken to ensure that the utilitarian calculations on which the argument is based fix only on personal and ignore external preferences. That is an important conclusion for political theory because it shows, for example, why the arguments of John Stuart Mill in *On Liberty* are not counterutilitarian but, on the contrary, serve the only defensible form of utilitarianism.

Important as that conclusion is at the level of political philosophy, however, it is in itself of limited practical significance because it will be impossible to devise political procedures that will accurately discriminate between personal and external preferences. Representative democracy is widely thought to be the institutional structure most suited, in a complex and diverse society, to the identification and achievement of utilitarian policies. It works imperfectly at this, for the familiar reason that majoritarianism cannot sufficiently take account of the intensity, as distinct from the number, of particular preferences, and because techniques of political persuasion, backed by money, may corrupt the accuracy with which votes represent the genuine preferences of those who have voted. Nevertheless, democracy seems to enforce utilitarianism more satisfactorily, in spite of these imperfections, than any alternative general political scheme would.

But democracy cannot discriminate, within the overall preferences imperfectly revealed by voting, distinct personal and external components, so as to provide a method for enforcing the former while ignoring the latter. An actual vote in an election or referendum must be taken to represent an overall preference rather than some component of the preference that a skillful cross-examination of the individual voter, if time and expense permitted, would reveal. Personal and external preferences are sometimes so inextricably combined, moreover, that the discrimination is psychologically as well as institutionally impossible. That will be true, for example, in the case of the associational preferences that many people have for members of one race, or people of one talent or quality, over another, for this is a personal preference so parasitic upon external preferences that it is impossible to say, even as a

matter of introspection, what personal preferences would remain if the underlying external preference were removed. It is also true of certain self-denying preferences that many individuals have; that is, preferences for less of a certain good on the assumption, or rather proviso, that if they have less, other people, equally deserving, will have more. That is also a preference, however noble, that is parasitic upon external preferences, in the shape of political and moral theories, and though we might resist this conclusion, such preferences may no more be counted in a defensible utilitarian argument than less attractive preferences rooted in prejudice rather than altruism.

I wish now to propose the following general theory of rights. The concept of an individual political right, in the strong antiutilitarian sense I distinguished earlier, is a response to the philosophical defects of a utilitarianism that counts external preferences and the practical difficulties of a utilitarianism that does not. It allows us to enjoy the institutions of political democracy, institutions which enforce overall or unrefined utilitarianism, and yet protect the fundamental right of citizens to equal concern and respect by prohibiting decisions that seem, antecedently, very likely to have been reached by virtue of the external components of the preferences democracy reveals.

It should be plain how this theory of rights might be used to support the idea, which is the subject of this essay, that we have distinct rights to certain liberties like the liberty of free expression and of free choice in personal sexual moralities. It might be shown that any utilitarian constraint on these liberties must be based on overall preferences in the community that we know, from our general knowledge of society, are likely to contain large components of external preferences, in the shape of political or moral theories, which the political process cannot discriminate and eliminate. As I have said, my present purpose is not to frame the arguments that would have to be made to defend particular rights to liberty in this way, but only to show the general character such arguments might have.

I do wish, however, to mention one alleged right that might be called into question by my general argument, which is the supposed individual right to the free use of property. I have elsewhere complained about the argument, popular in certain quarters, that it is inconsistent for liberals to defend a liberty of speech, for example, and not also concede a parallel right of some sort to property and its use. There might be force in that argument if the claim that we have a right to speech depended on the more general proposition that we have a right to something called liberty as such. But, as I said earlier, that general idea is untenable and incoherent; there is no such thing as any general right to liberty. The argument for any given specific liberty may therefore be entirely independent of the argument for any other, and there is no antecedent inconsistency or even implausibility in contending for one while disputing the other.

What can be said, on the general theory of rights I offer, for any particular right of property? What can be said, for example, in favor of the right to liberty of contract sustained by the Supreme Court in the famous Lochner case and later regretted not only by the Court but by liberals generally? I cannot think of any argument that a political decision to limit such a right, in the way in which minimum-wage laws limited it, is antecedently likely to have given effect to external preferences and in that way offended the right of those whose liberty is curtailed to equal concern and respect. If, as I think, no such argument can be made out, then the alleged right may not exist; in any case, there can be no inconsistency in denying that it exists while warmly defending a right to other liberties.

Notes

1. I use *liberty* in this essay in the sense Isaiah Berlin called "negative."
2. See "Taking Rights Seriously," *New York Review of Books* (17 December 1970).
3. "The DeFunis Case: The Right to Go to Law School," *New York Review of Books* (5 February 1976).

Suggested Further
Reading

Attig, Thomas, et. al., eds. "The Restraint of Liberty." In *Bowling Green Studies in Applied Philosophy,* vol. 8. Bowling Green, Ohio: Bowling Green University Press, 1985.

Barry, N. P. *On Classical Liberalism and Libertarianism.* London: Macmillan, 1986.

Bay, Christian. *The Structure of Freedom.* Stanford: Stanford University Press, 1958.

Benn, S. I. *A Theory of Freedom.* New York: Cambridge University Press, 1988.

Bergmann, Frithjof. *On Being Free.* Notre Dame, Ind.: University of Notre Dame Press, 1977.

Berlin, Isaiah. *Four Essays on Liberty.* New York: Oxford University Press, 1969.

Bauman, Zygmunt. *Freedom.* Milton Keynes: Open University Press, 1988.

Brenkert, George G. *Political Freedom.* New York: Routledge, 1991.

Buchanan, James M. *The Limits of Liberty.* Chicago: University of Chicago Press, 1975.

Carritt, E. F. "Liberty and Equality." In *Political Philosophy,* edited by Anthony Quinton. New York: Oxford University Press, 1967.

Cohen, G. A. "The Structure of Proletarian Unfreedom." *Philosophy and Public Affairs* 12 (1983): 3–33.

Cohen, Joshua. "Freedom of Expression." *Philosophy and Public Affairs* 22 (1993): 207–263.

Cranston, Maurice. *Freedom: A New Analysis.* 3rd ed. New York: Basic Books, 1967.

Crocker, Lawrence. *Positive Liberty.* The Hague: Martinus Nijhoff, 1980.

Day, J. P. *Liberty and Justice.* London: Croom Helm, 1986.

Devlin, Patrick. *The Enforcement of Morals.* Oxford: Oxford University Press, 1959.

Dietze, Gottfried. *Liberalism Proper and Proper Liberalism.* Baltimore, Md.: Johns Hopkins University Press, 1985.

Douglas, Jack D. *The Myth of the Welfare State.* New Brunswick, N.J.: Transaction Publishers, 1989.

Dworkin, Gerald. "Paternalism." *Monist* 56 (1972): 64–84.

Dworkin, Ronald. *Taking Rights Seriously.* Cambridge, Mass.: Harvard University Press, 1977.

Feinberg, Joel. *Harm to Others.* Vol. 1 of *The Moral Limits of the Criminal Law.* New York: Oxford University Press, 1984.

———. *Harm to Self.* Vol. 3 of *The Moral Limits of the Criminal Law.* New York: Oxford University Press, 1986.

———. *Harmless Wrongdoing.* Vol. 4 of *The Moral Limits of the Criminal Law.* New York: Oxford University Press, 1990.

———. *Offense to Others.* Vol. 2 of *The Moral Limits of the Criminal Law.* New York: Oxford University Press, 1985.

———. *Rights, Justice, and the Bounds of Liberty.* Princeton: Princeton University Press, 1980.

———. *Social Philosophy.* Englewood Cliffs, N.J.: Prentice-Hall, 1973.

Flathman, Richard E. *The Philosophy and Politics of Freedom.* Chicago: University of Chicago Press, 1987.

Friedrich, Carl J., ed. *Nomos IV: Liberty.* New York: Atherton, 1962.

Galipeau, Claude J. *Isaiah Berlin's Liberalism.* Oxford: Clarendon Press, 1994.

Gray, John. *Beyond the New Right: Markets, Government, and the Common Environment.* London: Routledge, 1993.

———. *Hayek on Liberty.* Oxford: Basil Blackwell, 1984.

———. *Liberalism.* Milton Keynes: Open University Press, 1986.

———. *Mill on Liberty: A Defence.* London: Routledge & Kegan Paul, 1983.

———. *Post-Liberalism: Studies in Political Theory.* New York: Routledge, 1993.

Gray, Tim. *Freedom.* London: Macmillan, 1991.

Griffiths, A. P., ed. *Of Liberty.* Cambridge: Cambridge University Press, 1983.

Hart, H. L. A. *Law, Liberty, and Morality.* Stanford, Calif.: Stanford University Press, 1963.

Hayek, F. A. *The Constitution of Liberty.* Chicago: University of Chicago Press, 1960.

Hodson, John D. *The Ethics of Legal Coercion.* Boston: D. Reidel, 1983.

Justman, Stewart. *The Hidden Text of Mill's Liberty.* Savage, Md.: Rowman and Littlefield, 1991.

Langton, Rae. "Whose Right? Ronald Dworkin, Women, and Pornographers." *Philosophy and Public Affairs* 19 (1990): 331–359.

Lee, J. Roger. "Choice and Harms." In *Rights and Regulation,* edited by T. R. Machan and R. B. Johnson. Cambridge, Mass.: Ballinger, 1983.

Lyons, David. *Rights, Welfare, and Mill's Moral Theory.* New York: Oxford University Press, 1994.

MacCallum, Gerald C. "Negative and Positive Freedom." *Philosophical Review* 76 (1962): 312–334.

MacFarlane, L. J. "On Two Concepts of Liberty." *Political Studies* 11 (1963): 77–81.

Machan, Tibor, ed. *The Libertarian Reader.* Totowa, N.J.: Rowman & Littlefield, 1982.

Mendus, Susan. *Toleration and the Limits of Liberalism.* London: Macmillan, 1989.

Miller, David, ed. *Liberty.* New York: Oxford University Press, 1991.

Narveson, Jan. *The Libertarian Idea.* Philadelphia, Pa.: Temple University Press, 1988.

Nicholls, David. "Positive Liberty, 1880–1914." *American Political Science Review* 56 (1962): 114–128.

Nozick, Robert. "Coercion." In *Philosophy, Science, and Method,* edited by S. Morgenbesser, P. Suppes, and M. White. New York: St. Martin's Press, 1969.

Oppenheim, Felix. *Dimensions of Freedom.* New York: St. Martin's Press, 1961.

———. *Political Concepts.* Chicago: University of Chicago Press, 1981.

Pelczynski, Z., and J. Gray, eds. *Conceptions of Liberty in Political Theory.* London: Athlone, 1984.

Pennock, J. R. "Hobbes's Confusing 'Clarity'—The Case of 'Liberty'." In *Hobbes Studies,* edited by Keith C. Brown. London: Oxford University Press, 1965.

Pennock, J. R., and J. W. Chapman, eds. *Nomos XIV: Coercion.* Chicago: Aldine-Atherton, 1972.

Popper, Karl. *The Open Society and Its Enemies,* 5th ed. Princeton: Princeton University Press, 1966.

Raz, Joseph. *The Morality of Freedom.* Oxford: Clarendon Press, 1986.

Ryan, Alan. *J. S. Mill.* London: Routledge & Kegan Paul, 1974.

Ryan, Alan, ed. *The Idea of Freedom.* New York: Oxford University Press, 1979.

Sampson, Geoffrey. *An End To Allegiance: Individual Freedom and the New Politics.* London: Temple Smith, 1984.

———. *Liberty and Language.* New York: Oxford University Press, 1974.

Sartorius, Rolf, ed. *Paternalism.* Minneapolis: University of Minnesota Press, 1983.

Scanlon, Thomas. "A Theory of Freedom of Expression." *Philosophy and Public Affairs* 1 (1972): 204–226.

Schauer, Frederick. *Free Speech: A Philosophical Enquiry.* Cambridge: Cambridge University Press, 1982.

Schoeman, F. D. *Privacy and Social Freedom*. New York: Cambridge University Press, 1992.
Steiner, Hillel. "Individual Liberty." *Proceedings of the Aristotelian Society* 75 (1974–75): 33–50.
Stephen, J. F. *Liberty, Equality, Fraternity*. Cambridge: University Press, 1967.
Sunstein, Cass R. *Democracy and the Problem of Free Speech*. New York: Free Press, 1993.
Taylor, Charles. *Sources of the Self: The Making of the Modern Identity*. Cambridge, Mass.: Harvard University Press, 1989.
Ten, C. L. *Mill on Liberty*. Oxford: Clarendon, 1980.
Weinstein, W. L. "The Concept of Liberty in Nineteenth Century English Political Thought." *Political Studies* 13 (1965): 145–162.
Woodward, James. "Paternalism and Justification." *Canadian Journal of Philosophy,* suppl. vol. 8 (1982): 67–85.
Zvesper, John. *Nature and Liberty*. New York: Routledge, 1993.

III
JUSTICE AND
EQUALITY

Questions of distributive justice have been the major focus of recent political philosophy, particularly among writers who share egalitarian commitments. Yet one cannot find a more forceful and stimulating treatment of the causes and evils of inequality than Rousseau's *Discourse on the Origin of Inequality*, first published in 1755. He begins with a conception of human beings as capable of progress or improvement, not vicious by nature—in fact, possessing the natural virtue of pity—and able to exercise free choice in acting to satisfy their simple, limited needs. It would be virtually impossible to make another one's slave in the state of nature, for natural inequalities are insignificant compared to social ones, which are the product of education, position, and wealth. The true founder of civil society was the first to claim land as his. Crimes, wars, and misery are the eventual result of systems of private property, in Rousseau's view, and he offers a fascinating, quasi-historical account of the conditions which lead to its institution. Government is the tool of the rich, who invented it to protect their interests, fix the laws of property permanently, and subject the rest of humankind to perpetual labor and servitude. Rousseau relates the various forms of government to the degrees of inequality present at the time of their founding and traces the progress of inequality through a series of worsening stages. Readers will be struck by the ways in which Rousseau anticipates later thinkers, particularly Marx.

John Rawls's egalitarian theory of justice has its origins in the classical contract theories of Locke, Rousseau, and Kant. He employs the idea of a hypothetical contract between persons denied knowledge of their particular abilities, talents, social position, and conception of the good—differences that set individuals at odds and are irrelevant from the point of view presupposed by morality—in his argument for a set of principles of justice. Deprived of knowledge of their particular identities to the extent necessary to guarantee fairness, yet rational and self-interested, the parties in this "original position" must choose a conception of justice to regulate the basic structure of their society, to determine the distribution of the benefits and burdens, the rights and responsibilities, of social cooperation. These hypothetical contractors may be regarded as free and equal moral persons, and the fairness of the original position, in which no party has any bargaining advantages, is taken to ensure the fairness of the principles agreed upon. Rawls believes that the parties, whose ignorance of their individual assets and inclinations is balanced by a full knowledge of general facts of economic and social behavior, will unanimously adopt principles that protect the fundamental liberties of everyone, establish conditions of equal opportunity, and produce an acceptable level of social and economic equality. Thus, Rawls argues, they will reject utilitarianism and other alternatives, accepting instead the following principles: (1) each person has an equal right to the most extensive scheme of equal basic liberties compatible with a similar scheme of liberties for all, and (2) social and economic inequalities must meet two conditions: they must be (a) to the greatest expected benefit of the least advantaged, and (b) attached to offices and positions open to all under conditions of fair opportunity. In the first of his essays included here, Rawls explains some of the basic assumptions and motivations behind his theory without going into the details of the contract argument (for which the reader is referred to *A Theory of Justice*). The second essay addresses specific problems of distributive justice and provides a more elaborate discussion of the Difference Principle.

Robert Nozick's libertarian theory of distributive justice is significantly influenced by Locke's theory of property and represents an important alternative to the "end-result" theories of Rawls and of the utilitarians. Unlike their conceptions, Nozick's "historical entitlement" theory does not assume some particular end state or pattern of distribution to be realized, whether one of equality or maximal welfare. Nozick's principles of acquisition, transfer, and rectification of holdings emphasize instead the ways in which people obtain things; if a distribution arises in accordance with the principles, it is just, regardless of who has what amount. In fact, Nozick observes that it requires constant governmental intervention to maintain a particular pattern, since liberty to give and exchange tends to upset all but the very weakest prescribed patterns. Coercive redistribution of income and wealth for purposes of greater equality, for example, is unjust on Nozick's view. Indeed, he contends, "Taxation of earnings from labor is on a par with forced labor." Nozick develops Lockean ideas of original acquisition and concludes with some criticisms of Rawls's theory—that it cannot explain why social cooperation in production creates new or special problems of distributive justice that cannot be handled by a historical entitlement conception, and further, that Rawls's egalitarian social order would not be acceptable to the better endowed. (For a fuller discussion of the difficulties with Rawls's conception and other theories favoring redistribution, the reader is referred to Nozick's *Anarchy, State, and Utopia*. His more recent views are presented in the essay "The Zigzag of Politics," in his book, *The Examined Life*.)

Thomas Scanlon distinguishes natural property rights from the right to noninterference; the former go beyond noninterference and need special justification. He considers the libertarian argument that freedom requires minimization of nonvoluntary obligations and maximization of market-type arrangements, and he suggests that this and similar views often rest on a failure to distinguish different forms of political and economic unfreedom. Scanlon proposes three bases for evaluating obligations imposed by social institutions: the possibility of renunciation of citizenship, the amount of control over one's own life and activities, and the extent of control of the form of obligations. He then proceeds to argue against the view attributed to Nozick—that recognition of a right to opt out of, for example, egalitarian institutions implies a right of internal emigration. Thomas Nagel distinguishes instrumental reasons favoring equality from the claim that it has intrinsic value, and he offers an assessment of three different conceptions of moral equality, including those of Rawls and of utilitarianism. The next two selections confront the questions of whether broadly liberal theories of justice and rights are compatible with objective theories of the human good and with our common convictions about responsibility and desert.

Jeffrey Paul and Fred D. Miller, Jr., examine the critiques of liberalism developed by Alasdair MacIntyre and Michael Sandel, whose communitarian perspectives assume that an objective or common good would undermine the case for a priority of negative liberty and other individual rights over other social values. Paul and Miller argue that these philosophers fail to provide an adequate account of the objective human good and, more important, do not establish that such an account cannot serve as the foundation for a liberal theory; the authors attempt to demonstrate the possibility of this kind of derivation in their conclusion. Samuel Scheffler suggests that some common objections to political liberalism—that it undermines personal responsibility and does not give people what they deserve—are not satisfactorily answered by any of the leading philosophical theories of liberalism. The significance of these concerns, he believes, is not sufficiently appreciated by liberals generally, and he suggests that this could be a major part of the reason for the declining popularity of liberalism in the United States.

John Rawls's more recent work is represented by his essay "The Domain of the Political and Overlapping Consensus." He maintains that viable pluralistic democracy requires the general acceptance of certain fundamental rights and freedoms, an "overlapping consensus," despite different comprehensive moral and political conceptions. Rawls tries to show that such a consensus is not a mere political compromise devoid of moral import; rather, it is constituted of principles of justice that all reasonable members of society can accept. If he is correct, then he has explained how a political conception of justice can unify and encourage tolerance in a pluralistic society without undue coercion or violation of the liberal requirement of moral neutrality among competing comprehensive theories of the good.

From *Discourse on the Origin of Inequality*

JEAN-JACQUES ROUSSEAU

Second Part

The first man, who after enclosing a piece of ground, took it into his head to say, *this is mine,* and found people simple enough to believe him, was the real founder of civil society. How many crimes, how many wars, how many murders, how many misfortunes and horrors, would that man have saved the human species, who pulling up the stakes or filling up the ditches should have cried to his fellows: Beware of listening to this impostor; you are lost, if you forget that the fruits of the earth belong equally to us all, and the earth itself to nobody! But it is highly probable that things had by then already come to such a pass, that they could not continue much longer as they were; for as this idea of property depends on several prior ideas which could only spring up gradually one after another, it was not formed all at once in the human mind: men must have made considerable progress; they must have acquired a great stock of industry and knowledge, and transmitted and increased it from age to age before they could arrive at this last point of the state of nature. Let us therefore take up things at an earlier stage, and collect into one point of view, and in their most natural order, the slow succession of events and discoveries.[. . .]

As long as men remained satisfied with their rustic huts; as long as they were content with clothes made of the skins of animals, sewn with thorns and fish bones; as long as they continued to consider feathers and shells as sufficient ornaments, and to paint their bodies different colors, to improve or ornament their bows and arrows, to fashion with sharp-edged stones some little fishing boats, or clumsy instruments of music; in a word, as long as they undertook such works only as a single person could finish, and stuck to such arts as did not require the joint endeavors of several hands, they lived free, healthy, honest and happy, as much as their nature would admit, and continued to enjoy with each other all the pleasures of an independent intercourse; but from the moment one man began to stand in need of another's assistance; from the moment it appeared an advantage for one man to possess enough provisions for two, equality vanished; property was introduced; labor became necessary; and boundless forests became smiling fields, which had to be watered with human sweat, and in which slavery and misery were soon seen to sprout out and grow with the harvests.

Metallurgy and agriculture were the two arts whose invention produced this great revolution. With the poet, it is gold and silver, but with the philosopher, it is iron and corn, which have civilized men, and ruined mankind. Accordingly both one and the other were unknown to the savages of America, who for that very reason have still remained savages; nay, other nations seem to have continued in a state of barbarism, as long as they continued to exercise one only of these arts without the other; and perhaps one of the best reasons, that can be assigned, why Europe has been, if not earlier, at least more constantly and highly civilized than the other quarters of the world, is that it both abounds most in iron and is most fertile in corn.

It is very difficult to conjecture how men came to know anything of iron, and of the art of employing it: for we are not to suppose that they should of themselves think of digging the ore out of the mine, and preparing it for smelting, before they knew what could be the result of such a process. On the other hand, there is the less reason to attribute this discovery to any accidental fire, as mines are formed nowhere but in barren places, bare of trees and plants, so that it looks as if nature had taken pains to keep from us so mischievous a secret. Nothing therefore remains but the extraordinary chance of some volcano, which belching forth metallic substances already fused might have given the spectators the idea of imitating that operation of nature. And we must further suppose in them great courage and foresight to undertake so laborious a work, and have, at so great a distance, an eye to the advantages they might derive from it; qualities scarcely suitable but to minds more advanced than those can be supposed to have been.

As to agriculture, the principles of it were known a long time before the practice of it took place, and it is hardly possible that men, constantly employed in drawing their subsistence from trees and plants, should not have early hit on the means employed by nature for the generation of vegetables; but in all probability it was very late before their industry took a turn that way, either because trees which with hunting and fishing supplied them with food, did not require their attention; or because they did not know the use of grain; or because they had no instruments to cultivate it; or because they were destitute of foresight in regard to

future necessities; or lastly, because they lacked means to hinder others from running away with the fruit of their labors. We may believe that on their becoming more industrious they began their agriculture by cultivating with sharp stones and pointed sticks a few vegetables or roots about their cabins; and that it was a long time before they knew the method of preparing wheat, and were provided with instruments necessary to raise it in large quantities; not to mention the necessity there is, in order to follow this occupation and sow lands, to consent to lose something now to gain a great deal later on; a precaution very foreign to the turn of man's mind in a savage state, in which, as I have already remarked, he can hardly foresee in the morning what he will need at night.

For this reason the invention of other arts must have been necessary to oblige mankind to apply themselves to that of agriculture. As soon as some men were needed to smelt and forge iron, others were wanted to maintain them. The more hands were employed in manufactures, the fewer hands were left to provide subsistence for all, though the number of mouths to be supplied with food continued the same; and as some required commodities in exchange for their iron, the rest at last found out the method of making iron serve for the multiplication of commodities. Thus were established on the one hand husbandry and agriculture, and on the other the art of working metals and of multiplying the uses of them.

The tilling of the land was necessarily followed by its distribution; and property once acknowledged, the first rules of justice ensued: for to secure every man his own, every man had to be able to own something. Moreover, as men began to extend their views toward the future, and all found themselves in possession of goods capable of being lost, there was none without fear of reprisals for any injury he might do to others. This origin is so much the more natural, as it is impossible to conceive how property can flow from any other source but work; for what can a man add but his labor to things which he has not made, in order to acquire a property in them? It is the labor of the hands alone, which giving the husbandman a title to the produce of the land he has tilled gives him a title to the land itself, at least until he has gathered in the fruits of it, and so on from year to year; and this enjoyment forming a continued possession is easily transformed into property. The ancients, says Grotius, by giving to Ceres the epithet of legislatrix, and to a festival celebrated in her honor the name of Thesmophoria, insinuated that the distribution of lands produced a new kind of right; that is the right of property different from that which results from the law of nature.

Things thus circumstanced might have remained equal, if men's talents had been equal, and if, for instance, the use of iron and the consumption of commodities had always held an exact proportion to each other; but as nothing preserved this balance, it was soon broken. The man that had most strength performed most labor; the most dexterous turned his labor to best account; the most ingenious found out methods of lessening his labor; the husbandman required more iron, or the smith more grain, and while both worked equally, one earned a great deal by his labor, while the other could scarcely live by his. Thus natural inequality insensibly unfolds itself with that arising from men's combining, and the differences among men, developed by the differences of their circumstances, become more noticeable, more permanent in their effects, and begin to influence in the same proportion the condition of individuals.

Matters once having reached this point, it is easy to imagine the rest. I shall not stop to describe the successive inventions of other arts, the progress of language, the trial and employment of talents, the inequality of fortunes, the use or abuse of riches, nor all the details which follow these, and which every one may easily supply. I shall just give a glance at mankind placed in this new order of things.

Behold then all our faculties developed; our memory and imagination at work; egoism involved; reason rendered active; and the mind almost arrived at the utmost bounds of that perfection it is capable of. Behold all our natural qualities put in motion; the rank and lot of every man established, not only as to the amount of property and the power of serving

or hurting others, but likewise as to genius, beauty, strength or skill, merits or talents; and as these were the only qualities which could command respect, it was found necessary to have or at least to affect them. It became to the interest of men to appear what they really were not. To be and to seem became two very different things, and from this distinction sprang haughty pomp and deceitful knavery, and all the vices which form their train. On the other hand, man, heretofore free and independent, was now, in consequence of a multitude of new needs, brought into subjection, as it were, to all nature, and especially to his fellows, whose slave in some sense he became, even by becoming their master; if rich, he stood in need of their services, if poor, of their assistance; even mediocrity itself could not enable him to do without them. He must therefore have been continually at work to interest them in his happiness, and make them, if not really, at least apparently find their advantage in laboring for his: this rendered him sly and artful in his dealings with some, imperious and cruel in his dealings with others, and laid him under the necessity of using ill all those whom he stood in need of, as often as he could not awe them into compliance and did not find it his interest to be useful to them. In fine, an insatiable ambition, the rage of raising their relative fortunes, not so much through real necessity as to overtop others, inspires all men with a wicked inclination to injure each other, and with a secret jealousy so much the more dangerous, as to carry its point with the greater security it often puts on the mask of benevolence. In a word, competition and rivalry on the one hand, and an opposition of interests on the other, and always a secret desire of profiting at the expense of others. Such were the first effects of property, and the inseparable attendants of nascent inequality.

Riches, before the invention of signs to represent them, could scarcely consist in anything but lands and cattle, the only real goods which men can possess. So, when estates increased so much in number and in extent as to take in whole countries and touch each other, it became impossible for one man to aggrandize himself but at the expense of some other; at the same time, the supernumerary inhabitants, who were too weak or too indolent to make such acquisitions in their turn, impoverished without having lost anything, because while everything about them changed they alone remained the same, were obliged to receive or force their subsistence from the hands of the rich. And from that began to arise, according to their different characters, domination and slavery, or violence and rapine. The rich on their side scarcely began to taste the pleasure of commanding, when they preferred it to every other; and making use of their old slaves to acquire new ones, they no longer thought of anything but subduing and enslaving their neighbors; like those ravenous wolves, who having once tasted human flesh, despise every other food, and thereafter want only men to devour.

It is thus that the most powerful or the most wretched, respectively considering their power and wretchedness as a kind of right to the possessions of others, equivalent in their minds to that of property, the equality once broken was followed by the most terrible disorders. It is thus that the usurpations of the rich, the pillagings of the poor, and the unbridled passions of all, by stifling the cries of natural compassion, and the still feeble voice of justice, rendered men avaricious, wicked and ambitious. There arose between the title of the strongest and that of the first occupier a perpetual conflict, which always ended in battle and bloodshed. The new state of society became the most horrible state of war: Mankind thus debased and harassed, and no longer able to retrace its steps, or renounce the fatal acquisitions it had made; laboring, in short, merely to its confusion by the abuse of those faculties, which in themselves do it so much honor, brought itself to the very brink of ruin.

Attonitus novitate mali, divesque miserque, effugere optat opes; et quae modo voverat, odit.[1]

But it is impossible that men should not sooner or later have made reflections on so wretched a situation, and upon the calamities with which they were overwhelmed. The rich in particular must have soon perceived how much they suffered by a perpetual war, of which they alone supported all the expense, and in which, though all risked life, they alone risked any property. Besides, whatever color they might pretend to give their usurpations, they sufficiently saw that these usurpations were in the main founded upon false and precarious titles, and that what they had acquired by mere force, others could again by mere force wrest out of their hands, without leaving them the least room to complain of such a proceeding. Even those, who owed all their riches to their own industry, could scarce ground their acquisitions upon a better title. It availed them nothing to say, It was I built this wall; I acquired this spot by my labor. Who traced it out for you, another might object, and what right have you to expect payment at our expense for doing that we did not oblige you to do? Don't you know that numbers of your brethren perish, or suffer grievously for want of what you have too much of, and that you should have had the express and unanimous consent of mankind to appropriate to yourself more of the common subsistence, more than you needed for yours? Destitute of valid reasons to justify, and sufficient forces to defend himself; crushing individuals with ease, but with equal ease crushed by banditti; one against all, and unable, on account of mutual jealousies, to unite with his equals against enemies united by the common hopes of pillage; the rich man, thus pressed by necessity, at last conceived the deepest project that ever entered the human mind: this was to employ in his favor the very forces that attacked him, to make allies of his enemies, to inspire them with other maxims, and make them adopt other institutions as favourable to his pretensions, as the law of nature was unfavorable to them.

With this view, after laying before his neighbors all the horrors of a situation, which armed them all one against another, which rendered their possessions as burdensome as their wants, and in which no one could expect any safety either in poverty or riches, he easily invented specious arguments to bring them over to his purpose. "Let us unite," said he, "to secure the weak from oppression, restrain the ambitious, and secure to every man the possession of what belongs to him: Let us form rules of justice and of peace, to which all may be obliged to conform, which shall give no preference to anyone, but may in some sort make amends for the caprice of fortune, by submitting alike the powerful and the weak to the observance of mutual duties. In a word, instead of turning our forces against ourselves, let us collect them into a sovereign power, which may govern us by wise laws, may protect and defend all the members of the association, repel common enemies, and maintain a perpetual concord and harmony among us.''

Many fewer words of this kind would have sufficed to persuade men so uncultured and easily seduced, who had besides too many quarrels among themselves to live without arbiters, and too much avarice and ambition to live long without masters. All gladly offered their necks to the yoke, thinking they were securing their liberty; for though they had sense enough to perceive the advantages of a political constitution, they had not experience enough to see beforehand the dangers of it. Those among them who were best qualified to foresee abuses were precisely those who expected to benefit by them; even the soberest judged it requisite to sacrifice one part of their liberty to insure the rest, as a wounded man has his arm cut off to save the rest of his body.

Such was, or must have been, the origin of society and of law, which gave new fetters to the weak and new power to the rich; irretrievably destroyed natural liberty, fixed for ever the laws of property and inequality; changed an artful usurpation into an irrevocable right; and for the benefit of a few ambitious individuals subjected the rest of mankind to perpetual labor, servitude, and misery. We may easily conceive how the establishment of a single society rendered that of all the rest absolutely necessary, and how, to withstand united forces, it became necessary for the rest of mankind to unite in their turn. Societies once formed in this manner, soon multiplied or spread to such a degree, as to cover the face of the earth; and not to leave a corner in the whole universe, where a man could throw off the yoke, and withdraw his head from under the often ill-conducted sword which he saw perpetually hanging over it. The civil law being thus be-

come the common rule of citizens, the law of nature no longer obtained except between the different societies, where under the name of the law of nations, it was modified by some tacit conventions to render commerce possible, and supply the place of natural compassion, which, losing by degrees all that influence over societies which it originally had over individuals, no longer exists but in some great souls, who consider themselves as citizens of the world, force the imaginary barriers that separate people from people, after the example of the sovereign being from whom we all derive our existence, and include the whole human race in their benevolence.

Political bodies, thus remaining in a state of nature among themselves, soon experienced the inconveniencies which had obliged individuals to quit it; and this state became much more fatal to these great bodies, than it had been before to the individuals which now composed them. Hence those national wars, those battles, those murders, those reprisals, which make nature shudder and shock reason; hence all those horrible prejudices, which make it a virtue and an honor to shed human blood. The worthiest men learned to consider cutting the throats of their fellows as a duty; at length men began to butcher each other by thousands without knowing for what; and more murders were committed in a single action, and more horrible disorders at the taking of a single town, than had been committed in the state of nature during ages together upon the whole face of the earth. Such are the first effects we may conceive to have arisen from the division of mankind into different societies. Let us return to their institution.

I know that several writers have assigned other origins to political society; as for instance, the conquests of the powerful, or the union of the weak; and it is no matter which of these causes we adopt in regard to what I am going to establish. That which I have just laid down, however, seems to me the most natural, for the following reasons. First, because, in the first case, the right of conquest being in fact no right at all, it could not serve as a foundation for any other right, the conqueror and the conquered ever remaining with respect to each other in a state of war, unless the conquered, restored to the full possession of their liberty, should freely choose their conqueror for their chief. Until then, whatever capitulations might have been made between them being founded upon violence, and thus ipso facto null and void, there could not have existed in this hypothesis either a true society, or a political body, or any other law but that of the strongest. Secondly, because these words *strong* and *weak,* are, in the second case, ambiguous; for during the interval between the establishment of the right of property or prior occupancy, and that of political government, the meaning of these terms is better expressed by the words *poor* and *rich,* as before the establishment of laws men in reality had no other means of subjecting their equals, but by invading their property, or by parting with some of their own property to them. Thirdly, because the poor having nothing but their liberty to lose, it would have been the height of madness in them to give up willingly the only blessing they had left without obtaining some consideration for it; whereas the rich being sensitive, if I may say so, in every part of their possessions, it was much easier to do them mischief, and therefore more incumbent upon them to guard against it; and because, in fine, it is but reasonable to suppose that a thing has been invented by him to whom it could be of service, rather than by him to whom it must prove detrimental.

Government in its infancy had no regular and permanent form. For want of a sufficient fund of philosophy and experience, men could see no further than the present inconveniencies, and never thought of providing for future ones except as they arose. In spite of all the labors of the wisest legislators, the political state still continued imperfect, because it was in a manner the work of chance; and, as the foundations of it were ill laid, time, though sufficient to reveal its defects and suggest the remedies for them, could never mend its original faults. It was always being mended; whereas they should have begun as Lycurgus did at Sparta, by clearing the ground and removing all the old materials, so that they could then put up a good edifice. Society at first consisted merely

of some general conventions which all the members bound themselves to observe, and the performance of which the whole body guaranteed to every individual. Experience was necessary to show the great weakness of such a constitution, and how easy it was for those who infringed it to escape the conviction or chastisement of faults, of which the public alone was to be both the witness and the judge; the laws could not fail of being eluded a thousand ways; inconveniencies and disorders could not but multiply continually, until it was at last found necessary to think of committing to private persons the dangerous trust of public authority, and to magistrates the care of enforcing obedience to the decisions of the people. For to say that chiefs were elected before the confederacy was formed, and that the ministers of the laws existed before the laws themselves, is a supposition too ridiculous to deserve serious refutation.

It would be equally unreasonable to imagine that men at first threw themselves into the arms of an absolute master, without any conditions or consideration on his side; and that the first means contrived by jealous and unconquered men for their common safety was to run headlong into slavery. In fact, why did they give themselves superiors, if it was not to be defended by them against oppression, and protected in their lives, liberties, and properties, which are in a manner the elements of their being? Now in the relations between man and man, the worst that can happen to one man being to see himself at the mercy of another, would it not have been contrary to the dictates of good sense to begin by making over to a chief the only things they needed his assistance to preserve? What equivalent could he have offered them for so great a right? And had he presumed to exact it on pretense of defending them, would he not have immediately received the answer in the fable: What worse will an enemy do to us? It is therefore past dispute, and indeed a fundamental maxim of all political law, that people gave themselves chiefs to defend their liberty and not to be enslaved by them. *If we have a Prince,* said Pliny to Trajan, *it is in order that he may keep us from having a master.*

Politicians argue in regard to the love of liberty with the same sophistry that philosophers do in regard to the state of nature; by the things they see they judge of things very different which they have never seen, and they attribute to men a natural inclination to slavery, on account of the patience with which the slaves within their notice bear the yoke; not reflecting that it is with liberty as with innocence and virtue, the value of which is not known but by those who possess them, and the taste for which is lost when they are lost. I know the charms of your country, said Brasidas to a satrap who was comparing the life of the Spartans with that of the Persepolites; but you cannot know the pleasures of mine.

As an unbroken courser erects his mane, paws the ground, and rages at the bare sight of the bit, while a trained horse patiently suffers both whip and spur, just so the barbarian will never reach his neck to the yoke which civilized man carries without murmuring, but prefers the most stormy liberty to a peaceful slavery. It is not therefore by the servile disposition of enslaved nations that we must judge of the natural dispositions of man for or against slavery, but by the prodigies done by every free people to secure themselves from oppression. I know that the former are constantly crying up that peace and tranquility they enjoy in their irons, and that *miserrimam servitutem pacem appellant:*[2] But when I see the latter sacrifice pleasures, peace, riches, power, and even life itself to the preservation of that one treasure so disdained by those who have lost it; when I see freeborn animals through a natural abhorrence of captivity dash their brains out against the bars of their prison; when I see multitudes of naked savages despise European pleasures, and brave hunger, fire and sword, and death itself to preserve their independence, I feel that it is not for slaves to argue about liberty.

As to paternal authority, from which several have derived absolute government and every other mode of society, it is sufficient, without having recourse to Locke and Sidney, to observe that nothing in the world differs more from the cruel spirit of despotism than the gentleness of that authority, which looks more to the advantage of him who obeys than to the utility of him who commands; that by the law of nature the father continues master of his child no longer than the child stands in need of his assistance; that after that term they become equal, and that then the son, entirely independent of the father, owes him no obedience, but only respect. Gratitude is indeed a duty which we are bound to pay, but which benefactors cannot exact. Instead of saying that civil society is derived from paternal authority, we should rather say that it is to the former that the latter owes its principal force. No one individual was acknowledged as the father of several other individuals, until they settled about him. The father's goods, which he can indeed dispose of as he pleases, are the ties which hold his children to their dependence upon him, and he may divide his substance among them in proportion as they shall have deserved by a continual deference to his commands. Now the subjects of a despotic chief, far from having any such favor to expect from him, as both themselves and all they have are his property, or at least are considered by him as such, are obliged to receive as a favor what he relinquishes to them of their own property. He does them justice when he strips them; he treats them with mercy when he suffers them to live.

By continuing in this manner to test facts by right, we should discover as little solidity as truth in the voluntary establishment of tyranny; and it would be a hard matter to prove the validity of a contract which was binding only on one side, in which one of the parties should take everything and the other nothing, and which could only turn out to the prejudice of him who had bound himself. This odious system is even today far from being that of wise and good monarchs, and especially of the kings of France, as may be seen by divers passages in their edicts, and particularly by that of a celebrated piece published in 1667 in the name and by the orders of Louis XIV. "Let it therefore not be said that the Sovereign is not subject to the laws of his Realm, since the contrary is a maxim of the law of nations which flattery has sometimes attacked, but which good princes have always defended as the tutelary divinity of their Realms. How much more reasonable is it to say with the sage Plato, that the perfect happiness of a State consists in the subjects obeying their prince, the prince obeying the laws, and the laws being equitable and always directed to the good of the public?'' I shall not stop to consider whether, liberty being the noblest faculty of man, it is not degrading our nature, lowering ourselves to the level of brutes, who are the slaves of instinct, and even offending the author of our being, to renounce without reserve the most precious of his gifts, and to submit to committing all the crimes he has forbidden us, merely to gratify a mad or a cruel master; and whether that sublime craftsman must be more irritated at seeing his work dishonored than at seeing it destroyed. I shall only ask what right those, who were not afraid thus to degrade themselves, could have to subject their posterity to the same ignominy, and renounce for them, blessings which come not from their liberality, and without which life itself must appear a burden to all those who are worthy to live.

Pufendorf says that, as we can transfer our property from one to another by contracts and conventions, we may likewise divest ourselves of our liberty in favor of other men. This, in my opinion, is a very poor way of arguing; for, in the first place, the property I cede to another becomes a thing quite foreign to me, and the abuse of which can no way affect me; but it concerns me greatly that my liberty is not abused, and I cannot, without incurring the guilt of the crimes I may be forced to commit, expose myself to become the instrument of any. Besides, the right of property being of mere human convention and institution, every man may dispose as he pleases of what he possesses: but the case is otherwise with regard to the essential gifts of nature, such as life and liberty, which every man is permitted to enjoy, and of which it is doubtful at least whether any man has a right to divest himself: by giving up the one, we degrade our being; by giving up the other we annihilate it as much as it is our power to do so; and as no temporal enjoyments can indemnify us for the loss of either, it would be an offense against both nature and reason to renounce them for any consideration. But

though we could transfer our liberty as we do our property, it would be quite different with regard to our children, who enjoy the father's property only by the transmission of his right; whereas liberty being a blessing, which as men they hold from nature, their parents have no right to strip them of it; so that, just as to establish slavery it was necessary to do violence to nature, so it was necessary to alter nature to perpetuate such a right; and the jurisconsults, who have gravely pronounced that the child of a slave is born a slave, have in other words decided that a man will not be born a man.

It therefore appears to me incontestibly true, that not only governments did not begin by arbitrary power, which is but the corruption and extreme term of government, and at length brings it back to the law of the strongest against which governments were at first the remedy; but even that, supposing they had begun in this manner, such power being illegal in itself could never have served as a foundation for social law, nor of course for the inequality it instituted.

Without embarking now upon the inquiries which still remain to be made into the nature of the fundamental pact underlying every kind of government, I shall accept the common opinion, and confine myself here to holding the establishment of the political body to be a real contract between the multitude and the chiefs elected by it. A contract by which both parties oblige themselves to the observance of the laws that are therein stipulated, and form the ties of their union. The multitude having, in regard to their social relations, concentrated all their wills in one, all the articles, in regard to which this will expresses itself, become so many fundamental laws, which oblige without exception all the members of the State, and one of which regulates the choice and power of the magistrates appointed to look to the execution of the rest. This power extends to everything that can maintain the constitution, but extends to nothing that can alter it. To this power are added honors, that may render the laws and their ministers respectable; and the ministers are distinguished by certain prerogatives, which may recompense them for the heavy burdens inseparable from a good administration. The magistrate, on his side, obliges himself not to use the power with which he is entrusted except in conformity to the intention of his constituents, to maintain every one of them in the peaceable possession of his property, and upon all occasions to prefer the public good to his own private interest.

Before experience had shown, or knowledge of the human heart had made the abuses inseparable from such a constitution foreseeable, it must have appeared so much the more perfect, as those appointed to look to its preservation had themselves had most interest in it; for magistracy and its rights being built solely on the fundamental laws, as soon as these ceased to exist, the magistrates would cease to be legitimate, the people would no longer be bound to obey them, and, as the essence of the State did not consist in the magistrates but in the laws, each one would rightfully regain his natural liberty.

A little reflection would afford us new arguments in confirmation of this truth, and the nature of the contract might alone convince us that it cannot be irrevocable: for if there were no superior power capable of guaranteeing the fidelity of the contracting parties and of obliging them to fulfill their mutual engagements, they would remain sole judges in their own cause, and each of them would always have a right to renounce the contract, as soon as he discovered that the other had broke the conditions of it, or that these conditions ceased to suit his private convenience. Upon this principle, the right of abdication may probably be founded. Now, to consider, as we do, only what is human in this institution, if the magistrate, who has all the power in his own hands, and who appropriates to himself all the advantages of the contract, has nonetheless a right to renounce his authority; how much better a right should the people, who pay for all the faults of its chief, have to renounce their dependence upon him. But the shocking dissensions and disorders without number, which would be the necessary consequence of so dangerous a privilege, show more than anything else how much human governments stood in need of a more solid basis than that of mere reason, and how necessary it was for the public tranquillity, that

the will of the Almighty should interpose to give to sovereign authority a sacred and inviolable character, which should deprive subjects of the fatal right to dispose of it. If mankind had received no other advantages from religion, this alone would be sufficient to make them adopt and cherish it, since it is the means of saving more blood than fanaticism has been the cause of spilling. But let us resume the thread of our hypothesis.

The various forms of government owe their origin to the various degrees of inequality which existed between individuals at the time of their institution. Where a man happened to be preeminent in power, virtue, riches, or credit, he became sole magistrate, and the State assumed a monarchical form. If several of pretty equal eminence stood out over all the rest, they were jointly elected, and this election produced an aristocracy. Those whose fortune or talents were less unequal, and who had deviated less from the state of nature, retained in common the supreme administration, and formed a democracy. Time demonstrated which of these forms suited mankind best. Some remained altogether subject to the laws; others soon bowed their necks to masters. The former labored to preserve their liberty; the latter thought of nothing but invading that of their neighbors, jealous at seeing others enjoy a blessing which they themselves had lost. In a word, riches and conquest fell to the share of the one, and virtue and happiness to that of the other.

In these various modes of government the offices at first were all elective; and when riches did not decide, the preference was given to merit, which gives a natural ascendancy, and to age, which is the parent of deliberateness in council, and experience in execution. The ancients among the Hebrews, the Gerontes of Sparta, the Senate of Rome, nay, the very etymology of our word *Seigneur,* show how much grey hairs were formerly respected. The oftener the choice fell upon old men, the oftener it became necessary to repeat it, and the more the trouble of such repetitions became sensible; intrigues took place; factions arose, the parties grew bitter; civil wars blazed forth; the lives of the citizens were sacrificed to the pretended happiness of the State; and things at last came to such a pass, as to be ready to relapse into their primitive confusion. The ambition of the principal men induced them to take advantage of these circumstances to perpetuate the hitherto temporary offices in their families; the people already inured to dependence, accustomed to ease and the conveniences of life, and too much enervated to break their fetters, consented to the increase of their slavery for the sake of securing their tranquillity; and it is thus that chiefs, become hereditary, contracted the habit of considering their offices as a family estate, and themselves as proprietors of those communities, of which at first they were but mere officers; of calling their fellow-citizens their slaves; of numbering them, like cattle, among their belongings; and of calling themselves the peers of gods, and kings of kings.

By pursuing the progress of inequality in these different revolutions, we shall discover that the establishment of laws and of the right of property was the first term of it; the institution of magistrates the second; and the third and last the changing of legal into arbitrary power; so that the different states of the rich and poor were authorized by the first epoch; those of the powerful and weak by the second; and by the third those of master and slave, which formed the last degree of inequality, and the term in which all the rest at last end, until new revolutions entirely dissolve the government, or bring it back nearer to its legal constitution.

To conceive the necessity of this progress, we are not so much to consider the motives for the establishment of the body politic, as the forms it assumes in its realization; and the faults with which it is necessarily attended: for those vices, which render social institutions necessary, are the same which render the abuse of such institutions unavoidable. And as laws (Sparta alone excepted, whose laws chiefly regarded the education of children, and where Lycurgus established such manners and customs, as made laws almost needless) are in general less strong than the passions, and restrain men without changing them, it would be no hard matter to prove that every government, which carefully guarding against all alteration

and corruption should scrupulously comply with the purpose of its establishment, was set up unnecessarily; and that a country, where no one either eluded the laws, or made an ill use of magistracy, required neither laws nor magistrates.

Political distinctions are necessarily led in with civil distinctions. The inequality between the people and the chiefs increases so fast as to be soon felt by individuals, and appears among them in a thousand shapes according to their passions, their talents, and circumstances. The magistrate cannot usurp any illegal power without making himself creatures with whom he must share it. Besides, citizens only allow themselves to be oppressed in proportion as hurried on by a blind ambition, and looking rather below than above them, they come to love authority more than independence. When they submit to fetters, it is only to be the better able to fetter others in their turn. It is no easy matter to reduce to obedience a man who does not wish to command; and the most astute politician would find it impossible to subdue those men who only desire to be independent. But inequality easily gains ground among base and ambitious souls, ever ready to run the risks of fortune, and almost indifferent whether they command or obey, as she proves either favorable or adverse to them. Thus then there must have been a time, when the eyes of the people were bewitched to such a degree, that their rulers needed only to have said to the lowest of men, "Be great you and all your posterity," to make him immediately appear great in the eyes of everyone as well as in his own; and his descendants took still more upon them, in proportion to their distance from him: the more distant and uncertain the cause, the greater the effect; the longer line of drones a family produced, the more illustrious it was reckoned.

Were this a proper place to enter into details, I could easily explain in what manner inequalities of credit and authority become unavoidable among private persons the moment that, united into one body, they are obliged to compare themselves one with another, and to note the differences which they find in the continual intercourse every man must have with his neighbor. These differences are of several kinds; but riches, nobility or rank, power and personal merit, being in general the principal distinctions, by which men in society measure each other, I could prove that the harmony or conflict between these different forces is the surest indication of the good or bad original constitution of any State: I could show that among these four kinds of inequality, personal qualities being the source of all the rest, riches are that in which they ultimately terminate, because, being the most immediately useful to the prosperity of individuals, and the most easy to communicate, they are made use of to purchase every other distinction. By this observation we are enabled to judge with tolerable exactness, how much any people has deviated from its primitive institution, and what steps it has still to make to the extreme term of corruption. I could show how much this universal desire of reputation, of honors, of preference, with which we are all devoured, exercises and compares our talents and our forces; how much it excites and multiplies our passions; and, by creating an universal competition, rivalry, or rather enmity among men, how many disappointments, successes, and catastrophes of every kind it daily causes among the innumerable aspirants whom it engages in the same competition. I could show that it is to this itch of being spoken of, to this fury of distinguishing ourselves which seldom or never gives us a moment's respite, that we owe both the best and the worst things among us, our virtues and our vices, our sciences and our errors, our conquerors and our philosophers; that is to say, a great many bad things and a very few good ones. I could prove, in short, that if we behold a handful of rich and powerful men seated on the pinnacle of fortune and greatness, while the crowd grovel in obscurity and want, it is merely because the first prize what they enjoy but in the same degree that others are deprived of it; and that, without changing their condition, they would cease to be happy the minute the people ceased to be miserable.

But these details would alone furnish sufficient matter for a more considerable work, in which we might weigh the advantages and disadvantages of every species of government, relatively to the rights of man in a state of na-

ture, and might likewise unveil all the different faces under which inequality has appeared to this day, and may hereafter appear to the end of time, according to the nature of these several governments, and the revolutions which time must unavoidably occasion in them. We should then see the multitude oppressed by domestic tyrants in consequence of those very precautions taken by them to guard against foreign masters. We should see oppression increase continually without its being ever possible for the oppressed to know where it would stop, nor what lawful means they had left to check its progress. We should see the rights of citizens, and the liberties of nations extinguished by slow degrees, and the groans and protestations and appeals of the weak treated as seditious murmurings. We should see policy confine to a mercenary portion of the people the honor of defending the common cause. We should see taxes made necessary, the disheartened husbandman desert his field even in time of peace, and quit the plough to gird on the sword. We should see fatal and whimsical rules laid down for the code of honor. We should see the champions of their country sooner or later become her enemies, and perpetually holding their daggers to the breasts of their fellow-citizens. Nay the time would come when they might be heard to say to the oppressor of their country:

Pectore si fratris gladium juguloque parentis Condere me jubeas, gravidaeque in viscera partu Conjungis, invita peragam tamen omnia dextra.[3]

From the vast inequality of conditions and fortunes, from the great variety of passions and of talents, of useless arts, of pernicious arts, of frivolous sciences, would issue clouds of prejudices equally contrary to reason, to happiness, to virtue. We should see the chiefs foment everything that tends to weaken men united in societies by dividing them; everything that, while it gives society an air of apparent harmony, sows in it the seeds of real dissension; everything that can inspire the different classes with mutual distrust and hatred by an opposition of their rights and interests, and so strengthen that power which controls them all.

It is from the midst of this disorder and these revolutions, that despotism, gradually rearing themselves as having, a right to equal respect and consideration in determining the principles by which the basic arrangements of their society are to be regulated. Finally, we express their being free by stipulating that they each have, and view themselves as having, fundamental aims and higher-order interests (a conception of their good) in the name of which it is legitimate to make claims on one another in the design of their institutions. At the same time, as free persons they do not think of themselves as inevitably bound to, or as identical with, the pursuit of any particular array of fundamental interests that they may have at any given time; instead, they conceive of themselves as capable of revising and altering these final ends and they give priority to preserving their liberty in this regard.

In addition, I assume that a well-ordered society is stable relative to its conception of justice. This means that social institutions generate an effective supporting sense of justice. Regarding society as a going concern, its members acquire as they grow up an allegiance to the public conception and this allegiance usually overcomes the temptations and strains of social life.

Now we are here concerned with a conception of justice and the idea of equality that belongs to it. Thus, let us suppose that a well-ordered society exists under circumstances of justice. These necessitate some conception of justice and give point to its special role. First, moderate scarcity obtains. This means that although social cooperation is productive and mutually advantageous (one person's or group's gain need not be another's loss), natural resources and the state of technology are such that the fruits of joint efforts fall short of the claims that people make. And second, persons and associations have contrary conceptions of the good that lead them to make conflicting claims on one another; and they also hold opposing religious, philosophical, and moral convictions (on matters the public conception leaves open) as well as different ways of evaluating arguments and evidence in many important cases. Given these circumstances, the members of a well-ordered society are not indifferent as to how the benefits pro-

duced by their cooperation are distributed. set of principles is required to judge betwee social arrangements that shape this division advantages. Thus the role of the principles justice is to assign rights and duties in the ba structure of society and to specify the mann in which institutions are to influence the ov all distribution of the returns from social c operation. The basic structure is the prima subject of justice and that to which the pr ciples of justice in the first instance apply.

It is perhaps useful to observe that the noti of a well-ordered society is an extension of idea of religious toleration. Consider a plur istic society, divided along religious, ethnic, cultural lines in which the various groups ha reached a firm understanding on the scheme principles to regulate their fundamental stitutions. While they have deep differen about other things, there is public agreem on this framework of principles and citiz are attached to it. A well-ordered society not attained social harmony in all things, if deed that would be desirable; but it achieved a large measure of justice and es lished a basis for civic friendship, which ma people's secure association together possib

II

The notion of a well-ordered society assu that the basic structure, the fundamental s institutions and their arrangement into institutions and their arrangement into scheme, is the primary subject of justice. V is the reason for this assumption? First of any discussion of social justice must take nature of the basic structure into account. pose we begin with the initially attractive that the social process should be allowe develop over time as free agreements fairl rived at and fully honoured require. Stra away we need an account of when agreem are free and the conditions under which are reached are fair. In addition, while conditions may be satisfied at an earlier the accumulated results of agreements in junction with social and historical contir cies are likely to change institutions opportunities so that the conditions for fre fair agreements no longer hold. The

up her hideous head, and devouring in every part of the State all that still remained sound and untainted, would at last succeed in trampling upon the laws and the people, and establish itself upon the ruins of the republic. The times immediately preceding this last alteration would be times of calamity and trouble; but at last everything would be swallowed up by the monster; and the people would no longer have chiefs or laws, but only tyrants. From this fatal moment all regard to virtue and manners would likewise disappear; for despotism, *cui ex ho nesto nulla est spes,*[4] tolerates no other master, wherever it reigns; the moment it speaks, probity and duty lose all their influence, and the blindest obedience is the only virtue to slaves.

This is the last term of inequality, the extreme point which closes the circle and meets that from which we set out. It is here that all private men return to their primitive equality, because they are nothing; and that, subjects having no longer any law but the will of their master, nor the master any other law but his passions, all notions of good and principles of justice again disappear. This is when everything returns to the sole law of the strongest, and of course to a new state of nature different from that with which we began, inasmuch as the first was the state of nature in its purity, and this one the consequence of excessive corruption. There is, in other respects, so little difference between these two states, and the contract of government is so much dissolved by despotism, that the despot is master only so long as he continues the strongest, and that, as soon as they can expel him, they may do it without his having the least right to complain of their violence. The insurrection, which ends in the death or deposition of a sultan, is as juridical an act as any by which the day before he disposed of the lives and fortunes of his subjects. Force alone upheld him, force alone overturns him. Thus all things take place and succeed in their natural order; and whatever may be the upshot of these hasty and frequent revolutions, no one man has reason to complain of another's injustice, but only of his own indiscretion or bad fortune.

By thus discovering and following the lost and forgotten road, which man must have fol-

lowed in going from the state of nature to the social state, by restoring, together with the intermediate positions which I have been just indicating, those which want of time obliges me to omit, or which my imagination has failed to suggest, every attentive reader must unavoidably be struck at the immense space which separates these two states. In this slow succession of things he may meet with the solution of an infinite number of problems in morality and politics, which philosophers are puzzled to solve. He will perceive that, the mankind of one age not being the mankind of another, the reason why Diogenes could not find a man was, that he sought among his contemporaries the man of a bygone period: Cato, he will then see, fell with Rome and with liberty, because he did not suit the age in which he lived; and the greatest of men served only to astonish that world, which would have cheerfully obeyed him, had he come into it five hundred years earlier. In a word, he will find himself in a condition to understand how the soul and the passions of men by insensible alterations change as it were their very nature; how it comes to pass, that in the long run our wants and our pleasures seek new objects; that, original man vanishing by degrees, society no longer offers to the eyes of the sage anything but an assemblage of artificial men and factitious passions, which are the work of all these new relations, and have no foundation in nature. What reflection teaches us on that score, observation entirely confirms. Savage man and civilized man differ so much at the bottom of their hearts and in their inclinations, that what constitutes the supreme happiness of the one would reduce the other to despair. The first sighs for nothing but repose and liberty; he desires only to live, and to be exempt from labor; nay, the ataraxy of the most confirmed Stoic falls short of his profound indifference to every other object. Civilized man, on the other hand, is always in motion, perpetually sweating and toiling, and racking his brains to find out occupations still more laborious: he continues a drudge to his last minute; nay, he courts death to be able to live, or renounces life to acquire immortality. He pays court to men in power whom he hates, and to rich men whom he de-spises; he sticks at nothing to have the honor of serving them; he boasts proudly of his baseness and their protection; and proud of his slavery, he speaks with disdain of those who have not the honor of sharing it. What a spectacle must the painful and envied labors of a European minister of state form in the eyes of a Caribbean! How many cruel deaths would not this indolent savage prefer to such a horrid life, which very often is not even sweetened by the pleasure of doing good? But to see the purpose of so many cares, his mind would first have to affix some meaning to these words *power* and *reputation;* he should be apprised that there are men who set value on the way they are looked on by the rest of mankind, who know how to be happy and satisfied with themselves on the testimony of others rather than upon their own. In fact, the real source of all those differences is that the savage lives within himself, whereas social man, constantly outside himself, knows only how to live in the opinion of others; and it is, if I may say so, merely from their judgment of him that he derives the consciousness of his own existence. It is foreign to my subject to show how this disposition engenders so much indifference toward good and evil, notwithstanding such fine discourses on morality; how everything, being reduced to appearances, becomes mere art and mummery; honor, friendship, virtue, and often vice itself, of which we at last learn the secret of boasting; how, in short, ever asking others what we are, and never daring to ask ourselves, in the midst of so much philosophy, humanity and politeness, and such sublime moral codes, we have nothing but a deceitful and frivolous exterior, honor without virtue, reason without wisdom, and pleasure without happiness. It is sufficient that I have proved that this is certainly not the original state of man, and that it is merely the spirit of society, and the inequality which society engenders, that thus

change and transform all our natural inclinations.

I have endeavored to reveal the origin and progress of inequality, the institution and abuse of political societies, as far as these things are capable of being deduced from the nature of man by the mere light of reason, and independently of those sacred maxims which give the sanction of divine right to sovereign authority. It follows from this survey that inequality, almost non-existent among men in the state of nature, derives its force and its growth from the development of our faculties and the progress of the human mind, and at last becomes permanent and lawful by the establishment of property and of laws. It likewise follows that moral[5] inequality, authorized, solely by positive right,[6] clashes with natural right, whenever it is not in proportion to physical[7] inequality; a distinction which sufficiently determines what we are to think of that kind of inequality which obtains in all civilized nations, since it is evidently against the law of nature that children should command old men, and fools lead the wise, and that a handful should gorge themselves with superfluities, while the starving masses lack the barest necessities of life.

Notes

1. Both rich and poor, shocked at their newfound ills, would fly from wealth, and hate what they had sought. (Ovid *Metamorphoses* 11. 127.)
2. "They call the most wretched slavery peace." (Tacitus *Histories* 4. 17.)
3. "If you order me to plunge my sword into my brother's breast and into my father's throat and into the vitals of my wife heavy with child, I shall do, nevertheless, all these things even though my hand is unwilling." (Lucan *Pharsalia* 1. 376–8.)
4. "in which there is no hope afforded by honesty."
5. "Moral" should here be interpreted as meaning "social," or "artificial."
6. I.e., established laws.
7. I.e., "natural."

A Kantian Conception of Equality

JOHN RAWLS

My aim in these remarks is to give a brief account of the conception of equality that underlies the view expressed in *A Theory of Justice* and the principles considered there. I hope to state the fundamental intuitive idea simply and informally; and so I make no attempt to sketch the argument from the original position. In fact, this construction is not mentioned until the end and then only to indicate its role in giving a Kantian interpretation to the conception of equality already presented.[1]

I

When fully articulated, any conception of justice expresses a conception of the person, of the relations between persons, and of the general structure and ends of social cooperation. To accept the principles that represent a conception of justice is at the same time to accept an ideal of the person; and in acting from these principles we realize such an ideal. Let us begin, then, by trying to describe the kind of person we might want to be and the form of society we might wish to live in and to shape our interests and character. In this way we arrive at the notion of a well-ordered society. I shall first describe this notion and then use it to explain a Kantian conception of equality.

First of all, a well-ordered society is effectively regulated by a public conception of justice. That is, it is a society all of whose members accept, and know that the others accept, the same principles (the same conception) of justice. It is also the case that basic social institutions and their arrangement into one scheme (the basic structure) actually satisfy, and are on good grounds believed by everyone to satisfy, these principles. Finally, publicity also implies that the public conception is founded on reasonable beliefs that have been established by generally accepted methods of inquiry; and the same is true of the application of its principles to basic social arrangements. This last aspect of publicity does not mean that everyone holds the same religious, moral, and theoretical beliefs; on the contrary, there are assumed to be sharp and indeed irreconcilable differences on such questions. But at the same time there is a shared understanding that the principles of justice, and their application to the basic structure of society, should be determined by considerations and evidence that are supported by rational procedures commonly recognized.

Secondly, I suppose that the members of a well-ordered society are, and view themselves as, free and equal moral persons. They are moral persons in that, once they have reached the age of reason, each has, and views the others as having, a realized sense of justice; and this sentiment informs their conduct for the most part. That they are equal is expressed by the supposition that they each have, and view

John Rawls, "A Kantian Conception of Equality," from *The Cambridge Review* (February 1975). Reprinted by permission of the author and publisher.

up her hideous head, and devouring in every part of the State all that still remained sound and untainted, would at last succeed in trampling upon the laws and the people, and establish itself upon the ruins of the republic. The times immediately preceding this last alteration would be times of calamity and trouble; but at last everything would be swallowed up by the monster; and the people would no longer have chiefs or laws, but only tyrants. From this fatal moment all regard to virtue and manners would likewise disappear; for despotism, *cui ex honesto nulla est spes*,[4] tolerates no other master, wherever it reigns; the moment it speaks, probity and duty lose all their influence, and the blindest obedience is the only virtue to slaves.

This is the last term of inequality, the extreme point which closes the circle and meets that from which we set out. It is here that all private men return to their primitive equality, because they are nothing; and that, subjects having no longer any law but the will of their master, nor the master any other law but his passions, all notions of good and principles of justice again disappear. This is when everything returns to the sole law of the strongest, and of course to a new state of nature different from that with which we began, inasmuch as the first was the state of nature in its purity, and this one the consequence of excessive corruption. There is, in other respects, so little difference between these two states, and the contract of government is so much dissolved by despotism, that the despot is master only so long as he continues the strongest, and that, as soon as they can expel him, they may do it without his having the least right to complain of their violence. The insurrection, which ends in the death or deposition of a sultan, is as juridical an act as any by which the day before he disposed of the lives and fortunes of his subjects. Force alone upheld him, force alone overturns him. Thus all things take place and succeed in their natural order; and whatever may be the upshot of these hasty and frequent revolutions, no one man has reason to complain of another's injustice, but only of his own indiscretion or bad fortune.

By thus discovering and following the lost and forgotten road, which man must have followed in going from the state of nature to the social state, by restoring, together with the intermediate positions which I have been just indicating, those which want of time obliges me to omit, or which my imagination has failed to suggest, every attentive reader must unavoidably be struck at the immense space which separates these two states. In this slow succession of things he may meet with the solution of an infinite number of problems in morality and politics, which philosophers are puzzled to solve. He will perceive that, the mankind of one age not being the mankind of another, the reason why Diogenes could not find a man was, that he sought among his contemporaries the man of a bygone period: Cato, he will then see, fell with Rome and with liberty, because he did not suit the age in which he lived; and the greatest of men served only to astonish that world, which would have cheerfully obeyed him, had he come into it five hundred years earlier. In a word, he will find himself in a condition to understand how the soul and the passions of men by insensible alterations change as it were their very nature; how it comes to pass, that in the long run our wants and our pleasures seek new objects; that, original man vanishing by degrees, society no longer offers to the eyes of the sage anything but an assemblage of artificial men and factitious passions, which are the work of all these new relations, and have no foundation in nature. What reflection teaches us on that score, observation entirely confirms. Savage man and civilized man differ so much at the bottom of their hearts and in their inclinations, that what constitutes the supreme happiness of the one would reduce the other to despair. The first sighs for nothing but repose and liberty; he desires only to live, and to be exempt from labor; nay, the ataraxy of the most confirmed Stoic falls short of his profound indifference to every other object. Civilized man, on the other hand, is always in motion, perpetually sweating and toiling, and racking his brains to find out occupations still more laborious: he continues a drudge to his last minute; nay, he courts death to be able to live, or renounces life to acquire immortality. He pays court to men in power whom he hates, and to rich men whom he de-spises; he sticks at nothing to have the honor of serving them; he boasts proudly of his baseness and their protection; and proud of his slavery, he speaks with disdain of those who have not the honor of sharing it. What a spectacle must the painful and envied labors of a European minister of state form in the eyes of a Caribbean! How many cruel deaths would not this indolent savage prefer to such a horrid life, which very often is not even sweetened by the pleasure of doing good? But to see the purpose of so many cares, his mind would first have to affix some meaning to these words *power* and *reputation;* he should be apprised that there are men who set value on the way they are looked on by the rest of mankind, who know how to be happy and satisfied with themselves on the testimony of others rather than upon their own. In fact, the real source of all those differences is that the savage lives within himself, whereas social man, constantly outside himself, knows only how to live in the opinion of others; and it is, if I may say so, merely from their judgment of him that he derives the consciousness of his own existence. It is foreign to my subject to show how this disposition engenders so much indifference toward good and evil, notwithstanding such fine discourses on morality; how everything, being reduced to appearances, becomes mere art and mummery; honor, friendship, virtue, and often vice itself, of which we at last learn the secret of boasting; how, in short, ever asking others what we are, and never daring to ask ourselves, in the midst of so much philosophy, humanity and politeness, and such sublime moral codes, we have nothing but a deceitful and frivolous exterior, honor without virtue, reason without wisdom, and pleasure without happiness. It is sufficient that I have proved that this is certainly not the original state of man, and that it is merely the spirit of society, and the inequality which society engenders, that thus change and transform all our natural inclinations.

I have endeavored to reveal the origin and progress of inequality, the institution and abuse of political societies, as far as these things are capable of being deduced from the nature of man by the mere light of reason, and independently of those sacred maxims which give the sanction of divine right to sovereign authority. It follows from this survey that inequality, almost non-existent among men in the state of nature, derives its force and its growth from the development of our faculties and the progress of the human mind, and at last becomes permanent and lawful by the establishment of property and of laws. It likewise follows that moral[5] inequality, authorized, solely by positive right,[6] clashes with natural right, whenever it is not in proportion to physical[7] inequality; a distinction which sufficiently determines what we are to think of that kind of inequality which obtains in all civilized nations, since it is evidently against the law of nature that children should command old men, and fools lead the wise, and that a handful should gorge themselves with superfluities, while the starving masses lack the barest necessities of life.

Notes

1. Both rich and poor, shocked at their newfound ills, would fly from wealth, and hate what they had sought. (Ovid *Metamorphoses* 11. 127.)
2. "They call the most wretched slavery peace." (Tacitus *Histories* 4. 17.)
3. "If you order me to plunge my sword into my brother's breast and into my father's throat and into the vitals of my wife heavy with child, I shall do, nevertheless, all these things even though my hand is unwilling." (Lucan *Pharsalia* 1. 376–8.)
4. "in which there is no hope afforded by honesty."
5. "Moral" should here be interpreted as meaning "social," or "artificial."
6. I.e., established laws.
7. I.e., "natural."

A Kantian Conception of Equality

JOHN RAWLS

My aim in these remarks is to give a brief account of the conception of equality that underlies the view expressed in *A Theory of Justice* and the principles considered there. I hope to state the fundamental intuitive idea simply and informally; and so I make no attempt to sketch the argument from the original position. In fact, this construction is not mentioned until the end and then only to indicate its role in giving a Kantian interpretation to the conception of equality already presented.[1]

I

When fully articulated, any conception of justice expresses a conception of the person, of the relations between persons, and of the general structure and ends of social cooperation. To accept the principles that represent a conception of justice is at the same time to accept an ideal of the person; and in acting from these principles we realize such an ideal. Let us begin, then, by trying to describe the kind of person we might want to be and the form of society we might wish to live in and to shape our interests and character. In this way we arrive at the notion of a well-ordered society. I shall first describe this notion and then use it to explain a Kantian conception of equality.

First of all, a well-ordered society is effectively regulated by a public conception of justice. That is, it is a society all of whose members accept, and know that the others accept, the same principles (the same conception) of justice. It is also the case that basic social institutions and their arrangement into one scheme (the basic structure) actually satisfy, and are on good grounds believed by everyone to satisfy, these principles. Finally, publicity also implies that the public conception is founded on reasonable beliefs that have been established by generally accepted methods of inquiry; and the same is true of the application of its principles to basic social arrangements. This last aspect of publicity does not mean that everyone holds the same religious, moral, and theoretical beliefs; on the contrary, there are assumed to be sharp and indeed irreconcilable differences on such questions. But at the same time there is a shared understanding that the principles of justice, and their application to the basic structure of society, should be determined by considerations and evidence that are supported by rational procedures commonly recognized.

Secondly, I suppose that the members of a well-ordered society are, and view themselves as, free and equal moral persons. They are moral persons in that, once they have reached the age of reason, each has, and views the others as having, a realized sense of justice; and this sentiment informs their conduct for the most part. That they are equal is expressed by the supposition that they each have, and view

John Rawls, "A Kantian Conception of Equality," from *The Cambridge Review* (February 1975). Reprinted by permission of the author and publisher.

themselves as having, a right to equal respect and consideration in determining the principles by which the basic arrangements of their society are to be regulated. Finally, we express their being free by stipulating that they each have, and view themselves as having, fundamental aims and higher-order interests (a conception of their good) in the name of which it is legitimate to make claims on one another in the design of their institutions. At the same time, as free persons they do not think of themselves as inevitably bound to, or as identical with, the pursuit of any particular array of fundamental interests that they may have at any given time; instead, they conceive of themselves as capable of revising and altering these final ends and they give priority to preserving their liberty in this regard.

In addition, I assume that a well-ordered society is stable relative to its conception of justice. This means that social institutions generate an effective supporting sense of justice. Regarding society as a going concern, its members acquire as they grow up an allegiance to the public conception and this allegiance usually overcomes the temptations and strains of social life.

Now we are here concerned with a conception of justice and the idea of equality that belongs to it. Thus, let us suppose that a well-ordered society exists under circumstances of justice. These necessitate some conception of justice and give point to its special role. First, moderate scarcity obtains. This means that although social cooperation is productive and mutually advantageous (one person's or group's gain need not be another's loss), natural resources and the state of technology are such that the fruits of joint efforts fall short of the claims that people make. And second, persons and associations have contrary conceptions of the good that lead them to make conflicting claims on one another; and they also hold opposing religious, philosophical, and moral convictions (on matters the public conception leaves open) as well as different ways of evaluating arguments and evidence in many important cases. Given these circumstances, the members of a well-ordered society are not indifferent as to how the benefits produced by their cooperation are distributed. A set of principles is required to judge between social arrangements that shape this division of advantages. Thus the role of the principles of justice is to assign rights and duties in the basic structure of society and to specify the manner in which institutions are to influence the overall distribution of the returns from social cooperation. The basic structure is the primary subject of justice and that to which the principles of justice in the first instance apply.

It is perhaps useful to observe that the notion of a well-ordered society is an extension of the idea of religious toleration. Consider a pluralistic society, divided along religious, ethnic, or cultural lines in which the various groups have reached a firm understanding on the scheme of principles to regulate their fundamental institutions. While they have deep differences about other things, there is public agreement on this framework of principles and citizens are attached to it. A well-ordered society has not attained social harmony in all things, if indeed that would be desirable; but it has achieved a large measure of justice and established a basis for civic friendship, which makes people's secure association together possible.

II

The notion of a well-ordered society assumes that the basic structure, the fundamental social institutions and their arrangement into one scheme, is the primary subject of justice. What is the reason for this assumption? First of all, any discussion of social justice must take the nature of the basic structure into account. Suppose we begin with the initially attractive idea that the social process should be allowed to develop over time as free agreements fairly arrived at and fully honoured require. Straightaway we need an account of when agreements are free and the conditions under which they are reached are fair. In addition, while these conditions may be satisfied at an earlier time, the accumulated results of agreements in conjunction with social and historical contingencies are likely to change institutions and opportunities so that the conditions for free and fair agreements no longer hold. The basic structure specifies the background conditions against which the actions of individuals, groups, and associations take place. Unless this structure is regulated and corrected so as to be just over time, the social process with its procedures and outcomes is no longer just, however free and fair particular transactions may look to us when viewed by themselves. We recognize this principle when we say that the distribution resulting from voluntary market transactions will not in general be fair unless the antecedent distribution of income and wealth and the structure of the market is fair. Thus we seem forced to start with an account of a just basic structure. It's as if the most important agreement is that which establishes the principles to govern this structure. Moreover, these principles must be acknowledged ahead of time, as it were. To agree to them now, when everyone knows their present situation, would enable some to take unfair advantage of social and natural contingencies, and of the results of historical accidents and accumulations.

Other considerations also support taking the basic structure as the primary subject of justice. It has always been recognized that the social system shapes the desires and aspirations of its members; it determines in large part the kind of persons they want to be as well as the kind of persons they are. Thus an economic system is not only an institutional device for satisfying existing wants and desires but a way of fashioning wants and desires in the future. By what principles are we to regulate a scheme of institutions that has such fundamental consequences for our view of ourselves and for our interests and aims? This question becomes all the more crucial when we consider that the basic structure contains social and economic inequalities. I assume that these are necessary, or highly advantageous, for various reasons: they are required to maintain and to run social arrangements, or to serve as incentives; or perhaps they are a way to put resources in the hands of those who can make the best social use of them; and so on. In any case, given these inequalities, individuals' life-prospects are bound to be importantly affected by their family and class origins, by their natural endowments and the chance contingencies of

their (particular early) development, and by other accidents over the course of their lives. The social structure, therefore, limits people's ambitions and hopes in different ways, for they will with reason view themselves in part according to their place in it and take into account the means and opportunities they can realistically expect.

The justice of the basic structure is, then, of predominant importance. The first problem of justice is to determine the principles to regulate inequalities and to adjust the profound and long-lasting effects of social, natural, and historical contingencies, particularly since these contingencies combined with inequalities generate tendencies that, when left to themselves, are sharply at odds with the freedom and equality appropriate for a well-ordered society. In view of the special role of the basic structure, we cannot assume that the principles suitable to it are natural applications, or even extensions, of the familiar principles governing the actions of individuals and associations in everyday life which take place within its framework. Most likely we shall have to loosen ourselves from our ordinary perspective and take a more comprehensive viewpoint.

III

I shall now state and explain two principles of justice, and then discuss the appropriateness of these principles for a well-ordered society. They read as follows:

(1) Each person has an equal right to the most extensive scheme of equal basic liberties compatible with a similar scheme of liberties for all.

(2) Social and economic inequalities are to meet two conditions: they must be (a) to the greatest expected benefit of the least advantaged; and (b) attached to offices and positions open to all under conditions of fair opportunity.

The first of these principles is to take priority over the second; and the measure of benefit to the least advantaged is specified in terms of an index of social primary goods. These goods I define roughly as rights, liberties, and opportunities, income and wealth, and the social bases of self-respect. Individuals are assumed to want these goods whatever else they want, or whatever their final ends. The least advantaged are defined very roughly, as the overlap between those who are least favoured by each of the three main kinds of contingencies. Thus this group includes persons whose family and class origins are more disadvantaged than others, whose natural endowments have permitted them to fare less well, and whose fortune and luck have been relatively less favourable, all within the normal range (as noted below) and with the relevant measures based on social primary goods. Various refinements are no doubt necessary, but this definition of the least advantaged suitably expresses the link with the problem of contingency and should suffice for our purposes here.

I also suppose that everyone has physical needs and psychological capacities within the normal range, so that the problems of special health care and of how to treat the mentally defective do not arise. Besides prematurely introducing difficult questions that may take us beyond the theory of justice, the consideration of these hard cases can distract our moral perception by leading us to think of people distant from us whose fate arouses pity and anxiety. Whereas the first problem of justice concerns the relations among those who in the normal course of things are full and active participants in society and directly or indirectly associated together over the whole course of their life.

Now the members of a well-ordered society are free and equal; so let us first consider the fittingness of the two principles to their freedom, and then to their equality. These principles reflect two aspects of their freedom, namely, liberty and responsibility, which I take up in turn. In regard to liberty, recall that people in a well-ordered society view themselves as having fundamental aims and interests which they must protect, if this is possible. It is partly in the name of these interests that they have a right to equal consideration and respect in the design of their society. A familiar historical example is the religious interest; the interest in the integrity of the person, freedom

from psychological oppression and from physical assault and dismemberment is another. The notion of a well-ordered society leaves open what particular expression these interests take; only their general form is specified. But individuals do have interests of the requisite kind and the basic liberties necessary for their protection are guaranteed by the first principle.

It is essential to observe that these liberties are given by a list of liberties; important among these are freedom of thought and liberty of conscience, freedom of the person and political liberty. These liberties have a central range of application within which they can be limited and compromised only when they conflict with other basic liberties. Since they may be limited when they clash with one another, none of these liberties is absolute; but however they are adjusted to form one system, this system is to be the same for all. It is difficult, perhaps impossible, to give a complete definition of these liberties independently from the particular circumstances, social, economic, and technological, of a given well-ordered society. Yet the hypothesis is that the general form of such a list could be devised with sufficient exactness to sustain this conception of justice. Of course, liberties not on the list, for example, the right to own certain kinds of property (e.g., means of production), and freedom of contract as understood by the doctrine of laissez-faire, are not basic; and so they are not protected by the priority of the first principle.[2]

One reason, then, for holding the two principles suitable for a well-ordered society is that they assure the protection of the fundamental interests that members of such a society are presumed to have. Further reasons for this conclusion can be given by describing in more detail the notion of a free person. Thus we may suppose that such persons regard themselves as having a highest-order interest in how all their other interests, including even their fundamental ones, are shaped and regulated by social institutions. As I noted earlier, they do not think of themselves as unavoidably tied to any particular array of fundamental interests; instead they view themselves as capable of revising and changing these final ends. They wish, therefore, to give priority to their liberty to do this, and so their original allegiance and continued devotion to their ends are to be formed and affirmed under conditions that are free. Or, expressed another way, members of a well-ordered society are viewed as responsible for their fundamental interests and ends. While as members of particular associations some may decide in practice to yield much of this responsibility to others, the basic structure cannot be arranged so as to prevent people from developing their capacity to be responsible, or to obstruct their exercise of it once they attain it. Social arrangements must respect their autonomy and this points to the appropriateness of the two principles.

IV

These last remarks about responsibility may be elaborated further in connection with the role of social primary goods. As already stated, these are things that people in a well-ordered society may be presumed to want, whatever their final ends. And the two principles assess the basic structure in terms of certain of these goods: rights, liberties, and opportunities, income and wealth, and the social bases of self-respect. The latter are features of the basic structure that may reasonably be expected to affect people's self-respect and self-esteem (these are not the same) in important ways.[3] Part (a) of the second principle (the difference principle, or as economists prefer to say, the maximum criterion) uses an index of these goods to determine the least advantaged. Now certainly there are difficulties in working out a satisfactory index, but I shall leave these aside. Two points are particularly relevant here: first, social primary goods are certain objective characteristics of social institutions and of people's situation with respect to them; and second, the same index of these goods is used to compare everyone's social circumstances. It is clear, then, that although the index provides a basis for interpersonal comparisons for the purposes of justice, it is not a measure of individuals' overall satisfaction or dissatisfaction. Of course, the precise weights adopted in such an index cannot be laid down ahead of time, for these should be adjusted, to some degree at

least, in view of social conditions. What can be settled initially is certain constraints on these weights, as illustrated by the priority of the first principle.

Now, that the responsibility of free persons is implicit in the use of primary goods can be seen in the following way. We are assuming that people are able to control and to revise their wants and desires in the light of circumstances and that they are to have responsibility for doing so, provided that the principles of justice are fulfilled, as they are in a well-ordered society. Persons do not take their wants and desires as determined by happenings beyond their control. We are not, so to speak, assailed by them, as we are perhaps by disease and illness, so that wants and desires fail to support claims to the means of satisfaction in the way that disease and illness support claims to medicine and treatment.

Of course, it is not suggested that people must modify their desires and ends whatever their circumstances. The doctrine of primary goods does not demand the stoic virtues. Society for its part bears the responsibility for upholding the principles of justice and secures for everyone a fair share of primary goods (as determined by the difference principle) within a framework of equal liberty and fair equality of opportunity. It is within the limits of this division of responsibility that individuals and associations are expected to form and moderate their aims and wants. Thus among the members of a well-ordered society there is an understanding that as citizens they will press claims for only certain kinds of things, as allowed for by the principles of justice. Passionate convictions and zealous aspirations do not, as such, give anyone a claim upon social resources or the design of social institutions. For the purposes of justice, the appropriate basis of interpersonal comparisons is the index of primary goods and not strength of feeling or intensity of desire. The theory of primary goods is an extension of the notion of needs, which are distinct from aspirations and desires. One might say, then, that as citizens the members of a well-ordered society collectively take responsibility for dealing justly with one another founded on a public and objective measure of (extended) needs, while as individuals and members of associations they take responsibility for their preferences and devotions.

V

I now take up the appropriateness of the two principles in view of the equality of the members of a well-ordered society. The principles of equal liberty and fair opportunity (part (b) of the second principle) are a natural expression of this equality; and I assume, therefore, that such a society is one in which some form of democracy exists. Thus our question is: by what principle can members of a democratic society permit the tendencies of the basic structure to be deeply affected by social chance, and natural and historical contingencies?

Now since we are regarding citizens as free and equal moral persons (the priority of the first principle of equal liberty gives institutional expression to this), the obvious starting point is to suppose that all other social primary goods, and in particular income and wealth, should be equal: everyone should have an equal share. But society must take organizational requirements and economic efficiency into account. So it is unreasonable to stop at equal division. The basic structure should allow inequalities so long as these improve everyone's situation, including that of the least advantaged, provided these inequalities are consistent with equal liberty and fair opportunity. Because we start from equal shares, those who benefit least have, so to speak, a veto; and thus we arrive at the difference principle. Taking equality as the basis of comparison those who have gained more must do so on terms that are justifiable to those who have gained the least.

In explaining this principle, several matters should be kept in mind. First of all, it applies in the first instance to the main public principles and policies that regulate social and economic inequalities. It is used to adjust the system of entitlements and rewards, and the standards and precepts that this system employs. Thus the difference principle holds, for example, for income and property taxation, for fiscal and economic policy; it does not apply to particular transactions or distributions, nor, in general, to small scale and local decisions, but rather to the background against which these take place. No observable pattern is required of actual distribution, nor even any measure of the degree of equality (such as the Gini coefficient) that might be computed from these.[4] What is enjoined is that the inequalities make a functional contribution to those least favoured. Finally, the aim is not to eliminate the various contingencies, for some such contingencies seem inevitable. Thus even if an equal distribution of natural assets seemed more in keeping with the equality of free persons, the question of redistributing these assets (were this conceivable) does not arise, since it is incompatible with the integrity of the person. Nor need we make any specific assumptions about how great these variations are; we only suppose that, as realized in later life, they are influenced by all three kinds of contingencies. The question, then, is by what criterion a democratic society is to organize co-operation and arrange the system of entitlements that encourages and rewards productive efforts? We have a right to our natural abilities and a right to whatever we become entitled to by taking part in a fair social process. The problem is to characterize this process.[5]

At first sight, it may appear that the difference principle is arbitrarily biased towards the least favoured. But suppose, for simplicity, that there are only two groups, one significantly more fortunate than the other. Society could maximize the expectations of either group but not both, since we can maximize with respect to only one aim at a time. It seems plain that society should not do the best it can for those initially more advantaged; so if we reject the difference principle, we must prefer maximizing some weighted mean of the two expectations. But how should this weighted mean be specified? Should society proceed as if we had an equal chance of being in either group (in proportion to their size) and determine the mean that maximizes this purely hypothetical expectation? Now it is true that we sometimes agree to draw lots but normally only to things that cannot be appropriately divided or else cannot be enjoyed or suffered in common.[6]

And we are willing to use the lottery principle even in matters of lasting importance if there is no other way out. (Consider the example of conscription.) But to appeal to it in regulating the basic structure itself would be extraordinary. There is no necessity for society as an enduring system to invoke the lottery principle in this case; nor is there any reason for free and equal persons to allow their relations over the whole course of their life to be significantly affected by contingencies to the greater advantage of those already favoured by these accidents. No one had an antecedent claim to be benefited in this way; and so to maximize a weighted mean is, so to speak, to favour the more fortunate twice over. Society can, however, adopt the difference principle to arrange inequalities so that social and natural contingencies are efficiently used to the benefit of all, taking equal division as a benchmark. So while natural assets cannot be divided evenly, or directly enjoyed or suffered in common, the results of their productive efforts can be allocated in ways consistent with an initial equality. Those favoured by social and natural contingencies regard themselves as already compensated, as it were, by advantages to which no one (including themselves) had a prior claim. Thus they think the difference principle appropriate for regulating the system of entitlements and inequalities.

VI

The conception of equality contained in the principles of justice I have described as Kantian. I shall conclude by mentioning very briefly the reasons for this description. Of course, I do not mean that this conception is literally Kant's conception, but rather that it is one of no doubt several conceptions sufficiently similar to essential parts of his doctrine to make the adjective appropriate. Much depends on what one counts as essential. Kant's view is marked by a number of dualisms, in particular, the dualisms between the necessary and the contingent, form and content, reason and desire, and noumena and phenomena. To abandon these dualisms as he meant them is, for many, to abandon what is distinctive in his

theory. I believe otherwise. His moral conception has a characteristic structure that is more clearly discernible when these dualisms are not taken in the sense he gave them but reinterpreted and their moral force reformulated within the scope of an empirical theory. One of the aims of *A Theory of Justice* was to indicate how this might be done.

To suggest the main idea, think of the notion of a well-ordered society as an interpretation of the idea of a kingdom of ends thought of as a human society under circumstances of justice. Now the members of such a society are free and equal and so our problem is to find a rendering of freedom and equality that it is natural to describe as Kantian; and since Kant distinguished between positive and negative freedom, we must make room for this contrast. At this point I resorted to the idea of the original position: I supposed that the conception of justice suitable for a well-ordered society is the one that would be agreed to in a hypothetical situation that is fair between individuals conceived as free and equal moral persons, that is, as members of such a society. Fairness of the circumstances under which agreement is reached transfers to the fairness of the principles agreed to. The original position was designed so that the conception of justice that resulted would be appropriate.

Particularly important among the features of the original position for the interpretation of negative freedom are the limits on information, which I called the veil of ignorance. Now there is a stronger and a weaker form of these limits. The weaker supposes that we begin with full information, or else that which we possess in everyday life, and then proceed to eliminate only the information that would lead to partiality and bias. The stronger form has a Kantian explanation: we start from no information at all; for by negative freedom Kant means being able to act independently from the determination of alien causes; to act from natural necessity is to subject oneself to the heteronomy of nature. We interpret this as requiring that the conception of justice that regulates the basic structure, with its deep and long-lasting effects on our common life, should not be adopted on grounds that rest on a knowledge of the various contingencies. Thus when this conception is agreed to, knowledge of our social position, our peculiar desires and interests, or of the various outcomes and configurations of natural and historical accident is excluded. One allows only that information required for a rational agreement. This means that, so far as possible, only the general laws of nature are known together with such particular facts as are implied by the circumstances of justice.

Of course, we must endow the parties with some motivation, otherwise no acknowledgement would be forthcoming. Kant's discussion in the *Groundwork* of the second pair of examples indicates, I believe, that in applying the procedure of the categorical imperative he tacitly relied upon some account of primary goods. In any case, if the two principles would be adopted in the original position with its limits on information, the conception of equality they contain would be Kantian in the sense that by acting from this conception the members of a well-ordered society would express their negative freedom. They would have succeeded in regulating the basic structure and its profound consequences on their persons and mutual relationships by principles the grounds for which are suitably independent from chance and contingency.

In order to provide an interpretation of positive freedom, two things are necessary: first, that the parties are conceived as free and equal moral persons must play a decisive part in their adoption of the conception of justice; and second, the principles of this conception must have a content appropriate to express this determining view of persons and must apply to the controlling institutional subject. Now if correct, the argument from the original position seems to meet these conditions.

The assumption that the parties are free and equal moral persons does have an essential role in this argument; and as regards content and application, these principles express, on their public face as it were, the conception of the person that is realized in a well-ordered society. They give priority to the basic liberties, regard individuals as free and responsible masters of their aims and desires, and all are to share equally in the means for the attainment of ends unless the situation of everyone can be improved, taking equal division as the starting point. A society that realized these principles would attain positive freedom, for these principles reflect the features of persons that determined their selection and so express a conception they give to themselves.

Notes

1. Sections I, III, and IV of this discussion draw upon sections I and III of "Reply to Alexander and Musgrave," *Quarterly Journal of Economics* (November 1974). Sections II, V, and VI of that paper take up some questions about the argument from the original position.
2. This paragraph confirms H. L. A. Hart's interpretation. See his discussion of liberty and its priority in "Rawls on Liberty and its Priority," *Chicago Law Review* (April 1973): 536–540.
3. I discuss certain problems in interpreting the account of primary goods in "Fairness to Goodness," *Philosophical Review* (October 1975): 536–554.
4. For a discussion of such measures, see A. K. Sen, *On Economic Inequality* (New York: Oxford University Press, 1973), chap. 2.
5. The last part of this paragraph alludes to some objections raised by Robert Nozick in his *Anarchy, State, and Utopia* (New York: Basic Books, 1974), esp. pp. 213–229.
6. At this point I adapt some remarks of Hobbes. See *Leviathan,* chap. 15, under the thirteenth and fourteenth laws of nature.

Distributive Justice[1]

JOHN RAWLS

I

We may think of a human society as a more or less self-sufficient association regulated by a common conception of justice and aimed at advancing the good of its members. As a co-operative venture for mutual advantage, it is characterized by a conflict as well as an identity of interests. There is an identity of interests since social co-operation makes possible a better life for all than any would have if everyone were to try to live by his own efforts; yet at the same time men are not indifferent as to how the greater benefits produced by their joint labours are distributed, for in order to further their own aims each prefers a larger to a lesser share. A conception of justice is a set of principles for choosing between the social arrangements which determine this division and for under-writing a consensus as to the proper distributive shares.

Now at first sight the most rational conception of justice would seem to be utilitarian. For consider: each man in realizing his own good can certainly balance his own losses against his own gains. We can impose a sacrifice on ourselves now for the sake of a greater advantage later. A man quite properly acts, as long as others are not affected, to achieve his own greatest good, to advance his ends as far as possible. Now, why should not a society act on

precisely the same principle? Why is not that which is rational in the case of one man right in the case of a group of men? Surely the simplest and most direct conception of the right, and so of justice, is that of maximizing the good. This assumes a prior understanding of what is good, but we can think of the good as already given by the interests of rational individuals. Thus just as the principle of individual choice is to achieve one's greatest good, to advance so far as possible one's own system of rational desires, so the principle of social choice is to realize the greatest good (similarly defined) summed over all the members of society. We arrive at the principle of utility in a natural way: by this principle a society is rightly ordered, and hence just, when its institutions are arranged so as to realize the greatest sum of satisfactions.

The striking feature of the principle of utility is that it does not matter, except indirectly, how this sum of satisfactions is distributed among individuals, any more than it matters, except indirectly, how one man distributes his satisfactions over time. Since certain ways of distributing things affect the total sum of satisfactions, this fact must be taken into account in arranging social institutions; but according to this principle the explanation of common-sense precepts of justice and their seemingly stringent character is that they are those rules

John Rawls, "Distributive Justice," from *Philosophy, Politics and Society,* 3rd series, ed. P. Laslett and W. G. Runciman. Copyright © Basil Blackwell, 1967. Reprinted by permission of the author and publisher.

which experience shows must be strictly respected and departed from only under exceptional circumstances if the sum of advantages is to be maximized. The precepts of justice are derivative from the one end of attaining the greatest net balance of satisfactions. There is no reason in principle why the greater gains of some should not compensate for the lesser losses of others; or why the violation of the liberty of a few might not be made right by a greater good shared by many. It simply happens, at least under most conditions, that the greatest sum of advantages is not generally achieved in this way. From the standpoint of utility the strictness of common-sense notions of justice has a certain usefulness, but as a philosophical doctrine it is irrational.

If, then, we believe that as a matter of principle each member of society has an inviolability founded on justice which even the welfare of everyone else cannot over-ride, and that a loss of freedom for some is not made right by a greater sum of satisfactions enjoyed by many, we shall have to look for another account of the principles of justice. The principle of utility is incapable of explaining the fact that in a just society the liberties of equal citizenship are taken for granted, and the rights secured by justice are not subject to political bargaining nor to the calculus of social interests. Now, the most natural alternative to the principle of utility is its traditional rival, the theory of the social contract. The aim of the contract doctrine is precisely to account for the strictness of justice by supposing that its principles arise from an agreement among free and independent persons in an original position of equality and hence reflect the integrity and equal sovereignty of the rational persons who are the contractees. Instead of supposing that a conception of right, and so a conception of justice, is simply an extension of the principle of choice for one man to society as a whole, the contract doctrine assumes that the rational individuals who belong to society must choose together, in one joint act, what is to count among them as just and unjust. They are to decide among themselves once and for all what is to be their conception of justice. This decision is thought of as being made in a suitably

defined initial situation one of the significant features of which is that no one knows his position in society, nor even his place in the distribution of natural talents and abilities. The principles of justice to which all are forever bound are chosen in the absence of this sort of specific information. A veil of ignorance prevents anyone from being advantaged or disadvantaged by the contingencies of social class and fortune; and hence the bargaining problems which arise in everyday life from the possession of this knowledge do not affect the choice of principles. On the contract doctrine, then, the theory of justice, and indeed ethics itself, is part of the general theory of rational choice, a fact perfectly clear in its Kantian formulation.

Once justice is thought of as arising from an original agreement of this kind, it is evident that the principle of utility is problematical. For why should rational individuals who have a system of ends they wish to advance agree to a violation of their liberty for the sake of a greater balance of satisfactions enjoyed by others? It seems more plausible to suppose that, when situated in an original position of equal right, they would insist upon institutions which returned compensating advantages for any sacrifices required. A rational man would not accept an institution merely because it maximized the sum of advantages irrespective of its effect on his own interests. It appears, then, that the principle of utility would be rejected as a principle of justice, although we shall not try to argue this important question here. Rather, our aim is to give a brief sketch of the conception of distributive shares implicit in the principles of justice which, it seems, would be chosen in the original position. The philosophical appeal of utilitarianism is that it seems to offer a single principle on the basis of which a consistent and complete conception of right can be developed. The problem is to work out a contractarian alternative in such a way that it has comparable if not all the same virtues.

II

In our discussion we shall make no attempt to derive the two principles of justice which we shall examine; that is, we shall not try to show that they would be chosen in the original position.[2] It must suffice that it is plausible that they would be, at least in preference to the standard forms of traditional theories. Instead we shall be mainly concerned with three questions: first, how to interpret these principles so that they define a consistent and complete conception of justice; second, whether it is possible to arrange the institutions of a constitutional democracy so that these principles are satisfied, at least approximately; and third, whether the conception of distributive shares which they define is compatible with common-sense notions of justice. The significance of these principles is that they allow for the strictness of the claims of justice; and if they can be understood so as to yield a consistent and complete conception, the contractarian alternative would seem all the more attractive.

The two principles of justice which we shall discuss may be formulated as follows: first, each person engaged in an institution or affected by it has an equal right to the most extensive liberty compatible with a like liberty for all; and second, inequalities as defined by the institutional structure or fostered by it are arbitrary unless it is reasonable to expect that they will work out to everyone's advantage and provided that the positions and offices to which they attach or from which they may be gained are open to all. These principles regulate the distributive aspects of institutions by controlling the assignment of rights and duties throughout the whole social structure, beginning with the adoption of a political constitution in accordance with which they are then to be applied to legislation. It is upon a correct choice of a basic structure of society, its fundamental system of rights and duties, that the justice of distributive shares depends.

The two principles of justice apply in the first instance to this basic structure, that is, to the main institutions of the social system and their arrangement, how they are combined together. Thus this structure includes the political constitution and the principal economic and social institutions which together define a person's liberties and rights and affect his life-prospects, what he may expect to be and how well he may expect to be and how well he may expect to fare. The intuitive idea here is that those born into the social system at different positions, say in different social classes, have varying life-prospects determined, in part, by the system of political liberties and personal rights, and by the economic and social opportunities which are made available to these positions. In this way the basic structure of society favours certain men over others, and these are the basic inequalities, the ones which affect their whole life-prospects. It is inequalities of this kind, presumably inevitable in any society, with which the two principles of justice are primarily designed to deal.

Now the second principle holds that an inequality is allowed only if there is reason to believe that the institution with the inequality, or permitting it, will work out for the advantage of every person engaged in it. In the case of the basic structure this means that all inequalities which affect life prospects, say the inequalities of income and wealth which exist between social classes, must be to the advantage of everyone. Since the principle applies to institutions, we interpret this to mean that inequalities must be to the advantage of the representative man for each relevant social position; they should improve each such man's expectation. Here we assume that it is possible to attach to each position an expectation, and that this expectation is a function of the whole institutional structure: it can be raised and lowered by reassigning rights and duties throughout the system. Thus the expectation of any position depends upon the expectations of the others, and these in turn depend upon the pattern of rights and duties established by the basic structure. But it is not clear what is meant by saying that inequalities must be to the advantage of every representative man, and hence our first question.

III

One possibility is to say that everyone is made better off in comparison with some historically relevant benchmark. An interpretation of this kind is suggested by Hume.[3] He sometimes says that the institutions of justice, that is, the rules regulating property and contracts, and so on, are to everyone's advantage, since each man can count himself the gainer on balance when he considers his permanent interests. Even though the application of the rules is sometimes to his disadvantage, and he loses in the particular case, each man gains in the long-run by the steady administration of the whole system of justice. But all Hume seems to mean by this is that everyone is better off in comparison with the situation of men in the state of nature, understood either as some primitive condition or as the circumstances which would obtain at any time if the existing institutions of justice were to break down. While this sense of everyone's being made better off is perhaps clear enough, Hume's interpretation is surely unsatisfactory. For even if all men including slaves are made better off by a system of slavery than they would be in the state of nature, it is not true that slavery makes everyone (even a slave) better off, at least not in a sense which makes the arrangement just. The benefits and burdens of social co-operation are unjustly distributed even if everyone does gain in comparison with the state of nature; this historical or hypothetical benchmark is simply irrelevant to the question of justice. In fact, any past state of society other than a recent one seems irrelevant offhand, and this suggests that we should look for an interpretation independent of historical comparisons altogether. Our problem is to identify the correct hypothetical comparisons defined by currently feasible changes.

Now the well-known criterion of Pareto[4] offers a possibility along these lines once it is formulated so as to apply to institutions. Indeed, this is the most natural way of taking the second principle (or rather the first part of it, leaving aside the requirement about open positions). This criterion says that group welfare is at an optimum when it is impossible to make any one man better off without at the same time making at least one other man worse off. Applying this criterion to allocating a given bundle of goods among given individuals, a particular allocation yields an optimum if there is no redistribution which would improve one individual's position without worsening that of

another. Thus a distribution is optimal when there is no further exchange which is to the advantage of both parties, or to the advantage of one and not to the disadvantage of the other. But there are many such distributions, since there are many ways of allocating commodities so that no further mutually beneficial exchange is possible. Hence the Pareto criterion, as important as it is, admittedly does not identify the best distribution, but rather a class of optimal, or efficient, distributions. Moreover, we cannot say that a given optimal distribution is better than any non-optimal one; it is only superior to those which it dominates. The criterion is at best an incomplete principle for ordering distributions.

Pareto's idea can be applied to institutions. We assume, as remarked above, that it is possible to associate with each social position an expectation which depends upon the assignment of rights and duties in the basic structure. Given this assumption, we get a principle which says that the pattern of expectations (inequalities in life-prospects) is optimal if and only if it is impossible to change the rules, to redefine the scheme of rights and duties, so as to raise the expectations of any representative man without at the same time lowering the expectations of some other representative man. Hence the basic structure satisfies this principle when it is impossible to change the assignment of fundamental rights and duties and to alter the availability of economic and social opportunities so as to make some representative man better off without making another worse off. Thus, in comparing different arrangements of the social system, we can say that one is better than another if in one arrangement all expectations are at least as high, and some higher, than in the other. The principle gives grounds for reform, for if there is an arrangement which is optimal in comparison with the existing state of things, then, other things equal, it is a better situation all around and should be adopted.

The satisfaction of this principle, then, defines a second sense in which the basic structure makes everyone better off; namely, that from the standpoint of its representative men in the relevant positions, there exists no change which would improve anyone's condition without worsening that of another. Now we shall assume that this principle would be chosen in the original position, for surely it is a desirable feature of a social system that it is optimal in this sense. In fact, we shall suppose that this principle defines the concept of efficiency for institutions, as can be seen from the fact that if the social system does not satisfy it, this implies that there is some change which can be made which will lead people to act more effectively so that the expectations of some at least can be raised. Perhaps an economic reform will lead to an increase in production with given resources and techniques, and with greater output someone's expectations are raised.

It is not difficult to see, however, that while this principle provides another sense for an institution's making everyone better off, it is an inadequate conception of justice. For one thing, there is the same incompleteness as before. There are presumably many arrangements of an institution and of the basic structure which are optimal in this sense. There may also be many arrangements which are optimal with respect to existing conditions, and so many reforms which would be improvements by this principle. If so, how is one to choose between them? It is impossible to say that the many optimal arrangements are equally just, and the choice between them a matter of indifference, since efficient institutions allow extremely wide variations in the pattern of distributive shares.

Thus it may be that under certain conditions serfdom cannot be significantly reformed without lowering the expectations of some representative man, say that of landowners, in which case serfdom is optimal. But equally it may happen under the same conditions that a system of free labour could not be changed without lowering the expectations of some representative man, say that of free labourers, so that this arrangement likewise is optimal. More generally, whenever a society is relevantly divided into a number of classes, it is possible, let's suppose, to maximize with respect to any one of its representative men at a time. These maxima give at least this many optimal positions, for none of them can be departed from

to raise the expectations of any man without lowering those of another, namely, the man with respect to whom the maximum is defined. Hence each of these extremes is optimal. All this corresponds to the obvious fact that, in distributing particular goods to given individuals, those distributions are also optimal which give the whole stock to any one person; for once a single person has everything, there is no change which will not make him worse off.

We see, then, that social systems which we should judge very differently from the standpoint of justice may be optimal by this criterion. This conclusion is not surprising. There is no reason to think that, even when applied to social systems, justice and efficiency come to the same thing. These reflections only show what we knew all along, which is that we must find another way of interpreting the second principle, or rather the first part of it. For while the two principles taken together incorporate strong requirements of equal liberty and equality of opportunity, we cannot be sure that even these constraints are sufficient to make the social structure acceptable from the standpoint of justice. As they stand the two principles would appear to place the burden of ensuring justice entirely upon these prior constraints and to leave indeterminate the preferred distributive shares.

IV

There is, however, a third interpretation which is immediately suggested by the previous remarks, and this is to choose some social position by reference to which the pattern of expectations as a whole is to be judged, and then to maximize with respect to the expectations of this representative man consistent with the demands of equal liberty and equality of opportunity. Now, the one obvious candidate is the representative man of those who are least favoured by the system of institutional inequalities. Thus we arrive at the following idea: the basic structure of the social system affects the life-prospects of typical individuals according to their initial places in society, say the various income classes into which they are born, or depending upon certain natural attributes, as when institutions make discriminations between men and women or allow certain advantages to be gained by those with greater natural abilities. The fundamental problem of distributive justice concerns the differences in life-prospect which come about in this way. We interpret the second principle to hold that these differences are just if and only if the greater expectations of the more advantaged, when playing a part in the working of the whole social system, improve the expectations of the least advantaged. The basic structure is just throughout when the advantages of the more fortunate promote the well-being of the least fortunate, that is, when a decrease in their advantages would make the least fortunate even worse off than they are. The basic structure is perfectly just when the prospects of the least fortunate are as great as they can be.

In interpreting the second principle (or rather the first part of it which we may, for obvious reasons, refer to as the difference principle), we assume that the first principle requires a basic equal liberty for all, and that the resulting political system, when circumstances permit, is that of a constitutional democracy in some form. There must be liberty of the person and political equality as well as liberty of conscience and freedom of thought. There is one class of equal citizens which defines a common status for all. We also assume that there is equality of opportunity and a fair competition for the available positions on the basis of reasonable qualifications. Now, given this background, the differences to be justified are the various economic and social inequalities in the basic structure which must inevitably arise in such a scheme. These are the inequalities in the distribution of income and wealth and the distinctions in social prestige and status which attach to the various positions and classes. The difference principle says that these inequalities are just if and only if they are part of a larger system in which they work out to the advantage of the most unfortunate representative man. The just distributive shares determined by the basic structure are those specified by this constrained maximum principle.

Thus, consider the chief problem of distributive justice, that concerning the distribution of wealth as it affects the life-prospects of those starting out in the various income groups. These income classes define the relevant representative men from which the social system is to be judged. Now, a son of a member of the entrepreneurial class (in a capitalist society) has a better prospect than that of the son of an unskilled labourer. This will be true, it seems, even when the social injustices which presently exist are removed and the two men are of equal talent and ability; the inequality cannot be done away with as long as something like the family is maintained. What, then, can justify this inequality in life-prospects? According to the second principle it is justified only if it is to the advantage of the representative man who is worst off, in this case the representative unskilled labourer. The inequality is permissible because lowering it would, let's suppose, make the working man even worse off than he is. Presumably, given the principle of open offices (the second part of the second principle), the greater expectations allowed to entrepreneurs has the effect in the longer run of raising the life-prospects of the labouring class. The inequality in expectation provides an incentive so that the economy is more efficient, industrial advance proceeds at a quicker pace, and so on, the end result of which is that greater material and other benefits are distributed throughout the system. Of course, all of this is familiar, and whether true or not in particular cases, it is the sort of thing which must be argued if the inequality in income and wealth is to be acceptable by the difference principle.

We should now verify that this interpretation of the second principle gives a natural sense in which everyone may be said to be made better off. Let us suppose that inequalities are chain-connected: that is, if an inequality raises the expectations of the lowest position, it raises the expectations of all positions in between. For example, if the greater expectation of the representative entrepreneur raises that of the unskilled labourer, it also raises that of the semi-skilled. Let us further assume that inequalities are close-knit: that is, it is impossible to raise (or lower) the expectation of any representative man without raising (or lowering) the expectations of every other representative man, and in particular, without affecting one way or the other that of the least fortunate. There is no loose-jointedness, so to speak, in the way in which expectations depend upon one another. Now, with these assumptions, everyone does benefit from an inequality which satisfies the difference principle, and the second principle as we have formulated it reads correctly. For the representative man who is better off in any pairwise comparison gains by being allowed to have his advantage, and the man who is worse off benefits from the contribution which all inequalities make to each position below. Of course, chain-connection and close-knitness may not obtain; but in this case those who are better off should not have a veto over the advantages available for the least advantaged. The stricter interpretation of the difference principle should be followed, and all inequalities should be arranged for the advantage of those in middle positions. Should these conditions fail, then, the second principle would have to be stated in another way.

It may be observed that the difference principle represents, in effect, an original agreement to share in the benefits of the distribution of natural talents and abilities, whatever this distribution turns out to be, in order to alleviate as far as possible the arbitrary handicaps resulting from our initial starting places in society. Those who have been favoured by nature, whoever they are, may gain from their good fortune only on terms that improve the well-being of those who have lost out. The naturally advantaged are not to gain simply because they are more gifted, but only to cover the costs of training and cultivating their endowments and for putting them to use in a way which improves the position of the less fortunate. We are led to the difference principle if we wish to arrange the basic social structure so that no one gains (or loses) from his luck in the natural lottery of talent and ability, or from his initial place in society, without giving (or receiving) compensating advantages in return. (The parties in the original position are not said to be attracted by this idea and so agree to it; rather, given the symmetries of their situation, and particularly their lack of knowledge, and so on, they will find it to their interest to agree to a

principle which can be understood in this way.) And we should note also that when the difference principle is perfectly satisfied, the basic structure is optimal by the efficiency principle. There is no way to make anyone better off without making someone else worse off, namely, the least fortunate representative man. Thus the two principles of justice define distributive shares in a way compatible with efficiency, at least as long as we move on this highly abstract level. If we want to say (as we do, although it cannot be argued here) that the demands of justice have an absolute weight with respect to efficiency, this claim may seem less paradoxical when it is kept in mind that perfectly just institutions are also efficient.

V

Our second question is whether it is possible to arrange the institutions of a constitutional democracy so that the two principles of justice are satisfied, at least approximately. We shall try to show that this can be done provided the government regulate a free economy in a certain way. More fully, if law and government act effectively to keep markets competitive, resources fully employed, property and wealth widely distributed over time, and to maintain the appropriate social minimum, then if there is equality of opportunity underwritten by education for all, the resulting distribution will be just. Of course, all of these arrangements and policies are familiar. The only novelty in the following remarks, if there is any novelty at all, is that this framework of institutions can be made to satisfy the difference principle. To argue this, we must sketch the relations of these institutions and how they work together.

First of all, we assume that the basic social structure is controlled by a just constitution which secures the various liberties of equal citizenship. Thus the legal order is administered in accordance with the principle of legality, and liberty of conscience and freedom of thought are taken for granted. The political process is conducted, so far as possible, as a just procedure for choosing between governments and for enacting just legislation. From the standpoint of distributive justice, it is also essential that there be equality of opportunity in several senses. Thus, we suppose that, in addition to maintaining the usual social overhead capital, government provides for equal educational opportunities for all either by subsidizing private schools or by operating a public school system. It also enforces and underwrites equality of opportunity in commercial ventures and in the free choice of occupation. This result is achieved by policing business behaviour and by preventing the establishment of barriers and restrictions to the desirable positions and markets. Lastly, there is a guarantee of a social minimum which the government meets by family allowances and special payments in times of unemployment, or by a negative income tax.

In maintaining this system of institutions the government may be thought of as divided into four branches. Each branch is represented by various agencies (or activities thereof) charged with preserving certain social and economic conditions. These branches do not necessarily overlap with the usual organization of government, but should be understood as purely conceptual. Thus the allocation branch is to keep the economy feasibly competitive, that is, to prevent the formation of unreasonable market power. Markets are competitive in this sense when they cannot be made more so consistent with the requirements of efficiency and the acceptance of the fact of consumer preferences and geography. The allocation branch is also charged with identifying and correcting, say by suitable taxes and subsidies wherever possible, the more obvious departures from efficiency caused by the failure of prices to measure accurately social benefits and costs. The stabilization branch strives to maintain reasonably full employment so that there is no waste through failure to use resources and the free choice of occupation and the deployment of finance is supported by strong effective demand. These two branches together are to preserve the efficiency of the market economy generally.

The social minimum is established through the operations of the transfer branch. Later on we shall consider at what level this minimum should be set, since this is a crucial matter; but

for the moment, a few general remarks will suffice. The main idea is that the workings of the transfer branch take into account the precept of need and assign it an appropriate weight with respect to the other common-sense precepts of justice. A market economy ignores the claims of need altogether. Hence there is a division of labour between the parts of the social system as different institutions answer to different common-sense precepts. Competitive markets (properly supplemented by government operations) handle the problem of the efficient allocation of labour and resources and set a weight to the conventional precepts associated with wages and earnings (the precepts of each according to his work and experience, or responsibility and the hazards of the job, and so on), whereas the transfer branch guarantees a certain level of well-being and meets the claims of need. Thus it is obvious that the justice of distributive shares depends upon the whole social system and how it distributes total income, wages plus transfers. There is with reason strong objection to the competitive determination of total income, since this would leave out of account the claims of need and of a decent standard of life. From the standpoint of the original position it is clearly rational to insure oneself against these contingencies. But now, if the appropriate minimum is provided by transfers, it may be perfectly fair that the other part of total income is competitively determined. Moreover, this way of dealing with the claims of need is doubtless more efficient, at least from a theoretical point of view, than trying to regulate prices by minimum wage standards and so on. It is preferable to handle these claims by a separate branch which supports a social minimum. Henceforth, in considering whether the second principle of justice is satisfied, the answer turns on whether the total income of the least advantaged, that is, wages plus transfers, is such as to maximize their long-term expectations consistent with the demands of liberty.

Finally, the distribution branch is to preserve an approximately just distribution of income and wealth over time by affecting the background conditions of the market from period to period. Two aspects of this branch may be distinguished. First of all, it operates a system of inheritance and gift taxes. The aim of these levies is not to raise revenue, but gradually and continually to correct the distribution of wealth and to prevent the concentrations of power to the detriment of liberty and equality of opportunity. It is perfectly true, as some have said,[5] that unequal inheritance of wealth is no more inherently unjust than unequal inheritance of intelligence; as far as possible the inequalities founded on either should satisfy the difference principle. Thus, the inheritance of greater wealth is just as long as it is to the advantage of the worst off and consistent with liberty, including equality of opportunity. Now by the latter we do not mean, of course, the equality of expectations between classes, since differences in life-prospects arising from the basic structure are inevitable, and it is precisely the aim of the second principle to say when these differences are just. Instead, equality of opportunity is a certain set of institutions which assures equally good education and chances of culture for all and which keeps open the competition for positions on the basis of qualities reasonably related to performance, and so on. It is these institutions which are put in jeopardy when inequalities and concentrations of wealth reach a certain limit; and the taxes imposed by the distribution branch are to prevent this limit from being exceeded. Naturally enough where this limit lies is a matter for political judgment guided by theory, practical experience, and plain hunch; on this question the theory of justice has nothing to say.

The second part of the distribution branch is a scheme of taxation for raising revenue to cover the costs of public goods, to make transfer payments, and the like. This scheme belongs to the distribution branch since the burden of taxation must be justly shared. Although we cannot examine the legal and economic complications involved, there are several points in favour of proportional expenditure taxes as part of an ideally just arrangement. For one thing, they are preferable to income taxes at the level of common-sense precepts of justice, since they impose a levy according to how much a man takes out of the common store of goods and not according to how much he contributes (assuming that income is fairly earned in return for productive efforts). On the other hand, proportional taxes treat everyone in a clearly defined uniform way (again assuming that income is fairly earned) and hence it is preferable to use progressive rates only when they are necessary to preserve the justice of the system as a whole, that is, to prevent large fortunes hazardous to liberty and equality of opportunity, and the like. If proportional expenditure taxes should also prove more efficient, say because they interfere less with incentives, or whatever, this would make the case for them decisive provided a feasible scheme could be worked out.[6] Yet these are questions of political judgment which are not our concern; and, in any case, a proportional expenditure tax is part of an idealized scheme which we are describing. It does not follow that even steeply progressive income taxes, given the injustice of existing systems, do not improve justice and efficiency all things considered. In practice we must usually choose between unjust arrangements and then it is a matter of finding the lesser injustice.

Whatever form the distribution branch assumes, the argument for it is to be based on justice: we must hold that once it is accepted the social system as a whole—the competitive economy surrounded by a just constitutional and legal framework—can be made to satisfy the principles of justice with the smallest loss in efficiency. The long-term expectations of the least advantaged are raised to the highest level consistent with the demands of equal liberty. In discussing the choice of a distribution scheme we have made no reference to the traditional criteria of taxation according to ability to pay or benefits received; nor have we mentioned any of the variants of the sacrifice principle. These standards are subordinate to the two principles of justice; once the problem is seen as that of designing a whole social system, they assume the status of secondary precepts with no more independent force than the precepts of common sense in regard to wages. To suppose otherwise is not to take a sufficiently comprehensive point of view. In setting up a just distribution branch these precepts may or may not have a place depending upon the demands of the two principles of justice when applied to the entire system.

VI

Our problem now is whether the whole system of institutions which we have described, the competitive economy surrounded by the four branches of government, can be made to satisfy the two principles of justice. It seems intuitively plausible that this can be done, but we must try to make sure. We assume that the social system as a whole meets the demands of liberty; it secures the rights required by the first principle and the principle of open offices. Thus the question is whether, consistent with these liberties, there is any way of operating the four branches of government so as to bring the inequalities of the basic structure in line with the difference principle.

Now, quite clearly the thing to do is to set the social minimum at the appropriate level. So far we have said nothing about how high this minimum should be. Common sense might be content to say that the right level depends on the average wealth of the country, and that, other things equal, the minimum should be higher if this average is higher; or it might hold that the proper level depends on customary expectations. Both of these ideas are unsatisfactory. The first is not precise enough since it does not state how the minimum should depend on wealth and it overlooks other relevant considerations such as distribution; and the second provides no criterion for when customary expectations are themselves reasonable. Once the difference principle is accepted, however, it follows that the minimum should be set at the level which, taking wages into account, maximizes the expectations of the lowest income class. By adjusting the amount of transfers, and the benefits from public goods which improve their circumstances, it is possible to increase or decrease the total income of the least advantaged (wages plus transfers plus benefits from public goods). Controlling the sum of transfers and benefits, thereby raising or lowering the social minimum, gives sufficient leeway in the whole scheme to satisfy the difference principle.

Now, offhand it might appear that this arrangement requires a very high minimum. It is easy to imagine the greater wealth of those better off being scaled down until eventually all stand on nearly the same level. But this is a misconception. The relevant expectation of the least advantaged is their long-term expectation extending over all generations; and hence over any period of time the economy must put aside the appropriate amount of real capital accumulation. Assuming for the moment that this amount is given, the social minimum is determined in the following way. Suppose, for simplicity, that transfer payments and the benefits from public goods are supported by expenditure (or income) taxes. Then raising the minimum entails raising the constant proportion at which consumption (or income) is taxed. Now presumably as this proportion is increased there comes a point beyond which one of two things happens: either the savings required cannot be made or the increased taxes interfere so much with the efficiency of the economy that the expectations of the lowest class for that period no longer improve but begin to decline. In either case the appropriate level for the minimum has been reached and no further increase should be made.

In order to make the whole system of institutions satisfy the two principles of justice, a just savings principle is presupposed. Hence we must try to say something about this difficult question. Unfortunately there are no very precise limits on what the rate of saving should be; how the burden of real saving should be shared between generations seems to admit of no definite answer. It does not follow, however, that certain general bounds cannot be prescribed which are ethically significant. For example, it seems clear that the classical principle of utility, which requires us to maximize total well-being over all generations, results in much too high a rate of saving, at least for the earlier generations. On the contract doctrine the question is approached from the standpoint of the parties in the original position who do not know to which generation they belong, or what comes to the same thing, they do not know the stage of economic advance of their society. The veil of ignorance is complete in this respect. Hence the parties ask themselves how much they would be willing to save at each stage on the assumption that other generations save at the same rates. That is, a person is to consider his willingness to save at every phase of development with the understanding that the rates he proposes will regulate the whole span of accumulation. Since no one knows to which generation he belongs, the problem is looked at from the standpoint of each. Now it is immediately obvious that all generations, except possibly the first, gain from a reasonable rate of accumulation being maintained. Once the saving process is begun, it is to the advantage of all later generations. Each generation passes on to the next a fair equivalent in real capital as defined by a just savings principle, this equivalent being in return for what is received from previous generations and enabling the later ones to have a higher standard of life than would otherwise be possible. Only those in the first generation do not benefit, let's suppose; while they begin the whole process, they do not share in the fruits of their provision. At this initial stage, then, in order to obtain unanimity from the point of view of generations, we must assume that fathers, say, are willing to save for the sake of their sons, and hence that, in this case at least, one generation cares for its immediate descendants. With these suppositions, it seems that some just savings principle would be agreed to.

Now a just savings principle will presumably require a lower rate of saving in the earlier stages of development when a society is poor, and a greater rate as it becomes wealthier and more industrialized. As their circumstances become easier men would find it reasonable to agree to save more since the real burden is less. Eventually, perhaps, there will come a point beyond which the rate of saving may decline or stop altogether, at least if we suppose that there is a state of affluence when a society may concentrate on other things and it is sufficient that improvements in productive techniques be introduced only to the extent covered by depreciation. Here we are referring to what a society must save as a matter of justice; if it wishes to save for various grand projects, this is another matter.

We should note a special feature of the reciprocity principle in the case of just savings. Normally this principle applies when there is an exchange of advantages, that is, when each party gives something to the other. But in the accumulation process no one gives to those from whom he has received. Each gives to subsequent generations and receives from his predecessors. The first generation obtains no benefits at all, whereas the last generations, those living when no further saving is required, gain the most and give the least. Now this may appear unjust; and contrary to the formulation of the difference principle, the worst off save for those better off. But although this relation is unusual, it does not give rise to any difficulty. It simply expresses the fact that generations are spread out in time and exchanges between them can take place in only one direction. Therefore, from the standpoint of the original position, if all are to gain, they must agree to receive from their predecessors and to pass along a fair equivalent to those who come after them. The criterion of justice is the principle which would be chosen in the original position; and since a just savings principle would, let's suppose, be agreed to, the accumulation process is just. The savings principle may be reconciled with the difference principle by assuming that the representative man in any generation required to save belongs to the lowest income class. Of course, this saving is not done so much, if at all, by taking an active part in the investment process; rather it takes the form of approving of the economic arrangements which promote accumulation. The saving of those worse off is undertaken by accepting, as a matter of political judgment, those policies designed to improve the standard of life, thereby abstaining from the immediate advantages which are available to them. By supporting these arrangements and policies the appropriate savings can be made, and no representative man regardless of generation can complain of another for not doing his part.

Of the nature of the society at which the saving process aims we can give only the most general description. It is a society of persons with the greatest equal talent enjoying the benefits of the greatest equal liberty under economic conditions reached immediately after the highest average income per capita at which any saving at all is required. There is no longer a lowest income class in the traditional sense; such differences in wealth as exist are freely chosen and accepted as a price of doing things less in demand. All of this is, unfortunately, terribly vague. But, in any case, this general conception specifies a horizon of sorts at which the savings process aims so that the just savings principle is not completely indeterminate. That is, we suppose that the intention is to reach a certain social state, and the problem of the proper rate of accumulation is how to share fairly in the burdens of achieving it. The contractarian idea is that if we look at this question from the perspective of those in the original position, then, even though the savings principle which results is inevitably imprecise, it does impose ethically significant bounds. What is of first importance is that the problem of just savings be approached in the right way; the initial conception of what we are to do determines everything else. Thus, from the standpoint of the original position, representatives of all generations, so to speak, must agree on how to distribute the hardships of building and preserving a just society. They all gain from adopting a savings principle, but also they have their own interests which they cannot sacrifice for another.

VII

The sketch of the system of institutions satisfying the two principles of justice is now complete. For once the just rate of savings is determined, at least within broad limits, we have a criterion for setting the level of the social minimum. The sum of transfers should be that which maximizes the expectations of the lowest income class consistent with the appropriate saving being undertaken and the system of equal liberties maintained. This arrangement of institutions working over time results in a definite pattern of distributive shares, and each man receives a total income (wages plus transfers) to which he is entitled under the rules upon which his legitimate expectations are founded. Now an essential feature of this

whole scheme is that it contains an element of pure procedural justice. That is, no attempt is made to specify the just distribution of particular goods and services to particular persons, as if there were only one way in which, independently of the choices of economic agents, these things should be shared. Rather, the idea is to design a scheme such that the resulting distribution, whatever it is, which is brought about by the efforts of those engaged in cooperation and elicited by their legitimate expectations, is just.

The option of pure procedural justice may be explained by a comparison with perfect and imperfect procedural justice. Consider the simplest problem of fair division. A number of men are to divide a cake: assuming that a fair division is an equal one, which procedure will give this outcome? The obvious solution is to have the man who divides the cake take the last piece. He will divide it equally, since in this way he assures for himself as large a share as he can. Now in this case there is an independent criterion for which is the fair division. The problem is to devise a procedure, a set of rules for dividing the cake, which will yield this outcome. The problem of fair division exemplifies the features of perfect procedural justice. There is an independent criterion for which outcome is just—and we can design a procedure guaranteed to lead to it.

The case of imperfect procedural justice is found in a criminal trial. The desired outcome is that the defendant should be declared guilty if and only if he has committed the offence as charged. The trial procedure is framed to search for and to establish this result, but we cannot design rules guaranteed to reach it. The theory of trial procedures examines which rules of evidence, and the like, are best calculated to advance this purpose. Different procedures may reasonably be expected in different circumstances to yield the right result, not always, but at least most of the time. Hence a trial is a case of imperfect procedural justice. Even though the law may be carefully followed, and the trial fairly and properly conducted, it may reach the wrong outcome. An innocent man may be found guilty, a guilty man may be set free. In such cases we speak of a miscarriage of justice: the injustice springs from no human fault but from a combination of circumstances which defeats the purpose of the rules.

The notion of pure procedural justice is illustrated by gambling. If a number of persons engage in a series of fair bets, the distribution of cash after the last bet is fair, or at least not unfair, whatever this distribution is. (We are assuming, of course, that fair bets are those which define a zero expectation, that the bets are made voluntarily, that no one cheats, and so on.) Any distribution summing to the initial stock of cash held by everyone could result from a series of fair bets; hence all of these distributions are, in this sense, equally fair. The distribution which results is fair simply because it is the outcome. Now when there is pure procedural justice, the procedure for determining the just result must actually be carried out; for in this case there is no independent criterion by reference to which an outcome can be known to be just. Obviously we cannot say that a particular state of affairs is just because it could have been reached by following a just procedure. This would permit far too much and lead to absurdly unjust consequences. In the case of gambling, for example, it would entail that any distribution whatever could be imposed. What makes the final outcome of the betting fair, or not unfair, is that it is the one which has arisen after a series of fair gambles.

In order, therefore, to establish just distributive shares a just total system of institutions must be set up and impartially administered. Given a just constitution and the smooth working of the four branches of government, and so on, there exists a procedure such that the actual distribution of wealth, whatever it turns out to be, is just. It will have come about as a consequence of a just system of institutions satisfying the principles to which everyone would agree and against which no one can complain. The situation is one of pure procedural justice, since there is no independent criterion by which the outcome can be judged. Nor can we say that a particular distribution of wealth is just because it is one which could have resulted from just institutions although it has not, as this would be to allow too much. Clearly there are

many distributions which may be reached by just institutions, and this is true whether we count distributions of particular goods and services among particular individuals. There are indefinitely many outcomes and what makes one of these just is that it has been achieved by actually carrying out a just scheme of co-operation as it is publicly understood. It is the result which has arisen when everyone receives that to which he is entitled given his and others' actions guided by their legitimate expectations and their obligations to one another. We can no more arrive at a just distribution of wealth except by working together within the framework of a just system of institutions than we can win or lose fairly without actually betting.

This account of distributive shares is simply an elaboration of the familiar idea that economic rewards will be just once a perfectly competitive price system is organized as a fair game. But in order to do this we have to begin with the choice of a social system as a whole, for the basic structure of the entire arrangement must be just. The economy must be surrounded with the appropriate framework of institutions, since even a perfectly efficient price system has no tendency to determine just distributive shares when left to itself. Not only must economic activity be regulated by a just constitution and controlled by the four branches of government, but a just saving-function must be adopted to estimate the provision to be made for future generations. Thus, we cannot, in general, consider only piecewise reforms, for unless all of these fundamental questions are properly handled, there is no assurance that the resulting distributive shares will be just; while if the correct initial choices of institutions are made, the matter of distributive justice may be left to take care of itself. Within the framework of a just system men may be permitted to form associations and groupings as they please so long as they respect the like liberty of others. With social ingenuity it should be possible to invent many different kinds of economic and social activities appealing to a wide variety of tastes and talents; and as long as the justice of the basic structure of the whole is not affected, men may be allowed, in accordance with the principle of free association, to enter into and to take part in whatever activities they wish. The resulting distribution will be just whatever it happens to be. The system of institutions which we have described is, let's suppose, the basic structure of a well-ordered society. This system exhibits the content of the two principles of justice by showing how they may be perfectly satisfied; and it defines a social ideal by reference to which political judgment among second-bests, and the long range direction of reform, may be guided.

VIII

We may conclude by considering the third question: whether this conception of distributive shares is compatible with common-sense notions of justice. In elaborating the contract doctrine we have been led to what seems to be a rather special, even eccentric, conception the peculiarities of which centre in the difference principle. Clear statements of it seem to be rare, and it differs rather widely from traditional utilitarian and intuitionist notions.[7] But this question is not an easy one to answer, for philosophical conceptions of justice, including the one we have just put forward, and our common-sense convictions, are not very precise. Moreover, a comparison is made difficult by our tendency in practice to adopt combinations of principles and precepts the consequences of which depend essentially upon how they are weighted; but the weighting may be undefined and allowed to vary with circumstances, and thus relies on the intuitive judgments which we are trying to systematize.

Consider the following conception of right: social justice depends positively on two things, on the equality of distribution (understood as equality in levels of well-being) and total welfare (understood as the sum of utilities taken over all individuals). On this view one social system is better than another without ambiguity if it is better on both counts, that is, if the expectations it defines are both less unequal and sum to a larger total. Another conception of right can be obtained by substituting the principle of a social minimum for the principle of equality; and thus an arrangement of institu-

tions is preferable to another without ambiguity if the expectations sum to a larger total and it provides for a higher minimum. The idea here is to maximize the sum of expectations subject to the constraint that no one be allowed to fall below some recognized standard of life. In these conceptions the principles of equality and of a social minimum represent the demands of justice, and the principle of total welfare that of efficiency. The principle of utility assumes the role of the principle of efficiency the force of which is limited by a principle of justice.

Now in practice combinations of principles of this kind are not without value. There is no question but that they identify plausible standards by reference to which policies may be appraised, and given the appropriate background of institutions, they may give correct conclusions. Consider the first conception: a person guided by it may frequently decide rightly. For example, he would be in favour of equality of opportunity, for it seems evident that having more equal chances for all both improves efficiency and decreases inequality. The real question arises, however, when an institution is approved by one principle but not by the other. In this case everything depends on how the principles are weighted, but how is this to be done? The combination of principles yields no answer to this question, and the judgment must be left to intuition. For every arrangement combining a particular total welfare with a particular degree of inequality one simply has to decide, without the guidance from principle, how much of an increase (or decrease) in total welfare, say, compensates for a given decrease (or increase) in equality.

Anyone using the two principles of justice, however, would also appear to be striking a balance between equality and total welfare. How do we know, then, that a person who claims to adopt a combination of principles does not, in fact, rely on the two principles of justice in weighing them, not consciously certainly, but in the sense that the weights he gives to equality and total welfare are those which he would give to them if he applied the two principles of justice? We need not say, of course, that those who in practice refer to a combination of principles, or whatever, rely on the contract doctrine, but only that until their conception of right is completely specified the question is still open. The leeway provided by the determination of weights leaves the matter unsettled.

Moreover, the same sort of situation arises with other practical standards. It is widely agreed, for example, that the distribution of income should depend upon the claims of entitlement, such as training and experience, responsibility and contribution, and so on, weighed against the claims of need and security. But how are these common-sense precepts to be balanced? Again, it is generally accepted that the ends of economic policy are competitive efficiency, full employment, an appropriate rate of growth, a decent social minimum, and a more equal distribution of income. In a modern democratic state these aims are to be advanced in ways consistent with equal liberty and equality of opportunity. There is no argument with these objectives; they would be recognized by anyone who accepted the two principles of justice. But different political views balance these ends differently, and how are we to choose between them? The fact is that we agree too little when we acknowledge precepts and ends of this kind; it must be recognized that a fairly detailed weighting is implicit in any complete conception of justice. Often we content ourselves with enumerating common-sense precepts and objectives of policy, adding that on particular questions we must strike a balance between them having studied the relevant facts. While this is sound practical advice, it does not express a conception of justice. Whereas on the contract doctrine all combinations of principles, precepts, and objectives of policy are given a weight in maximizing the expectations of the lowest income class consistent with making the required saving and maintaining the system of equal liberty and equality of opportunity.

Thus despite the fact that the contract doctrine seems at first to be a somewhat special conception, particularly in its treatment of inequalities, it may still express the principles of justice which stand in the background and control the weights expressed in our everyday judgments. Whether this is indeed the case can be decided only by developing the consequences of the two principles in more detail and noting if any discrepancies turn up. Possibly there will be no conflicts; certainly we hope there are none with the fixed points of our considered judgments. The main question perhaps is whether one is prepared to accept the further definition of one's conception of right which the two principles represent. For, as we have seen, common sense presumably leaves the matter of weights undecided. The two principles may not so much oppose ordinary ideas as provide a relatively precise principle where common sense has little to say.

Finally, it is a political convention in a democratic society to appeal to the common good. No political party would admit to pressing for legislation to the disadvantage of any recognized social interest. But how, from a philosophical point of view, is this convention to be understood? Surely it is something more than the principle of efficiency (in its Paretian form) and we cannot assume that government always affects everyone's interests equally. Yet since we cannot maximize with respect to more than one point of view, it is natural, given the ethos of a democratic society, to single out that of the least advantaged and maximize their long-term prospects consistent with the liberties of equal citizenship. Moreover, it does seem that the policies which we most confidently think to be just do at least contribute positively to the well-being of this class, and hence that these policies are just throughout. Thus the difference principle is a reasonable extension of the political convention of a democracy once we face up to the necessity of choosing a complete conception of justice.

Notes

1. In this essay I try to work out some of the implications of the two principles of justice discussed in "Justice as Fairness" which first appeared in the *Philosophical Review* in 1958 and which is reprinted in *Philosophy, Politics and Society,* Series 2, pp. 132–57.

2. This question is discussed very briefly in "Justice as Fairness," pp. 138–41. The intuitive idea is as follows. Given the circumstances of the original po-

234

JUSTICE AND EQUALITY

sition, it is rational for a man to choose as if he were designing a society in which his enemy is to assign him his place. Thus, in particular, given the complete lack of knowledge (which makes the choice one under uncertainty), the fact that the decision involves one's life-prospects as a whole and is constrained by obligations to third parties (e.g., one's descendants) and duties to certain values (e.g., to religious truth), it is rational to be conservative and so to choose in accordance with an analogue of the maximin principle. Viewing the situation in this way, the interpretation given to the principles of justice in Section IV is perhaps natural enough. Moreover, it seems clear how the principle of utility can be interpreted: it is the analogue of the Laplacean principle for choice uncertainty. (For a discussion of these choice criteria, see R. D. Luce and H. Raiffa, *Games and Decisions* [1957], pp. 275–298).

3. For this observation I am indebted to Brian Barry.
4. Introduced by him in his *Manuel d'économie politique* (1909) and long since a basic principle of welfare economics.
5. See, for example, F. von Hayek, *The Constitution of Liberty* (1960), p. 90.
6. See N. Kaldor, *An Expenditure Tax* (1955).
7. The nearest statement known to me is by Santayana. See the last part of chap. 4 in *Reason and Society* (1906) on the aristocratic ideal. He says, for example, "... an aristocratic regimen can only be justified by radiating benefit and by proving that were less given to those above, less would be attained by those beneath them." But see also Christian Bay, *The Structure of Freedom* (1958), who adopts the principle of maximizing freedom, giving special attention to the freedom of the marginal, least privileged man. Cf. pp. 59, 374f.

Distributive Justice

ROBERT NOZICK

The term "distributive justice" is not a neutral one. Hearing the term "distribution," most people presume that some thing or mechanism uses some principle or criterion to give out a supply of things. Into this process of distributing shares some error may have crept. So it is an open question, at least, whether redistribution should take place; whether we should do again what has already been done once, though poorly. However, we are not in the position of children who have been given portions of pie by someone who now makes last-minute adjustments to rectify careless cutting. There is no *central* distribution, no person or group entitled to control all the resources, (jointly) deciding how they are to be doled out. What each person gets, he gets from others who give to him in exchange for something, or as a gift. In a free society, diverse persons control different resources, and new holdings arise out of the voluntary exchanges and actions of persons. There is no more a distributing or distribution of shares than there is a distributing of mates in a society in which persons choose whom they shall marry. The total result is the product of many individual decisions which the different individuals involved are entitled to make. Some uses of the term "distribution," it is true, do not imply a previous distributing appropriately judged by some criterion (e.g., "probability distribution"); nevertheless, de-spite the title of this essay, it would be best to use a terminology that clearly is neutral. We shall speak of people's holdings; a principle of justice in holdings describes (part of) what justice tells us (requires) about holdings. I shall state first what I take to be the correct view about justice in holdings, and then turn to the discussion of alternative views.[1]

1. The Entitlement Theory

The subject of justice in holdings consists of three major topics. The first is the *original acquisition of holdings,* the appropriation of un-held things. This includes the issues of how unheld things may come to be held, the process(es) by which unheld things may come to be held, the things that may come to be held by these processes, the extent of what comes to be held by a particular process, and so on. We shall refer to the complicated truth about this topic, which we shall not formulate here, as the principle of justice in acquisition. The second topic concerns the *transfer of holdings* from one person to another. By what processes may a person transfer holdings to another? How may a person acquire a holding from another who holds it? Under this topic come general descriptions of voluntary exchange, and gift, and (on the other hand) fraud, as well as reference to particular conventional details fixed upon a given society. The complicated truth about this subject (with placeholders for conventional details) we shall call the principle of justice in transfer. (And we shall suppose it also includes principles governing how a person may divest himself of a holding, passing it into an unheld state.)

If the world were wholly just, the following inductive definition would exhaustively cover the subject of justice in holdings.

(1) A person who acquires a holding in accordance with the principle of justice in acquisition is entitled to that holding.
(2) A person who acquires a holding in accordance with the principle of justice in transfer, from someone else entitled to the holding, is entitled to the holding.
(3) No one is entitled to a holding except by (repeated) applications of (1) and (2).

The complete principle of distributive justice would say simply that a distribution is just if everyone is entitled to the holdings they possess under the distribution.

A distribution is just if it arises from another (just) distribution by legitimate means. The legitimate means of moving from one distribution to another are specified by the principle of justice in transfer. The legitimate first "moves" are specified by the principle of justice in acquisition.[2] Whatever arises from a just situation by just steps is itself just. The means of change specified by the principle of justice in transfer, preserve justice. As correct rules of inference are truth preserving, and any conclusion deduced via repeated application of such rules from only true premises is itself true, so the means of transition from one situation to another specified by the principle of justice in transfer are justice preserving, and any situation actually arising from repeated transitions in accordance with the principle from a just situation is itself just. The parallel between justice-preserving transformations and truth-preserving transformations illuminates where it fails as well as where it holds. That a conclusion could have been deduced by truth-preserving means from premises that are true suffices to show its truth. That from a just sit-

uation a situation *could* have arisen via justice-preserving means does *not* suffice to show its justice. The fact that a thief's victims voluntarily *could* have presented him with gifts, does not entitle the thief to his ill-gotten gains. Justice in holdings is historical; it depends upon what actually has happened. We shall return to this point later.

Not all actual situations are generated in accordance with the two principles of justice in holdings: the principle of justice in acquisition and the principle of justice in transfer. Some people steal from others, or defraud them, or enslave them seizing their product and preventing them from living as they choose, or forcibly exclude others from competing in exchanges. None of these are permissible modes of transition from one situation to another. And some persons acquire holdings by means not sanctioned by the principle of justice in acquisition. The existence of past injustice (previous violations of the first two principles of justice in holdings) raises the third major topic under justice in holdings: the rectification of injustice in holdings. If past injustice has shaped present holdings in various ways, some identifiable and some not, what now, if anything, ought to be done to rectify these injustices? What obligations are the performers of injustice under to their victims? What obligations do the beneficiaries of injustice have to those whose position is worse than it would have been had the injustice not been done? Or, than it would have been had compensation been paid promptly? How, if at all, do things change if the beneficiaries and those made worse off are not the direct parties in the act of injustice, but, for example, their descendants? Is an injustice done to someone whose holding was itself based upon an unrectified injustice? How far back must one go in wiping clean the historical slate of injustices? What may victims of injustice permissibly do in order to rectify the injustices being done to them, including the many injustices done by persons acting through their government? I do not know of a thorough or theoretically sophisticated treatment of such issues. Idealizing greatly, let us suppose theoretical investigation will produce a principle of rectification. This principle uses historical information about previous situations and injustices done in them (as defined by the first two principles of justice, and rights against interference), and information about the actual course of events that flowed from these injustices, up until the present, and it yields a description (or descriptions) of holdings in the society. The principle of rectification presumably will make use of (its best estimate of) subjunctive information about what would have occurred (or a probability distribution over what might have occurred, using the expected value) if the injustice had not taken place. If the actual description of holdings turns out not to be one of the descriptions yielded by the principle, then one of the descriptions yielded must be realized.[3]

The general outlines of the theory of justice in holdings are that the holdings of a person are just if he is entitled to them by the principles of justice in acquisition and transfer, or by the principle of rectification of injustice (as specified by the first two principles). If each person's holdings are just then the total set (distribution) of holdings is just. To turn these general outlines into a specific theory we would have to specify the details of each of the three principles of justice in holdings: the principle of acquisition of holdings, the principle of transfer of holdings, and the principle of rectification of violations of the first two principles. I shall not attempt that task here. (Locke's principle of justice in acquisition is discussed below.)

1. Historical Principles and End-Result Principles

The general outlines of the entitlement theory illuminate the nature and defects of other conceptions of distributive justice. The entitlement theory of justice in distribution is *historical;* whether a distribution is just depends upon how it came about. In contrast, *current time-slice principles* of justice hold that the justice of a distribution is determined by how things are distributed (who has what) as judged by some *structural* principle(s) of just distribution. A utilitarian who judges between any two dis-

tributions by seeing which has the greater sum of utility and, if these tie, who applies some fixed equality criterion to choose the more equal distribution would hold a current time-slice principle of justice. As would someone who had a fixed schedule of trade-offs between the sum of happiness and equality. All that needs to be looked at, in judging the justice of a distribution, according to a current time-slice principle, is who ends up with what; in comparing any two distributions one need look only at the matrix presenting the distributions. No further information need be fed into a principle of justice. It is a consequence of such principles of justice that any two structurally identical distributions are equally just. (Two distributions are structurally identical if they present the same profile, but perhaps have different persons occupying the particular slots. My having ten and your having five, and my having five and your having ten, are structurally identical distributions.) Welfare economics is the theory of current time-slice principles of justice. The subject is conceived as operating on matrices representing only current information about distribution. This, as well as some of the usual conditions (e.g., the choice of distribution is invariant under relabeling of columns), guarantees that welfare economics will be a current time-slice theory, with all of its inadequacies.

Most persons do not accept current time-slice principles as constituting the whole story about distributive shares. They think it relevant in assessing the justice of a situation to consider not only the distribution it embodies, but also how that distribution came about. If some persons are in prison for murder or war crimes, we do not say that to assess the justice of the distribution in the society we must look only at what this person has, and that person has, and that person has . . . , at the current time. We think it relevant to ask whether someone did something so that he *deserved* to be punished, deserved to have a lower share. Most will agree to the relevance of further information with regard to punishments and penalties. Consider also desired things. One traditional socialist view is that workers are entitled to the product and full fruits of their labor; they have earned it; a distribution is unjust if it does not give the workers what they are entitled to. Such entitlements are based upon some past history. No socialist holding this view would find it comforting to be told that because the actual distribution A happens to coincide structurally with the one he desires D, A therefore is no less just than D; it differs only in that the "parasitic" owners of capital receive under A what the workers are entitled to under D, and the workers receive under A what the owners are entitled to (under D), namely very little. Rightly in my view, this socialist holds onto the notions of earning, producing, entitlement, desert, etc. and he rejects (current time-slice) principles that look only to the structure of the resulting set of holdings. (The set of holdings resulting from what? Isn't it implausible that how holdings are produced and come to exist has no effect at all on who should hold what?) His mistake lies in his view of what entitlements arise out of what sorts of productive processes.

We construe the position we discuss too narrowly by speaking of *current* time-slice principles. Nothing is changed if structural principles operate upon a time sequence of current time-slice profiles and, for example, give someone more now to counterbalance the less he has had earlier. A utilitarian or an egalitarian or any mixture of the two over time will inherit the difficulties of his more myopic comrades. He is not helped by the fact that *some* of the information others consider relevant in assessing a distribution is reflected, unrecoverably, in past matrices. Henceforth, we shall refer to such unhistorical principles of distributive justice, including the current time-slice principles, as *end-result principles* or *end-state principles.*

In contrast to end-result principles of justice, *historical principles* of justice hold that past circumstances or actions of people can create differential entitlements or differential deserts to things. An injustice can be worked by moving from one distribution to another structurally identical one, for the second, in profile the same, may violate people's entitlements or deserts; it may not fit the actual history.

2. *Patterning*

The entitlement principles of justice in holdings that we have sketched are historical principles of justice. To better understand their precise character, we shall distinguish them from another subclass of the historical principles. Consider, as an example, the principle of distribution according to moral merit. This principle requires total distributive shares to vary directly with moral merit; no person should have a greater share than anyone whose moral merit is greater. (If moral merit could be not merely ordered but measured on an interval or ratio scale, stronger principles could be formulated). Or consider the principle that results by substituting "usefulness to society" for "moral merit" in the previous principle. Or instead of "distribute according to moral merit," or "distribute according to usefulness to society," we might consider "distribute according to the weighted sum of moral merit, usefulness to society, and need," with the weights of the different dimensions equal. Let us call a principle of distribution *patterned* if it specifies that a distribution is to vary along with some natural dimension, weighted sum of natural dimensions, or lexicographic ordering of natural dimensions. And let us say a distribution is patterned if it accords with some patterned principle. (I speak of natural dimensions, admittedly without a general criterion for them, because for any set of holdings some artificial dimensions can be gimmicked up to vary along with the distribution of the set.) The principle of distribution in accordance with moral merit is a patterned historical principle, which specifies a patterned distribution. "Distribute according to I.Q." is a patterned principle that looks to information not contained in distributional matrices. It is not historical, however, in that it does not look to any past actions creating differential entitlements to evaluate a distribution; it requires only distributional matrices whose columns are labeled by I.Q. scores. The distribution in a society, however, may be composed of such simple patterned distributions, without itself being simply patterned. Different sectors may operate different patterns, or some combination of patterns may operate in different proportions across a society. A distribution composed in this manner, from a small number of patterned distributions, we also shall term patterned. And we extend the use of "pattern" to include the overall designs put forth by combinations of end-state principles.

Almost every suggested principle of distributive justice is patterned: to each according to his moral merit, or needs, or marginal product, or how hard he tries, or the weighted sum of the foregoing, and so on. The principle of entitlement we have sketched is *not* patterned.[4] There is no one natural dimension or weighted sum or combination of (a small number of) natural dimensions that yields the distributions generated in accordance with the principle of entitlement. The set of holdings that results when some persons receive their marginal products, others win at gambling, others receive a share of their mate's income, others receive gifts from foundations, others receive interest on loans, others receive gifts from admirers, others receive returns on investment, others make for themselves much of what they have, others find things, and so on, will not be patterned. Heavy strands of patterns will run through it; significant portions of the variance in holdings will be accounted for by pattern variables. If most people most of the time choose to transfer some of their entitlements to others only in exchange for something from them, then a large part of what many people hold will vary with what they held that others wanted. More details are provided by the theory of marginal productivity. But gifts to relatives, charitable donations, bequests to children, and the like, are not best conceived, in the first instance, in this manner. Ignoring the strands of pattern, let us suppose for the moment that a distribution actually gotten by the operation of the principle of entitlement is random with respect to any pattern. Though the resulting set of holdings will be unpatterned, it will not be incomprehensible, for it can be seen as arising from the operation of a small number of principles. These principles specify how an initial distribution may arise (the principle of acquisition of holdings) and how distributions may be transformed into others (the principle

of transfer of holdings). The process whereby the set of holdings is generated will be intelligible, though the set of holdings itself that results from this process will be unpatterned.[. . .]

3. How Liberty Upsets Patterns

It is not clear how those holding alternative conceptions of distributive justice can reject the entitlement conception of justice in holdings. For suppose a distribution favored by one of these nonentitlement conceptions is realized. Let us suppose it is your favorite one and call this distribution D_1; perhaps everyone has an equal share, perhaps shares vary in accordance with some dimension you treasure. Now suppose that Wilt Chamberlain is greatly in demand by basketball teams, being a great gate attraction. (Also suppose contracts run only for a year, with players being free agents.) He signs the following sort of contract with a team: In each home game, twenty-five cents from the price of each ticket of admission goes to him. (We ignore the question of whether he is "gouging" the owners, letting them look out for themselves.) The season starts, and people cheerfully attend his team's games; they buy their tickets, each time dropping a separate twenty-five cents of their admission price into a special box with Chamberlain's name on it. They are excited about seeing him play; it is worth the total admission price to them. Let us suppose that in one season one million persons attend his home games, and Wilt Chamberlain winds up with $250,000, a much larger sum than the average income and larger even than anyone else has. Is he entitled to this income? Is this new distribution D_2 unjust? If so, why? There is *no* question about whether each of the people was entitled to the control over the resources they held, in D_1, because that was the distribution (your favorite) that (for the purposes of argument) we assumed was acceptable. Each of these persons *chose* to give twenty-five cents of their money to Chamberlain. They could have spent it on going to the movies, or on candy bars, or on copies of *Dissent* magazine, or of *Monthly Review*. But they all, at least one million of them, converged on giving it to Wilt Chamberlain in exchange for watching him play basketball. If D_1 was a just distribution, and people voluntarily moved from it to D_2, transferring parts of their shares they were given under D_1 (what was it for if not to do something with?), isn't D_2 also just? If the people were entitled to dispose of the resources to which they were entitled (under D_1), didn't this include their being entitled to give it to, or exchange it with, Wilt Chamberlain? Can anyone else complain on grounds of justice? Each other person already has his legitimate share under D_1. Under D_1 there is nothing that anyone has that anyone else has a claim of justice against. After someone transfers something to Wilt Chamberlain, third parties *still* have their legitimate shares; *their* shares are not changed. By what process could such a transfer among two persons give rise to a legitimate claim of distributive justice on a portion of what was transferred, by a third party who had no claim of justice on any holding of the others *before* the transfer?[5] To cut off objections irrelevant here, we might imagine the exchanges occurring in a socialist society, after hours. After playing whatever basketball he does in his daily work, or doing whatever other daily work he does, Wilt Chamberlain decides to put in *overtime* to earn additional money. (First his work quota is set; he works time over that.) Or imagine it is a skilled juggler people like to see, who puts on shows after hours.

Why might some people work overtime in a society in which it is assumed their needs are satisfied? Perhaps because they care about things other than needs. I like to write in books that I read, and to have easy access to books for browsing at odd hours. It would be very pleasant and convenient to have the resources of Widener Library in my back yard. No society, I assume, will provide such resources close to each person who would like them as part of his regular allotment (under D_1). Thus, persons either must do without some extra things that they want, or be allowed to do something extra to get (some of) these things. On what basis could the inequalities that would eventuate be forbidden? Notice also that small factories would spring up in a socialist society,

unless forbidden. I melt down some of my personal possessions (under D_1) and build a machine out of the material. I offer you, and others, a philosophy lecture once a week in exchange for your cranking the handle on my machine, whose products I exchange for yet other things, and so on. (The raw materials used by the machine are given to me by others who possess them under D_1, in exchange for hearing lectures.) Each person might participate to gain things over and above their allotment under D_1. Some persons even might want to leave their job in socialist industry, and work full time in this private sector. I say something more about these issues elsewhere. Here I wish merely to note how private property, even in means of production, would occur in a socialist society that did not forbid people to use as they wished some of the resources they are given under the socialist distribution D_1. The socialist society would have to forbid capitalist acts between consenting adults.[6]

The general point illustrated by the Wilt Chamberlain example and the example of the entrepreneur in a socialist society is that no end-state principle or distributional pattern principle of justice can be continuously realized without continuous interference in people's lives. Any favored pattern would be transformed into one unfavored by the principle, by people choosing to act in various ways; e.g., by people exchanging goods and services with other people, or giving things to other people, things the transferrers are entitled to under the favored distributional pattern. To maintain a pattern one must either continuously interfere to stop people from transferring resources as they wish to, or continually (or periodically) interfere to take from some persons resources that others for some reason chose to transfer to them. (But if some time limit is to be set on how long people may keep resources others voluntarily transfer to them, why let them keep these resources for *any* period of time? Why not have immediate confiscation?) It might be objected that all persons voluntarily will choose to refrain from actions which would upset the pattern. This presupposes unrealistically (a) that all will most want to maintain the pattern (are those who don't, to be "reeducated" or forced to undergo "self-criticism"?); (b) that each can gather enough information about his own actions and the ongoing activities of others to discover which of his actions will upset the pattern; and (c) that diverse and farflung persons can coordinate their actions to dovetail into the pattern. Compare the manner in which the market is neutral among persons' desires, as it reflects and transmits widely scattered information via prices, and coordinates persons' activities.

It puts things perhaps a bit too strongly to say that every patterned (or end-state) principle is liable to be thwarted by the voluntary actions of the individual parties transferring some of their shares they receive under the principle. For perhaps some *very* weak patterns are not so thwarted.[7] Any distributional pattern with any egalitarian component is overturnable by the voluntary actions of individual persons over time; as is every patterned condition with sufficient content so as actually to have been proposed as presenting the central core of distributive justice. Still, given the possibility that some weak conditions or patterns may not be unstable in this way, it would be better to formulate an explicit description of the kind of (interesting and contentful) patterns under discussion, and to prove a theorem about their instability. Since the weaker the patterning, the more likely it is that the entitlement system itself satisfies it, a plausible conjecture is that any patterning either is unstable or is satisfied by the entitlement system.[. . .]

5. Redistribution and Property Rights

Apparently patterned principles allow people to choose to expend upon themselves, but not upon others, those resources they are entitled to (or rather, receive) under some favored distributional pattern D_1. For if each of several persons chooses to expend some of his D_1 resources upon one other person, then that other person will receive more than his D_1 share, disturbing the favored distributional pattern. Maintaining a distributional pattern is individualism with a vengeance! Patterned distributional principles do not give people what entitlement principles do, only better distrib-

uted. For they do not give the right to choose what to do with what one has; they do not give the right to choose to pursue an end involving (intrinsically, or as a means) the enhancement of another's position. To such views, families are disturbing; for within a family occur transfers that upset the favored distributional pattern. Either families themselves become units to which distribution takes place, the column occupiers (on what rationale?), or loving behavior is forbidden. We should note in passing the ambivalent position of radicals towards the family. Its loving relationships are seen as a model to be emulated and extended across the whole society, while it is denounced as a suffocating institution to be broken, and condemned as a focus of parochial concerns that interfere with achieving radical goals. Need we say that it is not appropriate to enforce across the wider society the relationships of love and care appropriate within family, relationships which are voluntarily undertaken?[8] Incidentally, love is an interesting instance of another relationship that is historical, in that (like justice) it depends upon what actually occurred. An adult may come to love another because of the other's characteristics; but it is the other person, and not the characteristics, that is loved. The love is not transferable to someone else with the same characteristics, even to one who "scores" higher for these characteristics. And the love endures through changes of the characteristics that gave rise to it. One loves the particular person one actually encountered. Why love is historical, attaching to persons in this way and not to characteristics, is an interesting and puzzling question.

Proponents of patterned principles of distributive justice focus upon criteria for determining who is to receive holdings; they consider the reasons for which someone should have something, and also the total picture of holdings. Whether or not it is better to give than to receive, proponents of patterned principles ignore giving altogether. In considering the distribution of goods, income, etc., their theories are theories of recipient-justice; they completely ignore any right a person might have to give something to someone. Even in exchanges where each party is simultaneously giver and recipient, patterned principles of justice focus only upon the recipient role and its supposed rights. Thus discussions tend to focus on whether people (should) have a right to inherit, rather than on whether people (should) have a right to bequeath or on whether persons who have a right to hold also have a right to choose that others hold in their place. I lack a good explanation of why the usual theories of distributive justice are so recipient-oriented; ignoring givers and transferrers and their rights is of a piece with ignoring producers and their entitlements. But why is it *all* ignored?

Patterned principles of distributive justice necessitate *re*distributive activities. The likelihood is small that any actual freely arrived at set of holdings fits a given pattern; and the likelihood is nil that it will continue to fit the pattern as people exchange and give. From the point of view of an entitlement theory, redistribution is a serious matter indeed, involving, as it does, the violation of people's rights. (An exception is those takings that fall under the principle of the rectification of injustices.) From other points of view, also, it is serious.

Taxation of earnings from labor is on a par with forced labour.[9] Some persons find this claim obviously true: taking the earnings of n hours labor is like taking n hours from the person; it is like forcing the person to work n hours for another's purpose. Others find the claim absurd. But even these, *if* they object to forced labor, would oppose forcing unemployed hippies to work for the benefit of the needy.[10] And they also would object to forcing each person to work five extra hours each week for the benefit of the needy. But a system that takes five hours' wages in taxes does not seem to them like one that forces someone to work five hours, since it offers the forcee a wider range of choice in activities than does taxation in kind with the particular labor specified. (But we can imagine a gradation of systems of forced labor, from one that specifies a particular activity, to one that gives a choice among two activities, to . . . ; and so on up.) Furthermore, people envisage a system with something like a proportional tax on everything above the amount necessary for basic needs. Some think this does not force someone to

work extra hours, since there is no fixed number of extra hours he is forced to work, and since he can avoid the tax entirely by earning only enough to cover his basic needs. This is a very uncharacteristic view of forcing for those who *also* think people are forced to do something *whenever* the alternatives they face are considerably worse. However, *neither* view is correct. The fact that others intentionally intervene, in violation of a side-constraint against aggression, to threaten force to limit the alternatives, in this case to paying taxes or (presumably the worse alternative) bare subsistence, makes the taxation system one of forced labor, and distinguishes it from other cases of limited choices which are not forcings.[11]

The man who chooses to work longer to gain an income more than sufficient for his basic needs prefers some extra goods or services to the leisure and activities he could perform during the possible non-working hours; whereas the man who chooses not to work the extra time prefers the leisure activities to the extra goods or services he could acquire by working more. Given this, if it would be illegitimate for a tax system to seize some of a man's leisure (forced labor) for the purpose of serving the needy, how can it be legitimate for a tax system to seize some of a man's goods for that purpose? Why should we treat the man whose happiness requires certain material goods or services differently from the man whose preferences and desires make such goods unnecessary for his happiness? Why should the man who prefers seeing a movie (and who has to earn money for a ticket) be open to the required call to aid the needy, while the person who prefers looking at a sunset (and hence need earn no extra money) is not? Indeed, isn't it surprising that redistributionists choose to ignore the man whose pleasures are so easily attainable without extra labor, while adding yet another burden to the poor unfortunate who must work for his pleasures? If anything, one would have expected the reverse. Why is the person with the nonmaterial or nonconsumption desire allowed to proceed unimpeded to his most favored feasible alternative, whereas the man whose pleasures or desires involve material things and who must work for extra money (thereby serving whoever considers his activities valuable enough to pay him) is constrained in what he can realize? Perhaps there is no difference in principle. And perhaps some think the answer concerns merely administrative convenience. (These questions and issues will not disturb those who think forced labor to serve the needy or realize some favored end-state pattern acceptable.) In a fuller discussion we would have (and want) to extend our argument to include interest, entrepreneurial profits, etc. Those who doubt that this extension can be carried through, and who draw the line here at taxation of income from labor, will have to state rather complicated patterned *historical* principles of distributive justice; since end-state principles would not distinguish *sources* of income in any way. It is enough for now to get away from end-state principles and to make clear how various patterned principles are dependent upon particular views about the sources or the illegitimacy or the lesser legitimacy of profits, interest, etc.; which particular views may well be mistaken.

What sort of right over others does a legally institutionalized end-state pattern give one? The central core of the notion of a property right in X, relative to which other parts of the notion are to be explained, is the right to determine what shall be done with X; the right to choose which of the constrained set of options concerning X shall be realized or attempted.[12] The contraints are set by other principles or laws operating in the society; in our theory by the Lockean rights people possess (under the minimal state). My property rights in my knife allow me to leave it where I will, but not in your chest. I may choose which of the acceptable options involving the knife is to be realized. This notion of property helps us to understand why earlier theorists spoke of people as having property in themselves and their labor. They viewed each person as having a right to decide what would become of himself and what he would do, and as having a right to reap the benefits of what he did.

This right of selecting the alternative to be realized from the constrained set of alternatives may be held by an *individual* or by a *group*

with some procedure for reaching a joint decision; or the right may be passed back and forth, so that one year I decide what's to become of X, and the next year you do (with the alternative of destruction, perhaps, being excluded). Or, during the same time period, some types of decisions about X may be made by me, and others by you. And so on. We lack an adequate, fruitful, analytical apparatus for classifying the *types* of constraints on the set of options among which choices are to be made, and the *types* of ways decision powers can be held, divided, and amalgamated. A *theory* of property would, among other things, contain such a classification of constraints and decision modes, and from a small number of principles would follow a host of interesting statements about the *consequences* and effects of certain combinations of constraints and modes of decision.

When end-result principles of distributive justice are built into the legal structure of a society, they (as do most patterned principles) give each citizen an enforcible claim to some portion of the total social product; that is, to some portion of the sum total of the individually and jointly made products. This total product is produced by individuals laboring, using means of production others have saved to bring into existence, by people organizing production or creating means to produce new things or things in a new way. It is on this batch of individual activities that patterned distributional principles give each individual an enforcible claim. Each person has a claim to the activities and the products of other persons, independently of whether the other persons enter into particular relationships that give rise to these claims, and independently of whether they voluntarily take these claims upon themselves, in charity or in exchange for something.

Whether it is done through taxation on wages or on wages over a certain amount, or through seizure of profits, or through there being a big *social pot* so that it's not clear what's coming from where and what's going where, patterned principles of distributive justice involve appropriating the actions of other persons. Seizing the results of someone's labor is equivalent to seizing hours from him and directing him to carry on various activities. If people force you to do certain work, or unrewarded work, for a certain period of time, they decide what you are to do and what purposes your work is to serve apart from your decisions. This process whereby they take this decision from you makes them a *part owner* of you; it gives them a property right in you. Just as having such partial control and power of decision, by right, over an animal or inanimate object would be to have a property right in it.

End-state and most patterned principles of distributive justice institute (partial) ownership by others of people and their actions and labor. These principles involve a shift from the classical liberals' notion of self-ownership to a notion of (partial) property rights in *other* people.

Considerations such as these confront end-state and other patterned conceptions of justice with the question of whether the actions necessary to achieve the selected pattern don't themselves violate moral side-constraints. Any view holding that there are moral side-constraints on actions, that not all moral considerations can be built into end-states that are to be achieved,[13] must face the possibility that some of its goals are not achievable by any morally permissible available means. An entitlement theorist will face such conflicts in a society that deviates from the principles of justice for the generation of holdings, if and only if the only actions available to realize the principles themselves violate some moral constraints. Since deviation from the first two principles of justice (in acquisition and transfer) will involve other persons' direct and aggressive intervention to violate rights, and since moral constraints will not exclude defensive or retributive action in such cases, the entitlement theorist's problem rarely will be pressing. And whatever difficulties he has in applying the principle of rectification to persons who did not themselves violate the first two principles, are difficulties in balancing the conflicting considerations so as correctly to formulate the complex principle of rectification itself; he will not violate moral side-constraints by applying the principle. Proponents of patterned conceptions of justice, however, often will face head-on clashes (and poignant ones if they cherish each party to the clash) between moral side-constraints on how individuals may be treated on the one hand and, on the other, their patterned conception of justice that presents an end-state or other pattern that *must* be realized.

May a person emigrate from a nation that has institutionalized some end-state or patterned distributional principle? For some principles (e.g., Hayek's) emigration presents no theoretical problem. But for others it is a tricky matter. Consider a nation having a compulsory scheme of minimal social provision to aid the neediest (or one organized so as to maximize the position of the worst-off group); no one may opt out of participating in it. (None may say, "don't compel me to contribute to others and don't provide for me via this compulsory mechanism if I am in need.") Everyone above a certain level is forced to contribute to aid the needy. But if emigration from the country were allowed, anyone could choose to move to another country that did not have compulsory social provision but otherwise was (as much as possible) identical. In such a case, the person's only motive for leaving would be to avoid participating in the compulsory scheme of social provision. And if he does leave, the needy in his initial country will receive no (compelled) help from him. What rationale yields the result that the person be permitted to emigrate, yet forbidden to stay and opt out of the compulsory scheme of social provision? If providing for the needy is of overriding importance, this does militate against allowing internal opting out; but it also speaks against allowing external emigration. (Would it also support, to some extent, the kidnapping of persons living in a place without compulsory social provision, who could be forced to make a contribution to the needy in your community?) Perhaps the crucial component of the position that allows emigration solely to avoid certain arrangements, while not allowing anyone internally to opt out of them, is a concern for fraternal feelings within the country. "We don't want anyone here who doesn't contribute, who doesn't care enough about the others to contribute." That concern, in this case, would have to be tied to the view that forced aiding tends to produce fraternal feelings between the aided and the aider (or perhaps merely to the view that the knowledge that someone or other voluntarily is not aiding produces unfraternal feelings).

6. Locke's Theory of Acquisition

Before we turn to consider another theory of justice in detail, we must introduce an additional bit of complexity into the structure of the entitlement theory. This is best approached by considering Locke's attempt to specify a principle of justice in acquisition. Locke views property rights in an unowned object as originating through someone's mixing his labor with it. This gives rise to many questions. What are the boundaries of what labor is mixed with? If a private astronaut clears a place on Mars, has he mixed his labor with (so that he comes to own) the whole planet, the whole uninhabited universe, or just a particular plot? Which plot does an act bring under ownership? The minimal (possibly disconnected) area such that an act decreases entropy in that area, and not elsewhere? Can virgin land (for the purposes of ecological investigation by high-flying airplanes) come under ownership by a Lockean process? Building a fence around a territory presumably would make one the owner of only the fence (and the land immediately underneath it).

Why does mixing one's labor with something make one the owner of it? Perhaps because one owns one's labor, and so one comes to own a previously unowned thing that becomes permeated with what one owns. Ownership seeps over into the rest. But why isn't mixing what I own with what I don't own a way of losing what I own rather than a way of gaining what I don't? If I own a can of tomato juice, and spill it in the sea so that its molecules (radioactive, so I can check this) mingle evenly throughout the sea, do I thereby come to own the sea, or have I foolishly dissipated my tomato juice? Perhaps the idea, instead, is that laboring on something improves it and makes it more valuable; and anyone is entitled to own a (thing whose) value he has created. (Reinforcing this, perhaps, is the view that laboring is unpleasant. If some people made things ef-

fortlessly, as the cartoon characters in *The Yellow Submarine* trail flowers in their wake, would they have lesser claim to their own products whose making didn't *cost* them anything?) Ignore the fact that laboring on something may make it less valuable (spraying pink enamel paint on a found piece of driftwood). Why should one's entitlement extend to the whole object rather than just to the *added value* one's labor has produced? (Such reference to value might also serve to delimit the extent of ownership; e.g., substitute "increases the value of" for "decreases entropy in" in the above entropy criterion.) No workable or coherent value-added property scheme has yet been devised, and any such scheme presumably would fall to objections (similar to those) that fell the theory of Henry George.

It will be implausible to view improving an object as giving full ownership to it, if the stock of unowned objects that might be improved is limited. For an object's coming under one person's ownership changes the situation of all others. Whereas previously they were at liberty (in Hohfeld's sense) to use the object, they now no longer are. This change in the situation of others (by removing their liberty to act on a previously unowned object) need not worsen their situation. If I appropriate a grain of sand from Coney Island, no one else may now do as they will with *that* grain of sand. But there are plenty of others left for them to do the same with. Or if not grains of sand, then other things. Alternatively, the things I do with the grain of sand I appropriate might improve the position of others, counterbalancing their loss of the liberty to use that grain. The crucial point is whether appropriation of an unowned object worsens the situation of others.

Locke's proviso that there be "enough and as good left in common for others" (sec. 27) is meant to ensure that the situation of others is not worsened. (If this proviso is met, is there any motivation for his further condition of nonwaste?) It is often said that this proviso once held but now no longer does. But there appears to be an argument for the conclusion that if the proviso no longer holds, then it cannot ever have held so as to yield permanent and inheritable property rights. Consider the first person Z for whom there is not enough and as good left to appropriate. The last person Y to appropriate left Z without his previous liberty to act on an object, and so worsened Z's situation. So Y's appropriation is not allowed under Locke's proviso. Therefore the next to last person X to appropriate left Y in a worse position, for X's act ended permissible appropriation. Therefore X's appropriation wasn't permissible. But then the appropriator two from last, W, ended permissible appropriation and so, since it worsened X's position, W's appropriation wasn't permissible. And so on back to the first appropriator A of a permanent property right.

This argument, however, proceeds too quickly. Someone may be made worse off by another's appropriation in two ways: first, by losing the opportunity to improve his situation by a particular appropriation or any one; and second, by no longer being able to use freely (without appropriation) what he previously could. A *stringent* requirement that another not be made worse off by an appropriation would exclude the first way if nothing else counterbalances the diminution in opportunity, as well as the second. A *weaker* requirement would exclude the second way though not the first. With the weaker requirement, we cannot zip back so quickly from Z to A, as in the above argument; for though person Z can no longer *appropriate,* there may remain some for him to *use* as before. In this case Y's appropriation would not violate the weaker Lockean condition. (With less remaining that people are at liberty to use, users might face more inconvenience, crowding, etc; in that way the situation of others might be worsened, unless appropriation stopped far short of such a point.) It is arguable that no one legitimately can complain if the weaker provision is satisfied. However, since this is less clear than in the case of the more stringent proviso, Locke may have intended this stringent proviso by "enough and as good" remaining, and perhaps he meant the non-waste condition to delay the end point from which the argument zips back.

Is the situation of persons who are unable to appropriate (there being no more accessible and useful unowned objects) worsened by a system allowing appropriation and permanent property? Here enter the various familiar social considerations favoring private property: it increases the social product by putting means of production in the hands of those who can use them most efficiently (profitably); experimentation is encouraged, because with separate persons controlling resources, there is no one person or small group whom someone with a new idea must convince to try it out; private property enables people to decide on the pattern and types of risks they wish to bear, leading to specialized types of risk bearing; private property protects future persons by leading some to hold back resources from current consumption for future markets; it provides alternate sources of employment for unpopular persons who don't have to convince any one person or small group to hire them, and so on. These considerations enter a Lockean theory to support the claim that appropriation of private property satisfies the intent behind the "enough and as good left over" proviso, *not* as a utilitarian justification of property. They enter to rebut the claim that because the proviso is violated, no natural right to private property can arise by a Lockean process. The difficulty in working such an argument to show the proviso is satisfied is in fixing the appropriate baseline for comparison. Lockean appropriation makes people no worse off than they would be *how?*[14] This question of fixing the baseline needs more detailed investigation than we are able to give it here. It would be desirable to have an estimate of the general economic importance of original appropriation for a society, in order to see how much leeway there is for differing theories of appropriation and of the location of the baseline. Perhaps this importance can be measured by the percentage of all income that is based upon untransformed raw materials and given resources (rather than human actions), mainly rental income representing the unimproved value of the land, and the price of raw materials in situ, and by the percentage of current wealth that represents such income in the past.[15]

We should note that it is not only persons favoring *private* property who need a theory of how property rights legitimately originate.

Those believing in collective property—for example, those believing that a group of persons living in an area jointly own the territory, or its mineral resources—also must provide a theory of how such property rights arise, of why the persons living there have rights to determine what is done with the land and resources there that persons living elsewhere don't have (with regard to the same land and resources).

7. The Proviso

Whether or not Locke's particular theory of appropriation can be spelled out so as to handle various difficulties, I assume that any adequate theory of justice in acquisition will contain a proviso similar to the weaker of the ones we have attributed to Locke. A process normally giving rise to a permanent bequeathable property right in a previously unowned thing, will not do so if the position of others no longer at liberty to use the thing is thereby worsened. It is important to specify *this* particular mode of worsening the situation of others, for the proviso does not encompass other modes. It does not include the worsening due to more limited opportunities to appropriate (the first way above, corresponding to the more stringent condition), and it does not include how I "worsen" a seller's position if I appropriate materials to make some of what he is selling, and enter into competition with him. Someone whose appropriation (otherwise) would violate the proviso still may appropriate provided he compensates the others so that their situation is not thereby worsened; unless he does compensate these others, his appropriation will violate the (proviso of the) principle of justice in acquisition and will be an illegitimate one.[16] A theory of appropriation incorporating this Lockean proviso will handle correctly the cases (objections to the theory lacking the proviso) where someone appropriates the total supply of something necessary for life.[17]

A theory that includes this proviso in its principle of justice in acquisition, also must contain a more complex principle of justice in transfer. Some reflection of the proviso about appropriation constrains later actions. If my appropriating all of a certain substance violates the Lockean proviso, then so does my appropriating some and purchasing all the rest from others who obtained it without (otherwise) violating the Lockean proviso. If the proviso excludes someone's appropriating all the drinkable water in the world, it also excludes his purchasing it all. (More weakly, and messily, it may exclude his charging certain prices for some of his supply.) This proviso (almost?) never will come into effect; the more someone acquires of a scarce substance that others want, the higher the price of the rest will go, and the more difficult it will become for him to acquire it all. But still, we can imagine, at least, that something like this occurs: someone makes simultaneous secret bids to the separate owners of a substance, each of whom sells assuming he can easily purchase more from the other owners; or some natural catastrophe destroys all of the supply of something except that in one person's possession. The total supply could not be all permissibly appropriated by one person at the beginning. His later acquisition of it all does not show that the original appropriation violated the proviso (even by a reverse argument similar to the one above that tried to zip back from Z to A). Rather, it is the combination of the original appropriation *plus* all the later transfers and actions that violates the Lockean proviso.

Each owner's title to his holding includes the historical shadow of the Lockean proviso in appropriation. This excludes his transferring it into an agglomeration that does violate the Lockean proviso, and excludes his using it in a way, in coordination with others or independently of them, so as to violate the proviso by making the situation of others worse than their baseline situation. Once it is known that someone's ownership runs afoul of the Lockean proviso, there are stringent limits on what he may do with (what it is difficult any longer unreservedly to call) "his property." Thus a person may not appropriate the only water hole in a desert and charge what he will. Nor may he charge what he will if he possesses one, and unfortunately it chances that all the water holes in the desert dry up, except for his. This unfortunate circumstance, admittedly no fault of his, brings into operation the Lockean proviso and limits his property rights.[18] Similarly, an owner's property right in the only island in an area does not allow him to order a castaway from a shipwreck off his island as a trespasser, for this would violate the Lockean proviso.

Notice that the theory does not say that owners do have these rights but that the rights are overridden to avoid some catastrophe. (Overridden rights do not disappear; they leave a trace of a sort absent in the cases under discussion.)[19] There is no such external (and ad hoc?) overriding. Considerations internal to the theory of property itself, to its theory of acquisition and appropriation, provide the means for handling such cases. The results, however, may be coextensive with some condition about catastrophe, since the baseline for comparison is so low as compared to the productiveness of a society with private appropriation, that the question of the Lockean proviso being violated arises only in the case of catastrophe (or a desert-island situation).

The fact that someone owns the total supply of something necessary for others to stay alive does *not* entail that his (or anyone's) appropriation of anything left some people (immediately or later) in a situation worse than the baseline one. A medical researcher who synthesizes a new substance that effectively treats a certain disease and who refuses to sell except on his terms, does not worsen the situation of others by depriving them of whatever he has appropriated. The others (easily can) possess the same materials he appropriated; the researcher's appropriation or purchase of chemicals didn't make those chemicals scarce in a way so as to violate the Lockean proviso. Nor would someone else's purchasing the total supply of the synthesized substance from the medical researcher. The fact that the medical researcher uses easily available chemicals to synthesize the drug no more violates the Lockean proviso than does the fact that the only surgeon able to perform a particular operation eats easily obtainable food in order to stay alive and have the energy to work. This shows that the Lockean proviso is not an "end-state principle"; it focuses on a particular way that appropriative acts affect others, and not on the structure of the situation that results.

Intermediate between someone who takes all of the public supply, and someone who makes the total supply out of easily obtainable substances, is someone who appropriates the total supply of something in a way that does not deprive the others of it. For example, someone finds a new substance in an out-of-the-way place. He discovers that it effectively treats a certain disease, and appropriates the total supply. He does not worsen the situation of others; if he did not stumble upon the substance no one else would have, and the others would remain without it. However, as time passes, the likelihood increases that others would have come across the substance; upon this fact might be based a limit to his property right in the substance so that others are not below their baseline position, e.g., its bequest might be limited. The theme of someone worsening another's situation by depriving him of something he otherwise would possess, may also illuminate the example of patents. An inventor's patent does not deprive others of an object which would not exist if not for the inventor. Yet patents would have this effect on others who independently invent the object. Therefore, these independent inventors, upon whom the burden of proving independent discovery may rest, should not be excluded from utilizing their own invention as they wish (including selling it to others). Furthermore, a known invention drastically lessens the chances of actual independent invention. For persons who know of an invention usually will not try to reinvent it, and the notion of independent discovery here would be murky at best. Yet we may assume that in the absence of the original invention, sometime later someone else would have come up with it. This suggests placing a time limit on patents, as a rough rule of thumb to approximate how long it would have taken, in the absence of knowledge of the invention, for independent discovery.

I believe that the free operation of a market system will not actually run afoul of the Lockean proviso. If this is correct, the proviso will not provide a significant opportunity for future state action. Indeed, were it not for the effects of previous *illegitimate* state action, people would not think the possibility of the proviso's being violated as of more interest than any other logical possibility. (Here I make an empirical historical claim; as does someone who disagrees with this.) This completes our indication of the complication in the entitlement theory introduced by the Lockean proviso.

II. Rawls' Theory

We can bring our discussion of distributive justice into sharper focus by considering in some detail John Rawls' recent contribution to the subject. *A Theory of Justice*[20] is a powerful, deep, subtle, wide-ranging, systematic work in political and moral philosophy which has not seen its like since the writings of John Stuart Mill, if then. It is a fountain of illuminating ideas, integrated together into a lovely whole. Political philosophers now must either work within Rawls' theory or explain why not. The considerations and distinctions we have developed are illuminated by, and help illuminate, Rawls' masterful presentation of an alternative conception. Even those who remain unconvinced after wrestling with Rawls' systematic vision will learn much from its close study. I do not speak only of the Millian sharpening of one's views in combatting (what one takes to be) error. It is impossible to read Rawls' book without incorporating much, perhaps transmuted, into one's own deepened view. And it is impossible to finish his book without a new and inspiring vision of what a moral theory may attempt to do and unite, of how *beautiful* a whole theory can be. I permit myself to concentrate here on disagreements with Rawls' theory only because I am confident that my readers will have discovered for themselves its many virtues.

1. Social Cooperation

In considering the role of the principles of justice, Rawls says:

Let us assume, to fix ideas, that a society is a more or less self-sufficient association of persons who in their relations to one another recognize certain rules of conduct as binding and who for the most part act in accordance with them. Suppose further that these rules specify a system of cooperation designed to advance the good of those taking part in it. Then, although a society is a cooperative venture for mutual advantage, it is typically marked by a conflict as well as by an identity of interests. There is an identity of interests since social cooperation makes possible a better life for all than any would have if each were to live solely by his own efforts. There is a conflict of interests since persons are not indifferent as to how the greater benefits produced by their collaboration are distributed, for in order to pursue their ends they each prefer a larger to a lesser share. A set of principles is required for choosing among the various social arrangements which determine this division of advantages and for underwriting an agreement on the proper distributive shares. These principles are the principles of social justice: they provide a way of assigning rights and duties in the basic institutions of society and they define the appropriate distribution of the benefits and burdens of social cooperation (p. 4).

Let us imagine n individuals who do not cooperate together and who each live solely by their own efforts. Each person i receives a payoff, return, income, etc. S_i; the sum total of what all the separately acting individuals got is $S = \sum_{n}^{i} = 1 \, S_i$. By cooperating together they can obtain a larger sum total T. The problem of distributive social justice, according to Rawls, is how these benefits of cooperation are to be distributed or allocated. This problem might be conceived of in two ways: how is the total T to be allocated?; or, how is the incremental amount due to social cooperation, that is, the benefits of social cooperation $T - S$, to be allocated? The latter formulation assumes that each individual i receives from the subtotal S of T, his share S_i. The two statements of the problem differ. When combined with the noncooperative distribution of S (each i getting S_i), a "fair-looking" distribution of $T - S$ under the second version may not yield a "fair-looking" distribution of T (the first version). Alternatively, a fair-looking distribution of T may give a particular individual i less than his share S_i. (The constraint $T_i \geqslant S_i$ on the answer to the first formulation of the problem, where T_i is the share in T of the ith individual, would exclude this possibility.) Rawls, without distinguishing these two formulations of the problem, writes as though his concern is the first one of how the total sum T is to be distributed. One might claim, to support a focus on the first issue, that due to the enormous benefits of social cooperation, the noncooperative shares S_i are so small in comparison to any cooperative ones T_i that they may be ignored in setting up the problem of social justice. Though we should note that this certainly is not how people entering into cooperation with each other would agree to conceive of the problem of dividing up cooperation's benefits.

Why does social cooperation *create* the problem of distributive justice? Would there be no problem of justice and no need for a theory of justice, if there was no social cooperation at all, if each person got his share solely by his own efforts? If we suppose, as Rawls seems to, that this situation does *not* raise questions of distributive justice, then in virtue of what facts about social cooperation do these questions of justice emerge? What is it about social cooperation that gives rise to issues of justice? It cannot be said that there will be conflicting claims only where there is social cooperation; that individuals who produce independently and (initially) fend for themselves will not make claims of justice on each other. If there were ten Robinson Crusoes, each working alone for two years on separate islands, who discovered each other and the facts of their different allotments by radio communication via transmitters left twenty years earlier, could they not make claims on each other, supposing it were possible to transfer goods from one island to the next?[21] Wouldn't the one with least make a claim on ground of need, or on the ground that his island was naturally poorest, or on the ground that he was naturally least capable of fending for himself? Mightn't he say that justice demanded he be given some more by the others, claiming it unfair that he should receive so much less and perhaps be destitute, perhaps starving? He might go on to say that the different individual noncooperative shares stem from differential natural endowments, which are not deserved, and that the task of justice is to rectify these arbitrary facts and inequities. Rather than its being the case that one *will* make such claims in the situation lacking

social cooperation, perhaps the point is that such claims clearly would be without merit. Why would they clearly be without merit? In the social noncooperation situation, it might be said, each individual deserves what he gets unaided by his own efforts; or rather, no one else can make a claim *of justice* against this holding. It is pellucidly clear in this situation who is entitled to what, so no theory of justice is needed. On this view social cooperation introduces a muddying of the waters that makes it unclear or indeterminate who is entitled to what. Rather than saying that no theory of justice applies to this noncooperative case (wouldn't it be unjust if someone stole another's products in the noncooperative situation?), I would say that it is a clear case of application of the correct theory of justice: the entitlement theory.

How does social cooperation change things so that the same entitlement principles that apply to the noncooperative cases become inapplicable or inappropriate to cooperative ones? It might be said that one cannot disentangle the contributions of distinct individuals who cooperate; everything is everyone's joint product. On this joint product, or on any portion of it, each person plausibly will make claims of equal strength; all have an equally good claim, or at any rate no person has a distinctly better claim than any other. Somehow (this line of thought continues), it must be decided how this total product of joint social cooperation (to which individual entitlements do not apply differentially) is to be divided up: this is the problem of distributive justice.

Don't individual entitlements apply to parts of the cooperatively produced product? First, suppose that social cooperation is based upon division of labor, specialization, comparative advantage, and exchange; each person works singly to transform or transport his product until it reaches its ultimate consumer. People cooperate in making things but they work separately; each person is a miniature firm.[22] The products of each person are easily identifiable, and exchanges are made in open markets with prices set competitively, given informational constraints, etc. In such a system of social cooperation, what is the task of a theory of justice? It might be said that whatever holdings result will depend upon the exchange ratios or prices at which exchanges are made, and therefore that the task of a theory of justice is to set criteria for "fair prices." This is hardly the place to trace the serpentine windings of theories of a just price. It is difficult to see why these issues should even arise here. People are choosing to make exchanges with other people and to transfer entitlements, with no restrictions on their freedom to trade with any other party at any mutually acceptable ratio.[23] Why does such sequential social cooperation, linked together by people's voluntary exchanges, raise any special problems about how things are to be distributed? Why isn't the appropriate (a not inappropriate) set of holdings just the one which *actually occurs* via this process of mutually agreed to exchanges whereby people choose to give to others what they are entitled to give or hold?

Let us now drop our assumption that people work independently, cooperating only in sequence via voluntary exchanges, and instead consider people who work together jointly to produce something. Is it now impossible to disentangle people's respective contributions? The question here is not whether marginal productivity theory is an appropriate theory of fair or just shares, but whether there is some coherent notion of identifiable marginal product. It seems unlikely that Rawls' theory rests on the strong claim that there is no such reasonably serviceable notion. Anyway, once again we have a situation of a large number of bilateral exchanges: owners or resources reaching separate agreements with entrepreneurs about the use of their resources, entrepreneurs reaching agreements with individual workers, or groups of workers first reaching some joint agreement and then presenting a package to an entrepreneur, etc. People transfer their holdings or labor in free markets, with the exchange ratios (prices) determined in the usual manner. If marginal productivity theory is reasonably adequate, people will be receiving, in these voluntary transfers of holdings, (roughly) their marginal products.[24]

But if the notion of marginal product were so ineffective that factors' marginal products

in actual situations of joint production could not be identified by hirers or purchasers of the factors, then the resulting distribution to factors would not be patterned in accordance with marginal product. Someone who viewed marginal productivity theory, where it was applicable, *as a patterned theory of justice,* might think such situations of joint production and indeterminate marginal product provided an opportunity for some theory of justice to enter to determine appropriate exchange ratios. But an entitlement theorist would find acceptable whatever distribution resulted from the party's voluntary exchanges.[25] The questions about the workability of marginal productivity theory are intricate ones.[26] Let us merely note here the strong personal incentive for owners of resources to converge to the marginal product, and the strong market pressures tending to produce this result. Employers of factors of productions are not all dolts who don't know what they're doing, transferring holdings they value to others on an irrational and arbitrary basis. Indeed, Rawls' position on inequalities requires that separate contributions to joint products be isolable, to some extent. For Rawls goes out of his way to argue that inequalities are justified if they serve to raise the position of the worst-off group in the society; if without the inequalities the worst-off group would be even more worse off. These serviceable inequalities stem, at least in part, from the necessity to provide incentives to certain people to perform various activities or fill various roles that not everyone can do equally well. (Rawls is *not* imagining that inequalities are needed to fill positions that everyone can do equally well, or that the most drudgery-filled positions that require the least skill will command the highest income.) But *to whom* are the incentives to be paid? To which performers of what activities? When it is necessary to provide incentives to some to perform their productive activities, there is no talk of a joint social product from which no individual's contribution can be disentangled. If the product was all that inextricably joint, it couldn't be known that the extra incentives were going to the crucial persons; and it couldn't be known that the additional product produced by these now motivated people is greater than the expenditure to them in incentives. So it couldn't be known whether the provision of incentives was efficient or not, whether it involved a net gain or a net loss. But Rawls' discussion of justifiable inequalities presupposes that these things can be known. And so the claim we have imagined about the indivisible nonpartitionable nature of the joint product is seen to dissolve, leaving the reasons for the view that social cooperation creates special problems of distributive justice otherwise not present, unclear if not mysterious.

2. Terms of Cooperation and the Difference Principle

Another entry into the issue of the connection of social cooperation with distributive shares brings us to grips with Rawls' actual discussion. Rawls imagines rational, mutually disinterested, individuals meeting in a certain situation, or abstracted from their other features not provided for in this situation. In this hypothetical situation of choice, which Rawls calls "the original position," they choose the first principles of a conception of justice that is to regulate all subsequent criticism and reform of their institutions. While making this choice, no one knows his place in society, his class position or social status, or his natural assets and abilities, his strength, intelligence, etc.

The principles of justice are chosen behind a veil of ignorance. This ensures that no one is advantaged or disadvantaged in the choice of principles by the outcome of natural chance or the contingency of social circumstances. Since all are similarly situated and no one is able to design principles to favor his particular condition, the principles of justice are the result of a fair agreement or bargain (sec. 3).

What would persons in the original position agree to?

Persons in the initial situation would choose two . . . principles: the first requires equality in the assignment of basic rights and duties, while the second holds that social and economic inequalities, for example, inequalities of wealth and authority are just only if they result in compensating benefits for everyone, and in particular for the least advantaged members of society. These principles rule out justifying institutions on the grounds that the hardships of some are offset by a greater good in the aggregate. It may be expedient but it is not just that some should have less in order that others may prosper. But there is no injustice in the greater benefits earned by a few provided that the situation of persons not so fortunate is thereby improved. The intuitive idea is that since everyone's well-being depends upon a scheme of cooperation without which no one could have a satisfactory life, the division of advantages should be such as to draw forth the willing cooperation of everyone taking part in it, including those less well situated. Yet this can be expected only if reasonable terms are proposed. The two principles mentioned seem to be a fair agreement on the basis of which those better endowed, or more fortunate in their social position, neither of which we can be said to deserve, could expect the willing cooperation of others when some workable scheme is a necessary condition of the welfare of all (sec. 3).

This second principle, which Rawls specifies as the difference principle, holds that the institutional structure is to be so designed that the worst-off group under it is at least as well off as the worst-off group (not necessarily the same group) would be under any alternative institutional structure. If persons in the original position follow the minimax policy in making the significant choice of principles of justice, Rawls argues, they will choose the difference principle. Our concern here is not whether persons in the position Rawls describes actually would minimax and actually would choose the particular principles Rawls specifies. Still, we should question why individuals in the original position would choose a principle that focuses upon groups, rather than individuals. Won't application of the minimax principle lead each person in the original position to favor maximizing the position of the worst-off *individual?* To be sure, this principle would reduce questions of evaluating social institutions to the issue of how the unhappiest depressive fares. Yet avoiding this by moving the focus to groups (or representative individuals) seems ad hoc, and is inadequately motivated for those in the original position (see p. 98 and sec. 16 generally). Nor is it clear which groups are appropriately considered; why exclude the group of depressives or alcoholics or the representative paraplegic?

If the difference principle is not satisfied by some institutional structure J, then under J some group G is worse off than it would be under another institutional structure I that satisfies the principle. If another group F is better off under J than it would be under the I favored by the difference principle, is this sufficient to say that under J "some . . . have less in order that others may prosper"? (Here one would have in mind that G has less in order that F prosper. Could one also make the same statement about I? Does F have less under I in order that G may prosper?) Suppose that in a society

(1) Group G has amount A and group F has amount B, with B greater than A. Also things could be arranged differently so that G would have more than A, and F would have less than B. (The different arrangement might involve a mechanism to transfer some holdings from F to G.)

Is this sufficient to say

(2) G is poorly off *because* F is well off; G is poorly off *in order that* F be well off; F's being well off *makes* G poorly off; G is poorly off *on account of* F's being well off; G is not better off *because of* how well off F is?

If so, does the truth of (2) depend on G's being in a worse position than F? There is yet another possible institutional structure K that transfers holdings from the worse-off group G to F, making G even more worse off. Does the possibility of K make it true to say that under J, F is not (even) better off because of how well off G is?

We do not normally hold that the truth of a subjunctive as in (1) is alone sufficient for the truth of some indicative causal statement as in (2). It would improve my life in various ways if you were to choose to become my devoted slave, supposing I could get over the initial discomfort. Is the cause of my present state your

not becoming my slave? Because your enslaving yourself to a poorer person would improve his lot and worsen yours, are we to say that that poor person is badly off because you are as well off as you are; has he less in order that you may prosper? From

(3) If P were to do act A then Q would not be in situation S,

we will conclude

(4) P's not doing A is responsible for Q's being in situation S; P's not doing A causes Q to be in S

only if we *also* believe that

(5) P ought to do act A, or P has a duty to do act A, or P has an obligation to do act A, etc.[27]

Thus the inference from (3) to (4), in this case, *presupposes* (5). One cannot argue from (3) to (4) as one step in order *to get to* (5). The statement that in a particular situation some have less in order that others may prosper is often based upon the very evaluation of a situation or an institutional framework that it is introduced to support. Since this evaluation does *not* follow merely from the subjunctive (e.g., [1] or [3]) an *independent* argument must be produced for it.[28]

Rawls holds, as we have seen, that

since everyone's well-being depends upon a scheme of cooperation without which no one could have a satisfactory life, the division of advantages should be such as to draw forth the willing cooperation of everyone taking part in it, including those less well situated. Yet this can be expected only if reasonable terms are proposed. The two principles mentioned seem to be a fair agreement on the basis of which those better endowed or more fortunate in their social position . . . could expect the willing cooperation of others when some workable scheme is a necessary condition of the welfare of all (sec. 3).

No doubt, the difference principle presents terms on the basis of which those less well endowed would be willing to cooperate. (What *better* terms could they propose for themselves?) But is this a fair agreement on the basis of which those *worse* endowed could expect the *willing* cooperation of others? With regard to the existence of gains from social cooperation, the situation is symmetrical. The better endowed gain by cooperating with the worse endowed, *and* the worse endowed gain by cooperating with the better endowed. Yet the difference principle is not neutral between the better and the worse endowed. Whence the assymmetry?

Perhaps the symmetry is upset if one asks *how much* each gains from the social cooperation. This question might be understood in two ways: How much do people benefit from social cooperation, as compared to their individual holdings in a *non*cooperative scheme? That is, how much is $T_i - S_i$, for each individual *i?* Or, alternatively, how much does each individual gain from general social cooperation, as compared (not with *no* cooperation but) with more limited cooperation? The latter is the more appropriate question with regard to general social cooperation. For failing general agreement on the principles to govern how the benefits of general social cooperation are to be held, not everyone will remain in a noncooperative situation if there is some other beneficial cooperative arrangement involving some (but not all) people, whose participants *can* agree. These people will participate in this more narrow cooperative arrangement. To focus upon the benefits of the better and the worse endowed cooperating together, we must try to imagine less extensive schemes of partitioned social cooperation in which the better endowed cooperate only among themselves and the worse endowed cooperate only among themselves, with no cross-cooperation. The members of both groups gain from the internal cooperation within their respective groups, and have larger shares than they would if there were no social cooperation at all. An individual benefits from the wider system of extensive cooperation between the better and the worse endowed, to the extent of his incremental gain from this wider cooperation; the amount by which his share under a scheme of general cooperation is greater than it would be under one of limited intragroup (but not cross-group) cooperation. *General* cooperation will be of more benefit to the better or to the worse endowed if (to pick a simple criterion) the mean incremental gain from general cooperation (over against limited intragroup cooperation) is greater in one group than it is in the other.

One might speculate about whether there is an inequality between the groups' mean incremental gains and, if so, which way it goes. If the better endowed includes those who manage to accomplish something of great economic advantage to others, such as new inventions, new ideas about production or ways of doing things, skill at economic tasks, etc.,[29] it is difficult to avoid concluding that the *less* well endowed gain *more* than the better endowed do from the scheme of general cooperation. What follows from this conclusion? I do *not* mean to imply that the better endowed should get even more than they get under the entitlement system of general social cooperation.[30] What *does* follow from the conclusion is a deep suspicion of imposing, in the name of fairness, constraints upon voluntary social cooperation (and the set of holdings that arises from it) so that those already benefitting most from this general cooperation benefit even more!

Rawls would have us imagine the worse endowed persons saying something like the following: "Look, better endowed, you gain by cooperating with us. If you want our cooperation you'll have to accept reasonable terms. We suggest these terms: We'll cooperate with you only if we get *as much as possible.* That is, the terms of our cooperation should give us that maximal share such that, if it was tried to give us more, we'd end up with less." How generous these proposed terms are might be seen by imagining that the better endowed make the (almost) symmetrical opposite proposal: "Look, worse endowed, you gain by cooperating with *us.* If you want our cooperation you'll have to accept reasonable terms. We propose these terms: We'll cooperate with you so long as *we* get as much as possible. That is, the terms of our cooperation should give us the maximal share such that, if it was tried to give us more, we'd end up with less." If these terms seem outrageous, as they are, why don't the terms proposed by those worse endowed seem the same? Why shouldn't the better endowed treat this latter proposal as beneath consideration, supposing someone to have the nerve explicitly to state it?

Rawls devotes much attention to explaining why those less well favored should not complain at receiving less. His explanation, simply put, is that because the inequality works for his advantage, someone less well favored shouldn't complain about it; he receives *more* in the unequal system than he would in an equal one. (Though he might receive still more in another unequal system that placed someone else below him.) But Rawls discusses the question of whether those *more* favored will or should find the terms satisfactory *only* in the following passage, where A and B are any two representative men with A being the more favored:

The difficulty is to show that A has no grounds for complaint. Perhaps he is required to have less than he might since his having more would result in some loss to B. Now what can be said to the more favored man? To begin with, it is clear that the well-being of each depends on a scheme of social cooperation without which no one could have a satisfactory life. Secondly, we can ask for the willing cooperation of everyone only if the terms of the scheme are reasonable. The difference principle, then, seems to be a fair basis on which those better endowed, or more fortunate in their social circumstances, could expect others to collaborate with them when some workable arrangement is a necessary condition of the good of all (p. 103).

What Rawls imagines being said to the more favored men does *not* show that these men have no grounds for complaint, nor does it at all diminish the weight of whatever complaints they have. That the well-being of all depends on social cooperation without which no one could have a satisfactory life could also be said to the less well endowed by someone proposing any other principle, including that of maximizing the position of the best endowed. Similarly for the fact that we can ask for the willing cooperation of everyone only if the terms of the scheme are reasonable. The question is: what terms *would be* reasonable? What Rawls imagines being said thus far merely sets up his problem; it doesn't distinguish his pro-

posed difference principle from the (almost) symmetrical counterproposal that we imagined the better endowed making, or from any other proposal. Thus, when Rawls continues, "The difference principle, then, seems to be a fair basis on which those best endowed, or more fortunate in their social circumstances, could expect others to collaborate with them when some workable arrangement is a necessary condition of the good of all," the presence of the "then" in his sentence is puzzling. Since the sentences which precede it are neutral between his proposal and any other proposal, the conclusion that the difference principle presents a fair basis for cooperation *cannot* follow from what precedes it in this passage. Rawls is merely repeating that it seems reasonable; hardly a convincing reply to anyone to whom it doesn't seem reasonable. Rawls has not shown that the more favored man A has no grounds for complaint at being required to have less in order that another B might have more than he otherwise would. And he can't have shown this, since A *does* have grounds for complaint. Doesn't he?[. . .]

Notes

1. The reader who has looked ahead and seen that the second part of this essay discusses Rawls' theory, mistakenly may think that every remark or argument in the first part against alternative theories of justice is meant to apply to or anticipate a criticism of his theory. This is not so; there are other theories also worth criticizing.

2. Applications of the principle of justice in acquisition, may also occur as part of the move from one distribution to another. You may find an unheld thing now, and appropriate it. Acquisitions also are to be understood as included when, to simplify, I speak only of transitions by transfers.

3. If the principle of rectification of violations of the first two principles yields more than one description of holdings, then some choice must be made as to which of these is to be realized. Perhaps the sort of considerations about distributive justice and equality I argue against play a legitimate role in *this* subsidiary choice. Similarly, there may be room for such considerations in deciding which otherwise arbitrary features a statute will embody, when such features are unavoidable because other considerations do not specify a precise line, yet one must be drawn.

4. One might try to squeeze a patterned conception of distributive justice into the framework of the enti-

tlement conception, by formulating a gimmicky obligatory "principle of transfer" that would lead to the pattern. For example, the principle that if one has more than the mean income, one must transfer everything one holds above the mean to persons below the mean so as to bring them up to (but not over) the mean. We can formulate a criterion for a "principle of transfer" to rule out such obligatory transfers, or we can say that no correct principle of transfer, no principle of transfer in a free society will be like this. The former is probably the better course, though the latter also is true.

Alternatively, one might think to make the entitlement conception instantiate a pattern, by using matrix entries that express the relative strength of a person's entitlements as measured by some real-valued function. But even if the limitation to natural dimensions failed to exclude this function, the resulting edifice would *not* capture our system of entitlements to *particular* things.

5. Might not a transfer have instrumental effects on a third party, changing his feasible options? (But what if the two parties to the transfer independently had used their holdings in this fashion?) I discuss this question elsewhere, but note here that this question concedes the point for distributions of ultimate intrinsic noninstrumental goods (pure utility experiences, so to speak) that are transferrable. It also might be objected that the transfer might make a third party more envious because it worsens his position relative to someone else. I find it incomprehensible how it can be thought that this involves a claim of justice. On envy, see *Anarchy, State, and Utopia,* chap. 8.

Here and elsewhere in this essay, a theory which incorporates elements of pure procedural justice might find what I say acceptable, *if* kept in its proper place; that is, if background institutions exist to ensure the satisfaction of certain conditions on distributive shares. But if these institutions are not themselves the sum or invisible-hand result of people's voluntary (nonaggressive) actions, the constraints they impose require justification. At no point does *our* argument assume any background institutions more extensive than those of the minimal night-watchman state, limited to protecting persons against murder, assault, theft, fraud, etc.

6. See the selection from John Henry MacKay's novel, *The Anarchists,* reprinted in Leonard Krimmerman and Lewis Perry, eds., *Patterns of Anarchy* (New York, 1966), pp. 16–33, in which an individualist anarchist presses upon a communist anarchist the question: "Would you, in the system of society which you call 'free Communism', prevent individuals from exchanging their labor among themselves by means of their own medium of exchange? And further: Would you prevent them from occupying land for the purpose of personal use?" The novel continues: "[the] question was not to be escaped. If he answered 'Yes!' he admitted that society had the right of control over the individual and threw

overboard the autonomy of the individual which he had always zealously defended; if on the other hand, he answered 'No!' he admitted the right of private property which he had just denied so emphatically. . . . Then he answered 'In Anarchy any number of men must have the right of forming a voluntary association, and so realizing their ideas in practice. Nor can I understand how any one could justly be driven from the land and house which he uses and occupies . . . every serious man must declare himself: for Socialism, and thereby for force and against liberty, or for Anarchism, and thereby for liberty and against force.' " In contrast, we find Noam Chomsky writing, "Any consistent anarchist must oppose private ownership of the means of production," and "the consistent anarchist then . . . will be a socialist . . . of a particular sort" (Introduction to Daniel Guerin, *Anarchism: From Theory to Practice* [New York, 1970], pp. xiii, xv).

7. Is the patterned principle stable that requires merely that a distribution be Pareto-optimal? One person might give another a gift or bequest that the second could exchange with a third to their mutual benefit. Before the second makes this exchange, there is not Pareto-optimality. Is a stable pattern presented by a principle choosing that among the Pareto-optimal positions that satisfies some further condition *C?* It may seem there cannot be a counterexample, for won't any voluntary exchange made away from a situation show that the first situation wasn't Pareto-optimal? (Ignore the implausibility of this last claim for the case of bequests.) But principles are to be satisfied over time, during which new possibilities arise. A distribution that at one time satisfies the criterion of Pareto-optimality might not do so when some new possibilities arise (Wilt Chamberlain grows up and starts playing basketball); and though people's activities will tend to move then to a new Pareto-optimal position, *this* new one need not satisfy the contentful condition *C.* Continual interference will be needed to insure the continual satisfaction of *C.* (The theoretical possibility should be investigated of a pattern's being maintained by some invisible-hand process that brings it back to an equilibrium that fits the pattern when deviations occur.)

8. One indication of the stringency of Rawls' difference principle, which we attend to in the second part of this essay, is its inappropriateness as a governing principle even within a family of individuals who love one another. Should a family devote its resources to maximizing the position of its least well off and talented child, holding back the other children or using resources for their education and development only if they will follow a policy throughout their lifetimes of maximizing the position of their least fortunate sibling? Surely not. How then can this even be considered as the appropriate policy for enforcement in the wider society? (I discuss below what I think would be

Rawls' reply: that some principles apply at the macro-level which do not apply to microsituations.)

9. I am unsure as to whether the arguments I present below show that such taxation just *is* forced labor; so that "is on a par with" means "is one kind of." Or alternatively, whether the arguments emphasize the great similarities between such taxation and forced labor, to show it is plausible and illuminating to view such taxation in the light of forced labor. This latter approach would remind one of how John Wisdom conceives of the claims of metaphysicians.

10. Nothing hangs on the fact that here and elsewhere I speak loosely of *needs;* since I go on, each time, to reject the criterion of justice which includes it. If, however, something did depend upon the notion, one would want to examine it more carefully. For a skeptical view, see Kenneth Minogue, *The Liberal Mind* (New York, 1963), pp. 103–112.

11. Further details that this statement should include are contained in my essay, "Coercion," in *Philosophy, Science, and Method*, ed. S. Morgenbesser, P. Suppes, and M. White (New York, 1969).

12. On the themes in this and the next paragraph, see the writings of Armen Alchian.

13. See *Anarchy, State, and Utopia*, chap. 3.

14. Compare sec. 2 of Robert Paul Wolff's "A Refutation of Rawls' Theorem on Justice," *Journal of Philosophy* 63 (March 1966): 179–190. Wolff's criticism does not apply to Rawls' conception under which the baseline is fixed by the difference principle.

15. I have not seen a precise estimate. David Friedman discusses this issue in *The Machinery of Freedom* (New York, 1973), pp. xiv, xv, and suggests one twentieth (of national income) as an upper limit for the first two factors mentioned. However, he does not attempt to estimate the percentage of current wealth that is based upon such income in the past.

16. Fourier held that since the process of civilization had deprived the members of society of certain liberties (to gather, pasture, engage in the chase), a socially guaranteed minimum provision for persons was justified as compensation for the loss. Alexander Gray, *The Socialist Tradition* (New York, 1968), p. 188. But this puts the point too strongly. This compensation would be due those persons, if any, for whom the process of civilization was a *net loss*, for whom the benefits of civilization did not counterbalance being deprived of these particular liberties.

17. For example, Rashdall's case of someone who comes upon the only water in the desert several miles ahead of others who also will come to it, and appropriates it all. Hastings Rashdall, "The Philosophical Theory of Property," in *Property, Its Duties and Rights* (London, 1915).

18. The situation would be different if his water hole didn't dry up, due to special precautions he took to prevent this. Compare our discussion of the case in the text with Hayek's, *The Constitution of Liberty*,

(p. 136); and also with Ronald Hamowy's "Hayek's Concept of Freedom; A Critique," *New Individualist Review* (April 1961): 28–31.

19. I discuss overriding and its moral traces in "Moral Complications and Moral Structures," *Natural Law Forum* 13 (1968): 1–50.

20. (Cambridge, Mass., 1971). Otherwise unidentified references in the text that follows are to this volume.

21. See Milton Friedman, *Capitalism and Freedom* (Chicago, 1962), p. 165.

22. On the question of why the economy contains firms (of more than one person), and each individual does not contract and recontract with others, see Ronald H. Coase, "The Nature of the Firm," reprinted in *Readings in Price Theory*, ed. George Stigler and Kenneth Boulding (Homewood, Ill., 1952); and Armen A. Alchian and Harold Demsetz, "Production, Information Costs and Economic Organization," *American Economic Review*, 1972.

23. We do not, however, assume here or elsewhere the satisfaction of those conditions specified in economists' artificial model of "perfect competition." One appropriate mode of analysis is presented in Israel M. Kirzner, *Market Theory and the Price System* (Princeton, N.J., 1963).

24. Receiving this, we should note, is not the same as receiving the equivalent of what the person *causes* to exist, or *produces*. The marginal product of a unit of F_1 with respect to factor $F_2, \ldots, F_n$ is a *subjunctive* notion; it is the difference between the total product of $F_2, \ldots, F_n$ used most efficiently (as efficiently as known how, given prudence about many costs in finding out the most efficient use of factors), and the total product of the most efficient uses of $F_2, \ldots, F_n$ along with a unit less of F_1. But these two different most efficient uses of $F_2, \ldots, F_n$ along with a unit less of F_1 (one with the additional unit of F_1 the other without it) will use them differently. And F_1's marginal product (with respect to the other factors), what everyone reasonably would pay for an additional unit of F_1, will not be what it *causes* (it causes) combined with $F_2, \ldots, F_n$ and the other units of F_1, but rather the difference it makes, the difference there would be if this unit of F_1 were absent and the remaining factors were organized most efficiently to cope with its absence. Thus marginal productivity theory is not best thought of as a theory of actual produced product, of those things whose causal pedigree includes the unit of the factor; but rather as a theory of the difference (subjunctively defined) made by the presence of a factor. If such a view were connected with justice, it would seem to fit best with an entitlement conception.

25. Readers who believe that Marx's analysis of exchange relations between owners of capital and laborers undercuts the view that the set of holdings which results from voluntary exchange is legitimate, or who believe it a distortion to term such exchanges "voluntary," will find some relevant

considerations adduced in *Anarchy, State, and Utopia,* chap. 8.

26. See Marc Blaug, *Economic Theory in Retrospect,* chap. 2, and the references cited therein. For a recent survey of issues about the marginal productivity of capital, see G. C. Harcourt, "Some Cambridge Controversies in the Theory of Capital," *Journal of Economic Literature* 7 (June 1969): 369–405.

27. Here we simplify the content of (5), but not to the detriment of our present discussion. Also, of course, beliefs other than (5), when conjoined with (3) would justify the inference to (4); for example belief in the material conditional "If (3) then (4)." It is something like (5), though, that is relevant to our discussion here.

28. Though Rawls does not clearly distinguish (2) from (1) and (4) from (3), I do not claim that he makes the illegitimate step of sliding from the latter subjunctive to the former indicative. Even so, the mistake is worth pointing out because it is an easy one to fall into, and it might appear to prop up positions we argue against.

29. They needn't be *better endowed,* from birth. In the context in which Rawls uses it, all "better endowed" means is: accomplishes more of economic value, able to do this, has a high marginal product, etc. (The role played in this by unpredictable factors complicates imagining a prior partitioning of the two groups.) The text follows Rawls in categorizing persons as "better" and "worse" endowed only in order to criticize the considerations *he* adduces for his theory. The entitlement theory does not rest upon any assumption that the classification is an important one or even a possible one, or upon any elitist presupposition.

Since the entitlement theorist does not accept the patterned principle "to each according to his natural endowment," he can easily grant that what an exercised endowment brings in the market will depend upon the endowments of others and how they choose to exercise them, upon the market-expressed desires of buyers, upon the alternate supply of what he offers and of what others may substitute for what he offers, and upon other circumstances summing the myriad choices and actions of others. Similarly, we saw earlier that the similar considerations Rawls adduces about upon what social factors the marginal product of labor depends (p. 308) will not faze an entitlement theorist, even though they might undercut the rationale put forth by a proponent of the patterned principle of distribution according to marginal product.

30. Supposing they could identify themselves and each other, they might *try* to exact a larger share by banding together as a group and bargaining jointly with the others. Given the large numbers of persons involved and the incentive for some of the better endowed individuals to break ranks and reach separate agreements with the worse endowed, if such a coalition of the better endowed is unable to impose sanctions on its defectors it will dissolve. The better endowed remaining in the coalition may use boycott as a "sanction," and refuse to cooperate with a defector. To break the coalition, those less well endowed would have to (be able to) offer someone better endowed sufficient incentive to defect to make up for his loss through no longer being able to cooperate with the other better endowed persons. Perhaps it would pay for someone to defect from the coalition only as part of a sizable group of defectors, which defecting group the initial coalition might try to keep small by special offers to individuals to defect *from it,* etc. The problem is a complicated one, further complicated by the obvious fact (despite our use of Rawls' classificatory terminology) that there is no sharp line of cleavage between the endowments of people, to determine which groups would form.

Liberty, Contract, and Contribution

THOMAS M. SCANLON, JR.

There is a natural prima facie case for the inclusion of market exchange within any distributive system. For, given any distribution of goods taken as just, if two parties would prefer the result of a bilateral exchange to the status quo why not allow them to trade? Institutions that do not allow or do not provide for such exchanges seem to involve objectionable restrictions on the liberty of those to whom they apply. They appear to be inefficient as well, since each such trade, by moving the trading parties to preferred positions and, we may suppose, leaving others unaffected, moves the whole situation closer to Pareto optimality.

This argument is only prima facie because of several presuppositions only alluded to in this chapter. The first of these is the assumption that no one other than the trading parties is affected by the exchange. As just stated, this is obviously too strong a requirement. A better alternative would be something closer to "no one other than the trading parties is affected in ways one has a right to be protected against." But what are these ways? A whole theory seems to be required to set the threshold of illegitimate interference. A second way of approaching the limitations of the argument, one which may present this problem in a more manageable form, focuses on the justice of the preexisting distribution. If the distribution of goods prior to the exchange is legitimate, then,

it would seem, those who hold these goods are entitled to redistribute them as they please. Thus, by appeal to the justice of this distribution (or of the institutions producing it) we may avoid the messy problem of considering and weighing all the possible side effects of each exchange. But this advance is more apparent than real. Virtually any plausible set of institutions will impose some limitations on what one may do with the goods one acquires through the legal forms those institutions specify, and the nature and extent of these limitations is certain to be an important factor in determining the moral acceptability of those institutions. Thus, all the problems involved in setting the threshold of illegitimate interference will reappear in arguments for and against the justifiability of particular sets of institutions and the complexes of rights and limitations they involve.

But there is some advantage in thus pushing the problem one step back—from consideration of the merits of particular transactions to the justification of institutions that allow or limit them. The preference appealed to in the prima facie argument presented above—a preference for the results of exchange over the status quo, given institutions that make such exchange possible—does not by itself suffice to establish the preferability of such institutions, even under the assumption that no one other than the trading parties is affected by the transaction. For it is possible that having institutions that allow for transactions of the kind in question involves costs that outweigh the advantages of the opportunity they provide. Arguments appealing to such costs are in some cases arguments for justifiable paternalism, i.e., claims that the opportunity in question is so likely to be used unwisely that it is rational to prefer not to have this opportunity at all. But to argue against market institutions by appealing to their costs one need not argue paternalistically. One nonpaternalistic argument is that advanced by Peter Singer: Having a system in which certain goods and services are exchangeable and can be purchased may foster attitudes toward these goods, toward others, and toward ourselves that one may rationally wish to avoid.[1] The argument I will be considering later in this chapter is also nonpaternalistic, but it does not concern the attitudes and motives engendered by market institutions.

Institutions of Voluntary Agreement

I have so far been concerned with a case for including market exchange within any institution of property, production, and distribution. Markets have been considered as a kind of topping-off mechanism for moving the result of any distributive system closer to Pareto optimality. But market exchange is often conceived as having a more fundamental role. Indeed, the notion of free exchange as represented in the ideal of the market may seem to be *the* fundamental notion of social cooperation. This will seem to be so if one sees such cooperation as freely entered into by individuals who establish the terms of their cooperation through a process of bargaining on the basis of the particular assets—energy, talents, information, and perhaps also transferable goods previously acquired—that they "bring with them." Any other conception of social arrangements, any conception that is not at the fundamental level a market conception, will, it may be argued, portray at least some of the participants in social institutions to some degree as unwilling contributors; and, to this degree, the institutions in question must be seen as illegitimate.

But, insofar as it suggests that under ideal market institutions all obligations would derive from specific voluntary undertakings, this argument rests on a mistake. Market institutions themselves—the rules specifying, e.g., how contracts are to be made, that contracts duly made are to be fulfilled, and that contractually acquired property rights are to be respected—cannot derive their authority from particular contracts. Certainly, they do not do so in practice; for persons born into a market society, these institutions and the specific property rights already established under them represent fixed features of social life, factors that apply to them without their consent, constraining and determining the opportunities they will have to enter into truly voluntary arrangements with their contemporaries. The point here is an old one, familiar at least since Hume. Arguing against attempts to see political authority as founded on a promise by the subjects to obey the sovereign, Hume contended that such a theory could not account for the obligations of present subjects of existing states, since it was simply not the case that every citizen who was supposed to be obligated could be found to have made such a promise.[2] Further, he argued, the appeal to a promise would, in any case, be theoretically idle, since promising is itself a social institution defined by conventional rules, and the moral requirement of fidelity to that institution (in particular, fidelity to the rule specifying that promises duly made are to be kept) stands just as much in need of philosophical explanation as does the requirement of obedience to political authority.

Now one might argue here, in opposition to Hume, that there is an important sense in which the principle of fidelity to agreements is a natural moral requirement, not dependent on any preexisting social framework. To be sure, two strangers in a state of nature could not exchange *promises* in the strict sense; i.e., they could not invoke our particular institution. But one such person might get another to do something by causing the other to form an expectation of reciprocal service on some specific, future occasion; and the two might even come to an understanding over exactly what conditions attach to this arrangement, e.g., what intervening circumstances would excuse the second party from performance of his part of the bargain. This one encounter hardly makes a social institution, yet it does seem to create a moral obligation. The person who benefits from the first performance is, from a moral point of view, no more free to refuse to perform in turn than he would be had he promised to do so. One might infer from this that the role of a conventionally established system of rules like our institution of promising is merely to serve as an aid in helping us create mutual expectations without having to work out anew, on each occasion, exactly what the form and limits of those expectations are to be. Such an institution has obvious usefulness. Its usefulness increases the motivation to fulfill agreements made under it since people will not want to risk being excluded from its use. But this additional motivation is not essential to the moral force of agreements, which derives from the voluntary creation of mutual expectations.

If this argument is accepted, then Hume's own analysis of the moral basis of fidelity to contracts must be rejected.[3] But something remains of his thesis that promising must be seen as a social institution and appraised as such. Even if the role of social institutions in generating binding agreements is confined to that of providing a ready-made matrix for the formation of mutual expectations, the fact remains that there are many different systems of rules that might fulfill this role. These practices may differ from one another, and from our own institution of promising, in trivial ways, e.g., in the ritual or form of words through which obligations are undertaken, or in more substantial ways, e.g., in the conditions recognized as voiding obligation. If we live in a society in which one of these practices is conventionally established, then, unless we are unusually circumspect and explicit, the provisions of that practice will determine the nature and scope of the obligations we undertake.

But can just any system of rules, or any system that is generally accepted in a community, define morally binding obligations? It seems that there are independent moral requirements

which such practices must satisfy. Consider, for example, an institution of "vicarious agreement" according to which some people, say men, could make agreements on behalf of other capable adults, say women, without their consent, and could modify and abrogate agreements already made by them. Such an institution would be morally flawed. Would the fact that it was generally accepted in a society by men and women alike be sufficient to make agreements it sanctions morally binding on women who have not consented to them? Whether this is so will depend, I think, on the nature of this "general acceptance." We would be inclined to regard a woman as morally bound by agreements made in her name only if her acceptance of the institution was not mere acquiescence but was of such a nature as to constitute a willing authorization of men to make agreements on her behalf. Given the blanket nature of this authorization, however, it would take clear, positive evidence to convince us that it was freely and knowingly given, as it would have to be to have moral force. Similar remarks would apply to agreements arising from force or fraud under systems of agreement-making that failed to recognize force or fraud as voiding obligations. Such agreements would not in general be morally binding, but it is conceivable that they might be so if the "strict liability" system was something people entered into freely.

These examples all concern moral requirements designed to protect those who make agreements. This is why it seems that these requirements could be set aside by genuine consent. If all moral requirements on systems of agreement-making were of this kind then it might be true, as this discussion has at times suggested, that any agreement is morally binding as long as it is entered into freely by promisor and promisee. But promises can affect third parties. A binding promise creates in the promisee a right which others ought not interfere with. Further, the rights created by a promise can conflict with other claims on the promisor. If I am bound by a promise to help you build your barn tomorrow morning, then I may not be free to help Jones fight his brush fire. If we arrived at our understanding by invoking some social institution of agreement-making, the rules of this institution may provide some guide as to the conditions under which I am released from my obligation because of someone else's claim on me. But a given system of rules may get these conditions wrong, e.g., by specifying that I am bound where in fact I am not. If they do this then the rules are in that respect simply void because they conflict with the relevant moral requirements. These requirements, if they can be set aside at all by voluntary agreement, cannot be amended merely by consent of promisor and promisee. At the very least more general consent would be required.

Institutions of Property

Much of what I have just said about institutions of voluntary agreement applies *mutatis mutandis* to institutions of property. There are many different ways in which the mechanisms of acquisition and exchange of property, and the rights and prerogatives of property owners, may be constituted. As in the previous case, what our rights as property owners are will, in general, depend on the system of rules conventionally established in our community. And again, as in the previous case, there are moral requirements which these rules must satisfy if the rights and prerogatives they prescribe are to be the basis of legitimate claims under the conditions prevailing in our society. But while the moral limitations on systems of agreement-making that concern effects on third parties are easily overlooked,[4] the corresponding limitations on systems of property are obvious and crucial. To acquire property in an object is to acquire rights that one may press, not only against a particular person with whom one has entered into agreement in order to acquire the property, but also against anyone else who may come along and be in a position to interfere with one's use or disposal of that object. This will include a large number of people with whom the possessor has never come in contact at all. The rights in question therefore exceed the scope of actual face to face agreements.

Now it might be argued here that the obligation not to interfere with the property of oth-

ers no more needs to be founded on a past agreement than does the obligation not to murder or assault. These are natural moral requirements, which social institutions may make precise and enforce but which they do not create. After all, is it not clear that a person could be wronged by being deprived of his land and crops, even in the absence of any social institutions establishing rights to property? I cannot give a complete answer to this objection here, but I believe that what is violated in cases of the kind just mentioned is not, strictly speaking, a property right. It is rather some general right to noninterference, which covers only a small part of what are usually thought of as property rights. This is shown by the fact that what happens in such an example strikes us as clearly wrong only if we suppose, first, that what is taken is of use to the person from whom it is taken (i.e., that the taking really constitutes an interference with that person's life and activities), and second, that the appropriation and use of this thing by the supposedly wronged party did not already constitute an interference with others, e.g., with the person who did the taking.[5] But in real systems of property (as this notion has generally been understood), at least the first of these limits is dropped: One's property rights are violated if some object over which one has established title through the conventionally established procedure is removed, whether or not the loss of that object affects one at all.[6] Thus, the conventions establishing forms of appropriation, if they are legitimate, extend a person's rights to the forebearance of others beyond what the primitive right to noninterference establishes. And these extended rights stand in need of justification, particularly since the main interest people have in acquiring title to goods that are not of direct use in satisfying those needs protected by the primitive right of noninterference lies in the power those goods bring to command the services of others.

Thus, a system of property is a nonvoluntary social institution in a strong sense. The problem of explaining how a system of rights and prerogatives can be morally binding on people even without their actual consent has most often been confronted as the problem of political obligation; but the interest of Hume's analysis, presented above, lies just in the observation that the state is only one among many institutions presenting this same difficulty. One approach to this problem that is familiar from discussions of the political case is the notion of hypothetical agreement. Suppose we could establish that, if the participants in a given institution were in a position freely to decide whether or not to cooperate on the terms that institution provides, then it would be rational for them to agree to these terms. This might be taken to provide some reason for believing that institution to be legitimate and for regarding complaints against its requirements as unjustified. Suppose, on the other hand, it were conceded that some of the persons to whom a given institution applies would have no reason to accept cooperation on the terms it offers them if they had a chance to choose. In that case, we would have to admit that the institution was not wholly legitimate and that it rested to some degree on mere coercion or on some members' taking advantage of the inability of others to refuse to participate.[7] Such an argument, by appeal to hypothetical agreement, is inescapably contrary to fact; it relies on claims about what would be the case if some admittedly false assumption were to hold. But the argument is not essentially concerned with an imaginary convocation of fictional persons. The question at issue remains, what do present persons regard as reasonable terms of cooperation? The function of the notion of a hypothetical contract is merely to serve as a framework within which arguments about what terms are reasonable can be set forth in a general way. It is useful to the degree to which it leads arguments about terms of cooperation to be formulated in helpful and enlightening ways.

The Hypothetical Contract Model

The idea of possible unanimous agreement on terms of cooperation as even a necessary condition for the legitimacy of social institutions already embodies a certain moral point of view, a kind of formal egalitarianism. This moral standpoint is not wholly uncontroversial,

but it need not be taken as a matter of controversy in our consideration of market institutions, since most of the relevant arguments for or against markets, e.g., those intuitive arguments for markets considered at the outset of this chapter, are ones which could be offered within a hypothetical contract framework. The moral content of the idea of hypothetical agreement is increased as we move beyond mere formal egalitarianism—beyond the idea that institutions must be justified to each of their members—to include particular judgments as to what considerations should or should not be recognized as legitimate grounds on which members may refuse to accept given terms of cooperation. In the forms of hypothetical contract argument that rely heavily upon the device of a hypothetical contractual situation, judgments about the relevant grounds for accepting or rejecting such principles may be built in, in the form of restrictions on the knowledge and motivation of the parties to the contract.[8] Thus, for example, the parties, assumed to be self-interested, may be assumed not to know what talents or disabilities they may have, the idea being that they are thereby deprived of any grounds for favoritism towards the able or the disabled. As we will see later, however, once such "improper" influences are screened out it may still not be clear how the proper weighting of various conflicting interests is to be determined. Further, such restrictions on knowledge require justification, and it seems that an adequate justification would have to address directly the moral points at issue, namely why it is that some claims are morally relevant and others are not and why some morally relevant claims take precedence over others.

There is a dilemma here for the advocate of the hypothetical contract model. If one sticks closely to the position I have called *formal egalitarianism*, then the model appears quite weak. On the other hand, as more content is built into the model, and the conditions under which hypothetical agreement is reached become more and more different from the point of view of actual citizens, the model itself becomes increasingly difficult to justify, and whatever controversy surrounds the particular conclusions reached is transferred to the controversial features of the model. In what follows I will stay closer to the former alternative, trying to show how the weaker form of the hypothetical-contract model can be used to deal with one argument in favor of markets. This will mean that problems of balancing competing interests must be faced as independent moral issues rather than brought within the contract framework in the form of assumptions about the knowledge or motivation of the contracting parties. The result may be, however, that the hypothetical contract is left with a severely diminished role.

Our concern, then, is with those basic institutions of a society that apply to all of its members without their consent. Very roughly, the benefits and burdens associated with these institutions can be thought of as falling into the following broad categories: On the side of benefits, the basic institutions of a society will, first, define the personal and property rights of individual members, their rights to the forebearance of others, and their powers to alter their relationship to others through voluntary undertakings. Second, these institutions may provide for the enforcement of these rights by creating positions of special authority and responsibility, e.g., the police, the judicial system, etc. Finally, institutions may create agencies to provide other goods and services, including both public goods and distributable goods such as health care, guaranteed income, etc., and may specify what rights individual members have to claim shares in these goods. Obviously, none of these goods can be provided without corresponding contributions. The legitimacy of institutions, in the sense in which we have been discussing it, is just their moral title to require such contributions without prior consent (i.e., to require of those to whom the institutions apply that they refrain from invasion of the personal and property rights which those institutions specify, that they acknowledge and not interfere with the authority assigned to its officials, and that they contribute in those ways required by the institutions to the maintenance of the system of enforcement and to the provision of whatever other benefits the institutions provide.)

Markets, Obligations, and Liberty

Proponents of market institutions typically advocate that the nonvoluntarily incurred obligations of members of society be kept to a minimum by keeping to a minimum those benefits guaranteed to all members simply qua members. Of course market proponents divide over just where the appropriate minimum of benefits lies—whether, for example, roads or schools should be provided for all via compulsory taxation or left to individual initiative. But, without getting into the details of these particular controversies, we can consider in general some arguments raised in favor of leaving a larger sphere to the operation of the market. Some of these arguments appeal to considerations of efficiency, to the alleged efficiency of market mechanisms as means of allocating factors of production or as methods for distributing the social product. I will touch briefly on distributive considerations, but I will focus my main attention on a different and, I think, more fundamental argument. This is the claim that considerations of liberty require the minimization of nonvoluntarily incurred obligations and, correspondingly, the maximization of the sphere left to truly voluntary arrangements, i.e., to the market. This claim is the natural successor to the argument, considered earlier, that took free contract as the basis of all legitimate social obligations, once that argument is trimmed back in recognition of the fact that the basic institutions of society are bound to involve some nonvoluntary component.[9]

To properly appraise this argument it is important to distinguish various bases on which one may object to the obligations imposed by given social institutions. I will argue that the force of many arguments in favor of market institutions, in particular that of some arguments recently offered by Robert Nozick,[10] depends on a failure to distinguish different forms of political and economic unliberty. Once these are distinguished one can, if one wishes, accept in quite a strong form the libertarian intuitions to which these arguments appeal without being forced to accept their conclusions. A subsidiary effect of the following discussion is to point out the degree to which we stand in need of a set of categories of economic liberty adequate to modern conditions. Political liberty is commonly conceived (both in the philosophical tradition and in public discussion) in terms of a highly developed set of categories: freedom of speech and of the press, specific forms of political participation and representation, etc. One can debate the degree to which these notions are adequate to conditions in the modern state, but at least they provide us with starting points for discussion that have a firm place in the public mind and have been thoroughly explored and carefully articulated over a long period of time. But neither the tradition of political philosophy nor common understanding provides us with a comparable set of categories of economic liberty. Perhaps the notions of property rights and freedom of contract constitute a set of categories that once played this role, but as I shall argue below these do not constitute an adequate conception of economic liberty. To move beyond laissez faire we need to develop such a conception, but at present none has established itself either in the public mind or in political philosophy. Arguments in this area frequently rely on familiar notions imported from politics and law such as due process, representation, etc. These are no doubt relevant, but they need to be justified and perhaps circumscribed by being placed within a more general theory of liberty in the economic sphere.

I am not going to present or even sketch a theory of economic liberty here. I will merely consider three different ways in which the obligations imposed by various social institutions can be compared and criticized. These are:

(1) To what extent are the citizens of an institution legally free to avoid the obligations it imposes by renouncing their citizenship altogether?

(2) How deeply do the obligations imposed by an institution interfere with the ability of members to exercise control over their lives and activities?

(3) To what extent are present citizens able (e.g., through political mechanisms) to control the form that their obligations take?

I will comment briefly on each of these in turn.

Renunciation of Citizenship

Certainly one way in which institutions can fail to meet the requirements of moral legitimacy is by being overly restrictive of the right of citizens to opt out. The extent of this right is a question that has been insufficiently explored in the literature of political philosophy. I do not know what a complete account of this matter would look like, but a few points seem reasonably clear. Presumably, a state could legitimately restrict exit when this was necessary to enforce private contracts. To this end, if circumstances required it, perhaps a state could enforce a short waiting period after one's announced intention to leave, in order to give possible creditors an opportunity to state their claims. It also seems plausible that some social benefits, such as special forms of training, could legitimately carry requirements of service that would have to be fulfilled before exit would be permitted. (If this is true, it is uncontroversially so only where the goods in question figure in the lives of members of the society in such a way that their acceptance can be regarded as truly voluntary. Some forms of education may meet this requirement, but others will not.) A more controversial question is whether in some emergency situations a government could legitimately restrict exit in order to retain enough able citizens to meet a present threat. Is some explicit "fair warning" required before such a restriction on exit can be enforced? If not, then the legitimacy of the restriction seems to involve an appeal to the idea that remaining in the society involves a voluntary acceptance of the risk of being unable to leave should an emergency arise. These unsystematic observations suggest to me that the right of exit can legitimately be restricted only as a result of a voluntary undertaking whose consequences are publicly known. For citizens who have made no such undertaking this right is virtually absolute.

Imposition of Obligations

Contributions required of members as a condition for their continued receipt of benefits may vary in the degree to which they intrude into the members' lives and interfere with their control over their activities and over the development and exercise of their talents. For example, the contribution required of members may be more or less specific in the form of activity it requires. One reason why taxation is generally thought of as a more acceptable form of required contribution than, say, a system of required tasks or a requirement of payments in kind is that it leaves citizens with greater latitude in deciding how to arrange their lives while still meeting their social obligations.[11] Of course, the enforcement of such required contributions is only one of the ways in which institutions may restrict or enhance the ability of their members to exercise effective control over their productive lives (and over how much of their lives is devoted to production). If we are appraising institutions on this score we should therefore be concerned not merely with this one obligation but rather with the total effect that a set of institutions has on the de facto ability of its members to exercise this kind of effective self-regulation.

To give a systematic account of when some institutions are to be preferred to others on this basis, or even an analysis of the various dimensions along which comparisons of this kind should be carried out, would require at least the beginnings of a theory of this particular form of liberty. I have no such theory. It seems likely that the relative importance generally attached to avoiding various forms of intrusion and to maintaining particular forms of control may be quite different in different societies (and the forms of control and intrusion with which people are concerned will vary too). Searching for a single general principle in this area, perhaps one might try a modified version of Rawls' claim about the priority of political liberty: Once the level of material well-being in a society reaches a point at which the most urgent needs are met and the development of one's capacities and pursuit of one's special interests for their own sake becomes a

possibility, people will have an increasing marginal preference for effective control over their own productive activities relative to competing considerations of economic efficiency.[12] The claim that such a preference would be rational is at least no less plausible in the economic case than in the political case where Rawls employed it. Moreover, such a general preference seems at first to be more promising as a theoretical basis for economic than for political liberty. But this contrast now seems doubtful. Rawls' appeal to increasing marginal preference, taken as a complete theory of political liberty, would be unsatisfying, quite apart from any doubts about the reality of this preference, because it leaves the object of the preference— the liberties themselves—unaccounted for. A list of such liberties is more or less taken as given. But a large part of what one wants from a philosophical account of political liberty is an explanation of what liberties are or should be included on the list, what structure they have, and why. In the economic case we bring with us no such list of liberties to be explained and analyzed, hence this dissatisfaction does not come immediately to mind. But dissatisfaction reemerges once we ask what the preference asserted is a preference *for*. Certainly it is not simply a preference for, say, more leisure time over a greater output of material goods (or vice versa), or one for a redefinition of tasks in order to make jobs more varied and less tedious even if longer hours are then required to produce the same goods. Rather, it is a preference for mechanisms that enable one to affect such choices.

Citizens' Control of Obligations

This brings us to the third question mentioned above, namely the extent to which the current citizens of a given institution are able, through political processes or otherwise, to control and modify the form that their institutional obligations take. Even if the requirements that citizenship imposes on us at any given time are to a large extent inherited from previous generations, the degree to which we (or a majority of us) are empowered to modify them if we so choose is an important factor in their acceptability. Political power that, even under ideal conditions, can be controlled by a mere majority, does not have the legitimizing force of consent. It does make some difference, however, as is shown in the widespread feeling that there is a special objection to the conscription of citizens who have not yet reached voting age.

To turn now to the particular question at issue, suppose that we are considering a set of institutions that constitute a full-blown welfare state, guaranteeing education, health care, and an assured minimum standard of living to all its citizens. These benefits can be offered only on the basis of some regular contributions, part of which, we may suppose, take the form of a tax system that diminishes the rate at which citizens can benefit from voluntary commercial arrangements with one another. Suppose that there will be some members of such a society whose income is less than what they could command if they could bargain with their fellow citizens on an unregulated market, holding out for the maximum others would be willing to pay to secure their services. If some of these members are able, from a practical point of view, to exercise their right to opt out, then they may have a choice between remaining members on the terms now offered them or bargaining with the society from without as free agents and, thereby, let us suppose, obtaining a higher income.

This possibility may be seen as posing a practical problem for nonmarket institutions, namely the problem that they may be unstable, or at least inefficient, because they are continually subject to the defection of their most talented and valuable members.[13] But the problem also has a theoretical form, which is of greater interest for our present purposes. Whether or not anyone ever overcomes his own inertia and becomes a ''free agent'' (or is bargained away by a competing society), the fact, if it were a fact, that it would always be rational for those members of a cooperative system who have economically valuable talents to drop out of the system, and irrational for them to stay, would raise a question about even the theoretical viability of that system. Here one may argue that this objection rests on an artificially narrow view of the relevant grounds of rational preference. Membership in a cooperative association of equals, in which the needs of all are provided for and in which each is motivated to contribute by his perception of the needs of the group and his obligations to it, may itself count as an important and valuable good. When this good, and other particular values for which this kind of association may be a precondition, are taken into account, it is by no means obvious that even rigorously egalitarian nonmarket institutions will be subject to the theoretical charge of irrationality in a damaging form, provided that such institutions are able to provide their members with the material requirements of a decent life.

But reasonable people may differ over the value to be attached to such goods of community and over the exact price it is rational to pay for their enjoyment. This poses a problem for our application of the hypothetical contract model. Despite the fact that there are plausible, or even very generally shared, ends and values relative to which participation in given institutions is a rational choice, there may be some people who find themselves living under these institutions for whom such participation is not worth its costs, given the ends and values they actually hold. For such people, the fact that their institutions are the object of *possible* hypothetical consent on the basis of other postulated goals may be small comfort. Where opting out is a practical as well as a legal possibility, this problem does not seem pressing; these people can always emigrate. But what of those for whom emigration may not be a practical alternative?

Internal Emigration

As long as there are some people in this position of would-be emigrants, the contractualists' claim that it would be rational for everyone, given a free choice, to consent to the prevailing institutions is literally false: There are some members whose cooperation rests, finally, on their inability to leave. This theoretical difficulty could be eased, and the would-be emigrants given as much as they could ask for, if they were given the chance to opt out legally, without leaving home physically; i.e., to transfer directly to a special status of resident aliency with rights and duties they might obtain by emigrating, and to deal with their former compatriots as foreigners.[14] Indeed, one could argue that if the right to opt out is as absolute as suggested above then it requires us to recognize such a right of "internal emigration." Essentially this claim is advanced by Nozick.[15] Acceptance of this argument might well aggravate the practical instability mentioned earlier. More interesting, however, is its apparent theoretical effect of turning all legitimate institutions into ones that approximate a system of free contract of the type favored by market advocates. Through the institutions of a welfare state the members of a society can offer one another whatever terms of cooperation they choose but, if this argument is accepted, members would have to be free to take those terms or to reject them if they felt they could do better for themselves by bargaining with their fellows as social emigrés-at-home.

But must this argument be accepted? I think not. The distinction between free external emigration and free internal emigration has an importance that goes beyond the practical differences between these two forms of exiting. In both cases it is important to ask what is the source of the system of contract relations and property rights under which the free agents deal with their former associates and legally own what they gain as a result of these transactions? In examples of external emigration, what is usually appealed to is some supposed "natural" system of contract and property rights. In practice, of course, an emigré would have to go somewhere; presumably, therefore, he would be bound by the specific institutions of contract and property prevailing in his new society (and with respect to these, the questions of legitimacy with which we began could be raised anew). But the examples as they are usually presented seem to presuppose a kind of Howard Hughes or Robert Vesco who is always able to find a haven from which he can deal with the rest of us on whatever terms he can get us to accept. What we have in such examples is thus not a fixed system of property and exchange, but some ad hoc extrainstitutional arrangement.

The case of internal emigration, however, presents quite a different situation. As long as the emigrés remain at home, their profits, if truly *theirs,* must be so under the system of property rights enforced by the prevailing institutions of their (old) society. So the argument for the right of internal emigration, if it is successful, does not merely require that the nonmarket society enter into ad hoc bargains with external "pirates," but also that it become a market society itself, enforcing contracts with the emigrés and enforcing their rights to keep what they gain through these transactions. To do this involves not only releasing some people from their obligations but at the same time enforcing a system of rights that gives the would-be emigrés new economic power over their fellow citizens. A justification of such a move must, therefore, involve justification of this power; it will have to involve consideration of, on the one hand, the claims of the emigrés—not claims to be allowed to leave, but to create new terms of cooperation—and, on the other hand, the claims of the other citizens—not claims to command the services of the emigrés, but claims to be free from, e.g., the kind of domination that results from great concentration of wealth in a few hands. By contrast, in considering a genuine right to leave, we would be concerned with, on the one hand, the liberty of the emigrés to free themselves altogether of unwanted institutional ties and, on the other, whatever claims on their services other members of society may have. As I have suggested above, it seems likely that this question is relatively easy to resolve.

Thus a right of internal emigration of the sort that would turn all legitimate institutions into market institutions cannot be derived from the right to opt out (even if this right is virtually absolute). The case for internal emigration would have to be made on the basis of arguments about the forms of control that those who are and remain citizens should be allowed to exercise over their own contributions and those of others.

Conclusions

This brings me back to parts (2) and (3) of my analysis of the obligation to contribute. Enforcement, either of a pure system of free contract or of a system of highly qualified property rights, will involve restricting some alternatives that might otherwise be open to people. Can we say that a system of free contract is clearly preferable to a nonmarket system on the ground that the restrictions involved intrude less on citizens' control over the development and exercise of their talents? I do not see that this is so.

I begin with a purely negative philosophical point, which I hope is clear from what has gone before. From the fact that institutions of a certain form involve a minimum of nonvoluntary obligations it does not follow that such institutions are to be preferred to others on the grounds that they best promote the relevant forms of liberty. To settle this issue of liberty one must take up the complex empirical question of what the consequences will be, under given social and economic conditions, of the adoption of various institutional arrangements. In particular, it must be shown what the consequences are for the ability of various individuals in the society to maintain control over their own lives and pursuits.

Under a range of possible and, in our experience, not uncommon circumstances, establishment of a system of property rights based on free contract means that some people, in order to gain the means to life, have to devote virtually all their productive energies to whatever tasks and pursuits are desired by those who control the goods necessary for life in their society. The claim of nonmarket institutions is that they can prevent this kind of domination through restrictions on distribution and ownership. Doing this may involve placing limits on how much people can come to own and will also involve decreasing, through taxation, the rate at which people can benefit from the scarcity of their particular talents. It may also involve requiring a certain minimum contribution from every able member of the society as a condition for continued rights to social benefits.[16] Even institutions involving obligations of this sort need not involve direct restrictions on citizens' choice of occupations. Nor is it immediately apparent that such a system would represent a diminution rather than an enlargement of people's ability to choose forms of productive activity that they find re-

warding. Certainly, there is much to be learned about the difficult empirical question of how such control can be preserved and enhanced within large-scale economic institutions. I cannot here defend a claim about what the best answer to this question is in any particular case or about the role that restricted market mechanisms might play in such an answer. Instead, I will offer in closing one further philosophical remark about the form that the argument for such an answer should take.

The argument presented here suggests that in choosing between nonmarket institutions and market institutions we face a choice between institutions that restrict the liberty of some people—those who would do well to become "emigrés" or those for whom the values of community rank relatively low—and institutions that restrict the liberty of others—those who would be subject to the control of others in a market society or those who set a high value on the goods of community. There is no way to frame institutions so as to satisfy both of these groups. Thus, assuming that each generation will include some representatives of each group, no matter how we frame our institutions, some people will be faced, without their consent, with institutions that, in a most obvious sense, they would not have chosen.

As mentioned earlier, one way to deal with this difficulty within the hypothetical-contract framework is to say that institutions are legitimate if they are in accord with principles which parties would choose if forced to make their choice without knowing which of the two groups they belonged to. I want to suggest here another way of understanding the argument. This approach may reach the same conclusions as the "veil of ignorance" method, but it may avoid at least some of its apparent problems.

Suppose we face the fact that there is no way to resolve our conflict that will be literally acceptable to both sides. Nevertheless, we will try to preserve the idea that we must be able to *justify* our choice to all of the parties concerned. If the choice goes against the potential emigrés, we can say to them: We realize that this system denies you opportunities you would like to have, but adopting a system that involved the general enforcement of the rights you seek would mean asking some people to accept a system that made them, to a very high degree, subservient to your wishes. On the other hand, if the choice goes in favor of the potential emigrés and against the remaining residents, we can say to them: We are sorry, but we could not do better for you without asking others to accept limits on the degree to which they can benefit from the scarcity of their talents, an upper limit on wealth, and the possibility of a required minimum contribution to society.

Of course, the exact form of these responses will depend on prevailing circumstances and the nature and consequences of the institutions they require. But in general, in the kind of circumstances we are most familiar with, it seems to me that the second response is in a clear sense going to be the weaker one. If this is so, then it provides us with a kind of contractualist argument in favor of nonmarket institutions— a ground for claiming that such institutions are justifiable to all concerned, in a way that pure market institutions are not.

A few remarks about this argument are in order. First, it involves a kind of balancing of interests; it appeals to our intuitive judgment that what one group stands to lose is weightier than what the other stands to gain. What kind of weighing is going on here?[17] One interpretation of the hypothetical contract argument suggests that it is a comparison of the strength of individual preferences. What is claimed is that individuals on both sides of the controversy must admit that *they* set a higher value on avoiding certain intrusions into their lives than on avoiding others. But would we modify our conclusion if the parties on one side of the dispute had genuinely different preferences (e.g., if they cared about nothing so much as keeping open the chance to strike it really rich)? If we would not, then what is appealed to in our argument is not mere preference but a judgment with moral content that requires explanation and defense. Even if it is individual preferences that are being balanced, however, the argument is not a utilitarian one. This is shown by the fact that it involves no appeal to the relative sizes of the two groups. If a genuine summing of interests were involved, these numbers would be crucial.

There are several ways in which my conclusion could be avoided. One would be to maintain that the forms of acquisition that the would-be emigrés wish their institutions to recognize are part of a natural right of property; therefore, the decision against the emigrés does not merely deny the fulfillment of an interest (as a decision against the other members of the society would), but also infringes on a right.[18] I have argued briefly against this position. Another way to deny my conclusion would be to maintain that, as a matter of distributive justice, there is a specific level of return to which the holders of scarce talents are entitled and that nonmarket institutions are unjust insofar as they interfere with these just returns. This does not strike me as a plausible line for a defender of market institutions to take. Given the degree to which the distributions effected by markets are dependent on chance considerations involving the distribution of talents and the pattern of tastes in a society, it seems unlikely that there is any plausible distributive pattern to which the outcome of market institutions will generally conform. But I have not dealt with such distributive considerations here. My argument has been, rather, that insofar as one moves away from particular distributive criteria and focuses instead on considerations of liberty, the case for pure market institutions does not appear to be as strong as is sometimes supposed.

Acknowledgments

Since the Battelle Conference I have had the opportunity to read later versions of this paper for a number of audiences to whom I am indebted for many comments and suggestions. I am also grateful to Charles Beitz, G. A. Cohen, Adam Morton, and William Talbott for written comments which have helped me to improve the paper.

Notes

1. "Altruism and Commerce: A Defense of Titmuss Against Arrow," *Philosophy and Public Affairs* 2 (1973):312–323; and "Freedoms and Utilities in the Distribution of Health Care," in G. Dworkin et al., eds., *Markets and Morals* (Washington, D.C.: Hemisphere, 1977), chap. 9.
2. "Of the Original Contract" [reprinted in this vol-

ume] in *David Hume's Political Essays,* ed. C. W. Hendel (New York: Liberal Arts, 1953), pp. 43–61.

3. As given in Hume, *A Treatise of Human Nature,* ed. L. A. Selby-Bigge (Oxford: Oxford University Press, 1888), bk. 3, pt. 2, sec. 5.

4. In an earlier version of this paper I was myself inclined to overlook it and to contrast institutions of promising and institutions of property more sharply in this regard. For clarification on this point I am indebted to G. A. Cohen.

5. Compare these with the two restrictions on the acquisition of property in the state of nature set forth by John Locke in *Second Treatise of Government* [reprinted in part in this volume] (ed. T. P. Peardon [New York: Liberal Arts, 1952]), viz., first, that the goods actually be used and not wasted by the possessor, and, second, that there be "enough and as good" left for others. Locke himself distinguishes (sec. 50) between the primitive notion of property so restricted and systems of property founded on consent in which these restrictions are relaxed.

6. As is shown by the fact that those who deny that any right is violated in such cases commonly describe themselves as rejecting property. W. Godwin in *Enquiry Concerning Political Justice,* 3rd abridged ed. (ed. K. C. Carter [Oxford: Oxford University Press, 1971]), for example, so describes his doctrine that a person has no right to an object if that person's possession of it produces less utility than its possession by someone else to whom it could be transferred. But he sees his further doctrine that people have a right not to have their possessions forcibly removed (even when they have no right to retain them) as constituting a reintroduction of property rights. It is, of course, not obvious that these two doctrines can be made consistent.

7. This statement of the intuitive basis of the appeal to a hypothetical contract is close to that given by John Rawls (see, e.g., "Justice as Fairness," in *Philosophy, Politics and Society,* 2nd series, ed. P. Laslett and W. G. Runciman [Oxford: Basil Blackwell, 1969] pp. 132–157, and especially pp 144–145). The idea of *possible* unanimous agreement as a necessary condition for the legitimacy of coercive institutions was clearly stated by Kant in *The Metaphysics of Morals* (trans J. Ladd as *Metaphysical Elements of Justice* [Indianapolis: Bobbs-Merrill, 1965]), sec. 47.

8. This is the form of Rawls' theory, as presented in *A Theory of Justice* (Cambridge, Mass.: Harvard University Press, 1971), especially sec. 24.

9. Milton Friedman [with J. Vaizey, "Equality and Income," *The Listener* 91 (May 1974): 688–690] emphasizes the primacy of liberty in the case for market institutions. Considerations of liberty are also central to Robert Nozick's antiredistributive arguments in "Distributive Justice" [reprinted in this volume] *Philosophy and Public Affairs* 3

(1973): 45–126; and *Anarchy, State, and Utopia* (New York: Basic Books, 1974).

10. Ibid.

11. Nozick ("Distributive Justice," pp. 65–66; and *Anarchy, State, and Utopia,* p. 169) makes light of the attempt to distinguish between taxation and forced labor on this basis, pointing out that there is a "gradation of systems of forced labor, from one that specifies a particular activity, to one that gives a choice among two activities, to . . . ; and so on up." But this does not seem to me to show that some systems in this series are not morally preferable to others.

12. *A Theory of Justice,* sec. 82.

13. For an interesting discussion of an actual instance of this problem, see P. Bernstein in "Run Your Own Business: Worker-owned Plywood Firms," *Working Papers for a New Society* 2 (1974): 24–34. The question at issue is how worker-owned firms, organized on the basis of equal distribution of profits, cope with the fact that certain specialty jobs generally command a wage higher than the equal monthly advance against profits that cooperative firms can offer. The answer is, generally, by hiring these specialists as outside "free agents" rather than sacrificing the principle of equal sharing among members. The example is particularly appropriate for the promarket argument considered here, since the firms are operating within a larger market economy that provides a framework within which the free agents can deal with the firms.

14. "A status of resident alien" rather than "the status," since I am here supposing that the emigrés are granted the economic status of free agents, and resident aliens are not generally accorded such privileges. For a philosophical discussion of the status of resident aliens in historical societies, and an argument for the recognition of such status as a refuge from some obligations to contribute (particularly from conscription), see M. Walzer in *Obligations: Essays on Disobedience, War, and Citizenship,* (Cambridge, Mass.: Harvard University Press, 1970), chap. 5.

15. "Distributive Justice," p. 70; and *Anarchy, State, and Utopia,* pp. 173–174.

16. "As a condition," since I think institutions might well allow people to opt out of the economic system without leaving the country if they wished to be genuine nonparticipants in the economy. Such persons would not raise the difficulties presented by resident free agents since they would not exercise economic power over other members of the society.

17. I discuss the problem raised in the next few sentences more fully in "Preference and Urgency," *Journal of Philosophy* 72 (1975): 655–670.

18. This is an important part of Nozick's argument as I understand it.

Equality

THOMAS NAGEL

I

It is difficult to argue for the intrinsic social value of equality without begging the question. Equality can be defended up to a point in terms of other values like utility and liberty. But some of the most difficult questions are posed when it conflicts with these.

Contemporary political debate recognizes four types of equality: political, legal, social, and economic. The first three cannot be defined in formal terms. Political equality is not guaranteed by granting each adult one vote and the right to hold public office. Legal equality is not guaranteed by granting everyone the right to a jury trial, the right to bring suit for injuries, and the right to counsel. Social equality is not produced by the abolition of titles and official barriers to class mobility. Great substantive inequalities in political power, legal protection, social esteem and self-respect are compatible with these formal conditions. It is a commonplace that real equality of every kind is sensitive to economic factors. While formal institutions may guarantee a minimum social status to everyone, big differences in wealth and income will produce big distinctions above that—distinctions that may be inherited as well.

So the question of economic equality cannot be detached from the others, and this complicates the issue, because the value of the other types of equality may be of a very different kind. To put it somewhat paradoxically, their value may not be strictly egalitarian. It may depend on certain rights, like the right to fair treatment by the law, that must be impartially protected, and that cannot be protected without a measure of substantive equality. Rights are in an extended sense egalitarian, because everyone is supposed to have them; but this is not a matter of distributive justice. The equal protection of individual rights is usually thought to be a value independent of utility and of equality in the distribution of advantages. Later I shall comment on the relation among these values, but for now let us assume their distinctness. This means that the defense of economic equality on the ground that it is needed to protect political, legal, and social equality may not be a defense of equality per se— equality in the possession of benefits in general. Yet the latter is a further moral idea of great importance. Its validity would provide an independent reason to favor economic equality as a good in its own right. If, *per impossibile,* large economic inequalities did not threaten political, legal, and social equality, they would be much less objectionable. But there might still be something wrong with them.

In addition to the arguments that depend on its relation to other types of equality, there is

Thomas Nagel, ''Equality,'' delivered as the Tanner Lecture on Human Values at Stanford University, 1977. Printed with permission of the Tanner Lectures on Human Values, a Corporation, University of Utah, Salt Lake City, Utah.

at least one nonegalitarian, instrumental argument for economic equality itself, on grounds of utility. The principle of diminishing marginal utility states that for many goods, a particular further increment has less value to someone who already possesses a significant amount of the good than to someone who has less.[1] So if the total quantity of such a good and the number of recipients remains constant, an equal distribution of it will always have greater total utility than a less equal one.

This must be balanced against certain costs. First, attempts to reduce inequality may also reduce the total quantity of goods available, by affecting incentives to work and invest. For example, a progressive income tax and diminishing marginal utility make it more expensive to purchase the labor of those whose services are most in demand. Beyond a certain point, the pursuit of equality may sacrifice overall utility, or even the welfare of everyone in the society.

Second, the promotion of equality may require objectionable means. To achieve even moderate equality it is necessary to restrict economic liberty, including the freedom to make bequests. Greater equality may be attainable only by more general coercive techniques, including ultimately the assignment of work by public administration instead of private contracts. Some of these costs may be unacceptable not only on utilitarian grounds but because they violate individual rights. Opponents of the goal of equality may argue that if an unequal distribution of benefits results from the free interactions and agreements of persons who do not violate each other's rights, then the results are not objectionable, provided they do not include extreme hardship for the worst off.

II

So there is much to be said about the instrumental value and disvalue of equality; the question of its intrinsic value does not arise in isolation. Yet the answer to that question determines what instrumental costs are acceptable. If equality is in itself good, then producing it may be worth a certain amount of inefficiency and loss of liberty.

There are two types of argument for the intrinsic value of equality, communitarian and individualistic. According to the communitarian argument, equality is good for a society taken as a whole. It is a condition of the right kind of relations among its members, and of the formation in them of healthy fraternal attitudes, desires, and sympathies. This view analyzes the value of equality in terms of a social and individual ideal. The individualistic view, on the other hand, defends equality as a correct *distributive* principle—the correct way to meet the conflicting needs and interests of distinct people, whatever those interests may be, more or less. It does not assume the desirability of any particular kinds of desires, or any particular kinds of interpersonal relations. Rather it favors equality in the distribution of human goods, whatever these may be—whether or not they necessarily include goods of community and fraternity.

Though the communitarian argument is very influential, I am going to explore only the individualistic one, because that is the type of argument that I think is more likely to succeed. It would provide a moral basis for the kind of liberal egalitarianism that seems to me plausible. I do not have such an argument. This essay is a discussion of the form such an argument would have to take, what its starting points should be, and what it must overcome.

A preference for equality is at best one component in a theory of social choice, or choice involving numbers of people. Its defense does not require the rejection of other values with which it may come into conflict. However, it is excluded by theories of social choice which make certain other values dominant. Egalitarianism may once have been opposed to aristocratic theories, but now it is opposed in theoretical debate by the adherents of two nonaristocratic values: utility and individual rights. I am going to examine the dispute in order to see how equality might be shown to have a value that can resist these to some extent, without replacing them.

Though I am interested in the most general foundation for such a principle, I shall begin by discussing a more specialized egalitarian view, the position of John Rawls.[2] It applies specifically to the design of the basic social institutions, rather than to distributive choices, and perhaps it cannot be extended to other cases. But it is the most developed liberal egalitarian view in the field, and much debate about equality focuses on it. So I will initially pose the opposition between equality, utility, and rights in terms of his position. Later I shall explain how my own egalitarian view differs from his.

Rawls' theory assigns more importance to equal protection of political and personal liberties than to equality in the distribution of other benefits. Nevertheless it is strongly egalitarian in this respect also. His principle of distribution for general goods, once equality in the basic liberties is secure, is that inequalities are justified only if they benefit the worst-off group in the society (by yielding higher productivity and employment, for example).

This so-called Difference Principle is used not to determine allocation directly, but only for the assessment of economic and social institutions, which in turn influence the allocation of goods. While it is counted a good thing for anyone to be made better off, the value of improving the situation of those who are worse off takes priority over the value of improving the situation of those who are better off. This is largely independent of the relative quantities of improvement involved, and also of the relative numbers of persons. So given a choice between making a thousand poor people somewhat better off and making two thousand middle class people considerably better off, the first choice would be preferred. It should be added that people's welfare for these purposes is assessed in terms of overall life prospects, not just prosperity at the moment.

This is a very strong egalitarian principle, though it is not the most radical we can imagine. It is constructed by adding to the general value of improvement a condition of priority to the worst off. A more egalitarian position would hold that some inequalities are bad even if they benefit the worst off, so that a situation in which *everyone* is worse off may be preferable if the inequalities are reduced enough. So long as the argument remains individualistic such a position could seem attractive only for reasons stemming from the connection between economic and social equality.[3]

Later I shall discuss Rawls' arguments for the view, and offer some additional ones, but first let me say something about the two positions to which it is naturally opposed, and against which it has to be defended. They are positions that do not accord intrinsic value to equality but admit other values whose pursuit or protection may require the acceptance of considerable inequality. Those values, as I have said, are utility and individual rights.

From a utilitarian point of view, it does not make sense to forego greater benefits for the sake of lesser, or benefits to more people for the sake of fewer, just because the benefits to the worst off will be greater. It is better to have more of what is good and less of what is bad, no matter how they are distributed.

According to a theory of individual rights, it is wrong to interfere with people's liberty to keep or bequeath what they can earn merely in order to prevent the development of inequalities in distribution. It may be acceptable to limit individual liberty to prevent grave evils, but inequality is not one of those. Inequalities are not wrong if they do not result from wrongs of one person against another. They must be accepted if the only way to prevent them is to abridge individual rights to the kind of free action that violates no one else's rights.

Both types of theory point out the costs of pursuing distributive equality, and deny that it has independent value that outweighs these costs. More specifically, the pursuit of equality is held to require the illegitimate sacrifice of the rights or interests of some individuals to the less important interests of others. These two theories are also radically opposed to one another. Together with egalitarianism they form a trio of fundamentally different views about how to settle conflicts among the interests of different people.

III

What is the nature of the dispute between them? The units about which the problem arises are individual persons, individual human lives. Each of them has a claim to consideration. In some sense the distinctness of these claims is at the heart of the issue. The question is whether (a) the worst off have a prior claim, or (b) the enforcement of that claim would ignore the greater claim of others not among the worst off, who would benefit significantly more if a less egalitarian policy were adopted instead, or (c) it would infringe the claims of other persons to liberty and the protection of their rights.

Now this looks like a dispute about the value of equality. But it can also be viewed as a dispute about *how* people should be treated equally, not about whether they should be. The three views share an assumption of moral equality between persons, but differ in their interpretations of it. They agree that the moral claims of all persons are, at a sufficiently abstract level, the same, but disagree over what these are.[4]

The defender of rights locates them in the freedom to do certain things without direct interference by others. The utilitarian locates them in the requirement that each person's interests be fully counted as a component in the calculation of utility used to decide which states of affairs are best and which acts or policies are right. The egalitarian finds them in an equal claim to actual or possible advantages. The issue remains acute even though most social theories do not fall squarely into one of these categories, but give primacy to one interpretation of moral equality and secondary status to the others.

All three interpretations of moral equality attempt to give equal weight, in essential respects, to each person's point of view. This might even be described as the mark of an enlightened ethic, though some theories that do not share it still qualify as ethical. If the opposition of views about distributive equality can be regarded as a disagreement about the proper interpretation of this basic requirement of moral equality, that provides a common reference against which the opposing positions may be measured. It should be possible to compare the quality of their justifications, instead of simply registering their mutual incompatibility.

What it means to give equal weight to each person's point of view depends on what is morally essential to that point of view, what it is in each of us that must be given equal weight. It also depends on how the weights are combined. And these two aspects of the answer are interdependent. Let us consider each of the positions from this point of view.

IV

The moral equality of utilitarianism is a kind of majority rule: each person's interests count once, but some may be outweighed by others. It is not really a majority of *persons* that determines the result, but a majority of interests suitably weighted for intensity. Persons are equal in the sense that each of them is given a "vote" weighted in proportion to the magnitude of his interests. Although this means that the interests of a minority can sometimes outweigh the interests of a majority, the basic idea is majoritarian because each individual is accorded the same (variable) weight and the outcome is determined by the largest total.

In the simplest version, all of a person's interests or preferences are counted, and given a relative weight depending on their weight for him. But various modifications have been suggested. One doubt voiced about utilitarianism is that it counts positively the satisfaction of evil desires (sadistic or bigoted ones, for example). Mill employed a distinction between higher and lower pleasures, and gave priority to the former. (Could there be a corresponding distinction for pains?) Recently, Thomas Scanlon has argued that any distributive principle, utilitarian or egalitarian, must use some objective standard of interest, need, or urgency distinct from mere subjective preference to avoid unacceptable consequences. Even if the aim is to maximize the total of some quantity of benefit over all persons, it is necessary to pick a single measure of that quantity that applies fairly to everyone, and pure preference is not a good measure. "The fact that someone would be willing to forego a decent diet in order to build a monument to his god does not mean that his claim on others for aid in his project has the same strength as a claim for aid in obtaining enough to eat (even assuming that the sacrifices required of others would be the same)."[5]

Even if a standard of objectivity is introduced, the range of morally relevant interests can still be quite broad, and it will vary from person to person. The individual as moral claimant continues to be more or less the whole person. On the other hand, anyone's claims can in principle be completely outvoted by the claims of others. In the final outcome a given individual's claims may be met hardly at all, though they have been counted in the majoritarian calculation used to arrive at that outcome.

Utilitarianism takes a generous view of individual moral claims and combines them aggregatively. It applies the resulting values to the assessment of overall results or states of affairs, and derives the assessment of actions from this as a secondary result. One is to do what will tend to promote the results that appear best from a point of view that combines all individual interests. The moral equality of utilitarianism consists in letting each person's interests contribute in the same way to determining what in sum would be best overall.

V

Rights are very different, both in structure and in content. They are not majoritarian or in any other way aggregative, and they do not provide an assessment of overall results. Instead, they determine the acceptability of actions directly. The moral equality of persons under this conception is their equal claim against each other not to be interfered with in specified ways. Each person must be treated equally in certain definite respects by each other person.

In a sense, these claims are not combined at all. They must be respected individually. What anyone may do is restricted to what will not violate the rights of anyone else. Since the designated aspect of each person's point of view sets this limit *by itself,* the condition is a kind of unanimity requirement.

Rights may be absolute, or it may be permissible to override them when a significant threshold is reached in the level of harm that can be prevented by doing so. But however they are defined, they must be respected in every case where they apply. They give every person a limited veto over how others may treat him.

This kind of unanimity condition is possible only for rights that limit what one person may

do to another. There cannot in this sense be rights to *have* certain things—a right to medical care, or to a decent standard of living, or even a right to life. The language of rights is sometimes used in this way, to indicate the special importance of certain human goods. But I believe that the true moral basis of such claims is the priority of more urgent over less urgent individual needs, and this is essentially an egalitarian principle. To preserve distinctions I shall use the term "right" only for a claim that gives its possessor a kind of veto power, so that if everyone has the right, that places a condition of unanimous acceptability, in this respect, on action. There can be no literal right to life in that sense, because there are situations in which any possible course of action will lead to the death of someone or other; and if everyone had a right to stay alive, nothing would be permissible in those situations.[6]

Rights of the kind I am considering escape this problem because they are agent-centered. A right not to be killed, for example, is not a right that everyone do what is required to insure that you are not killed. It is merely a right not to be killed, and it is correlated with other people's duty not to *kill* you.

Such an ethic does not enjoin that violations of rights be minimized. That would be to count them merely as particularly grave evils in the assessment of outcomes. Instead, rights limit action directly: each person is forbidden to violate directly the rights of others even if he could reduce the overall number of violations of rights indirectly by violating a few himself. It is hard to account for such agent-centered restrictions. One thing to say about them by way of interpretation is that they represent a higher degree of moral inviolability than principles requiring us to do whatever will minimize the violation of rights. For if that were the principle, then violation of the right would not always be wrong. The moral claim of a right not to be murdered even to prevent several other murders is stronger than the claim which merely counts murder as a great evil, for the former prohibits murders that the latter would permit. That is true even though the latter might enable one to prevent more murders than the former. But this does not go very far toward explaining agent-centered rights. A serious account would have to consider not only the protected interests but the relation between the agent and the person he is constrained not to treat in certain ways, even to achieve very desirable ends. The concern with what one is doing to whom, as opposed to the concern with what happens, is an important primary source of ethics that is poorly understood.

Having noted that rights yield an assessment in the first instance of actions rather than of outcomes, we can see that they also define individual moral claims more narrowly than does utilitarianism, and combine them differently. The utilitarian constructs an impersonal point of view in which those of all individuals are combined to give judgments of utility, which in turn are to guide everyone's actions. For a defender of rights, the respects in which each person is inviolable present a direct and *independent* limit to what any other person may do to him. There is no single combination of viewpoints which yields a common goal for everyone, but each of us must limit our actions to a range that is not unacceptable to anyone else in certain respects. Typically, the range of what may be done because it violates no rights is rather large.

For this reason the morality of rights tends to be a limited, even a minimal morality. It leaves a great deal of human life ungoverned by moral restrictions or requirements. That is why, if unsupplemented, it leads naturally to political theories of limited government, and, in the extreme, to the libertarian theory of the minimal state. The justification of broad government action to promote all aspects of the general welfare requires a much richer set of moral requirements.[7]

This type of limited morality also has the consequence that the numbers of people on either side of an issue do not count. In a perfectly unanimous morality the only number that counts is one. If moral acceptability is acceptability in a certain respect from each person's point of view, then even if in other respects one course of action is clearly more acceptable to most but not all of the people involved, no further moral requirement follows.[8]

The moral equality of rights, then, consists in assigning to each person the same domain of interests with respect to which he may not be directly interfered with by anyone else.

VI

Oddly enough, egalitarianism is based on a more obscure conception of moral equality than either of the less egalitarian theories. It employs a much richer version of each person's point of view than does a theory of rights. In that respect it is closer to utilitarianism. It also resembles utilitarianism formally, in being applied first to the assessment of outcomes rather than of actions. But it does not combine all points of view by a majoritarian method. Instead, it establishes an order of priority among needs and gives preference to the most urgent, regardless of numbers. In that respect it is closer to rights theory.

What conception of moral equality is at work here, i.e., what equal moral claim is being granted to everyone and how are these claims combined? Each individual's claim has a complex form: it includes more or less all his needs and interests, but in an order of relative urgency or importance. This determines both which of them are to be satisfied first and whether they are to be satisfied before or after the interests of others. Something close to unanimity is being invoked. An arrangement must be acceptable first from the point of view of everyone's most basic claims, then from the point of view of everyone's next most basic claims, etc. By contrast with a rights theory, the individual claims are not limited to specific restrictions on how one may be treated. They concern whatever may happen to a person, and in appropriate order of priority they include much more than protection from the most basic misfortunes. This means that the order of priority will not settle all conflicts, since there can be conflicts of interest even at the most basic level, and therefore unanimity cannot be achieved. Instead, one must be content to get as close to it as possible.

One problem in the development of this idea is the definition of the order of priority: whether a single, objective standard of urgency should be used in construing the claims of each person, or whether his interests should be ranked at his own estimation of their relative importance. In addition to the question of objectivity, there is a question of scale. Because moral equality is equality between persons, the individual interests to be ranked cannot be momentary preferences, desires, and experiences. They must be aspects of the individual's life taken as a whole: health, nourishment, freedom, work, education, self-respect, affection, pleasure. The determination of egalitarian social policy requires some choice among them, and the results will be very different depending on whether material advantages or individual liberty and self-realization are given priority.

But let me leave these questions aside. The essential feature of an egalitarian priority system is that it counts improvements to the welfare of the worse off as more urgent than improvements to the welfare of the better off. These other questions must be answered to decide who is worse off and who is better off, and how much, but what makes a system egalitarian is the priority it gives to the claims of those whose overall life prospects put them at the bottom, irrespective of numbers or of overall utility. Each individual with a more urgent claim has priority, in the simplest version of such a view, over each individual with a less urgent claim. The moral equality of egalitarianism consists in taking into account the interests of each person, subject to the same system of priorities of urgency, in determining what would be best overall.

VII

It is obvious that the three conceptions of moral equality with which we are dealing are extremely different. They define each person's equal moral claim differently, and they derive practical conclusions from sets of such claims in different ways. They seem to be radically opposed to one another, and it is very difficult to see how one might decide among them.

My own view is that we do not have to. A plausible social morality will show the influence of them all. This will certainly not be conceded by utilitarians or believers in the dominance of rights. But to defend liberal egalitarianism it is not necessary to show that moral equality *cannot* be interpreted in the

ways that yield rights or utilitarianism. One has only to show that an egalitarian interpretation is also acceptable. The result then depends on how these disparate values combine.

Though my own view is somewhat different from that of Rawls, I shall begin by considering his arguments, in order to explain why another account seems to me necessary.[9] He gives two kinds of argument for his position. One is intuitive and belongs to the domain of ordinary moral reasoning. The other is theoretical and depends on the construction by which Rawls works out his version of the social contract and which he calls the Original Position. I shall begin with two prominent examples of the first kind of argument and then go on to a brief consideration of the theoretical construction.

One point Rawls makes repeatedly is that the natural and social contingencies that influence welfare—talent, early environment, class background—are not themselves deserved. So differences in benefit that derive from them are morally arbitrary.[10] They can be justified only if the alternative would leave the least fortunate even worse off. In that case everyone benefits from the inequalities, so the extra benefit to some is justified as a means to this. A less egalitarian principle of distribution, whether it is based on rights or on utility, allows social and natural contingencies to produce inequalities justified neither because everyone benefits nor because those who get more deserve more.

The other point is directed specifically against utilitarianism. Rawls maintains that utilitarianism applies to problems of social choice—problems in which the interests of many individuals are involved—a method of decision appropriate for one individual.[11] A single person may accept certain disadvantages in exchange for greater benefits. But no such compensation is possible when one person suffers the disadvantages and another gets the benefits.

So far as I can see, neither of these arguments is decisive. The first assumes that inequalities need justification, that there is a presumption against permitting them. Only that would imply that undeserved inequalities are morally arbitrary in an invidious sense, unless otherwise justified. If they were arbitrary only in the sense that there were no reasons for or against them, they would require no justification, and the aim of avoiding them could provide no reason to infringe on anyone's rights. In any case the utilitarian has justification to offer for the inequalities that his system permits: that the sum of advantages is greater than it would be without the inequality. But even if an inequality were acceptable only if it benefited everyone, that would not have to imply anything as strong as the Difference Principle. More than one deviation from equality may benefit everyone to some extent, and it would require a specific egalitarian assumption to prefer the one that was most favorable to the worst off.

The second argument relies on a diagnosis of utilitarianism that has recently been challenged by Derek Parfit.[12] But even if the diagnosis is correct, it does not supply an argument for equality, for it does not say why this method of summation is not acceptable for the experiences of many individuals. It certainly cannot be justified simply by extension from the individual case, but it has enough prima facie appeal to require displacement by some better alternative. It merely says that more of what is good is better than less, and less of what is bad is better than more. Someone might accept this conclusion without having reached it by extending the principle of individual choice to the social case. There is no particular reason to think that the principle will be either the same or different in the two cases.

In utilitarianism intrapersonal compensation has no special significance. It acquires significance only against the background of a refusal *in general* to accept the unrestricted summation of goods and evils—a background to which it provides the exception. This background must be independently justified. By itself, the possibility of intrapersonal compensation neither supports nor undermines egalitarian theories. It implies only that *if* an egalitarian theory is accepted, it should apply only across lives rather than within them. It is a reason for taking individual human lives, rather than individual experiences, as the units over which any dis-

tributive principle should operate. But it could serve this function for anti-egalitarian as well as for egalitarian views. This is the reverse of Rawls' argument: no special distributive principle should be applied *within* human lives because that would be to extend to the individual the principle of choice appropriate for society. Provided that condition is met, intrapersonal compensation is neutral among distributive principles.

Next let me consider briefly Rawls' contractarian argument. Though he stresses that his theory is about the morality of social institutions, its general ideas about equality can I think be applied more widely. The Original Position, his version of the social contract, is a constructed unanimity condition which attributes to each person a schematic point of view that abstracts from the differences between people, but allows for the main categories of human interest. The individual is expected to choose principles for the assessment of social institutions on the assumption that he may be anyone, but without assuming that he has an equal chance of being anyone, or that his chance of being in a certain situation is proportional to the number of people in that situation.

The resulting choice brings out the priorities that are generally shared, and combines interests ranked by these priorities without regard to the numbers of people involved. The principles unanimously chosen on the basis of such priorities grant to each person the same claim to have his most urgent needs satisfied prior to the less urgent needs of anyone else. Priority is given to individuals who, taking their lives as a whole, have more urgent needs, rather than to the needs that more individuals have.

There has been much controversy over whether the rational choice under the conditions of uncertainty and ignorance that prevail in the Original Position would be what Rawls says it is, or even whether any choice could be rational under those conditions. But there is another question that is prior. Why does what it would be rational to agree to under those conditions determine what is right?

Let us focus this question more specifically on the features of the Original Position that are responsible for the egalitarian result. There are two of them. One is that the choice must be unanimous, and therefore everyone must be deprived of all information about his conception of the good or his position in society. The other is that the parties are not allowed to choose as if they had an equal chance of being anyone in the society, because in the absence of any information about probabilities it is not, according to Rawls, rational to assign some arbitrarily, using the Principle of Insufficient Reason. The Original Position is constructed by subtracting information without adding artificial substitutes. This results directly in the maximin strategy of choice, which leads to principles that favor the worst off in general and impose even more stringent equality in the basic liberties.

Suppose Rawls is right about what it would be rational to choose under those conditions. We must then ask why a unanimous choice under conditions of ignorance, without an assumption that one has an equal chance of being anyone in the society, correctly expresses the constraints of morality. Other constructions also have a claim to counting all persons as moral equals. What makes these conditions of unanimity under ignorance the right ones? They insure that numbers do not count[13] and urgency does, but that is the issue. A more fundamental type of argument is needed to settle it.

VIII

The main question is whether a kind of unanimity should enter into the combination of different points of view when evaluative judgments are being made about outcomes. This is an issue between egalitarian and utilitarian theories, both of which concern themselves with outcomes. Rights theories are opposed to both, because although they use a kind of unanimity condition, it is a condition on the acceptability of actions rather than of outcomes. In defending an interpretation of moral equality in terms of unanimity applied in the assessment of outcomes, I am therefore denying that either utilitarianism or rights theories, or both, represent the whole truth about ethics.

As I have said, acceptance of egalitarian values need not imply total exclusion of the others. Egalitarians may allow utility independent weight, and liberal egalitarians standardly acknowledge the importance of certain rights, which limit the means that may be used in pursuing equality and other ends.[14] I believe that rights exist and that this agent-centered aspect of morality is very important. The recognition of individual rights is a way of accepting a requirement of unanimous acceptability when weighing the claims of others in respect to what one may do. But a theory based exclusively on rights leaves out too much that is morally relevant, even if the interests it includes are among the most basic. A moral view that gives no weight to the value of overall outcomes cannot be correct.[15]

So let me return to the issue of unanimity in the assessment of outcomes. The essence of such a criterion is to try in a moral assessment to include each person's point of view separately, so as to achieve a result which is in a significant sense acceptable to each person involved or affected. Where there is conflict of interests, no result can be competely acceptable to everyone. But it is possible to assess each result from each point of view to try to find the one that is least unacceptable to the person to whom it is most unacceptable. This means that any other alternative will be more unacceptable to someone than this alternative is to anyone. The preferred alternative is in that sense the least unacceptable, considered from each person's point of view separately. A radically egalitarian policy of giving absolute priority to the worst off, regardless of numbers, would result from always choosing the least unacceptable alternative, in this sense.

This ideal of individual acceptability is in fundamental opposition to the aggregative ideal, which constructs a special moral point of view by combining those of individuals into a single conglomerate viewpoint distinct from all of them. That is done in utilitarianism by adding them up. Both the separate and the conglomerate methods count everyone fully and equally. The difference between them is that the second moves beyond individual points of view to something more comprehensive than any of them, though based on them. The first stays closer to the points of view of the individuals considered.

It is this ideal of acceptability to each individual that underlies the appeal of equality. We can see how it operates even in a case involving small numbers. Suppose I have two children, one of which is normal and quite happy, and the other of which suffers from a painful handicap. Call them respectively the first child and the second child. I am about to change jobs. Suppose I must decide between moving to an expensive city where the second child can receive special medical treatment and schooling, but where the family's standard of living will be lower and the neighborhood will be unpleasant and dangerous for the first child—or else moving to a pleasant semi-rural suburb where the first child, who has a special interest in sports and nature, can have a free and agreeable life. This is a difficult choice on any view. To make it a test for the value of equality, I want to suppose that the case has the following feature: the gain to the first child of moving to the suburb is substantially greater than the gain to the second child of moving to the city. After all, the second child will also suffer from the family's reduced standard of living and the disagreeable environment. And the educational and therapeutic benefits will not make him happy but only less miserable. For the first child, on the other hand, the choice is between a happy life and a disagreeable one. Let me add as a feature of the case that there is no way to compensate either child significantly for its loss if the choice favoring the other child is made. The family's resources are stretched, and neither child has anything else to give up that could be converted into something of significant value to the other.

If one chose to move to the city, it would be an egalitarian decision. It is more urgent to benefit the second child, even though the benefit we can give him is less than the benefit we can give the first child. This urgency is not necessarily decisive. It may be outweighed by other considerations, for equality is not the only value. But it is a factor, and it depends on the worse off position of the second child. An improvement in his situation is more im-

portant than an equal or somewhat greater improvement in the situation of the first child.

Suppose a third child is added to the situation, another happy, healthy one, and I am faced with the same choice in allocation of indivisible goods. The greater urgency of benefiting the second child remains. I believe that this factor is essentially unchanged by the addition of the third child. It remains just as much more urgent to benefit the second child in this case as it was when there were only two children.[16]

The main point about a measure of urgency is that it is done by pairwise comparison of the situations of individuals. The simplest method would be to count *any* improvement in the situation of someone worse off as more urgent than any improvement in the situation of someone better off; but this is not especially plausible. It is more reasonable to accord greater urgency to large improvements somewhat higher in the scale than to very small improvements lower down. Such a modified principle could still be described as selecting the alternative that was least unacceptable from each point of view. This method can be extended to problems of social choice involving large numbers of people. So long as numbers do not count it remains a type of unanimity criterion, defined by a suitable measure of urgency. The problem of justifying equality then becomes the problem of justifying the pursuit of results that are acceptable to each person involved.

Before turning to a discussion of this problem, let me say why I think that even if it were solved, it would not provide the foundation for a correct egalitarian theory. It seems to me that no plausible theory can avoid the relevance of numbers completely. There may be some disparities of urgency so great that the priorities persist whatever numbers are involved. But if the choice is between preventing severe hardship for some who are very poor and deprived, and preventing less severe but still substantial hardship for those who are better off but still struggling for subsistence, then it is very difficult for me to believe that the numbers do not count, and that priority of urgency goes to the worse off however many more there are of the better off. It might be suggested that this is a case where equality is outweighed by utility. But if egalitarian urgency is itself sensitive to numbers in this way, it does not seem that any form of unanimity criterion could explain the foundation of the view. Nor does any alternative foundation suggest itself.

IX

For a view of the more uncompromising type, similar in structure to that of Rawls, we need an explanation of why individual pairwise comparison to find the individually least unacceptable alternative is a good way to adjudicate among competing interests. What would it take to justify this method of combining individual claims? I think the only way to answer this question is to ask another: what is the source of morality? How do the interests of others secure a hold on us in moral reasoning, and does this imply a way in which they must be considered in combination?

I have a view about the source of other-regarding moral reasons that suggests an answer to this question. The view is not very different from the one I defended in *The Possibility of Altruism,*[17] and I will only sketch it here. I believe that the general form of moral reasoning is to put yourself in other people's shoes. This leads to acceptance of an impersonal concern for them corresponding to the impersonal concern for yourself that is needed to avoid a radical incongruity between your attitudes from the personal and impersonal standpoints, i.e., from inside and outside your life. Some considerable disparity remains, because the personal concerns remain in relation to yourself and your life: they are not to be replaced or absorbed by the impersonal ones that correspond to them.[18] (One is also typically concerned in a personal way for the interests of certain others to whom one is close.) But we derive moral reasons by forming in addition a parallel impersonal concern corresponding to the interests of all other individuals. It will be as strong or as weak, as comprehensive or as restricted, as the impersonal concern we are constrained by the pressures of congruency to feel about ourselves. In

a sense, the requirement is that you love your neighbor as yourself: but only as much as you love yourself when you look at yourself from outside, with fair detachment.

The process applies separately to each individual and yields a set of concerns corresponding to the individual lives. There may be disparities between a person's objective interests and his own subjectively perceived interests or wishes, but apart from this, his claims enter the impersonal domain of reasons unchanged, as those of an individual. They do not come detached from him and go into a big hopper with all the others. The impersonal concern of ethics is an impersonal concern for oneself and all others as individuals. It derives from the necessary generalization of an impersonal concern for one's own life and interests, and the generalization preserves the individualistic form of the original.

For this reason the impersonal concern that results is fragmented: it includes a separate concern for each person, and it is realized by looking at the world from each person's point of view separately and individually, rather than by looking at the world from a single comprehensive point of view. Imaginatively one must split into all the people in the world, rather than turn oneself into a conglomeration of them.

This, it seems to me, makes pairwise comparison the natural way to deal with conflicting claims. There may be cases where the policy chosen as a result will seek to maximize satisfaction rather than equalizing it, but this will only be where all individuals have an equal chance of benefiting, or at least not a conspicuously unequal chance.[19] At the most basic level, the way to choose from many separate viewpoints simultaneously is to maintain them intact and give priority to the most urgent individual claims.

As I have said, equality is only one value and this is only one method of choice. We can understand a radically egalitarian system just as we can understand a radical system of rights, but I assume neither is correct. Utility is a legitimate value, and the majoritarian or conglomerate viewpoint on which it depends is an allowable way of considering the conflicting interests of numbers of different people at once. Still, the explanation of egalitarian values in terms of separate assessment from each point of view is a step toward understanding; and if it does not imply that these values are absolute, that is not necessarily a drawback.

Notes

1. This is obviously not true of things in which interest varies greatly, like recordings of bird songs, or horror comic books.
2. *A Theory of Justice* (Cambridge, Mass.: Harvard University Press, 1971).
3. The argument would be that improvements in the well-being of the lowest class as a result of material productivity spurred by wage differentials are only apparent: damage to their self-respect outweighs the material gains. And even inequalities that genuinely benefit the worst off may destroy nondistributive values like community or fraternity. See Christopher Ake, "Justice as Equality," *Philosophy & Public Affairs* 5 (Fall 1975): 69–89, esp. 76–77.
4. This way of looking at the problem was suggested to me by a proposal of Rawls (personal communication, January 31, 1976): Suppose we distinguish between the equal treatment of persons and their (equal) right to be treated as equals. (Here persons are *moral* persons.) The *latter* is more basic: Suppose the Original Position represents the latter re moral persons when they agree on principles and suppose they *would* agree on *some* form of equal treatment. What more is needed?
5. T. M. Scanlon, "Preference and Urgency," *Journal of Philosophy* 72 (November 6 1975): 659–660.
6. There may be circumstances in which nothing is permissible—true moral dilemmas in which every possible course of action is wrong. But these arise only from the clash of distinct moral principles and not from the application of one principle.
7. The issue over the *extent* of morality is one of the deepest in ethical theory. Many have felt it an objection to utilitarianism that it makes ethics swallow up everything, leaving only one optimal choice, or a small set of equally optimal alternatives, permissible for any person at any time. Those who offer this objection differ over the size and shape of the range of choices that should be left to individual inclination after the ethical boundaries have been drawn.
8. John Taurek has recently defended essentially this position in his paper, "Should the Numbers Count?" *Philosophy & Public Affairs* 6 (Summer 1977): 293 316. He holds that given a choice between saving one life and saving five others, one is not required to save the five: one may save either the one or the five. I believe that he holds this because there is at least one point of view from which saving the five is not the better choice. Taurek does believe that some moral requirements derive from special rights and obligations, but in cases like this, where there are fundamental conflicts of interest, it is impossible to define a condition of universal acceptability, and the choice is therefore not governed by any moral requirement.
9. Some of my comments are developed in "Rawls on Justice," *Philosophical Review* 83 (1973): 220–233.
10. *Theory of Justice,* pp. 74, 104.
11. *Theory of Justice,* pp. 27, 187.
12. "Later Selves and Moral Principles," in *Philosophy & Personal Relations,* ed. A. Montefiore (London: Routledge & Kegan Paul, 1973). Parfit suggests that utilitarianism could express the dissolution of temporally extended individuals into experiential sequences rather than the conflation of separate individuals into a mass person.
13. Since the Difference Principle is applied not to individuals but to social classes, conflicts of interest within the worst off or any other groups are absorbed in a set of average expectations. This means that the numbers count in a sense *within* a social class, in determining which policy benefits it most on average. But numbers do not count in determining priority among classes in the urgency of their claims. That is why the problems of this conception of social justice are similar to those of a more individually tailored egalitarianism.
14. Such a view is defended by Ronald Dworkin in *Taking Rights Seriously* (Cambridge, Mass.: Harvard University Press, 1977).
15. I have said more about this in "Libertarianism Without Foundations," *Yale Law Journal* 85 (1975), a review of Robert Nozick's *Anarchy, State, and Utopia* (New York: Basic Books, 1974).
16. Note that these thoughts do not *depend* on any idea of personal identity over time, though they can *employ* such an idea. All that is needed to evoke them is a distinction between persons at a time. The impulse to distributive equality arises so long as we can distinguish between two experiences being had by two persons and their being had by one person. The criteria of personal identity over time merely determine the size of the units over which a distributive principle operates. That, briefly, is what I think is wrong with Parfit's account of the relation between distributive justice and personal identity.
17. Oxford: Clarendon Press, 1970.
18. In this respect my present view differs from the one in *The Possibility of Altruism.*
19. I leave aside the question when the equality of chances can be counted as real enough to supersede the inequality of actual outcomes. Perhaps that applies only to certain kinds of outcomes, and certain ways of determining chances.

Communitarian and
Liberal Theories
of the Good

JEFFREY PAUL and

FRED D. MILLER, JR.

I

A major thesis of contemporary liberal philosophy is that its theory of justice, which incorporates strong rights to negative liberty, must be prior to and independent of a theory of the good.[1] This priority is necessary, according to liberal theorists, in view of the requirement that any adequate theory accommodate a plurality of contending views of the good, no one of which is capable of eliciting public assent to it.[2] Recent critics of liberalism have disputed this thesis,[3] maintaining instead that there is indeed an objective good, rather than a plurality of contending goods, which at least seriously compromises and possibly undermines the negative liberty with which liberals traditionally associated their theories. Variously called communitarians, virtue theorists, or republicans, these critics have presented an important challenge to contemporary liberalism whether of the individualist or welfare state variety.

In this essay we will argue that while this challenge fails, because the critics' particular theories of the objective good are not successfully defended by them, liberals were mistaken even to have felt threatened by the possibility that such theories might succeed. It is our contention that the objective good, properly understood, is entirely compatible with the liberal theory of justice. Indeed, we will argue that this very theory of justice can be derived from a conception of the objective good, a result unanticipated by the theories of liberals like John Rawls and Ronald Dworkin. Our essay will not include such a derivation, but only demonstrate that such a derivation is possible.

II

The liberal theory of justice, with its correlative conception of human ends or goods, has certain essential features which have been the subjects of the extraordinary critique that has surfaced in recent political theory. In order to appreciate the contours of that critique, the elements of the liberal theory that it opposes need to be more fully described.

John Rawls identifies the distinctive feature of this liberalism as its derivation of principles of justice that can accommodate the practice of a variety of conceptions of the good life.

... liberalism as a political doctrine supposes that there are many conflicting and incommensurable conceptions of the good, each compatible with the full rationality of human persons, so far as we can ascertain within a workable conception of justice. As a consequence of this supposition, liberalism assumes that it is a characteristic feature of a free democratic culture that a plurality of conflicting and

Jeffrey Paul and Fred E. Miller, Jr., ''Communitarian and Liberal Conceptions of the Good,'' from *Review of Metaphysics*, 63 (June 1990). Reprinted by permission of the authors and publisher.

incommensurable conceptions of the good are affirmed by its critics.[4]

The capaciousness of liberal principles of justice appropriate to such axiological pluralism is necessary, according to Rawls, just because of the failure of ethicists to derive a conception of the good which is objective and, thereby, sufficiently authoritative to command the universal assent of rational individuals. Therefore, principles of justice must be derived antecedent to and independent of any putative theory of the good. Such principles will typically include strong protections for negative liberty, as such liberty is required for the practice of varying and incommensurable conceptions of the good. It will additionally exclude practices which are incompatible with such value pluralism, practices which coercively interfere with the peaceable strivings of citizens. Therefore, those conceptions of the good which require for their practice continual interference with the freedom of action of others are not protected and indeed, by implication, are proscribed by the liberal theory of justice:

The principles of right, and so of justice, put limits on which satisfactions have value; they impose restrictions on what are reasonable conceptions of one's good. In drawing up plans and in deciding on aspirations men are to take those constraints into account. Hence, in justice as fairness one does not take the propensity and inclinations as given, whatever they are, and then seek the best way to fill them. Rather, their desires and aspirations are restricted from the outset by the principles of justice which specify the boundaries that men's systems of ends must respect. We can express this by saying that in justice as fairness the concept of right is prior to that of the good.[5]

This priority involves not only the practical requirement of constraining the intrusive and obstructive actions of citizens, but consists as well of the necessity to constrain the philosophical effects of a good antecedently derived upon any principles of justice that would then have to conform to it. That is, on the liberal view, principles of justice derived from some antecedent conception of the good would be overly narrow and, thereby, exclude competing conceptions. Liberal principles of justice, then,

would appear to be both conceptually and practically incompatible with an antecedently derived theory of a good which claimed to be objective and, therefore, uniquely desirable. The utilitarian theory of the good is illustrative of this incompatibility:

Seeking the greatest satisfaction of desire may, then, justify harsh repressive measures against actions that cause no social injury. To defend individual liberty in this case the utilitarian has to show that given the circumstances the real advantage in the long run lies on the side of freedom; and this argument may or may not be successful.[6]

The incompatibility of an objective theory of the good with a theory of justice that incorporates a strong principle of negative liberty[7] is viewed by the communitarian critics of liberalism as a reason to jettison the latter. These critics share among themselves the view that there is a single objective good and share with their liberal adversaries the conviction that such a good is profoundly subversive of rights to negative liberty. The derivation of such a good, they conclude, signals at least the dilution of those rights and perhaps their ultimate demise. The particular theories of the good embraced by these critics will next be analyzed in order, first, to demonstrate in what their alleged incompatibility with liberal rights consists, and second, to assess the arguments which they advance on behalf of these theories.

The arguments which we shall consider here affirm the existence of some common good which can be advanced apart from and frequently at the expense of the interests of individuals and which, therefore, may require the sacrifice of their liberty.[8] In the next two sections, we take up two examples of this argument, as found in Alasdair MacIntyre (in section III) and Michael Sandel (in section IV).

III

Alasdair MacIntyre's *After Virtue* includes an argument that the theory of the objective good, understood as a common good, is incompatible with liberal theory. It is impossible for us to examine in detail MacIntyre's complex and wide-ranging argument, which includes the exegesis of a series of philosophical positions and literary works spanning two millenia. Our discussion will of necessity focus on what is directly relevant to our topic, specifically, his argument that the objective good as defined by the virtue tradition is incompatible with the liberal theory of negative rights.

We take this alleged incompatibility to be at the core of MacIntyre's conclusion that "the crucial moral opposition is between liberal individualism in some version or other and the Aristotelian tradition in some version."[9] According to MacIntyre, Aristotle's account of the virtues "decisively constitutes the classical tradition as a tradition of moral thought."[10] Because Aristotle occupies a central place in MacIntyre's own account of the virtues, we need to review briefly his account of Aristotle's theory, concentrating on the elements which he finds problematic and those which are preserved in his own reconstruction. (We shall not be concerned here with the correctness of MacIntyre's interpretation of Aristotle.)

Aristotle's ethics is grounded in his metaphysical biology, according to which human beings like other species have a specific *telos* or end defined by their human nature. This biology supports a teleological ethics: The objective good for man, or *eudaimonia* (flourishing, happiness, well-being), consists in the realization of this *telos*. The virtues are defined as "precisely those qualities the possession of which will enable an individual to achieve *eudaimonia* and the lack of which will frustrate his movement toward that *telos*."[11] However, the virtues are not merely instrumental means to that end; the exercise of the virtues is intrinsically valuable because it is a constitutive means, that is, "a necessary and central part" of the good life.[12] Further, Aristotle claims that a human being is a political animal (*politikon zōon*).[13] Hence, individuals can achieve their *telos* only within a *polis,* which is "a community whose shared aim is the realisation of the human good," presupposing "a wide range of agreement in that community on goods and virtues." This necessitates civic friendship, "the sharing of all in the common project of creating and sustaining the life of the city." MacIntyre remarks that "this notion of the po-

litical community as a common project is alien to the modern liberal individualist world."[14] Aristotle would regard a modern liberal political society not as a genuine *polis* but "only as a collection of citizens of nowhere who have banded together for their common protection."[15] For he conceives of the *polis* as a community "in which men in company pursue *the* human good and not merely as—what the modern liberal state takes itself to be—providing the arena in which each individual seeks his or her own private good."[16] Hence, there is no room on his view for the modern liberal distinction between law and morality: a major task of the *polis* and its laws is to make the citizens virtuous.[17]

Although MacIntyre holds that Aristotle's theory of the virtues plays a most significant role in the historical development of moral theory, he also finds that it contains serious flaws.[18] The first of these is that Aristotle's teleological view of the good presupposes a metaphysical biology which has been invalidated by modern science. Second, Aristotle is criticized because his understanding of human nature and of the virtues is, according to MacIntyre, mistakenly ahistorical. Aristotle's understanding of human nature as a biological constant is erroneous, and he fails to appreciate the importance of culture in shaping human identity. Nor does he recognize that his own conception of the virtues is dependent upon a particular historical setting and that tables of the virtues other than his might be required for other social and political systems. Moreover, the medieval versions of Aristotelianism compound these errors by locating the source of its veracity in supernatural teleology, a foundation ill-suited to our current secular age. For these reasons, MacIntyre undertakes a reconstruction of the Aristotelian theory of the virtues without its original or medieval foundations.[19]

He offers a "unitary core concept" of the virtues which is intended to apply to any adequate conception of the virtues and to accommodate historical and cultural variations.[20] He develops this concept through three stages. First, he defines a virtue as "an acquired human quality the possession and exercise of which tends to enable us to achieve those goods which are internal to practices and the lack of which effectively prevents us from achieving any such goods."[21] This definition shares some important formal features with the Aristotelian virtues,[22] but it is not satisfactory because it allows for too much arbitrariness and incompleteness in the moral life. This can be relieved only if there is "a *telos* which transcends the limited goods of practices by constituting the good of a whole human life, the good of a human life conceived as a unity."[23] In his second stage, MacIntyre suggests that this unity can be defined in terms of a narrative quest: "the good life for man is the life spent in seeking for the good life for man, and the virtues necessary for the seeking are those which will enable us to understand what more and what else the good life for man is."[24] In his final stage, MacIntyre argues that what it is to live the good life concretely varies from one particular social context to another, in which individuals are "bearers of a particular social identity."[25] My social roles "constitute the given of my life, my moral starting point."[26] MacIntyre's argument seems to be that the objective good for an individual must be a *telos* which transcends the particular goods the individual seeks and which makes the individual's life a unity, but such a *telos* cannot be justified in terms of Aristotle's metaphysical teleology or medieval supernatural teleology. There remains only one alternative: the justification must be "socially teleological."[27]

On the basis of this social teleology MacIntyre advances the following general claims: The self is historically and socially defined—"the self has to find its moral identity in and through its membership in communities such as those of the family, the neighborhood, the city and the tribe," and as a bearer of their traditions.[28] The good is also socially defined: "goods, and with them the only grounds for the authority of laws and virtues, can only be discovered by entering into those relationships which constitute communities whose central bond is a shared vision of an understanding of goods."[29] The good is common and not individually realizable: "my good as a man is one and the same as the good of those others with whom I am bound up in human community.

There is no way of my pursuing my good which is necessarily antagonistic to you pursuing yours because *the* good is neither mine peculiarly nor yours peculiarly—goods are not private property."[30] MacIntyre emphasizes that these doctrines are inimical to modern political philosophies,[31] and especially to modern liberal individualism.

We do not dispute MacIntyre's claim that his communitarian view of the good has anti-liberal implications, for example, the denial of the distinction between law and morality[32] and the assignation to individuals of collective responsibility and of guilt for historical injustices.[33] We do, however, question whether he has provided a persuasive case that the objective good must be understood in communitarian terms, even if it is supposed to include the exercise of the virtues. Let us consider first his argument for the central claim that the human good must be socially defined:

For I am never able to seek for the good or exercise the virtues only *qua* individual. This is partly because what it is to live the good life concretely varies from circumstance to circumstance even when it is one and the same conception of the good life and one and the same set of virtues which are being embodied in a human life. What the good life is for a fifth-century Athenian general will not be the same as what it was for a medieval nun or a seventeenth-century farmer. But it is not just that different individuals live in different social circumstances; it is also that we all approach our own circumstances as bearers of a particular social identity. I am someone's son or daughter, someone else's cousin or uncle; I am a citizen of this or that city, a member of this or that guild or profession; I belong to this clan, that tribe, this nation. Hence what is good for me has to be the good for one who inhabits these roles. As such, I inherit from the past of my family, my city, my tribe, my nation, a variety of debts, inheritances, rightful expectations and obligations. These constitute the given of my life, my moral starting point. This is in part what gives my life its own moral particularity.[34]

We question whether MacIntyre's premises support his conclusion. Suppose we grant the premise that "I am never able to seek for the good or exercise the virtues only *qua* individual." Philoctetes stranded by himself on an island for years in Sophocles' tragedy was not able to exercise the virtues or seek the good.[35] A child raised by wolves would not learn a language or presumably have any conception of "the good" or "the virtues." Different people with a different cultural history will exercise the virtues in quite different ways, and the fact that they have different social roles helps to explain this difference. These examples suggest that having a social and cultural tradition is a necessary condition for attaining the good. But from the fact that A requires X as a necessary condition for the attainment of the good, it does not follow that X constitutes or defines the good for A. Further, even if we accept Aristotle's claim that "someone presumably does not have a good of his own without participation in the management of a household and without a polity,"[36] it does not follow that the objective good of that individual is defined by his particular household and *polis*. For even if it were true that the objective good of individuals required certain societal and political arrangements for its attainment, it would not follow that the objective good must be defined by the particular society in which the individuals happened to live. Indeed, as we shall argue in section IV, the liberal may maintain that it is a necessary condition for individual attainment of the good that social and political institutions include the principle of equal liberty or negative rights. But it would surely be consistent with this to maintain that the good could be specified independently of particular social and political contexts.

MacIntyre represents his theory that the good is defined by social traditions as the only way to escape from the moral dilemmas of "the modern self with its criterionless choices."[37] He regards his social teleology as the only available alternative to the no longer credible biological teleology of Aristotle and the supernatural teleology of the medievals. However, he has not provided a compelling argument that these three teleologies are the only possible accounts of the objective good. His argument that "the Enlightenment project had to fail" depends upon the undefended claim that once a teleological view of human nature, in the classical or medieval sense, is rejected,

it is impossible to provide a rational justification of morality based on a conception of human nature. But even if MacIntyre were correct about the Enlightenment project, it is unclear that his social teleology is a genuine alternative to the subjective good which he is trying to escape. In a society isolated from others, like the heroic world of the Homeric epics, the members may have no doubt that "reality is as they represent it to themselves," so that their epistemology can be "a thoroughgoing realism."[38] But from the point of view of another society, the good of the heroic society is subjective, "i.e., what *they* think is good." The fact that some degree of intersubjective agreement may be attained within these communities does not obviate the fact that each of their conceptions of the good is subjective and arbitrary when viewed from the standpoint of the others.[39]

When we survey alternative communities, the view that the good is socially determined has disturbing implications, especially where there is a manifest conflict between what is good for a person and what is socially approved. For example, if I were a slave in ancient Athens, or a serf in a medieval manor, should these socially assigned roles "constitute the given of my life, my moral starting point?" MacIntyre denies that his view entails "that the self has to accept the moral *limitations* of the particularity of those forms of community."[40] But this implies that there is an answer to the question, "On what grounds can I as a member of a community challenge the socially determined good?" It should be possible to criticize the institutions and practices of a community as morally flawed, even if the community provides no moral basis or opening for criticism. The grounds for criticism of a community must ultimately be independent of the good socially determined by that community or by any other one, and it is difficult to see how such a nonsubjectivist standard could be forthcoming given MacIntyre's theory.

Moreover, why is it necessarily the case that a good derived from a social tradition should be incompatible with the liberal theory of negative rights? One reason might be found in

MacIntyre's claim that modern individualism could find no use for the notion of tradition except as an adversary notion, and therefore cannot have a tradition-based genesis and derivation.[41] However, as John Gray has remarked, liberal thinkers such as Tocqueville, Constant, and Hayek have come to appreciate the conservative insight that "the maintenance of moral and cultural traditions is a necessary condition of lasting progress."[42]

Another reason that MacIntyre offers in defense of his contention that negative liberty is incompatible with an objective good is that its origin in the shared understandings of communities implies that it must be a common or shared good. Such a common or shared good would require, presumably, the abrogation of the negative liberties of those persons who failed to pursue, in requisite ways, the common good, following instead their own deviant inclinations. But, from the fact that the good is a product of shared understandings, it certainly does not follow that the good so derived must be a shared or common good. The claim that it must be is a non-sequitur, as well as an example of the genetic fallacy, for the vision of the social good so shared might be of a pluralistic society in which a variety of final ends, both commensurable and incommensurable, are practiced. According to such a view, the community becomes, a la Rawls and contra MacIntyre, "a cooperative venture for the mutual advantage."[43]

The conception of the good as a shared good is also defended by MacIntyre because of its alleged practical necessity:

In a society where there is no shared conception of the community's good as specified by the good for man, there can no longer either be any very substantial concept of what it is to contribute more or less to the achievement of that good.[44]

But this is merely asserted, not argued for. Theories which define the good as individual self-realization, appropriately specified and qualified, can produce a lucid account of what will count as a contribution to the achievement of that good.

Nevertheless, MacIntyre seems to hold that his virtue ethic provides him with the resources for an internal critique of liberalism, demonstrating that liberalism permits the virtues in only a very degenerate sense. Capitalism and the acquisitiveness allied with liberal individualism are, he contends, antithetical to the virtue tradition, because the virtues are valued simply as means to the production and acquisition of commodities in the market.[45] However, neither liberalism nor individualism entails acquisitiveness in such a strong sense as to crowd out the virtues. It is true that one can become so fixated on acquisitive, goal-directed activities such as earning money or accumulating goods that one loses sight of the virtues, which are for MacIntyre excellences concerned with intrinsically valuable activities. But it is also possible for individuals in a liberal, capitalist society to maintain a proper balance in their lives between goal-directed and intrinsically valuable activities. Furthermore, the same activity can be intrinsically valuable as well as productive; thus, in a free society a philosopher or artist can simultaneously lead the good life and make a living.

The precise source and nature of the alleged moral antithesis between economic individualism and its counterparts are delineated by MacIntyre as follows:

So long as productive work occurs within the structure of households, it is easy and right to understand that work as part of the sustaining of the community of the household and of those wider forms of community which the household in turn sustains. As, and, to the extent that, work moves outside the household and is put to the service of impersonal capital, the realm of work tends to become separated from everything but the service of biological survival and the reproduction of the labour force, on the one hand, and that of institutionalized acquisitiveness, on the other. *Pleonexia*, a vice in the Aristotelian scheme, is now the driving force of modern productive work. The means-end relationships embodied for the most part in such work—on a production line, for example—are necessarily external to the goods which those who work seek; such work too has consequently been expelled from the realm of practices with goods internal to themselves. And correspondingly practices have in turn been removed to the margins of social and cultural life.

Arts, sciences and games are taken to be *work* only for a minority of specialists: the rest of us may receive incidental benefits in our leisure time only as spectators or consumers.[46]

MacIntyre supposes the introduction of commodity production to be antithetic to the maintenance of the household and communal values. However, the very opposite is the case. The division of labor implied in commodity production in fact widens community bonds by rewarding individuals who successfully fulfill the economic preferences of those members of the community who reside beyond their own household. Indeed, it immerses the entrepreneur in a web of economically reciprocal relationships with geographically diverse elements of the population in which investment and production will be sustained only to the extent that they satisfy the preferences of others.[47]

MacIntyre's depiction of capitalism neglects the central role played by the entrepreneur. It is instructive to contrast the position of entrepreneurs in a capitalist society with that of the planning classes in noncapitalist societies in which capital investment is a state monopoly and private investment is proscribed. The capitalist entrepreneur must attend to the preferences of those whose purchases he must elicit in order to recover his investment and pay for his operating costs. In doing so, he is motivated by the personal rewards of successfully satisfying those preferences and the personal costs of failing to satisfy them. The planning classes of noncapitalist societies have insulated themselves from the requirement of satisfying consumer preference through their coercive monopoly of the investment function and their ability to subsidize through taxation their failures to satisfy consumers. They are neither enticed by the rewards of success nor threatened by the risk of failure. The consequence has been a pattern of failure on the part of noncapitalist regimes throughout the world to meet consumer demands for food, clothing, housing, and other commodities.[48]

It would seem more natural to admire the virtue of attending to the preferences of others, which is inculcated by the institutions of private capital markets and investor ownership of production, rather than the indifference to consumer preference which typifies the monopolized capital markets of noncapitalist societies. But the compatibility of self-regarding and other-regarding economic activity within a market, an insight at least as old as Adam Smith, is mysteriously never grasped by MacIntyre.

In conclusion, MacIntyre's "shared vision" is an insufficient justification for a good alleged to be common and not individual. Moreover, the historical and social genesis of his moral philosophy leave it vulnerable to the charge of subjectivism, a fatal indictment for a theory which aspires to objectivity. Another communitarian theory can be viewed as an attempt to overcome by metaphysical analysis the limitations of MacIntyre's position. To that theory, advanced by Michael Sandel, we now turn.

IV

An objective theory of the good can require the sacrifice of someone's negative liberty for two sorts of reasons (aside from paternalism). First, one's negative liberty could be constrained for the benefit of another. An economic regulation which restricts the liberty of some in order to benefit the least economically advantaged and is justified by Rawl's difference principle exemplifies this sort of restriction. Second, it may be argued that limitations on the exercise of one's negative liberty are justified neither to promote one's own interests nor those of other individuals, but for the good of society as a whole, the thesis advanced by MacIntyre and defended in a quite different manner by Michael Sandel in *Liberalism and the Limits of Justice.*

Sandel considers a rigid adherence to a principle of equal liberty incompatible with a theory of the objective good. Moreover, he believes that an important version of contemporary liberalism, notably that of Rawls, has implicitly acknowledged its attachment to such a good, thereby compromising its otherwise unqualified allegiance to a principle of equal liberty. According to Sandel, Rawls's theory is involved in a fatal inconsistency which can only be resolved in one of two ways: by the abandonment of the difference principle or by the acknowledgement that the real subject of this principle must be a social organism superior to and inclusive of individuals, the good of which may require the rejection of negative liberty. Because Sandel believes that Rawls has given us good independent grounds for retaining the difference principle, he suggests that we adopt the latter alternative and in so doing endorse a theory of the objective social good.

In this part of the essay we examine the grounds for Sandel's claims about the incoherence of Rawlsian liberalism as well as the basis for his radical revision of it. In so doing, we will impugn the alleged foundation of that revision and, therefore, urge that it is the difference principle, not the principle of equal liberty, that Rawls should reject. Once the difference principle is removed, we will argue, Rawlsian liberalism becomes invulnerable to the charge that it must subscribe to a theory of an organic social good which should shape and limit the principles of justice.

Sandel's thesis is that the grounds from which Rawls derives his first principle of justice, the principle of greatest equal liberty, must be rejected in order to retain the first part of his second principle of justice, the difference principle, given that the latter requires a radically different foundation than the former. According to Rawls, both principles have a common point of derivation in the original position. Here, hypothetical mutually disinterested persons are situated behind the well-known veil of ignorance. While they have ends that they seek to advance, they have no knowledge of them nor of their respective capacities to realize them. Thus situated in circumstances of moderate scarcity, the parties know only that they prefer certain primary goods, goods which are instrumental to one's purposes whatever these happen to be. And these goods include the requirement that each person "have the fullest liberty to realize his aims and purposes compatible with an equal liberty for others,"[49] which is Rawl's first principle of justice. The second principle derived

by the parties in the original position specifies that:

Social and economic inequalities are to be arranged so that they are both (a) to the greatest benefit of the least advantaged and (b) attached to offices and positions open to all under conditions of fair equality of opportunity.[50]

It is part (a), which Rawls calls the difference principle, that Sandel believes is incompatible with the assumptions Rawls makes about the original position. This incompatibility, according to Sandel, is traceable to the supposition that the original position is inhabited by plural and mutually disinterested persons. These two assumptions about the inhabitants of the original position, Sandel argues, embody for Rawls the Kantian maxim that everyone is to be treated as an end in himself and not the means for the ends of another; and this maxim clashes with the prescription of the difference principle. If this principle is unchallengeable, then, it is Sandel's conclusion that Rawls must abandon the atomistic social ontology of the original position.

In order to take the full measure of Sandel's charge of incoherence, we must now explicate Rawls's defense of the difference principle as well as the conclusions that Sandel wishes to draw from it. Rawls adopts the difference principle on the grounds that alternative conceptions of distributive justice assign benefits based upon unwarranted grounds. The principle of natural liberty, for example, allows individuals to accumulate economic benefits based upon their talents and holdings. But the prior accumulation of the latter may be affected by a variety of contingencies which will unfairly advantage some over others. A meritocratic distributive principle which attempts to rectify this unfairness by correcting for social and cultural inequities will be little better than its natural libertarian predecessor, according to Rawls:

Even if it works to perfection in eliminating the influence of social contingencies, it still permits the distribution of wealth and income to be determined by the natural distribution of abilities and talents. Within the limits allowed by the background arrangements, distributive shares are divided by the outcome of the natural lottery; and this outcome is arbitrary from a moral perspective. There is no more reason to permit the distribution of income and wealth to be settled by the distribution of natural assets than by historical and social fortune.[51]

Because no one can be said to deserve what has been arbitrarily distributed, according to Rawls, no one can be said to deserve his assets nor the benefits that flow from their productive use:

Those who have been favored by nature, whoever they are, may gain from their good fortune only on terms that improve the situation of those who have lost out.[52]

Such terms are those specified by the difference principle, which "... represents, in effect, an agreement to regard the distribution of natural talents as a common asset and to share in the benefits of this distribution whatever it turns out to be."[53] And this decision according to Rawls assures that embodied "... in the basic structure of society [is] men's desire to treat one another not as means only but as ends in themselves."[54]

If the decision to regard the attributes of individuals as common property appears, as Nozick has argued,[55] to flout the Kantian injunction which the principles of justice are supposed to embody, then Rawls can respond in one of two ways, according to Sandel. First, Rawls could argue that it is not *persons* who are being used as means to the betterment of others, but only their *attributes.* Since these attributes are not mine in any strong or constitutive sense, as I am merely the site at which these attributes are contingently gathered, the sharing of them with others does not use me as a means to the ends of others. Sandel concludes that:

Only on a theory of the person that held these endowments to be essential *constituents* rather than alienable *attributes* of the self could the sharing of assets be viewed as using *me* as a means to others' ends. But on Rawls' account all endowments are contingent and in principle detachable from the self. ...[56]

While Rawls could avail himself of this solution, according to Sandel, it so depletes the self

of assets as to leave it utterly contentless. The "person" who is thereby rescued from being used as a means to the welfare of others can hardly be said to exist at all. The invention of this characterless person, then, saves Rawls as a Kantian at the expense of the intelligibility of his theory, says Sandel.

However, Sandel puts forth an alternative solution to this dilemma which instead of radically severing an individual from his characteristics, seeks to reintegrate the two while obliterating boundaries between persons so that "... the relevant description of the self may embrace more than a single empirically-individuated human being."[57] Such an intersubjective self, Sandel argues, is precisely what Rawls is committed to by the difference principle. The treatment of natural endowments as a common asset, then, would not violate the Kantian maxim, since what Sandel calls "the intersubjective self" would only be using what belongs to it as an integral part of its identity. Sandel claims further that we are individuated fundamentally not by the boundaries of our bodies,[58] but by our socially derived self-understandings which are not separable from our identities:

And in so far as our self-understandings comprehend a wider subject than the individual alone, whether a family or tribe or city or class or nation or people, to this extent they define a community in the constitutive sense. And what marks such a community is not merely a spirit of benevolence, or the prevalence of communitarian values, or even 'shared final ends' alone but a common vocabulary of discourse and a background of implicit practices and understandings within which the opacity of the participants is reduced if never finally dissolved. In so far as justice depends for its pre-eminence on the separations, or boundedness of persons in the cognitive sense its priority would diminish as that opacity faded and this community deepened.[59]

Justice—meaning in this context, the principle of equal liberty, not the difference principle—would be subordinated to a principle of the social good which would replace it in priority and thereby weaken (perhaps eliminate?) the legitimacy of its constraints.

But this subordination is only required if

what we might call the holistic conception of society is called upon to salvage the difference principle. If the difference principle itself rests on questionable foundations, then it rather than the atomistic conception of society is an expendable part of Rawlsian liberalism. To these foundations, then, we next turn our attention.

The difference principle rests on the assumption that the natural endowments of persons have been arbitrarily distributed from the moral point of view. But what does it mean to say that our endowments have been arbitrarily distributed to us? Rawls's metaphors give us several clues. For example, he refers to the well-endowed as beneficiaries of ". . . the outcome of the natural lottery; and this outcome is arbitrary from a moral perspective."[60] He contrasts "those who have been favored by nature" with "those who have lost out."[61] And he recommends the difference principle if ". . . we wish to set up the social system so that no one gains or loses from his *arbitrary place in the distribution of natural assets.*"[62]

The features of natural endowments which require that we regard them as common assets are the (1) arbitrariness of (2) their distribution and (3) the benefit this confers upon some *only at the expense of others.* This suggests that Rawls conceives of the origination of human beings in terms of a lottery in which a limited number of natural assets of varying quality are assigned randomly to a finite number of pre-existing contentless selves. Suppose for example that at some time t_1 there are 10 such empty selves being prepared for the reception of attributes. A distributor of attributes stands before a container marked Intelligence Quotients, in which there are 5 IQs exceeding 140 and 5 more below 105. The distributor is blindfolded and reaches into his container to retrieve and successively assign IQs to each of the waiting selves who are labeled "1" through "10." 1, 3, 4, 7, and 10 receive the high IQs while 2, 5, 6, 8, and 9 receive the low ones. The reason that 2, 5, 6, 8, and 9 do not have IQs above 140 is because 1, 3, 4, 7, and 10 were given them instead. That is, the latter five benefited *at the expense of* the former five, so that the benefits accorded to one group impose

losses on the other. And these benefits and costs were distributed randomly, without reasons which could justify each of the assignments.

From this example we can discern the general conditions for the alleged moral arbitrariness of our differential capacities and talents. First, they were *assigned* or *distributed* to pre-existing *selves.* For, if there were no such pre-existing contentless selves we could not explain the distinctions between actual persons as the outcome of a distribution or lottery. Second, there must be, at the time of the assignments, a fixed number of detached attributes of a certain type (say, IQ), which is at least as large as the number of contentless individuals. Of these attributes, at least one must be different from the others, so that at least one person in receiving it is benefited or deprived by someone else's loss or gain. Third, the method of assigning attributes to individuals must be arbitrary, that is, not done because someone merited some attribute, or had been promised some attribute or had earned some attribute. "Arbitrary," in this context, means without a sufficient reason and the random means of making assignments satisfies this definition. Where those three conditions have been fulfilled, we can say that self-subsisting natural endowments have indeed been *distributed* to self-subsisting contentless people in an *arbitrary* fashion and that some have benefited at the expense of others.

The selves so endowed would not be said to deserve their productive output as it would have resulted not from *their* efforts *alone* (*they* being essentially contentless), but rather from *their* use of *natural assets* which were randomly received at the expense of others and, therefore, are not deserved by them. Nothing *they* have done could count as a basis for desert. Perhaps they are entitled to their assets by virtue of a principle of self-ownership. And perhaps this entitlement (as distinguished from desert) would justify their claims to the fruits of their labor. But, such a principle could not have entitled them to the natural endowments which are not constitutive of their identities, and which they receive after their individuation as contentless selves. Individually, then, persons can neither be alleged to deserve nor be entitled to their assets nor to the benefits which flow from their use. Therefore, Sandel concludes, we must be committed to a principle which treats those assets as common property.

One of us has argued previously that from Rawls's inference that no person is entitled to his natural assets it does not follow, therefore, that everyone is.[63] But if everyone is not jointly entitled to personal endowments, and if each person individually is not entitled to his own endowments, then no one is entitled to any of them. If no one is entitled to any natural endowments, then no one either individually or as a part of a collective, is entitled to what is produced through their use. But if this is so, we would argue, there is no warrant for any principle of distributive justice at all, including, obviously, the difference principle. Rawls, of course, wants to have his cake after he has swallowed it. He wants to place in doubt the entitlement of any particular person to his assets without imperiling his own favored conclusion, namely the entitlement of all persons to their aggregated endowments. But this cannot be done. His own view of endowments as arbitrarily possessed provides no warrant for their ownership by anyone, whether defined as an individual person(s), or a community, or holistic self. And if there is no warrant for the ownership of natural assets by anyone, there is no warrant for any principle which allocates their use by anyone, nor any warrant for a principle which allocates the fruits of their use. The difference principle is wholly without justification and, consequently, the problem of its consistency with Rawls's social ontology never arises.

To this nihilistic scenario two alternatives remain. The first is the aforementioned favored solution of Sandel. It requires that a collective self of which (presumably) natural assets would be integral features is the proper claimant of all such assets and, therefore, the rightful beneficiary of their fruits. Any principle which redistributed those fruits to the constituent personalities of a larger social self would not thereby violate the Kantian maxim, for the justice dispensed under this principle would be

intrasubjective and, hence, *could not* violate the autonomy of individuals. There is another plausible solution to this dilemma, but before stating it we might briefly assess Sandel's proposal.

Sandel maintains that what essentially determines the identity of this intersubjective superself or community are the understandings that its constituent members share of themselves collectively considered.[64] But if these understandings *alone* are what is constitutive of communal identity and, therefore, essential to it, then natural endowments remain as contingently related to Sandel's enlarged self as they are to Rawls's atomistic self. Sandel, then, provides no better justification for the shared ownership of such endowments than Rawls does.

There is another solution to this dilemma which emerges from the essential falseness of the metaphorical portrait that Rawls gives us of the way in which human beings are initially endowed with their talents and capacities. This portrait, we should recall, presents a set of preexisting contentless selves which are arbitrarily assigned a set of finite differentiated attributes so that the acquisitions of one person are made at the expense of others. But there *are* no preexisting selves nor any limited set of characteristic elements which might possibly be distributed to any of them. Persons come into being *with* their genes, not without them. Indeed, there is no contentless self that can be distinguished from its biological inheritance. People just *are* the physical entities that are created by the uniting of an egg and a sperm, not the contentless receptacles that Rawls's portrait suggests that they are. They are not treated fairly or unfairly by being endowed in certain ways, because there *is* no preendowment *they* to be so treated. Nor are they benefited at the expense of others due to the limited number of attributes available. Parents produce children with endowments, they do not select potential recipients of some finite subset of their genes and in doing so, deny those genes to others.

Rawls erroneously separates individuals into their real contentless selves and their contingently held endowments. But people just *are* their endowments. Peel all of their characteristics away and nothing at all remains (or nothing but a philosopher's fiction). If people are inseparable from their endowments in that they do not preexist them as contentless selves but are initially constituted by them and are indistinguishable from them, then there is no reason to construct some super-individuated self. Persons are already individuated by their physical boundaries.

But if people are essentially constituted by their natural endowments then there are no grounds for distinguishing between what *they* accomplish and what is accomplished by their *assets*. Nor are there any grounds for distinguishing between the instrumental treatment of *them* and of their assets. To use their *assets* as means will just be to use *them* as means. Moreover, to say that someone else is entitled to use my endowments will be to say that someone else is entitled to use *me*. And to say that something is produced with my endowments is just to say that it is produced by me. If, then, I am entitled to what I produce and if I am essentially identifiable with my endowments, then no distributive principle of justice may transgress this entitlement.

Now if I am therefore entitled to what *I* produce, then the difference principle must be given up as potentially in violation of this entitlement. In giving it up a Rawlsian will avoid the charge rightly made by Sandel and Nozick that this principle flouts the Kantian maxim which any liberal theory of justice must evince. What remains after it is discarded is the principle of equal liberty, the negative libertarian principle.

V

Clearly either of the two conceptions of the objective good previously examined would, if successfully defended by its proponent, have eviscerated or eliminated altogether a principle of negative liberty. That each conception evinces an incompatibility with liberal justice is uncontestable. By successfully challenging their claims to objective status one relieves liberal justice of the threat which they, cumulatively and individually, posed to its preeminence. However, that these particular contenders have proven vulnerable to criticism in no way implies that future candidates will be as fragile. An invincible future candidate would, presumably, jeopardize the principle of negative liberty once again. Must Rawls and other liberals continue to insist that the derivation of justice take place prior to and independent of theories of the good in order to insulate their theories of justice from possible threats of this kind? Is it the case that liberal justice is jeopardized whenever an alleged objective good is adduced antecedent to justice and is said to comprise the foundation from which justice is to be derived? Clearly Rawls believes that there would be such a threat. For he believes that any principle of justice derived from a prior conception of the good will be so formulated as to exclude the practice of competing theories.

In this section we will argue that Rawls is unnecessarily alarmed by the prospect that the principles of justice must be subordinated to the requirements of the good, rather than the other way around. More specifically, we will argue that for a certain category of purported goods, should any of them turn out to be *the* objective good, the same principle of equal liberty derived within the original position is deducible from that good.

This result may in fact be directly inferred from what Rawls has to say about the relationship of the right to the good. The principle of equal liberty adopted in the original position is accepted by the participants in advance of knowing their particular ends:

They implicitly agree, therefore, to conform their conceptions of their good to what the principles of justice require, or at least not to press claims which directly violate them.[65]

The principles of right, and so of justice, put limits on which satisfactions have value; they impose restrictions on what are reasonable conceptions of one's good.[66]

In other words, the principle of equal liberty provides the requisite moral space for the pursuit of any members of this set of reasonable conceptions of the good. Enlarge that space so that previously excluded conceptions of the good can now be pursued within its confines and you will find that there is a net decrease in the number eventually practiced. For the previously excluded conceptions all require that their adherents infringe upon the liberty of others to pursue their conceptions of the good. And this infringement will reduce the number of conceptions of the good actually followed. The reason for this diminution is that the previously excluded conceptions are just those which require that liberty be unequally distributed, while the smaller original group of conceptions included only those that require an equal distribution of liberty. For the smaller original set of goods, equal liberty is a necessary condition of their compossible pursuit. Therefore, for any member g of that set S_g, the greatest equal liberty principle of justice is a necessary condition of its pursuit. If g_1 is a conception which is a member of S_g, any principle of justice j_x which is a necessary condition of all members of S_g will be a necessary condition of any of them, for example, g_1, which is a proper subset of S_g. Thus, if g_1 is *the* objective good, then it follows that its necessary social condition j_x is *the* objective principle of justice. But j_x is the same principle which permitted the compossible pursuit of all members of S_g. Therefore, we can conclude that there is a set of proposed goods such that if any one of them should be claimed as the one objective good, then the principle(s) of justice derived from it is sufficiently capacious to permit the practice of all members of the set but sufficiently restricted so as to exclude the pursuit of goods which cannot be compossibly practiced with the other members of the set. If any member of the set is claimed as objective, its pursuit will not exclude the practice of the other members of that set, and so the incompatibility thesis does not hold for members of the set. More important, if any member of the set turns out to be *the* objective good, liberal principles of justice which permit a variety of competing goods to be practiced can be deduced from it. That is, the good can be deduced prior to liberal principles of justice and the liberal principle can be derived from the good, so long as we assume that there is an entailment relationship between a thing and its necessary conditions.

This result will not seem terribly surprising to many critics of Rawls who have frequently accused him of introducing a liberal theory of the good prior to the derivation of the principles of justice. Thomas Nagel was among the earliest to have done so,[67] and Sandel has expressed similar misgivings.[68] What Rawls calls the thin theory of the good incorporates the primary social goods which are necessary for agency regardless of a person's particular purposes. The parties in the original position are supposed to be motivated by desires to obtain the primary social goods, but not by final ends or purposes, and so they choose principles of justice which include only the former. Nagel has objected that principles of justice which depend upon a refusal to rank final ends are weighted in favor of individual inclination. Moreover, the primary social goods will not be equally effective in advancing different sorts of plans and are consequently biased toward some and against others. Those ends particularly favored by Rawls's list of primary social goods are "individualistic" according to Nagel.

We are inclined to agree with this assessment. But, while the antecedent derivation of the good may be viewed by some liberals as a defect in a theory of justice, we believe that it is an unavoidable aspect of the origination of such theories and does not adversely affect the pluralism which they are intended to support. What such theories of the good rule out are conceptions of final ends which require that the personal liberty of some be compromised, in order to advance the views of others. Leninism and Fascism are ruled out as acceptable plans of life for just this reason. For the realization of such plans will require the obstruction of the plans of most other people. The thin theory of the good prevents such interference by insisting that among its catalog of primary social goods is the greatest equal liberty of each agent, a requirement which may not be traduced by the plans of any individual.

It is our contention that what Rawls calls the thin theory of the good is a sufficiently full conception so as to place his claim that his theory of justice is developed prior to his theory of the good in considerable doubt. What the participants in the original position do not know are their particular final ends. But most theories do not equate *the* good with the particular ends of individuals which are said to realize or embody it. *The* good is a generic concept which may be instantiated in a variety of particular ends. That the participants do not know what their final ends are does not make Rawls's initial conception of the good any thinner than many theories of the good (such as Bentham's) which refuse to specify the particular ends that satisfy *the good*, but rather set forth general criteria which these ends must meet. Indeed, a sufficiently comprehensive "thin" theory of the good which fully sets forth the social and individual antecedents of agency will clearly demarcate not only just and unjust ends, but of the just ends, specify which are more and less worthy. A less morally worthy end which does not require the constriction of another's liberty for its fulfillment will not be prohibited by any principle of justice. For a less worthy end on this view is one which insufficiently supplies to its agent the necessary goods required for its realization by him. It is certainly less worthy in terms of *his* ends, but because it does not require the sacrifice of another's liberty, it is not the sort of end that must be ruled out by a principle of justice. Objective theories of the good, then, can be defined in terms of the necessary conditions of purpose fulfillment (whatever those purposes happen to be), without thereby entailing the demise of a principle of equal liberty.

This conclusion is consistent with both the more distant as well as the recent history of varieties of individualist liberalism. Locke's natural law embodies a theory of the good which implies the rights necessary to its satisfaction. Herbert Spencer specifically endorses a theory of the good from which he derives a principle of equal liberty.[69] Several examples of recent individualistic liberal theory have first deduced a theory of *the* good and then derived a principle of justice which incorporates rights to negative liberty.[70] The notion, then, that liberty is jeopardized by theories which purport

to have validated an objective conception of the good prior to their derivation of principles of justice is not supported by examples such as these.

What any conception of the good from which strong rights to negative liberty are derivable must supply in order to avoid such a threat are four components. First, it must avoid impersonal theories of the good (like utilitarianism) which may require for their realization the sacrifice of the liberty and good of some people in order to amplify an impersonally defined good. That is, goods must be agent-relative. Second, it must avoid either implicit or explicit theories of human hierarchy, which require the sacrifice of the liberty of alleged inferior members of the hierarchy to the interests of its putative superior members. Or, conversely, it must exclude the sacrificing of purported superior members to the interests of the alleged inferior. Third, it must incorporate a strong fallibility principle to avoid the claims of aspiring paternalists. And finally, among those possible ends which do not conflict with the requirements of agency, the individual must be free to select or identify which final ends he will pursue.[71]

Notes

1. See John Rawls, *A Theory of Justice* (Cambridge, Mass.: Harvard University Press, 1971), 31.
2. Ronald Dworkin, *A Matter of Principle* (Cambridge, Mass.: Harvard University Press, 1985), 191.
3. Benjamin R. Barber, *Strong Democracy* (Berkeley: University of California Press, 1984); Alasdair MacIntyre, *After Virtue* (Notre Dame: University of Notre Dame Press, 1981); Alasdair MacIntyre, *Whose Justice? Which Rationality?* (Notre Dame: University of Notre Dame Press, 1988); Frank I. Michelman, "Foreword: Traces of Self-Government," The Supreme Court: 1985 Terms, *Harvard Law Review* 100, no. 4 (1986): 4–77; Michael J. Sandel, "Democrats and Community," *The New Republic* 198, no. 8 (February 22, 1988): 20–23; Michael J. Sandel, *Liberalism and the Limits of Justice* (Cambridge: Cambridge University Press, 1982); Geoffrey R. Stone, et al., *Constitutional Law* (Boston: Little, Brown and Company, 1986); Cass R. Sunstein, "Disrupting Voluntary Transactions" (unpublished paper presented at a Liberty Fund Conference, "Liberty and Commu-

nity,'' Tucson, Arizona, June 2–5, 1988); Cass R. Sunstein, ''Interest Groups in American Public Law,'' *Stanford Law Review* 38, no. 29 (November 1985): 29–87; Cass R. Sunstein, ''Legal Interference with Private Preferences,'' *The University of Chicago Law Review* 53, no. 4 (Fall 1986): 1129–1174; Cass R. Sunstein, ''Naked Preferences and the Constitution,'' *Columbia Law Review* 84, no. 7 (November 1984): 1689–1732. We criticize Sunstein's position in a forthcoming essay, ''Sunstein's New Legal Paternalism.''

4. Rawls, ''Justice as Fairness: Political not Metaphysical,'' *Philosophy & Public Affairs* 14, no. 3 (Summer 1985): 248–249.

5. *A Theory of Justice*, 31.

6. *A Theory of Justice*, 450.

7. In *A Theory of Justice*, 201–205, Rawls connects his equal liberty principle with the notion of negative liberty as characterized by Berlin and Constant. It encompasses ''freedom of thought and liberty of conscience, freedom of the person and the civil liberties.'' Rawls does not count ''the inability to take advantage of one's rights and opportunities as a result of poverty and ignorance, and a lack of means generally . . . among the constraints definitive of liberty.''

8. In ''Sunstein's New Legal Paternalism'' (cited in note 3 above), we criticize another set of arguments, namely, those which presuppose conceptions of an objective good which is qualitatively, but not numerically, the same for all persons and which, therefore, may be separately realized by each of them. These arguments allege that each person has a real interest which makes him in this respect like his fellows, but which can be realized by him separately from them. These arguments may provide a justification for paternalistic interferences with negative liberty.

9. *After Virtue*, 241.

10. Ibid., 138.

11. Ibid., 139; compare 152, 172.

12. Ibid., 140.

13. *After Virtue*, 141. MacIntyre regards Aristotle on this point as in basic agreement with other classical Greeks, including Sophocles. See *After Virtue*, 127.

14. Ibid., 146.

15. Ibid., 147.

16. Ibid., 160.

17. Ibid., 160, 182.

18. Ibid., 152–153.

19. *After Virtue*, 152, 183. He finds similar difficulties with the medieval theory based upon supernatural teleology; see 172.

20. Ibid., ch. 14–15.

21. Ibid., 178.

22. Ibid., 183–186.

23. Ibid., 189.

24. Ibid., 204. Critics have objected that this somewhat Delphic claim does not strictly follow from what precedes it, and seems unjustifiedly partial towards the philosophical life.

25. Ibid., 204.

26. Ibid., 205.

27. *After Virtue*, 183.

28. Ibid., 205–206.

29. Ibid., 240.

30. Ibid., 213; compare MacIntyre's interpretation of Aristotle's notion of the common good on 146.

31. See ibid., 215, 219f. Apparent exceptions are the Jacobins and republicans for whom he evinces some sympathy (Ibid., 219–221).

32. Ibid., 160.

33. Ibid., 205.

34. *After Virtue*, 204–205.

35. See *After Virtue*, 127.

36. *Nicomachean Ethics* 6.8.1142a9–10 (MacIntyre trans.).

37. See *After Virtue*, 187–189.

38. Ibid., 121.

39. MacIntyre uses a similar methodology in *Whose Justice? Which Rationality?* (Notre Dame: Notre Dame University Press, 1988). T. H. Irwin advances powerful objections against this methodology in ''Tradition and Reason in the History of Ethics,'' *Social Philosophy & Policy* 7, no. 1 (1989): 45–68.

40. *After Virtue*, 205.

41. Ibid., 206.

42. John Gray, *Liberalism* (Minnesota: University of Minnesota Press, 1986), 87.

43. See *After Virtue*, 233; *A Theory of Justice*, 14.

44. *After Virtue*, 211.

45. Compare *After Virtue*, 237.

46. *After Virtue*, 211.

47. The opposition that MacIntyre discerns between practices with goods internal to themselves and commodity production is also illusory. The aeronautical engineer, computer designer, or pharmaceutical scientist in a market economy who would satisfy the preferences of consumers through his discoveries must, in order to make them, adhere to the internal disciplines and goods of his science.

48. See Nicholas Eberstadt, *The Poverty of Communism* (New Brunswick: Transaction Publishers, 1988); and Peter Rutland, *The Myth of the Plan* (LaSalle: Open Court, 1985).

49. *Liberalism and the Limits of Justice*, 25.

50. *A Theory of Justice*, 83.

51. *A Theory of Justice*, 73–74.

52. Ibid., 101.

53. Ibid., 101.

54. Ibid., 179.

55. Robert Nozick, *Anarchy, State, and Utopia* (New York: Basic Books, 1974), 228.

56. *Liberalism and the Limits of Justice*, 78.

57. Ibid., 80.

58. Ibid., 80.

59. *Liberalism and the Limits of Justice*, 172, 173.

60. *A Theory of Justice*, 74.

61. Ibid., 101.

62. Ibid., 102; emphasis added.

63. Fred D. Miller, Jr., ''The Natural Right to Private

Property,'' in *The Libertarian Reader,* ed. Tibor Machan (Totowa, N.J.: Rowman and Littlefield, 1982), 278.

64. Sandel presents no argument to demonstrate that from the fact that our self-understandings are to some extent determined by community ties and practices, it follows that all of those who share in these communal bonds and practices belong to a superindividual social organism. In order to allege plausibly the existence of such an intersubjective self comprised of individuals but greater than them, Sandel would have to demonstrate that a new ontological entity is produced from these shared understandings such that it is able to *do* the things which are commonly attributable to individuals. For example, he would have to show that the emergent entity is capable of initiating action and that this action is causally determinative of the characteristics and behavior of individuals. For unless Sandel can at least attribute *agency* to such an organism, no basis exists for alleging that it has the ontological status of individuals. Moreover, their agency could not be a *pseudo-agency* of the following sort: e.g., because the government of the society was willing to traduce and override the preferences of individual citizens in order to mobilize the population and direct it toward some social goal, it could not thereby be claimed that the "social organism" had initiated action on behalf of its constitutive and dependent citizens. That is, a genuine social action would have to be initiated by the social entity rather than by any of its constituents.

65. *A Theory of Justice,* 31.

66. *A Theory of Justice,* 31.

67. Thomas Nagel, ''Rawls on Justice,'' *Reading Rawls,* ed. Norman Daniels (New York: Basic Books, 1974), 849.

68. *Liberalism and the Limits of Justice,* 25–28, 60, 61.

69. Herbert Spencer, ''The Great Political Superstition,'' in *The Man Versus the State,* ed. Donald Macrae (New York: Penguin Books, 1969), 151–183.

70. See Eric Mack, ''How to Derive Ethical Egoism,'' *The Personalist* 52, no. 4 (Autumn 1971): 735–743; Eric Mack, ''Egoism and Rights,'' *The Personalist* 54, no. 1 (Winter 1973): 5–33; and Loren E. Lomasky, *Persons, Rights, and the Moral Community* (Oxford: Oxford University Press, 1987).

71. This essay was presented in an earlier draft at a Liberty Fund Conference on Liberty and Community in Tucson, Arizona, June 2–5, 1988, directed by Jules Coleman. We are grateful to Douglas Rasmussen and Neera Badhwar for helpful criticisms of the earlier draft.

Responsibility, Reactive Attitudes, and Liberalism in Philosophy and Politics

SAMUEL SCHEFFLER

History will record that, during the 1980s, liberalism came under sustained and politically devastating attack in the United States.[1] The bearing of this attack, if any, on contemporary liberal philosophical theories, such as those advanced by John Rawls and others, is not obvious. In part, this is because the relation between American political liberalism and contemporary philosophical liberalism is not a simple one.[2] On the one hand, nobody would wish seriously to suggest that the United States, during the period that began when Franklin Roosevelt became president and ended when Ronald Reagan did, was a well-ordered Rawlsian society, or that the social welfare programs implemented during that period gave full expression to the difference principle. Yet, at the same time, Rawl's work is naturally understood as providing a theoretical justification for many of the sorts of programs advocated by political liberals, and it would surely be a mistake to think of liberalism in the philosophical context as entirely unrelated to the liberal politics of the day. Thus it is reasonable to wonder about the philosophical relevance of the political repudiation of liberalism represented by the "Reagan revolution."

The conservatives who came to power during the 1980s are standardly interpreted as having tapped into two different sources of dis-

satisfaction with political liberalism. The first was primarily economic, and focused on liberal taxation and social welfare policies. The second was primarily social, and focused on liberal policies with respect to issues like abortion, pornography, and the role of religion in society. To the extent that social conservatives emphasized traditional values of family and community, their concerns had something in common with the opposition by communitarian philosophers to the purportedly excessive individualism of liberalism. At the same time, however, much of the dissatisfaction with political liberalism in the 1980s was due not to the belief that it was excessively individualistic but rather to the belief that it was, in an important respect, not individualistic enough. In saying this, I do not mean merely that liberalism was perceived as insufficiently individualistic in economic terms. It is certainly true, as everyone agrees and as I have said, that the overwhelming success of the political right was due to its capacity to appeal both to social conservatives and to economic conservatives. It is also true, and it has been widely noted, that the alliance between these two groups was sometimes an uneasy one, precisely because of the tension between the libertarian spirit of laissez-faire capitalism and the broadly communitarian tendency of much social conservatism. But when I say that liberalism came under attack partly because it was perceived as insufficiently individualistic, I am not just alluding to the conservative criticism of liberal economic policies. Rather, I mean that a more general conception of individual responsibility, a conception whose appeal cuts across political lines, was perceived as under threat both from liberal programs of economic redistribution and from liberal policies on certain social issues. Both types of liberal position were perceived, in effect, as resting on a reduced conception of individual agency and responsibility. And so resistance to this diminished conception of responsibility helped to fuel opposition to both parts of the liberal agenda.

Of course, many liberals would vigorously deny that the programs and policies they favor rely on a reduced conception of responsibility, as opposed to a proper understanding of the standard conception. These liberals might expect that support for their position could be found in contemporary liberal philosophical theories. I will argue in this article, however, that the reason various liberal programs may appear incompatible with ordinary thinking about responsibility is that they assign important benefits and burdens on the basis of considerations other than individual desert.[3] And, I will argue, it is noteworthy that none of the most prominent contemporary versions of philosophical liberalism assigns a significant role to desert at the level of fundamental principle. Moreover, contemporary philosophical defenses of liberalism appear to underestimate the importance of the human attitudes and emotions that find expression through our practices with respect to desert. If these claims are correct, then contemporary philosophical liberalism may provide little support for the view that liberal policies can be reconciled with ordinary notions of responsibility. Indeed, if these claims are correct, then there are deeply entrenched ideas about responsibility that have contributed to the political repudiation of liberalism, and that leading contemporary versions of philosophical liberalism simply do not accept. This suggests that, far from helping political liberals to rebut the charge of incompatibility with ordinary notions of responsibility, contemporary philosophical liberalism may itself be vulnerable to such a charge.

I

There are a variety of liberal political positions that have been perceived as incompatible with ordinary beliefs about the responsibility of an individual agent for his or her actions. For example, liberals have long been accused of responding to crime by advocating policies that emphasize the social causes of criminal behavior while neglecting the responsibility of the individual who engages in such behavior. In the area of criminal justice in particular, this emphasis is said to have manifested itself in interpretations of the insanity defense and related pleas that treat an excessively broad range of conditions and circumstances as nullifying an individual's responsibility for his or her criminal conduct. Liberalism has also been blamed, relatedly, for the growing tendency in our culture to reinterpret what were previously viewed as vices—excessive drinking or gambling, for example—as diseases or addictions, thus relocating them outside the ambit of personal responsibility. Liberal social welfare programs, meanwhile, have been accused of undermining individual responsibility by making society bear the cost of meeting its poorest members' most urgent needs. This is said to provide the poor with strong incentives to avoid making efforts to support themselves, thus producing a permanent class of dependent citizens who view social welfare programs as "entitlements," and who see no need to take responsibility for improving their own material position. Finally, liberal affirmative action programs have been perceived as implying a reduced conception of individual responsibility insofar as they award social positions and opportunities on the basis of membership in targeted social groups rather than on the basis of individual effort, merit, or achievement. Thus, on some of the most important and intensely controversial social issues of the day, the liberal position has met with resistance at least in part because of a perception that it rests on an attenuated conception of personal responsibility.

To avoid misunderstanding, let me emphasize that I am not endorsing the criticisms of liberalism that I have mentioned. I am merely calling attention to the range of liberal positions and policies that have been subject to political attack on the ground of their supposed incompatibility with ordinary principles of personal responsibility. In so doing, I am trying to focus attention on an important question that arises for liberals about the form that their response to such criticisms should take. Should liberals dispute the charge that the policies they advocate are incompatible with the standard conception of personal responsibility, or should they instead concede that the alleged incompatibility is genuine, but argue that this reveals a flaw in the standard conception rather than in liberalism?

As a matter of political strategy, liberals may well be reluctant to present their position as resting on a reduced conception of responsibility. For any such conception would appear to run counter to the dominant ethos of American society. The extraordinary litigiousness of modern-day America has been widely commented upon. In combination with other features of the prevailing cultural climate, it has led some observers to conclude that Americans no longer believe in simple bad luck, but think instead that any misfortune that befalls a person must be somebody's fault. Offhand, this would not seem to be a promising climate in which to argue the virtues of a reduced conception of responsibility. Admittedly, it may be argued that much of the litigiousness of American society has been made possible by developments in tort law that have themselves been taken to illustrate the erosion of traditional standards of responsibility. Yet the erosion of those standards cannot plausibly be said to explain the prevalence of the underlying litigious impulse, still less the wider impulse to blame and find fault. It is true, as earlier noted, that there has been a growing tendency in our society to extend the concept of *disease* to certain patterns of behavior that were previously regarded as vices, thus narrowing the scope of individual responsibility in some areas. Yet, at the same time, countervailing tendencies have also developed, including, interestingly enough, a sharply increased level of moralizing about personal health itself: with the individual's habits of diet and exercise, for example, treated increasingly as appropriate objects of moral approval or disapproval. Thus, in short, although the perceived boundaries of individual responsibility are to some extent in flux, and although, as the political controversies we are discussing indicate, there is a widespread sense that traditional notions of responsibility are under attack and that their influence is eroding, there is no evidence that the impulse to employ the concepts and categories of responsibility is disappearing or even diminishing significantly in strength.

In view of these considerations, it would seem that the more promising political strategy for liberals would be to present the policies they advocate as compatible with traditional notions of responsibility. This would presumably mean arguing that any appearance of incompatibility is due to a failure properly to interpret the implications of those notions. The question, however, is whether this argument can be successfully made. In the case of each of the liberal policies I have mentioned, the appearance of incompatibility arises, as I have said, from the fact that the policy in question assigns important benefits or burdens on the basis of considerations other than those of individual desert. In order to reconcile these policies with ordinary notions of responsibility, what liberals would need to argue is not that we should, in general, be skeptics about desert, but rather that ordinary principles of desert, properly understood, do not have the policy implications in these cases that critics of liberalism suppose them to have. Many liberals would undoubtedly say that they are fully prepared to offer such arguments. As I shall attempt to show, however, it is a striking fact that, according to the dominant philosophical defenses of liberalism that are current today, desert has no role whatsoever to play in the fundamental normative principles that apply to the basic social, political, and economic institutions of society. This suggests that political liberals can expect to receive little assistance from contemporary liberal philosophers as they attempt to demonstrate the compatibility of their agenda with ordinary notions of desert and responsibility. And this cannot but raise the question of whether there is any theoretically defensible interpretation of liberalism that would support such a demonstration.

Of course, philosophical defenses of liberalism continue to be offered, as they always have been, from a variety of importantly different perspectives. My claim, however, is that none of the major strands in contemporary liberal philosophy assigns a significant role to desert at the level of fundamental principle. This is most obvious in the case of the utilitarian strand. Although Rawlsian liberalism explicitly defines itself in opposition to utilitarianism, there is of course an important tradition of utilitarian support for liberal institutions that extends from Mill to the present day. Yet there is no form of utilitarianism that treats desert as a basic moral concept. Indeed, utilitarianism as it is most naturally interpreted presents a radical challenge to ordinary notions of responsibility. On the one hand, utilitarianism greatly widens the scope of individual responsibility, insofar as it treats the outcomes that one fails to prevent as no less important in determining the rightness or wrongness of one's actions than the outcomes that one directly brings about. On the other hand, the responsibility whose scope is thus widened is also quite shallow, on the utilitarian view, for assignments of responsibility carry no direct implications of blame or desert, and amount to little more in themselves than judgments about the optimality of acts. The shallowness of utilitarian responsibility is reflected in J. J. C. Smart's well-known comment that "the notion of *the* responsibility [for an outcome] is a piece of metaphysical nonsense."[4] This does not mean that utilitarians are incapable of recognizing that, in order to function efficiently, a social institution or cooperative scheme may need to assign distinct functions and roles to different individuals, thus producing a clear division of responsibility among the participants in that institution or scheme. Nor need utilitarians deny that there are often sound reasons for social institutions to distribute benefits and burdens

of certain types in accordance with publicly acknowledged standards of individual merit or demerit, or that when they do so, individuals who meet the relevant criteria or standards may be said to deserve the benefit or burden in question. But here desert is understood as an institutional artifact rather than as one of the normative bases of institutional design.

For the purposes of my argument, it is an important fact that the most influential contemporary proponent of a purely institutional view of desert is not a utilitarian at all, but is rather Rawls himself. As is well known, Rawls maintains in *A Theory of Justice* that it is "one of the fixed points of our considered judgments that no one deserves his place in the distribution of native endowments any more than one deserves one's initial starting point in society."[5] He takes this uncontroversial judgment to imply that the better endowed also do not deserve the greater economic advantages that their endowments might enable them to amass under certain possible institutional arrangements. According to Rawls, the "principles of justice that regulate the basic structure [of society] and specify the duties and obligations of individuals do not mention moral desert," or desert of any other kind for that matter.[6] Nevertheless, he says:

It is perfectly true that given a just system of cooperation as a scheme of public rules and the expectations set up by it, those who, with the prospect of improving their condition, have done what the system announces that it will reward are entitled to their advantages. In this sense the more fortunate have a claim to their better situation; their claims are legitimate expectations established by social institutions, and the community is obligated to meet them. But this sense of desert presupposes the existence of the cooperative scheme; it is irrelevant to the question . . . [of how] in the first place the scheme is to be designed.[7]

On this way of understanding desert, the idea that social institutions should be designed in such a way as to ensure that people get what they deserve makes about as much sense as the idea that universities were created so that professors would have somewhere to turn in their grades, or that baseball was invented in order to ensure that batters with three strikes would always be out.

The fact that Rawlsian and utilitarian liberals agree about the derivative status of desert suffices to establish this view as the prevailing liberal orthodoxy in philosophy. This does not mean, however, that it has attracted no opposition. The best-known criticism of Rawls's position on desert is the one developed by Robert Nozick in *Anarchy, State, and Utopia*.[8] Nozick is especially critical of the way Rawls moves from the premise that people do not deserve their "natural assets" to the conclusion that they do not deserve the advantages that those assets may enable them to amass. "It needn't be," Nozick writes, "that the foundations underlying desert are themselves deserved, *all the way down*."[9] Yet when Nozick develops his own conception of distributive justice, the concept of desert once again plays no role. Instead, he argues that individuals are "entitled" to their natural assets whether or not they can be said to deserve them, and that they are also entitled, within limits, to the "holdings" that those assets enable them to acquire.

Although Nozick's libertarian conception of justice is not a liberal position in the sense we are discussing, it does of course belong to the older tradition of Lockean liberalism, to which the version of liberalism that we are considering stands in a complex relationship both historically and conceptually. And if there is any position capable of laying claim to the term *liberal* that might be expected to assign an important role to the concept of desert, it is surely this type of Lockean libertarianism. It is therefore a remarkable fact that the most conspicuous contemporary proponent of such a position makes no more use of the notion of desert in elaborating his own view of distributive justice than do the Rawlsian and utilitarian positions he so severely criticizes. It is even more remarkable when one considers that these three positions—Nozick's, Rawls's, and the utilitarian's—represent three of the four viewpoints that, taken together, have dominated American political philosophy for the last twenty years.

Nor do things look very different when we consider the fourth position, communitarianism. Readers of Michael Sandel's influential book *Liberalism and the Limits of Justice*[10] might be tempted to think otherwise. In that book, Sandel provides an extended critique of Rawlsian liberalism from a communitarian perspective, and he devotes considerable attention both to Rawls's treatment of desert and to Nozick's criticism of that treatment. The main thrust of Sandel's argument is that Rawls's treatment of desert is an outgrowth of his reliance on an unsatisfactory conception of the self: a conception that leaves the self "too thin to be capable of desert."[11] In Sandel's view, the Rawlsian self is a "pure subject of possession," whose identity is fixed independently of the aims, attributes, and attachments that it happens to have.[12] Conceived of in this way, the self is said to lack any features by virtue of which it could be thought to deserve anything; it is a mere "condition of agency standing beyond the objects of its possession."[13] "Claims of desert," by contrast, "presuppose thickly-constituted selves," whose very identity is in part determined by their particular aims, attachments, and loyalties.[14]

Since Sandel thinks that we "cannot coherently regard ourselves"[15] in the way that he believes Rawls requires us to do, but must instead regard ourselves as "thickly-constituted," one might expect that he would then go on to assign a more important role to desert than Rawls does. Yet that is just what he does not do. In the course of a discussion of affirmative action, he considers the "meritocratic" position "that the individual possesses his attributes in some unproblematic sense and therefore deserves the benefits that flow from them, and that part of what it means for an institution or distributive scheme to be just is that it rewards individuals antecedently worthy of reward."[16] Rather than endorsing these propositions, Sandel says that "Rawls and Dworkin present powerful arguments against these assumptions which defenders of meritocracy would be hard-pressed to meet."[17] And although Sandel reiterates his claim that the liberal vision provided by philosophers like Rawls and Dworkin nevertheless depends on unsatisfactory notions of community and the self, nowhere does he actually argue that a proper understanding of community and self would vindicate the conception of desert that Rawls and Dworkin reject.[18]

Not only, then, do the main lines of contemporary philosophical liberalism agree in avoiding any appeal to a preinstitutional conception of desert—any appeal, that is, to an independent standard of desert by reference to which the justice of institutional arrangements is to be measured—but, moreover, some of the most prominent critics of contemporary liberalism also shy away from such appeals. And they do so even when, like Sandel, they see the liberal rejection of preinstitutional desert as associated with an unsatisfactory conception of the self, and even when, like Nozick, they are clearly sympathetic to the idea of preinstitutional desert. How is this surprising degree of convergence to be explained? Doubtless there are a number of factors at work, no single one of which will suffice to explain the thinking of each and every philosopher. However, I believe that there is one factor that any adequate explanation of the general phenomenon will need to cite, and that is the influence of naturalism. The widespread reluctance among political philosophers to defend a robust notion of preinstitutional desert is due in part to the power in contemporary philosophy of the idea that human thought and action may be wholly subsumable within a broadly naturalistic view of the world. The reticence of these philosophers—their disinclination to draw on any preinstitutional notion of desert in their theorizing about justice—testifies in part to the prevalence of the often unstated conviction that a thoroughgoing naturalism leaves no room for a conception of individual agency substantial enough to sustain such a notion. This problem, the problem of the relation between naturalism and individual agency, is of course a descendant of the problem of determinism and free will. Or, more accurately perhaps, it is the variant of that problem that seems most urgent from a contemporary standpoint. Thus my suggestion is that the reluctance of many contemporary political philosophers to rely on a preinstitutional notion of desert results in part from a widespread though often implicit skepticism about individual agency, a form of skepticism that is the contemporary descendant of skepticism about freedom of the will.

It might be thought an objection to this diagnosis that the same contemporary philosophers who avoid any reliance on desert nevertheless make heavy use of other moral notions, including notions of rights, justice, equality, and the like. As in the case of free will and determinism, however, the moral notions that seem most directly threatened by modern naturalistic outlooks are the notions of desert and responsibility. That is because the threat to morality posed by such outlooks proceeds via their threat to individual agency, and of all moral notions, the notions of desert and responsibility are the ones that depend most obviously and immediately on an understanding of what human agency involves. Thus if the internalization of a broadly naturalistic outlook were going to produce skepticism about any single aspect of morality, this would surely be the one. Of course, it might be argued that, in the end, naturalism supports skepticism about desert only if it also supports skepticism about moral thought more generally, so that it is ultimately inconsistent to forswear any reliance on desert while continuing to use other moral notions as before. Even if this is correct, however, it does not impugn the diagnosis I have offered. For, as I have said, desert and responsibility are the moral notions that are most conspicuously threatened by a thoroughgoing naturalism. So whether or not their position is ultimately consistent, it is not implausible that political philosophers whose justificatory ambitions give them every reason to resist skepticism about morality in general, but who have also absorbed a broadly naturalistic view of the place of human beings in the world, should register their uneasiness about the implications of naturalism through a reluctance to rely on any preinstitutional notion of desert.

II

If the diagnosis just offered is correct, then the project of reconciling the policies advocated by political liberals with traditional ideas about individual responsibility is one that contemporary philosophical liberals are poorly equipped to undertake. For they reject the preinstitutional notion of desert on which the traditional ideas rely, and, if I am right, they do so, at least in part, out of a sense that, given our best current understanding of how the world works, that preinstitutional notion can no longer be taken seriously. The defense of political liberalism would therefore appear to require either a liberal theory unlike those that dominate contemporary political philosophy or a frank repudiation of traditional ideas about responsibility, at least insofar as those ideas rely on a preinstitutional notion of desert. I have already argued that such a repudiation is unlikely to be popular politically. However, this invites a further question. If indeed the repudiation of traditional ideas about responsibility would be politically unpopular, is that owing to contingent features of the present political climate, or do those ideas have a deeper and more securely entrenched hold on our thought?

There is at least some reason to think that the latter may be the case. This can be seen most readily by considering the relation between the conception of desert advocated by contemporary philosophical liberals and some of the attitudes recommended by a familiar form of ''compatibilism'' about free will and determinism. As against those who believe that the truth of determinism would leave no room for traditional notions of desert and responsibility, and would, therefore, undermine our existing practices of moral praise and blame, one standard version of compatibilism holds that even if determinism were true, such practices would continue to be justified by virtue of their social efficacy or utility. As P. F. Strawson has noted,[19] however, far from reassuring those ''pessimists'' who see determinism as posing a threat to our practices of praise and blame, this compatibilist argument seems to them not to provide ''a sufficient basis, . . . or even the right *sort* of basis, for these practices as we understand them.''[20] For the argument represents the practices in question ''as instruments of policy, as methods of individual treatment and social control.''[21] And, Strawson says, pessimists react to this representation with both

conceptual and emotional shock: conceptual shock, because the compatibilist construal omits an important feature of our actual concepts of praise and blame, and emotional shock, because this omission suggests that compatibilism, if accepted, would require a drastic change in human attitudes and personal relations. What the compatibilist construal leaves out is any acknowledgment of the fact that our actual practices of moral praise and blame, in addition to having social utility, serve to express a variety of feelings and attitudes, such as gratitude, resentment, and indignation, liability to which is essential to participation in most of the types of human relationship that we value most deeply.[22] Strawson refers to these emotions as ''reactive attitudes,'' because, he says, they are reactions to the attitudes and intentions of others, either toward ourselves or toward third parties. When we do not regard an individual as capable of participating in ordinary human relationships, because, for example, of some extreme psychological abnormality, then the reactive attitudes tend to be inhibited and replaced by an ''objective attitude'' in which the person is viewed, in a clinical spirit, as someone to be managed or treated or controlled. The compatibilist construal of our practices of moral praise and blame is unnerving because the exclusively instrumental role that it assigns to those practices would be appropriate only in a relationship in which the reactive attitudes were absent and a thoroughgoing objectivity of attitude prevailed. Thus the effect of that construal is to convince pessimists that determinism may threaten not only our existing practices of praise and blame but also the wide range of ordinary human relationships that could not exist if, as this version of compatibilism appears to require, the reactive attitudes were systematically suspended.

Strawson himself believes that, in the end, such pessimism is unwarranted, for the reactive attitudes as a whole neither need nor admit of any justification, and so no thesis of determinism could possibly give us a reason to suspend them, still less ''require'' us to do so. If certain influential compatibilist formulations treat our practices of praise and blame in isolation from their connections to the reactive attitudes, that is just a defect in those formulations. It does not testify to any genuine incompatibility between determinism and the attitudes themselves.

Much as I admire Strawson's article, I find myself more persuaded by his diagnosis of what troubles pessimists about the form of compatibilism he discusses than by his conclusion that pessimism is in the end unwarranted. My aim here, however, is not to argue against that conclusion. It is rather to call attention to the way in which the issues Strawson raises are relevant to debates about liberalism. What makes them relevant is the close connection between the compatibilist construal of praise and blame to which Strawson objects and the purely institutional conception of desert favored by liberal philosophers. Strawson's compatibilist seeks to justify the practices whereby we hold people responsible or accountable for their actions by reference to the social utility of such practices. Liberal philosophers, meanwhile, regard the defensibility of the practices whereby we treat individuals who behave in certain ways as deserving certain rewards or penalties as entirely dependent on the prior defensibility of the social institutions that are said to give rise to those practices.[23] In each case, the assignment of benefits and burdens in accordance with a conception of merit or desert is seen as requiring justification by reference to something putatively more fundamental: either to the utility of such assignments or to their placement within a larger institutional framework that is thought of as independently justifiable. In neither case is a conception of merit or desert treated as morally fundamental or as an independent normative constraint on the design of social institutions.

It is true that liberal philosophers, or at least those liberal philosophers whose orientation is not utilitarian, need not conceive of our practices with respect to merit and desert in the narrowly instrumental way that is characteristic of what Strawson calls "the objective attitude." In this respect, their position differs from the type of compatibilist position that Strawson criticizes. Yet it resembles that position in the ways that I have described, and

this is sufficient to raise the question of whether it too is insufficiently sensitive to the role of the relevant practices in giving expression to our reactive attitudes. Admittedly, some liberal philosophers who reject the idea of preinstitutional desert in favor of the notion of legitimate institutional expectations would nevertheless agree that punishment, at least, has an important "expressive function."[24] Yet these philosophers need to show that the reactive attitudes whose expression through the institution of punishment they acknowledge do not rest on just the sorts of assumptions about preinstitutional desert that they reject. Offhand, it would seem that if the punishment of a murderer or a rapist, say, serves to express the community's outrage and indignation, it does so by answering to the thought that the perpetrator *deserves* a severe penalty, where this does not mean merely that he has reason to expect one. Furthermore, the liberal philosophers I am discussing do not treat desert-based judgments about the assignment of social and economic benefits as serving to express significant interpersonal reactions at all. Yet it is clear that judgments to the effect that certain individuals do or do not deserve certain benefits have an important expressive function in many contexts. This might not present a problem for liberals if the reactive attitudes were sufficiently plastic that they were capable of finding full expression via whatever system of institutional expectations and entitlements happened to be in place. To the extent that those attitudes are less than fully flexible, however, any purely institutional conception of desert runs the risk of conflicting with them, and hence of presenting itself as incompatible with a web of fundamental interpersonal responses. Thus, if liberalism proposes to replace our ordinary notion of desert with the idea of legitimate institutional expectations, and if that proposal meets with political resistance, the possibility cannot be excluded that such resistance is responsive in part to an underlying tension between liberalism and the reactive attitudes, rather than stemming exclusively from contingent features of the prevailing political climate.

The upshot of the discussion to this point

may be summarized as follows. Political liberalism has come under heavy attack in this country owing in part to a perception that many of the programs and policies advocated by liberals rest on a reduced conception of individual responsibility. Although some liberals might wish to reject this perception as erroneous, it is a striking fact that the dominant contemporary philosophical defenses of liberalism, by virtue of their reliance on a purely institutional notion of desert, do indeed advocate a reduced conception of responsibility. And in so doing, they may to some extent be underestimating the significance of the human attitudes and emotions that find expression through our practices with respect to desert and responsibility. If so, then two conclusions seem to follow. The first is that contemporary philosophical liberalism may be vulnerable to a criticism not unlike the one that has been directed at contemporary political liberalism. The second is that the prospects of political liberalism might best be served, not by additional arguments in favor of a purely institutional conception of desert, but rather by a demonstration that liberal programs and policies do not in fact require such a conception.

As I have indicated, these conclusions could perhaps be avoided, at least in the case of liberal principles of distributive justice, if it could be shown that the reactive attitudes were sufficiently plastic as to render them fully compatible with an institutional system of economic expectations that was insensitive to any independent considerations of desert. It is unclear whether a convincing argument to this effect is available. To the best of my knowledge, the closest thing to such an argument that one finds in contemporary liberal theory is Rawls's argument for the stability of his conception of justice.[25] That argument turns on the claim that citizens in a well-ordered society regulated by Rawlsian principles would acquire a more effective sense of justice than would citizens in societies ordered by other conceptions of justice, most notably utilitarianism. In order to establish this claim, Rawls sketches an account of the development of the moral sentiments with the aim of demonstrating that an effective sense of justice would be

the normal outcome of the processes of moral development in a Rawlsian society. Rawls's account emphasizes the intimate relation between the sense of justice and reactive attitudes like shame, guilt, and resentment, and he takes pains to argue that these attitudes would tend to develop in a well-ordered society in such a way that, in their mature form, they would naturally come to be regimented by the Rawlsian principles of justice. That is, people would feel guilty if they violated those principles, they would feel resentful of violations committed by others, and so on. Rawls takes the psychological plausibility of his account to depend on the idea that his principles of justice embody an ideal of reciprocity or mutuality, and it is therefore natural that he should contrast his account primarily with the moral psychology of utilitarianism. For the ideas of reciprocity and mutuality have no fundamental ethical significance for utilitarianism, and as a result utilitarian moral psychology seems forced to make implausibly heavy demands on the human capacity for sympathetic identification. In so doing, utilitarianism seems to underestimate the psychological constraints on the design of stable social and political institutions, and Rawls's account has great force by comparison. Yet Rawls never explicitly addresses the question whether his own repudiation of preinstitutional desert may not itself involve such an underestimation, albeit one of a less extreme sort. In other words, he never explicitly considers, and thus never convincingly rules out, the possibility, first, that our judgments about the proper distribution of benefits and burdens in society may, in addition to regimenting our reactive attitudes, serve as a vehicle for expressing those attitudes; and, second, that the attitudes in question may rest on an assumption that individuals are responsible agents in a sense that implies that their distributive shares ought to be influenced in certain ways by their behavior.[26] Here it seems relevant to note that, whereas Strawson says that resentment and other reactive attitudes are "essentially reactions to the quality of others' wills toward us,"[27] resentment in political contexts—whether it arises on the left or on the right—is more often a reaction to (what are perceived as) the *undeserved advantages* of others, and not to the quality of their wills at all.

III

There is some irony in the fact that the difficulty to which I have been calling attention arises for nonutilitarian versions of contemporary liberal theory. For such theories tend to appeal to people who regard utilitarianism's aggregative character as rendering it incapable of providing a tolerably secure foundation for individual rights, and who regard its instrumental, goal-oriented structure as rendering it incapable of attaching sufficient weight, or the right kind of weight, to those features of human life and personal relations about which we care most. Many such people would view the failure of familiar forms of compatibilism to appreciate either the role of our practices of praise and blame in giving expression to our reactive attitudes or the role of the reactive attitudes in human interpersonal relations as an unsurprising consequence of the instrumental, utilitarian character of those compatibilist formulations. In this way, they would see the failings of such formulations as serving to illustrate the very sorts of considerations that make nonutilitarian versions of liberal theory look attractive. Hence the irony in the fact that those versions of liberalism may themselves be insufficiently sensitive to the significance of the reactive attitudes in relation to our notions of desert and responsibility.

Even if this is granted, of course, it may be thought to reveal nothing more important than the existence of an internal tension in the views of a certain group of people. However, I believe that the tension between philosophical liberalism and ordinary notions of desert and responsibility has wider significance, for three main reasons. The first reason, which I have already emphasized, is that the prospects of political liberalism may depend in part on how this tension is resolved. This will be so, at any rate, at least insofar as it is contemporary philosophical liberalism, with its disavowal of preinstitutional desert, that is seen as providing the theoretical foundation for the positions and policies advocated by political liberals.

The second reason is that an appreciation of the tension between liberalism and desert helps to illuminate the intense philosophical controversy surrounding liberalism's alleged ''neutrality'' among competing ''conceptions of the good.'' Liberalism's claims to neutrality have always struck critics of varying persuasions as involving a certain degree of bad faith. There are a number of reasons for this, but one of the most important is that liberalism seems to many of its critics to presuppose a conception of human life and an understanding of the place of human beings in the world that is itself in conflict with many conceptions of the good. To these critics, the difficulty is not that liberalism directly endorses some particular conception of the good or directly condemns some other conception. The fundamental problem arises much earlier, at the stage at which liberalism defines the ''individuals'' among whose conceptions of the good it purports to be neutral. To its critics, the liberal framework itself seems to incorporate an understanding of what it is to be a human individual that is highly contentious, and that leads inevitably to the design of institutions and the creation of conditions that are far more hospitable to some ways of life than to others. The argument I have been developing in this article reveals one of the bases for this criticism. For, as I have said, the unwillingness of liberal philosophers to rely on any preinstitutional conception of desert is due in part to their internalization of a broadly naturalistic outlook, and to their skeptical understanding of how robust a notion of individual agency is compatible with such an outlook. Yet a purely naturalistic understanding of human life *is* contentious. The modern world is deeply divided in its attempt to come to terms with the power of naturalism, and one of the defining features of modern life is a deep uneasiness about what place there may be for our selves and our values in the world that science is in the process of discovering. It is clear, moreover, that different conceptions of the good respond to this uneasiness in very different ways. Thus if liberalism does presuppose a naturalistically based skepticism about individual agency, it is hardly surprising that its claims to neutrality among diverse conceptions of the good should seem suspect. Moreover, although the political prospects of liberalism might be improved if liberal policies could be defended by appeal to a more robust conception of agency and responsibility, there would be no gain in neutrality if liberalism were seen to rest upon such a conception. For as long as a purely naturalistic understanding of human life remains controversial—as long as the place of human beings in the world of science is subject to debate—*no* conception of agency and responsibility can claim to be neutral among conceptions of the good. This may seem to imply that, in order to preserve its neutrality, liberalism should refrain from endorsing any conception of individual agency or responsibility. However, even if such absti nence were a conceptual possibility, as it almost certainly is not,[28] it would have the peculiar effect of reducing liberalism to silence on the very subject that was supposed to be its specialty, namely, the nature and moral importance of the individual human agent.

The third reason why the tension between philosophical liberalism and ordinary notions of desert and responsibility is significant is that it raises a philosophically and politically important question about the moral psychology of liberalism. I have already argued that the question of the plasticity of the reactive attitudes assumes great importance for liberal philosophers in view of their reliance on a purely institutional conception of desert. However, this is really but an instance of a more general challenge facing liberalism. The more general challenge is to allay the suspicion that the interpersonal attitudes that liberals value in the private sphere may be psychologically continuous with social and political attitudes whose implications are uncongenial to liberalism. The suggestion that our reactive attitudes may presuppose a preinstitutional notion of desert that is incompatible with liberal principles of justice represents one way in which this suspicion can arise. Another way in which it can arise is via the suggestion that the very same psychological proclivities that lead people to develop personal loyalties and attachments may also lead them to develop forms of group identifi-

cation and allegiance that liberalism cannot easily accommodate. The suggestion, in other words, is that the psychology of friendship and close personal relations is also the psychology of communal solidarity and partiality. This suggestion receives support from communitarianism in the domain of theory, and from the rise of nationalism and multiculturalism in the domain of political practice. Indeed, it is at this point that the communitarian criticism of liberalism and the desert-based criticism begin to converge. For each sees liberalism as demanding, at the level of political interaction, an individual psychology of bland impartiality: a psychology that is thoroughly unrealistic, and that would be incapable, even if it *were* realistic, of sustaining the rich interpersonal relations that liberals are prepared to celebrate in the realm of private life.[29]

IV

I should emphasize that my aim in this article has not been to defend the preinstitutional notion of desert that is embedded in traditional conceptions of responsibility. Indeed, liberals (among whom I number myself) may well be right to be skeptical of this notion, and, hence, of the traditional conceptions that rely on it. My aim has merely been to call attention to the extent of such skepticism among liberals, and to its significance. Before concluding, however, let me address two objections to my argument that will long since have occurred to the reader. The first objection is that my characterization of contemporary liberal philosophy as having internalized a naturalistically based skepticism about individual agency and responsibility cannot possibly be correct, at least as applied to the liberalism of Rawls. For, especially in those writings that postdate *A Theory of Justice,* Rawls takes pains to emphasize the Kantian roots of his theory, and to highlight the role played in that theory by a conception of citizens as "free and equal moral persons." Moreover, he says it is a feature of that conception that citizens "are regarded as taking responsibility for their ends and [that] this affects how their various claims are assessed.''[30] Thus it may seem clearly inaccurate to represent Rawls as relying on an attenuated conception of agency and responsibility.

In response, however, I would make two points. First, the doctrine of "responsibility for ends," as Rawls presents it, does not involve any preinstitutional conception of desert, nor is it intended as an independent constraint on the design of just institutions. Instead, it simply amounts to the claim that

given just background institutions and the provision for all of a fair index of primary goods (as required by the principles of justice), citizens are capable of adjusting their aims and ambitions in the light of what they can reasonably expect and of restricting their claims in matters of justice to certain kinds of things. They recognize that the weight of their claims is not given by the strength or intensity of their wants and desires, even when they are rational.[31]

Rawls's argument in this passage is that people have the capacity to adjust their aims and aspirations in light of their institutional expectations, provided that the institutions in question are just. The purpose of this argument is to explain why a reliance on primary goods as an index of well-being is not inappropriate, despite the fact that someone with unusually expensive tastes and preferences may derive less satisfaction from a given bundle of those goods than someone with more modest tastes and preferences. Rawls's claim is that just institutions need make no special provision for expensive preferences, not because individuals are responsible in some preinstitutional sense for their own preferences, but rather because people living in a just society have the capacity to adjust their preferences in light of the resources they can expect to have at their command. To be sure, this capacity may itself be preinstitutional in some sense. However, there is an important difference between the claim that people possess preinstitutional capacities that would enable them to adapt to a certain institutional assignment of responsibility and the claim that the assignment of responsibility is itself preinstitutional. Thus, whatever one thinks of Rawls's argument, there is, as far as

I can see, nothing in it that has any tendency to vindicate traditional notions of responsibility or desert.[32]

A similar conclusion applies, incidentally, to Ronald Dworkin's treatment of expensive tastes. Dworkin appears at one point to express sympathy for the position that people do not *deserve* compensation for expensive tastes, or at least for those expensive tastes that they have deliberately cultivated. However, it quickly emerges that, for Dworkin, the claim that some individual does not deserve compensation for his expensive tastes may be legitimate only insofar as it is based on a judgment that the individual in question has already received what has independently been identified as his fair share of social resources.[33] For Dworkin, in other words, there is no prior standard of desert that determines what counts as a fair share or as a just institutional arrangement. Thus Dworkin does not appeal to a preinstitutional conception of desert any more than do the other liberal theorists we have discussed.[34]

Returning to Rawls, the other point I want to make is simply that, although his broadly Kantian conception of the person may well be incompatible with the attenuated notion of individual agency to which I have referred, explicit endorsement of the former is compatible with tacit reliance on the latter. Insofar as Rawls's unwillingness to accept preinstitutional desert gives rise to a reduced conception of individual responsibility, any tension between such a conception and Rawls's Kantian ideal of the person must be viewed as a tension internal to his theory. Moreover, a tension of this sort seems likely to afflict any form of liberalism that defers at crucial points to the authority of a naturalistic outlook, while seeking simultaneously to situate itself within the philosophical tradition of Kant.[35]

The second objection that I wish very briefly to address may be put as follows. If, as I have argued, there is a surprising degree of agreement among contemporary philosophical liberals and their critics about the advisability of avoiding any appeal to preinstitutional desert, then why should it be a special problem for political liberalism if it too avoids any such appeal? The answer is that although liberalism's most prominent philosophical critics may be reluctant to appeal to preinstitutional desert, its most prominent political critics certainly are not. On the contrary, conservative politicians do not hesitate to invoke traditional notions of desert and responsibility in attacking liberal positions. Thus if political liberalism does require the rejection of preinstitutional desert, then although it will be in tune with the prevailing philosophical consensus, that may not suffice to prevent its political isolation. Indeed, if one takes the view that our reactive attitudes require a preinstitutional conception of desert that is incompatible with a broadly naturalistic outlook, then, to the extent that political liberalism reflects the prevailing philosophical consensus, pessimism about the philosophical implications of naturalism may translate into pessimism about the political prospects of liberalism.

Notes

Earlier versions of this article were presented to audiences at the University of Arizona, the University of California at Davis, the University of California at Santa Barbara, the University of Washington, and the Boalt Hall School of Law at the University of California at Berkeley. I am grateful to all of these audiences for valuable discussion, which prompted numerous improvements. In addition, I received enormously helpful written comments, for which I am greatly indebted, from G. A. Cohen, Eric Rakowski, T. M. Scanlon, and the Editors of *Philosophy & Public Affairs*.

1. Similar developments also occurred, to one degree or another, in some of the other western democracies, most notably Great Britain. But I will limit my discussion to the United States, which is where the philosophical debate about liberalism was most active during the period in question.

2. In recent work Rawls has distinguished between "political liberalism," which is said not to depend on any "comprehensive moral doctrine," and "comprehensive liberalism," which does so depend. See "Justice as Fairness: Political Not Metaphysical," *Philosophy & Public Affairs* 14, no. 3 (Summer 1985): 223–51, and "The Idea of an Overlapping Consensus," *Oxford Journal of Legal Studies* 7 (1987): 1–25. His own view is said to be an instance of the former, while those of Kant and Mill are cited as examples of the latter. The distinction I am drawing is, as should be evident, a different one. I am concerned with the relations be-

tween liberalism as a position in American political life and liberalism as a view in contemporary political philosophy. In this sense, Rawls's view is an example of philosophical liberalism.

3. For illuminating discussion of many issues concerning desert, see Joel Feinberg, "Justice and Personal Desert," in his *Doing and Deserving* (Princeton: Princeton University Press, 1970), pp. 55–94; and George Sher, *Desert* (Princeton: Princeton University Press, 1987).

4. J. C. C. Smart, "An Outline of a System of Utilitarian Ethics," in J. C. C. Smart and Bernard Williams, *Utilitarianism: For and Against* (Cambridge: Cambridge University Press, 1973), p. 54.

5. John Rawls, *A Theory of Justice* (Cambridge, Mass.: Harvard University Press, 1971), p. 104.

6. Ibid., p. 311.

7. Ibid., p. 103. Curiously, Rawls appears to suggest (on pp. 314–15) that reliance on a preinstitutional conception of desert *is* appropriate in the case of retributive justice, despite the fact that it is inappropriate in the case of distributive justice. As Michael Sandel argues (in *Liberalism and the Limits of Justice* [Cambridge: Cambridge University Press, 1982], pp. 89–92), it is very difficult to see what basis Rawls has for making this distinction, since the considerations that lead him to reject preinstitutional desert in the case of distributive justice seem to apply with equal force to the case of retributive justice. And, as T. M. Scanlon observes, "Rawls' theory of distributive justice" employs "a general philosophical strategy" that is equally available in the retributive case:

In approaching the problems of justifying both penal and economic institutions we begin with strong pretheoretical intuitions about the significance of choice: voluntary and intentional commission of a criminal act is a necessary condition of just punishment, and voluntary economic contribution can make an economic reward just and its denial unjust. One way to account for these intuitions is by appeal to a preinstitutional notion of desert: certain acts deserve punishment, certain contributions merit rewards, and institutions are just if they distribute benefits and burdens in accord with these forms of desert.

The strategy I am describing makes a point of avoiding any such appeal. The only notions of desert which it recognizes are internal to institutions and dependent upon a prior notion of justice: if institutions are just then people deserve the rewards and punishments which those institutions assign them. In the justification of institutions, the notion of desert is replaced by an independent notion of justice; in the justification of specific actions and outcomes it is replaced by the idea of legitimate (institutional) expectations. ("The Significance of Choice," in *The Tanner Lectures on Human Values VIII*, ed. Sterling McMurrin [Salt Lake City: University of Utah Press, 1988], p. 188)

Scanlon himself is generally sympathetic to the strategy he describes, and his own account of the "significance of choice" also avoids any reliance on a preinstitutional notion of desert. Because Rawls's view of retributive justice is not developed at any length and plays virtually no role in the overall argument of his book, and because it is dubiously consistent with his account of distributive justice, I will not devote any further attention to it. I regard it as a small and insufficiently motivated departure from the general attitude toward desert that dominates his work and the work of the other liberal theorists with whom I am concerned.

8. Robert Nozick, *Anarchy, State, and Utopia* (New York: Basic Books, 1974).

9. Ibid., p. 225.

10. Cited in note 7.

11. Sandel, *Liberalism and the Limits of Justice*, p. 178.

12. Ibid., p. 85.

13. Ibid., p. 93.

14. Ibid., p. 178.

15. Ibid., p. 65.

16. Ibid., p. 139.

17. Ibid.

18. Alasdair MacIntyre may be cited as a critic of liberalism who endorses a robust notion of desert and who does so within the context of a broadly communitarian framework. It is certainly true that MacIntyre calls attention to the absence in contemporary theories of justice, especially those of Rawls and Nozick, of any significant role for desert, and that he attaches great significance to this omission. However, it cannot be said that MacIntyre develops a rival theory of justice for our society that does assign a fundamental role to desert. He is more concerned to persuade us of how far-reaching a repudiation of modern political thought would be necessary in order to embrace such a conception. Indeed, he believes that the tradition of thought in which the concept of desert is most securely situated requires "a rejection of the modern political order" altogether (*After Virtue*, 2d ed. [Notre Dame, Ind.: University of Notre Dame Press, 1984], p. 237). His argument therefore provides not a counterexample to, but rather additional support for, my thesis about the extent of skepticism within contemporary political philosophy about the concept of desert.

19. In "Freedom and Resentment," *Proceedings and Addresses of the British Academy* 48 (1962): 1–25, reprinted in *Free Will*, ed. Gary Watson (Oxford: Oxford University Press, 1982), pp. 59–80. References to Strawson's essay will be to the reprinting in Watson's volume.

20. Ibid., p. 62.

21. Ibid., p. 76.

22. Feinberg makes some closely related points in "Justice and Personal Desert" and in "The Expressive Function of Punishment" (in his *Doing and Deserving*, pp. 95–118), although he is not concerned in those essays with questions about freedom of the will.

23. As noted earlier, Rawls would apparently take this view only of our practices with respect to distributive justice, and not of our practices with respect to retributive justice. Other liberal philosophers would take the same view of both. Although I doubt that Rawls can consistently restrict his rejection of preinstitutional desert to the distributive case alone, the problem I am describing arises even on the assumption that he can.

24. An example is Scanlon in "The Significance of Choice."

25. In chapter 8 of *A Theory of Justice*.

26. In an unpublished manuscript ("Justice as Fairness: A Restatement" [Cambridge, Mass., 1990], pp. 58–64), Rawls says that he does not reject preinstitutional desert altogether; he merely denies that it can play any role in a "political" conception of justice designed for a modern, pluralistic democracy, and believes that it must be replaced for the purposes of such a conception by the idea of legitimate expectations. This seems to me to represent a significant departure from the views expressed in *A Theory of Justice*, at (for example) pp. 312–13. And, in any case, it leaves the question I have raised in the text unanswered.

27. Strawson, "Freedom and Resentment," p. 70.

28. The "almost" is a mark of my respect for the "method of avoidance" employed by Rawls in "Justice as Fairness: Political Not Metaphysical" and subsequent writings. The "certainly" is a measure of my skepticism about whether that method can successfully be extended to the issue at hand.

29. In "Foundations of Liberal Equality" (in *The Tanner Lectures on Human Values XI*, ed. Grethe Peterson [Salt Lake City: University of Utah Press, 1990], pp. 3–119, esp. sec. 2), Ronald Dworkin addresses the apparent discontinuity between what he calls the "personal" and "political" perspectives in liberal thought.

30. Rawls, "Justice as Fairness: Political Not Metaphysical," p. 243.

31. John Rawls, "Kantian Constructivism in Moral Theory: The Dewey Lectures 1980," *Journal of Philosophy* 77 (1980): 545. See also his "Fairness to Goodness," *Philosophical Review* 84 (1975): 551–54; "A Kantian Conception of Equality," *Cambridge Review* 96 (1975): 96–97; "Social Unity and Primary Goods," in *Utilitarianism and Beyond*, ed. Amartya Sen and Bernard Williams (Cambridge: Cambridge University Press, 1982), pp. 167–70; and "Justice as Fairness: Political Not Metaphysical," pp. 243–44.

32. For a discussion of Rawls's argument that I take to support this conclusion, see Scanlon, "The Significance of Choice," pp. 197–201. (See also Scanlon's "Preference and Urgency," *Journal of Philosophy* 72 [1975]: 655–69.) G. A. Cohen would apparently disagree with my reading of Rawls, for he says, in commenting on a passage similar to the one I have quoted in the text, that Rawls's "picture of the individual as responsibly

guiding his own taste formation is hard to reconcile with . . . the skepticism which he expresses about extra reward for extra benefit'' ("On the Currency of Egalitarian Justice," *Ethics* 99 [1989]: 914). If, as I believe, Rawls's doctrine of responsibility for ends does not rely on a preinstitutional conception of desert or responsibility, then it need not conflict with his refusal to reward effort per se.

33. Ronald Dworkin, "What Is Equality? Part I: Equality of Welfare," *Philosophy & Public Affairs* 10, no. 3 (Summer 1981): 237–40.

34. G. A. Cohen argues that we should "distinguish among expensive tastes according to whether or not their bearer can reasonably be held responsible for them" ("On the Currency of Egalitarian Justice," p. 923). He also argues that although Dworkin's solution to the problem of expensive tastes rests explicitly on a distinction between preferences and resources, nevertheless Dworkin's position owes what plausibility it has to the fact that the notions of choice and responsibility lie in the background of his discussion, "doing a good deal of unacknowledged work" (ibid., p. 928). Indeed, Cohen concludes that, despite his reliance on the preferences/resources distinction, "Dworkin has, in effect, performed for egalitarianism the considerable service of incorporating within it the most powerful idea in the arsenal of the anti-egalitarian right: the idea of choice and responsibility. But that supreme effect of his contribution needs to be rendered more explicit" (ibid., p. 933). In my view, Dworkin's

avoidance of preinstitutional desert, especially when combined with his explicit reliance on the preferences/resources distinction, casts serious doubt on the idea that he has incorporated the same conception of responsibility relied on by the "anti-egalitarian right." Of course, this is compatible with Cohen's claim that, "insofar as [Dworkin] succeeds in making his cut [between preferences and resources] plausible, it is by obscuring . . . the differences between it" and a distinction that emphasizes the importance of responsibility (ibid., p. 922).

35. Rawls's recent assertion (see note 26) that he does not *reject* preinstitutional desert, but merely believes that it is too controversial to play any role in a political conception of justice designed for a modern pluralistic democracy, may seem to provide another reason for thinking that my claim about the influence of naturalism cannot be correct. As I indicated in note 26, however, I believe that Rawls's recent discussion understates the extent of the skepticism about preinstitutional desert that is expressed in *A Theory of Justice*. Nor is there any hint in *A Theory of Justice* that Rawls's reason for avoiding preinstitutional desert is that he believes the notion to be too controversial to play a role in a political conception of justice. In any event, my claim about the influence of naturalism is not a claim about the explicit premises of liberal arguments, nor does it purport to be an exhaustive statement of the factors responsible for the liberal aversion to preinstitutional desert.

The Domain of the Political and Overlapping Consensus

JOHN RAWLS

In this article, I shall examine the idea of an overlapping consensus[1] and its role in a political conception of justice for a constitutional regime. A political conception, I shall suppose, views the political as a special domain with distinctive features that call for the articulation within the conception of the characteristic values that apply to that domain. Justice as fairness, the conception presented in my book *A Theory of Justice* [*Theory*][2], is an example of a political conception and I refer to it to fix ideas. By going over these matters I hope to allay misgivings about the idea of an overlapping consensus, especially the misgiving that it makes political philosophy political in the wrong way.[3] That is, this idea may suggest to some the view that consensus politics is to be taken as regulative and that the content of first principles of justice should be adjusted to the claims of the dominant political and social interests.

This misgiving may have resulted from my having used the idea of an overlapping consensus without distinguishing between two stages in the exposition of justice as fairness and without stressing that the idea of an overlapping consensus is used only in the second. To explain: in the first stage justice as fairness should be presented as a free-standing political conception that articulates the very great values

applicable to the special domain of the political, as marked out by the basic structure of society. The second stage consists of an account of the stability of justice as fairness, that is, its capacity to generate its own support,[4] in view of the content of its principles and ideals as formulated in the first stage. In this second stage the idea of an overlapping consensus is introduced to explain how, given the plurality of conflicting comprehensive religious, philosophical, and moral doctrines always found in a democratic society—the kind of society that justice as fairness itself enjoins—free institutions may gain the allegiance needed to endure over time.

I. Four General Facts

I begin with some background. Any political conception of justice presupposes a view of the political and social world, and recognizes certain general facts of political sociology and human psychology. Four general facts are especially important.

The first fact is that the diversity of comprehensive religious, philosophical, and moral doctrines found in modern democratic societies is not a mere historical condition that may soon pass away; it is a permanent feature of the public culture of democracy. Under the political

John Rawls, ''The Domain of the Political and Overlapping Consensus,'' 64 N.Y.U. L. Rev. 233 (1989). Reprinted by permission of the author and *New York University Law Review*.

and social conditions that the basic rights and liberties of free institutions secure, a diversity of conflicting and irreconcilable comprehensive doctrines will emerge, if such diversity does not already exist. Moreover, it will persist and may increase. The fact about free institutions is the fact of pluralism.

A second and related general fact is that only the oppressive use of state power can maintain a continuing common affirmation of one comprehensive religious, philosophical, or moral doctrine. If we think of political society as a community when it is united in affirming one and the same comprehensive doctrine, then the oppressive use of state power is necessary to maintain a political community. In the society of the Middle Ages, more or less united in affirming the Catholic faith, the Inquisition was not an accident; preservation of a shared religious belief demanded the suppression of heresy. The same holds, I believe, for any comprehensive philosophical and moral doctrine, even for secular ones. A society united on a form of utilitarianism, or on the liberalism of Kant or Mill, would likewise require the sanctions of state power to remain so.

A third general fact is that an enduring and secure democratic regime, one not divided into contending doctrinal confessions and hostile social classes, must be willingly and freely supported by at least a substantial majority of its politically active citizens. Together with the first general fact, this means that for a conception of justice to serve as the public basis of justification for a constitutional regime, it must be one that widely different and even irreconcilable comprehensive doctrines can endorse. Otherwise the regime will not be enduring and secure. As we shall see later, this suggests the need for what I have referred to as a political conception of justice.[5]

A fourth fact is that the political culture of a reasonably stable democratic society normally contains, at least implicitly, certain fundamental intuitive ideas from which it is possible to work up a political conception of justice suitable for a constitutional regime. This fact is important when we come to specify the general features of a political conception of

justice and to elaborate justice as fairness as such a view.

II. The Burdens of Reason

These facts, especially the first two—namely, the fact that a diversity of comprehensive doctrines is a permanent feature of a society with free institutions, and that this diversity can be overcome only by the oppressive use of state power—call for explanation. For why should free institutions with their basic rights and liberties lead to diversity, and why should state power be required to suppress it? Why does our sincere and conscientious attempt to reason with one another fail to lead us to agreement? It seems to lead to agreement in science, or if disagreement in social theory and economics often seems intractable, at least—in the long run—in natural science.

There are, of course, several possible explanations. We might suppose that most people hold views that advance their own more narrow interests; and since their interests are different, so are their views. Or perhaps people are often irrational and not very bright, and this mixed with logical errors leads to conflicting opinions.

But such explanations are too easy, and not the kind we want. We want to know how reasonable disagreement is possible, for we always work at first within ideal theory. Thus we ask: how might reasonable disagreement come about?

One explanation is this. We say that reasonable disagreement is disagreement between reasonable persons, that is, between persons who have realized their two moral powers[6] to a degree sufficient to be free and equal citizens in a democratic regime, and who have an enduring desire to be fully cooperating members of society over a complete life. We assume such persons share a common human reason, similar powers of thought and judgment, a capacity to draw inferences and to weigh evidence and to balance competing considerations, and the like.

Now the idea of reasonable disagreement involves an account of the sources, or causes, of disagreement between reasonable persons. These sources I shall refer to as the "burdens of reason." The account of these burdens must be such that it is fully compatible with, and so does not impugn, the reasonableness of those who disagree among themselves.

What, then, goes wrong? If we say it is the presence of prejudice and bias, of self- and group-interest, of blindness and willfulness—not to mention irrationality and stupidity (often main causes of the decline and fall of nations)—we impugn the reasonableness of at least some of those who disagree. We must discover another explanation.

An explanation of the right kind is that the burdens of reason, the sources of reasonable disagreement among reasonable persons, are the many hazards involved in the correct (and conscientious) exercise of our powers of reason and judgment in the ordinary course of political life. Except for the last two sources below, the ones I mention now are not peculiar to reasoning about values; nor is the list I give complete. It covers only the more obvious sources of reasonable disagreement:

(a) The evidence—empirical and scientific—bearing on the case may be conflicting and complex, and hence hard to assess and evaluate.

(b) Even where we agree fully about the kinds of considerations that are relevant, we may disagree about their weight, and so arrive at different judgments.

(c) To some extent all of our concepts, not only our moral and political concepts, are vague and subject to hard cases; this indeterminacy means that we must rely on judgment and interpretation (and on judgments about interpretations) within some range (not itself sharply specifiable) wherein reasonable persons may differ.

(d) To some unknown extent, our total experience, our whole course of life up to now, shapes the way we assess evidence and weigh moral and political values, and our total experiences surely differ. Thus, in a modern society with its numerous offices and positions, its various divisions of labor, its many social groups and often their ethnic variety, the total experiences of citizens are disparate enough for their judgments to diverge, at least to some degree, on many if not most cases of any significant complexity.

(e) Often there are different kinds of normative considerations of different force on both sides of a question and it is difficult to make an overall assessment.[7]

(f) Finally, since any system of social institutions can admit only a limited range of values, some selection must be made from the full range of moral and political values that might be realized. This is because any system of institutions has, as it were, but a limited social space. In being forced to select among cherished values, we face great difficulties in setting priorities, and other hard decisions that may seem to have no clear answer.[8]

These are some sources of the difficulties in arriving at agreement in judgment, sources that are compatible with the full reasonableness of those judging. In noting these sources—these burdens of reason—we do not, of course, deny that prejudice and bias, self- and group-interest, blindness and willfulness, play an all-too-familiar part in political life. But these sources of unreasonable disagreement stand in marked contrast to sources of disagreement compatible with everyone's being fully reasonable.

I conclude by stating a fifth general fact: we make many of our most important judgments subject to conditions which render it extremely unlikely that conscientious and fully reasonable persons, even after free discussion, can exercise their powers of reason so that all arrive at the same conclusion.

III. Precepts of Reasonable Discussion

Next I consider how, if we are reasonable, we should conduct ourselves in view of the plain facts about the burdens of reason. I suppose that, as reasonable persons, we are fully aware of these burdens, and try to take them into account. On this basis we recognize certain precepts to govern deliberation and discussion. A few of these follow.

First, the political discussion aims to reach reasonable agreement, and hence so far as possible it should be conducted to serve that aim. We should not readily accuse one another of self- or group-interest, prejudice or bias, and of such deeply entrenched errors as ideological blindness and delusion. Such accusations arouse resentment and hostility, and block the way to reasonable agreement. The disposition to make such accusations without compelling grounds is plainly unreasonable, and often a declaration of intellectual war.

Second, when we are reasonable we are prepared to find substantive and even intractable disagreements on basic questions. The first general fact means that the basic institutions and public culture of a democratic society specify a social world within which opposing general beliefs and conflicting comprehensive doctrines are likely to flourish and may increase in number. It is unreasonable, then, not to recognize the likelihood—indeed the practical certainty—of irreconcilable reasonable disagreements on matters of the first significance. Even when it seems that agreement should in principle be possible, it may be unattainable in the present case, at least in the foreseeable future.[9]

Third, when we are reasonable, we are ready to enter discussion crediting others with a certain good faith. We expect deep differences of opinion, and accept this diversity as the normal state of the public culture of a democratic society. To hate that fact is to hate human nature, for it is to hate the many not unreasonable expressions of human nature that develop under free institutions.[10]

I have suggested that the burdens of reason sufficiently explain the first two general facts—the facts of pluralism, given free institutions, and the necessity of the oppressive use of state power to maintain a political community (a political society united on a comprehensive doctrine)—whatever further causes those facts might have. Those facts are not, then, mere historical contingencies. Rather, they are rooted in the difficulties of exercising our reason under the normal conditions of human life.

IV. Features of a Political Conception of Justice

Recall that the third general fact was that an enduring and stable democratic regime is one that at least a substantial majority of its politically active citizens freely support. Given this fact, what are the more general features of a political doctrine underlying a regime able to gain such allegiance? Plainly, it must be a doctrine that a diversity of comprehensive religious, philosophical, and moral doctrines can endorse, each from its own point of view.[11] This follows not only from the third general fact but also from the first, the fact of pluralism: for a democratic regime will eventually, if not from the outset, lead to a pluralism of comprehensive doctrines.

Let us say that a political conception of justice (in contrast to a political regime) is stable if it meets the following condition: those who grow up in a society well-ordered by it—a society whose institutions are publicly recognized to be just, as specified by that conception itself—develop a sufficient allegiance to those institutions, that is, a sufficiently strong sense of justice guided by appropriate principles and ideals, so that they normally act as justice requires, provided they are assured that others will act likewise.[12]

Now what more general features of a political conception of justice does this definition of stability suggest? The idea of a political conception of justice includes three such features:[13]

First, while a political conception of justice is, of course, a moral conception, it is worked out for a specific subject, namely, the basic structure of a constitutional democratic regime. This structure consists in society's main political, social, and economic institutions, and how they fit together into one unified system of social cooperation.

Second, accepting a political conception of justice does not presuppose accepting any particular comprehensive doctrine. The conception presents itself as a reasonable conception for the basic structure alone.[14]

Third, a political conception of justice is formulated so far as possible solely in terms of certain fundamental intuitive ideas viewed as implicit in the public political culture of a democratic society. Two examples are the idea of society as a fair system of social cooperation over time from one generation to the next, and the idea of citizens as free and equal persons fully capable of engaging in social cooperation over a complete life. (That there are such ideas is the fourth general fact.) Such ideas of society and citizen are normative and political ideas; they belong to a normative political conception, and not to metaphysics or psychology.[15]

Thus the distinction between political conceptions of justice and other moral conceptions is a matter of scope, that is, of the range of subjects to which a conception applies, and of the wider content which a wider range requires. A conception is said to be general when it applies to a wide range of subjects (in the limit, to all subjects); it is comprehensive when it includes conceptions of what is of value in human life, ideals of personal virtue and character, and the like, that inform much of our nonpolitical conduct (in the limit, our life as a whole).

Religious and philosophical conceptions tend to be general and fully comprehensive; indeed, their being so is sometimes regarded as a philosophical ideal to be attained. A doctrine is fully comprehensive when it covers all recognized values and virtues within one rather precisely articulated scheme of thought; whereas a doctrine is partially comprehensive when it comprises certain, but not all, nonpolitical values and virtues and is rather loosely articulated. By definition, then, for a conception to be even partially comprehensive it must extend beyond the political and include nonpolitical values and virtues.

Keeping these points in mind, political liberalism tries to articulate a workable political conception of justice. The conception consists in a view of politics and of the kind of political institutions which would be most just and appropriate when we take into account the five general facts. From these facts rises the need to found social unity on a political conception that can gain the support of a diversity of comprehensive doctrines. Political liberalism is not, then, a view of the whole of life: it is not a (fully or partially) comprehensive doctrine.

Of course, as a liberalism, it has the kind of content we historically associate with liberalism. It affirms certain basic political and civil rights and liberties, assigns them a certain priority, and so on. Justice as fairness begins with the fundamental intuitive idea of a well-ordered society as a fair system of cooperation between citizens regarded as free and equal. This idea together with the five general facts shows the need for a political conception of justice, and such a conception in turn leads to the idea of "constitutional essentials," as we may refer to them.

A specification of the basic rights and liberties of citizens—rights and liberties they are to have in their status as free and equal—falls under those essentials. For such rights and liberties concern the fundamental principles that determine the structure of the political process—the powers of the legislative, executive and the judiciary, the limits and scope of majority rule, as well as the basic political and civil rights and liberties legislative majorities must respect, such as the right to vote and to participate in politics, freedom of thought and liberty of conscience, and also the protections of the rule of law.

These matters are a long story; I merely mention them here. The point is that a political understanding of the constitutional essentials is of utmost urgency in securing a workable basis of fair political and social cooperation between citizens viewed as free and equal. If a political conception of justice provides a reasonable framework of principles and values for resolving questions concerning these essentials—and this must be its minimum objective—then a diversity of comprehensive doctrines may endorse it. In this case a political conception of justice is already of great significance, even though it may have little specific to say about innumerable economic and social issues that legislative bodies must regularly consider.

V. The Special Domain of the Political

The three features of a political conception[16] make clear that justice as fairness is not applied moral philosophy. That is, its content—its principles, standards, and values—is not presented as an application of an already elaborated moral doctrine, comprehensive in scope and general in range. Rather, it is a formulation of a family of highly significant (moral) values that properly apply to basic political institutions; it gives a specification of those values which takes account of certain special features of the political relationship, as distinct from other relationships.

The political relationship has at least two significant features:

First, it is a relationship of persons within the basic structure of society, a structure of basic institutions we enter only by birth and exit only by death (or so we may appropriately assume).[17] Political society is closed, as it were; and we do not, and indeed cannot, enter or leave it voluntarily.

Second, the political power exercised within the political relationship is always coercive power backed by the state's machinery for enforcing its laws. In a constitutional regime political power is also the power of equal citizens as a collective body. It is regularly imposed on citizens as individuals, some of whom may not accept the reasons widely thought to justify the general structure of political authority (the constitution), some of whom accept that structure, but do not regard as well grounded many of the statutes and other laws to which they are subject.

Political liberalism holds, then, that there is a special domain of the political identified by at least these features. So understood, the political is distinct from the associational, which is voluntary in ways that the political is not; it is also distinct from the personal and the familial, which are affectional domains, again in ways the political is not.[18]

Taking the political as a special domain, let us say that a political conception formulating its basic values is a "free-standing" view. It is a view for the basic structure that formulates its values independent of non-political values and of any specific relationship to them. Thus a political conception does not deny that there are other values that apply to the associational, the personal, and the familial; nor does it say that the political is entirely separate from those values. But our aim is to specify the special domain of the political in such a way that its main institutions can gain the support of an overlapping consensus.

As a form of political liberalism, then, justice as fairness holds that, with regard to the constitutional essentials, and given the existence of a reasonably well-ordered constitutional regime, the family of very great political values expressed by its principles and ideals normally will have sufficient weight to override all other values that may come into conflict with them. Justice as fairness also holds, again with respect to constitutional essentials, that so far as possible, questions about those essentials should be settled by appeal to those political values alone. For it is on those questions that agreement among citizens who affirm opposing comprehensive doctrines is most urgent.

Now, in holding these convictions we clearly imply some relation between political and non-political values. Thus, if it is said that outside the church there is no salvation,[19] and that hence a constitutional regime, with its guarantees of freedom of religion, cannot be accepted unless it is unavoidable, we must make some reply. From the point of view of political liberalism, the appropriate reply is to say that the conclusion is unreasonable:[20] it proposes to use the public's political power— a power in which citizens have an equal share—to enforce a view affecting constitutional essentials about which citizens as reasonable persons, given the burdens of reason, are bound to differ uncompromisingly in judgment.

It is important to stress that this reply does not say that a doctrine *Extra ecclesiam nulla salus* is not true. Rather, it says that it is unreasonable to use the public's political power to enforce it. A reply from within an alternative comprehensive view—the kind of reply we should like to avoid in political discussion—

would say that the doctrine in question is incorrect and rests on a misapprehension of the divine nature. If we do reject the enforcement by the state of a doctrine as unreasonable we may of course also regard that doctrine itself as untrue. And there may be no way entirely to avoid implying its lack of truth, even when considering constitutional essentials.[21]

Note, however, that in saying it is unreasonable to enforce a doctrine, we do not necessarily reject it as incorrect, though we may do so. Indeed, it is vital to the idea of political liberalism that we may with perfect consistency hold that it would be unreasonable to use political power to enforce our own comprehensive religious, philosophical or moral views—views which we must, of course, affirm as true or reasonable (or at least as not unreasonable).

VI. How Is Political Liberalism Possible?

The question now arises, how, as I have characterized it, is political liberalism possible? That is, how can the values of the special domain of the political—the values of a subdomain of the realm of all values—normally outweigh any values that may conflict with them? Or put another way: how can we affirm our comprehensive doctrines as true or reasonable and yet hold that it would not be reasonable to use the state's power to gain the allegiance of others to them?[22]

The answer to this question has two complementary parts. The first part says that values of the political are very great values indeed and hence not easily overridden. These values govern the basic framework of social life, "the very groundwork of our existence,"[23] and specify the fundamental terms of political and social cooperation. In justice as fairness some of these great values are expressed by the principles of justice for the basic structure: the values of equal political and civil liberty, of fair equality of opportunity, of economic reciprocity, the social bases of mutual respect among citizens, and so on.

Other great values fall under the idea of free public reason, and are expressed in the guidelines for public inquiry and in the steps taken to secure that such inquiry is free and public, as well as informed and reasonable. These values include not only the appropriate use of the fundamental concepts of judgment, inference, and evidence, but also the virtues of reasonableness and fair-mindedness as shown in the adherence to the criteria and procedures of common sense knowledge, and to the methods and conclusions of science when not controversial, as well as respect for the precepts governing reasonable political discussion.[24]

Together these values give expression to the liberal political ideal that since political power is the coercive power of free and equal citizens as a corporate body, this power should be exercised, when constitutional essentials are at stake, only in ways that all citizens can reasonably be expected to endorse publicly in the light of their own common, human reason.[25]

So far as possible, political liberalism tries to present a free-standing account of these values as those of a special domain—the political. It is left to citizens individually, as part of their liberty of conscience, to settle how they think the great values of the political domain relate to other values within their comprehensive doctrine. We hope that by doing this we can, in working political practice, firmly ground the constitutional essentials in those political values alone, and that these values will provide a satisfactory shared basis of public justification.

The second part of the answer as to how political liberalism is possible complements the first. This part says that the history of religion and philosophy shows that there are many reasonable ways in which the wider realm of values can be understood so as to be either congruent with, or supportive of, or else not in conflict with, the values appropriate to the special domain of the political as specified by a political conception of justice for a democratic regime. History tells of a plurality of not unreasonable comprehensive doctrines. That these comprehensive doctrines are divergent makes an overlapping consensus necessary. That they are not unreasonable makes it possible. A model case of an overlapping consensus of the kind I have considered elsewhere shows how this is so.[26] Many other such cases could make the same point.

VII. The Question of Stability

Justice as fairness, as I have said, is best presented in two stages.[27] In the first stage it is worked out as a free-standing political (but of course moral) conception for the basic structure of society. Only when this is done and its content—its principles of justice and ideals—is provisionally on hand do we take up, in the second stage, the problem of stability and introduce the idea of an overlapping consensus: a consensus in which a diversity of conflicting comprehensive doctrines endorse the same political conception, in this case, justice as fairness.

In describing the second stage, let us agree that a political conception must be practicable, that is, must fall under the art of the possible. This contrasts with a moral conception that is not political; a moral conception may condemn the world and human nature as too corrupt to be moved by its precepts and ideals.

There are, however, two ways in which a political conception may be concerned with stability.[28] In one way, we suppose that stability is a purely practical matter: if a conception fails to be stable, it is futile to try to base a political structure upon it. Perhaps we think there are two separate tasks: one is to work out a political conception that seems sound, or reasonable, at least to us; the other is to find ways to bring others who reject the conception to share it in due course, or failing that, to act in accordance with it, prompted if need be by penalties enforced by state power. As long as the means of persuasion or enforcement can be found, the conception is viewed as stable; it is not utopian in the pejorative sense.

But as a liberal conception, justice as fairness is concerned with stability in a second, very different way. Finding a stable conception is not simply a matter of avoiding futility. Rather, what counts is the kind of stability and the nature of the forces that secure it. The idea is that, given certain assumptions specifying a reasonable human psychology[29] and the normal conditions of human life, those who grow up under basic institutions that are just—institutions that justice as fairness itself enjoins—acquire a reasoned and informed allegiance to those institutions sufficient to render the institutions stable. Put another way, the sense of justice of citizens, in view of their traits of character and interests as formed by living under a just basic structure, is strong enough to resist the normal tendencies to injustice. Citizens act willingly so as to give one another justice over time. Stability is secured by sufficient motivation of the appropriate kind acquired under just institutions.[30]

The kind of stability required of justice as fairness is based, then, on its being a liberal political view, one that aims at being acceptable to citizens as reasonable and rational, as well as free and equal, and so addressed to their free public reason. Earlier we saw how this feature of liberalism connects with the feature of political power in a constitutional regime, namely, that it is the power of equal citizens as a collective body. It follows that if justice as fairness were not expressly designed to gain the reasoned support of citizens who affirm reasonable although conflicting comprehensive doctrines—the existence of such conflicting doctrines being a feature of the kind of public culture which that conception itself encourages—it would not be liberal.[31]

The point, then, is that, as a liberal conception, justice as fairness must not merely avoid futility; the explanation of why it is practicable must be of a special kind. The problem of stability is not the problem of bringing others who reject a conception to share it, or to act in accordance with it, by workable sanctions if necessary—as if the task were to find ways to impose that conception on others once we are ourselves convinced it is sound. Rather, as a liberal political conception, justice as fairness relies for its reasonableness in the first place upon generating its own support in a suitable way by addressing each citizen's reason, as explained within its own framework.[32]

Only in this manner is justice as fairness an account of political legitimacy. Only so does it escape being a mere account of how those who hold political power can satisfy themselves, in the light of their own convictions, whether political or fully comprehensive, that they are acting properly—satisfy themselves, that is, and not citizens generally.[33] A conception of political legitimacy aims for a public basis of justification and appeals to free public reason, and hence to all citizens viewed as reasonable and rational.

VIII. Comparison with *A Theory of Justice*

It may seem that the idea of an overlapping consensus and related topics are a significant departure from *Theory*. They are some departure certainly; but how much? *Theory* never discusses whether justice as fairness is meant as a comprehensive moral doctrine or as a political conception of justice. In one place it says that if justice as fairness succeeds reasonably well, a next step would be to study the more general view suggested by the name "rightness as fairness."[34]

But *Theory* holds that even this view would not be fully comprehensive: it would not cover, for example, our relations to other living things and to the natural order itself.[35] *Theory* emphasizes the limited scope of justice as fairness, and the limited scope of the kind of view it exemplifies; the book leaves open the question of how far its conclusions might need revision once these other matters are taken into account. There is, however, no mention of the distinction between a political conception of justice and a comprehensive doctrine. The reader might reasonably conclude, then, that justice as fairness is set out as part of a comprehensive view that may be developed later were success to invite.

This conclusion is supported by the discussion of the well-ordered society of justice as fairness in Part III of *Theory*.[36] There it is assumed that the members of any well-ordered society, whether it be a society of justice as fairness or of some other view, accept the same conception of justice and also, it seems, the same comprehensive doctrine of which that conception is a part, or from which it can be derived. Thus, for example, all the members of a well-ordered society associated with utilitarianism (classical or average) are assumed to affirm the utilitarian view, which is by its nature (unless expressly restricted) a comprehensive doctrine.

Although the term was introduced in another context,[37] the idea of an overlapping consensus was first introduced to think of the well-ordered society of justice as fairness in a different and more realistic way.[38] Given the free institutions which that conception itself enjoins, we can no longer assume that citizens generally, even if they accept justice as fairness, also accept the particular comprehensive view in which it might seem to be embedded in *Theory*. We now assume citizens hold two distinct views; or perhaps better, we assume their overall view has two parts. One part can be seen to be, or to coincide with, a political conception of justice; the other part is a (fully or partially) comprehensive doctrine to which the political conception is in some manner related.[39]

The political conception may be simply a part of, or an adjunct to, a partially comprehensive view; or it may be endorsed because it can be derived within a fully articulated comprehensive doctrine. It is left to citizens individually to decide for themselves in what way their shared political conception is related to their wider and more comprehensive views. A society is well-ordered by justice as fairness so long as, first, citizens who affirm reasonable comprehensive doctrines generally endorse justice as fairness as giving the content of their political judgments; and second, unreasonable comprehensive doctrines do not gain enough currency to compromise the essential justice of basic institutions.

This is a better and no longer utopian way of thinking of the well-ordered society of justice as fairness. It corrects the view in *Theory,* which fails to take into account the condition of pluralism to which its own principles lead.

Moreover, because justice as fairness is now seen as a free-standing political conception that articulates fundamental political and constitutional values, endorsing it involves far less than is contained in a comprehensive doctrine. Taking such a well-ordered society as the aim of reform and change does not seem altogether impracticable; under the reasonably favorable conditions that make a constitutional regime possible, that aim is a reasonable guide and may be in good part realized. By contrast, a free democratic society well ordered by any comprehensive doctrine, religious or secular, is surely utopian in a pejorative sense. Achieving it would, in any case, require the oppressive use of state power. This is as true of the liberalism of rightness as fairness, as it is of the Christianity of Aquinas or Luther.

IX. In What Sense Political?

To trace our steps, I put before you this brief summary.[40] I have suggested that once we recognize the five general facts[41] and the inevitable burdens of reason even under favorable conditions,[42] and once we reject the oppressive use of state power to impose a single comprehensive doctrine as the way to achieve social unity, then we are led to democratic principles and must accept the fact of pluralism as a permanent feature of political life. Hence, to achieve social unity for a well-ordered democratic regime, what I have called political liberalism introduces the idea of an overlapping consensus and along with it the further idea of the political as a special domain. Political liberalism does this not only because its content includes the basic rights and liberties the securing of which leads to pluralism, but also because of the liberal ideal of political legitimacy, namely, that social cooperation, at least as it concerns the constitutional essentials, is to be conducted so far as possible on terms both intelligible and acceptable to all citizens as reasonable and rational. Those terms are best stated by reference to the fundamental political and constitutional values (expressed by a political conception of justice) that, given the diversity of comprehensive doctrines, all citizens may still be reasonably expected to endorse.

We must, however, be careful that a political conception is not political in the wrong way. It should aim to formulate a coherent view of the very great (moral) values applying to the political relationship and to set out a public basis of justification for free institutions in a manner accessible to free public reason. It must not be political in the sense of merely specifying a workable compromise between known and existing interests, nor political in looking to the particular comprehensive doctrines

known to exist in society and in then being tailored to gain their allegiance.

In this connection let us ensure that the assumptions about pluralism do not make justice as fairness political in the wrong way. Consider first the five general facts reviewed in Parts I and II. These we suppose are accepted from the point of view of you and me as we try to develop justice as fairness. When the original position is viewed as a device of representation, these facts are made available to the parties in that position as they decide which principles of justice to select. So if principles that require free democratic institutions are accepted in the first stage, then the account of the stability in the second stage must show how justice as fairness can be endorsed by an overlapping consensus. As we have seen, this follows because free institutions themselves lead to pluralism.

The crucial question, then, is whether the five general facts, along with other premises allowed by the constraints of the original position in the first stage, suffice to lead the parties to select the two principles of justice;[43] or whether certain further assumptions related to pluralism are also needed, assumptions that make justice as fairness political in the wrong way. I cannot settle this matter here; it would require a survey of the argument from the original position.

I believe we need only suppose in the first stage that the parties assume the fact of pluralism to obtain, that is, that a plurality of comprehensive doctrines exists in society.[44] The parties must then protect against the possibility that the person each party represents may be a member of a religious, ethnic, or other minority. This suffices for the argument for the equal basic liberties to get going. In the second stage, when stability is considered, the parties again assume that pluralism obtains. They confirm principles leading to a social world that allows free play to human nature and thus, we hope, encourages a diversity of reasonable rather than unreasonable comprehensive doctrines, given the burdens of reason.[45] This makes stability possible.

Now it is often said that the politician looks to the next election, the statesman to the next generation. To this we add that the student of philosophy looks to the standing conditions of human life, and how these affect the burdens of reason. Political philosophy must take into account the five general facts we noted, among them the fact that free institutions encourage a diversity of comprehensive doctrines. But in doing this we abstract from the particular content of these doctrines, whatever it may be, and from the many contingencies under which the doctrines exist. A political conception so arrived at is not political in the wrong way but suitably adapted to the public political culture that its own principles shape and sustain. And although such a conception may not apply to all societies at all times and places, this does not make it historicist, or relativist; rather, it is universal in virtue of its extending appropriately to specify a reasonable conception of justice among all nations.

X. Concluding Remarks

The foregoing shows, I think, that the freedoms discussed have a dual role. On the one hand, they are the result of the working out, at the most basic level (in what I called the first stage of justice as fairness), of the fundamental ideas of a democratic society as a fair system of cooperation between citizens as free and equal. On the other hand, in the second stage, we know on the basis of general facts and the historical condition of the age that a conception of political justice leading to free institutions must be acceptable to a plurality of opposing comprehensive doctrines. That conception must, therefore, present itself as independent of any particular comprehensive view and must firmly guarantee for all citizens the basic rights and liberties as a condition of their sense of security and their peaceful, mutual recognition.

As the first role is perhaps clearer than the second, I comment on the latter. We know from the burdens of reason that even in a well-ordered society, where the basic freedoms are secure, sharp political disagreement will persist on their more particular interpretation. For instance, where exactly should the line be drawn between church and state? Or, granting there is no such crime as seditious libel, who pre-

cisely belongs to the class of public persons in regard to whom the law of libel is relaxed? Or, what are the limits of protected speech? So the question arises: if disagreements on such constitutional essentials always remain, what is gained by a publicly recognized political conception? Isn't the aim—to underwrite the basic rights and liberties of citizens by achieving an overlapping consensus, thereby giving everyone the sense that their rights are indeed secure—still unresolved?

There are two replies to this. First, by securing the basic rights and liberties, and assigning them a due priority, the most divisive questions are taken off the political agenda. This means that they are publicly recognized as politically settled, once and for all, and so contrary views on those questions are emphatically rejected by all political parties.[46] Though disagreements remain, as they must, they occur in areas of less central significance, where reasonable citizens equally attached to the political conception may reasonably be expected to differ. If liberty of conscience is guaranteed and separation of church and state is enjoined, we still expect there to be differences about what more exactly these provisions mean. Differences in judgment on the details in matters of any complexity even among reasonable persons are a condition of human life. But with the most divisive questions off the political agenda, it should be possible to reach a peaceful settlement within the framework of democratic institutions.

A second reply, complementing the first, is that the political conception, when properly formulated, should guide reflective judgment both to an agreed enumeration of the basic rights and liberties and to an agreement about their central range of significance. This it can do by its fundamental intuitive idea of society as a fair system of cooperation between citizens as free and equal persons, and by its idea of such persons as having the two moral powers, one a capacity for a sense of justice and the other a capacity for a conception of the good, that is, a conception of what is worthy of their devoted pursuit over a complete life.[47] Basic rights and liberties secure the conditions for the adequate development and exercise of those powers by citizens viewed as fully co-operating members of society. Citizens are thought to have and to want to exercise these powers whatever their more comprehensive religious, philosophical, or moral doctrine may be. Thus, the equal political liberties and freedom of speech and thought enable us to develop and exercise these powers by participating in society's political life and by assessing the justice and effectiveness of its laws and social policies; and liberty of conscience and freedom of association enable us to develop and exercise our moral powers in forming, revising, and rationally pursuing our conceptions of the good that belong to our comprehensive doctrines, and affirming them as such.[48]

But in view of the truism that no conception, whether in law, morals, or science, interprets and applies itself, we should expect various interpretations of even the constitutional essentials to gain currency. Does this jeopardize the rule of law? Not necessarily. The idea of the rule of law has numerous elements and it can be specified in a variety of ways. But however this is done, it cannot depend on the idea of a clear, unambiguous directive that informs citizens, or legislators, or judges what the constitution enjoins in all cases. There can be no such thing. The rule of law is not put in jeopardy by the circumstance that citizens, and even legislators and judges, may often hold conflicting views on questions of interpretation.

Rather, the rule of law means the regulative role of certain institutions and their associated legal and judicial practices. It may mean, among other things, that all officers of the government, including the executive, are under the law and that their acts are subject to judicial scrutiny, that the judiciary is suitably independent, and that civilian authority is supreme over the military. Moreover, it may mean that judges' decisions rest on interpreting existing law and relevant precedents, that judges must justify their verdicts by reference thereto and adhere to a consistent reading from case to case, or else find a reasonable basis for distinguishing them, and so on. Similar constraints do not bind legislators; while they may not

defy basic law and can try politically to change it only in ways the constitution permits, they need not explain or justify their vote, though their constituents may call them to account. The rule of law exists so long as such legal institutions and their associated practices (variously specified) are conducted in a reasonable way in accordance with the political values that apply to them: impartiality and consistency, adherence to law and respect for precedent, all in the light of a coherent understanding of recognized constitutional norms viewed as controlling the conduct of all government officers.[49]

Two conditions underwrite the rule of law so understood: first, the recognition by politically engaged citizens of the dual role of the basic rights and liberties; and second, its being the case that the main interpretations of those constitutional essentials take the most divisive matters off the political agenda and specify the central range of significance of the basic liberties in roughly the same way. The ideas of the domain of the political and of an overlapping consensus indicate how these conditions strengthen the stability of a political conception.

It is important for the viability of a just democratic regime over time for politically active citizens to understand those ideas. For in the long run, the leading interpretations of constitutional essentials are settled politically. A persistent majority, or an enduring alliance of strong enough interests, can make of the Constitution what it wants.[50] This fact is simply a corollary to the third general fact—that an enduring democratic regime must be freely supported by a substantial majority of its politically active citizens. As a fact, we must live with it and see it as specifying further one of the conditions of achieving a well-ordered constitutional state.

Notes

1. An overlapping consensus exists in a society when the political conception of justice that regulates its basic institutions is endorsed by each of the main religious, philosophical, and moral doctrines likely to endure in that society from one generation to the next. I have used this idea mainly in Rawls, "Jus-

tice as Fairness: Political not Metaphysical," *Philosophy and Public Affairs* 14, no. 223 (1985) [hereinafter "Justice as Fairness"], and Rawls, "The Idea of an Overlapping Consensus," *Oxford Journal of Legal Studies* 7, no. 1 (1987) [hereinafter "Overlapping Consensus"]. The idea is introduced in J. Rawls, *A Theory of Justice* [hereinafter *Theory*] (1971), pp. 387–88.

2. *Theory, supra* note 1.

3. For an awareness of these misgivings I am indebted to the comments of G. A. Cohen and Paul Seabright (soon after the lecture "Overlapping Consensus" was given at Oxford in May 1986); see "Overlapping Consensus," *supra* note 1, and to discussions with Jürgen Habermas (at Harvard the following October). For a better understanding of and suggestions for how to deal with the misgivings, I am greatly indebted to Ronald Dworkin, Thomas Nagel, and T. M. Scanlon. I also have gained much from Wilfried Hinsch, to whom I owe the important idea of a reasonable comprehensive doctrine, which I have simply elaborated a bit. This idea, when joined with suitable companion ideas such as the burdens of reason, see Part II infra, and the precepts of reasonable discussion, see Part III infra, imposes an appropriate limit on the comprehensive doctrines we may reasonably expect to be included in an overlapping consensus.

4. See Part VIII infra.

5. See Part VII infra.

6. These powers are those of a capacity for a sense of justice and a capacity for a conception of the good. *Theory, supra* note 1, p. 505; "Justice as Fairness," *supra* note 1, pp. 232–34.

7. This source of disagreement I have expressed in a somewhat flat way. It could be put more strongly by saying, as Thomas Nagel does, that there are basic conflicts of value in which there seem to be decisive and sufficient (normative) reasons for two or more incompatible courses of action; and yet some decision must be made. See T. Nagel, *Mortal Questions* (1979), pp. 128–41. Moreover, these normative reasons are not evenly balanced, and so it matters greatly what decision is made. The lack of even balance holds because in such cases the values are incomparable. They are each specified by one of the several irreducibly different perspectives within which values arise, in particular, the perspectives that specify obligations, rights, utility, perfectionist ends, and personal commitments. Put another way, these values have different bases which their different formal features reflect. These basic conflicts reveal what Nagel thinks of as the fragmentation of value. See id. I find much in Nagel's discussion very plausible, and I might endorse it were I stating my own (partially) comprehensive moral doctrine; since I am not doing that, but rather trying so far as possible to avoid controversial philosophical theses and to give an account of the difficulties of reason that rest on the plain facts open

to all, I refrain from any statement stronger than (e).

8. This point has often been stressed by Sir Isaiah Berlin, most recently in his article "On the Pursuit of the Ideal," *New York Review of Books,* Mar. 17, 1988; p. 11.

9. For instance, consider the questions of the causes of unemployment and the more effective ways to reduce it.

10. I have adapted this idea from Pliny the Younger's remark, "He who hates vice, hates mankind," quoted in J. Shklar, *Ordinary Vices* (1984), p. 192.

11. Here I assume that any substantial majority will include citizens who hold conflicting comprehensive doctrines.

12. Note that this is a definition of stability for a political conception of justice. It is not to be mistaken for a definition of stability, or of what I call the security, of a political regime (as a system of institutions).

13. The features of a political conception of justice are discussed in more detail in "Justice as Fairness," *supra* note 1, pp. 224–34.

14. A political conception for the basic structure must also generalize to, or else fit in with, a political conception for an international society of constitutionally democratic states; but here I put this important matter aside. See note 46 infra.

15. See "Justice as Fairness," *supra* note 1, pp. 239–40 & n. 22 (discussing a "political conception of the person").

16. See Part IV *supra.*

17. The appropriateness of this assumption rests in part on a point I shall only mention here, namely, that the right of emigration does not make the acceptance of political authority voluntary in the way that freedom of thought and liberty of conscience make the acceptance of ecclesiastical authority voluntary. This brings out a further feature of the domain of the political, one that distinguishes it from the associational.

18. The associational, the personal, and the familial are only three examples of the non-political; there are others.

19. The common medieval maxim *Extra ecclesiam nulla salus* ("Outside the church there is no salvation") was used, for example, in the famous bull "Unam sanctam" of Nov. 18, 1302, by Pope Boniface VIII, reprinted in *Enchiridion symbolorum definitionum et declarationum de rebus fidei et morum 870,* 33d ed., ed. H. Denzinger & A. Schönmetzer (1965), p. 279.

20. For clarity on this point I owe thanks to Wilfried Hinsch and Peter de Marneffe.

21. See Rawls, "Overlapping Consensus," *supra* note 1, p. 14.

22. Recall here the formulation of political liberalism a few lines back, namely, given the existence of a well-ordered constitutional democratic regime, the family of great values expressed by its principles and ideals, and realized in its basic institutions, nor-

mally has sufficient weight to override whatever other values may come into conflict with them. See Part IV *supra.*

23. J. S. Mill, *Utilitarianism,* ch.5, sec. 25 (3rd ed., 1867), reprinted in *John Stuart Mill: A Selection of His Works,* ed. J. Robson (1982), p. 216.

24. See Part III *supra.*

25. On this point see the instructive discussion by Jeremy Waldron, "Theoretical Foundations of Liberalism," *Philosophical Quarterly* no. 37, 127 (1987).

26. See "Justice as Fairness," *supra* note 1, p. 250. The model case of an overlapping consensus is one in which the political conception is endorsed by three comprehensive doctrines: the first endorses justice as fairness, say, because its religious beliefs and understanding of faith lead to the principle of toleration and support the basic equal liberties; the second doctrine affirms justice as fairness as a consequence of a comprehensive liberal conception such as that of Kant or Mill; while the third affirms justice as fairness as a political conception, that is, not as a consequence of a wider doctrine but as in itself sufficient to express very great values that normally outweigh whatever other values might oppose them, at least under reasonably favorable conditions. See also Rawls, "Overlapping Consensus," *supra* note 1, sec. III, pp. 9–12 (more fully discussing this model case).

27. These two stages correspond to the two parts of the argument from the original position for the two principles of justice contained in *Theory, supra* note 1. In the first part (pp. 118–93) the parties select principles without taking the effects of the special psychologies into account. In the second part (pp. 395–587) they ask whether a society well ordered by the principles selected in the first part would be stable, that is, would generate in its members a sufficiently strong sense of justice to counteract tendencies to injustice. The argument for the principles of justice is not complete until the principles selected in the first part are shown in the second part to be sufficiently stable. So in *Theory* the argument is not complete until the next to last section, section 86 (pp. 567–77). For these two parts, see pp. 144, 530–31.

28. In this and the next several paragraphs I am indebted to a very helpful discussion with T. M. Scanlon.

29. The assumptions of such a psychology are noted briefly in "Overlapping Consensus," *supra* note 1, pp. 22–23. In Section VI (pp. 18–22) of the same essay I also consider the way in which a political conception can gain an allegiance to itself that may to some degree shape comprehensive doctrines to conform to its requirements. This is plainly an important aspect of stability and strengthens the second part of the answer as to how political liberalism is possible. See Part VI *supra.*

I wish to thank Frances Kamm for pointing out to me several significant complications in the re-

lation between a political conception and the comprehensive doctrines it shapes to accord with it, and how far as a result the viability of political liberalism depends on the support of such doctrines. It seems best not to pursue these matters here but to postpone them until a more complete account of stability can be given.

30. As stated in *Theory,* the question is whether the just and the good are congruent. *Theory, supra* note 1, pp. 395, 567–77. In section 86 (pp. 567–77) of *Theory,* it is argued that a person who grows up in a society well ordered by justice as fairness, and who has a rational plan of life, and who also knows, or reasonably believes, that everyone else has an effective sense of justice, has sufficient reason, founded on that person's good (and not on justice) to comply with just institutions. These institutions are stable because the just and the good are congruent. That is, no reasonable and rational person in the well-ordered society of justice as fairness is moved by rational considerations of the good not to honor what justice requires.

31. Recall the reasonable comprehensive doctrines are ones that recognize the burdens of reason and accept the fact of pluralism as a condition of human life under free democratic institutions, and hence accept freedom of thought and liberty of conscience. See Parts II and III *supra.*

32. The force of the phrase "within its own framework" as used in the text emerges in the two parts of the argument from the original position in *Theory, supra* note 1. Both parts are carried out within the same framework and subject to the same conditions embedded in the original position as a device of representation.

33. For this distinction, see Nagel, *What Makes Political Theory Utopian?* (unpublished paper, dated Apr. 1988, on file at New York University Law Review).

34. Theory, *supra* note 1, p. 17.

35. Id. at p. 512.

36. Id. at pp. 453–62.

37. Id. at pp. 387–88.

38. "Justice as Fairness," *supra* note 1, pp. 248–51.

39. For example, in the well-ordered society of justice as fairness, some may hold a form of utilitarianism as their comprehensive doctrine, provided they understand that doctrine, as I believe J. S. Mill did, so as to coincide in its requirements with justice as fairness, at least for the most part. See J. S. Mill, *supra* note 23, ch. 3, sec. 10.

40. I am grateful to Erin Kelley for valuable discussion about how to put this summary.

41. See Parts I & II *supra.*

42. See Part II *supra.*

43. These two principles are:

1. Each person has an equal right to a fully adequate scheme of equal basic rights and liberties, which scheme is compatible with a similar scheme for all.

2. Social and economic inequalities are to satisfy two

conditions: first, they must be attached to offices and positions open to all under conditions of fair equality of opportunity; and second, they must be to the greatest benefit of the least advantaged members of society.

"Justice as Fairness," *supra* note 1, p. 227.

44. I should like to thank David Chow for very helpful comments on this point.

45. The reasons for thinking reasonable rather than unreasonable doctrines are encouraged are sketched briefly in "Overlapping Consensus," *supra* note 1, pp. 18–23.

46. For example, it is not on the political agenda whether certain groups are to have the vote, or whether certain religious or philosophical views have the protections of liberty of conscience and freedom of thought.

47. This conception of the person, which characterizes citizens, is also a political conception. "Justice as Fairness," *supra* note 1, pp. 239–44. I add that persons understand their own conceptions of the good against the background of their own comprehensive doctrines.

48. For further discussion of the basic rights and liberties, see Rawls, *Basic Liberties and Their Priority,* in Tanner Lectures on Human Values 3, ed. S. McMurrin (1982).

49. I owe thanks to T. M. Scanlon for helpful discussion of the rule of law as summarized in the last two paragraphs.

50. On this point, see A. Bickel, *The Least Dangerous Branch* (1962), pp. 244–72, discussing politics of *Dred Scott* v. *Sanford,* 60 U.S. (19 Haw.) 393 (1857), and the school segregation cases, notably *Brown* v. *Board of Education,* 347 U.S. 483 (1954).

Suggested Further Reading

Arrow, Kenneth J. *Social Choice and Justice*. Cambridge: Harvard University Press, 1984.

Baker, John. *Arguing for Equality*. London: Verso, 1987.

Barry, Brian. *The Liberal Theory of Justice*. Oxford: Clarendon, 1973.

———. *A Treatise on Social Justice*. Vol. I: *Theories of Justice*. Berkeley, Calif.: University of California Press, 1989.

Baynes, Kenneth. *The Normative Grounds of Social Criticism: Kant, Rawls, and Habermas*. Albany, N.Y.: State University of New York Press, 1992.

Becker, Lawrence C. "Too Much Property." *Philosophy and Public Affairs* 21 (1992): 196–206.

Bell, Daniel. *Communitarianism and its Critics*. New York: Oxford University Press, 1993.

Blackstone, W. T., ed. *The Concept of Equality*. Minneapolis: Burgess, 1969.

Blocker, H. G., and E. H. Smith, eds. *John Rawls' Theory of Social Justice: An Introduction*. Athens: Ohio University Press, 1980.

Brandt, R. B., ed. *Social Justice*. Englewood Cliffs, N.J.: Prentice-Hall, 1962.

Braybrooke, David. *Meeting Needs*. Princeton: Princeton University Press, 1987.

Brown, Henry Phelps. *Egalitarianism and the Generation of Inequality*. Oxford: Clarendon Press, 1988.

Buchanan, Allen E. "Justice as Reciprocity versus Subject-Centered Justice." *Philosophy and Public Affairs* 19 (1990): 227–252.

———. *Marx and Justice*. Totowa, N.J.: Rowman and Littlefield, 1982.

Buchanan, James M. "The Justice of Natural Liberty." In *Adam Smith and Modern Political Economy*, edited by Gerald P. O'Driscoll, Jr. Ames: Iowa State University Press, 1979.

Campbell, T. D. "Equality of Opportunity." *Proceedings of the Aristotelian Society* 75 (1974–75): 51–68.

Charvet, John. *A Critique of Freedom and Equality*. Cambridge: Cambridge University Press, 1981.

Christman, John. "Distributive Justice and the Complex Structure of Ownership." *Philosophy and Public Affairs* 23 (1994): 225–250.

Corlett, J. Angelo, ed. *Equality and Liberty: Analyzing Rawls and Nozick*. London: Macmillan, 1991.

Daniels, Norman, ed. *Reading Rawls*. New York: Basic Books, 1976.

Delaney, C. F., ed. *The Liberalism—Communitarianism Debate*. Lanham, Md.: Rowman and Littlefield, 1994.

Dworkin, Ronald. *Taking Rights Seriously*. Cambridge, Mass.: Harvard University Press, 1977.

———. "What is Equality?" *Philosophy and Public Affairs* 10 (1981): 185–246 (Part 1), 283–345 (Part 2).

Fernández de la Mora, Gonzalo. *Egalitarian Envy: The Political Foundations of Social Justice.* New York: Paragon House, 1987.

Fishkin, James. *Justice, Equal Opportunity, and the Family.* New Haven: Yale University Press, 1983.

Flew, Antony. *Equality in Liberty and Justice.* London: Routledge, 1989.

———. *The Politics of Procrustes.* London: Temple Smith, 1981.

Friedrich, C. J., and J. W. Chapman, eds. *Nomos VI: Justice.* Englewood Cliffs, N.J.: Prentice-Hall, 1963.

Galston, William A. *Justice and the Human Good.* Chicago: University of Chicago Press, 1980.

Gauthier, David P. *Morals by Agreement.* London: Oxford University Press, 1985.

Gibbard, Allan. "Constructing Justice." *Philosophy and Public Affairs* 20 (1991): 264–279.

———. "Human Evolution and the Sense of Justice." In *Midwest Studies in Philosophy,* vol. 7, edited by Peter A. French et al. Minneapolis: University of Minnesota Press, 1982.

Goodin, Robert E., and Andrew Reese, eds. *Liberal Neutrality.* London: Routledge, 1989.

Gordon, Scott. *Welfare, Justice, and Freedom.* New York: Columbia University Press, 1980.

Gutmann, Amy. "Communitarian Critics of Liberalism." *Philosophy and Public Affairs* 14 (1985): 308–322.

———. *Liberal Equality.* Cambridge: Cambridge University Press, 1980.

Hayek, F. A. *Law, Legislation, and Liberty.* Vol. 2: *The Mirage of Social Justice.* Chicago: University of Chicago Press, 1976.

Jacobs, Lesley A. *Rights and Deprivation.* Oxford: Clarendon Press, 1993.

Joseph, Keith, and Jonathan Sumption. *Equality.* London: John Murray, 1979.

Kukathas, Chandran, and Philip Pettit. *Rawls: A Theory of Justice and its Critics.* Stanford, Calif.: Stanford University Press, 1990.

Lakoff, Sanford A. *Equality in Political Philosophy.* Cambridge, Mass.: Harvard University Press, 1964.

Lucas, J. R. *On Justice.* Oxford: Clarendon Press, 1980.

Martin, Rex. *Rawls and Rights.* Lawrence: University Press of Kansas, 1985.

Miller, David. *Social Justice.* Oxford: Clarendon Press, 1976.

Moon, J. Donald, ed. *Responsibility, Rights, and Welfare: The Theory of the Welfare State.* Boulder, Colo.: Westview Press, 1988.

Nagel, Thomas. *Equality and Partiality.* New York: Oxford, 1991.

Nozick, Robert. *The Examined Life: Philosophical Meditations.* New York: Simon and Schuster, 1989.

Oppenheim, Felix. "Egalitarianism as a Descriptive Concept." *American Philosophical Quarterly* 7 (1970): 143–152.

Paul, E. F. *Property Rights and Eminent Domain.* New Brunswick, N.J.: Transaction Publishers, 1987.

Paul, E. F., and Howard Dickman, eds. *Liberty, Property, and the Foundations of the American Constitution.* Albany, N.Y.: SUNY Press 1989

Paul, E. F., et al., eds. *Liberty and Equality.* Oxford: Basil Blackwell, 1985.

Paul, Jeffrey, ed. *Reading Nozick.* Totowa, N.J.: Rowman and Allanheld, 1983.

Pennock, J. R., and J. W. Chapman, eds. *Nomos IX: Equality.* New York: Atherton, 1967.

Pettit, Philip. *Judging Justice.* London: Routledge and Kegan Paul, 1980.

Pogge, Thomas W. *Realizing Rawls.* Ithaca, N.Y.: Cornell University Press, 1989.

Posner, Richard A. *The Economics of Justice.* Cambridge, Mass.: Harvard University Press, 1981.

Rae, Douglas W. *Equalities.* Cambridge, Mass.: Harvard University Press, 1981.

Raphael, D. D. *Justice and Liberty.* London: Athlone Press, 1980.

Rawls, John. "Justice as Fairness: Political Not Metaphysical." *Philosophy and Public Affairs* 14 (1985): 223–251.

———. *Political Liberalism.* New York: Columbia University Press, 1993.

———. *A Theory of Justice.* Cambridge, Mass.: Harvard University Press, 1971.

Rees, J. C. *Equality.* New York: Macmillan, 1971.

Reese, Andrew. *Property*. London: Macmillan, 1986.

Rescher, Nicholas. *Distributive Justice*. Indianapolis: Bobbs-Merrill, 1966.

Ripstein, Arthur. "Equality, Luck, and Responsibility." *Philosophy and Public Affairs* 23 (1994): 3–23.

Roemer, John E. "A Pragmatic Theory of Responsibility for the Egalitarian Planner." *Philosophy and Public Affairs* 22 (1993): 146–166.

Ryan, Alan, ed. *Justice*. New York: Oxford University Press, 1993.

Sandel, Michael J. *Liberalism and the Limits of Justice*. New York: Cambridge University Press, 1982.

———. "The Procedural Republic and the Unencumbered Self," *Political Theory* 12 (1984): 81–96.

Sen, Amartya. *Inequality Reexamined*. Cambridge, Mass.: Harvard University Press, 1992.

Tawney, R. H. *Equality*. New York: Harcourt Brace, 1931.

Waldron, Jeremy. *Liberal Rights: Collected Papers 1981–1991*. Cambridge: Cambridge University Press, 1993.

———. *The Right to Private Property*. Oxford: Clarendon Press, 1988.

Walzer, Michael. *Spheres of Justice*. New York: Basic Books, 1983.

———. *Thick and Thin: Moral Argument at Home and Abroad*. Notre Dame, Ind.: University of Notre Dame Press, 1994.

Wellman, Carl. *Welfare Rights*. Totowa, N.J.: Rowman and Littlefield, 1982.

Westen, Peter. *Speaking of Equality: An Analysis of the Rhetorical Force of "Equality" in Moral and Legal Discourse*. Princeton: Princeton University Press, 1990.

Wildavsky, Aaron. *The Rise of Radical Egalitarianism*. Washington, D.C.: American University Press, 1991.

Wolff, R. P. *Understanding Rawls*. Princeton: Princeton University Press, 1977.

Wolgast, Elizabeth H. *The Grammar of Justice*. Ithaca, N.Y.: Cornell University Press, 1987.

IV
DEMOCRACY AND REPRESENTATION

The idea of government by the people has taken many different forms in political theory and practice. What kind of democratic government, if any, is justifiable, and why? Obviously, the feasibility and desirability of a given form of democracy are relative to a particular type of society and thus depend on its traditions, level of advancement, size, and so forth. What was suitable for a Greek polis or a New England town is not likely to be relevant for large modern nation-states. As suggested earlier with respect to the concept of liberty, the question of selecting a particular conception of democracy over others is not a linguistic one; rather, it involves examination of our basic values. Thus, we may be able to agree that democracy implies a kind of political decision-making procedure in which, in some sense, the people are ultimately sovereign. But such procedures may take many different forms, and some will be thought intrinsically desirable (e.g., because they allow everyone to participate in political decisions at some level or because they give every citizen an equal influence), while others will be justified primarily in terms of their tendency to produce good consequences—just or beneficial policies and laws.

Mill's theory of representative democracy involves the latter type of justification. Given that people mature in their faculties are most likely to know their interests and that democratic participation can be expected to develop and sustain the relevant capacities of judgment and character, the case that can be made for democracy on utilitarian grounds is clear. But direct democracy is not possible. Some form of representative government, in which the people have control yet do not engage in the business of governing, is the only viable arrangement. Mill served in Parliament himself, and the later chapters of his *Considerations on Representative Government* include proposals of a specific nature concerning elections and the suffrage. He also makes a case for proportional representation, to ensure that minority opinions be heard—the functions of the assembly being both legislative and deliberative. In the selections from early chapters included here, Mill discusses the tendency of democratic states to encourage people of active character, with its intellectual, practical, and moral excellences; the role of the Constitution and positive political morality; the delegation of administrative responsibilities by representatives; the need for a special Commission of Legislation to initiate bills; and the potential weaknesses of representative democracy.

William N. Nelson outlines a justification for democratic government that is in some important respects a development of Mill's thinking. Standard attempts to justify democracy on the grounds that it distributes political power equally or maximizes satisfaction of voters' desires, even if they are correct as far as they go, leave open the question of the desirability of these goals, Nelson points out. The same criticism can be made of most arguments in terms of participation—why is it morally significant? Nelson's instrumental case for democracy involves showing that it tends to produce just laws and policies. He begins by sketching a conception of moral justification that owes much to Rawls, providing a general idea of what conditions must be satisfied by acceptable moral principles. Nelson goes on to argue that the procedures of a constitutional democracy tend to create laws that are acceptable for analogous reasons, and he concludes with a comparison of his theory with others.

Richard Wollheim offers some remarks on the history of democratic ideas and formulates a thought-provoking paradox for proponents of democracy. How can one consistently believe that the outcome of a political decision process ought to be the democratic choice and yet also have a conviction that a different policy alternative should be adopted on its merits? David M. Estlund addresses the issue of how to interpret theoretically the idea of voting. Are votes just expressions of preferences or, as he insists, expressions of beliefs about what is right or good for society? Susan Mendus explains why many feminists, despite the suffrage, are disenchanted with contemporary democracy, and she offers some suggestions for what measures would be necessary to gain their allegiance.

We have been speaking primarily of representative democracy, but the very concept of representation is far from clear. Classic discussions of this idea, in the writings of Hobbes and Rousseau, Bentham and Burke, Mill and others, yield little agreement about what it is. Once again, we are in the frustrating position of trying to settle on a conception that will help us to understand and perhaps arrive at an answer to important questions, but the process of conceptual clarification and choice involves substantive commitments. We ask, for instance, what is the role of a representative, or what is occurring when one person represents others. Expressions such as "taking their place" and "acting on their behalf" come immediately to mind, but they are not very helpful. Somewhat narrower questions, such as whether a representative does or should do what his constituents want or what he thinks is best for them—what Hanna F. Pitkin refers to as the "mandate-independence" dispute—are similarly not resolvable on either linguistic or empirical bases. Pitkin's view is that the concept of representation imposes broad constraints within which many alternatives are possible. The conception we end up accepting is a reflection of what we believe about a number of factual and moral issues. For example, we may have a view about what constitutes an interest. Is it nothing more than a desire? An informed desire? One that is long-term and stable? Or is it something essentially different, largely independent of our wants, more "objective"? We must also arrive at a reasonable position concerning the relative capabilities of representatives and those whom they serve. How much knowledge and prudence, what sense of the good of the community as a whole, can be plausibly assumed on each side? The representative will be faced with apparent conflicts about obligations to supporters, to constituents, to party leaders, and to all those whom his or her decisions might affect. What basis is there for ordering these obligations in some rough scheme of priority? Even when it is certain what the interests of various people are, the representative must decide whose interests are most important. As Pitkin observes in her selection "Political Representation," representation is not an activity in which experts seek "scientific truths," yet neither is it a matter of making nonrational, arbitrary choices. Still other beliefs influence our specific conception of representation, for example, concerning the significance of elections and whether they give mandates under at least some circumstances. Pitkin discusses these and related issues in her examination of representation.

Bruce E. Cain and W. T. Jones, a political scientist and a philosopher, respectively, propose a conceptual framework to facilitate comparisons of the many different theories of representation and its implementation. They characterize their approach as pragmatic, in contrast to normative and empirical approaches, with a view to closing the logical gap between what is the case and what ought to be. They are mainly interested in substantive (as opposed to purely formal) theories of implementation, such as those of Aristotle, Madison, and Dahl. Why might one theorist favor lengthy terms for representatives, whereas another advocates relatively short terms? Why do writers on representation differ so widely on the issue of how much freedom a representative should have to exercise his or her own judgment? Answers to these sorts of questions usually refer to differences in the theorists' perceptions of their circumstances (times, customs, etc.), that is, to contextual variables, but Cain and Jones give reasons to focus instead on belief variables, for example, the theorists' political aims or values, their views of human nature, and so forth. Their framework has four components: the theorist's preferences concerning representatives' dispositions, the theorist's assumptions about human nature, the theorist's beliefs about what behavior is likely, given these assumptions, and finally, specific recommendations for implementation. The authors illustrate the usefulness of their framework by applying their categories to the proposals of Rousseau and Bentham.

From *Considerations on Representative Government*

JOHN STUART MILL

Chapter III. That the Ideally Best Form of Government Is Representative Government

[...] There is no difficulty in showing that the ideally best form of government is that in which the sovereignty, or supreme controlling power in the last resort, is vested in the entire aggregate of the community; every citizen not only having a voice in the exercise of that ultimate sovereignty, but being, at least occasionally, called on to take an actual part in the government, by the personal discharge of some public function, local or general.

To test this proposition, it has to be examined in reference to the two branches into which, as pointed out in the last chapter, the inquiry into the goodness of a government conveniently divides itself, namely, how far it promotes the good management of the affairs of society by means of the existing faculties, moral, intellectual, and active, of its various members, and what is its effect in improving or deteriorating those faculties.

The ideally best form of government, it is scarcely necessary to say, does not mean one which is practicable or eligible in all states of civilization, but the one which, in the circumstances in which it is practicable and eligible, is attended with the greatest amount of beneficial consequences, immediate and prospective. A completely popular government is the only polity which can make out any claim to this character. It is pre-eminent in both the departments between which the excellence of a political constitution is divided. It is both more favourable to present good government, and promotes a better and higher form of national character, than any other polity whatsoever.

Its superiority in reference to present well-being rests upon two principles, of as universal truth and applicability as any general propositions which can be laid down respecting human affairs. The first is, that the rights and interests of every or any person are only secure from being disregarded, when the person interested is himself able, and habitually disposed, to stand up for them. The second is, that the general prosperity attains a greater height, and is more widely diffused, in proportion to the amount and variety of the personal energies enlisted in promoting it.

Putting these two propositions into a shape more special to their present application; human beings are only secure from evil at the hands of others, in proportion as they have the power of being, and are, self-*protecting;* and they only achieve a high degree of success in their struggle with Nature, in proportion as they are self-*dependent,* relying on what they themselves can do, either separately or in concert, rather than on what others do for them.

The former proposition—that each is the only safe guardian of his own rights and interests—is one of those elementary maxims of prudence, which every person, capable of conducting his own affairs, implicitly acts upon, wherever he himself is interested. Many, indeed, have a great dislike to it as a political doctrine, and are fond of holding it up to obloquy, as a doctrine of universal selfishness. To which we may answer, that whenever it ceases to be true that mankind, as a rule, prefer themselves to others, and those nearest to them to those more remote, from that moment Communism is not only practicable, but the only defensible form of society; and will, when that time arrives, be assuredly carried into effect. For my own part, not believing in universal selfishness, I have no difficulty in admitting that Communism would even now be practicable among the élite of mankind, and may become so among the rest. But as this opinion is anything but popular with those defenders of existing institutions who find fault with the doctrine of the general predominance of self-interest, I am inclined to think they do in reality believe, that most men consider themselves before other people. It is not, however, necessary to affirm even thus much, in order to support the claim of all to participate in the sovereign power. We need not suppose that when power resides in an exclusive class, that class will knowingly and deliberately sacrifice the other classes to themselves: it suffices that, in the absence of its natural defenders, the interest of the excluded is always in danger of being overlooked; and, when looked at, is seen with very different eyes from those of the persons whom it directly concerns. In this country, for example, what are called the working classes may be considered as excluded from all direct participation in the government. I do not believe that the classes who do participate in it, have in general any intention of sacrificing the working classes to themselves. They once had that intention; witness the persevering attempts so long made to keep down wages by law. But in the present day, their ordinary disposition is the very opposite: they willingly make considerable sacrifices, especially of their pecuniary interest, for the benefit of the working classes, and err rather by too lavish and indiscriminating beneficence; nor do I believe that any rulers in history have been actuated by a more sincere desire to do their duty towards the poorer portion of their countrymen. Yet does Parliament, or almost any of the members composing it, ever for an instant look at any question with the eyes of a working man? When a subject arises in which the labourers as such have an interest, is it regarded from any point of view but that of the employers of labour? I do not say that the working men's view of these questions is in general nearer to the truth than the other: but it is sometimes quite as near; and in any case it ought to be respectfully listened to, instead of being, as it is, not merely turned away from, but ignored. On the question of strikes, for instance, it is doubtful if there is so much as one among the leading members of either House, who is not firmly convinced that the reason of the matter is unqualifiedly on the side of the masters, and that the men's view of it is simply absurd. Those who have studied the question, know well how far this is from being the case; and in how different, and how infinitely less superficial a manner the point would have to be argued, if the classes who strike were able to make themselves heard in Parliament.

It is an inherent condition of human affairs, that no intention, however sincere, of protecting the interests of others, can make it safe or salutary to tie up their own hands. Still more obviously true is it, that by their own hands only can any positive and durable improvement of their circumstances in life be worked out. Through the joint influence of these two principles, all free communities have both been more exempt from social injustice and crime, and have attained more brilliant prosperity, than any others, or than they themselves after they lost their freedom. Contrast the free states of the world, while their freedom lasted, with the contemporary subjects of monarchical or oligarchical despotism: the Greek cities with the Persian satrapies; the Italian republics, and the free towns of Flanders and Germany, with the feudal monarchies of Europe; Switzerland, Holland, and England, with Austria or anterevolutionary France. Their superior prosperity was too obvious ever to have been gainsaid: while their superiority in good government and social relations, is proved by the prosperity, and is manifest beside in every page of history. If we compare, not one age with another, but the different governments which coexisted in the same age, no amount of disorder which exaggeration itself can pretend to have existed amidst the publicity of the free states, can be compared for a moment with the contemptuous trampling upon the mass of the people which pervaded the whole life of the monarchical countries, or the disgusting individual tyranny which was of more than daily occurrence under the systems of plunder which they called fiscal arrangements, and in the secrecy of their frightful courts of justice.

It must be acknowledged that the benefits of freedom, so far as they have hitherto been enjoyed, were obtained by the extension of its privileges to a part only of the community; and that a government in which they are extended impartially to all is a desideratum still unrealized. But though every approach to this has an independent value, and in many cases more than an approach could not, in the existing state of general improvement, be made, the participation of all in these benefits is the ideally perfect conception of free government. In proportion as any, no matter who, are excluded from it, the interests of the excluded are left without the guarantee accorded to the rest, and they themselves have less scope and encouragement than they might otherwise have to that exertion of their energies for the good of themselves and of the community, to which the general prosperity is always proportioned.

Thus stands the case as regards present well-being; the good management of the affairs of the existing generation. If we now pass to the influence of the form of government upon character, we shall find the superiority of popular government over every other to be, if possible, still more decided and indisputable.

This question really depends upon a still more fundamental one—viz, which of two common types of character, for the general good of humanity, it is most desirable should predominate—the active, or the passive type; that which struggles against evils, or that which

endures them; that which bends to circumstances, or that which endeavours to make circumstances bend to itself.

The commonplaces of moralists, and the general sympathies of mankind, are in favour of the passive type. Energetic characters may be admired, but the acquiescent and submissive are those which most men personally prefer. The passiveness of our neighbours increases our sense of security, and plays into the hands of our wilfulness. Passive characters, if we do not happen to need their activity, seem an obstruction the less in our own path. A contented character is not a dangerous rival. Yet nothing is more certain, than that improvement in human affairs is wholly the work of the uncontented characters; and, moreover, that it is much easier for an active mind to acquire the virtues of patience, than for a passive one to assume those of energy.

Of the three varieties of mental excellence, intellectual, practical, and moral, there never could be any doubt in regard to the first two, which side had the advantage. All intellectual superiority is the fruit of active effort. Enterprise, the desire to keep moving, to be trying and accomplishing new things for our own benefit or that of others, is the parent even of speculative, and much more of practical, talent. The intellectual culture compatible with the other type is of that feeble and vague description, which belongs to a mind that stops at amusement, or at simple contemplation. The test of real and vigorous thinking, the thinking which ascertains truths instead of dreaming dreams, is successful application to practice. Where that purpose does not exist, to give definiteness, precision, and an intellible meaning to thought, it generates nothing better than the mystical metaphysics of the Pythagoreans or the Vedas. With respect to practical improvement, the case is still more evident. The character which improves human life is that which struggles with natural powers and tendencies, not that which gives way to them. The self-benefiting qualities are all on the side of the active and energetic character: and the habits and conduct which promote the advantage of each individual member of the community, must be at least a part of those which conduce most in the end to the advancement of the community as a whole.

But on the point of moral preferability, there seems at first sight to be room for doubt. I am not referring to the religious feeling which has so generally existed in favour of the inactive character, as being more in harmony with the submission due to the divine will. Christianity as well as other religions has fostered this sentiment; but it is the prerogative of Christianity, as regards this and many other perversions, that it is able to throw them off. Abstractedly from religious considerations, a passive character, which yields to obstacles instead of striving to overcome them, may not indeed be very useful to others, no more than to itself, but it might be expected to be at least inoffensive. Contentment is always counted among the moral virtues. But it is a complete error to suppose that contentment is necessarily or naturally attendant on passivity of character; and unless it is, the moral consequences are mischievous. Where there exists a desire for advantages not possessed, the mind which does not potentially possess them by means of its own energies, is apt to look with hatred and malice on those who do. The person bestirring himself with hopeful prospects to improve his circumstances, is the one who feels goodwill towards others engaged in, or who have succeeded in, the same pursuit. And where the majority are so engaged, those who do not attain the object have had the tone given to their feelings by the general habit of the country, and ascribe their failure to want of effort or opportunity, or to their personal ill luck. But those who, while desiring what others possess, put no energy into striving for it, are either incessantly grumbling that fortune does not do for them what they do not attempt to do for themselves, or overflowing with envy and ill-will towards those who possess what they would like to have.

In proportion as success in life is seen or believed to be the fruit of fatality or accident, and not of exertion, in that same ratio does envy develop itself as a point of national character. The most envious of all mankind are the Orientals. In Oriental moralists, in Oriental tales, the envious man is remarkably prominent.

In real life, he is the terror of all who possess anything desirable, be it a palace, a handsome child, or even good health and spirits: the supposed effect of his mere look constitutes the all-pervading superstition of the evil eye. Next to Orientals in envy, as in activity, are some of the Southern Europeans. The Spaniards pursued all their great men with it, embittered their lives, and generally succeeded in putting an early stop to their successes.[1] With the French, who are essentially a southern people, the double education of despotism and Catholicism has, in spite of their impulsive temperament, made submission and endurance the common character of the people, and their most received notion of wisdom and excellence: and if envy of one another, and of all superiority, is not more rife among them than it is, the circumstance must be ascribed to the many valuable counteracting elements in the French character, and most of all to the great individual energy which, though less persistent and more intermittent than in the self-helping and struggling Anglo-Saxons, has nevertheless manifested itself among the French in nearly every direction in which the operation of their institutions has been favourable to it.

There are, no doubt, in all countries, really contented characters, who not merely do not seek, but do not desire, what they do not already possess, and these naturally bear no ill-will towards such as have apparently a more favoured lot. But the great mass of seeming contentment is real discontent, combined with indolence or self indulgence, which, while taking no legitimate means of raising itself, delights in bringing others down to its own level. And if we look narrowly even at the cases of innocent contentment, we perceive that they only win our admiration, when the indifference is solely to improvement in outward circumstances, and there is a striving for perpetual advancement in spiritual worth, or at least a disinterested zeal to benefit others. The contented man, or the contented family, who have no ambition to make any one else happier, to promote the good of their country or their neighbourhood, or to improve themselves in moral excellence, excite in us neither admiration nor approval. We rightly ascribe this sort of contentment to mere unmanliness and want of spirit. The content which we approve, is an ability to do cheerfully without what cannot be had, a just appreciation of the comparative value of different objects of desire, and a willing renunciation of the less when incompatible with the greater. These, however, are excellences more natural to the character, in proportion as it is actively engaged in the attempt to improve its own or some other lot. He who is continually measuring his energy against difficulties, learns what are the difficulties insuperable to him, and what are those which though he might overcome, the success is not worth the cost. He whose thoughts and activities are all needed for, and habitually employed in, practicable and useful enterprises, is the person of all others least likely to let his mind dwell with brooding discontent upon things either not worth attaining, or which are not so to him. Thus the active, self-helping character is not only intrinsically the best, but is the likeliest to acquire all that is really excellent or desirable in the opposite type.

The striving, go-ahead character of England and the United States is only a fit subject of disapproving criticism, on account of the very secondary objects on which it commonly expends its strength. In itself it is the foundation of the best hopes for the general improvement of mankind. It has been acutely remarked, that wherever anything goes amiss, the habitual impulse of French people is to say "Il faut de la patience"; and of English people, "What a shame." The people who think it a shame when anything goes wrong—who rush to the conclusion that the evil could and ought to have been prevented, are those who, in the long run, do most to make the world better. If the desires are low placed, if they extend to little beyond physical comfort and the show of riches, the immediate results of the energy will not be much more than the continual extension of man's power over material objects; but even this makes room and prepares the mechanical appliances, for the greatest intellectual and social achievements; and while the energy is there, some persons will apply it, and it will be applied more and more, to the perfecting not of outward circumstances alone, but of man's

inward nature. Inactivity, unaspiringness, absence of desire, are a more fatal hindrance to improvement than any misdirection of energy; and are that through which alone, when existing in the mass, any very formidable misdirection by an energetic few becomes possible. It is this, mainly, which retains in a savage or semi-savage state the great majority of the human race.

Now there can be no kind of doubt that the passive type of character is favoured by the government of one or a few, and the active self-helping type by that of the Many. Irresponsible rulers need the quiescence of the ruled, more than they need any activity but that which they can compel. Submissiveness to the prescriptions of men as necessities of nature, is the lesson inculcated by all governments upon those who are wholly without participation in them. The will of superiors, and the law as the will of superiors, must be passively yielded to. But no men are mere instruments or materials in the hands of their rulers, who have will or spirit or a spring of internal activity in the rest of their proceedings: and any manifestation of these qualities, instead of receiving encouragement from despots, has to get itself forgiven by them. Even when irresponsible rulers are not sufficiently conscious of danger from the mental activity of their subjects to be desirous of repressing it, the position itself is a repression. Endeavour is even more effectually restrained by the certainty of its impotence, than by any positive discouragement. Between subjection to the will of others, and the virtues of self-help and self-government, there is a natural incompatibility. This is more or less complete, according as the bondage is strained or relaxed. Rulers differ very much in the length to which they carry the control of the free agency of their subjects, or the supersession of it by managing their business for them. But the difference is in degree, not in principle; and the best despots often go the greatest lengths in chaining up the free agency of their subjects. A bad despot, when his own personal indulgences have been provided for, may sometimes be willing to let the people alone; but a good despot insists on doing them good, by making them do their own business in a better way than they themselves know of. The regulations which restricted to fixed processes all the leading branches of French manufactures, were the work of the great Colbert.

Very different is the state of the human faculties where a human being feels himself under no other external restraint than the necessities of nature, or mandates of society which he has his share in imposing, and which it is open to him, if he thinks them wrong, publicly to dissent from and exert himself actively to get altered. No doubt, under a government partially popular, this freedom may be exercised even by those who are not partakers in the full privileges of citizenship. But it is a great additional stimulus to any one's self-help and self-reliance when he starts from even ground, and has not to feel that his success depends on the impression he can make upon the sentiments and dispositions of a body of whom he is not one. It is a great discouragement to an individual, and a still greater one to a class, to be left out of the constitution; to be reduced to plead from outside the door to the arbiters of their destiny, not taken into consultation within. The maximum of the invigorating effect of freedom upon the character is only obtained, when the person acted on either is, or is looking forward to becoming, a citizen as fully privileged as any other. What is still more important than even this matter of feeling, is the practical discipline which the character obtains, from the occasional demand made upon the citizens to exercise, for a time and in their turn, some social function. It is not sufficiently considered how little there is in most men's ordinary life to give any largeness either to their conceptions or to their sentiments. Their work is a routine; not a labour of love, but of self-interest in the most elementary form, the satisfaction of daily wants; neither the thing done, nor the process of doing it, introduces the mind to thoughts or feelings extending beyond individuals; if instructive books are within their reach, there is no stimulus to read them; and in most cases the individual has no access to any person of cultivation much superior to his own. Giving him something to do for the public, supplies, in a measure, all these deficiencies. If circumstances allow the amount of public duty

assigned him to be considerable, it makes him an educated man. Notwithstanding the defects of the social system and moral ideas of antiquity, the practice of the dicastery and the ecclesia raised the intellectual standard of an average Athenian citizen far beyond anything of which there is yet an example in any other mass of men, ancient or modern. The proofs of this are apparent in every page of our great historian of Greece; but we need scarcely look further than to the high quality of the addresses which their great orators deemed best calculated to act with effect on their understanding and will. A benefit of the same kind, though far less in degree, is produced on Englishmen of the lower middle class by their liability to be placed on juries and to serve parish offices; which, though it does not occur to so many, nor is so continuous, nor introduces them to so great a variety of elevated considerations, as to admit of comparison with the public education which every citizen of Athens obtained from her democratic institutions, must make them nevertheless very different beings, in range of ideas and development of faculties, from those who have done nothing in their lives but drive a quill, or sell goods over a counter. Still more salutary is the moral part of the instruction afforded by the participation of the private citizen, if even rarely, in public functions. He is called upon, while so engaged, to weigh interests not his own; to be guided, in case of conflicting claims, by another rule than his private partialities; to apply, at every turn, principles and maxims which have for their reason of existence the common good: and he usually finds associated with him in the same work minds more familiarized than his own with these ideas and operations, whose study it will be to supply reasons to his understanding, and stimulation to his feeling for the general interest. He is made to feel himself one of the public, and whatever is for their benefit to be for his benefit. Where this school of public spirit does not exist, scarcely any sense is entertained that private persons, in no eminent social situation, owe any duties to society, except to obey the laws and submit to the government. There is no unselfish sentiment of identification with the public. Every thought or feeling, either of interest or of duty, is absorbed in the individual and in the family. The man never thinks of any collective interest, of any objects to be pursued jointly with others, but only in competition with them, and in some measure at their expense. A neighbour, not being an ally or an associate, since he is never engaged in any common undertaking for joint benefit, is therefore only a rival. Thus even private morality suffers, while public is actually extinct. Were this the universal and only possible state of things, the utmost aspirations of the lawgiver or the moralist could only stretch to making the bulk of the community a flock of sheep innocently nibbling the grass side by side.

From these accumulated considerations it is evident, that the only government which can fully satisfy all the exigencies of the social state, is one in which the whole people participate; that any participation, even in the smallest public function, is useful; that the participation should everywhere be as great as the general degree of improvement of the community will allow; and that nothing less can be ultimately desirable, than the admission of all to a share in the sovereign power of the state. But since all cannot, in a community exceeding a single small town, participate personally in any but some very minor portions of the public business, it follows that the ideal type of a perfect government must be representative.

Chapter V. Of The Proper Functions of Representative Bodies

In treating of representative government, it is above all necessary to keep in view the distinction between its idea or essence, and the particular forms in which the idea has been clothed by accidental historical developments, or by the notions current at some particular period.

The meaning of representative government is, that the whole people, or some numerous portion of them, exercise through deputies periodically elected by themselves, the ultimate controlling power, which, in every constitution, must reside somewhere. This ultimate power they must possess in all its completeness. They must be masters, whenever they

please, of all the operations of government. There is no need that the constitutional law should itself give them this mastery. It does not, in the British Constitution. But what it does give, practically amounts to this. The power of final control is as essentially single, in a mixed and balanced government, as in a pure monarchy or democracy. This is the portion of truth in the opinion of the ancients, revived by great authorities in our own time, that a balanced constitution is impossible. There is almost always a balance, but the scales never hang exactly even. Which of them preponderates, is not always apparent on the face of the political institutions. In the British Constitution, each of the three co-ordinate members of the sovereignty is invested with powers which, if fully exercised, would enable it to stop all the machinery of government. Nominally, therefore, each is invested with equal power of thwarting and obstructing the others: and if, by exerting that power, any of the three could hope to better its position, the ordinary course of human affairs forbids us to doubt that the power would be exercised. There can be no question that the full powers of each would be employed defensively, if it found itself assailed by one or both of the others. What then prevents the same powers from being exerted aggressively? The unwritten maxims of the Constitution—in other words, the positive political morality of the country: and this positive political morality is what we must look to, if we would know in whom the really supreme power in the Constitution resides.

By constitutional law, the Crown can refuse its assent to any Act of Parliament, and can appoint to office and maintain in it any Minister, in opposition to the remonstrances of Parliament. But the constitutional morality of the country nullifies these powers, preventing them from being ever used; and, by requiring that the head of the Administration should always be virtually appointed by the House of Commons, makes the body the real sovereign of the State. These unwritten rules, which limit the use of lawful powers, are, however, only effectual, and maintain themselves in existence, on condition of harmonizing with the actual distribution of real political strength. There is in every constitution a strongest power—one which would gain the victory, if the compromises by which the Constitution habitually works were suspended, and there came a trial of strength. Constitutional maxims are adhered to, and are practically operative, so long as they give the predominance in the Constitution to that one of the powers which has the preponderance of active power out of doors. This, in England, is the popular power. If, therefore, the legal provisions of the British Constitution, together with the unwritten maxims by which the conduct of the different political authorities is in fact regulated, did not give to the popular element in the Constitution that substantial supremacy over every department of the government, which corresponds to its real power in the country, the Constitution would not possess the stability which characterizes it; either the laws or the unwritten maxims would soon have to be changed. The British Government is thus a representative government in the correct sense of the term: and the powers which it leaves in hands not directly accountable to the people, can only be considered as precautions which the ruling power is willing should be taken against its own errors. Such precautions have existed in all well-constructed democracies. The Athenian Constitution had many such provisions; and so has that of the United States.

But while it is essential to representative government that the practical supremacy in the state should reside in the representatives of the people, it is an open question what actual functions, what precise part in the machinery of government, shall be directly and personally discharged by the representative body. Great varieties in this respect are compatible with the essence of representative government, provided the functions are such as secure to the representative body the control of everything in the last resort.

There is a radical distinction between controlling the business of government, and actually doing it. The same person or body may be able to control everything, but cannot possibly do everything; and in many cases its control over everything will be more perfect, the less it personally attempts to do. The commander of an army could not direct its movements ef-

fectually if he himself fought in the ranks, or led an assault. It is the same with bodies of men. Some things cannot be done except by bodies; other things cannot be well done by them. It is one question, therefore, what a popular assembly should control, another what it should itself do. It should, as we have already seen, control all the operations of government. But in order to determine through what channel this general control may most expediently be exercised, and what portion of the business of government the representative assembly should hold in its own hands, it is necessary to consider what kinds of business a numerous body is competent to perform properly. That alone which it can do well, it ought to take personally upon itself. With regard to the rest, its proper province is not to do it, but to take means for having it well done by others.

For example, the duty which is considered as belonging more peculiarly than any other to an assembly representative of the people, is that of voting the taxes. Nevertheless, in no country does the representative body undertake, by itself or its delegated officers, to prepare the estimates. Though the supplies can only be voted by the House of Commons, and though the sanction of the House is also required for the appropriation of the revenues to the different items of the public expenditure, it is the maxim and the uniform practice of the Constitution that money can be granted only on the proposition of the Crown. It has, no doubt, been felt, that moderation as to the amount, and care and judgement in the detail of its application, can only be expected when the executive government, through whose hands it is to pass, is made responsible for the plans and calculations on which the disbursements are grounded. Parliament, accordingly, is not expected, nor even permitted, to originate directly either taxation or expenditure. All it is asked for is its consent, and the sole power it possesses is that of refusal.

The principles which are involved and recognized in this constitutional doctrine, if followed as far as they will go, are a guide to the limitation and definition of the general functions of representative assemblies. In the first place, it is admitted in all countries in which the representative system is practically understood, that numerous representative bodies ought not to administer. The maxim is grounded not only on the most essential principles of good government, but on those of the successful conduct of business of any description. No body of men, unless organized and under command, is fit for action, in the proper sense. Even a select board, composed of few members, and these specially conversant with the business to be done, is always an inferior instrument to some one individual who could be found among them, and would be improved in character if that one person were made the chief, and all the others reduced to subordinates. What can be done better by a body than by any individual, is deliberation. When it is necessary, or important to secure hearing and consideration to many conflicting opinions, a deliberative body is indispensable. Those bodies, therefore, are frequently useful, even for administrative business, but in general only as advisers; such business being, as a rule, better conducted under the responsibility of one. Even a joint-stock company has always in practice, if not in theory, a managing director; its good or bad management depends essentially on some one person's qualification, and the remaining directors, when of any use, are so by their suggestions to him, or by the power they possess of watching him, and restraining or removing him in case of misconduct. That they are ostensibly equal sharers with him in the management is no advantage, but a considerable set-off against any good which they are capable of doing: it weakens greatly the sense in his own mind, and in those of other people, of that individual responsibility in which he should stand forth personally and undividedly.

But a popular assembly is still less fitted to administer, or to dictate in detail to those who have the charge of administration. Even when honestly meant, the interference is almost always injurious. Every branch of public administration is a skilled business, which has its own peculiar principles and traditional rules, many of them not even known, in any effectual way, except to those who have at some time had a hand in carrying on the business, and none of them likely to be duly appreciated by

persons not practically acquainted with the department. I do not mean that the transaction of public business has esoteric mysteries, only to be understood by the initiated. Its principles are all intelligible to any person of good sense, who has in his mind a true picture of the circumstances and conditions to be dealt with: but to have this he must know those circumstances and conditions; and the knowledge does not come by intuition. There are many rules of the greatest importance in every branch of public business (as there are in every private occupation), of which a person fresh to the subject neither knows the reason or even suspects the existence, because they are intended to meet dangers or provide against inconveniences which never entered into his thoughts. I have known public men, ministers, of more than ordinary natural capacity, who on their first introduction to a department of business new to them, have excited the mirth of their inferiors by the air with which they announced as a truth hitherto set at naught, and brought to light by themselves, something which was probably the first thought of everybody who ever looked at the subject, given up as soon as he had got on to a second. It is true that a great statesman is he who knows when to depart from traditions, as well as when to adhere to them. But it is a great mistake to suppose that he will do this better for being ignorant of the traditions. No one who does not thoroughly know the modes of action which common experience has sanctioned, is capable of judging of the circumstances which require a departure from those ordinary modes of action. The interests dependent on the acts done by a public department, the consequences liable to follow from any particular mode of conducting it, require for weighing and estimating them a kind of knowledge, and of specially exercised judgement, almost as rarely found in those not bred to it, as the capacity to reform the law in those who have not professionally studied it. All these difficulties are sure to be ignored by a representative assembly which attempts to decide on special acts of administration. At its best, it is inexperience sitting in judgement on experience, ignorance on knowledge: ignorance which never suspecting the existence of what it does not know, is equally careless and supercilious, making light of, if not resenting, all pretensions to have a judgement better worth attending to than its own. Thus it is when no interested motives intervene: but when they do, the result is jobbery more unblushing and audacious than the worst corruption which can well take place in a public office under a government of publicity. It is not necessary that the interested bias should extend to the majority of the assembly. In any particular case it is often enough that it affects two or three of their number. Those two or three will have a greater interest in misleading the body, than any other of its members are likely to have in putting it right. The bulk of the assembly may keep their hands clean, but they cannot keep their minds vigilant or their judgements discerning in matters they know nothing about: and an indolent majority, like an indolent individual, belongs to the person who takes most pains with it. The bad measures or bad appointments of a minister may be checked by Parliament; and the interest of ministers in defending, and of rival partisans in attacking, secures a tolerably equal discussion: but *quis custodiet custodes?* who shall check the Parliament? A minister, a head of an office, feels himself under some responsibility. An assembly in such cases feels under no responsibility at all: for when did any member of Parliament lose his seat for the vote he gave on any detail of administration? To a minister, or the head of an office, it is of more importance what will be thought of his proceedings some time hence, than what is thought of them at the instant: but an assembly, if the cry of the moment goes with it, however hastily raised or artificially stirred up, thinks itself and is thought by everybody to be completely exculpated however disastrous may be the consequences. Besides, an assembly never personally experiences the inconveniences of its bad measures, until they have reached the dimensions of national evils. Ministers and administrators see them approaching, and have to bear all the annoyance and trouble of attempting to ward them off.

The proper duty of a representative assembly in regard to matters of administration, is not to decide them by its own vote, but to take care that the persons who have to decide them shall be the proper persons. Even this they cannot advantageously do by nominating the individuals. There is no act which more imperatively requires to be performed under a strong sense of individual responsibility than the nomination to employments. The experience of every person conversant with public affairs bears out the assertion, that there is scarely any act respecting which the conscience of an average man is less sensitive; scarcely any case in which less consideration is paid to qualifications, partly because men do not know, and partly because they do not care for, the difference in qualifications between one person and another. When a minister makes what is meant to be an honest appointment, that is when he does not actually job it for his personal connexions or his party, an ignorant person might suppose that he would try to give it to the person best qualified. No such thing. An ordinary minister thinks himself a miracle of virtue if he gives it to a person of merit, or who has a claim on the public on any account, though the claim or the merit may be of the most opposite description to that required. *Il fallait un calculateur, ce fut un danseur qui l'obtint,* is hardly more of a caricature than in the days of Figaro; and the minister doubtless thinks himself not only blameless but meritorious if the man dances well. Besides, the qualifications which fit special individuals for special duties can only be recognized by those who know the individuals, or who make it their business to examine and judge of persons from what they have done, or from the evidence of those who are in a position to judge. When these conscientious obligations are so little regarded by great public officers who can be made responsible for their appointments, how must it be with assemblies who cannot? Even now, the worst appointments are those which are made for the sake of gaining support or disarming opposition in the representative body: what might we expect if they were made by the body itself? Numerous bodies never regard special qualifications at all. Unless a man is fit for the gallows, he is thought to be about as fit as other people for almost anything for which he can offer himself as a candidate. When appointments made by a public body are not decided, as they almost always are, by party connexion or private jobbing, a man is appointed either because he has a reputation, often quite undeserved, for *general* ability, or frequently for no better reason than that he is personally popular.

It has never been thought desirable that Parliament should itself nominate even the members of a Cabinet. It is enough that it virtually decides who shall be prime minister, or who shall be the two or three individuals from whom the prime minister shall be chosen. In doing this it merely recognizes the fact that a certain person is the candidate of the party whose general policy commands its support. In reality, the only thing which Parliament decides is, which of two, or at most three, parties or bodies of men, shall furnish the executive government: the opinion of the party itself decides which of its members is fittest to be placed at the head. According to the existing practice of the British Constitution, these things seem to be on as good a footing as they can be. Parliament does not nominate any minister, but the Crown appoints the head of the administration in conformity to the general wishes and inclinations manifested by Parliament, and the other ministers on the recommendation of the chief; while every minister has the undivided moral responsibility of appointing fit persons to the other offices of administration which are not permanent. In a republic, some other arrangement would be necessary: but the nearer it approached in practice to that which has long existed in England, the more likely it would be to work well. Either, as in the American republic, the head of the Executive must be elected by some agency entirely independent of the representative body; or the body must content itself with naming the prime minister, and making him responsible for the choice of his associates and subordinates. To all these considerations, at least theoretically, I fully anticipate a general assent: though, practically, the tendency is strong in representative bodies to interfere more and more in the details of administration, by virtue of the general law, that whoever has

the strongest power is more and more tempted to make an excessive use of it; and this is one of the practical dangers to which the futurity of representative governments will be exposed.

But it is equally true, though only of late and slowly beginning to be acknowledged, that a numerous assembly is as little fitted for the direct business of legislation as for that of administration. There is hardly any kind of intellectual work which so much needs to be done not only by experienced and exercised minds, but by minds trained to the task through long and laborious study, as the business of making laws. This is a sufficient reason, were there no other, why they can never be well made but by a committee of very few persons. A reason no less conclusive is, that every provision of a law requires to be framed with the most accurate and long-sighted perception of its effect on all the other provisions; and the law when made should be capable of fitting into a consistent whole with the previously existing laws. It is impossible that these conditions should be in any degree fulfilled when laws are voted clause by clause in a miscellaneous assembly. The incongruity of such a mode of legislating would strike all minds, were it not that our laws are already, as to form and construction, such a chaos, that the confusion and contradiction seem incapable of being made greater by any addition to the mass. Yet even now, the utter unfitness of our legislative machinery for its purpose is making itself practically felt every year more and more. The mere time necessarily occupied in getting through Bills, renders Parliament more and more incapable of passing any, except on detached and narrow points. If a Bill is prepared which even attempts to deal with the whole of any subject (and it is impossible to legislate properly on any part without having the whole present to the mind), it hangs over from session to session through sheer impossibility of finding time to dispose of it. It matters not though the Bill may have been deliberately drawn up by the authority deemed the best qualified, with all appliances and means to boot; or by a select commission, chosen for their conversancy with the subject, and having employed years in considering and digesting the particular measure; it cannot be passed, because the House of Commons will not forgo the precious privilege of tinkering it with their clumsy hands. The custom has of late been to some extent introduced, when the principle of a Bill has been affirmed on the second reading, of referring it for consideration in detail to a Select Committee: but it has not been found that this practice causes much less time to be lost afterwards in carrying it through the Committee of the whole House: the opinions or private crotchets which have been overruled by knowledge, always insist on giving themselves a second chance before the tribunal of ignorance. Indeed, the practice itself has been adopted principally by the House of Lords, the members of which are less busy and fond of meddling, and less jealous of the importance of their individual voices, than those of the elective House. And when a Bill of many clauses does succeed in getting itself discussed in detail, what can depict the state in which it comes out of Committee! Clauses omitted, which are essential to the working of the rest; incongruous ones inserted to conciliate some private interest, or some crotchety member who threatens to delay the Bill; articles foisted in on the motion of some sciolist with a mere smattering of the subject, leading to consequences which the member who introduced or those who supported the Bill did not at the moment foresee, and which need an amending Act in the next session to correct their mischiefs. It is one of the evils of the present mode of managing these things, that the explaining and defending of a Bill, and of its various provisions, is scarcely ever performed by the person from whose mind they emanated, who probably has not a seat in the House. Their defence rests upon some minister or member of Parliament who did not frame them, who is dependent on cramming for all his arguments but those which are perfectly obvious, who does not know the full strength of his case, nor the best reasons by which to support it, and is wholly incapable of meeting unforeseen objections. This evil, as far as Government bills are concerned, admits of remedy, and has been remedied in some representative constitutions, by allowing the Government to be represented in

either House by persons in its confidence, having a right to speak, though not to vote.

If that, as yet considerable, majority of the House of Commons who never desire to move an amendment or make a speech, would no longer leave the whole regulation of business to those who do; if they would bethink themselves that better qualifications for legislation exist, and may be found if sought for, than a fluent tongue, and the faculty of getting elected by a constituency; it would soon be recognized, that in legislation as well as administration, the only task to which a representative assembly can possibly be competent, is not that of doing the work, but of causing it to be done; of determining to whom or to what sort of people it shall be confided, and giving or withholding the national sanction to it when performed. Any government fit for a high state of civilization, would have as one of its fundamental elements a small body, not exceeding in number the members of a Cabinet, who should act as a Commission of legislation, having for its appointed office to make the laws. If the laws of this country were, as surely they will soon be, revised and put into a connected form, the Commission of Codification by which this is effected should remain as a permanent institution, to watch over the work, protect it from deterioration, and make further improvements as often as required. No one would wish that this body should of itself have any power of *enacting* laws: the Commission would only embody the element of intelligence in their construction; Parliament would represent that of will. No measure would become a law until expressly sanctioned by Parliament; and Parliament, or either House, would have the power not only of rejecting but of sending back a Bill to the Commission for reconsideration or improvement. Either House might also exercise its initiative, by referring any subject to the Commission, with directions to prepare a law. The Commission, of course, would have no power of refusing its instrumentality to any legislation which the country desired. Instructions, concurred in by both Houses, to draw up a Bill which should effect a particular purpose, would be imperative on the Commissioners, unless they preferred to resign their office.

Once framed, however, Parliament should have no power to alter the measure, but solely to pass or reject it; or, if partially disapproved of, remit it to the Commission for reconsideration. The Commissioners should be appointed by the Crown, but should hold their offices for a time certain, say five years, unless removed on an address from the two Houses of Parliament, grounded either on personal misconduct (as in the case of judges), or on refusal to draw up a Bill in obedience to the demands of Parliament. At the expiration of the five years a member should cease to hold office unless reappointed, in order to provide a convenient mode of getting rid of those who had not been found equal to their duties, and of infusing new and younger blood into the body.

The necessity of some provision corresponding to this was felt even in the Athenian Democracy, where, in the time of its most complete ascendancy, the popular Ecclesia could pass Psephisms (mostly decrees on single matters of policy), but laws, so called, could only be made or altered by a different and less numerous body, renewed annually, called the Nomothetae, whose duty it also was to revise the whole of the laws, and keep them consistent with one another. In the English Constitution there is great difficulty in introducing any arrangement which is new both in form and in substance, but comparatively little repugnance is felt to the attainment of new purposes by an adaptation of existing forms and traditions. It appears to me that the means might be devised of enriching the Constitution with this great improvement through the machinery of the House of Lords. A Commission for preparing Bills would in itself be no more an innovation on the Constitution than the Board for the administration of the Poor Laws, or the Inclosure Commission. If, in consideration of the great importance and dignity of the trust, it were made a rule that every person appointed a member of the Legislative Commission, unless removed from office on an address from Parliament, should be a Peer for life, it is probable that the same good sense and taste which leave the judicial functions of the Peerage practically to the exclusive care of the law lords, would leave the business of legislation, except on questions involving political principles and interests, to the professional legislators; that Bills originating in the Upper House would always be drawn up by them; that the Government would devolve on them the framing of all its Bills; and that private members of the House of Commons would gradually find it convenient, and likely to facilitate the passing of their measures through the two Houses, if instead of bringing in a Bill and submitting it directly to the House, they obtained leave to introduce it and have it referred to the Legislative Commission. For it would, of course, be open to the House to refer for the consideration of that body not a subject merely, but any specific proposal, or a Draft of a Bill in extenso, when any member thought himself capable of preparing one such as ought to pass; and the House would doubtless refer every such draft to the Commission, if only as materials, and for the benefit of the suggestions it might contain: as they would, in like manner, refer every amendment or objection, which might be proposed in writing by any member of the House after a measure had left the Commissioners' hands. The alteration of Bills by a Committee of the whole House would cease, not by formal abolition, but by desuetude; the right not being abandoned, but laid up in the same armoury with the royal veto, the right of withholding the supplies, and other ancient instruments of political warfare, which no one desires to see used, but no one like to part with, lest they should at any time be found to be still needed in an extraordinary emergency. By such arrangements as these, legislation would assume its proper place as a work of skilled labour and special study and experience; while the most important liberty of the nation, that of being governed only by laws assented to by its elected representatives, would be fully preserved, and made more valuable by being detached from the serious, but by no means unavoidable, drawbacks which now accompany it in the form of ignorance and ill-considered legislation.

Instead of the function of governing, for which it is radically unfit, the proper office of a representative assembly is to watch and control the government: to throw the light of publicity on its acts: to compel a full exposition and justification of all of them which any one considers questionable; to censure them if found condemnable, and, if the men who compose the government abuse their trust, or fulfil it in a manner which conflicts with the deliberate sense of the nation, to expel them from office, and either expressly or virtually appoint their successors. This is surely ample power, and security enough for the liberty of the nation. In addition to this, the Parliament has an office, not inferior even to this in importance; to be at once the nation's Committee of Grievances, and its Congress of Opinions; an arena in which not only the general opinion of the nation, but that of every section of it, and as far as possible of every eminent individual whom it contains, can produce itself in full light and challenge discussion; where every person in the country may count upon finding somebody who speaks his mind, as well or better than he could speak it himself—not to friends and partisans exclusively, but in the face of opponents, to be tested by adverse controversy; where those whose opinion is overruled, feel satisfied that it is heard, and set aside not by a mere act of will, but for what are thought superior reasons, and commend themselves as such to the representatives of the majority of the nation; where every party or opinion in the country can muster its strength, and be cured of any illusion concerning the number or power of its adherents; where the opinion which prevails in the nation makes itself manifest as prevailing, and marshals its hosts in the presence of the government, which is thus enabled and compelled to give way to it on the mere manifestation, without the actual employment, of its strength; where statesmen can assure themselves, far more certainly than by any other signs, what elements of opinion and power are growing, and what declining, and are enabled to shape their measures with some regard not solely to present exigencies, but to tendencies in progress. Representative assemblies are often taunted by their enemies with being places of mere talk and *bavardage.* There has seldom been more misplaced derision. I know not how a representative assembly can more usefully employ itself than in talk, when the subject of talk is the great public interests of the country, and every sentence of it represents the opinion either of some important body of persons in the nation, or of an individual in whom some such body have reposed their confidence. A place where every interest and shade of opinion in the country can have its cause even passionately pleaded, in the face of the government and of all other interests and opinions, can compel them to listen, and either comply, or state clearly why they do not, is in itself, if it answered no other purpose, one of the most important political institutions that can exist anywhere, and one of the foremost benefits of free government. Such "talking" would never be looked upon with disparagement if it were not allowed to stop "doing"; which it never would, if assemblies knew and acknowledged that talking and discussion are their proper business, while *doing,* as the result of discussion, is the task not of a miscellaneous body, but of individuals specially trained to it; that the fit office of an assembly is to see that those individuals are honestly and intelligently chosen, and to interfere no further with them, except by unlimited latitude of suggestion and criticism, and by applying or withholding the final seal of national assent. It is for want of this judicious reserve, that popular assemblies attempt to do what they cannot do well—to govern and legislate—and provide no machinery but their own for much of it, when of course every hour spent in talk is an hour withdrawn from actual business. But the very fact which most unfits such bodies for a Council of Legislation, qualifies them the more for their other office—namely, that they are not a selection of the greatest political minds in the country, from whose opinions little could with certainty be inferred concerning those of the nation, but are, when properly constituted, a fair sample of every grade of intellect among the people which is at all entitled to a voice in public affairs. Their part is to indicate wants, to be an organ for popular demands, and a place of adverse discussion for all opinions relating to public matters, both great and small; and, along with this, to check by criticism, and eventually by withdrawing their support, those high public officers who really conduct the public business, or who appoint those by whom it is conducted. Nothing but the restriction of the function of representative bodies within these rational limits, will enable the benefits of popular control to be enjoyed in conjunction with the no less important requisites (growing ever more important as human affairs increase in scale and in complexity) of skilled legislation and administration. There are no means of combining these benefits, except by separating the functions which guarantee the one from those which essentially require the other; by disjoining the office of control and criticism from the actual conduct of affairs, and devolving the former on the representatives of the Many, while securing for the latter, under strict responsibility to the nation, the acquired knowledge and practised intelligence of a specially trained and experienced Few.

The preceding discussion of the functions which ought to devolve on the sovereign representative assembly of the nation, would require to be followed by an inquiry into those properly vested in the minor representative bodies, which ought to exist for purposes that regard only localities. And such an inquiry forms an essential part of the present treatise; but many reasons require its postponement, until we have considered the most proper composition of the great representative body, destined to control as sovereign the enactment of laws and the administration of the general affairs of the nation.

Chapter VI. Of the Infirmities and Dangers to Which Representative Government is Liable

The defects of any form of government may be either negative or positive. It is negatively defective if it does not concentrate in the hands of the authorities, power sufficient to fulfil the necessary offices of a government; or if it does not sufficiently develop by exercise the active capacities and social feelings of the individual citizens. On neither of these points is it necessary that much should be said at this stage of our inquiry.

The want of an amount of power in the gov-

ernment, adequate to preserve order and allow of progress in the people, is incident rather to a wild and rude state of society generally, than to any particular form of political union. When the people are too much attached to savage independence, to be tolerant of the amount of power to which it is for their good that they should be subject, the state of society (as already observed) is not yet ripe for representative government. When the time for that government has arrived, sufficient power for all needful purposes is sure to reside in the sovereign assembly; and if enough of it is not entrusted to the executive, this can only arise from a jealous feeling on the part of the assembly towards the administration, never likely to exist but where the constitutional power of the assembly to turn them out of office has not yet sufficiently established itself. Wherever that constitutional right is admitted in principle, and fully operative in practice, there is no fear that the assembly will not be willing to trust its own ministers with any amount of power really desirable; the danger is, on the contrary, lest they should grant it too ungrudgingly, and too indefinite in extent, since the power of the minister is the power of the body who make and who keep him so. It is, however, very likely, and is one of the dangers of a controlling assembly, that it may be lavish of powers, but afterwards interfere with their exercise; may give power by wholesale, and take it back in detail, by multiplied single acts of interference in the business of administration. The evils arising from this assumption of the actual function of governing, in lieu of that of criticizing and checking those who govern, have been sufficiently dwelt upon in the preceding chapter. No safeguard can in the nature of things be provided against this improper meddling, except a strong and general conviction of its injurious character.

The other negative defect which may reside in a government, that of not bringing into sufficient exercise the individual faculties, moral, intellectual, and active, of the people, has been exhibited generally in setting forth the distinctive mischiefs of despotism. As between one form of popular government and another, the advantage in this respect lies with that which most widely diffuses the exercise of public functions; on the one hand, by excluding fewest from the suffrage; on the other, by opening to all classes of private citizens, so far as is consistent with other equally important objects, the widest participation in the details of judicial and administrative business; as by jury trial, admission to municipal offices and above all by the utmost possible publicity and liberty of discussion, whereby not merely a few individuals in succession, but the whole public, are made, to a certain extent, participants in the government, and sharers in the instruction and mental exercise derivable from it. The further illustration of these benefits, as well as of the limitations under which they must be aimed at, will be better deferred until we come to speak of the details of administration.

The *positive* evils and dangers of the representative, as of every other form of government, may be reduced to two heads: first, general ignorance and incapacity, or, to speak more moderately, insufficient mental qualifications, in the controlling body; secondly, the danger of its being under the influence of interests not identical with the general welfare of the community.

The former of these evils, deficiency in high mental qualifications, is one to which it is generally supposed that popular government is liable in a greater degree than any other. The energy of a monarch, the steadiness and prudence of an aristocracy, are thought to contrast most favourably with the vacillation and short-sightedness of even a qualified democracy. These propositions, however, are not by any means so well founded as they at first sight appear.

Compared with simple monarchy, representative government is in these respects at no disadvantage. Except in a rude age, hereditary monarchy, when it is really such, and not aristocracy in disguise, far surpasses democracy in all the forms of incapacity supposed to be characteristic of the last. I say, except in a rude age, because in a really rude state of society there is a considerable guarantee for the intellectual and active capacities of the sovereign. His personal will is constantly encountering obstacles from the wilfulness of his subjects,

and of powerful individuals among their number. The circumstances of society do not afford him much temptation to mere luxurious self-indulgence; mental and bodily activity, especially political and military, are his principal excitements; and among turbulent chiefs and lawless followers he has little authority, and is seldom long secure even of his throne, unless he possesses a considerable amount of personal daring, dexterity, and energy. The reason why the average of talent is so high among the Henries and Edwards of our history, may be read in the tragical fate of the second Edward and the second Richard, and the civil wars and disturbances of the reigns of John and his incapable successor. The troubled period of the Reformation also produced several eminent hereditary monarchs, Elizabeth, Henri Quatre, Gustavus Adolphus; but they were mostly bred up in adversity, succeeded to the throne by the unexpected failure of nearer heirs, or had to contend with great difficulties in the commencement of their reign. Since European life assumed a settled aspect, anything above mediocrity in an hereditary king has become extremely rare, while the general average has been even below mediocrity, both in talent and in vigour of character. A monarchy constitutionally absolute now only maintains itself in existence (except temporarily in the hands of some active-minded usurper) through the mental qualifications of a permanent bureaucracy. The Russian and Austrian Governments, and even the French Government in its normal condition, are oligarchies of officials, of whom the head of the State does little more than select the chiefs. I am speaking of the regular course of their administration; for the will of the master of course determines many of their particular acts.

The governments which have been remarkable in history for sustained mental ability and vigour in the conduct of affairs, have generally been aristocracies. But they have been, without any exception, aristocracies of public functionaries. The ruling bodies have been so narrow, that each member, or at least each influential member, of the body, was able to make, and did make, public business an active profession, and the principal occupation of his life. The only aristocracies which have manifested high governing capacities, and acted on steady maxims of policy, through many generations, are those of Rome and Venice. But, at Venice, though the privileged order was numerous, the actual management of affairs was rigidly concentrated in a small oligarchy within the oligarchy, whose whole lives were devoted to the study and conduct of the affairs of the state. The Roman government partook more of the character of an open aristocracy like our own. But the really governing body, the Senate, was in general exclusively composed of persons who had exercised public functions, and had either already filled or were looking forward to fill the higher offices of the state, at the peril of a severe responsibility in case of incapacity and failure. When once members of the Senate, their lives were pledged to the conduct of public affairs; they were not permitted even to leave Italy except in the discharge of some public trust; and unless turned out of the Senate by the censors for character or conduct deemed disgraceful, they retained their powers and responsibilities to the end of life. In an aristocracy thus constituted, every member felt his personal importance entirely bound up with the dignity and estimation of the commonwealth which he administered, and with the part he was able to play in its councils. This dignity and estimation were quite different things from the prosperity or happiness of the general body of the citizens, and were often wholly incompatible with it. But they were closely linked with the external success and aggrandizement of the State: and it was, consequently, in the pursuit of that object almost exclusively, that either the Roman or the Venetian aristocracies manifested the systematically wise collective policy, and the great individual capacities for government, for which history has deservedly given them credit.

It thus appears that the only governments, not representative, in which high political skill and ability have been other than exceptional, whether under monarchical or aristocratic forms, have been essentially bureaucracies. The work of government has been in the hands of governors by profession; which is the essence and meaning of bureaucracy. Whether the work is done by them because they have been trained to it, or they are trained to it because it is to be done by them, makes a great difference in many respects, but none at all as to the essential character of the rule. Aristocracies, on the other hand, like that of England, in which the class who possessed the power derived it merely from their social position, without being specially trained or devoting themselves exclusively to it (and in which, therefore, the power was not exercised directly, but through representative institutions oligarchically constituted) have been, in respect to intellectual endowments, much on a par with democracies; that is, they have manifested such qualities in any considerable degree, only during the temporary ascendancy which great and popular talents, united with a distinguished position, have given to some one man. Themistocles and Pericles, Washington and Jefferson, were not more completely exceptions in their several democracies, and were assuredly much more splendid exceptions, than the Chathams and Peels of the representative aristocracy of Great Britain, or even the Sullys and Colberts of the aristocratic monarchy of France. A great minister, in the aristocratic governments of modern Europe, is almost as rare a phenomenon as a great king.

The comparison, therefore, as to the intellectual attributes of a government, has to be made between a representative democracy and a bureaucracy: all other governments may be left out of the account. And here it must be acknowledged that a bureaucratic government has, in some important respects, greatly the advantage. It accumulates experience, acquires well-tried and well-considered traditional maxims, and makes provision for appropriate practical knowledge in those who have the actual conduct of affairs. But it is not equally favorable to individual energy of mind. The disease which afflicts bureaucratic governments, and which they usually die of, is routine. They perish by the immutability of their maxims; and, still more, by the universal law that whatever becomes a routine loses its vital principle, and having no longer a mind acting within it, goes on revolving mechanically though the work it is intended to do remains undone. A bureaucracy always tends to become a pedantocracy. When the bureaucracy is the real government, the spirit of the corps (as with the Jesuits) bears down the individuality of its more distinguished members. In the profession of government, as in other professions, the sole idea of the majority is to do what they have been taught; and it requires a popular government to enable the conceptions of the man of original genius among them, to prevail over the obstructive spirit of trained mediocrity. Only in a popular government (setting apart the accident of a highly intelligent despot) could Sir Rowland Hill have been victorious over the Post Office. A popular government installed him *in* the Post Office, and made the body, in spite of itself, obey the impulse given by the man who united special knowledge with individual vigour and originality. That the Roman aristocracy escaped this characteristic disease of a bureaucracy, was evidently owing to its popular element. All special offices, both those which gave a seat in the Senate and those which were sought by senators, were conferred by popular election. The Russian Government is a characteristic exemplification of both the good and bad side of bureaucracy: its fixed maxims, directed with Roman perseverance to the same unflinchingly-pursued ends from age to age; the remarkable skill with which those ends are generally pursued; the frightful internal corruption, and the permanent organized hostility to improvements from without, which even the autocratic power of a vigorous-minded Emperor is seldom or never sufficient to overcome; the patient obstructiveness of the body being in the long run more than a match for the fitful energy of one man. The Chinese Government, a bureaucracy of Mandarins, is, as far as known to us, another apparent example of the same qualities and defects.

In all human affairs, conflicting influences are required, to keep one another alive and efficient even for their own proper uses; and the exclusive pursuit of one good object, apart from some other which should accompany it, ends not in excess of one and defect of the other, but in the decay and loss even of that which has been exclusively cared for. Government by trained officials cannot do, for a country, the things which can be done by a free government; but it might be supposed capable of doing some things which free government, of itself, cannot do. We find, however, that an outside element of freedom is necessary to enable it to do effectually or permanently even its own business. And so, also, freedom cannot produce its best effects, and often breaks down altogether, unless means can be found of combining it with trained and skilled administration. There could not be a moment's hesitation between representative government, among a people in any degree ripe for it, and the most perfect imaginable bureaucracy. But it is, at the same time, one of the most important ends of political institutions, to attain as many of the qualities of the one as are consistent with the other; to secure, as far as they can be made compatible, the great advantage of the conduct of affairs by skilled persons, bred to it as an intellectual profession, along with that of a general control vested in, and seriously exercised by, bodies representative of the entire people. Much would be done towards this end by recognizing the line of separation, discussed in the preceding chapter, between the work of government properly so called, which can only be well performed after special cultivation, and that of selecting, watching, and, when needful, controlling the governors, which in this case, as in others, properly devolves, not on those who do the work, but on those for whose benefit it ought to be done. No progress at all can be made towards obtaining a skilled democracy, unless the democracy are willing that the work which requires skill should be done by those who possess it. A democracy has enough to do in providing itself with an amount of mental competency sufficient for its own proper work, that of superintendence and check.

How to obtain and secure this amount, is one of the questions to be taken into consideration in judging of the proper constitution of a representative body. In proportion as its composition fails to secure this amount, the assembly will encroach, by special acts, on the province of the executive; it will expel a good, or elevate and uphold a bad, ministry; it will connive at, or overlook, in them, abuses of trust, will be deluded by their false pretences, or will withhold support from those who endeavour to fulfil their trust conscientiously; it will countenance, or impose, a selfish, a capricious and impulsive, a shortsighted, ignorant, and prejudiced general policy, foreign and domestic; it will abrogate good laws, or enact bad ones, let in new evils, or cling with perverse obstinacy to old; it will even, perhaps, under misleading impulses, momentary or permanent, emanating from itself or from its constituents, tolerate or connive at proceedings which set law aside altogether, in cases where equal justice would not be agreeable to popular feeling. Such are among the dangers of representative government, arising from a constitution of the representation which does not secure an adequate amount of intelligence and knowledge in the representative assembly.

We next proceed to the evils arising from the prevalence of modes of action in the representative body, dictated by sinister interests (to employ the useful phrase introduced by Bentham), that is, interests conflicting more or less with the general good of the community.

It is universally admitted, that, of the evils incident to monarchical and aristocratic governments, a large proportion arise from this cause. The interest of the monarch, or the interest of the aristocracy, either collective or that of its individual members, is promoted, or they themselves think that it will be promoted, by conduct opposed to that which the general interest of the community requires. The interest, for example, of the government is to tax heavily: that of the community is, to be as little taxed as the necessary expenses of good government permit. The interest of the king, and of the governing aristocracy, is to possess, and exercise, unlimited power over the people; to enforce, on their part, complete conformity to the will and preferences of the rulers. The interest of the people is, to have as little control exercised over them in any respect, as is consistent with attaining the legitimate ends of government. The interest, or apparent and supposed interest, of the king or aristocracy, is to permit no censure of themselves, at least in any

form which they may consider either to threaten their power, or seriously to interfere with their free agency. The interest of the people is that there should be full liberty of censure on every public officer, and on every public act or measure. The interest of a ruling class, whether in an aristocracy or an aristocratic monarchy, is to assume to themselves an endless variety of unjust privileges, sometimes benefiting their pockets at the expense of the people, sometimes merely tending to exalt them above others, or, what is the same thing in different words, to degrade others below themselves. If the people are disaffected, which under such a government they are very likely to be, it is the interest of the king or aristocracy to keep them at a low level of intelligence and education, foment dissensions among them, and even prevent them from being too well off, lest they should "wax fat, and kick"; agreeably to the maxim of Cardinal Richelieu in his celebrated "Testament Politique." All these things are for the interest of a king or aristocracy, in a purely selfish point of view, unless a sufficiently strong counter-interest is created by the fear of provoking resistance. All these evils have been, and many of them still are, produced by the sinister interests of kings and aristocracies, where their power is sufficient to raise them above the opinion of the rest of the community; nor is it rational to expect, as the consequence of such a position, any other conduct.

These things are superabundantly evident in the case of a monarchy or an aristocracy; but it is sometimes rather gratuitously assumed, that the same kind of injurious influences do not operate in a democracy. Looking at democracy in the way in which it is commonly conceived, as the rule of the numerical majority, it is surely possible that the ruling power may be under the dominion of sectional or class interests, pointing to conduct different from that which would be dictated by impartial regard for the interest of all. Suppose the majority to be whites, the minority negroes, or vice versa: is it likely that the majority would allow equal justice to the minority? Suppose the majority Catholics, the minority Protestants, or the reverse; will there not be the same danger? Or let the majority be English, the minority Irish, or the contrary: is there not a great probability of similar evil? In all countries there is a majority of poor, a minority who, in contradistinction, may be called rich. Between these two classes, on many questions, there is complete opposition of apparent interest. We will suppose the majority sufficiently intelligent to be aware that it is not for their advantage to weaken the security of property, and that it would be weakened by any act of arbitrary spoliation. But is there not a considerable danger lest they should throw upon the possessors of what is called realized property, and upon the larger incomes, an unfair share, or even the whole, of the burden of taxation, and having done so, add to the amount without scruple, expending the proceeds in modes supposed to conduce to the profit and advantage of the labouring class? Suppose, again, a minority of skilled labourers, a majority of unskilled: the experience of many Trade Unions, unless they are greatly calumniated, justifies the apprehension that equality of earnings might be imposed as an obligation, and that piece-work, payment by the hour, and all practices which enable superior industry or abilities to gain a superior reward, might be put down. Legislative attempts to raise wages, limitation of competition in the labour market, taxes or restrictions on machinery, and on improvements of all kinds tending to dispense with any of the existing labour—even, perhaps, protection of the home producer against foreign industry—are very natural (I do not venture to say whether probable) results of a feeling of class interest in a governing majority of manual labourers.

It will be said that none of these things are for the *real* interest of the most numerous class: to which I answer, that if the conduct of human beings was determined by no other interested considerations than those which constitute their "real" interest, neither monarchy nor oligarchy would be such bad governments as they are; for assuredly very strong arguments may be, and often have been, adduced to show that either a king or a governing senate are in much the most enviable position, when ruling justly and vigilantly over an active,

wealthy, enlightened, and high-minded people. But a king only now and then, and an oligarchy in no known instance, have taken this exalted view of their self-interest: and why should we expect a loftier mode of thinking from the labouring classes? It is not what their interest is, but what they suppose it to be, that is the important consideration with respect to their conduct: and it is quite conclusive against any theory of government, that it assumes the numerical majority to do habitually what is never done, nor expected to be done, save in very exceptional cases, by any other depositaries of power—namely, to direct their conduct by their real ultimate interest, in opposition to their immediate and apparent interest. No one, surely, can doubt that many of the pernicious measures above enumerated, and many others as bad, would be for the immediate interest of the general body of unskilled labourers. It is quite possible that they would be for the selfish interest of the whole existing generation of the class. The relaxation of industry and activity, and diminished encouragement to saving, which would be their ultimate consequence, might perhaps be little felt by the class of unskilled labourers in the space of a single lifetime. Some of the most fatal changes in human affairs have been, as to their more manifest immediate effects, beneficial. The establishment of the despotism of the Caesars was a great benefit to the entire generation in which it took place. It put a stop to civil war, abated a vast amount of malversation and tyranny by praetors and proconsuls; it fostered many of the graces of life, and intellectual cultivation in all departments not political; it produced monuments of literary genius dazzling to the imaginations of shallow readers of history, who do not reflect that the men to whom the despotism of Augustus (as well as of Lorenzo de' Medici and of Louis XIV) owes its brilliancy, were all formed in the generation preceding. The accumulated riches, and the mental energy and activity, produced by centuries of freedom, remained for the benefit of the first generation of slaves. Yet this was the commencement of a régime by whose gradual operation all the civilization which had been gained, insensibly faded away, until the Empire which had conquered and embraced the world in its grasp, so completely lost even its military efficiency, that invaders whom three or four legions had always sufficed to coerce, were able to overrun and occupy nearly the whole of its vast territory. The fresh impulse given by Christianity came but just in time to save arts and letters from perishing, and the human race from sinking back into perhaps endless night.

When we talk of the interest of a body of men, or even of an individual man, as a principle determining their actions, the question what would be considered their interest by an unprejudiced observer, is one of the least important parts of the whole matter. As Coleridge observes, the man makes the motive, not the motive the man. What it is the man's interest to do or refrain from, depends less on any outward circumstances, than upon what sort of man he is. If you wish to know what is practically a man's interest, you must know the cast of his habitual feelings and thoughts. Everybody has two kinds of interests, interests which he cares for, and interests which he does not care for. Everybody has selfish and unselfish interests, and a selfish man has cultivated the habit of caring for the former, and not caring for the latter. Every one has present and distant interests, and the improvident man is he who cares for the present interests and does not care for the distant. It matters little that on any correct calculation the latter may be the more considerable, if the habits of his mind lead him to fix his thoughts and wishes solely on the former. It would be vain to attempt to persuade a man who beats his wife and illtreats his children, that he would be happier if he lived in love and kindness with them. He would be happier if he were the kind of person who *could* so live; but he is not, and it is probably too late for him to become, that kind of person. Being what he is, the gratification of his love of domineering, and the indulgence of his ferocious temper, are to his perceptions a greater good to himself, than he would be capable of deriving from the pleasure and affection of those dependent on him. He has no pleasure in their pleasure, and does not care for their affection. His neighbour, who does, is probably

a happier man than he; but could he be persuaded of this, the persuasion would, most likely, only still further exasperate his malignity or his irritability. On the average, a person who cares for other people, for his country, or for mankind, is a happier man than one who does not; but of what use is it to preach this doctrine to a man who cares for nothing but his own ease, or his own pocket? He cannot care for other people if he would. It is like preaching to the worm who crawls on the ground, how much better it would be for him if he were an eagle.

Now it is an universally observed fact, that the two evil dispositions in question, the disposition to prefer a man's selfish interests to those which he shares with other people, and his immediate and direct interests to those which are indirect and remote, are characteristics most especially called forth and fostered by the possession of power. The moment a man, or a class of men, find themselves with power in their hands, the man's individual interest, or the class's separate interest, acquires an entirely new degree of importance in their eyes. Finding themselves worshipped by others, they become worshippers of themselves, and think themselves entitled to be counted at a hundred times the value of other people; while the facility they acquire of doing as they like without regard to consequences, insensibly weakens the habits which make men look forward even to such consequences as affect themselves. This is the meaning of the universal tradition, grounded on universal experience, of men's being corrupted by power. Every one knows how absurd it would be to infer from what a man is or does when in a private station, that he will be and do exactly the like when a despot on a throne; where the bad parts of his human nature, instead of being restrained and kept in subordination by every circumstance of his life and by every person surrounding him, are courted by all persons, and ministered to by all circumstances. It would be quite as absurd to entertain a similar expectation in regard to a class of men; the Demos, or any other. Let them be ever so modest and amenable to reason while there is a power over them stronger than they, we ought to expect a total change in this respect when they themselves become the strongest power.

Governments must be made for human beings as they are, or as they are capable of speedily becoming: and in any state of cultivation which mankind, or any class among them, have yet attained, or are likely soon to attain, the interests by which they will be led, when they are thinking only of self-interest, will be almost exclusively those which are obvious at first sight, and which operate on their present condition. It is only a disinterested regard for others, and especially for what comes after them, for the idea of posterity, of their country, or of mankind, whether grounded on sympathy or on a conscientious feeling, which ever directs the minds and purposes of classes or bodies of men towards distant or unobvious interests. And it cannot be maintained that any form of government would be rational, which required as a condition that these exalted principles of action should be the guiding and master motives in the conduct of average human beings. A certain amount of conscience, and of disinterested public spirit, may fairly be calculated on in the citizens of any community ripe for representative government. But it would be ridiculous to expect such a degree of it, combined with such intellectual discernment, as would be proof against any plausible fallacy tending to make that which was for their class interest appear the dictate of justice and of the general good. We all know what specious fallacies may be urged in defence of every act of injustice yet proposed for the imaginary benefit of the mass. We know how many, not otherwise fools or bad men, have thought it justifiable to repudiate the national debt. We know how many, not destitute of ability, and of considerable popular influence, think it fair to throw the whole burden of taxation upon savings, under the name of realized property, allowing those whose progenitors and themselves have always spent all they received, to remain, as a reward for such exemplary conduct, wholly untaxed. We know what powerful arguments, the more dangerous because there is a portion of truth in them, may

be brought against all inheritance, against the power of bequest, against every advantage which one person seems to have over another. We know how easily the uselessness of almost every branch of knowledge may be proved, to the complete satisfaction of those who do not possess it. How many, not altogether stupid men, think the scientific study of languages useless, think ancient literature useless, all erudition useless, logic and metaphysics useless, poetry and the fine arts idle and frivolous, political economy purely mischievous? Even history has been pronounced useless and mischievous by able men. Nothing but that acquaintance with external nature, empirically acquired, which serves directly for the production of objects necessary to existence or agreeable to the senses, would get its utility recognized if people had the least encouragement to disbelieve it. Is it reasonable to think that even much more cultivated minds than those of the numerical majority can be expected to be, will have so delicate a conscience, and so just an appreciation of what is against their own apparent interest, that they will reject these and the innumerable other fallacies which will press in upon them from all quarters as soon as they come into power, to induce them to follow their own selfish inclinations and short-sighted notions of their own good, in opposition to justice, at the expense of all other classes and of posterity?

One of the greatest dangers, therefore, of democracy, as of all other forms of government, lies in the sinister interest of the holders of power: it is the danger of class legislation; of government intended for (whether really effecting it or not) the immediate benefit of the dominant class, to the lasting detriment of the whole. And one of the most important questions demanding consideration, in determining the best constitution of a representative government, is how to provide efficacious securities against this evil.

If we consider as a class, politically speaking, any number of persons who have the same sinister interest—that is, whose direct and apparent interest points towards the same description of bad measures; the desirable object would be that no class, and no combination of classes likely to combine, should be able to exercise a preponderant influence in the government. A modern community, not divided within itself by strong antipathies of race, language, or nationality, may be considered as in the main divisible into two sections, which, in spite of partial variations, correspond on the whole with two divergent directions of apparent interest. Let us call them (in brief general terms) labourers on the one hand, employers of labour on the other: including however along with employers of labour, not only retired capitalists, and the possessors of inherited wealth, but all that highly paid description of labourers (such as the professions) whose education and way of life assimilate them with the rich, and whose prospect and ambition it is to raise themselves into that class. With the labourers, on the other hand, may be ranked those smaller employers of labour, who by interests, habits, and educational impressions, are assimilated in wishes, tastes, and objects to the labouring classes; comprehending a large proportion of petty tradesmen. In a state of society thus composed, if the representative system could be made ideally perfect, and if it were possible to maintain it in that state, its organization must be such, that these two classes, manual labourers and their affinities on one side, employers of labour and their affinities on the other, should be, in the arrangement of the representative system, equally balanced, each influencing about an equal number of votes in Parliament: since, assuming that the majority of each class, in any difference between them, would be mainly governed by their class interests, there would be a minority of each in whom that consideration would be subordinate to reason, justice, and the good of the whole;

and this minority of either, joining with the whole of the other, would turn the scale against any demands of their own majority which were not such as ought to prevail. The reason why, in any tolerably constituted society, justice and the general interest mostly in the end carry their point, is that the separate and selfish interests of mankind are almost always divided; some are interested in what is wrong, but some, also, have their private interest on the side of what is right: and those who are governed by higher considerations, though too few and weak to prevail against the whole of the others, usually after sufficient discussion and agitation become strong enough to turn the balance in favour of the body of private interests which is on the same side with them. The representative system ought to be so constituted as to maintain this state of things: it ought not to allow any of the various sectional interests to be so powerful as to be capable of prevailing against truth and justice and the other sectional interests combined. There ought always to be such a balance preserved among personal interests, as may render any one of them dependent for its successes, on carrying with it at least a large proportion of those who act on higher motives, and more comprehensive and distant views.

Note

1. I limit the expression to past time, because I would say nothing derogatory of a great, and now at last a free, people, who are entering into the general movement of European progress with a vigour which bids fair to make up rapidly the ground they have lost. No one can doubt what Spanish intellect and energy are capable of; and their faults as a people are chiefly those for which freedom and industrial ardour are a real specific.

Open Government and Just Legislation: A Defense of Democracy

WILLIAM N. NELSON

It is important to bear in mind the distinctions between the different parts of a complete theory of democracy. To reject a theory on the ground that the system it proposes is unfeasible, for example, is not necessarily to deny that it is an inspiring ideal. More important, to reject a theory on the ground that it embodies an inadequate justification of a system of democracy is not to deny the possibility that democracy, as defined, *can* be justified—that there are other good arguments in its favor. Thus, while I have criticized a number of theories of democracy, I have not said that there is no adequate theory. Indeed, I have not even denied that democracy, as defined in one of the theories I have criticized, might be given an adequate justification. With the exception of the theory of democracy as popular sovereignty, which I rejected partly on grounds of feasibility, I have objected to various theories primarily because of the justifications they embody. Before turning to my positive tasks in this chapter, I shall take another brief look at some of these criticisms.

My main point could be summarized in this way: none of the theories discussed in Chapters II, III or V take the problem of justifying democracy seriously enough. The theories discussed in these chapters all assume the desirability of what they are supposed to be justifying. Now, this way of putting my point

is itself misleading, but I hope it is also illuminating. Consider the argument from fairness discussed in Chapter II. To be sure, it is possible to offer a characterization of democracy in terms of majority rule and to argue for this system in terms of the further claim that majority rule distributes political power equally. To argue thus is not to claim that democracy, as characterized, is self justifying. Majority rule is justified only because it distributes power fairly and equally. But it would not seem particularly odd if someone were to *define* democracy as the type of system that distributes power equally. If the argument from fairness were an adequate justification for democracy, then, on at least one not unreasonable characterization of democracy, democracy *would* be self justifying. To put the point another way: when people ask whether democracy is a desirable system, precisely what they mean to ask, at least sometimes, is whether it is desirable that political power be distributed equally

What I have just said about the argument from fairness could also be said about the economic justification of democracy. Here again, the kind of theory I have actually discussed characterizes democracy in terms of certain voting rules and procedures and then goes on to argue that a government ought to operate according to these rules and procedures be-

William N. Nelson, "Open Government and Just Legislation: A Defense of Democracy," Chapter VI of *On Justifying Democracy* by William N. Nelson (Routledge & Kegan Paul, 1980). Reprinted by permission of the author and publisher.

cause of their predicted results. However, the result which is assumed desirable in this argument, namely, maximum feasible satisfaction of whatever desires people happen to have (''consumer sovereignty'' for the consumers of government's products), is just the kind of goal that people often mean to be questioning when they question the value of democracy. More important, it seems to me not unreasonable to question the desirability of the democratic goals in terms of which both the argument from fairness and the economic argument propose that we justify democracy. It does not seem wildly unreasonable to suggest that not all desires deserve satisfaction and that some desires do not even deserve to be taken into account. For related reasons, it does not seem unreasonable at least to question the idea that political power should be shared equally by everyone.

The theories that cluster around the idea of maximum political participation or the idea of a participatory society present a more complex picture. Some versions seem to define democracy in terms of participation and then do little more than assert that people have a right to participate or that participation is intrinsically desirable. Some versions argue for participation in terms of its effects, but the effects in question are simply the long term stability of the participatory system—hardly an independent justification of the system! But some versions of participation theory suggest that participation has beneficial effects on the moral quality both of citizens and governmental policy. This kind of argument was never fully developed by the theorists considered in Chapter III, but it does at least deserve further consideration.

What we need to do, if we are to offer an argument for democracy capable of convincing those who are not already convinced democrats, is to begin with an independent account of what is morally desirable and why it is morally desirable. If we can then argue, in terms of such an account, that democracy is desirable itself, or has desirable consequences, we will have made some progress. This is what I shall attempt to do in this chapter. The task will

require an excursion into moral theory, and then a discussion of how a representative democracy might be expected to work so as to produce government acceptable from the perspective of the kind of moral theory I shall sketch. Following this discussion I shall return once again to the theories I have discussed in earlier chapters in order to explore the similarities and differences between my own theory and these alternatives.

The theory I shall develop in this chapter will be an instrumental theory. I shall argue that democracy is desirable largely because of its good effects—because it tends to produce good laws and policies, or, at least, to prevent bad ones. But this kind of theory has been subjected to serious criticism, perhaps most notably by Robert Dahl in his widely read *Preface to Democratic Theory*.[1] Since some of Dahl's arguments can be taken to be general arguments against any justification of the type I shall attempt, I must discuss Dahl's critique of Madison before proceeding with the program I have outlined.

1. Dahl on Madison

The first chapter of *Preface to Democratic Theory* is a critique of what Dahl takes to be the Madisonian theory of democracy. Democracy, on this theory, is American constitutional democracy with its complex system of checks on the power of majorities. Madison's argument for this system, according to Dahl, is that a republican form of government, circumscribed by checks on the power of majorities, is necessary to prevent tyranny. The absence of either popular elections or constitutional checks and balances will lead to tyranny (Dahl, 11).[2] This is a justification of constitutional democracy in terms of its substantive effects, and Dahl argues that it fails. He criticizes it on two grounds. First, assuming that we know what tyranny is, Dahl argues that Madison's justification seems to be based on a false empirical generalization. Second, he argues that we cannot really even test this generalization since we cannot give an adequate account of what tyranny is. True, we could define 'tyranny' in such a way that any nonrepublican government or government without separation of powers, was, by definition, tyrannical. But that kind of definition makes the argument trivial and uninteresting. The argument is interesting only if we begin with an independent definition of "tyranny", but no such definition is adequate.

The first objection presupposes that the second is mistaken, so it is hard to see just how we are to take it. Still, it seems reasonable to say that, on any initially plausible account of tyranny, there are possible nontyrannical governments that lack the kind of constitutional restraints on the power of majorities that we find in the United States Constitution. Great Britain is a good enough example (Dahl, 13). Moreover, common sense, together with a good deal of social theory, suggests that non-institutional, psychological restraints can be just as effective as legal restraints in preventing abuse of power (Dahl, 17–19).[3] So, it seems doubtful that a constitutional democracy of the sort Madison had in mind is necessary to prevent tyranny.

The second objection is the more fundamental one. If it is successful, it will undermine any attempt to justify a system of government by reference to a substantive moral goal like the avoidance of tyranny. How exactly does the objection go? To define 'tyranny' in terms of the deprivation of natural rights is not to define it adequately unless we can "specify a process by which specific natural rights can be defined in the context of some political society" (Dahl, 23). Any attempt to do so in a way consistent with other elements of a theory like Madison's will fail, so, "tyranny seems to have no operational meaning in the context of political decision-making" (Dahl, 24). Now, the general point here presumably is not limited to definitions of 'tyranny' or definitions of 'natural rights'. The point, rather, is that a justification of a form of government based on the claim that that government will produce certain kinds of legislation requires a precise account of the kind of legislation in question. Otherwise, it will be impossible to determine the truth of the key premise in the argument. Dahl thinks he has an argument to rule out any ad-

equate account, but I believe his argument fails.

There are two problems with Dahl's argument. First, he demands more of an adequate definition than he needs to demand, and, second, even given his overly strong requirement, he fails to demonstrate that it cannot be met. The second point is the easier one to make. Dahl argues by elimination. He considers only three possible theories of natural rights: that each person has a right to do whatever he wants; that each has a right to do whatever is not unanimously condemned, and, that each has a right to do whatever is not condemned by a majority. Dahl holds each to these theories to be either impractical or inconsistent with other elements of a theory like Madison's. (The third, for example, seems to rule out the possibility of majority tyranny (Dahl, 23–4).) But these are not all the possible theories of natural rights; so we cannot conclude that there is *no* adequate theory. And what a strange collection of theories Dahl has chosen to discuss! Moral theorists do not generally take seriously accounts of moral rights that make those rights depend on how people happen to vote. (What if they are immoral?) But here Dahl seems to be a victim of his decision to require not just a clear and precise account of the ethical goals to be attained by the political process, but an account that determines, *by some decisive political process,* what those goals involve. This brings us back to the first of the two problems mentioned above: Dahl demands more of an adequate definition than he needs to demand.

At the very least, Dahl requires that a definition of natural rights be operational. There are serious philosophical problems about the requirement of operational definition in any area of inquiry.[4] But, even if we assume that something like the requirement of operational definition is reasonable, I think Dahl requires too much. Everyone would agree, I suppose, that reasonable clarity and precision is desirable. No doubt one idea associated with operational definition is just this idea. The proponents of operational definition want to be able to say what does and does not follow from this or that proposition—what its truth conditions are. But they also want the presence or absence of these truth conditions to be subject to public determination. They want an account of truth conditions such that there will be virtually no room for disagreement about whether or not they are satisfied. Most would agree, however, that verifiability *in principle* is the most we can require. The most we can require is that, for each proposition, if we had the time, resources and so on, we could get near universal agreement on the truth or falsity of the proposition. Consider, for example, the concepts that figured in the economic analyses of democracy discussed in the preceding chapter, concepts like 'Pareto optimality' and 'Pareto improvement'. Even supposing a reasonable operational account of 'P prefers x to y', it would be virtually impossible to determine in an actual case whether one situation was really Pareto better than another. Yet the notion of a Pareto improvement is generally conceded to be the kind of notion that satisfies reasonable requirements of operationality.[5] Dahl, however, wants more than this.

If we want a political system that will make laws, if we want these laws to be an effective determinant of conduct, and if we want to penalize those who violate the laws, we need clear criteria, about which there can be little disagreement, by means of which we can determine what the law requires and who has complied wit it. It is not enough that this be determinable merely *in principle*. We need procedures that will terminate in a reasonably short period of time. When we attach practical consequences to the truth or falsity of certain propositions, we need practical, decisive procedures by which to determine their truth or falsity. Dahl, I want to suggest, confuses the requirement of decisive procedures appropriate in political contexts with the weaker requirements of clarity and verifiability in principle which may be appropriate in some theoretical contexts. It is for this reason that Dahl considers only accounts of natural rights stated in terms of procedures like majority rule.

I do not want to deny the importance of decisive, practical procedures in political sys-

tems. The question how we should go about justifying our choice of procedures is an important one just because we need some procedures. It is a difficult question just because no procedure can capture the moral criteria by which we evaluate political decisions. But the question whether a given system or procedure is justified is not itself a political question; it is a theoretical question. We do not need a decisive procedure to settle the question of the justifiability of our political decision procedures. Still, if we are to defend democracy, as Madison evidently did, by arguing that it tends to have results of a certain kind, it is incumbent on us to give a reasonably clear account of the kind of result we have in mind. To this extent, I agree with Dahl. But when Dahl objects that there is no way to clarify Madison's goal of nontyranny, he bases his objection on a survey of an absurdly small and irrelevant sample of possible attempts to clarify this goal. Apparently, this is because he requires more than clarity, and more even than what is normally demanded by those who require operational definitions.

Conceivably, Dahl was dimly aware of this kind of problem when he allowed himself to assume, at the beginning of his discussion of Madison, that we do have a clear enough understanding of what constitutes tyranny to evaluate Madison's central empirical claim—the claim that republican government with separation of powers is necessary for nontyrannical government. Dahl thinks it obvious, indeed, that there are governments significantly different from Madison's constitutional democracy that nevertheless manage to be nontyrannical. But now we should look again at this criticism. I do not want to quibble about the interpretation of Madison's writings in *The Federalist;* but, clearly, some theories *like* the theory Dahl attributes to Madison are immune to Dahl's criticisms. Thus, one might argue for some form of constitutional democracy not on the ground that it is *necessary* for decent government, but on the ground that it is more likely than other forms of government to lead to decent government. In sum, then, Dahl's arguments fall far short of ruling out any attempt to justify democracy in terms of the moral quality of its likely substantive results.

2. Morality and Just Government

The most important question about the system of laws and institutions making up the state is whether they satisfy the conditions morality lays down for such systems. Morality determines the limits of the permissible for systems of laws and institutions as well as for individual conduct. It has been said that "justice is the first virtue of institutions."[6] If this is so, it is so because a reasonable moral theory assigns a kind of priority to considerations of justice or because, in such a theory, considerations referred to as considerations of justice are just those relevant to the assessment of institutions. I have no objection to this way of speaking, but it leaves us with the following question: when it is true that legal, political or economic institutions are just, what does this involve? This is a substantive moral question. It can be answered only within a substantive theory. I shall argue for democracy, here, on the ground that it tends to produce specific laws and policies that are just. I am assuming that this kind of argument is sufficient to justify a political system, or at least to create a strong presumption in its favor. Suppose someone says that this kind of argument is irrelevant—that the crucial question concerns not the effects of the system, but its intrinsic features, whether it is fair, for example. I have no *general* argument against this position. I have attempted to reply to specific theories of this type in earlier chapters. I hope to establish, in this chapter, at least the possibility of a coherent, plausible justification in terms of effects. Skepticism about the possibility of such a theory, as voiced by Dahl for example, may well be one reason for the prevalence of "procedural" theories.

If we are to argue that democracy satisfies principles of justice, and if this requires us to argue that democracy is well designed to produce just laws and policies, we clearly must say something about what justice, and morality in general, require. One way to carry out a defense of democracy along these lines would be

this: offer an account of which laws are morally good laws, and then try to show that democracies tend to have good laws and that other governments do not. (Dahl used something analogous to this procedure to discredit Madison's contention that democracy is necessary for good government.) There are other possibilities, however. When Buchanan and Tullock argue that certain kinds of democratic procedure will lead to Pareto optimal outcomes, or to Pareto improvements on the status quo, they do not proceed by examining governments of various kinds and establishing correlations. Instead, they begin with a reasonably precise, abstract specification of the goals to be achieved and of the system they have in mind, and then, given more or less standard motivational assumptions, *deduce* the consequence they seek from their definitions, assumptions, and certain well-known results in economic theory. Of course, their argument is not as formal as I make it sound here, and my argument will not be as formal as theirs; but my argument will be more like theirs than like the other alternative mentioned. The mechanics of democracy are such, I shall argue, that, given certain assumptions about human nature, democracy will automatically tend to produce morally acceptable results. Now this kind of argument, like the others I have mentioned, seems to presuppose a clear account of which laws are morally good laws. I shall have something to say along these lines, but most of my argument will proceed at a higher level of abstraction. Instead of offering anything like a complete account of what morality requires, I shall suggest an account of what a (reasonable) morality is. This account will embody conditions which must be satisfied by any acceptable moral principles. I shall then argue that, following the procedures of (a kind of) constitutional democracy, we will tend to come up with laws that are justifiable in terms of principles satisfying the conditions of acceptability for moral principles. The general idea is this: the tests that a law has to pass to be adopted in a constitutional democracy are analogous to the tests that a moral principle must pass in order to be an acceptable moral principle.

What conditions must a principle satisfy in order to be an acceptable moral principle? What conditions must a set of principles satisfy if they are to constitute an adequate morality? What principles are true moral principles? It is natural to think that the answer to these questions depends on an account of the function of morality: true moral principles are principles that perform the function of moral principles. Looking at the problem in this way generates difficult questions. If two distinct sets of principles would equally well perform the function of morality, for example, is each set a set of true principles? More fundamental, however, is the question whether there is any such thing as *the* function(s) of morality. And how do we know when we have found it (them)? I do not have definitive answers to these questions. Nevertheless, I shall propose an account of morality in terms of its functions. The account I offer is not the only possible account of its kind. Others have been, or might be, offered. But neither is my account idiosyncratic. My suggestions about the function of morality should seem familiar both to theorists (since it is borrowed from other theorists) and to ordinary people. I think they are plausible suggestions. More important, whether or not what I offer here correctly captures the "essence" of morality seems to me *relatively* unimportant. What is more important is that we have reason to be interested in morality as I conceive it. The functions of morality, on my account, are important functions. We have reason to be interested in principles or rules performing these functions, and we have reason to be interested in the truth or falsity of judgments made with respect to these rules. In any case, I believe it is better to leave off these preliminary discussions and turn to the account itself. We will be in a better position to decide what to do with the account when we have it before us.

3. A Conception of Morality

Minimally, a morality can be described by a system of rules or principles proscribing some kinds of harmful or dangerous conduct and enjoining certain kinds of beneficial conduct. Such rules constitute a system of constraints or boundaries determining the limits of the permissible. To speak of these rules as constraints is to emphasize their overriding character; when moral considerations conflict with other considerations, moral considerations take precedence. Moral rules, as so far described, can be usefully distinguished into two groups. (1) Some rules proscribe or enjoin actions that are either harmful or useful in themselves, regardless of what other people are doing; (2) Some rules enjoin actions which will either prevent harm or promote benefits just in case they are generally performed.[7] Rules of type (2) may be either direct rules, enjoining specific types of conduct, or indirect rules requiring simply that people adhere to whatever specific rules or conventions are being generally adhered to.[8] When I speak here of rules governing actions, I include actions establishing or altering institutional structures. When I speak of rules requiring that we benefit or refrain from harming people, I do not mean to exclude rules requiring that we benefit some at the expense of others. Thus, moral rules can include rules for settling disputes when one gains only at the expense of another, and they can also include rules governing the distribution or redistribution of goods.

Even if any morality includes rules of the sort described here, it does not follow that such rules exhaust the content of morality, nor, more importantly, does it mean that any such set of rules constitutes an *adequate* morality. What more is necessary? Let me begin by considering John Rawls's notion of a 'well-ordered society'. A society is well-ordered, he says, when it is "effectively regulated by a public conception of justice." More specifically, "(1) everyone accepts and knows that the others accept, the same principles of justice, and (2) the basic social institutions generally satisfy and are generally known to satisfy these principles." In a well-ordered society, "while men may put forth excessive demands on one another, they nevertheless acknowledge a common point of view from which their claims may be adjudicated." The shared, public system of principles constitutes "the fundamental charter of a well-ordered human association."[9]

Pretty clearly, the notion of a well-ordered

society admits of degrees. Consensus on principles can be more or less perfect, and institutions can vary in the degree to which they satisfy the conditions laid down in the shared moral principles. In a perfectly well-ordered society, though, there will be complete agreement on principles for evaluating actions and common institutions. Moreover, I take it, there will be agreement that these principles are final (Rawls, 135–6). These principles are the *fundamental charter* of a well-ordered association. When these principles apply to a specific decision, they are taken to override any other considerations that might also apply. Thus, the shared, public system of rules in a well-ordered society plays the same role in the life of the community earlier assigned to moral rules in general. It is regarded as a system of *constraints* determining the limits of the permissible.

When a proposal is agreed to be contrary to the shared system of principles, it will be rejected by all. On the other hand, there may well be disagreement about the acceptability, *all things considered,* of proposals consistent with the shared morality. Nor is this the only source of disagreement and strife. While there is agreement, in a well-ordered society, on fundamental principles, there may not be agreement on the consequences of their application to particular cases. Typically, there will be agreement on what is relevant to a given decision, but there may well be disagreement on the truth or falsity of some statement that all regard as relevant. Nevertheless, the knowledge that there is agreement on ends strengthens "the bonds of civic friendship" (Rawls, 5), and mitigates the otherwise divisive effects of disagreement on specific matters of policy.

I want to suggest that one important function of a morality is to serve as the public system of constraints on action agreed to by citizens in a well-ordered society. A test for an *adequate* morality is that its principles be able to perform this function. The more stable a system of principles—the greater its capacity to continue to perform this function as a society grows and changes—the more adequate it is.

In general, then, those parts of a morality relevant to the assessment of laws and institutions consist of a system of final rules compliance with which tends to prevent harm or produce benefits. An adequate morality is a system of such rules on which there could be an enduring consensus. It is a system of rules that could be accepted by all members of society as principles determining the absolute limits of the permissible. Now, the idea of focusing on what could be agreed to or on what could constitute a consensus is like the idea that seems to underlie much moral theory in the social contract tradition.[10] There are, of course, differences within that tradition. Some theorists, for example, see moral principles as principles that *would* be agreed to in more or less idealized situations. Others hold that moral principles are principles actually agreed to in actual situations. The position I have sketched here is like those theories emphasizing hypothetical agreement since it asserts that an adequate morality is a system of principles that could be accepted by everyone, even if none is accepted now. On the other hand, it is like theories emphasizing an actual agreement in that it says a morality constitutes a possible consensus among actual people. There is precedent for this kind of combination. Indeed, I believe there is a plausible interpretation of Rawls's contract theory in which the notion of a well-ordered society plays the central role it plays in mine. On this reading of Rawls, a morality (or, anyway, principles of justice) constitutes a possible, public conception of justice in a well-ordered society. The appeal to the original contract—to the 'original position' in Rawls's theory—is designed to establish the *possibility* of consensus on principles of justice. When we find out that people in the original position would agree to certain principles, we find out that consensus, at least for a time, among some people, is possible. When we find out what they would agree to, we find out something about what kind of principles might form the basis of an *enduring* consensus. Principles people would agree to, in an initial situation of equality, behind a veil of ignorance, will be the kind of principles they would continue to accept in spite of changes in their prospects or other circumstances. But *full* justification of moral principles, on this interpretation, requires more than a demonstration that these principles would be chosen in the original position. It requires a demonstration that people in real societies are, or could become, sufficiently like people in the original position that principles chosen by the latter people could constitute a consensus among the former.[11]

One way in which my theory resembles other contract theories is that it seems to be subject to some of the same criticisms. Consider this question: why should we believe that real people ought to comply with the principles that ideal people would agree to in some hypothetical situation? This objection corresponds to the question about my theory, why should we believe that people ought to comply with rules that could, or even do, constitute a consensus on fundamental constraints on conduct? This question could be interpreted in different ways. (1) It might be the question whether we have any reason to be interested in the requirements of such systems of rules. (2) It could be the question whether what people would agree to has anything to do with what *morality* requires of them, or (3) it could be the question how, logically speaking, we can *derive* an 'ought' judgment from the mere existence of some system of principles or rules. To this last question, I believe, the most plausible response is in terms of something like the theory of 'ought' judgments developed by Roger Wertheimer in *The Significance of Sense*.[12] According to Wertheimer, roughly, all 'ought' judgments refer implicitly to some system of rules or principles. To say that *x* ought to do *y* is to say: (1) There is an adequate and relevant system of rules; (2) According to some rule of that system, were *x* in some situation *s, x* would (ideally or actually) *y;* and (3) *x* is in situation *s*. A system is a relevant system if it is a system of the type to which the speaker means to refer. It is an adequate system if it satisfies the conditions of adequacy for systems of its type.[13] Now, given an account of 'ought' judgments along these lines, there is no particular logical problem about how we could derive such judgments, given a system of rules of the sort discussed here. But do we have reason to be interested in rules that constitute a possible consensus, and would

those rules be adequate moral rules? I shall comment first on the latter question and then turn to the former.

I have suggested that we think of a morality as a system of overriding constraints on action compliance with which tends to produce benefits or prevent harm and which could serve as the fundamental charter of a well-ordered society. I have not said that any system of rules with these two properties is an adequate morality. The properties mentioned are necessary conditions. Are there other necessary conditions? The question whether the rules imagined here would be a morality no doubt stems partly from the feeling that the class of acceptable rules needs to be narrowed down further. At the very least, one might say, a set of principles is an adequate morality only when it represents a possible consensus *among free and independent persons.* We could imagine a kind of slave society in which the slaves themselves are so dehumanized that they would accept the slaveholders' rationale for their common institutions. But, given the modification suggested here, that would not show that these institutions were morally acceptable. To show this, we would have to show that principles permitting such institutions *would* be acceptable to all concerned even if they were free from its dehumanizing effects.

The requirement that a set of principles be a potential *stable* consensus—a consensus that would endure over time—will tend to rule out some seemingly unfair sets of principles in some societies. When there is social mobility, so that any person (or any person's child) might occupy most any position in society, people will be reluctant to accept principles giving special, permanent advantages even to their own social class. And, if they do, consensus on those principles will tend to break down as people who have known those advantages come to occupy less advantageous positions. However, in a rigid caste society, we would find neither of these kinds of check on the adoption of principles that look grossly unfair. A caste society with a caste morality may be a stable, well-ordered society. It does make some difference, then, whether we make it a necessary condition for a morality's being adequate that it constitute a possible, stable consensus among free and independent persons. But should we say this?

I shall argue here that people generally have reason to promote and comply with principles satisfying the conditions I have so far laid down; and I shall argue that people generally have a greater interest in such principles when those principles would be acceptable under conditions of freedom and independence. I do not believe this is a *proof* that principles satisfying the conditions in question constitute an adequate morality. If one holds that, by definition, moral principles are principles on which people have a reason to act, then my argument is relevant to such a proof. Be that as it may, the argument does serve as a partial justification of the kind of principles I have in mind, at least to those who share a certain ideal of social cooperation. Moreover, if I am correct, morality as I conceive it can perform what might be regarded as one of its characteristic functions: people can successfully appeal to its principles in order to criticize the conduct of others or to justify their own.[14]

With or without the added requirement that principles be acceptable to free and independent persons, what reason do we have to take an interest in moral principles as described here? Suppose, to begin with, that we are in a well-ordered society. If so, there will be a set of fundamental principles on which people agree, and it will be agreed that these principles determine the limits of the permissible. They entail a set of constraints on conduct within which, it is agreed, we must confine ourselves. They will require that we refrain from harming one another in various ways, and they will require that we benefit one another in various ways. Also, in a well-ordered society, legal, political and economic institutions will be justifiable from the perspective of these shared principles, and it will be agreed that this is so. Now, on these assumptions, we will want others to comply with our shared principles insofar as we stand to benefit (or to avoid harm) as a result of their compliance. More interesting, it will generally be in the interest of each individual to conform to those shared principles himself and to develop the general dis-

position to do so. It will also generally be in the interest of each that basic institutions continue to be justifiable in terms of the society's shared principles. The argument for these conclusions is pretty straightforward. Given a general belief in certain fundamental constraints, and given a normal interest in the opinions of others, each will want to *appear* to limit his behavior by those constraints. But the easiest way to appear to conform to principles, usually, is to conform to them! And, if one has an interest in such general conformity, one has an interest in developing the general disposition to conform. Moreover, given an interest in conforming to shared principles, each has an interest in minimizing conflict between the requirements of these principles and the constraints and requirements of institutions. When one benefits from institutional constraints on others, one wants to be able to justify those constraints. When one is able to make use of institutions to his advantage, one wants to be able to justify one's conduct to others. All this requires, however, that the institutions themselves be justifiable in terms of shared, public principles.

In a well-ordered society, under plausible assumptions about human motives, people generally have a reason to conform to shared principles of morality. Do they have *more* reason to conform to principles acceptable to free and independent persons than to principles that are not? Most people are concerned about the opinions of others, and this concern, at the very least, makes them want to appear to conform to shared principles. The reasons for this will vary from person to person. Some, perhaps, will simply want to avoid criticism. Even then, they will do well to cultivate a general disposition to conform, since actual conformity virtually guarantees the appearance of conformity, and alternative strategies can involve costly calculation and planning. But most of us, to a greater or lesser degree, do not want merely to appear to comply with generally accepted standards. We want, in Philippa Foot's nice phrase, "to live openly and in good faith with [our] neighbors."[15] Not only do we want to avoid the consequences of hypocrisy (always being on guard, trying to keep our lies consistent and so on), but we find lying and deceit intrinsically unpleasant. We do not want to have to conceal; we want our lives to be able to stand inspection. All this, of course, strictly requires only that we comply with whatever restrictions people actually believe in. But if it makes us feel uncomfortable to have to conceal our conduct from others, it will hardly satisfy us to know that we can justify our conduct to others only because they have come to accept certain principles under duress or some psychological constraint. At least the latter attitude seems a natural extension of the former. For many of us, then, some of the same considerations that lead us to take an interest in the requirements of shared principles will lead us also to take a greater interest in requirements that would be acceptable to people choosing freely and independently.

I have argued so far only that people in a well-ordered society have a reason to comply with generally accepted principles. But I have said that a morality consists of a set of principles that *would* perform the function of the public conception of justice in a well-ordered society. Do we have a reason to take an interest in a morality—in principles that would serve this function—when we are not in a well-ordered society? Does this property of a morality give us a reason to take an interest in it when it is not generally accepted? Most of us, I think, do have a reason to want principles to be generally accepted, and to comply with principles that could be generally accepted even when no such principles are now accepted. So long as we wish to be able to justify our conduct to others, we have reason to comply with rules that others *could* be led to accept; we also have reason to try to get those principles accepted. To this point, the argument is like the argument for complying with rules actually accepted in a well-ordered society. But suppose many people accept principles—racist principles might be an example—that are *inconsistent* with principles that could be generally accepted. In this case, conduct that *could* be justified to everyone, in the long run, could not be justified to many people in the short run. In this kind of situation, it is far from clear that individuals have a reason to

care about what morality requires. At least, whether a given person has reason to act according to principles that could be generally accepted will depend to a far greater extent on particular motives and features of his situation that are likely to differ from those of others. It will depend on the extent to which he must deal with members of racial minorities, for example; and it will depend on whether his desire to be able to justify his conduct to others is based on a mere desire to avoid ostracism and reprisals, or on a respect for persons as persons.

Aside from the desire to be able to justify our conduct to others, it should be remembered, we have other reasons to want certain kinds of general principles adopted and complied with. According to the theory under consideration, a morality is not just any system of principles that can be generally accepted and publicly avowed. It is a system of principles requiring some beneficial conduct and proscribing some harmful conduct. But then, insofar as we stand to benefit (or avoid harm) from compliance on the part of others, we have reason to want them to comply. Thus, we have an additional, independent reason to push for the acceptance of principles that could gain general acceptance and that people could therefore have a reason to comply with. One reason people have for complying with rules depends on the acceptability of those rules to other people. So, our interest in compliance on the part of others also gives us an interest in the general acceptability of those rules. It leads us to try to find systems of constraints that are, intuitively speaking, fair as well as beneficial.

Let me summarize. An adequate morality, I have suggested, can be described by a set of principles or rules having, at least, the following properties: (1) Compliance with the principles tends to produce benefits or prevent harm; (2) The principles could serve as the shared, public principles constituting a stable, "fundamental charter of a well-ordered human association" as Rawls understands this notion; and (3) The principles could perform this function in a society of free and independent persons. The idea is that it is a necessary condition for a system's being an adequate morality that it satisfy these conditions, but I did not argue for this conclusion directly. What I argued is that we have reason to want *some* such set of principles accepted and generally complied with. If some set is accepted and complied with, we have reason to comply ourselves and to urge continued compliance on the part of others. We have reason to treat them with the seriousness normally accorded a morality.

It should be emphasized that the arguments in this section depend on empirical assumptions, and that the conclusions hold only other things being equal. First, the arguments depend clearly on assumptions about human motives and interests, like the assumption that we are not generally indifferent to the opinions of others; and they depend on assumptions about our circumstances, like the assumption that it is costly and difficult to conceal one's conduct. These assumptions *could* be false, but I think they are not. Second, the extent to which one has a reason to comply with the directives of morality (as conceived here) will depend on the extent to which others accept and comply with those directives. If no one accepted principles with the properties of an adequate morality, people would have much less reason to try to develop and comply with such principles. Still, it is hard to imagine a complete lack of consensus on principles within subgroups in a society anyhow; and, in the absence of a rigid caste structure, people would tend to comply with principles most widely accepted and therefore most widely acceptable. The long run tendency is toward general compliance with, and general acceptance of, principles that have the properties of an adequate morality. But, even if this is right, it does not follow at all that each person will always have an overriding reason to comply with such principles in particular cases.[16]

At the beginning of the section before this one, I asked what conditions a political system had to satisfy in order to be morally acceptable, and I said that this question is itself a substantive moral question. In this section, I have offered a partial account of the nature of an adequate morality, but I have said virtually nothing about its substantive content. If I am right, of course, the substantive requirements

of morality will depend on what kinds of principles people can agree to under certain conditions and for certain purposes. What I shall argue in the next two sections is that familiar institutions of representative democracy tend to foster consensus on adequate principles of morality, and consequently tend to produce law and policy decisions consistent with these principles. The argument will depend in part on the precise nature of representative institutions and it will also presuppose some of the motivational assumptions I have introduced in this section in arguing that people have reason to care about the requirements of an adequate morality. The idea that this argument constitutes a *justification* for democracy depends on an assumption about what the substantive requirements of an adequate morality would be. Specifically, I assume that an adequate morality will include requirements that laws and social policy must satisfy, and I assume that it will not require anything of political decision procedures other than that they tend to produce acceptable laws and policies.

4. Democracy and Just Government: Mill's Argument

In this section I shall offer an interpretation and defense of the theory of democracy John Stuart Mill presented in *Considerations on Representative Government*.[17] I think Mill's justification of representative government is, in its main lines, reasonable. Other philosophers have suggested similar arguments, and Mill's argument needs to be supplemented at certain points; but I shall begin with Mill here, partly because he has sometimes been misinterpreted, and partly because, properly interpreted, he makes the case about as well as anyone.

According to Mill, the "ideally best form of government," the "form of government most eligible in itself," is representative government (Mill, 35–6). What does Mill mean by "most eligible in itself," and what, in his view, are the criteria for good government in general? Basic to Mill's theory of government is the idea that different systems of government are appropriate in different societies and in different stages in the development of a given society. The form of government ideally best in itself, then, is not the form of government best under all circumstances. Instead, the idea is this: We consider all possible states of society, and we suppose that each is governed by the form of government best for that state of society. Each form of government, then, is operating in its most propitious circumstances, and we say that the society that is best governed has the form of government that is best in itself. In Mill's words, that government is "most eligible in itself . . . which, if the necessary conditions existed for giving effect to its beneficial tendencies, would, more than all others, favor and promote not some one improvement, but all forms and degrees of it" (Mill, 35).

That form of government is best in itself which, given propitious circumstances, has the best effects. Government, according to Mill, is a *means* to certain ends (Mill, 15). But to what ends? What is the function of government? In Mill's view, there are two *criteria* for a good government. On the one hand, government must "promote the virtue and intelligence of the people" in the community. On the other hand, the "machinery" of government must be "adapted to take advantage of the amount of good qualities which may at any time exist and make them instrumental to the right purposes" (Mill, 25–6). As many commentators have noted, Mill tends to emphasize the first of these criteria. What has not generally been noticed is that possession of these criteria—of these *marks* of good government—is not what *makes* the government good. What *makes* the government good is its having good effects. Virtuous citizens and appropriate governmental "machinery" are marks of good government because they are what makes it possible for government to produce the right effects. This is quite clear from the way in which Mill introduces the idea of concentrating on the personal qualities of the citizenry. He begins by considering the problem of the administration of justice. An effective and fair judicial system requires intelligent, honest and fair-minded citizens: witnesses must be reliable, judges must refrain from taking bribes, jurors must be willing and able to consider the merits of a case

dispassionately, and so on (Mill, 24). Mill uses the same example in order to explain the importance of the "machinery" of government.

The judicial system being given, the goodness of the administration of justice is in the compound ratio of the worth of the men composing the tribunals, and the worth of the public opinion which influences or controls them. But all the difference between a good and a bad system of judicature lies in the contrivances adopted for bringing whatever moral and intellectual worth exists in the community to bear upon the administration of justice and making it duly operative on the result (Mill, 26).

The tendency of a government to promote the virtue of its citizens, together with the quality of its "machinery," are *criteria* of good government because governments that promote virtue and have the right machinery tend to perform the function of governments well. But the *function* of a government is to produce good decisions and good legislation—in general, to promote "the aggregate interests of society" (Mill, 16). An ideal form of government, then, will be a government that is in harmony with itself. It will consist of institutions that affect people's character in such a way that people with that kind of character, operating those institutions, will tend to produce the best laws and decisions. To show that a form of government is desirable, one would need, in principle, to begin with an account of the goals to be achieved—an account of good legislation, for example. One would then have to demonstrate that, given the machinery of government, and given the effects of that form of government on the citizenry, we could expect good laws and policies.

Mill is a utilitarian. He holds, as noted above, that government should be so designed that it promotes "the aggregate interests of society." Why does he think that representative government is the form of government most likely to achieve this goal? In part, of course, the answer is that representative government is not the best form of government under *all* conditions. If, for example, citizens have acquired neither the willingness to acquiesce in *necessary* authority, nor sufficient will to take an active role in government, representative government will fail (Mill, Chapter 3). Nevertheless, Mill holds, once the requisite conditions have been satisfied, representative government is superior to any other form of government, under *any* conditions. Why?

The "ideally best form of government," Mill says,

is that in which the sovereignty, or supreme controlling power in the last resort, is vested in the entire aggregate of the community, every citizen not only having a voice in the exercise of that ultimate sovereignty, but being, at least occasionally, called on to take an actual part in the government by the personal discharge of some public function, local or general (Mill, 42).

This kind of government, Mill says, will both make good use of people as they are, and will tend to improve them in such a way that they will govern even better as time passes. People will be secure from bad government because they will be "self-*protecting*" and they will be able to improve their collective lot because they will become "self-*dependent*" (Mill, 43). In a popular form of government, the chance of injustice will be reduced because each person will stand up for his own rights. And no one stands up for a person's rights better than that person himself. Moreover, a system in which people have some control over their political situation breeds an active, vigorous citizenry. According to Mill, not only will active persons do a better job of protecting their rights, but also, active as opposed to passive persons will promote the long term interests of society. Self government protects people against abuses, it breeds the type of citizen who will be vigilant in protecting himself, and it breeds in everyone the attitudes that a society must have in its rulers if it is to advance (Mill, 43–52).

Parts of Mill's position—the idea that democracy protects individuals against injustice by giving them a chance to stand up for their own rights, for example—are familiar to most of us.[18] But the question is whether it is really *true* that individual rights are protected in a democracy. In what kind of a democracy, operating under what kinds of voting rules, do rights get protected? Throughout most of

Chapter 3, Mill seems to be thinking of a direct democracy. He concludes the chapter thus:

it is evident that the only government that can fully satisfy all the exigencies of the social state is one in which the whole people participate; that any participation, even in the smallest public function, is useful; that the participation should everywhere be as great as the general degree of improvement of the community will allow; and that nothing less can be ultimately desirable than the admission of all to a share in the sovereign power of the state. But since all cannot, in a community exceeding a single small town, participate personally in any but some very minor portions of the public business, it follows that the ideal type of a perfect government must be representative (Mill, 55).

This is a non sequitur. If direct democracy is ideal, but unfeasible, it does not follow that the feasible alternative most similar, namely representative democracy, is therefore the best of the feasible alternatives. It may be the best, but we need further argument to show this. Specifically, we would need to show that it will perform functions like that of protecting the rights of individuals as well as any alternative. There are clearly difficult questions here. For example, will everyone be represented, or represented equally well, in a representative democracy? And will it make a difference whether Parliament operates on a simple majority rule or on some alternative kind of rule?

Even if we imagine that some kind of direct democracy is possible, and assume that people are vigorous in the protection of what they take to be their own rights and interests, it does not follow that each person's rights *will* be protected in a direct democracy. In Chapter V, we looked at some attempts to predict the outcome of democratic decision-making processes under various assumptions about voting rules, and on the assumption that each individual would be vigorous in trying to achieve his own ends. Mill does not offer anything like this kind of analysis of democratic decision-making, but our earlier discussions should remind us that there is no guarantee that everyone will get his way. Quite the contrary. The problem of majority tyranny is still a serious problem.

As it happens, Mill does devote some later

chapters (Chapter 7, especially) to the problem of designing a method of representation in which all shades of opinion achieve representation in Parliament. However, everyone's being represented in Parliament does not guarantee that everyone's rights will be respected in parliamentary decisions. After all, even direct democracy does not guarantee protection for everyone, since people may have diametrically opposed opinions as to what their rights are, and there is no reason to believe, a priori, that the person who is correct will prevail.

Mill would reply, I believe, that this objection is based on a misunderstanding of the way in which democracy works to protect people's rights. It is not because everyone has a vote that each person's rights are protected. Having a vote does not guarantee being on the winning side. The important thing about democratic government—whether direct democracy or representative democracy—is that the processes of decision-making and administration are carried out in the *open*. It is not that everyone will always have his or her way, but that whatever is done will be done in *public*. Administrators and legislators will be forced to *defend* their actions in public.

The proper function of a representative parliament, according to Mill, is not to administer, nor even to legislate, if by this we mean to write bills and enact statutes. If only because it is too large and diverse, it is ill suited to these tasks (Mill, 71–7). Its proper function is:

to watch and control the government: to throw the light of publicity on its acts; [and] to compel a full exposition and justification of all of them which anyone considers questionable; ... Parliament [is] at once the nation's Committee of Grievances and its Congress of Opinions—an arena in which not only the general opinion of the nation, but that of every section of it, and as far as possible of every eminent individual whom it contains, can produce itself in full light and challenge discussion; where every person in the country may count upon finding somebody who speaks his mind, as well or better than he could speak it himself, not to friends and partisans exclusively, but in the face of opponents, to be tested by adverse controversy; where those whose opinion is overruled feel satisfied that it is

heard and set aside not by a mere act of will, but for what are thought superior reasons ... (Mill, 81–2).

Why think that this kind of open government, open debate of public policy, willingness to consider grievances seriously and respond to them, will lead to good government? Why think, for that matter, that representatives will properly discharge their responsibility to publicize the activities of government, to publicize criticism of the government, and to debate the issues seriously? Won't there be a temptation, for example, simply to ignore demands for justification when they proceed from small minorities? There are two kinds of questions here. On the one hand, there are questions about the likelihood that elected representatives will perform the functions expected of them according to the theory. On the other hand, there is the question whether, even if they do, the result will be morally good government. Mill offers, at best, only partial answers to these questions.

In a way, each of the two questions I have raised here is a question concerning the character of citizens. How will they respond to demands for justification from others? What will they regard as an acceptable justification? When will they be willing to limit their demands on others? To what extent will they feel that they need to justify their conduct to others? The questions I have raised above are also questions about what morality requires. What is the relation between a policy's being acceptable to members of a community—its being justifiable in the sense that it is acceptable—and its being *morally* justifiable?

Now, in Mill's view, a major advantage of democracy is that it improves the character of its citizens. On the one hand, he thinks it will produce active, self assertive persons concerned with improving their environment. Perhaps more important, when citizens are required "to exercise, for a time and in their turn, some social function," this mitigates the fact that there is little "in most men's ordinary life to give any largeness either to their conceptions or to their sentiments." When a person is required to serve on juries, or to serve in local office, "[he] is called upon, while so engaged, to weigh interests not his own; to be guided, in case of conflicting claims, by another rule than his private partialities; to apply, at every turn, principles and maxims which have for their reason of existence the common good'' (Mill, 53–4).

As I read Mill, assumptions something like these are crucial to his theory. The open and public character of government in a representative democracy is a *desirable* feature of that kind of government only if we assume that open discussion of governmental policy tends to result in good policy choices, or at least tends to prevent bad choices. The plausibility of this assumption depends, in turn, on assumptions about the kind of policy that citizens will find acceptable. What Mill wants to claim is that the very process of open discussion leads people to adopt reasonable moral principles. It works both directly and indirectly. To the extent that citizens already have good character, public discussion of governmental policy alternatives results in good policy. To the extent that citizens lack good character, public discussion and debate tends to improve their character by leading them, for example, to appreciate the situation of others.

The question is whether any of this is true. If Mill wishes to claim that participating in government, listening to public debate of political issues, discussing these issues with acquaintances and so forth, will lead people to adopt any specific set of moral principles—utilitarian principles, for example—it is not clear how he could defend his claim. But it may be possible to provide a plausible defense of a less specific claim. Recall Rawls's conception of a 'well-ordered society' discussed in the preceding section: A well-ordered society is a society governed by commonly accepted principles of justice. Now, it does seem plausible that, when matters of public policy are subject to frequent public debate, and when most individuals are called upon, from time to time, ''to exercise some public function,'' that citizens will attempt to formulate principles in terms of which they will be able to defend their positions to others. Similarly, to the extent that political leaders must defend their positions publicly, they will have to formulate principles

and conceptions of the common good in terms of which they can justify their positions. At least, given open institutions, and given the kind of motivational assumptions discussed in the preceding section, public functionaries will attempt to formulate coherent justifications for their policies; and these justifications will have to be capable of gaining widespread public acceptance. Such justifications will have to represent a kind of possible consensus—a possible ''fundamental charter of a well-ordered society.'' But principles like this satisfy at least a necessary condition for adequate moral principles. And if we assume a populace sufficiently well educated to understand the consequences of legislative proposals, laws that can pass the test of public justifiability will tend to be morally justifiable laws.

5. Summary, Objections and Qualifications

Mill's theory of representative government, I have claimed, embodies a justification of the kind appropriate for a system of government. The argument is that representative government tends to produce morally acceptable laws and policies. At least, it tends to produce laws and policies within the bounds of the permissible as determined by reasonable moral principles. The argument needs to be filled out with a general account of moral principles; and I have attempted to provide a partial account which, when conjoined with Mill's argument, makes the argument plausible. The idea is this: Morality is a system of constraints on conduct which people could jointly acknowledge as the constraints determining the form of their association together. Thus, a good system of government is a system that leads people to formulate mutually agreeable conceptions of fundamental constraints, and it is a system that leads them to adopt laws and policies compatible with such constraints.[19] A system of representative government with an educated, responsible citizenry, and with representatives who understand their responsibility to promote serious, open discussion of governmental policy—a *public* government, we might call it— should have these consequences.

Is public government, as conceived here, feasible? This question could have different meanings. Many recent disputes about the feasibility of democratic institutions have focused on the difference between representative systems and direct democracy of one kind or another. Thus, those more or less sympathetic to current institutions have objected to advocates of greater participation—the town meeting model—that it is just impossible to operate a national government that way.[20] But clearly there is no such problem about a system of representative government. We already have one. On the other hand, existing institutions and practices are not above criticism from the perspective of the kind of theory suggested here. If there is a single idea that is central to Mill's theory, it is the idea of *open* government. In a society of any great size it is clear that the ideal of open government depends for its realization on a variety of institutions. A vigorous free press, free not only from legal limitations, but also from more subtle forms of intimidation, is clearly essential. Open meetings laws—"Sunshine Laws"—are also a natural step toward this ideal, as are proposals to broadcast congressional hearings and even sessions of congress. Such changes, evidently desirable in terms of this theory, are also possible.

The real problems of feasibility are not problems about the possibility of necessary institutions. They have to do with whether people—both citizens and officials of government—will comply with the spirit of open government. There is a nest of problems here. People, I have claimed, naturally want to be able to justify their conduct to others. They want their own actions and their institutions to be acceptable from the perspective of mutually acceptable principles. If Mill is right, the institutions of representative government, especially when they require some citizen participation at least at some level, tend to foster the development of this natural desire. When this desire is prevalent, open government conducted in a spirit of candor and openness tends to be good government. But, the prevalence of this desire does not itself guarantee that government will be so conducted. Quite simply,

well-meaning elected officials, wanting to enact justifiable policies, may lack faith in the public, and thus may decide to act undemocratically. In the short run, at least, they will not necessarily be acting wrongly. The argument for democracy, as conceived here, is an argument in terms of its long run tendencies. In the short run, it requires faith. Even in a society of well-meaning persons, democracy is not necessarily stable; it is liable to degenerate into nondemocratic alternatives.

Another kind of instability afflicts democracies. The advantage of democracy is that it *moralizes* the process of government.[21] It encourages both citizens and representatives to think of legislation and policy-making in terms of what can be justified; and it leads them to formulate principles and conceptions of the common good in terms of which they can carry out the process of justification. The result, at best, is a stable, well-ordered society, as Rawls understands this notion, with virtual unanimity on fundamental principles underwriting common laws and institutions. But another possibility is a politics built around entrenched, irreconcilable ideologies: a society divided into warring camps. What *morality* requires in a case like this cannot be specified in the abstract. Perhaps one of the ideologies is actually a reasonable morality. Perhaps neither is. In any case, there is no guarantee that the democratic process will result in reasonable laws and policies under these conditions, and it is possible that democracy itself will not long survive.[22]

A good question for empirical study is the question under what conditions the "moralizing" tendencies of democratic politics will tend to produce desirable results and under what conditions they will not. One might think that a crucial variable would be the method of voting. Specifically, one might think a simple majority rule, either in the election of representatives or in the legislative process itself, would encourage the development of ideologies with less than universal appeal. Something closer to a unanimity rule seems more appropriate, given the emphasis on unanimity in my theory. But, as we have seen in earlier chapters, the unanimity rule is equivalent to the rule of one when that one happens to favor the status quo. Unless we assume that the status quo has some privileged status in morality, the unanimity rule is not clearly preferable to the majority rule. The ideal of democratic politics sketched here is that, whatever policies we adopt, they will have to be *justifiable* in terms of widely acceptable principles. Under majority rule, a decision *not* to change is subject to the same requirement.

Variables other than voting rules may well be even more important. The size of the community and the quality of communications, the character and educational level of citizens, and the presence or absence of castes or patterns of segregation are all likely to influence the quality of political debate and, hence, the quality of legislation. Again, it will take empirical investigation to determine just what variables affect the *moral* quality of legislation as I understand this notion here. It seems to me likely, for example, that the pressures for just legislation will be greater in a society to which people feel committed than in a society from which emigration is easy or attractive. But this conjecture requires verification.[23]

It is worth recalling, briefly, Dahl's criticism of Madison. Madison claimed, according to Dahl, that American constitutional procedures are strictly *necessary* if we are to avoid tyranny, and Dahl ridiculed that idea. I think it is also clear that no system of political institutions, by itself, is *sufficient* to prevent tyranny. I suspect Dahl would agree fully. But if there is reason to believe that democratic institutions are morally preferable to nondemocratic alternatives, they must increase the likelihood that laws and policies will conform to the requirements of an adequate morality. Whether they will do so in a particular case probably depends on factors of the kinds I have mentioned.

Many theorists have argued for democracy on the ground that it tends to protect the rights of individuals, and, in general, to produce just laws and policies. But the arguments tend to be weak. True, people have a chance to exercise their grievances, argue for their rights, and exercise their franchise in defense of their positions. But what we need to know is whether legitimate claims will tend to prevail and illegitimate claims to lose. Why think that? I have offered a way to strengthen the argument by suggesting assumptions about human motivation, about the dynamics of representative government, and about the nature of morality. The argument depends especially on these assumptions about morality. I have assumed that an adequate morality constitutes a kind of possible point of agreement among people concerning the limits of the permissible in their common affairs. At the beginning of this chapter, I suggested that other attempted justifications of democracy tend to assume the value of what they are trying to justify. When they assume a moral theory, for example, the moral theory is just what critics of democracy are likely to regard as in need of justification. Now, I can imagine someone objecting to the conception of morality advanced here in much the same way: The idea that what is morally right has anything to do with what people believe, or are willing to accept, or whatever, might well seem to be presupposed by a belief in democracy; and that presupposition is what bothers critics of democracy. I have some sympathy with this objection. It is probably correct, and worth noting, that unless there is *some* systematic connection between people's needs, preferences, etc., and what morality requires, then it is doubtful that democracy can be morally justified. On the other hand, we need not assume, and I do not assume here, that morality simply requires doing what the majority prefers, or that all preferences and desires need to be given equal weight, or even that they be weighted in proportion to their subjective intensity. It is more complicated than that. Moreover, I have made at least some effort to show that the conception of morality assumed here is reasonable on independent grounds.

6. Comparisons and Contrasts

A. Participation Theory

Theories stressing the role of political participation in the democratic ideal have enjoyed a certain vogue in recent years, and some theorists of participatory democracy have appealed to the authority of John Stuart Mill. But, if I am right, participation plays a role in Mill's theory different from the role sometimes assigned to it by participation theorists. In any case, it certainly plays a different role in the theory I have sketched here and which I *claim* to find in Mill's work. Political participation, in my view, is not intrinsically good, whether we define "politics" broadly or narrowly. It is desirable neither because it tends to stabilize government (by making people *feel* committed to political decisions), nor because the act of participation somehow gives rise to a moral obligation, on the part of citizens, to comply with political decisions. I argued in Chapter III that participation does not have the latter effect, and whether or not it has the former, that effect is not necessarily desirable. Whether it is depends on the moral acceptability of the government's substantive policies.

In his critique of revisionist theory, Jack Walker said "public policy should result from extensive, informed discussion and debate."[24] In my view, and I believe in Mill's, a system of government is to be evaluated in terms of its legislative and policy decisions. Nevertheless, the conception of democracy defended in this chapter is like Walker's in its emphasis on open government, though I go beyond anything Walker says by offering a defense of this conception of democracy grounded in moral theory.

The idea of open and public debate can be distinguished from the idea of a participatory society as described in the work of Bachrach or Pateman, but this latter idea can also be given a defense in the context of the theory developed here. The defense parallels the elaboration of participation theory adumbrated at the conclusion of Chapter III. To the extent that popular participation in government is desirable, it is desirable because it contributes either directly or indirectly to the quality of government. However, in a representative democracy, the quality of government depends to a large extent on the character of citizens, since the policies adopted tend to be those that can be justified in public debate. Thus, if experience in the exercise of public functions, in group decision-making, and the like, leads people to take an interest in the general accepta-

bility of their actions and decisions, and if it leads them to adopt reasonable moral principles, then participation of these kinds contributes to the quality of democratic government. Mill speculates that participation has consequences like these, and so regards such participation as a desirable aspect of a system of representative government. This is not implausible, but neither is it obvious. It requires the kind of empirical confirmation discussed in Pateman's *Participation and Democratic Theory*.[25] Specifically, it is worth asking what kind of principles people will come to accept as a result of participatory decision-making in their work or in local affairs. When they turn from local to national issues, what attitudes will they bring with them? Will the experience of participatory decision-making in local or professional affairs leave them with a desire to seek policies acceptable to ever widening circles of people, or will it leave them with a firm commitment to ideologies favoring narrow local, class or professional interests?

B. Procedural Fairness

A direct appeal to the idea of fair procedures plays no role in the argument for democratic government sketched here. Consequently, it is not *necessarily* an objection to a specific system of representative government that it is unfair or unequal in some respect. Nevertheless, some features of systems of government that could be defended in terms of a demand for fairness can also be defended in terms of my theory. I noted in Chapter II that the idea of fairness seems to yield an argument for simple majority rule as opposed to unanimity or 2/3 majority rules. But, if we want a system in which all policies and institutions must be justifiable in terms of generally acceptable principles, then we have another argument in favor of simple majority rule. Since simple majority rule does not give any preference to existing institutions over new proposals, it subjects all institutions to the test of justifiability. Again, while there is no *direct* argument for equal (or proportional) representation of all classes, or interests, or geographical entities, there is an argument against policies that systematically prevent certain groups from making their concerns known. We need to encourage the development of principles acceptable to *everyone,* and of legislation justifiable in terms of those principles.

One qualification is in order. The conception of morality I have suggested in this chapter is that a morality is a system of constraints on conduct acceptable to everyone. This conception of morality makes it seem at least plausible that institutions of representative democracy will result in *morally* acceptable substantive laws and policies. But, as noted in Chapter II, it is *conceivable* that agreement on constraints will include, but be limited to, an agreement on fair procedures for assessing institutions or rules of conduct. In that case, there would be a direct argument for fair procedures.

C. Autonomy and Popular Sovereignty

How does the position outlined in this chapter differ from the theory of democracy as popular sovereignty—the theory that democracy secures individual autonomy because citizens in a democracy are self governing? The idea behind the latter theory seems to be this: We take people as they are, each person having a certain system of preferences over possible social arrangements. If people are in complete agreement, there is no problem. Democratic government legislates according to their (unanimous) will. However, we cannot expect this kind of unanimity in general. Hence, the idea of self government requires that we develop an account of *the will of the people.* Such an account defines the will of the people as some function of individual preferences, no matter what they happen to be. A democratic form of government is simply a form of government designed to legislate in accordance with the will of the people, as defined.

What this kind of theory requires, I argued in Chapter IV, is a conception of the will of the people satisfying a number of conditions of various types. Arrow's theorem suggests that we will not find any such conception, since he shows that no rule amalgamating individual preferences into a social preference can satisfy what he regards as minimal conditions. But,

even if we allow ourselves to weaken or alter some of his conditions, the resulting account will not lead to a theory of democracy as self government that gives rise to a justification of democracy. It is hard to see why self government, defined in terms of the kind of conception of the people's will in question, is desirable.

I argue in this chapter that government ought to accord with the unanimous will of the people, when this unanimity consists of agreement on principles constituting the basis of a stable, well-ordered society. Of course, we will ordinarily not have this kind of unanimity, but one aim of government, as conceived here, is to try to create it. And when there is a lack of agreement, governmental policy should accord with principles that *could* be generally accepted. Policy should be justifiable in terms of a possible consensus. Democratic government, ideally, prevents the adoption of policies that cannot be justified to most people; and the process of open discussion and debate leads individuals to adopt standards which, in turn, can gain wider and wider acceptance. The long-run result should be consensus on principles, and laws and policies consistent with those principles.

D. Economic Theories

Economics tells us that even people with largely conflicting aims and purposes can often strike mutually beneficial bargains. Economic theories of democracy treat a political system, on analogy with the market, as a set of institutions mediating the process of bargaining and exchange. It amalgamates individual choices and produces a social decision. Economists interested in *describing* political institutions ask the same questions that they ask when studying different economic institutions: Do these institutions favor certain preferences over others? How do they respond to changes in tastes or preferences? Do they lead to optimal patterns of preference satisfaction? Theorists concerned with the *evaluation* of democratic institutions tend to argue for them on the ground that they do result in such optimal levels of satisfaction and thus that they embody an analog of consumer sovereignty.

Like theories based on popular sovereignty, economic theories take preferences as given, though these theories do not claim that democracy guarantees self government or autonomy in any strong sense. With some plausibility, economic theorists can claim that democratic institutions result in a kind of optimal preference satisfaction. But the precise pattern of satisfaction—whose preferences will be satisfied to what degree—will depend on the precise structure of the bargaining problem facing citizens. The pattern of satisfaction will depend in part on factors like the intensity of different desires, but it will also depend on a variety of other factors.

The theory I defend in this chapter is similar to an economic theory in its abstract, quasi-deductive character. I begin with a general idea about the nature of democratic politics, an abstract account of morality, and an assumption about the motives of typical people. What I then argue is that democracy will result, given these assumptions, in a set of laws and policies consistent with the requirements of an adequate morality. Prima facie, there are two basic differences between my theory and the kind of economic theory discussed in Chapter V. First, by stressing the role of public debate and open justification, I argue for a different conception of the actual operation of democratic governments. I suggest that certain factors overlooked in economic theories have a significant impact on the actual outcome of democratic decision-making. Second, I offer a different account of the standards by which governmental decisions are to be judged.

One question about my own theory, from the perspective of economic theories, is whether I (and others writers like Mill) are right about the efficacy of factors like open and public debate. Will representative government in fact tend to produce something more like the kind of bargain or compromise among interest groups suggested by economic theories? How important this question is will depend on the answer to another question, namely, to what extent do the requirements of an adequate morality, as I have defined this notion, diverge

from the requirements of Pareto efficiency? If an adequate morality requires nothing more than Pareto optimality, then, even if the economic theorists' conception of the dynamics of democratic politics is correct, democracy will still be justified on my view. Now, this question seems especially pressing since, on my view, an adequate morality is (in part) a system of constraints defining a possible society-wide consensus. But the economic theorists have suggested that the only standard unanimously acceptable is the standard of Pareto optimality.

It is worth noting these points because it reminds us that the critique of economic theories, like, for example, the critique of the theory based on the idea of fair procedures, depends ultimately on the substantive content of an adequate moral theory. However, the idea that the Pareto criterion does not exhaust the content of an adequate social morality is not implausible on the conception of morality defended here. An adequate morality is not just any consensus. It is a consensus on certain overriding constraints that can be publicly avowed by free and independent persons, and that will be stable over time. My assumption is that these further conditions put some limits on the range of possible, adequate moralities.

Any morality, including one based on some version of the Pareto principle, will require or permit that some gain at the expense of others—that some desires be frustrated and others satisfied. Any morality will require that people refrain, on occasion, from even attempting to satisfy their desires in certain ways. Sooner or later sacrifices will be required of most everyone. The question is what constraints, based on what considerations, people will be willing to accept over time. Any set of principles, I suggest, incorporates, in effect, a *proposal* that certain interests, desires, or preferences are to be regarded as more important than others.[26] Thus, it may propose, as Rawls's principles of justice do, that desires for a certain share of "primary goods" (rights and opportunities, income and wealth) be given priority. Such principles will constitute an adequate morality to the extent that people already give priority to these goods in their own calculations, or will be willing to adopt this scheme of priorities on reflection, in the interest of having a commonly acceptable standard of justification. Given agreement on the central importance of some such goods in each person's life, it is not implausible that there could be consensus on principles requiring, say, an equal distribution of those goods. What I doubt is that people would agree, under any circumstances, to principles making one's right to a certain benefit any simple function of the intensity of one's subjective preference for that benefit or of one's "bargaining position" in the market distributing that benefit. According to the economic analysis of democratic institutions, such factors will tend to determine the allocation of benefits. Hence, the economic analysis of democracy fails to provide us in any direct way with a justification of democracy.

E. Pluralism in Political Sociology

Much of the modern work on democratic theory is the work of political sociologists. It is this work against which the theorists of participatory democracy reacted. The main aim of this sociological work, evidently, is to describe the operation of modern, democratic systems of government. Society is seen as a collection of interest groups and coalitions of interest groups striving to attain their several goals within the constraints of political institutions. The democratic political system provides interest groups with channels through which they can attempt to achieve their political goals. But, while these channels are open to most everyone, success is guaranteed to no group. Instead, any one group's ability to achieve its political goals is determined by the extent to which other groups have contrary goals, by the relative political power of these groups, by their willingness to compromise and so forth.

Given this general picture of society and of democratic politics, there seem to be a number of interesting problems for empirical study. Some theorists study the effects on this process of different institutional forms, strong presidential systems, and parliamentary systems with or without proportional representation, for example.[27] Other theorists have studied the effects of various social, economic, demographic and psychological factors on the development of interest groups and on the distribution of their membership. Theorists then combine the results of investigations like these and attempt to specify the conditions under which democratic systems will manage to retain the loyalty of citizens and remain stable over time without ceasing to be democratic. In general, it seems to be held, there is a range of possible democratic systems, and a range of possible configurations of classes of interest groups such that, given any of those systems and any of those configurations of interests, there is a good chance of stable democratic government.[28] Conflicting interest groups, though seldom able to gain everything they want through the political process, nevertheless remain loyal if only because they doubt that they can do better in any other system.

The sociological theorists under discussion here are notable for their apparent lack of interest in questions of justification or evaluation. To be sure, it is quite clear that they want to avoid authoritarian systems, either of the left or of the right. But, given this dominant concern, they seem to be mainly interested in specifying the prerequisites for stability in democratic systems. We attempt to extract a justification of democracy from their work only at our peril. But I suspect they would argue for democracy, if forced to do so, in roughly the way in which the economic theorists might: democracy makes it possible for the diverse groups in a pluralistic society to achieve their sometimes conflicting goals to the greatest extent possible.

The function of a just political system, I have argued, is to produce laws and policies consistent with the requirements of an adequate morality. A just political system will tend to satisfy those interests whose satisfaction is required by morality, and it will tend to ignore those interests whose satisfaction is inconsistent with morality. But there is nothing in the conception of democratic pluralism discussed here to lead us to expect these results. To the extent that governmental policy is determined *simply* by chance configurations of interest groups, by which groups make the most noise or have the most clout, or by chance quirks of a particular system of voting or representation, there is a clear danger of injustice. But even when policy represents something like a compromise or bargain among conflicting groups, there is no reason to believe that it is just. Hence, I reject the (implicit or explicit) justification of democracy found in either the economic or sociological theories of democracy. But to do this is not to reject the institutions they seek to justify, nor is it to deny that they are democratic institutions. In an open system of representative government, I have suggested, policies tend to be rejected when they cannot be justified publicly. Moreover, the process of open and public discussion leads to the development of conceptions of justice and the public good that have the capacity to be widely accepted. Hence, policy proposals tend to be rejected when they are inconsistent with such conceptions.

What I offer here is an *hypothesis* about the operation of constitutional democracy. If it is right, however, there is an important check on the influence of (some) interest groups. Groups that cannot find a way to justify their demands in terms of generally acceptable principles will tend to be ignored. Political parties that cannot find a way, consistent with their professed principles, to appeal to certain groups, will not appeal to them. Political parties do not simply assemble a platform that will appeal to groups representing any 51 percent of the electorate. They seek a platform that they are willing to defend before the whole electorate. The tendency, again, is to subject political activity to moral constraints. But not only does this tend to preclude political recognition of certain interests; it may well also, in the long run, lead people to alter their own conceptions of their interests. The long run equilibrium is, in Rawls's phrase, "a well-ordered society."

I have said that this is an hypothesis. If it is a correct hypothesis, then there is an argument in favor of (roughly) the institutions of modern constitutional democracy that has been overlooked. But there is a great deal of room for empirical investigation. First, does this hypothesis explain anything? How well can we explain legislation and governmental policy without making reference to the kind of appeal

to principle and demand for justification described here? Second, what kind of democratic system (parliamentary, multiparty, two-party, etc.) does most to encourage this aspect of democratic politics? Third, what social and psychological conditions must obtain if democracy is to work as it should?

Conclusions

This chapter is far too long to summarize. My central aim has been to argue for the political institution of modern constitutional democracies on the ground that they tend to produce just government, or, at least, to prevent serious injustice. An argument like this presupposes some kind of account of what justice requires. The requirements of justice are among the requirements of morality, and a morality, I suggest, is a set of principles capable of serving as the public charter of a well-ordered society of free and independent persons. It is a basis for consensus on the evaluation of shared institutions and practices. What makes democracy desirable is that it is a system of *open* government in which those who govern are called upon, from time to time, to account for their actions, to justify and defend them, in public. Open debate, in turn, fosters the development of a public morality. General acceptance of such a morality, in a democracy, precludes legislation and policies contrary to the morality.

Problems remain. First, at a number of points in this chapter I have indicated the need for empirical investigation. The basic question is just whether (or, better, under what conditions) democratic government will work as I have suggested it might work ideally. Second, even if it does work as I suggest, does this make it legitimate? Again and again, I have argued that this question is ambiguous. The argument here is that democracy is a desirable form of government, in the sense that it is a good solution to the problem of constitutional design. Under favorable conditions, at least, I would recommend the adoption of a democratic constitution to people establishing a government.

Notes

1. Robert Dahl, *Preface to Democratic Theory* (Chicago: University of Chicago Press, 1956). (Subsequent references in the text to "Dahl" are to this volume.)

2. Control of "factions" is also supposed to be necessary, but that is irrelevant to my argument here.

3. We have seen that some of the participation theorists, as well as those with whom they disagree, have been concerned with the psychological prerequisites of stable, decent government. Some of the former, of course, argue that extensive participation contributes to the development of the relevant psychological conditions.

4. See Carl Hempel, "Empiricist Criteria of Cognitive Significance: Problems and Changes" in his *Aspects of Scientific Explanation* (Chicago: Free Press, 1956).

5. It is supposed to be an advantage of the Pareto criterion that it makes conceptual demands weaker than those of some other welfare criteria, specifically those that presuppose interpersonal comparisons of levels of utility. The Pareto criterion, unlike some others, *is* operational.

6. John Rawls, *A Theory of Justice* (Cambridge, Mass.: Harvard University Press, 1971), p. 3.

7. Trivial examples include such rules as "everyone stop on red and go on green." Some examples are instances of coordination problems in which everyone gains *if and only if* everyone follows some rule. Other examples are analogous to the prisoners' dilemma in which universal cooperation is sufficient, but not necessary for the production of some shared benefit. The latter cases, of course, present serious problems of instability. For an interesting discussion of coordination problems, see David Lewis, *Convention* (Cambridge, Mass.: Harvard University Press, 1969). For the prisoners' dilemma, see Luce and Raiffa, *Games and Decisions* (New York: Wiley, 1957), chap. 5. On the relation between these problems and the requirements of morality, see David Gauthier, "Morality and Advantage," *Philosophical Review* 76 (October 1967): 460–475.

8. The so-called 'Principle of Fairness' is an example of such a rule. See Rawls, *A Theory of Justice,* sec. 18.

9. Rawls, *A Theory of Justice,* p. 5. (Subsequent references in the text to "Rawls" are to this volume.)

10. Among modern writers, Rawls is the best known proponent of a kind of hypothetical contract theory, though there are others. Gilbert Harman conceives of morality as a kind of actual agreement among actual persons. See "Moral Relativism Defended," *Philosophical Review* 84 (January 1975); *The Nature of Morality* (New York: Oxford University Press, 1977), chaps. 5–8; and "Relativistic Ethics: Morality as Politics," *Midwest Studies in Philosophy,* 3 (University of Minnesota: Morris, 1978), pp. 109–121.

11. Thomas Nagel has criticized Rawls on the ground that decisions reached in the original position are not neutral with respect to all conceptions of the good. The "primary goods," a fair distribution of which is required by the principles chosen in the original position, "are not equally valuable in pursuit of all conceptions of the good." Thus, what may seem agreeable to those in the original position may not be mutually acceptable to actual people in an actual society (See "Rawls on Justice," *Philosophical Review* 82 (April 1973): 228.) Rawls agrees that his theory incorporates a certain ideal of the person and is not neutral among different persons with different conceptions of the good. He argues, however, that no theory is completely neutral in these respects. (Rawls, "Fairness to Goodness," *Philosophical Review* 84 (October 1975): sec. 6, esp. p. 549.) If this is so, then it would seem that morality, conceived as a kind of public consensus, will be possible only to the extent that some people are willing either to alter their conceptions of the good or, at least, to treat some of their interests as not constituting a valid claim on others. (For some further remarks on this point, see the discussion of economic theories later in this chapter.)

12. Roger Wertheimer, *The Significance of Sense* (Ithaca, New York: Cornell University Press 1972), chap. 3.

13. Ibid. The definition of 'ought' is on p. 109. I suspect Wertheimer would not accept the account of adequacy I offer here. See his chap. 4.

14. For the distinction between *proof* and *justification* I have in mind, see Rawls, *A Theory of Justice,* sec. 87, esp. pp. 580–581.

15. Philippa Foot, "Morality as a System of Hypothetical Imperatives," *Philosophical Review* 81 (July 1972), p. 314. The argument in the text relies heavily on Mrs Foot's work, especially on the concluding pages of her "Moral Beliefs," *Proceedings of the Aristotelian Society* 58 (1958–9). See also Rawls, *A Theory of Justice,* sec. 86.

16. One person's belief that others comply with the rules does not, in itself, necessarily give that person a reason to comply himself. For some people, at least, complying with the rules, by itself, is not a convention in David Lewis's sense of the term. (See "Languages, Language and Grammar" in *On Noam Chomsky: Critical Essays* ed. G. Harman (New York: Doubleday 1974), p. 255.) Conformity to some moral rules is unstable, at least among some people: while each benefits if everyone complies, universal conformity is not necessary. (See the references in note 7 above, together with the accompanying text.) But, it may well be true, in most groups, that, if each complies with *and* professes belief in the rules, each thereby has reason to profess belief in *and* comply with the rules. This conjunctive regularity may come to have the status of a convention.

17. [Chapters 3, 5, and 6 reprinted in this volume.] Ref-

erences in the text to Mill are to the Bobbs-Merrill edition (Indianapolis and New York, 1958).

18. See, for example, Benn and Peters, *The Principles of Political Thought* (New York: Free Press, 1965), p. 414ff; and Carl Cohen, *Democracy* (Athens, Ga: University of Georgia Press, 1971), sec. 14.3.

19. Compare Rawls, *A Theory of Justice:* "Justice as fairness begins with the idea that where common principles are necessary and to everyone's advantage, they are to be worked out from the viewpoint of a suitably defined initial situation of equality . . . the constitutional process should preserve the equal representation of the original position to the degree that this is feasible" (pp. 221–222).

20. See Robert Dahl, *After the Revolution* (New Haven and London: Yale University Press, 1970) and "Democracy and the Chinese Boxes" in *Frontiers of Democratic Theory,* ed. H. Kariel (New York: Random House, 1970).

21. Benn and Peters, *The Principles of Political Thought,* p. 416.

22. Some writers, it seems to me, are excessively concerned about this prospect and hold that moralizing or ideological tendencies should be resisted in favor of the politics of compromise among (mere) interest groups. At least, this is the impression I get from S. M. Lipset, "The Paradox of American Politics," *The Public Interest* 41 (Fall 1975).

23. For discussion of this idea, see Albert Hirschman, *Exit, Voice and Loyalty* (Cambridge, Mass.: Harvard University Press, 1970).

24. "A Critique of the Elitist Theory of Democracy," reprinted as "Normative Consequences of 'Democratic' Theory" in *Frontiers of Democratic Theory* ed. H. Kariel (New York: Random House, 1970), p. 227.

25. Carole Pateman, *Participation and Democratic Theory* (Cambridge: Cambridge University Press, 1970), chap. 5.

26. Here I adopt one of the alternatives suggested by Scanlon in "Preference and Urgency," *Journal of Philosophy* 72 (November 1975): 668. The standard of urgency in a morality, he suggests, might not correspond to an actual consensus on what is important and what is not, but might be "the best available standard of justification that is mutually acceptable to people whose preferences diverge." For why a standard based on subjective intensity is not likely to work, see Scanlon, p. 659; and Rawls, "Fairness to Goodness," 7.

27. Anthony Downs, *An Economic Theory of Democracy* (New York: Harper and Row, 1957), chap. 9.

28. S. M. Lipset, *Political Man* (New York: Doubleday, 1960); R. Dahl, *Pluralist Democracy in the United States* (Chicago: Rand McNally, 1967).

A Paradox in the Theory of Democracy

RICHARD WOLLHEIM

The invention of Democracy is traditionally attributed to Cleisthenes. Many will object to this attribution, not so much on factual grounds, as because it savours too much of a heroic or Promethean view of history. But in this case at least such a view might seem justified. We know little enough of the motives or sentiments of the great reformer, but of the enduring significance of what he achieved there can be no reasonable doubt. The institutions that he devised survived with only minor modifications as the political structure of Athens; around them there developed a creed or theory of popular government, of which only fragments have come down to us; and, finally, it was to those institutions that the word Δημοκρχτία was initially applied. By the middle of the fifth century B.C. Democracy existed as a set of institutions, as a theory of government, and as a word. Since the institutions came first and prompted the rest, he who devised them may with good reason be celebrated as the inventor of Democracy.

From the days of Cleisthenes onwards Democracy has enjoyed a continuous, if often exiguous, history in Western culture. The political experience of Athens has never been forgotten and never totally dismissed if only because it is recorded in texts that for quite extraneous reasons have made a sustained claim upon the attention or reverence of the educated.

However, although there has been continuity, there has also been change. In several important respects the Democracy of Antiquity differs, and should be distinguished, from the Democracy of the modern world: and this not just in practice, but also in theory. To take an obvious case: to the classical mind Democracy was linked *in an essential way* with certain specific political institutions. These links no longer exist. For the institutions with which the Ancients so intimately connected Democracy either are no longer held to be connected, or even consistent, with Democracy, as in the case of public scrutiny or the lot, or else *are* still held to be connected with Democracy but not in a way which can be directly derived from the nature of Democracy, as, for instance, with the Rule of Law.

But the most important respect in which modern Democracy differs from classical Democracy is that whereas classical Democracy was a form of sectional government, to the modern mind Democracy is opposed to all forms of sectional government. The etymology of the word Democracy gives a clue to what the Ancients meant by it. For Democracy was regarded as a form of government parallel to, though different from, other forms of government designated by names having a parallel

Richard Wollheim, "A Paradox in the Theory of Democracy," from *Philosophy, Politics and Society,* 2nd Series, ed. P. Laslett and W. G. Runciman. Copyright © Basil Blackwell, 1962. Reprinted by permission of the author and publisher.

structure: Aristocracy, Oligarchy, Plutocracy, Ochlocracy. In each case power lay with a certain section of the population: the forms differed from one another according to the section with which power lay: and in each case the section was indicated by the prefix. In Aristocracy, it was the *aristoi* or the best: in Oligarchy, it was the *oligoi* or the few: in Plutocracy it was the *plutoi* or the rich: in Ochlocracy it was the *ochlos* or mob: in Democracy it was the *demos*. And the *demos* in the Greek city-state was a specific or determinate section of the population: the populace or the poor.

By contrast the modern conception of Democracy is of a form of government in which no restriction is placed upon the governing body: the governing body is identical with the citizen body. We might put the difference between the ancient and modern conceptions of Democracy like this: in both cases Democracy is the rule of the people: but in the classical theory the people is identified with a section or part of the population, whereas in modern theory the people is identified with the population as a whole.

Immediately a problem arises: if Democracy means the rule of the people *as a whole,* how can it be realized? For in any modern state the people is bound to be both *numerous* and *diverse,* and either of these characteristics by itself—let alone the conjunction of the two—surely must make a group of individuals incapable of effective rule. In antiquity, or at any rate in the political theory of antiquity, the problem does not arise. For the *demos* of the Greek city-state was, in the first place, relatively small: and, secondly, it was, or was supposed to be, united in interest, and therefore uniform in desire or want.

One solution to this problem is to suggest a return to the Greek conditions: or the suggestion is, rather, that the conditions which hold for the Greek *demos* should be made to hold for the population of a modern democracy. This population should, in the first place, be considerably reduced in size. And when it is no longer numerous, it will automatically cease to be diverse. Or if any diversity remains, this diversity will be purely phenomenal or apparent. This solution—which can roughly be equated with Rousseau's ideal of 'legitimate rule'—is obviously unacceptable. The restriction upon population is Utopian: and the 'true' or 'real' uniformity that it advocates, which is consistent with any degree of conscious diversity, is worthless.

Another solution consists in weakening the criteria attached to the notion of effective rule. For if we mean by 'ruling' 'devising and composing laws'—as the Greeks did—then it is clearly impossible for a numerous and diverse population to exercise collective rule. One answer, as we have seen, is that we should bring it about that the population in a Democracy is neither numerous nor diverse. Another answer is that we should mean something different by 'ruling': or that in elucidating Democracy we should employ a different concept of 'rule'. And it is this second answer that is, explicitly or implicitly, incorporated in most modern democratic theories. If modern theory insists that in a democracy the people in the sense of the whole population, not just a section of the population, should rule, it also insists that the people should rule in the sense not of devising or initiating legislation but of choosing or controlling it. And the significance of this is that it permits a people to rule despite its size and its diversity.

That size is no obstacle to the people ruling in what might be called this weakened sense should be evident. Since the control or choice of legislation does not require that the people should meet in general assembly, numbers do not impair its effectiveness. That diversity is equally no obstacle may be less apparent. That it is not derived directly from the fact that whereas to say that the people rule in the strong sense entails that everyone assents to the legislation enacted, to say that the people rule in the weak sense has no such entailment: popular rule, where rule means control, can be said to hold, even if a sizeable proportion of the population dissents from what is enacted.

However, even if popular rule is consistent with some degree of dissent, there must also be a degree with which it is inconsistent. Or to put it another way: for legislation to be said to be by the people, it must stand in some positive relation to what the individual citizens would like legislation to be like. How is this relation to be characterized?

In practice, of course, we say that legislation is democratic if (1) it concurs with what the majority of the population would like and (2) it is enacted because of this concurrence. It has however been argued that though the majority principle may be all right in practice, it certainly is inadequate to any ideal construction of Democracy: and since any justification of Democracy is most likely to relate to an ideal construction, this is important.

Before the inadequacies of the majority principle can be brought out, an ambiguity in its formulation needs to be resolved. For the principle may be insisting on a concurrence of the legislation with an absolute majority, or merely with a plurality, of citizens' choices. If an absolute majority is intended, then the majority principle is acceptable in that it never selects legislation that is intuitively unacceptable, given the choices of the individual citizens: the trouble is, however, that over too large a range not just of possible but of likely cases the majority principle selects no absolute majority legislation at all. Accordingly if government is to be continuous, the absolute-majority principle needs to be supplemented by another principle, and for this role the obvious candidate is the plurality principle. This principle in all likely cases at any rate *does* select specific legislation, but the trouble is that the legislation it selects is in some cases counter intuitive—given, that is, the choice of the citizens.[1] An example will illustrate this.

Let us suppose that there are three policies from which the population must choose: A, B, C. Forty percent choose A, 35 percent choose B, and 25 percent choose C. On the simple majority principle A is selected. However, those who choose B prefer C to A, and those who choose C prefer B to A. In the light of this information, it is far from clear that A is the right selection if democratic rule is to be observed. For 60 percent prefer both B and C to A.

What this example brings out is that it is not always clear which policy or legislation should be enacted in a democracy, given the choices of the individual citizens—if all we take into account are the first choices of the citizens. We need to go below this and consider the whole preference-schedule of the individual citizens.

Following up this kind of criticism of the majority principle, political scientists have envisaged the problem of Democracy as that of devising a function which would allow us to derive what might be called the 'democratic choice' from the ordered choices or preference-schedules of the individual citizens. It is only if we can construct such a function—the argument runs—that we can claim to have explicated the weak sense of 'rule' in which, according to *modern* theory, the people rule in a Democracy.

Recently, however, this approach has met with a reverse. For in his *Social Choice and Individual Values,* Arrow[2] has proved that it is impossible to construct a function that satisfies certain intuitive criteria. Arrow's specific concern was with what he called a 'social welfare function' whose task was to determine a complete 'social' preference schedule given the individual preference-schedules. However, it has more recently been shown[3] that Arrow's Impossibility Theorem also applies to the less ambitious project, which is more directly relevant to democracy, of constructing a function which would merely give us a 'social' first choice on the basis of the individual preference-schedules.

I mention this problem, however, solely *en passant:* not because I intend to tackle it, but because I intend to ignore it. For the purpose of this paper, I intend to assume that the so-called problem of aggregation has been solved: that there exists a method or rule[4] for going from individual choices to some specific legislation such that we can justifiably call the enactment of that legislation an instance of democratic rule.

Having made this assumption, I now want to go on and envisage Democracy in terms of a certain machine which operates according to this method or rule. The machine—which we may for convenience call the democratic machine—operates in a discontinuous fashion. Into it are fed at fixed intervals the choices of the individual citizens. The machine then aggregates them according to the pre-established rule or method, and so comes up with what may be called a 'choice' of its own. Democratic rule is said to be achieved if throughout the period when the machine is not working, the most recent choice of the machine is acted upon. The question now arises: What is the authority of the choice expressed by the machine? More specifically, why should someone who has fed his choice into the machine and then is confronted by the machine with a choice nonidentical with his own, feel any obligation to accept it?

In order however to advance the inquiry we must now note a distinction. For the choices that the individual citizen feeds into the democratic machine and on the basis of which the democratic 'choice' is made, are susceptible of two very different interpretations.

On the one hand, we may regard the choices as expressions of *want*. To say that a certain citizen chooses policy A or that he prefers policy A to policy B, is to say that he wants policy A more than any other policy or that he wants it more than policy B. The wants which the citizens' choices express need not, of course, be selfish or egotistical wants. When a man decides that he wants policy A more than policy B, he may well be moved not just by his own narrow interests but by a concern for the welfare of others. But all the same, in choosing A he is not asserting that the others want A, nor that A is in their interests, nor that A would be an ideal solution, nor that A ought to be realized; he would be asserting *tout court* that he wants A.

If we conceive the democratic machine as operating on choices in the sense of expressed wants, then our question resolves into something approximating to the old Utilitarian problem: Why should a man who wants A think that B ought to be the case, when B is not consistent with A but is arrived at by considering the wants of all the other citizens of the society? And I think that in this connexion it is only necessary to make two quite brief observations.

In the first place, there is no inconsistency whatsoever in wanting A and thinking that B ought to be the case, even when A and B are themselves inconsistent. We may well have a

desire and a moral belief that runs counter to that desire. Indeed there are moral philosophers who have held that morality would be inconceivable unless *some* of our moral beliefs ran counter to our desires.

However, though there is no inconsistency between wanting A and thinking that B ought to be the case, it should be equally obvious that the former could not serve as a reason for the latter nor the latter be derived from the former. Yet there seems a presumption in the question that just this is what is to be shown. Paradoxically though, Utilitarians (and I use the expression in a rather general way) seem to have held both that there was a prima facie inconsistency between wanting A and thinking that B ought to be the case, and also that this inconsistency was to be removed by showing that the belief that B ought to be the case was grounded in the want for A. But of course this last demand is an absurdity. It springs either from an absurdly exaggerated conception of what it is to prove consistency, i.e. that to prove two propositions are consistent one must show that one can be derived from the other, or else from a fundamentally egotistic conception of the basis of morality, i.e. that all one's moral beliefs are grounded in wants.

In fact the citizen who expresses a want for A and then, in deference to the operation of the democratic machine, thinks that B ought to be the case, thinks that B ought to be the case as the result of applying some higher-order principle to the effect that what the democratic machine chooses ought to be the case. He consults, in other words, his principles, he does not go back and consult again his wants. All he needs to be certain of is that his principles and his wants, though they may lead in different directions, are not actually inconsistent: and it seems very difficult to attach any sense even to the *possibility* that they could be.

However, it is now time to turn to another interpretation that can be put on the material which is characteristically fed into the democratic machine. On this view when the citizen chooses a certain policy or prefers one policy to another, he is expressing not a want but an *evaluation*. He chooses A or prefers A to B, because he thinks that A is the best policy, is the policy that ought to be enacted, or, alternatively, that A is a better policy than B or ought to be enacted in preference to B—not because he wants A more or needs it more than B. If it is objected at this stage that evaluations are based upon wants and therefore not to be contrasted with them, I can only reply that this may well be true if what is meant is that a man will often enough take his wants into account in arriving at his evaluations. But it does not follow from this that his evaluations are not different from his wants, nor that they cannot be placed in contrast to them. Indeed, the fact that evaluations may be based on wants is no more germane to our present discussion than it was to our earlier discussion that wants can be affected by evaluations.

Let us then regard the democratic machine as being fed with choices in the sense of evaluations. The evaluations are then aggregated by the machine in accordance with its established rule, and the machine comes up with a choice of its own. Anyone who accepts democracy is then obliged to think that the policy that the machine selects is the policy that ought to be enacted.

But immediately a difficulty arises. Let us imagine a citizen who feeds his choice for, say, A, or for A over B into the democratic machine. On the present interpretation, he is to be regarded as thereby expressing his opinion that A ought to be enacted. And now let us further suppose that the machine into which this and other choices have been fed comes up with its own choice, and its choice is for B. How can the citizen accept the machine's choice, which involves his thinking that B ought to be enacted when, as we already know, he is of the opinion, of the declared opinion, that A ought to be enacted?

Observe that we are confronted with a far more serious problem now when we interpret choices as evaluations than we were when we interpreted them as expressions of wants. For on the original interpretation the problem was (it will be remembered) that the acceptance of the machine's choice did not follow from one's own choice, which one had fed into the machine: the problem on this new interpretation is that the acceptance of the machine's choice

seems to be incompatible with—not just not to follow from, but to be incompatible with—one's own original choice. For if a man expresses a choice for A and the machine expresses a choice for B, then the man, if he is to be a sound democrat, seems to be committed to the belief that A ought to be the case *and* to the belief that B ought to be the case.

Now, this is a serious matter. For I think it is fairly self-evident that, even if the dichotomy of 'expressed want' 'evaluation' is somewhat harsh, the choices that the citizens of a democracy make when they are called upon to make a choice are far closer to evaluations than to expressions of want. And I hold this not because of any particularly elevated view I have of political behaviour but because I think that the ordinary citizen, confronted by a political choice, is far more likely to know which of the two policies he thinks *ought to be* enacted than which of them he *wants* enacted. Accordingly he is more likely to vote in a way that reflects his evaluations than in a way that reflects his wants. If this is so, then the difficulty that I have described would seem to constitute a paradox in the very heart of democratic theory.

There are two obvious ways in which the paradox might be broken. One is by denying that in the circumstances the man is committed to the belief that A (i.e. the policy of his choice) ought to be enacted: the other is by denying that the man is committed to the belief that B (i.e. the policy of the machine's choice) ought to be enacted. Either of these two ways would be effective in resolving the paradox: both have considerable plausibility: but neither, I submit, is ultimately acceptable. Let me review the arguments:

1. It might be claimed that the man who feeds his choice for A into the democratic machine is not in fact committed to believing that A ought to be the case in the face of the machine's verdict, since, though the choice that he feeds into the machine is certainly an evaluation, it is an *interim,* not a final or definitive, evaluation. When he expresses his preference for A or for A over B, his preference (properly understood) is hypothetical. Written out it would be formulated in some such way as "I think that A ought to be enacted, provided that

other people, or enough other people, are of the same opinion.'' The preference, the argument runs, is necessarily hypothetical, because when it is expressed, the man cannot know the preferences that will be expressed by his fellow-citizens. It is only when all these preferences have been fed into the machine, and the machine has operated on them and has come up with a preference of its own, that he has the requisite information on which to base a final as opposed to a provisional or interim choice. And then when he is in this position what he does is to reiterate the preference of the machine: he chooses as it has chosen—that is to say, in the present case he chooses B.

Once we understand this—the argument runs—the paradox disappears. No longer is there any temptation to think of the unfortunate citizen as committed both to the belief that A ought to be enacted and to the belief that B ought to be enacted—for it should now be clear that he continues to hold that A ought to be enacted only up to the moment when he has reason to think that B ought to be enacted: as soon as he has reason to commit himself to B, i.e. as soon as the machine has expressed *its* choices on the basis of all the choices in the community, his commitment to A dissolves. The man, in other words, withdraws his support from A and gives it to B.

The argument has some plausibility; but not, I think, enough. For, to begin with, it cannot be correct to interpret the choices fed into the democratic machine as interim or hypothetical, i.e. as of the form ''I think that A ought to be enacted if other people or enough other people are of the same opinion.'' And this for two reasons. First, a hypothetical choice, or a choice hypothetically expressed, generally implies some doubt whether the condition upon which the choice is dependent is or is not fulfilled. It would be inappropriate to express a choice hypothetically if one knew that the protasis was fulfilled: and it would be pointless to express it so if one knew that the protasis was unfulfilled. And yet in politics people sometimes vote knowing how the vote as a whole will go: sometimes, indeed, knowing full well that it will go in the opposite direction to that in which they cast their own vote. And we

don't think that the behaviour of such people is irrational. Suppose that a man votes Liberal, knowing full well that only a rather small minority of the population is of his opinion. We may disagree with his behaviour, but surely we don't think it irrational. Yet surely we ought to do so, if in casting his vote for the Liberals he was in effect saying ''I want a Liberal policy to be enacted if other people or enough other people are of my opinion,'' though he was quite certain that there was no chance whatsoever of there being enough people who were of his opinion.

Secondly, to interpret the citizens' choices as hypothetical is to imply that there is a dependence between what policy the citizen prefers and some other condition—in this case, how he thinks that others will vote: so that the citizen allows this consideration effectively to enter into his calculations when he decides which policy he supports. But this implication is surely, in many cases at least, unfounded. The citizen who votes for A cannot, without further qualification, be understood as expressing a view that A ought to be enacted if enough other people think so: because he may well be of the opinion that whether A ought to be enacted or not is *in some sense or other* independent of what other people think. Or even if he thinks that there is some dependence between what ought to be enacted and what others think, he may not think that there is a *total* dependence: so that if a policy is outvoted, then it automatically follows that it ought not to be enacted. Indeed, it would seem that democracy not merely allows but positively demands that our political preferences have a certain constancy to them and that they do not fluctuate with the preferences of others. In other words, when the machine's choice has been declared and we have given our adherence to it, there is a sense in which we still do and should stand by our original choice. What this sense is is still unclear, but that such a sense exists is surely indubitable.

However, suppose we allow that the citizen's choices are really hypothetical. Once we make this admission it is far from clear why a choice which is reached by aggregating them on the assumption that they are categorical or unconditional should have any particular appeal or authority. It is not very difficult to see why a choice which is based upon what are genuinely the unconditional choices of individual citizens should have authority: for such a choice would have been arrived at by considering what the citizens of the society actually think ought to be done. But if the democratic choice is the result of aggregating hypothetical choices, then it is arrived at merely by considering what the citizens of the society think ought to be done *under a certain set of conditions,* i.e. when other people agree with them. But why is this of such paramount significance? For is it not possible—indeed, is it not suggested by the form of words employed—that under a different set of conditions the citizens might well want something different done? Why then should we attach special prestige to what they think ought to be done if other people agree with them? Why is this a privileged condition? And, as far as I can see, the only reason for regarding any condition as privileged—in the sense that we are justified in detaching the remaining part of the preference and aggregating it—is that we are of the opinion that the condition is actually fulfilled. But it is quite clear that not in all cases of hypothetical choices will the condition be fulfilled. In some cases it will be, in others it will not be.

Moreover, if we take this suggestion for resolving the paradox of democracy *as a whole* we shall find a far stronger reason for thinking that a choice reached by aggregating hypothetical choices, where these hypothetical choices are choices conditional upon general agreement with the voter, has no natural authority. For it will be remembered that the voter who votes "A if enough others agree with this," switches to B when the democratic machine comes up with B. Now if this is so, surely he might equally well in the first place have voted B—for in voting B he would on this view merely have been expressing the view (which *is* surely his) that B ought to be enacted if enough people are of that opinion. Indeed it now seems as if the voter could quite legitimately have voted for *any* of the policies placed before him—provided only, of course,

that he neither knows that enough other people would prefer that policy nor knows that not enough other people will prefer that policy, i.e. if the uncertainty proviso, which, as we have seen, is necessary for the making of a hypothetical choice, is fulfilled. In other words, if the vote for A is interpreted as "A ought to be enacted if enough people are of the same opinion," and the voter is prepared to switch to support B if enough people are of that opinion, it is obvious that "A" as it appeared in his original vote was a variable, not a constant: a variable ranging over all the policies that are not obviously either winners or losers, not a constant designating one particular policy. If this is so, then it would be quite improper to take his vote literally, as meaning what it says—as one surely would do if one accepted a choice arrived at by aggregating it and similar votes. Accordingly the first attempt to solve our paradox must be rejected.

2. The other obvious way of breaking the paradox of Democracy would be by denying the other limb of the offending conjunction. Democracy—the argument would run—is government by compromise, and the role of the democratic machine is to function as a kind of impersonal arbitrator. In so far as the machine chooses a policy, it chooses a policy that it would be wise or prudent to follow, not a policy that the citizen ought to follow. And in so far as to believe in Democracy is to be prepared or disposed to accept the machine's choice, it is to accept it as the most sensible thing to do. The functioning of the democratic machine influences one's behaviour, actual and potential: what it does not do is increase one's obligations. On this view what one feeds into the machine are one's evaluations to the effect that this or that policy ought to be enacted: and these evaluations one continues to adhere to even after the machine has operated upon them. What the machine comes up with is the choice of a policy that it would be prudential for all to support, and there is no reason to postulate any incompatibility between the acceptance of such a policy, on the one hand, and, on the other, the continued adherence to one's own political beliefs. So once again the paradox disappears.

Once again the argument is plausible, but I do not think that ultimately it carries conviction. For, in the first place, it seems to me unrealistic to say that our commitment to the machine's choice, when the machine's choice does not concur with ours, is purely tactical or prudential. For if it were, then some argument analogous to that of Gyges's ring would apply. Suppose, once again, that our choice is for A and that of the machine is for B. Then if our support for B were purely tactical or prudential, we should surely be content if the B government were somehow outwitted and they found themselves, contrary to their own inclinations but with the continued support of their electors, putting through policy A. Yet I think it is fairly clear that if this happened in reality, we should be displeased and would think that something undesirable had occurred. If the machine chooses B, there is a sense in which we think that B ought to be enacted whether or not A could be. And this is more than tactical or prudential support.

Secondly it does not seem correct to equate—as the present argument does—belief in Democracy with a disposition to accept the successive choices of the democratic machine. For surely a man could be so disposed without believing in Democracy. He might, for instance, be prepared to go along with Democracy, because he thought that he could achieve power by no other means: although once he had achieved power he would probably try to end the democratic process. The problem, then, arises how we are to distinguish such a man from the genuine believer in Democracy. Surely the disposition to accept democratic results is common, and what must distinguish one from the other is the reason that each has for his acceptance. The genuine believer in Democracy is disposed to accept the successive choices of the democratic machine *because he believes that what the democratic machine chooses ought to be enacted.*

But once we make this concession the present solution to the paradox stands condemned. For if the believer in Democracy believes that what the democratic machine chooses ought to be enacted, then, whenever the machine actually chooses a policy, he must believe that that

policy ought to be enacted: not just that it would be wise or tactical to support its enactment, but that it ought to be enacted. In other words, the believer in Democracy is in our example committed to the belief that B ought to be enacted.

So we must abandon this solution to the paradox: which, it might be said, requires the same sort of systematic reinterpretation of our ordinary behaviour that Hobbes (on the traditional interpretation, at any rate) found himself committed to when he asserted an analogous theory about the obligation or commitment we have not just simply to Democracy but to government as such.

The paradox of Democracy cannot, it seems, be resolved by denying either of the limbs of the offending conjunction that gives rise to it. The only remaining way of resolving it is to show that the two limbs are, contrary to appearances, not inconsistent, and therefore their conjunction is not offensive. In other words, what is now required is to show that in our example it is perfectly in order for one and the same citizen to assert that A ought to be enacted, where A is the policy of his choice, and B ought to be enacted, where B is the policy chosen by the democratic machine, even when A and B are not identical.

Now, if my arguments have been sound so far, it is evident that either the two assertions *are* compatible, or else Democracy is inconsistent. I doubt that any of us are prepared to regard Democracy as inconsistent: in consequence we are committed to the view that, in the circumstances of my example, A ought to be enacted and B ought to be enacted are compatible. What we need to see, though, is *how* they are compatible, and the rest of this paper I shall devote to expounding, I fear rather sketchily, one explanation.

The explanation I proffer presupposes a distinction between direct and oblique moral principles. Direct principles refer to the morality of actions, policies, motives, etc., where these are picked out or designated by means of some general descriptive expressions, e.g. *murder, envy, benevolence, birth-control, telling lies,* etc. Oblique principles, by contrast, refer to the morality of actions, policies, motives, etc., where these actions, policies, motives, etc., are not picked out by reference to some common quality or characteristic that they possess, but are identified by means of an artificial property bestowed upon them either as the result of an act of will of some individual or in consequence of the corporate action of some institution. This is a far from satisfactory formulation of the distinction, neither very clear nor very precise, but I think that it will do for my present purposes. Examples of direct principles would be *Murder is wrong, Birth-control is permissible.* Examples of oblique principles would be *What is commanded by the sovereign ought to be done,* or *What is willed by the people is right.*

Now, my suggestion is that two judgements of the form "A ought to be the case" and "B ought to be the case" are not incompatible even though A and B cannot be simultaneously realized *if* one of these judgements is asserted as a direct principle whereas the other is asserted as a derivation from an oblique principle—provided that the direct and the oblique principle are not themselves incompatible. Now, I am aware that the proviso might give rise to some difficulty, for it might be natural to think that A ought to be enacted was incompatible with any oblique principle from which B ought to be enacted could be derived, ipso facto. For my principle to have any area of operation, it is of course important to exclude incompatibility of this kind and to permit as relevant only incompatibility of a more immediate kind. And I hope that this restriction will be seen to be less artificial when it is realized that a judgement of the kind B ought to be enacted is derived from an oblique principle only by the introduction of certain further factual premises, e.g. B has been commanded by the Sovereign, B is the will of the people, etc.

Now I think it should be clear that my suggestion, if accepted, would resolve our paradox by the only means still available to us, i.e. by showing that the two limbs of the conjunction are not inconsistent. For—to return to the example—"A ought to be enacted" is asserted by the citizen who has been outvoted as a direct principle, whereas "B ought to be enacted" is asserted by him as a derivation from

an oblique principle, i.e. the principle of Democracy.

But the question now arises, What reason have I for putting forward my suggestion? How is its truth to be established? And the only answer I can give is, I am afraid, disappointing. The most I can do is to try to dispose of two reasons, two reasons which I am sure are misguided, for rejecting it.

1. Someone might maintain that "A ought to be the case" and "B ought to be the case" are clearly incompatible, and being incompatible they are incompatible in all circumstances: a fortiori, they are incompatible no matter what reasons may be adduced in favour of either of them. Against this forth-right position I would like to urge a more sceptical attitude. It seems to me fairly evident that any judgement of the form "X ought to be the case" acquires a different meaning when it is asserted as a derivation from an oblique principle from that which it has when it is asserted directly, cf., e.g. Jews ought to be given privileged treatment asserted in the 1930s as a derivation from some principle to the effect that victims of persecution should be given exceptional treatment, and the same proposition asserted simply as an expression of Jewish chauvinism. Now if this is so, if the meaning of a principle can vary with the reasons for which it is asserted, and if—as is usually admitted—incompatibility is intimately associated with meaning, there seems, at the very least, good reason not to be dogmatic that of the two principles it is true that, once incompatible, always incompatible.

2. Again, it might be argued against my suggestion that "A ought to be the case" and "B ought to be the case" can never be consistently conjoined by anyone because the assertion of the first commits one to the implementation of A and the assertion of the second commits one to the implementation of B, and *ex hypothesi* this is impossible: for one cannot simultaneously commit oneself to the implementation of two policies that cannot be simultaneously realized.

Now this objection rests upon the identification of asserting (honestly asserting) that A ought to be the case with committing oneself to the implementation of A. And the identification is by no means self-evident. *Perhaps* honestly asserting "I ought to do A" does commit one to the implementation of A—but it is surely megalomania further to identify "A ought to be the case" with "I ought to do A" or to think that belief in the one commits one to belief in the other.

However, even if we do allow that there *is* an element of commitment in any evaluation to the effect that, e.g. A ought to be the case, it is by no means clear in the present case that the degree of commitment is such as to preclude any commitment to the other. For it is surely evident that the commitment cannot be total. The democrat who believes in his political heart that A ought to be enacted cannot be totally committed to A. And if the commitment is short of totality, then there is in principle room for some commitment to B, even when B diverges from A. Indeed, when we think of the actual situation, it seems that our degree of commitment to the political policy we directly support never goes beyond arguing on its behalf, persuading others of its truth, etc.—

whereas the degree of commitment we can plausibly be said to have to the choice of the democratic machine extends only to not resisting its implementation or perhaps to resisting any attempt to resist its implementation—and it seems perfectly possible to be simultaneously committed in these two different directions. Hence I conclude that the second objection to my suggestion fails.

Notes

1. Duncan Black, *Theory of Committees and Elections* (London, 1958), pp. 67–68.
2. Kenneth J. Arrow, *Social Choice and Individual Values* (New York, 1951), chap. 5.
3. R. D. Luce and H. Raiffa, *Games and Decisions* (New York, 1957), chap. 14.
4. "Rule" or "method" here are to be understood in some very general sense that will satisfy even those who hold that "the essence of democracy is something which must escape definition in terms of any functional relation between decisions and individual preference." I. M. D. Little, "Social Choice and Individual Values," *Journal of Political Economy* 60 (October 1952), p. 432.

Democracy Without Preference

DAVID M. ESTLUND

Is democracy fundamentally a competitive or a cooperative endeavor?[1] Some voters, both elected representatives and private citizens, base their votes on parochial interests or desires, while the votes of others are shaped by the apparent best interests of the whole political community. Which of these, if either, is the proper task of the democratic voter? It is a separate question how one morally ought to vote, since it is a separate question whether and how democracy imposes any moral requirements or bestows any moral legitimacy. I do not address the moral question directly in this paper. Instead, I want to ask which of these tasks, if either, is given by the idea of democracy.

The idea of democracy is a contested matter, but I shall take its core to be rule by the people by way of voting. This is not to say that voting is the most important democratic political activity practically, but only conceptually. Other features of democratic life, such as free expression, political participation, and equal consideration get their democratic credentials (though these are not their only moral ground) from an association with popular rule through voting.

Is the Wisconsin senator's task to promote, say, the dairy industry without taking into account the impact on the economies of other states? It could reasonably be argued that the public interest is best served if voters (repre-

sentatives or direct voters) do not try, individually, to promote it. Perhaps they should, instead, do the best that can be done for themselves or their constituency, and the competition between the interests of constituencies will, if power is distributed equally, produce the socially best outcome.

At least in some contexts, the adversarial (or Invisible Hand) argument is plausible. Recently, the predominant models of democratic choice have been of this variety. Social choice theory, in fact, has been developed largely by liberal welfare economists, whose stock in trade is the Invisible Hand of the perfect free market and its close, imperfect, variants.[2] Some of their work is meant to apply mainly in the economic sphere, but much of it is explicitly meant as a contribution to the theory of democratic, political, social choice where one participates by voting rather than trading.[3]

Most of the many theoretical interpretations currently employed describe a vote as an expression of a *preference*. This reflects, in many cases, adherence to something like an Invisible Hand model of democratic social choice. However, different theorists use "preference" to mean different things. I shall argue that under any acceptable interpretation, votes must be aggregable, advocative, and active. *The heart of the argument below is the attempt to demonstrate the failure of preference interpreta-*

David Estlund, "Democracy without Preference," from *Philosophical Review*, 99, no. 3 (July 1990): 397–423. Copyright Cornell University Press, 1990. Reprinted by permission of the author and publisher.

tions to meet these three conditions. The paper ends with arguments in favor of interpreting votes not as any sort of expression of individual preferences, but rather as statements that certain policies are in the common interest. This distinctively Rousseauean proposal may not be acceptable in every way; that is not my claim. This interpretation is shown to succeed where several of the most tempting interpretations could not, namely in meeting the three conditions, Aggregability, Advocacy, and Activity. Should this concluding positive argument be thought to fail, the prospects for an acceptable understanding of the task of the voter are all the more dim. Before enunciating and defending the three conditions on theoretical interpretations of voting, it must be considered whether such interpretation is necessary at all.

We may distinguish two senses of "interpretation of voting": *empirical* and *theoretical.* An empirical interpretation of voting is an interpretation of actual performances of the act of voting. There will be many true descriptions of any act of voting, some of which would be more relevant for democratic theory than others. The kind of interpretation I shall be considering, however, is not empirical, but theoretical.[4]

A theoretical interpretation asks, "what kind of action is referred to in a good theory of democracy by the term 'vote'?" A theorist of democracy, working before anyone had ever voted on anything, would have no voting acts which could be empirically interpreted. Still, the theory would include voting, and we might reasonably ask what sort of action voting should be in that theory. This cannot be assumed to be the same as what the voter ought to do. That is a separate question, whose answer depends on a prior theoretical interpretation of voting. Whether one ought, morally or prudentially, to vote honestly, or even vote at all, partly depends on what voting is—on the theoretical interpretation of voting.

This second, theoretical kind of interpretation of voting is, however, parasitic on the first, empirical kind. For example, to interpret votes theoretically as being expressions of interests is to assert that *in a properly working democracy* votes would be (empirically interpretable as) expressions of interest. Theoretical interpretations assert the appropriateness of certain empirical interpretations in a properly working democracy. These are not, however, empirical claims; they are claims about what sorts of social choice procedures are democratic.

Why does democratic theory need a theoretical interpretation of voting? It is important, first, whether *any* adequate interpretation is possible. If no adequate interpretation were possible, or consistent with the concept of democracy, then no argument could be made that a policy's being passed by majority vote conveys any justification or legitimacy on it. If votes express interests, desires, choices, ought-judgments, opinions or some such thing, then one can sensibly investigate the relation between majority rule and moral or other normative requirements. Suppose we said a vote is just a tool; it can be used by the voter in any way he or she pleases, to express desires, opinions, etc. All that matters is the bottom line— voting for x merely increases the chances of x's being enacted. This account of the matter shows that we can still *imagine* democratic social choice without assuming any interpretation. Still, it is difficult to see what could be said in favor of democratic choice on this account unless we know what a person is supposed to be doing in voting.

Consider two kinds of argument that votes need no interpretation in order to engage with moral theory.[5] The first argument notes that we needn't interpret votes in order to see that a system of making social decisions by voting will result in less outright physical conflict than would be seen in a system where each individual simply exerts whatever force is available in order to influence the course of events. A similar rationale might support giving two continually fighting children mallets made out of foam rubber, in order to channel their violence into a less destructive form. According to this view, it is this reduction of violent conflict that morally recommends democratic choice, and no interpretation of voting seems to be implied or required.

Yet, this view cannot really do without any interpretation of voting. Under what conditions can the combatants be expected to contain their efforts within these less violent bounds? Those who fare better under the restricted form of battle can be expected to stay with it as long as others do, but those who fare less well than they would if they resorted to more forceful means might be expected expeditiously to return to their wooden bats while the others are still fighting with only toys. Why would the physically and otherwise more powerful members of a society limit themselves to voting when they can apparently do better with a real fight? A powerful state, whatever its form, can reduce conflict as compared with the level of conflict in the mythical state of nature. However, to whatever extent democratic procedures are *especially* effective at preempting violent struggle, it must be owing to the prevalence in the society of a certain view, or theory of democracy according to which voting can be expected to yield outcomes that are fair, or optimal, or some such thing. Unless the participants believe that democratic choice has something else to recommend it, it will not have the virtue of preempting violent conflict, and there can be nothing else to recommend it without some interpretation of voting. So far, of course, this says little about what the *proper* interpretation is; that is the question I propose to take up.

The second way of denying the need for any theoretical interpretation of voting is to argue that majority rule, or some similar voting procedure, can be shown to be a *fair or just* way of making social choices, even without worrying about what votes mean. For example, in Rawlsian fashion, perhaps such a method would be agreed to in an initial position of fairness. However, on Rawls's view (which is the most fully articulated version of the sort of theory in question) this would be plausible only if there were no alternative under which all groups could expect to do better. What about the alternative of having choices made by experts in, say, economics and sociology? In order to be recommended to those in the original position, democratic choice must be shown to have a certain tendency to improve the situation of all groups, or at least a greater tendency than such alternatives. How could such a claim

about a voting procedure be sustained without a theory of the nature of voting? Indeed, Rawls himself denies that the democratic pedigree of a decision gives it any special authority. Democratic choice is to be recommended to the extent that it has the property of arriving at arrangements which themselves are just on independent grounds. Democratic choice, in Rawls's view (and in his terminology) yields no pure procedural justice.[6] Democracy's credentials as a perfect or imperfect procedure must, it seems, include a theoretical interpretation of voting.

These considerations support the need for a theoretical interpretation of voting. However, it is not only important that *some* interpretation of voting be possible. The adequate interpretation(s) will almost certainly have further consequences for both political theory and our understanding of actual democratic practice (though I do not consider any in this paper). If, for example, the only adequate interpretation of a vote is that it is a statement on the common interest (though this is stronger than the claim I defend below), then further questions are raised about what common interests are, their possibility and likelihood, their discoverability (in theory and practice), the justification of pursuing them contrary to the minority's opinion, etc. It is not as though there were a theory of democratic social choice into which one could simply plug any desired interpretation of voting without significantly affecting the rest of the theory. The interpretation of voting is an important part of a theory of democracy.

The Three A's

The following three conditions are constraints placed by the concept of democracy on any adequate theoretical interpretation of voting.

The Aggregability Condition

Democratic social choices must be determined by the cumulative impact of multiple inputs.[7] Consider a rule which is constructed by listing all possible sets of inputs in one column, and then in an adjacent column randomly entering various possible social choices. A rule that assigns to each set of inputs the social choice which happens to be next to it in the random list does not consider similar inputs cumulatively, and this alone disqualifies it as a democratic choice procedure.

Relevantly similar inputs should be considered cumulatively in a democratic procedure, but inputs which are similar in some ways can be different in others. Being cast on the same day, or in the same town, are extraneous sorts of similarity from the standpoint of democratic social choice. While votes could be aggregated, in the sense of being counted, according to some such criterion of similarity, votes which addressed the issue at hand in the same way would not necessarily be counted together. The appropriate kind of similarity is similarity with regard to the issue at hand in a given case of social choice. Inputs are similar in the relevant way if they stand in the same relation to the issue they address.

For any two votes that are aggregable they take either the same position or different positions on the issue, and votes that take the same position as each other are relevantly similar for the purposes of democratic choice. Two votes cannot be said to take the same or different positions on an issue unless they both take *some* position on that issue. The Aggregability Condition requires just this: *there must be some single issue on which, for any pair of the inputs, they take either the same or a different position.* This can be less awkwardly, though also less accurately, stated as follows: two inputs are relevantly similar if they constitute the same answer to the question posed by the choice procedure, and they are aggregable as long as they constitute answers to the same socially posed question at all. This "social question" analogy is useful but only approximate since desires, for example, can address the same issue, and so can be aggregable in the present sense, even though desires, not being acts at all, are never themselves answers to questions. The question analogy also supposes that there *is* a socially posed question, and this need not be literally true. The "social question" analogy, then, is intended only as a

shorthand device for representing what it is for inputs to address the same issue.

The Advocacy Condition

Democratic inputs must be for or against certain choices, as distinct from being just opinions that something is the case. Later I will argue that some opinions can be for or against things in the required way, but the opinion that the moon is made of green cheese, for example, is not for or against anything, and so cannot be a democratic input. A survey is often different from a voting procedure in this way. Votes, I shall say for now, advocate certain choices (though this gloss of the Advocacy Condition will be refined in Section V). To advocate something, say x, is to be *for* it, and to be against x is to be for not-x. Therefore, inputs can be advocative by being *either* for or against some policy.

If democratic inputs were not advocative, then even a unanimous outcome would be indeterminate as to which social choice is called for. Consider this example: there is a tribe whose social choice of where to dig a well is based on a poll of individual opinions as to where there is water. This may seem democratic, but only if we assume that the social choice would be to dig where the people expected water to lie. But suppose the governors' choice were intentionally to dig far away from the suspected location of water, perhaps out of meanness, or as an attempt to undo the regime by creating a shortage. This choice, too, would be *based on* the individuals' opinions on the location of water. If the inputs are only opinions on the location of water, neither choice is any more faithful to the inputs than the other. There is no way to judge the faithfulness of a social choice to these inputs because opinions on the location of water are not, *by themselves,* for or against anything. It may be objected that in such a case as the tribe in search of water, the context could make it clear that a statement on the location of water is also an act of advocating digging there. However, these inputs *would* then be advocative; they would not be counter-examples to the Advocacy Condition, since they *meet* it.

The presence of advocative inputs, those which are for or against some choice, does not immediately solve the sort of problem raised by the case of the tribe and the water. A social choice could still be based on acts which advocate some choice by choosing to do the opposite of what is advocated. It is a condition on democratic social choice procedures that the social choice is based on the votes *in the sense of doing what is advocated* (rather than, say, the opposite). This condition on democratic social choice *procedures* necessitates an Advocacy Condition on democratic *inputs*.

The Advocacy Condition, then, requires just this: that the inputs be "off the fence" that most simple statements are on. If this can be accomplished without inputs being straightforward acts of advocacy, that will suffice. The name "Advocacy Condition" will be retained in any case to recognize the measure of truth in the association in ordinary language of "voting" with advocacy.[8]

Ballots in real social choice procedures could perhaps include the possibility of something labelled "none of the above," and it might be thought that this is a problem for the Advocacy Condition. If this option received a large majority, either the social choice would be not to enact any of the other alternatives (and perhaps hold another vote with other alternatives), or the next most supported alternative would be considered to see if it received enough votes to win (for example, majority, plurality, etc.). In the first case, where none of the alternatives is enacted, "none of the above" functions as the name of a policy, a vote for which is an act of advocating it, namely, the policy of doing none of the above. This raises no problem for the Advocacy Condition.[9]

In the second case, those supporting the "none of the above" option are ignored from the standpoint of social choice. Whether they *should* be ignored or not in the procedure is not the question here. Given that they are ignored there is no reason to regard their acts as inputs, since, regardless of their number, they

could not win. Such responses as "none of the above" could have political significance of various kinds in the larger political system, but the present study is confined to democratic social choice, and from that standpoint such responses are irrelevant unless "none of the above" names an actual possible social choice (as above). The case of "none of the above" is different from that of abstention, which is treated below, under the Activity Condition.

The Activity Condition

Suppose there were a method, perhaps involving some amazing machine, for discovering the preferences of people without the individuals performing any acts at all (this is a coherent idea only on certain understandings of "preference"). Could a procedure with these individual characteristics as its inputs be a democratic social choice procedure? The question is not whether the passive method is as morally defensible as a real voting procedure, but rather whether such a passive procedure is democratic. The third condition on the theoretical interpretation of democratic inputs is that *they must be acts*. The concept of democracy requires this, whether or not morality even requires that social choice be democratic.

Appealing to the concept of democracy is problematic, since there is little agreement on the details of the concept. The term has acquired such positive moral connotations that if some political procedure is justified, some are tempted to say that it thereby counts as democratic. This use of the term has the disadvantage of preventing the very formulation of the question whether the property of being democratic ever justifies political procedures. A more common use of the term is to cover any procedure of making social choices in accordance with the interests and desires of the citizens, regardless of whether the citizens are in any way agents or authors of the social choice. This at least allows the question to arise whether democratic procedures are justified by their being democratic. However, by failing to distinguish government *for the people* from government *by the people* it suppresses the question whether there is any important moral difference between them. It is clear that these two ways of using the term both fail to recognize important distinctions. Thus, these uses may be agreed to be unfortunate. "Republicanism" might be a useful term for referring to government, or social choice, in the interests of the people. If the word "democracy" is to be reserved for government by, and not just government for, the people, the quintessential democratic entity, a vote, ought to be conceived as an act.

Voting procedures are often sensitive in various ways to inactivity. *Abstentions* can block enactments, for example. Is abstention a kind of democratic input which is not active, and therefore a difficulty for the proposed condition that democratic inputs must be acts? Abstention, whether or not it is an act itself, is abstention *from* some act. The act abstained from must surely be the act of voting, of offering one's input to the social choice procedure. It is true that failing to vote can affect the procedure, and one might abstain for that very reason, but abstaining does not thereby become a democratic *input*. Abstention, like bribery, can be a way of intentionally influencing the procedure, but neither is aggregated by democratic choice procedures. One might still object by demonstrating that some procedures actually aggregate abstentions. Some procedures may distinguish an abstention from the failure to vote at all by, for example, asking individuals to make their abstentions known. For example, a system in which voting was legally required of citizens might nonetheless allow them to specify by their vote that they endorse none of the proposed alternatives. However, this would be no counterexample to the Activity Condition, since abstentions of this sort are clearly acts.[10]

Democracy essentially involves the activity of the people in the process of governing. Democratic social choice must therefore be regarded as aggregating acts of some sort.

Varieties of Preference

In contemporary discussions of voting procedures, where any interpretation of votes is offered at all, votes are usually said to express *preferences.*[11] The term "preference" is unfortunately vague, and seems to mean different things in the works of different writers. Even though "preference" is somewhat vague, its popularity as an interpretation of democratic inputs may reflect an implicit recognition of what I am calling the Advocacy Condition. It is difficult (though, as I shall argue later, not impossible) to see how votes which could not be described as expressing a preference could be votes for or against anything, as votes must be, and this may account for the prominence of preference interpretations of voting.

The everyday usage of the word "prefer" is of little help in understanding the use of the word by theorists of social choice. For in everyday usage, to prefer chocolate to vanilla, or Mozart to Beethoven, is to like one better than the other. This usage is apparently not adopted by any social choice theorist. A use that is, in some ways, close to the everyday use is that to prefer A to B is to want it more. Wanting something more is distinct from liking it better, since one can, for various reasons, want A more than B even while liking B better than A. For example, one may want the food that is more nutritious, despite liking junk food better.

One might well wonder why anyone who means to discuss wants or desires (I shall use the terms interchangeably) would speak of preferences. There is perhaps the following justification. Given a choice between one kick in the shins or two, which do you prefer? Strictly speaking it is probably false to say you want one kick more than two; you probably do not want either, at all. Even if you have no other choice, you do not come to desire a kick in the shins. We can, however, phrase the situation in terms of desire: you want not-two-kicks-in-the-shins more than you want not-one-kick-in-the-shins. Or we can speak of a desire/aversion continuum, where strength of desire runs in the same direction on the continuum as weakness of aversion. The whole thing is made simpler by using "is preferred to" to mean "is higher on the desire/aversion continuum" or some similar formula. A theorist who wishes to speak of desires for or against, or of desires and aversions, may choose the term "preferences" for the sake of simplicity of expression. One of the interpretations of votes to be considered, then, is that they express *desires*.

In the work of some writers, social choice is closely associated with utilitarianism. The term "preference" is used, apparently univocally, in both contexts. Modern utilitarians who recommend maximizing preference satisfaction may, of course, mean desire satisfaction. However, "preference satisfaction" is often intended rather to mean "(objective) interest satisfaction" or more simply "welfare." For example, John Harsanyi[12] espouses a form of utilitarianism which operates on the "real interest" of individuals, and "what is really good" for them. Still, he uses the term "preferences" since he argues that a person's interests are best understood as what she rationally prefers, or what she would manifestly prefer under certain ideal conditions. Utilitarian moral theorists who speak of preferences often have in mind *interests,* and so this is a second likely meaning of "preference" in some social choice and democratic theory as well.

Behaviorists in the philosophy of psychology understand mental states as nothing more than dispositions to behave in certain ways under certain circumstances. Social choice theorists with behaviorist leanings[13] define a preference for A over B as a disposition to choose A over B in certain circumstances. A complete individual preference ranking is a summary, on this account, of all of an individual's dispositions to choose. By interpreting votes as preference rankings these theorists mean to interpret inputs as complete lists of the individuals' dispositions to choose between the available alternatives in a given instance of social choice. Therefore, I will also take up the interpretation of democratic inputs as *dispositions to choose.*

It might be thought appropriate also to consider the interpretation of votes as choices themselves, and not only dispositions to choose. However, it is a common mistake to assume that the voter's alternatives are certain social states, or policies. The social states, or government policies that are named on the ballot are alternatives confronting the society, not the individual. The society must choose between policy A and policy B; the choice is properly called a social choice. Except in the case of a dictator a social choice is never also an individual choice.[14] The individual's only choice in this procedure is between different ways of *voting.* How voting is to be interpreted remains an open question. Voters do have to make choices of a certain kind, but voting is not choosing.

Where votes are interpreted as preferences, then, this can be more precisely understood as interpreting them as desires, interests, dispositions to choose (or, as we shall see, individual reports of one of these three). Under which of these interpretations, if any, do votes meet the three conditions on democratic inputs, Aggregability, Advocacy, and Activity? The answer, I shall now argue, is that none of the six interpretations passes this test.

Preference Interpretations Disqualified

Interpretations of votes as desires, interests, or dispositions to choose do meet the Aggregability Condition. My desire for funding of the arts seems intuitively to be aggregable with your desire either for *or* against such funding (though the details of such aggregation remain unclear) and the same would seem to go for interests in it, or dispositions to choose it. They are also advocative in the required sense. That is, they are "for or against" certain choices; they are "off the fence." In themselves, however, all of them fail as democratic inputs, since none is an act. No argument is required here beyond what has already been offered in defense of the Activity Condition itself.

Desires, interests and dispositions to choose are not themselves acts, as democratic inputs must be, but desire *reports,* interest *reports,* and disposition-to-choose *reports* (hereafter "disposition reports") *are* acts and so they seem to succeed where desires and interests themselves fail. This adds three more possible versions of the view that votes are or express preferences. However, reports fail where the states themselves succeed, namely in the area of aggregability. First, we can grant, for now, that such reports are advocative in the required way. Second, it is true that unlike the desires, interests and dispositions themselves, reports are acts. They may meet the Advocacy Condition, as did the states themselves, and they clearly meet the Activity Condition, which desires, interests, and dispositions failed. However, they fail the Aggregability Condition since they are never reports on some single issue. This claim requires some expansion.

Reports (like desires, interests, statements, beliefs, etc.) are not aggregable with other reports unless they all address the same issue. The notion of an aggregate report is somewhat obscure even where the component reports do address the same issue, but if I am reporting on the weather, and you are reporting on the score of a baseball game, no real aggregate report is possible. The problem with interpreting democratic inputs as individual reports of one's own desires, interests, or dispositions is that each voter is reporting on a different issue: Smith reports on Smith's desires, interests or dispositions, Jones reports on Jones's states, and so on.

It is no good to say that there is a single issue here, represented by the single question,[15] "What is your desire (interest, disposition)?" When a school teacher places at the top of each student's printed exam the question, "What is your name?" there is, it is true, a sense in which each person faces the same issue. The issue faced by one student is *formally,* or *syntactically,* of the same type as that faced by each of the others, but this is not the sort of similarity that is required in order for the answers to be aggregable. Aggregability requires that the students face the same issue in the distinct sense that their answers all represent the same person as having a certain name. They must face the same issue in a *semantic,* rather than a syntactic sense, or in virtue of *content* rather than form. If the question at the top of each exam were, "What is your *teacher's* name?" the students would all face the same issue in the way required for aggregation, in a way that would allow us to imagine deriving an aggregate answer from the individual answers.[16] Similarly, if the issue faced by all voters were the nature of Smith's desires, their answers would be aggregable. But voters who are asked about their own desires face the same issue only in the irrelevant formal sense; in the required semantic, or content-based sense, each voter faces a different issue from that of every other voter. Because of the inevitable indexicals, "I," or "my," individual reports of desires, interests, or dispositions are, for this reason, not aggregable.[17] Let us call this the *Indexical Problem.*

It may seem surprising that the aggregability of desires themselves cannot somehow be worked into desire reports. Clearly, if the content of a desire were aggregable and could, without change, serve as a desire report, then both would be aggregable. But since the content of a desire is just a proposition or a state of affairs, it does not exhibit the nature of its "container," desire. It could as well be the content of a belief rather than a desire; the differences between the two types of mental state do not lie in their contents. Since they don't, themselves, exhibit the kind of state of which they are the contents, desire contents cannot ever provide all that is needed in a desire *report,* which must be partly *about* desire. So the aggregability of desires themselves cannot be appropriated by desire reports in this direct way.

While the content of a desire can be merely [that *p*], a desire report must include this desire content, *and* that it is the content of a desire. While this shows that the desire content cannot be the whole of a desire report, it doesn't yet show how the indexical problem arises. That is in virtue of a third required component of a desire report: *whose* desire it is. Again, this is not a necessary feature of the *desire* that is reported, but a necessary feature of a desire *report.* Whatever words, gestures, or other actions are used to report desires, interpreting them as desire reports involves taking all three components to be present—the desire *content,* its being the content of a *desire,* and its being the desire *of* the person reporting. My desire [that *p*] is not about me at all, but my statement or report [that I have a desire that *p*] clearly is.

That is why reports, unlike desires themselves, are subject to the Indexical Problem and are not, therefore, aggregable in the required sense.

The point about aggregability has a philosophically substantial role in the critique of Invisible Hand views of democracy. Democracy involves multiple individuals addressing some single issue, but the Invisible Hand view does not. Indeed, the hand that shapes such public issues is supposed to be invisible in just that sense—it is not the hand of any individual. This is a pivotal conflict between democratic and Invisible Hand views of social choice.[18]

Of the following interpretations of democratic inputs—desires, desire reports, interests, interest reports, dispositions to choose, and disposition reports—none is at the same time active and aggregable. Desires, interests, and dispositions are not active, while reports are not aggregable. But, it may be asked, why not regard the Activity Condition as being met by the report, and the Aggregability Condition met by the interests or desires themselves? The desires, interests, and dispositions themselves are, admittedly, aggregable when they are on the same issue, so if I report a desire for x, and you report a desire either for x or not-x, our desires themselves are in principle aggregable. The Activity Condition, as stated, says that the input must itself *be an act,* and the present objection does not meet that requirement. However, the requirement itself needs further defense in this context.

The Activity Condition is an implication of the fact that "democracy" refers to rule by the people, as argued above, and rule by the people is a stronger requirement in the present context than *participation* by the people. Consider an example of participation which is not rule by the people. Suppose that in some society, the social choices are made in accordance with astrological doctrines. The positions of various planets and stars are consulted and interpreted according to canons of astrology, and social choices are made by a king in accordance with what the heavens "indicate." Our question is this: if the astrological data were gathered and presented by the citizens, even all citizens, would their participation in this procedure con-

stitute rule by the people? Clearly it would not. The astrology case is like the objector's proposal in that in both cases the only activity of the citizens is their actively *delivering or presenting* the procedure's inputs. The inputs themselves are facts which could, in principle, have been discovered in some other way. It is these facts that determine the social choice, and not the citizens. At best it is the king who, constrained by the astrological facts, makes the social choice. The people participate, but they do not rule in any way. Therefore, participation does not always meet the Activity Condition.

An objector might say that the case is a bad analogy. In the astrological case it might be said that the king is not basing the decision on any *facts about the citizens,* and this is where it strays from true democracy. On the model of democratic choice proposed by the objector, where desires or interests are reported by individuals, the government does base the decision on facts about the citizens. However, this objection misses the point, as we can see if we simply suppose that astrology is a reliable indicator of the interests of the citizens. This would give the king access to relevant facts about the citizens, and they would be known through citizen participation. However, the procedure remains undemocratic.

The issue here is, at root, the agency of the voter in the social decision. If the king, or the social choice mechanism simply aggregates facts about the voter, and bases the social decision on these facts, we may (or may not) have a case of rule for the people, but we certainly do not have rule by them. It is not that they are not agents at all; surely they all are agents, in some acts. Rather, what is lacking is any ground for thinking of them as agents *of the social decision.* Altering the story so that these facts about them are actively presented by them ensures that they are agents in at least one act, but we never doubted this. We may grant this much; we might now be willing to say that what is done *depends* on an action of theirs (though this needn't be true since the facts they present are, in principle, independently obtainable). But it does not provide any new reason for thinking that what gets done is an action of theirs. The argument is not about whether rule by the people is superior to rule for the people in any way. The point is that rule by the people is a necessary condition (it may also be sufficient, but that does not matter here) of a system's being democratic. The Activity Condition, then, legitimately requires that the very thing which is aggregated by the social choice procedure is an act, so that the people can be agents or authors of the social choice (though this is not guaranteed merely by meeting the Activity Condition). Desires, interests, dispositions to choose, and reports of each, all therefore fail since none is both active and aggregable.

Votes As Common-Interest Statements

Self-interest statements have already been discussed (under the description "interest reports"), and they were found not to be aggregable with one another, since they are not all statements on the same issue. Statements about the interests of others ("other-interest statements" for brevity) would, however, be aggregable if the statements were all about the same interests of the same others (for example, "x is in Smith's interest"). Other-interest statements can in principle be aggregable, and, as with all statements, active as well.

Other-interest statements, however, are not advocative. This is consistent with holding that one can advocate a policy for the sake of others. But merely saying that something is in the interest of certain others is not necessarily to make an advocative statement. A white South African businessman's statement that foreign disinvestment is in the interest of members of the black majority is not necessarily an advocative statement, even though there is no reason to think it impossible for him to advocate disinvestment for the sake of the blacks. One can advocate certain things for the sake of others alone, and in the proper context saying that it is in their interest can be an act of advocacy. Still, the statement is not advocative in itself (or "intrinsically"), and this is what is required of democratic inputs by the Advocacy Condition.

Intrinsic advocacy may look like a new, un-

defended condition. In fact, however, if we distinguish "intrinsic" from "contextual" advocacy, we see that it *must* be intrinsic advocacy that is at issue in the Advocacy Condition. We're not considering the act of voting itself, but rather the interpretations of it.[19] Actual acts of voting are typically not speech acts at all, but hand raisings, box markings, and the like. If some voting act is properly interpreted as, for example, an other-interest statement, it is in virtue of the *context* of the real, non-linguistic voting act. If the voting act were itself thought to be advocative, then it could be accurately interpreted only by a statement that is *intrinsically* advocative. But, by hypothesis, we're considering voting acts that are accurately interpreted as other-interest statements. If these statements are not intrinsically advocative, then the acts they accurately interpret are not advocative intrinsically or contextually. It is irrelevant to ask at this stage whether other-interest statements can themselves be contextually advocative. There is no relevant context left to consider once we've arrived at the proper interpretation of the voting act. If voting acts must be advocative either contextually or intrinsically, they must admit of an interpretation that is advocative *intrinsically*. As for acts which, in the context, are interpretable as other-interest statements, they remain on the fence—they are not advocative. And saying so does not deny that a speech act which is an other-interest statement might be advocative in some contexts.

Self-interest statements are not aggregable, and other-interest statements are not advocative. This may seem to establish that *no* interest statements can be both advocative and aggregable. However, that would require the additional premise that *all* interest statements are either self-interest statements or other-interest statements. Interest statements are of *three* kinds: self-interest, other-interest, and *common*-interest. A common-interest statement is one which says that something is or is not in *our* interest, in the interest of those in some group which includes the speaker. Recall that self-interest statements were shown to be inaggregable, though perhaps advocative, and other-interest statements shown to be aggregable, though not advocative. In the space that remains I will argue that common-interest statements, while keeping the activity possessed by any statement, combine the advocacy of the self-interest statements with the aggregability of common-interest statements. Hence, common-interest statements can be shown to be aggregable, advocative, and active. Therefore, inputs which, in context, are interpretable as common-interest statements will meet all three conditions.

The first step is to show that *self*-interest statements meet the Advocacy Condition. If they do, then since common-interest statements effectively include a self-interest statement, common-interest statements will be shown to meet it as well. It is important at this stage to keep in mind that the goal is not to find an interpretation of voting under which voting is an *act of advocacy*. To meet the Advocacy Condition an interpretation need only be "off the fence," anything but solidly neutral, and that is all that will be shown. Indeed, interpretations of voting that are straightforward advocacy appear to be subject to separate serious difficulties.[20] Since common-interest statements include self-interest statements, if the latter puts one off the fence then so does the former. Of course, this would not be so if other parts of common-interest statements put one off the fence in the opposite direction. But the other parts are other-interest statements, and those are solidly on the fence. That is why the self-interest component is enough to put common-interest statements off the fence. It is an unanswered pressure in one direction.

The conclusion is not that one *advocates* the whole package for the beneficial bit, just that a common-interest statement is off the fence, advocative, in a way the other interpretations we have considered are not. As noted, it is dangerous unreflectively to assume that more advocacy would be better. The argument I will offer presently, that self-interest statements meet the Advocacy Condition, amounts to an important elaboration of that condition.

It is not necessary, in order for a statement to be advocative in the required way, that it be associated with any actual desire of the speaker. *What qualifies self-interest statements as advocative is a certain general relation such statements bear to desire.* While it is possible for such a statement not to be associated with a corresponding desire, such an absence of desire is anomalous. This can be shown in two steps. First, under normal conditions a statement that something is the case will be associated with a judgment or belief on the speaker's part that the alleged state of affairs obtains. In other words, a statement that *p*, in the absence of a speaker's belief that *p*, is an anomaly. Therefore, a statement that something is in one's own interest, without the speaker's believing it, is anomalous.

Second, under normal or ideal conditions a person's belief that something is in his or her interest is associated with a desire for that thing. The argument is not that people always, or even most of the time, want whatever they think best for them; I do not mean to take a stand either way on that question here. But when people do not want what they think best for themselves, however often it may occur, it is an anomaly. It is an event in need of special explanation. This much seems to be admitted if the phenomenon is described, as it usually is, as a *weakness* of a certain faculty, namely the will. Whatever the truth about whether one can fail to want what one thinks best for oneself, it would constitute, in a sense not to be pursued further here, a failure of a certain kind, and in that way it is an anomaly.

Consider the two steps together. (1) Self-interest statements are normally accompanied by self-interest judgments or beliefs, and (2) these are normally (as distinct from "frequently") associated in the subject with a desire for the thing judged to be good. By a reasonable sort of transitivity we find that self-interest statements are, in normal circumstances, associated with desires. Self-interest statements are, except in anomalous cases, accompanied by desire, and *even in these anomalous cases the statements are advocative,* since even in these cases their nature is such that if circumstances had been normal they would have been accompanied by desire.

Self-interest is here held to be specially related to motivation in a way that other-interest is not. However, this does not entail psychological egoism or any view about how rare or common other-interested motivation is. However common it may be, the connection in a given case between the motivation and the *particular* "other" will be contingent in a way that the connection between motivation and the believed interests of the self is not. This is so even if it is not just contingent that one will have many other-interested motives.

Is this admittedly weak sense of advocacy consistent with the original statement of the Advocacy Condition? As mentioned earlier, it is clearly a condition on democratic social choice that the social choice must be according to what the inputs are "for" rather than what they are "against." No such condition can be formulated for inputs that are not advocative in the sense of being "off the fence." We can see that the present weak sort of advocacy serves the purpose embodied in the Advocacy Condition. Inputs must, in the context, have a certain directionality. *The condition does not require that they count as advocating a policy in a straightforward way.* The property of being advocative in this special sense is, in this way, weaker than (though described by analogy with) simple acts of advocating some action. Common-interest statements are not necessarily acts of advocacy, but they have the kind of directionality which is exemplified by usual acts of advocating something. They are, I shall say, *weakly advocative,* and this is all that is required by the Advocacy Condition.

I have said that a common-interest statement effectively includes a self-interest statement, but this would not be true if "common interest" were understood as the interest of the group *as a group.* If there is thought to be such a thing as an interest of a group where the interest is not reducible to the interests of the individuals of the group, opinions on this matter would not be (even weakly) advocative. They would be special cases of other-interest statements, even where the speaker is a member of the group. I do not doubt that groups have irreducible interests of this kind, at least in the sense that a group can thrive apart from whether any of its members are thriving (for example, a political action organization in sup-

port of and made up of AIDS patients). Similarly, it is possible for the group to be in danger of extinction without any members being in such danger; they may just go their separate ways. What I do doubt is that an opinion about the irreducible interest of any group, even one of which the subject is a member, constitutes advocacy of the sort required of a vote.[21] It is not always, or even normally, associated with any desire.

The case of South Africa is again convenient here. The nation is a group whose very existence is threatened by demonstrations of members of the black population. Repressive measures may well be necessary for the survival of the nation, and are in that sense in its interest. However, this is not to say it is in the interest of any of its members; it may be in the interest of some, or it may be against the interests of all if, for example, repression will lead to bloody rioting and mayhem despite the survival of the nation. The statement of a black South African that repressive measures are in the interest of the nation is not intrinsically advocative of those measures in the manner required of a vote. For these reasons, common-interest statements are acceptable inputs only where a common-interest includes the interest of the individual whose opinion it is, for only then is the Advocacy Condition met.

The common-interest statement interpretation is, I believe, similar to Rousseau's interpretation of votes as statements on the General Will. However, some may read the General Will as the singular will of the group. Space precludes criticism of that interpretation here, but for present purposes it suffices to note that only on the less collectivistic reading I favor are Rousseau's inputs advocative, for reasons given in the preceding few paragraphs.[22]

Common-interest statements, those that address the issue of whether something is in the interest of every member of a certain group which includes the speaker, are aggregable with common-interest statements of other members of the group. If you and I each report our own interests, the reports are not aggregable. But if I report our interests, and you report our interests, we address the same issue—

the interests common to every member of a group in which you and I are both members. Common-interest statements are therefore *aggregable*. They are *advocative* since they include self-interest judgments, which are normally accompanied by desires, and they are *active* since all statements are acts.

The interpretation of votes as common-interest statements succeeds where the preference interpretations fail. Two disclaimers are in order: first, the six preference interpretations of voting which I have discussed (desires, interests, dispositions to choose, and reports of each of these) are not exhaustive of preference interpretations, and so I do not pretend to have explicitly defeated all such interpretations. Still, the arguments against these six appear to have more general force against various possible preference interpretations. If, as is likely in a preference interpretation, votes are interpreted as either individual states, or reports by individuals of their states, they will not be both active and aggregable.

Second, even among non-preference interpretations, the common-interest statement interpretation is not held to be the only one which meets the three conditions. For example, interpreting votes as ought statements or prescriptions may also meet them. I leave it for another paper to argue that these interpretations are subject to serious difficulties which do not afflict the common-interest statement interpretation.[23]

The arguments I have given for common-interest statements seem also to work for common-desire statements, and so from the standpoint of meeting the three conditions, common-interest statements and common-desire statements are equally successful. However, if we look beyond the three conditions we can see at least one respect in which common-interest statements have a certain primacy. On the usual understanding of desire, it is highly unlikely that there could be social policies of any specificity that are desired by every member of a political community.

The chances are somewhat improved under a theory which allows that real wants differ from apparent wants. If a certain policy is in fact best for all, then it might be argued that, since everyone wants what is best for them, everyone really wants this policy whether they realize it or not. However, this view achieves plausibility for common desires partly by assuming common interests. A statement that x is really desired by everyone virtually amounts to a statement that x is in everyone's interest. This is, of course, no objection to a theory's distinguishing real from apparent wants. However, it militates for the primacy of common-interest statements over common-desire statements, since the latter are plausible only when they virtually amount to the former.

The interpretation of votes as common-desire statements is closer than the common-interest interpretation to Rousseau's interpretation of votes as General Will statements. However, I would argue (if space allowed) that Rousseau's theory rests common will or common desire on common interests in the way just discussed. As he says, "We always want what is good for us, but we do not always see what it is. The populace is never corrupted, but it is often tricked, and only then does it *appear* to want what is bad."[24] Unless desires have this close relation to interest, the sheer improbability of a policy being desired by everyone is sufficient to relegate common-desire statements to the back burner as an interpretation of votes. Of course, it is far from obvious that there are any common interests, but this possibility cannot be dismissed immediately, by inspection, as in the case of common desires.

If the argument of this paper is correct, then to the extent that voters in the real world address only their own interests, the method of social choice is less than fully democratic. But how real-world votes are to be interpreted, I cannot say. If it were thought that only self-interested voting is psychologically possible, then the present argument would bode ill for the possibility of democracy. Some say common sense favors that view of voting. In political science it is subject to empirical challenge.[25]

However it is that actual voters do or could vote, the concept of democracy places con-

straints on what is to count as proper democratic voting. These constraints preclude the
interpretation of voting that is most influential
in the social sciences and in the general public,
that votes express preferences.

Notes

1. This paper is a revised version of Chapter Two of
   my doctoral dissertation, *The Theoretical Interpretation of Voting,* University of Wisconsin, 1986.
   For a year's financial support during that project I
   am grateful to the Charlotte Newcombe National
   Fellowship Foundation. I have benefitted from discussions of this material with many people, but beyond those named in separate notes I wish to thank
   in particular Dale Brant, Gerald Cohen, Haskell
   Fain, Alon Har El, Lester Hunt, Andrew Levine,
   Geoffrey Sayre-McCord, Dennis Stampe, and the
   editors of *The Philosophical Review.*
2. I have in mind, for example, the work of Kenneth
   Arrow, *Social Choice and Individual Values* (New
   Haven, Conn.: Yale University Press, 1951, 1963
   (First and Second Editions)); I. M. D. Little, "Social Choice and Individual Values," *Journal of Political Economy* 60 (1952), pp. 422–432; A. K. Sen,
   Collective Choice and Social Welfare (San Francisco, Calif.: Holden-Day, 1970, currently published by North-Holland, Amsterdam).
3. "First, it will be assumed that we wish to treat
   candidates equally.... Second, we wish that all
   voters should be treated equally; *we are seeking to
   model democracy.*" Kenneth Arrow, "Current Developments in the Theory of Social Choice," *Social Research* 44 (1977), pp. 607–622. Reprinted
   in Brian Barry and Russell Hardin, eds., *Rational
   Man and Irrational Society?* (Beverly Hills, Calif.:
   Sage Publications, 1982), pp. 252–263. Quotation
   from p. 252 in Barry and Hardin, my emphasis.
4. The idea of an interpretation of a vote is not just
   mine. Rousseau offers a theory which sees votes as
   opinions on the General Will. Arrow assumes that
   votes express preferences. Wollheim argues that
   votes are ought-judgments. (J.J. Rousseau, *On The
   Social Contract* (Indianapolis, Ind.: Hackett Publishing Co., 1983); Arrow, 1951, 1963, op. cit.;
   Richard Wollheim, "A Paradox in the Theory of
   Democracy," *Philosophy, Politics, and Society,*
   2nd series, ed. P. Laslett and W. G. Runciman
   (Oxford, England: Basil Blackwell, 1962).) Still,
   these say nothing about what an interpretation of
   a vote is.
5. The importance of these alternatives was made
   clear to me in a discussion with Robert Adams and
   Marilyn Adams.
6. *A Theory of Justice* (Cambridge, Mass.: Harvard
   University Press, 1971), pp. 356–381.
7. "Cumulative" does not imply that the inputs are
   in any sense "cardinal," since the number of those

voters with a certain ordinal ranking can be compared with the number of those with another ordinal ranking. This is to consider these rankings
cumulatively. In the present sense, even Arrow's
thorough ordinalism (op. cit., 1951, 1963) treats
similar inputs cumulatively.

8. The view that votes advocate choices finds support
   in J.L. Austin, *How To Do Things With Words*
   (Cambridge, Mass.: Harvard University Press,
   1962), pp. 151ff. In his tentative classification of
   types of illocutionary force, the second category is
   called Exercitives: "An exercitive is the giving of
   a decision in favour of or against a certain course
   of action, or advocacy of it.... It is a very wide
   class; examples are,... command, fine, vote
   for...."
9. The story goes (in this case via Martha Gibson) that
   a candidate for governor of a southern state had his
   name legally changed to "none of the above" and
   won a majority of votes. Clearly in this case a vote
   for "none of the above" could be advocative.
10. They are, however, apparently not advocative, and
    so are not allowable as an interpretation of demo-
    cratic inputs.
11. Arrow, 1951, op. cit.; Duncan Black, *The Theory
    of Committees and Elections* (Cambridge, England:
    Cambridge University Press, 1953), and their suc-
    cessors in the theory of voting explicitly connect
    voting and preferences. Not all of them explicitly
    relate their views to democracy, though Arrow is
    unambiguous (see Arrow, 1977, op. cit.; p. 257 in
    Barry and Hardin, 1982, op. cit.: "... we are seek-
    ing to model democracy." See also Arrow, 1963,
    op. cit., pp. 23, 85, 90, 120). Some others in the
    Arrow tradition are similarly explicit: for example,
    Robert Dahl, *A Preface to Democratic Theory*
    (Chicago, Ill.: University of Chicago Press, 1956);
    Kurt Baier, "Welfare and Preference," in *Human
    Values and Economic Policy,* ed. S. Hook (New
    York, N.Y.: New York University Press, 1967);
    William Riker, *Liberalism Against Populism* (San
    Francisco, Calif.: W. H. Freeman and Company,
    1982), esp. Chapter One; Michael Dummett, *Voting
    Procedures* (Oxford, England: Clarendon Press of
    Oxford University Press, 1984), p. 1.
        Since the argument of this paper was originally
    composed there has emerged a small literature on
    "epistemic" or "cognitive" or "deliberational"
    models of democracy. Even though the attempt is
    to develop an alternative to the standard economic
    understandings of social choice, Elster, at least, re-
    tains a preference interpretation of voting. See p.
    112 of "The Market and the Forum" in Elster and
    Aanund Hylland, eds., *Foundations of Social
    Choice Theory* (Cambridge, England: Cambridge
    University Press, 1986). Joshua Cohen seems, so
    far, to be leaving the issue open by describing in-
    puts to deliberative-democratic procedures as
    "preferences and convictions." See "The Eco-
    nomic Basis of Deliberative Democracy," *Social
    Philosophy and Policy* 6 (1988), and "Deliberation

and Democratic Legitimacy,'' in Hamlin and Pettit, eds., *The Good Polity* (London, England: Basil Blackwell, 1988). Cohen also discusses Coleman and Ferejohn's treatment of an unambiguous ''judgment'' interpretation of voting. See Jules Coleman and John Ferejohn, ''Democracy and Social Choice,'' and Cohen, ''An Epistemic Conception of Democracy,'' both in *Ethics* 97 (1986). In ''Rousseau's General Will: A Condorcetian Perspective,'' *American Political Science Review* 82 (1988), Bernard Grofman and Scott Feld interpret Rousseau as holding judgment-based voting to have profound epistemic value. See also the separate replies by Jeremy Waldron and David Estlund along with a rejoinder by Grofman and Feld collectively titled ''Democracy and the Common Interest: Rousseau and Condorcet Revisited,'' in *American Political Science Review* 83 (1989). In her recent book, *Natural Reasons* (Oxford, England: Oxford University Press, 1989) Susan Hurley briefly suggests some advantages that cognitive interpretations of voting may possess over preference interpretations.

12. John Harsanyi, ''Morality and the Theory of Rational Behavior,'' in A. Sen and B. Williams, eds., *Utilitarianism and Beyond* (Cambridge, England: Cambridge University Press, 1982).

13. Arrow, 1963, op. cit., shows behaviorist leanings when he says on pages 109–110, ''The essential point of the modern insistence on ordinal utility is the application of Leibniz's principle of the identity of indiscernibles. Only observable differences can be used as a basis for explanation. . . . [W]elfare judgements [are] to be based only on interpersonally observable behavior.''

14. The connection between choice and power is reflected in *Funk and Wagnall's* first definition of ''choose'': ''. . . take by preference.'' There is a situation which might be described as a vote which is at the same time a choice. That is the situation of a voter whose vote wholly determines the social choice regardless of the votes of others (what Arrow calls a dictator, in his technical use of that term). But at most one individual can be a dictator in this sense in any given instance of social choice. Therefore, there remains no ground for the theoretical interpretation of votes as choices, even if occasionally an individual's votes can be empirically interpreted as a choice. This point is seen clearly by Gibbard, Satterthwaite, and others who have emphasized that the question of which social alternative rationally to vote for is not the same as the question which social alternative rationally to choose. There may be good reasons to vote for a less preferred outcome. Gibbard and Satterthwaite prove a strong theorem about the pervasiveness of such situations. See Allan Gibbard, ''Manipulation of Voting Schemes: A General Result,'' *Econometrica* 41 (1973); and M. A. Satterthwaite, ''Strategy-Proofness and Arrow's Conditions,'' *Journal of Economic Theory* 10 (1975).

15. See the earlier discussion of the Aggregability Condition for more on this ''question analogy.''

16. ''What is your teacher's name?'' as a question to each of the members of a single class happens to address the same issue from the standpoint of form as well as content. If, however, the teacher were the father of one of the students, and that student were asked the name of her father, while the others were asked the name of their teacher, the issues faced would be different in form, but similar in content. Jerry Fodor, ''Methodological Solipsism,'' in *Representations* (Cambridge, Mass.: The MIT Press and Bradford Books, 1981) discusses these alternative criteria of similarity, but in the case of psychological attitudes, rather than what I call ''issues.'' I follow Fodor in characterizing the distinction in terms of form vs. content, and syntax vs. semantics. The distinction should be clear even if the aptness of these descriptions is doubted.

17. David Hume seems to deploy a similar point to preclude founding morals on certain views of self-love: ''Avarice, ambition, vanity, and all passions vulgarly, though improperly, comprised under the denomination of self-love, are here excluded from our theory concerning the origin of morals, not because *they are too weak,* but because *they have not a proper direction,* for that purpose. The notion of morals, implies some sentiment common to all mankind, which recommends the same object to general approbation. . . .'' Hume requires of the set of moral judgments, as I require of democratic inputs, that they have a common object. Hume seems further to be requiring agreement, but his main point here is the one about ''direction.'' See David Hume, *Enquiry Concerning Principles of Morals,* page 80 in Raphael, ed., *The British Moralists,* emphasis added.

18. The requirement that inputs be on a single issue turns up, for different reasons, in Rousseau's discussion of factionalization. For discussion see Grofman and Feld and replies and rejoinder cited in note 11.

19. ''Interpretation'' has a process-product ambiguity. Here and throughout it means the product.

20. There is the problem of how one can both strongly advocate a policy through voting, and also advocate that the majority rule when one is in the minority. The best-known discussion of this problem is Richard Wollheim, ''A Paradox in the Theory of Democracy,'' in Laslett and Runciman, op. cit. I discuss the significance of this problem in light of its many criticisms in ''The Persistent Puzzle of the Minority Democrat,'' *American Philosophical Quarterly* 26 (1989). See also note 23 of the present article.

21. If there is such a thing as the members ''identifying'' with the group this would involve a special conception of ''self'' in which the interest of the group would not be distinguished from the interests of the individuals. ''I'' gives way to ''we.'' In this case group-interest statements would be indistin-

guishable from common-interest statements, and so this is no clear alternative to my proposal despite the importantly different metaphysics.

22. Rousseau is sensitive to the feature of proper democratic voting which I represent in the Advocacy Condition: "... why do all want the happiness of each among them, if not because there is no person who does not apply this word *each* to himself, and does not think of himself while voting for all?" Rousseau, op. cit. Book II, Chapter IV, p. 33.

23. See my "The Persistent Puzzle of the Minority Democrat," op. cit. Ought statements and prescriptions are the most salient cases of intrinsically advocative statements other than interest statements. They are beyond the scope of the concentration on preference interpretations in the present paper. In the cited paper they fall victim to difficulties afflicting any "favoring" or *strongly* advocative interpretations of voting. That paper and this one, in conjunction, mark a fine line between too much and too little advocacy in the theoretical interpretation of voting. See also note 20.

24. Rousseau, op. cit., Book II, Chapter 111, p. 31, my emphasis.

25. See, for example, D. R. Kinder and D. R. Kiewiet, "Sociotropic Politics: The American Case," in R. G. Niemi and H. F. Weisberg, eds., *Controversies in Voting Behavior* (Washington, D.C.: Congressional Quarterly Press, 1984), and David Sears et al., "Self-Interest vs. Symbolic Politics in Policy Attitudes and Presidential Voting," *American Political Science Review* 74 (1980).

Losing the Faith: Feminism and Democracy

SUSAN MENDUS

Since Mary Wollstonecraft, generations of women and some men wove painstaking arguments to demonstrate that excluding women from modern public and political life contradicts the liberal democratic promise of universal emancipation and equality. They identified the liberation of women with expanding civil and political rights to include women on the same terms as men, and with the entrance of women into the public life dominated by men on an equal basis with them. After two centuries of faith that the ideal of equality and fraternity included women have still not brought emancipation for women, contemporary feminists have begun to question the faith itself.[1]

At a time when the Berlin Wall has been dismantled and Eastern Europe is embracing the values of Western liberal democracy, when an attempted coup in Moscow has been overthrown, and the republics of the former USSR have claimed independence and democratic freedoms, it may seem churlish to criticize democracy or to doubt its ability to live up to its own ideals. Democracy may indeed be an imperfect form of government, but all the others are far worse and this, surely, is a moment for recognizing the benefits which democracy brings, not a moment for drawing attention to its shortcomings. It is a moment for confirming our faith, not a moment for doubting it.

And yet, some feminists do doubt it. Moreover, the doubts run deep, and constitute an attack not only on the achievements of modern democratic states, but also on the underlying ideals of democratic theory itself. Feminists have long drawn attention to the facts of women's under-representation in political life, and of their over-representation amongst the unemployed, the low-paid, and the part-time work-force. They now suspect that these features, common to all modern democratic states, are not merely unfortunate contingencies, or remediable imperfections of specific states. Rather, they are an indication of deep gender bias in democratic theory itself. For feminists, democracy is not something which, as a matter of unfortunate fact, has failed to deliver on its promises to women. It embodies ideals which guarantee that it will never deliver unless it embarks upon extensive critical examination of its own philosophical assumptions. In brief, the charge made against democracy is that, for women, it was never more than an article of faith, and when two hundred years of democratization have failed (and are still failing) to deliver equality for women, even faith is giving out.

Susan Mendus, "Losing the Faith: Democracy and Feminism," from *Democracy: The Unfinished Journey 508 BC–AD 1993*, ed. John Dunn, by permission of Oxford University Press. Copyright Oxford University Press, 1992.

The uncharitable may interpret these remarks as nothing more than evidence of feminist paranoia and of women's general inability to recognize when they are well off. It is therefore important to stress that the charge is not simply that democratic *states* are, as a matter of fact, ones in which women are disadvantaged (though they are), but rather that democratic *theory* is, as a matter of principle, committed to ideals which guarantee that that will remain so. As a faith, democracy was always a false faith, and its prophets (including nearly all the major political philosophers of the past two hundred years) are now exposed as false prophets.

These are serious, depressing, and even dangerous charges. The more so if we have no preferred alternative to democracy, and no revised interpretation of its central ideals. The tasks for contemporary feminism are therefore twofold: first, to justify the claim that traditional democratic theory leads to undemocratic practice; secondly, to identify the ways in which that theory might be reinterpreted so as to come closer to democratic ideals. The former is feminism's critique of the faith; the latter is feminism's revision of the faith.

A Critique of the Faith

The belief that democratic theory condones undemocratic practice is not confined to feminist theorists. John Dunn has argued that there are 'two distinct and developed democratic theories loose in the world today—one dismally ideological and the other fairly blatantly utopian'. On the dismally ideological account democracy is simply the least bad mechanism for securing a measure of responsibility on the part of the governors to the governed. By contrast, the blatantly utopian account envisages a society in which all social arrangements represent the interests of all people. The former constitutes a practical proposal, but hardly an inspiring one; the latter may be inspiring, but is hardly practical. Despairing of finding anything which can reflect democracy's status as both a high ideal and a practical proposal, Dunn concludes that 'today, in politics, democracy is the *name* for what we cannot

have—yet cannot cease to want'.[2] On Dunn's analysis the grounds for scepticism about democracy lie largely in the circumstances of modern life: the social and economic differentiation which are characteristic of the modern world necessarily generate inequalities which fit ill with the democratic ideal of political equality. Connectedly, the sheer size of modern states creates a rift between the individual and the community which makes it impossible for individuals to perceive the state as a focus of common good. Thus, democracy is not attainable in large, modern, postindustrial societies: as an ideal, it promises human fulfilment and human freedom, but in the modern world this promise cannot be met and democracy has therefore become at best a method of curbing the excesses of rulers, and at worst an idle, or even a utopian dream.

But if Dunn fears that democracy cannot exist, given the nature of modern states, feminists note with some chagrin that democracy never did exist even prior to the growth of modern states: Carole Pateman briskly dismisses the subject, claiming that 'for feminists, democracy has never existed; women never have been and still are not admitted as full and equal members in any country known as a "democracy"'.[3] Put together, the two accounts are deeply unsettling: Dunn tells us that without small states and an undifferentiated public there cannot be democracy. Feminists tell us that even when there were small states and an undifferentiated public, still there never was democracy. For feminists, the facts of history—the denial of the vote to women, their historical confinement to a domestic realm, their incorporation within the interests of their husbands—prove beyond doubt that for women democracy has never existed. For them, therefore, Dunn's lament is not even a lament for times past, but only a reflection on what might have been but in fact never was.

Why was there never democracy for women, and why is there still no democracy for women? A number of modern writers implicitly assume that it is because women have historically been denied equality under the law and the formal, political right to vote. For example, Robert Dahl recognizes that almost all the major writers in the democratic tradition excluded women from their theories, but he implies that this is merely evidence of the fact that philosophers are children of their time, and that the problem may be solved simply by rewriting references to 'all men' as 'all men and women' or 'all adults'. Thus, indicating that all is now well, he writes: 'In most countries women gained the suffrage only in this century, and in a few only after the Second World War. In fact, not until our own century did democratic theory and practice begin to reflect a belief that all (or virtually all) adults should be included in the demos as a matter of right'.[4] And this completes his discussion of the role of women in modern democratic states.

Dahl's optimism is grounded in his recognition that women are now formally equal citizens, and in his belief that this formal equality need not be fatally undermined by social and economic inequalities. He accepts the general claim that political equality is comprised by lack of economic power, but argues that this should not lead to the pessimistic conclusion that democracy is 'something we cannot have yet cannot cease to want'. Rather, it suggests the more robust conclusion that the pursuit of democracy includes the removal of social and economic inequalities. He writes:

Though the idea of equal opportunity is often so weakly interpreted that it is rightly dismissed as too undemanding, when it is taken in its fullest sense it is extraordinarily demanding—so demanding, indeed, that the criteria for the democratic process would require a people committed to it to institute measures well beyond those that even the most democratic states have hitherto brought about.[5]

For Dahl, therefore, inequality is a practical problem which admits of practical solutions. Since it is a widespread and intransigent problem, there will be no 'quick fix', but there can be progress, and in tracing that progress Dahl does not see the need to make reference to any special feature of women's position beyond the recognition that they are, in general, amongst those who suffer from a lack of social and economic power. By implication, he denies that women constitute a special and intransigent problem for democratic theory. They are sim-

ply a specific example of a quite general, but remediable, problem, the problem of how to ensure that social and economic inequalities do not undermine the formal equality of the vote.

Many feminists dissent: although agreeing that there are practical problems, they also insist that, in the case of women, the problems have a theoretical origin which goes beyond mere social and economic inequality. Women, they argue, are different not simply because they lack economic and social power, but because historically they have been explicitly excluded from the category of citizen in the democratic state. So we might agree that democracy depends upon enlarging the economic power of those who are citizens, but so long as women (along with children, animals, and the insane) were excluded from that category, the question of enlarging their economic and social power frequently failed to arise. Indeed, women's economic power was normally identified with the economic power of their husbands, and the fact that wives themselves owned nothing was (and often still is) conveniently forgotten. Again, it is important to be clear about the status of this objection: usually, it is taken as simply a reflection on the historical facts of democratic societies, but it also contains the seeds of a criticism of democratic theory itself. The criticism may be made explicit by considering Dahl's two interpretations of what he calls 'the principle of inclusion' in democratic theory. This principle is the principle which dictates who shall count as a citizen in the democratic state, and therefore who shall have a say in determining the laws of the state.

Dahl notes that historically philosophers have vacillated between a contingent and a categorical principle of inclusion: thus, some urge that all adult members of a state are also, and thereby, citizens (the categorical criterion); others claim that only those who are qualified to rule may be citizens (the contingent claim). He concedes that the contingent criterion has been the most popular in the history of political philosophy, but urges that the categorical criterion is the appropriate one for modern democratic states. There should be no question of individuals having to prove their fitness to rule.

The criterion for being a full citizen is simply that one is an adult member of the state in question. This, and this alone, justifies according rights of citizenship.

There is, however, a worrying tension between the assumptions inherent in the demand for increased social and economic equality and the assumptions inherent in the demand for a categorical criterion of citizenship. For the former recognizes that if citizenship is to be meaningful, more than formal equality is required, whereas the latter is content with a formal criterion for being or becoming a citizen. The danger is that acceptance of the categorical principle of inclusion, with its requirement that we ignore differences between people at the formal level, may lead to minimizing differences between people in framing social policy. Most importantly, it may lead to an understanding of difference, specifically women's differences, as disadvantage, disability, or deviance. If difference is the problem at the level of inclusion, then the removal of difference may be thought to be the solution at the level of social policy.

Thus, to provide a concrete example, pregnancy is often treated as akin to illness, and maternity leave as a special case of sick-leave. Pregnant women are then equated with men who are ill or temporarily disabled, and the attempt to attain 'equality' for them rests on the assumption that they are, in effect, disabled men. By this strategy, inequalities are certainly reduced because women attain something by way of maternity benefit, and something is surely better than nothing. But the importance of the practical benefits should not disguise the fact that the theoretical assumptions of the strategy are assimilationist and patriarchal. Women attain a degree of equality only by conceding that the differences between themselves and men are differences which carry the implication of female inferiority. Moreover, this is not simply a complaint about the practical arrangements governing pregnancy and childbirth; it is a more general concern about the unspoken assumptions of many democratic theorists, specifically their assumption that equality is to be attained via the removal or

minimization of disadvantage, where what counts as disadvantage is held to be clear and uncontroversial, but is in fact determined by reference to a model which is intrinsically male.

Considerations of this sort highlight the fact that for women lack of social and economic power is only half the story: it is not simply bad luck that women, in general, lack economic power. It is the male model of normality which *guarantees* that that will be so. Iris Marion Young expresses the point forcefully:

In my view an equal treatment approach to pregnancy and childbirth is inadequate because it either implies that women do not have any right to leave and job security when having babies, or assimilates such guarantees under the supposedly gender-neutral category of 'disability'. . . . Assimilating pregnancy and disability tends to stigmatize these processes as 'unhealthy.'[6]

It is for this reason that many feminists have found it difficult to retain faith in democracy and democratic theory. And, as we have seen, the loss of faith occurs at several levels: historically, feminists are aware that the denial of difference at the level of inclusion has rarely been observed. Most philosophers have noted differences between men and women, and have argued that these differences support the exclusion of women from even the rights of formal political equality. More recently, feminists have drawn attention to the fact that even where the categorical criterion has been employed, it has not been accompanied by any strenuous efforts to remove the social and economic disadvantages suffered by women, and therefore formal political equality has been undermined by practical social and economic inequality. Finally, and most importantly, many feminists now doubt whether the denial or removal of difference is even an acceptable aim for political theory and practice. Again, the doubts arise on two levels. Anne Phillips has argued that the individualistic character of modern philosophy makes it inadequate for feminist purposes. She notes:

The anti-discrimination that informs much contemporary liberalism implies removing obstacles that block an individual's path and then applauding when that individual succeeds. The problem is still perceived in terms of previous *mis*-treatment, which judged and dismissed people because they had deviated from some prejudiced norm. The answer is presented in terms of treating them just as people instead.[7]

Where difference is interpreted as deviance or disadvantage, the response to it is to implement social policy which will minimize the effects of that disadvantage *in the specific case*. This individualistic response has been countered by the demand that what is required is recognition of *group* disadvantage. Far from asserting that it should not matter whether we are men or women, this strategy insists that men and women do have different degrees of power and that therefore policies should be implemented which take account of this fact and guarantee increased power to women as a group.

The second response is rather different. It denies that difference is always to be construed as disadvantage and, in the case of women, urges a restructuring of both political theory and political practice in such a way as to celebrate at least some differences. In other words, it denies that all difference is disability, and it objects to the strategy whereby the 'disadvantages' of pregnancy and childbirth are mitigated by assimilating them to male illness. So, where democratic theory characteristically urges that we should assume that everyone is the same, feminists urge a recognition that men and women are different. Similarly, where democratic theorists have urged that, in decisions about social policy, we should aim to minimize the disadvantages which spring from difference, feminists ask why such normal states as pregnancy should be categorized as disadvantages at all.

For feminists, therefore, losing the faith has been losing faith in the ability of doctrines of equality, understood as doctrines which advocate the minimization of difference, to deliver a political theory which will be sensitive to the realities of women's lives. The solution to this problem lies in a rewriting of democratic theory in such a way as to ensure that it acknowl-

edges and incorporates difference. Most importantly, it lies in a recognition that, in the case of women, the disadvantages which spring from difference are themselves politically significant. They are disadvantages inherent in not being male. So democratic theory falls at the first hurdle because it in fact employs a male, rather than a gender-neutral, standard by which to decide what counts as disadvantage.

The proposed solution is not without its dangers: oppressed and disadvantaged groups have long used a doctrine of equality as their most important single weapon, and have appealed to such concepts as 'common humanity' in their attempts to attain political and legal rights. Moreover, they have vigorously denied the significance of difference in political contexts, and urged that differences between them and other, more advantaged, groups should be ignored in the distribution of political rights. It is therefore a discomfiting about-face for feminist theorists now to insist on a politics of difference, and to pin their faith in the possibility that difference may be acknowledged, not construed as disadvantage.

To what extent do feminists wish to attack democratic ideals, and to what extent do they wish to reconstruct them? Is their argument that we should substitute an acceptance of difference for the demand for equality, or that the demand for equality itself requires a full and sensitive recognition of the practical significance of difference?

Revising the Faith

Some critics have argued that feminists do indeed reject the ideal of equality, and that they do so because they wrongly assume that equality is at odds with the recognition of difference. Thus, Richard Norman writes: 'Equality does not require the elimination of difference. Sexual equality, in particular, does not require a denial of the inescapable biological facts of sexual difference, and leaves open what further differences might follow from these'.[8] Certainly some feminists have spoken of equality in dismissive terms, and have urged that we should pay less attention to it. Virginia Held, for example says:

Occasionally, for those who give birth, equality will be an important concept as we strive to treat children fairly and have them treat each other with respect. But it is normally greatly overshadowed by such other concerns as that the relationship between ourselves and our children and each other be trusting and considerate.[9]

But this is simply the point that equality is not the only concept in moral and political life. It is not the complaint that equality necessarily conflicts with difference. And more generally, when feminists express reservations about equality, it is because they recognize that democratic theory itself has interpreted it as requiring the elimination or minimization of difference. In general, it is not feminists who urge that equality and difference are incompatible concepts; it is democratic theory which does that by its insistence on a specific understanding of equality—as something to be attained by the minimization of difference. The crucial debate in contemporary feminism is the debate between those who urge that sex should become irrelevant and those who believe that sex should not provide the basis for inequality. Neither of these strategies involves rejecting equality. Rather, the dispute is about how equality is to be attained.

However, the strategic problem is acute in the case of women for the simple reason that, unlike social and economic differences, sexual difference cannot be removed by social policy in quite the simple way which the theory requires. Where inequalities of power spring simply from social and economic inequalities, there is some hope of removing them by seeking to minimize them—though the task would be difficult. But where inequalities of power spring from sex, it may be morally undesirable, or even impossible, to attempt to remove them by this approach. Of course, such strategies have been used, and with great success, by early feminists in their attempt to secure equal legal and political rights for women. But feminists are now sceptical about such attempts, fearing that ultimately they leave for women

only the possibility of assimilation into a male world. Speaking about her own 'assimilation' feminism, Simone de Beauvoir said: 'the modern woman accepts masculine values: she prides herself on thinking, taking action, working, creating, on the same terms as men; instead of seeking to disparage them, she declares herself their equal'.[10] But the price of this form of feminism is high for, as Simone de Beauvoir herself concedes, it is incompatible with child care and mothering. This not only means that, for many women, it will be difficult, if not impossible, to 'win the game', it also means accepting the rules of the game— where those rules dictate that pregnancy is an illness and child care a disadvantage.

What is needed, therefore, is a way of conceptualizing difference which renders it compatible with equality, but also, and crucially, does not simply increase social differentiation. Yet more radically, what is needed is a recognition that in much traditional democratic theory the concepts of equality, difference, and disadvantage are themselves gender-biased: they assume a standard of normality which is inherently male.

What are the possibilities of reconceptualizing in this way? How can democratic states revise the ideal in a way which acknowledges difference as both ineliminable and valuable? At this stage, it is worth emphasizing that it is not only feminists who should have a strong interest in this question. Modern states are characterized by the heterogeneity of the people who inhabit them. Unlike fifth-century Athens, or Rousseau's ideal state, they are not gatherings of the like-minded, gentlemen's clubs writ large, where those who deviate may be excluded or required to conform. The denial of citizenship to all but white males is no longer an option, nor is the easy assumption that newcomers must earn their right to citizenship by becoming 'like us'. Difference is not going to go away, nor is it something for which those who are different feel disposed to apologize. Against this background, the insistence that equality is to be preserved via the minimization of difference, or via assimilation itself appears utopian and the complaint that the differentiation of modern life militates against democracy may elicit the response: 'so much the worse for democracy'.

However, before moving too rapidly to that pessimistic conclusion, I want to explore the possibility that such a re-conceptualization is possible, and that it is compatible with the democratic ideal of equality. One part of the answer lies in distinguishing between two levels of democratic interest: these answer to Dahl's two principles mentioned earlier—the principle of inclusion and the principle of equality. At the former level, difference is properly to be ignored, but at the latter level, it is to be recognized and accommodated. Thus, for purposes of deciding who is to count as a citizen of a democratic state, differences of class, race, and gender should not matter. But in adhering to a strong principle of equality, we are obliged to acknowledge these differences—to acknowledge them, but not thereby to eliminate them. For whereas traditional democratic theory tends to construe difference as an obstacle to the attainment of a truly democratic state, feminist theory should alert us to the possibility that difference is rather what necessitates the pursuit of democracy. Since it is the fact that we are not all the same which requires democracy, attempting to make us all the same will not deliver democracy. On the contrary, it will remove the rationale for democracy.

Perhaps this point can be made clearer by drawing attention to one very important rationale for a democratic order—its ability to accommodate variety and criticism. Famously, E. M. Forster once called for 'two cheers for democracy' and he explained 'one because it admits variety and two because it permits criticism'.[11] This argument is often interpreted as a claim about the ability of democracy, in the long run, to deliver truth: the free marketplace of ideas will, it is claimed, ensure that truth triumphs over error. But there may also be a different interpretation, which is that democratic societies are superior not because they deliver unity out of diversity, but simply because and in so far as they acknowledge diversity. The most famous exponent of this

view is, of course, John Stuart Mill, whose political theory began from the premiss that 'human beings are not like sheep, and even sheep are not indistinguishably alike'.[12] Mill's ideal political future was not one in which disagreement and difference are eradicated, for he did not believe that any such future was possible. Rather, his claim was that the existence of difference, and the recognition that difference was ineradicable, itself provided a major argument for democracy. Connectedly, Mill understood democracy not as a state, but rather as a process. There would be no end to disagreement, but this fact provided the reason for adopting a democratic order rather than a reason for doubting its practicality. Therefore, where some modern democratic theorists begin from a principle of equality, Mill begins from a recognition of difference. And where modern democratic theorists see their main aim as being to create equality by removing difference, Mill recognizes that it is difference which must be preserved lest the pursuit of equality simply degenerate into the imposition of uniformity. In brief, then, the significance of Mill's account is that he recognizes, and emphasizes, the priority of difference over equality and urges that equality must be pursued via the recognition of difference.

Historically, democratic theory guaranteed equality by according the rights of citizenship only to those who were already equal. Later, as in the philosophy of Kant, citizenship rights were theoretically allowed to those who were able to 'improve' themselves and thus earn the title 'citizen'. Recently, hope of equality (or despair about it) has rested upon the chances of employing social policy to obliterate the effects of arbitrary inequalities. In all these cases, difference has been perceived as an obstacle to equality, and the democratic aspiration has been to ignore or remove it. In so far, therefore, as the democratic faith has been a faith that difference may be ignored or removed, feminists have lost that faith.

But feminist concerns about democratic theory go beyond the insistence that equality must be attained without the elimination of difference. Feminists also highlight the extent to which difference itself is a value-laden concept, which takes male experience as the norm and interprets female experience as disadvantaged by comparison with it. If we view matters in this way, then we will see that what is asked for is not special treatment for women, but rather an end to the existing system of special treatment for men. Catharine MacKinnon writes:

> In reality . . . virtually every quality that distinguishes men from women is already affirmatively compensated in this society. Men's physiology defines most sports, their needs define auto and health insurance coverage, their socially defined biographies define workplace expectations and successful career patterns, their perspectives and concerns define quality in scholarship. . . . For each of their differences from women, what amounts to an affirmative action plan is in effect, otherwise known as the structure and values of American society.[13]

In Britain too, existing structures favour men's lifestyles. Thus, the demand that Parliamentary hours be changed in order to take account of women's domestic responsibilities is not a request for preferential treatment for women. It is simply a recognition that what already exists is a case of preferential treatment for men. In cases such as this there is often no happy medium, or mutually convenient compromise. But that fact should not lead us to the conclusion that what currently exists is neutral between men and women, or that when women ask for arrangements more suitable to them, they are asking for special favours.

The contribution which feminist theory makes to democratic theory is therefore twofold: by asserting that some differences are ineliminable, feminism searches for an understanding of democracy as something to be aimed at *through* difference, not something to be attained via the *removal* of difference. Specifically, it indicates that the pursuit of equality via the elimination of difference is not the route to a democratic society, but the route to an oppressive and exclusive society. Historically, societies which have claimed to 'represent the people' have in fact represented only that portion of the people which displays homogeneity. In modern theory 'representing the

people' must not be interpreted as representing that portion of the people who can be forced into the appropriate mould. If there is to be any hope for democracy, it must therefore cease to pursue equality by trying to eliminate difference and instead concentrate on pursuing it by recognizing difference more adequately.

This last claim, however, signals feminism's second contribution to the debate, which is that in modern democratic societies the concept of difference, and the connected concept of disadvantage, are themselves male-centred. To be different is to deviate from some norm and, in democratic societies, that norm is invariably a male norm. Debates about the need to encourage women to participate more fully in political life tend to take the form of requests for assistance for women who have child-care and domestic responsibilities. But, as we have seen, even this approach assumes not only that women are different, but that they require 'help' if they are to attain male standards. It assumes both that the male standard is correct, and that something more than justice is required if women are to attain it. Therefore, if democratic theory is to be sustained and improved, it must recognize not only that difference is sometimes ineliminable, but also that what counts as difference is not value-neutral. It must recognize its own gender-bias even (indeed especially) in cases where it seeks to 'assist' women. The faith that democracy can be transformed in this way is the faith to which feminists now cling.

Notes

1. Iris Marion Young, *Throwing Like a Girl and Other Essays in Feminist Philosophy and Social Theory* (Bloomington, Ind., 1990), p. 93.
2. John Dunn, *Western Political Theory in the Age of the Future* (Cambridge, 1979), pp. 26–27.
3. Carole Pateman, *The Disorder of Women* (Cambridge, 1989), p. 210.
4. Robert Dahl, *Democracy and Its Critics* (New Haven, Conn., and London, 1989), pp. 115–116.
5. Dahl, *Democracy*, p. 115.
6. Young, *Throwing Like a Girl*, p. 176.
7. Anne Phillips, *Engendering Democracy* (Cambridge, 1991), p. 150.
8. Peter Osborne, *Socialism and the Limits of Liberalism* (London and New York, 1991), p. 122.

9. Virginia Held, 'Liberty and Equality from a Feminist Perspective,' in N. MacCormick and Z. Bankowski, eds., *Enlightenment, Rights and Revolution: Essays in Legal and Social Philosophy* (Aberdeen, 1989), p. 225.

10. Michael Walzer, *The Company of Critics* (London, 1989), p. 164.

11. E. M. Forster, *Two Cheers for Democracy* (London, 1951), p. 79.

12. John Stuart Mill, *On Liberty.* In John Stuart Mill, *Three Essays,* edited by R. Wollheim (Oxford, 1975), p. 83.

13. Catharine MacKinnon, *Feminism Unmodified* (Cambridge, Mass., and London, 1987), p. 36.

Political Representation

HANNA F. PITKIN

Burkean and Liberal theories can be useful in more than one way for our view of representation as a substantive acting for others. Not only should they enrich and illustrate what has been said about the representative's role; but, since these writers are explicitly concerned with political representation, their ideas can serve to bring a rather abstract discussion into more direct confrontation with the realities of political life. Thus we should now be in a position to summarize what has been learned about the last view of representation, then to measure it against and relate it to what we know about the workings of politics. The formulation of the view we have arrived at runs roughly like this: representing here means acting in the interest of the represented, in a manner responsive to them. The representative must act independently; his action must involve discretion and judgment; he must be the one who acts. The represented must also be (conceived as) capable of independent action and judgment, not merely being taken care of. And, despite the resulting potential for conflict between representative and represented about what is to be done, that conflict must not normally take place. The representative must act in such a way that there is no conflict, or if it occurs an explanation is called for. He must not be found persistently at odds with the wishes of the represented without good reason

in terms of their interest, without a good explanation of why their wishes are not in accord with their interest.

This rather complex view only sets the outer limits of what will be acceptable as representing in the substantive sense. Within those limits a wide range of positions is possible, depending on the writer's views about what is represented; about the nature of interests, welfare, or wishes; about the relative capacities of representative and constituents; and about the nature of the issues with which the representative must deal. The first of these criteria is also the simplest. Where representation is conceived as being of unattached abstractions, the consultation of anyone's wishes or opinions is least likely to seem a significant part of representing. Burke did not think that representing had much to do with consulting the represented or doing what they wanted; that is because he was talking about the representation of unattached interests—interests to which no particular persons were so specially related that they could claim to be privileged to define the interest. But when people are being represented, their claim to have a say in their interest becomes relevant. At that point, the writer's conception of interest—or welfare, or wishes, or whatever terms of this kind he is working with—also becomes relevant to his position. The more he sees interests (or welfare or whatever) as objective, as determinable by people other than the one whose interest it is, the more possible it becomes for a representative to further the interest of his constituents without consulting their wishes. If they have a "true" interest about which they know very little, then the representative is justified in pursuing it even against their wishes. Burke's theory is the most extreme in this respect. But if such a view is pushed too far we leave the realm of representation altogether, and end up with an expert deciding technical questions and taking care of the ignorant masses as a parent takes care of a child.

In contrast, the more a writer sees interest, wants, and the like as definable only by the person who feels or has them, the more likely he is to require that a representative consult his constituents and act in response to what they ask of him. At the extreme, again, substantive acting for others becomes impossible, and a theorist must either fall back on other views of representation or declare the concept an illusion.

This range of possibilities is closely related to conceptions of the relative abilities and capacities of representative and represented. The more a theorist sees the representative as member of a superior elite of wisdom and reason, as Burke did, the less it makes sense for him to require the representative to consult the opinions or even the wishes of those for whom he acts. If superior wisdom and ability reside in the representative, then he must not subordinate them to the opinions of his ignorant, inferior constituents. Conversely, to the extent that a theorist sees representative and constituents as relatively equal in capacity and wisdom and information, he is likely to require that the views of the constituents be taken into account. If the representative is an ordinary, fallible man with no special knowledge or abilities, it seems highhanded and unjustifiable for him to ignore his constituents. Again the extremes are outside the concept altogether: a true expert taking care of a helpless child is no representative, and a man who merely consults and reflects without acting is not representing in the sense of substantively acting for others. But the intermediate range is broad.

These considerations, in turn, are related to the way in which theorists think of the representative's work—the kinds of issues and problems with which he has to deal. The more a theorist sees political issues as questions of knowledge, to which it is possible to find correct, objectively valid answers, the more inclined he will be to regard the representative as an expert and to find the opinion of the constituency irrelevant. If political issues are like scientific or even mathematical problems, it is foolish to try to solve them by counting noses in the constituency. On the other hand, the more a theorist takes political issues to be arbitrary and irrational choices, matters of whim or taste, the less it makes sense for a representative to barge ahead on his own, ignoring the tastes of those for whom he is supposed to be acting. If political choices are like the choice between, say, two kinds of food, the representative can only please either his own taste or theirs, and the latter seems the only justifiable choice. At the extremes, again, representation disappears. The expert scientist solving a technical problem is not representative at all, is not deciding anything, is not pursuing anybody's interest. The man choosing for others in matters of arbitrary taste is not acting for them in the substantive sense either; he can only substitute his will for theirs or else consult them and act as they wish. He cannot decide independently in their interest, for, where choice is a matter of taste, no interest is involved.

Political issues, by and large, are found in the intermediate range, where the idea of representing as a substantive acting for others does apply. Political questions are not likely to be as arbitrary as a choice between two foods; nor are they likely to be questions of knowledge to which an expert can supply the one correct answer. They are questions about action, about what should be done; consequently they involve both facts and value commitments, both ends and means. And, characteristically, the factual judgments, the value commitments, the ends and the means, are inextricably intertwined in political life. Often commitments to political values are deep and significant, unlike the trivial preferences of taste. Politics abounds with issues on which men are committed in a way that is not easily accessible to rational argument, that shapes the perception of arguments, that may be unchanged throughout a lifetime. It is a field where rationality is no guarantee of agreement. Yet, at the same time, rational arguments are sometimes relevant, and agreement can sometimes be reached. Political life is not merely the making of arbitrary choices, nor merely the resultant of bargaining between separate, private wants. It is always a combination of bargaining and compromise where there are irresolute and conflicting commitments, and common deliberation about public policy, to which facts and rational arguments are relevant.

But this is precisely the kind of context in which representation as a substantive activity is relevant. For representation is not needed where we expect scientifically true answers, where no value commitments, no decisions, no judgment are involved. And representation is impossible (except in a formalistic or symbolic or descriptive sense) where a totally arbitrary choice is called for, where deliberation and reason are irrelevant. We need representation precisely where we are not content to leave matters to the expert; we can have substantive representation only where interest is involved, that is, where decisions are not merely arbitrary choices.

And yet, if political issues involve partly irrational, deep, lasting value commitments, can our conception of representing as a substantive activity apply to them at all? We have said that the representative must pursue his constituents' interest, in a manner at least potentially responsive to their wishes, and that conflict between them must be justifiable in terms of that interest. But what becomes of terms like "interest" and "justifiable" if there can be lifelong, profound disagreement among men as to what their interest is—disagreement that remains despite deliberation and justification and argument? To the extent that this is so, the possibility of a substantive acting for others breaks down, and that view of the concept becomes irrelevant to politics. To the extent that this happens in practical political life, we seem then to fall back on descriptive representation; we choose a representative who shares our values and commitments and prevent the irresoluble conflict. Failing that, we can retreat to symbolic representation; we can let ourselves be influenced by emotional ties in spite of our doubts about whether our interests are being served. Or, failing even that, we can cling to our formal and institutional representative arrangements even when they seem devoid of substantive content. We can continue to obey, although we feel abused, or continue to remove a series of accountable representatives from office, although none of them serves our interest.

But if a theorist stays with the substantive activity of representing, he is likely to see that activity in relation to his conception of politics and political life. Indeed, there is some basis for arguing that the kinds of correlations we have been tracing here have significance not only conceptually but for empirical understanding of political systems as well. It may be that the more egalitarian a nation is in its general outlook, the more it feels that it is just as good as its rulers are, and perfectly capable of judging them, the less inclined it is to give them a wide range of discretion. Similarly, if there is sharp, deep-seated cleavage on important value commitments in the society, there will presumably be an increasing number of questions on which agreement cannot be reached by rational debate. Consequently we might expect an increasing desire in such a society for representativeness in its legislators, a desire to pick them from a particular group as the only safe guarantee of action in the interest of that group. Then more and more questions seem as arbitrary as a choice of candy, though they are by no means as trivial. Friedrich has pointed out that it is often the very countries for which proportional representation is most dangerous that insist on having it.[1] Even though it introduces into the legislature the irreconcilable antagonisms that pervade the society, they insist on it because they feel that only a member chosen from the particular group can act in its interest. And they may sometimes be right.

Within any functioning representative system, the same considerations apply to the personality of the legislator and to the particular issue before him. A representative who characteristically feels sure of his own knowledge and convictions is more likely to act on them; one who tends to feel skeptical and cautious about his own views is more likely to want to know what his constituents think. Some issues are more easily seen as having a right and a wrong side; others seem arbitrary, confusing, or a matter of opinion. Again, the more uncertain a representative feels about what he ought to do, the more likely he is to conceive of the issue as relevant to constituent feelings or opinions.[2] On such issues and to such men, politics seems more a matter of will than of right and wrong. This accounts for one of the difficulties in studying representation empirically. It will not do to examine voting on only a single issue; in the more extensive studies the issue sooner or later emerges as a relevant variable.[3] Again we can see why a simple choice: "Should he do what he thinks right or what you want?" is bound to produce equivocal answers.

All these elements—what is to be represented, whether it is objectively determinable, what the relative capacities of representative and constituents are, the nature of the issues to be decided, and so on—contribute to defining a theorist's position on the continuum between a "taking care of" so complete that it is no longer representation, and a "delivering their vote" so passive that it is at most a descriptive "standing for." But besides illustrating this observation, our examination of Burkean and Liberal theory has precipitated us into another dimension of substantive acting for others— the special features and problems of political representation: the distinction between private and public representing, between acting for a single principal or organization and acting for a constituency. It is now time to return to those political complications in the mandate-independence controversy which we earlier set aside, if only to show that our conceptual argument is even relevant to politics, and how it is relevant.

Representing as a substantive activity may often have seemed remote from the realities of political life. A political representative—at least the typical member of an elected legislature—has a constituency rather than a single principal; and that raises problems about whether such an unorganized group can even have an interest for him to pursue, let alone a will to which he could be responsive, or an opinion before which he could attempt to justify what he has done. These problems are further heightened when we consider what political science teaches about the members of such a constituency, at least in a modern mass democracy—their apathy, their ignorance, their malleability. Furthermore, the representative who is an elected legislator does not represent his constituents on just any business, and by himself in isolation. He works with other representatives in an institutionalized context at a specific task—the governing of a nation or a state. This reintroduces the familiar problem of local or partial interests versus the national interest, and the question of the political representative's role with respect to them.

Political representation need not raise any problems about the national interest; a symbolic head-of-state can stand for the nation without such a question even seeming relevant. Or the institutional context may be such that one person or body may act for the nation, while another body is composed of local representatives who do not govern or act for the whole nation.[4] The problem of the national interest arises only in the context of a representative legislature, a body composed of persons representing (as we say) various constituencies, and, at the same time, supposed to govern the nation and pursue the national interest. That context has often led theorists to formulate the classical dilemma: If a man represents a particular constituency in the legislature, is his duty to pursue its interest or the interest of the nation as a whole?

As with the mandate-independence controversy, theorists seem far too ready to accept this as a true dilemma, with mutually exclusive alternatives. But, as with the mandate-independence controversy, there is something to be said for both sides. If a man represents a certain constituency, then, according to the argument in the last four chapters, his obligation is to that constituency's interest. And in a practical sense, it is politically and socially important that local and partial interests should not be ruthlessly overridden and sacrificed in the name of the nation. On the other hand, someone has to govern and the national government must pursue the national interest. If the representatives as a group are given this task, they are thereby also given the national interest to look after. And, in a practical sense, it is politically and socially important that local and partial interests not be allowed to outweigh the needs and interests of the nation as a whole.

It is possible to avoid one horn of this dilemma by shifting ground on who or what is represented. If the legislator represents his constituency, the substantive "acting for" view of representation suggests that he must pursue its interest. So, if we want to show that his obligation is to the national interest, we say that it is really the nation he represents. A number of European constitutions can be cited as illustrations:

The members of the Reichstag are the representatives of the people as a whole, and shall not be bound by orders or instructions.

The members of Congress are representatives of the nation and not of the colleges which elect them.

The members of the two Houses shall represent the nation, and not the province alone, nor the subdivision of the province which elects them.

Deputies shall represent the nation as a whole, and not the several provinces from which they are chosen.[5]

But such formulations are no solution to our theoretical dilemma; they simply reject one of the alternatives, opting for the national interest instead of constituency interest. Such representatives might as well be elected at large, nation-wide.[6] This position is the obverse of the diehard defense of constituency interest; both tend to obscure the relationship between constituency and nation, between part and whole. They take the choice to be genuinely either-or, as if constituency and nation were mutually exclusive and unrelated units. They suggest that for a representative elected in California to have the duty of "representing" the interest of the whole nation is the same as if he had a

duty to "represent" the interest of New York. But of course this is not so; California is part of the nation. If we assume that a nation and its parts confront each other like two hostile nations, the problem is indeed insoluble. For then to admit that the national welfare is paramount would preclude representation of the locality. And, conversely, the locality could not be blamed for objecting to the emphasis on the national interest if that interest were necessarily hostile to its own.[7] But in fact, one of the most important features of representative government is its capacity for resolving the conflicting claims of the parts, on the basis of their common interest in the welfare of the whole.

A slightly more ambitious argument that frequently appears in the literature overcomes this weakness by postulating an automatic harmony between local and national interest. A sort of political "invisible hand" is supposed to prevent any real conflict. The nation is made up of its parts; so the national interest must be the sum of local or partial interests. The trouble with this argument is that it is false. We all know of cases in which the interest of some locality is in conflict with the national welfare. Moreover, this argument will not accomplish what its proponents expect from it, for it cuts both ways. A Congressman may say, "I'm here to represent my district. What is good for the majority of districts is good for the country,"[8] and take that to sanction his pursuit of his district's interest. But Burke can equally well maintain that every locality, being part of the whole, has a share in the national interest; and he can take that to sanction the representative's devotion to national welfare rather than constituency claims.

What is difficult here is the correct verbal formulation of the obvious facts: in a sense the nation is the sum of its parts, but in another sense the nation must sometimes ask some parts to sacrifice their welfare for its welfare. For a community to exist and persist, its members and subdivisions must benefit from its existence, have an interest in its perpetuation. In that sense each district is part of the whole, and the national interest is not a separate interest, hostile to its own. However, the national interest cannot just ignore or override the welfare of parts of the nation or even of individuals. In representative assemblies the national interest is often formulated out of the rival claims of interests and localities within the state. Yet sometimes a simple addition of these claims will not suffice; sometimes a direct, public-spirited attention to national welfare itself is required.

It would be useful to distinguish between what we might call initial-interest-claim, on the one hand, and final-objective-interest, on the other. The initial-interest-claim of a locality or group can be and often is opposed to the initial-interest-claim of the nation. But the nation also has an interest in the welfare of its parts and members, and they have an interest in its welfare. So, in theory, for each case there should exist an ideal final-objective-interest settlement (whether or not we can find it or agree on it), giving just the right weight to all considerations. A minor benefit to the whole nation purchased at the price of severe hardship to a part may not be justified. A minor benefit to a part purchased at the price of serious damage to the nation probably is not justified. About final-objective-interest one could say that the interest of the parts adds up to the interest of the whole, but such an optimistic formula must not be allowed to obscure the obvious conflicts in initial-interest-claim. Politics entails the reconciliation of conflicting claims, each usually with some justice on its side; the harmony of final-objective-interests must be *created*.[9]

The national unity that gives localities an interest in the welfare of the whole is not merely presupposed by representation; it is also continually re-created by the representatives' activities. As Charles E. Merriam has put it, "The generality of special interests must be woven into a picture" that is the national good.[10] There may be institutional systems in which this task is not performed by a representative body, where representatives plead their districts' cause before a monarch or other executive or national judge, who makes the final decisions. But this is not the typical situation in modern representative government.

The representative is, typically, both special pleader and judge, an agent of his locality as well as a governor of the nation. His duty is to pursue both local and national interest, the one because he is a representative, the other because his job as representative is governing the nation. That dual task is difficult, but it is neither practically nor theoretically impossible.

But there are other political realities to be considered, in addition to the problem of the national interest. The constituent, the voter who is to be represented, is not, of course, the rational, informed, interested, politically active citizen our formula seems to require.[11] Most people are apathetic about politics, and many do not bother to vote at all. Of those who do vote, the majority vote on the basis of a traditional party loyalty; sometimes personal characteristics of the candidate also play a role. But generally both personal characteristics and policy commitments are used to justify a preformed preference rather than as the basis for making a choice. The voters tend to ascribe to the candidate whatever policy they favor; few of them know anything about the Congressman's voting record. Decisions seem to be motivated mainly through contact with primary groups; people vote as their family, friends, and associates do. Thus voting decisions depend largely on habit, sentiment, and disposition rather than on rational, informed consideration of the candidate's or the party's stand on issues.

It would seem farfetched to imagine such voters in rational dialogue with their representative: "Why did you vote this way when we asked you to vote the opposite way?" "Ah, but I know certain facts of which you are ignorant, had you considered that . . . ?" "Well, yes, that does change matters. . . ." Surely nothing could be farther from what actually goes on in an election.

Similar problems exist when we turn to the representative and the realities of legislative behavior. Does the representative frequently consult his constituents' wishes, or, if not, does he apply his expert knowledge to a dispassionate, rational evaluation of what is best for them and the nation? Again, if these are one's assumptions, the facts would seem very disillusioning. For the legislator's position is far more complex than such a model would suggest. The modern representative acts within an elaborate network of pressures, demands, and obligations; and there is considerable disagreement among legislators about the proper way to perform their role.[12]

In the first place, the political representative has a constituency and constituents, not a principal. He is chosen by a great number of people; and, while it may be difficult to determine the interests or wishes of a single individual, it is infinitely more difficult to do so for a constituency of thousands. On many issues a constituency may not have any interest, or its members may have several conflicting interests.[13] And the representative knows of the voters' ignorance and apathy and irrationality, the diversity of their views and interests. Further, he seldom has access to accurate information about what views and interests they do have.[14]

In the second place, he is a professional politician in a framework of political institutions,[15] a member of a political party who wants to get reëlected, and a member of legislature along with other representatives. He must be sensitive to his political party (both local and national) and to various public and private groups and interests. As a member of the legislature, he occupies an office to which certain obligations and expectations are attached.[16] He must comply with its traditions and work within the framework of the rules and mores of the legislative body. He must get along with his colleagues, especially certain important ones among them.[17] To act effectively he must keep in mind not only the formal and informal rules of his legislative body but also its place in the whole structure of government.

In the third place, he will also have views and opinions, at least on some issues. He will feel that some measures are intrinsically unsound, immoral, or undesirable. At the same time, his opinions may, in turn, be shaped by those around him and his sources of information. His own opinion on a measure may be shaped by party leaders or other colleagues, by friends or effective lobbyists, or even by the mail. He himself may not be a reliable source of information as to just what shapes his opinion on some issue or even what determines his vote.[18] And issues do not come before him in isolation; issues are interrelated, and he may wish to compromise on some in order to gain on others.[19] A particular measure may have many parts, to which he responds in varying ways.[20] He also may see measures as having a significance beyond their immediate content, for example as part of an over-all party program.[21]

Thus in legislative behavior a great complexity and plurality of determinants are at work, any number of which may enter into a legislative decision. The legislator represents neither by a simple response to constituency desires nor by detached, Olympian judgment on the merits of a proposal. None of the analogies of acting for others on the individual level seems satisfactory for explaining the relationship between a political representative and his constituents. He is neither agent nor trustee nor deputy nor commissioner; he acts for a group of people without a single interest, most of whom seem incapable of forming an explicit will on political questions.

Must we then abandon the idea of political representation in its most common sense of "acting for"? This possibility has sometimes been suggested; perhaps representation in politics is only a fiction, a myth forming part of the folklore of our society. Or perhaps representation must be redefined to fit our politics; perhaps we must simply accept the fact that what we have been calling representative government is in reality just party competition for office. Yet, to "redefine" representation to equate it with the empirical reality of representative government, even if that reality displays no elements of what we would ordinarily call representation, seems pointless and misleading.

But perhaps it is a mistake to approach political representation too directly from the various individual-representation analogies— agent and trustee and deputy. Perhaps that approach, like descriptive or symbolic representation, leads us to expect or demand features in the representative relationship which are not there and need not be there. Perhaps when we conventionally speak of political representation, representative government, and the like, we do not mean or require that the representative stand in the kind of one-to-one, person-to-person relationship to his constituency or to each constituent in which a private representative stands to his principal.[22] Perhaps when we call a governmental body or system "representative," we are saying something broader and more general about the way in which it operates as an institutionalized arrangement. And perhaps even the representing done by an individual legislator must be seen in such a context, as embodied in a whole political system.

Political representation is primarily a public, institutionalized arrangement involving many people and groups, and operating in the complex ways of large-scale social arrangements. What makes it representation is not any single action by any one participant, but the over-all structure and functioning of the system, the patterns emerging from the multiple activities of many people. It is representation if the people (or a constituency) are present in governmental action, even though they do not literally act for themselves. Insofar as this is a matter of substantive acting for others, it requires independent action in the interest of the governed, in a manner at least potentially responsive to them, yet not normally in conflict with their wishes. And perhaps that can make sense and is possible even in politics, if we understand how and where to look for it.

Even if the representative does not examine his conscience as to the national interest on every issue, he may still be following a course of action designed to promote that interest. He may be playing his complicated role in the institutionalized political system in such a way that it strikes us as—that it *is*—representing. The mere fact that he is functioning within a representative system is, of course, no guarantee that he is truly representing; but it allows for more complex and long-range ways of representing than are possible for an isolated individual agent.

Similarly, although the political representative may ignore or even override constituency opinion, he may offer justifications, rationales, for doing so, in much the way that a substantive representative must be prepared to do. If we ask an American legislator whether he acts independently of constituents' wishes, and

why, he is likely to answer in terms of his knowledge and their ignorance and true interest.

The majority of my constituents occasionally lack knowledge of relevant facts and circumstances. For me not to take this into account would be a violation of my oath of office as a legislator, not to mention my obligation to my own conscience, judgment and sense of duty.

I knew full well and without the slightest question that had the five thousand people who had written me been in the possession of the knowledge which was mine, at least a majority of them would have taken [my] position.

Much sentiment is manufactured and the result of gross misinformation.

. . . he replied that he knew but one way to ascertain the public opinion of Connecticut; that was to ascertain what was right. When he found that out, he was quite sure that it would meet the approval of Connecticut.

. . . they do not really understand the matter.

. . . they don't even know what a tariff is. . . . Of course they don't know what they're talking about.

I understand the problems of that area. I know what is best for the farm section. . . . I vote my convictions and hope that the constituents will follow these. They expect this—unless a real organized group is excited about something. They generally expect that you have more information than they do. . . . I try to follow my constituents—to ignore them would be a breach of trust—but I use my judgment often because they are misinformed. I know that they would vote as I do if they had the facts that I have. . . . I figure if they knew what I know . . . they would understand my vote.[23]

These statements are not evidence but illustration. Indeed, they could not serve as evidence, for legislators make any number of statements about why they vote as they do, and none of them need be accurate. But the statements suggest that the view of representing as substantive activity may not, after all, be too abstract and idealized for application to real political life.

It may even make sense to speak of the people—the ignorant, apathetic, nonpolitical citizens—as being capable of collective action and judgment, as having, on occasion, a will or an opinion with which to confront their representative. But we must not succumb to an overly simplified picture of public opinion and the popular will. Political scientists have long known that "voting is essentially a group experience."[24] We vote, indeed we perceive political reality, through the people with whom we are in contact. Most of us are reached by the mass media only in a two-step process, by way of other people's perceptions of and reactions to them. There can be a good deal of latent opinion in the behavior of individuals who may not be able to articulate their opinions at all. As one recent study has put it:

The relation of Congressman to voter is not a simple bilateral one but is complicated by the presence of all manner of intermediaries: the local party, economic interests, the news media, racial and national organizations, and so forth. . . . Very often the Representative reaches the mass public through these mediating agencies, and the information about himself and his record may be considerably transformed as it diffuses out to the electorate in two or more stages. As a result, the public—or parts of it—may get simple positive or negative cues about the Congressman which were provoked by legislative action *but which no longer have a recognizable issue content.*[25]

The readiness of citizen A to vote for a certain candidate, derived from a casual conversation with B, who got it from overhearing C discuss an article in publication D—this readiness is, in a sense, a part of public opinion, even though A may not be able to muster a single reason for his vote, and may not care about the immediate issues. Perhaps it is to this kind of public opinion that the representative must be responsive, and can be responsible.

I am not suggesting an organic group mind. What the public does or thinks must (in theory) be translatable into the behavior or attitudes of individuals. I am only suggesting that this translation is not simple or obvious. The voting behavior of people in a representative democracy can respond to issues and policies, even if many individual voters do not respond directly to them. The process may be complex, involving an interaction among organizations, news media, and personal relationships. Even if most people vote in an irrational and uninformed response to primary group pressures,

this does not preclude the system as a whole from displaying a degree of "rational" response.

All this is only meant to sketch a framework on which one could maintain what seems to me in fact the case: that political representation is, in fact, representation, particularly in the sense of "acting for," and that this must be understood at the public level. The representative system must look after the public interest and be responsive to public opinion, except insofar as nonresponsiveness can be justified in terms of the public interest. At both ends, the process is public and institutional. The individual legislator does not act alone, but as a member of a representative body. Hence his pursuit of the public interest and response to public opinion need not always be conscious and deliberate, any more than the individual voter's role. Representation may emerge from a political system in which many individuals, both voters and legislators, are pursuing quite other goals. I am not suggesting that it must emerge from any particular system; there is no guarantee that it will. But it may emerge, and to the extent that it does we consider that system as being a representative government.

We must be cautious, also, about the absence of rational pursuit of the public interest by individuals. I do not wish to suggest that it is totally expendable, for I doubt whether any institutional framework could produce representation without conscious, rational, creative effort by some individuals. But there is latitude in a political system for apathy, ignorance, and self-seeking. That the social institution can produce a "rationality" most individual members seem to lack is easier to believe at the level of the voter than at the level of the legislator. And this may well be because a higher degree of individual rationality, of conscious representing and pursuit of the public interest is required in the legislative system than in the public. Undoubtedly, creative leadership is needed in any political system, and such leadership does not just happen. But when we speak of political representation, we are almost always speaking of individuals acting in an institutionalized representative system, and it is against the background of that system as a whole that their actions constitute representation, if they do.

We are now in a position to look back over the various "views" about the meaning and nature of representation, each persistent and plausible because it is founded in the familiar, valid, ordinary, unproblematic uses of some word in the "represent-" family. Despite their foundation in truth, these views are mutually incompatible and ultimately wrong, because they generalize too readily and too widely from a few examples, ignoring other equally valid examples. A correct and complete view of representation (the thing, "out there in the world"), of what representation is, depends on a correct and complete understanding of "representation" (the word, together with the other words in this family), what "representation" means. While we can, of course, redefine and revise the concept, it behooves us first to be clear on what it already means. For we are English speakers, and what it means in English is very likely what it means to us, what it is for us, in our world.

Each of the various views of representation makes some sense when applied to political life, and certain aspects of political life lend themselves to interpretation by each of the views. Heads of state, or elected legislative representatives, or government agents are, for certain purposes and under certain circumstances, authorized representatives, with authority to bind those in whose name they act. Elected political representatives, under certain circumstances, are "true" representatives only if they must eventually account for their actions to those for whom they act. It may be useful to think of an elected legislature as the image or reflection of the whole nation, or as a representative sample. When we deal with political ceremonial, or the role of political leaders in fostering loyalty and a sense of national unity through their own person, symbolic representation seems apropos, as it does for inanimate political symbols like the flag or the scales of justice. Under other conditions, in other contexts, representing as a substantive activity will seem the very essence of what is going on politically.

But although each of these views of representation has some relevance to political life, a mere recognition of that fact is not enough. It is not enough to say that representation means now one thing, now another; nor does it follow that each writer is entitled to his view and that all theories of representation are equally valid. For each view has its particular and peculiar assumptions and implications, deriving from examples of our ordinary use of words in the "represent-" family on which it is based. Think of the legislature as a pictorial representation or a representative sample of the nation, and you will almost inevitably concentrate on its composition rather than on its activities. Think of the same body as a symbol and you will almost inevitably be more concerned with its psychological impact on the minds of the people than with any accuracy of correspondence between it and the nation. Think of it, in turn, as an agent or collection of agents, and your interest will focus on other concerns. Thus it is necessary to know what each view implies and assumes, and which view is appropriate under the circumstances.

For to say that all the views are relevant to politics, and that all are related in the sense of being views of the same, single concept, is not to say that they are mutually interchangeable, or fit political life at the same point and in the same way. Something absent can be made present in many different ways, depending on what sort of thing it is; but not everything can be made present in every way. Although both descriptive and symbolic representation are representation, it does not follow that the best descriptive representative is the best symbolic representative, or that either will do the best job of representing as activity. Indeed, the perfection of one kind of representation, "making present," may preclude the perfection of other kinds in any particular case. And not every kind will even be possible in every context.

The aspects of political life that seem to embody representation are extremely various and diverse. A government as a whole may be said to represent its state, nation, country, or people. This assertion may be made concerning all governments, or it may be used to distinguish what we call "representative" government from other forms. Within a state, representation most commonly is ascribed to the legislature; but a theorist may find that each member represents the nation, or his own constituency, or his political party. In the case of proportional representation he may say that each member represents those who elected him; in the case of occupational representation, that he represents his profession; in the case of a geographic constituency, that he represents it or its residents or their interest. Nor is it necessary that a collegiate representative body be a legislature or have sovereign power; it can be an advisory body. But we can also speak of representation by the executive, whether he is a directly elected president or an indirectly chosen prime minister. We speak of representation by monarchs and titular heads of governments. Courts, judges, and juries have been discussed as representative organs of the state, and similarly we recognize administrative representation. Ambassadors represent a state abroad. Every government official or agent may sometimes be said to represent, in the sense that his actions are official state actions. We also recognize as political representation the activities of certain persons ''before'' government agencies. Thus we say that a lobbyist represents a certain group or interest before Congress, or before a Congressional committee. An agent or expert may represent an interest before an administrative tribunal. And a lawyer represents his client before the courts, although this is not usually regarded as political.

But these many persons and institutions do not all represent in the same sense or in the same way. Political representation is as wide and varied in range as representation itself will allow. The most that we can hope to do when confronted by such multiplicity is to be clear on what view of representation a particular writer is using, and whether that view, its assumptions and implications, really fit the case to which he is trying to apply them. Consider one of the most significant expressions in the realm of political representation—''representative government.'' There are many ways in which a government may be said to represent, but not all of them correspond to the idea of a representative government. Any number of theorists have gone wrong in this respect, no-

ticing only one sense in which a government may be said to represent, and immediately concluding that must be what ''representative government'' really means.

It is sometimes argued, particularly by authorization theorists, that every government represents its subjects in the sense that it has authority over them and makes laws for them.[26] Governments do have that authority; the authority to make laws seems part of the very meaning of government. Yet authority is not coextensive with representation; one need not represent in order to have authority to issue orders. But a government also acts in the name of its subjects. Thus a slightly modified position would be that all governments represent in the formalistic sense that their actions not only bind their subjects but are attributed *to* these subjects.[27] The government acts, and we say that the nation has acted. Yet this kind of representing will not enable us to distinguish representative government from other forms; it would make ''representative government'' a redundancy.

Other theorists supplement the *de jure* authority of a government to act in the name of its subjects as a nation, with its *de facto* capacity to win support and obedience from them.[28] They may then argue that a government represents only to the extent that its decrees are obeyed and it is accepted by its subjects. This doctrine is close to the views of de Grazia and Gosnell, that representing is a matter of pleasing the represented. A representative government could be distinguished from other forms, under such a notion, by the high degree of obedience or consent or support it received from its subjects. And, as with De Grazia and Gosnell, the way in which that consent or support is engineered and achieved seems totally irrelevant: one may adjust the ruler to the ruled, but one may equally adjust the ruled to what he wants of them. Representative governments defined by the degree of their popularity need not have elections or other democratic institutions.

The will on which a government rests may be democratic, even if oligarchic or plutocratic influences are powerful in creating it. It is quite possible that an interested minority may so control the avenues of information and suggestion that a majority will suffer persuasion contrary to their own interests. The decision of a leader may induce millions to support measures which they would have opposed if his prestige had been thrown to the other side.[29]

And all this seems perfectly compatible with representation and representative government.

Finally, some writers argue that a government is representative to the extent that it pursues the interest of its subjects and looks after their welfare, as distinct from merely being popular with them. "All government is somewhat representative," a writer tells us, "insofar as it identifies itself with the people's interests. . . ."[30] A representative government might, however, be distinguished, under such an approach, as one that pursues its subjects' interests to a very high degree.

But none of these senses in which one can say that (some) governments represent is what we mean when we speak of representative government. Whether governments have legitimate authority to bind their subjects, whether the subjects are obligated to obey, are largely philosophers' questions. For the ordinary layman or politician they simply are not problematical; laws are the kinds of things that ordinarily oblige and bind, just as promises are the kinds of things that one keeps. For anyone other than a speculative political philosopher, the right of government to bind its subjects is problematic only at times of resistance or revolution. Would-be revolutionaries might attempt to justify themselves by arguing that the government no longer represents them. And the international lawyer may have to decide which government is the legitimate spokesman for a nation, which in turn may depend on what government has effective control. Thus we may inquire whether the Peking government or that on Formosa properly represents China, or which government's delegation should represent the Congo in the United Nations.

There are occasions, also, when we become concerned with the "responsibility" of subjects for the actions of their government, meaning something different from the obligation to obey its laws. At the end of the Second World War and during the Nuremberg trials there was much speculation about the war guilt of the German people. Were they guilty of the atrocities committed in their name by the Hitler government? The kinds of arguments considered relevant here are undoubtedly familiar: How much popular support did Hitler have? How much resistance was there to him within Germany? How much did people know about what was being done? Did they approve of what they knew? But these questions are not coextensive with whether Nazi Germany was a representative government. We may agree that it was not. At most, the kind of information we want could be approximated by asking whether the German people would have supported a representative government that followed the same policies. Many people might argue the responsibility of the German people even though the Nazi government was not representative. We might agree, however, that in the case of a representative government the responsibility would be more clear-cut.[31]

But these are not at all the kinds of arguments we would normally consider relevant to deciding whether a particular government is or is not representative. By representative governments we mean to designate certain governments but not others. The United States, Great Britain, and Switzerland are usually regarded as representative governments. Dictatorships, true monarchies, and imposed colonial administrations are not usually so regarded. But is the Soviet Union a representative government? Is the Union of South Africa? Is Ghana? Is the United States, "really"? We know, at least in a general way, what the relevant arguments on such questions are. They probably begin with whether or not the rulers are elected. But they soon range beyond this. We want to know how genuine the elections are, who has the right to vote, whether the elected officials have the real governmental power, and how much opposition is permitted.

Note, first, what subjects these questions do not cover. To decide whether a government is representative, we do not ask whether it has the authority to make binding laws in the name of its citizens. Every legitimate government has this authority. Nor do we ask how effective this authority is; a country does not necessarily have a representative government because its crime rate is low and disobedience is infrequent. Could we show that a government is representative by demonstrating that its policies are beneficent and promote the welfare of its subjects? This criterion, at least, seems more tempting. But the actions of a benevolent dictatorship might be directed toward the welfare of the populace, and make no concessions to anything resembling democratic participation. Surely this would not be a representative government. We do expect a representative government to promote the popular welfare, and perhaps think it unlikely that other governments will do so. But the fact that a government looks after the interests of its subjects is at most a piece of evidence, a necessary but not a sufficient criterion for calling it representative.

How about a government which keeps its subjects happy, whose policies are widely accepted by them? Could we show that a government is representative by demonstrating its popularity among its subjects? Here I think the temptation is very great to say yes, but we must be cautious. Could we not imagine cases to the contrary? Suppose that a drowsy tropical island (before the Second World War, we had better say) is delightfully administered by a benevolent despot from the colonial office. The natives love him. But surely this is not a representative government. Or again, a dictator may perfect a new tranquilizing drug, and feed "happy-pills" to all his subjects so that they approve whole-heartedly of whatever he does. Surely not a representative government. Again, the contentment of the subjects is not sufficient to define representation.

Just as it is not enough to say that the individual representative who pleases his constituents represents them, so, at the level of government, it will not do to define representation by the acquiescence of the subjects. People may at times support a hereditary monarch; they may have nothing but good to say about a dictator (the critical members of the population having been removed). A dictatorship may have "active and preponderant" consent,

but that does not make it a representative government.

If support for the regime is manufactured by way of a monopoly of control over the media of mass communication, supplemented by severe coercion against oppositional elements. . . . If a political regime relies heavily on a highly organized propaganda monopoly, . . . and ruthlessly suppresses all political dissent, one must conclude that no amount of evidence of public support to the regime can prove that the people's genuine interests are not being exploited in the interest of the ruling few.[32]

By the same token, no amount of public support can then prove that the government is a representative one. When a ruler manipulates an inert mass of followers to accord with his will, we hesitate to say that he represents them. In the same way, if an interest group engages in a vast propaganda campaign to persuade the public in favor of some measure, we do not regard this activity as representation of the public.

It seems to me that we show a government to be representative not by demonstrating its control over its subjects but just the reverse, by demonstrating that its subjects have control over what it does. Every government's actions are attributed to its subjects formally, legally. But in a representative government this attribution has substantive content: the people really do act through their government, and are not merely passive recipients of its actions. A representative government must not merely be in control, not merely promote the public interest, but must also be responsive to the people. The notion is closely related to the view of representing as a substantive activity. For in a representative government the governed must be capable of action and judgment, capable of initiating government activity, so that the government may be conceived as responding to them. As in nonpolitical representation, the principal need not express his wishes, or even have formulated any, but he must be capable of doing so; when he does, his wishes should be fulfilled unless there is good reason (in terms of his interest) to the contrary. Correspondingly, a representative government requires that there be machinery for the expression of the wishes of the represented, and that the government respond to these wishes unless there are good reasons to the contrary. There need not be a constant activity of responding, but there must be a constant condition of responsive*ness*, of potential readiness to respond. It is not that a government represents only when it is acting in response to an express popular wish; a representative government is one which is responsive to popular wishes when there are some. Hence there must be institutional arrangements for responsiveness to these wishes. Again, it is incompatible with the idea of representation for the government to frustrate or resist the people's will without good reason, to frustrate or resist it systematically or over a long period of time. We can conceive of the people as "acting through" the government even if most of the time they are unaware of what it is doing, so long as we feel that they could initiate action if they so desired.[33]

Because this kind of political representation requires only potential responsiveness, access to power rather than its actual exercise, it is perfectly compatible with leadership and with action to meet new or emergency situations. It is incompatible, on the other hand, with manipulation or coercion of the public. To be sure, the line between leadership and manipulation is a tenuous one, and may be difficult to draw. But there undoubtedly *is* a difference, and this difference makes leadership compatible with representation while manipulation is not.[34] This is because leadership is, in a sense, at the mercy of the led. It succeeds only so long as they are willing to follow. Thus it is not incompatible with our requirement that the represented be able to get their way when they have an explicit will. Manipulation by a ruler, on the other hand, is imposed on the ruled, and threatens their capacity to reject a policy or initiate a new one. A person can be led and yet go of his own free will; something that is manipulated does not move itself. An inanimate object can be manipulated, but it cannot be led. Again, these are not just verbal games, but the right terms for naming a distinction in reality:

the difference between democratic and dictatorial relationships between ruler and ruled. Only if it seems right to attribute governmental action to the people in the substantive sense do we speak of representative government.[. . .]

Notes

1. Carl J. Friedrich, "Representation and Constitutional Reform in Europe," *Western Political Quarterly* 1 (June 1948): 128–129.
2. Lewis Anthony Dexter, "The Representative and His District," *Human Organization* 16 (Spring 1957): 3–4; George W. Hartmann, "Judgments," *Journal of Social Psychology* 21 (February 1945): 105, 113; Harold Foote Gosnell, *Democracy* (New York, 1948), p. 203.
3. This is seen most clearly by Warren E. Miller and Donald E. Stokes, "Constituency Influence in Congress," *American Political Science Review* 57 (March 1963): 45–56, and by Dexter, "The Representative," pp. 3–4; but also by L. E. Gleeck, "96 Congressmen Make Up Their Minds," *Public Opinion Quarterly* 4 (March 1940); Heinz Eulau et al., "The Role of the Representative," *American Political Science Review* 53 (September 1959): 745, 749; and Julius Turner, *Party and Constituency* (Baltimore, 1951), pp. 70, 79. It is overlooked by studies such as Wilder W. Crane's, which deal with only a single legislative measure. Crane found that "only one" legislator "deliberately voted on the merits" of the issue. But what was the issue? The instituting of Daylight Saving Time! "Do Representatives Represent?" *Journal of Politics* 22 (May 1960).
4. Thus American Congressmen sometimes defend their attention to local needs by saying that the national interest is properly the concern of the Senate and the President. "What snarls up the system is these so-called statesmen—Congressmen who vote for what they think is the country's interest . . . let the Senators do that . . . they're paid to be statesmen; we aren't," says a Congressman cited in Dexter, "The Representative," p. 3. Cf. Gerhard Leibholz, *Das Wesen der Repräsentation* (Berlin, 1929), p. 188.
5. Constitutions of Germany, Portugal, Belgium, and Italy, cited in Robert Luce, *Legislative Principles* (Boston, 1930), pp. 446–447; cf. Carl Schmitt, *The Necessity of Politics* (London, 1931), p. 69. Martin Drath points out that such clauses did not originate as moralistic admonitions to the representative, but had a real and practical political significance. *Die Entwicklung der Volksrepräsentation* (Bad Homburg, 1954), pp. 7–10.
6. Siéyès went so far as to argue that even the locally elected representative is really elected by the whole nation, and hence represents it. His speech in the

National Assembly of 1789 is cited in Karl Loewenstein *Volk und Parlament* (Munich, 1922), p. 199. Samuel Bailey in *The Rationale of Political Representation* (London, 1835), p. 137, argues that representatives should be elected nationally at large, if that were practical.

7. Misunderstanding of this distinction is common in the literature. Thus Luce cites the following passage from a speech by a delegate to the New Hampshire convention of 1902 *as an illustration of the way people prefer local to national interest:* "I had just as soon not be represented at all as to be represented by a man whose interests belong to another town, and who does not help our town." *Legislative Principles,* pp. 506–507.

8. Cited in Dexter, "The Representative," p. 3.

9. Drath, *Die Entwicklung,* p. 14; see also Sheldon S. Wolin, *Politics and Vision* (Boston, 1960), pp. 63–66.

10. *Systematic Politics* (Chicago, 1945), p. 140; also p. 145; Leibholz, *Das Wesen der Repräsentation,* pp. 47–58; Rudolf Smend, *Verfassung und Verfassungsrecht* (Munich, 1928), pp. 39–40.

11. On voting behavior see Joseph A. Schumpeter, *Capitalism, Socialism and Democracy* (New York, 1947), p. 261, and these empirical studies: Paul F. Lazarsfeld et al., *The People's Choice* (New York, 1948); Bernard R. Berelson et al., *Voting* (Chicago, 1954); Angus Campbell et al., *The Voter Decides* (White Plains, N.Y., 1954); Eugene Burdick and Arthur J. Brodbeck, eds., *American Voting Behavior* (Glencoe, Ill., 1959); Angus Campbell et al., *The American Voter* (New York, 1960).

12. Dexter, "The Representative," p. 3; John C. Wahlke and Heinz Eulau, eds., *Legislative Behavior* (Glencoe, Ill., 1959), pp. 298–304; John C. Wahlke et al., "American State Legislators' Role Orientation," *Journal of Politics* 22 (May 1960); Eulau, "The Role of the Representative"; Charles O. Jones, "Representation in Congress," *American Political Science Review* 55 (December 1961).

13. Sabine, "What Is the Matter?" in *The People, Politics and the Politician,* ed. A. N. Christensen and E. M. Kirkpatrick (New York, 1941); G. D. H. Cole, *Social Theory* (London, 1920), pp. 103–116; Dexter, "The Representative," pp. 4–5; Howard Lee McBain, *The Living Constitution* (New York, 1948), p. 233; Eulau, "The Role of the Representative," pp. 747, 751; Schumpeter, *Capitalism,* p. 261; Jones, "Representation in Congress," pp. 358–359, 365.

14. Dexter, "The Representative"; and "What Do Congressmen Hear: The Mail," *Public Opinion Quarterly* 20 (Spring 1956): 16–27; Eulau, "The Role of the Representative," p. 749; Frank Bonilla, "When Is Petition 'Pressure'?" *Public Opinion Quarterly* 20 (Spring 1956): 39–48; David B. Truman, *The Governmental Process* (New York, 1959), chap. 11; Jones, "Representation in Congress," pp. 366–367.

15. Henry B. Mayo, *An Introduction to Democratic Theory* (New York, 1960), p. 102; Wahlke and Eulau, *Legislative Behavior,* p. 117; Jones, "Representation in Congress," p. 359.

16. Robert M. MacIver, *The Modern State* (Oxford, 1926), p. 196; Joseph Tussman, *Obligation and the Body Politic* (New York, 1960), pp. 69, 75; Wahlke, "American State Legislators' Rule Orientation"; Wahlke and Eulau, *Legislative Behavior,* pp. 179–189, 284–293.

17. Dexter, "The Representative"; Wahlke and Eulau, *Legislative Behavior,* pp. 204–217.

18. Gleeck, "96 Congressmen," p. 7; Turner, *Party and Constituency,* p. 12; Dexter, "The Representative"; Truman, *The Governmental Process,* chap. 11.

19. Dexter, "The Representative," p. 5.

20. Jones, "Representation in Congress," pp. 363–364.

21. Wahlke and Eulau, *Legislative Behavior,* pp. 298–304.

22. "Obviously important changes take place which make the substitute assembly far different from the direct meeting of the people." Alfred De Grazia, *Public and Republic* (New York, 1951), p. 126.

"When one person represents a group, and still more when a number of persons represent different groups, the problem becomes much more complicated." John A. Fairlie, "The Nature of Political Representation," *American Political Science Review* 34 (June 1940), p. 466.

"My conclusion from this discussion is that the concepts connected with representation of individual persons by individual persons have no simple application to representative government." A. Phillips Griffiths and Richard Wollheim, "How Can One Person Represent Another?" Aristotelian Society, suppl. vol. 34 (1960), p. 207.

See also Peter Laslett, "The Face to Face Society," in *Philosophy, Politics and Society,* ed. Peter Laslett (New York, 1956).

23. The first three passages were elicited from New York State legislators by Hartmann, "Judgments," p. 111; the fourth passage is from the autobiography of Senator George F. Hoar, pp. 112–113, cited in Luce, *Legislative Principles,* p. 496; the fifth passage is a statement by a United States Congressman interviewed by Dexter, "The Representative," p. 3; the sixth is by a Congressman interviewed by Bonilla, "When Is Petition 'Pressure'?" pp. 46–47; the last is a statement by a senior member of the House Agriculture Committee interviewed by Jones, "Representation in Congress," p. 365.

24. Lazarsfeld, *The People's Choice,* p. 137. See also Elihu Katz and Paul F. Lazarsfeld, *Personal Influence* (Glencoe, Ill., 1955); Edward C. Banfield, *Political Influence* (Glencoe, Ill., 1961).

25. Miller and Stokes, "Constituency Influence in Congress," p. 55; italics mine.

26. For instance, Karl Loewenstein, *Political Power and the Governmental Process* (Chicago, 1957),

pp. 38–39; Eric Voegelin, *The New Science of Politics* (Chicago, 1952), p. 37.

27. For instance, Georg Jellinek, *Allgemeine Staatslehre* (Berlin, 1905), chap. 17.

28. For example, James Hogan, *Election and Representation* (1945), p. 114; John P. Plamenatz, *Consent, Freedom and Political Obligation* (London, 1938), p. 12; Eulau, "The Role of the Representative," p. 743; Fairlie, "Nature of Political Representation," p. 237; Avery Leiserson, *Administrative Regulation* (Chicago, 1942), pp. 3–9; Max Weber, *Wirtschaft und Gesellschaft* (Tübingen, 1956), chap. 1, pp. 25, 171–176. Gerhard Leibholz is particularly ambivalent between representation as authority and as effective authority: *Das Wesen der Repräsentation,* pp. 140–141, 163–164; and *Strukturprobleme der modernen Demokratie* (Karlsruhe, 1958), pp. 10–12.

29. MacIver, *The Modern State,* pp. 197–198.

30. W. D. Handcock, "What Is Represented in Representative Government?" *Philosophy* 22 (July 1947): 107; cf. John Dewey, *The Public and Its Problems* (New York, 1927), p. 76.

31. For instance, Plamenatz, *Consent,* p. 16.

32. Christian Bay, *The Structure of Freedom* (Stanford, 1958), p. 322.

33. For representative government to exist, "the *possibility* for opposition must be considered sufficient." Charles William Cassinelli, Jr., "The Concept of Representative Government" (unpubl. thesis, 1950), p. 62.

34. Five criteria for distinguishing a "process of consent" from a "process of manipulation" in political elections are suggested by Morris Janowitz and Dwaine Marvick, "Competitive Pressure and Democratic Consent," *Public Opinion Quarterly* 19 (Winter 1955–56): 381–400. See also their book of the same title (Ann Arbor, 1956) for an application. A useful discussion of the criteria of "free" elections is given in W. J. M. Mackenzie, *Free Elections* (New York, 1958), esp. the introduction and part 4.

Implementing Representation: A Framework and Two Applications

BRUCE E. CAIN and

W. T. JONES

This paper introduces a conceptual framework that makes possible a systematic comparison of the many contrasting proposals that theorists have put forward for implementing representation. We focus on the theorist (alternatively, on what classical theorists referred to as "the Legislator" or "the Law Giver"), and on his reasons for making the specific recommendations that he puts forward. Though for the purposes of exposition and illustration we limit our discussion to the recommendations of two theorists regarding representation, we believe the framework can be used to elucidate the many different proposals made by various theorists: The framework provides a standard structure and a standard vocabulary to which the varying arguments of individual theorists and their different vocabularies can be reduced for comparative purposes. The exposition of this framework is preceded by a short section that differentiates among possible approaches to the study of representation and that characterizes the one adopted here as "pragmatic." It is followed by a longer section that illustrates the value of the framework by comparing the proposals of Rousseau and Bentham.

I. Approaches to the Problem of Representation

In most political organizations the interests of some (the relatively many) are represented by others (the relatively few). The ends of any political organization cannot be realized unless the many are "well represented," that is, represented in ways that further those ends. Because political philosophers and political scientists have differed about ends, they have naturally differed about what it means to be well represented. Hobbes's conception of "authorized" rights, Locke's argument for accountable representatives, Burke's ideal of the representative as trustee, Hegel's notion of indirect and functional representation, are classical examples of this, the normative, approach to the problem of representation.

But political philosophers and political scientists also differ about how constituents and their representatives interact. What are the variables—structural, social, psychological—that affect these interactions, and how do changes in these variables explain the fact that constituents and their representatives behave differently in different circumstances? The attempt to answer such questions is the empirical approach to the study of representation. The Michigan studies of how voters perceive their electoral choice and Fenno's recent work on Congressional home styles are but two examples of the enormous literature that this approach has generated.[1]

Finally, since there is usually a gap between the way in which a given electorate and its representatives actually behave and the ways in which that electorate itself, its representatives, or some political philosophers believe they need to behave if the electorate are to be "well represented," a third approach to the study of representation, the "pragmatic," is possible. Here we distinguish between formal and substantive theories of implementation—between, to use Pitkin's language, the "standing for" and the "acting for" meanings of representation. In this paper we do not consider theories that hold citizens to be well represented if certain purely formal criteria—for instance, the one man-one vote rule—are satisfied; we concentrate on substantive theories. Aristotle's discussion of how to assure the preponderance of the middle class in a Greek city-state, Madison's ideas about constitutional engineering, Dahl's theory of polyarchy, are examples of this approach—they are studies of how "desirable" systems of representation can be achieved in various circumstances. Obviously, this third approach supplements the other two: the gap between what is and what ought to be can only be bridged by coming to understand the forces that affect the behavior of a given electorate and its representatives.

Political theorists have made an enormous number of different and often conflicting recommendations for implementing representation. Some, for instance, recommend very short terms for representatives; others, long terms. Some recommend imposing controls on the actions of representatives, others recommend allowing them a relatively free hand between elections. And so on.

Why are there these differences? To begin with, there are what may be called contextual variables—differences in the times and the customs or more precisely, differences in theorists' perceptions of the times and the customs. Thus some of the very great differences between Hobbes's and Locke's view of the social contract can surely be traced to the fact that whereas "Hobbes' opinions were formed in the years that led up to a bitter Civil War," Locke "was a participant in the organization of the Whig Party and an interested onlooker at its parliamentary triumph."[2] But other variables are also important—differences in the

kinds of goals that theorists have for the political process and differences in their conceptions of human nature. It is on the belief variables, in contrast to the contextual variables, that this study focuses.

We recognize, of course, that there are complex interactions between context variables and belief variables: on the one hand the success of the Glorious Revolution reinforced Locke's optimistic view of human nature; on the other, Hobbes's congenital pessimism may have led him to a gloomier view of Englishmen's potentiality for self-government than that reached by others who had lived through the Civil War. But we concentrate on the belief variables for two reasons. First, psychological theory is hardly sufficiently advanced to enable historians of political theory to reach firm conclusions about exactly how the opinions of political theorists were actually formed. Second, for comparative purposes, we want to bring into focus the various implicit logical structures that can relate a theorist's beliefs about human nature to his specific commendations. In a word, the paper offers a theory about the "good reasons" a theorist has, or might have, for the specific recommendations he makes, a theory that explains a theorist's recommendations by relating those recommendations to his underlying assumptions about human nature and about the ends of the state.

II. A Framework for Studying the Implementation of Representation

There are four components to the proposed framework: (1) the theorist's preferences regarding the dispositions that he hopes will guide representatives' actions, (2) the theorist's presuppositions about human nature, (3) his beliefs about likely behavioral regularities, given these presuppositions, and (4) specific recommendations for implementing representation.

First, as regards to dispositions: we use this term to refer to any tendency to respond in a specific, organized and distinctive pattern to given aspects of the environment, for instance, the tendency to be obedient, instead of disobedient, to commands, to be suspicious of, in-ad of cordial to, strangers, and so on. Here, of course, we are concerned only with dispositions that political theorists have thought to be especially relevant to the behavior of representatives, and we define a range of such dispositions (D_1–D_5) along five dimensions of representative action, the preferred set deriving in each case from the theorist's implicit or explicit notions about the desired ends for the state. Though the position a theorist adopts can fall anywhere on the continuum between the extremes and though a systematic study of any theorist's view could require us to specify his exact position on each of the five spectrums, it is enough, for the purpose of this illustrative essay, to identify the theorist's position as being on one end or the other of the spectrum (i.e., *a* or *b*). A profile of the dispositions a theorist wants representatives to have or acquire is simply the set of positions the theorist takes on each of these five dimensions. (See Table 1.)

Second, we define a set of beliefs about human nature (HN_1–HN_5) which consists of five pairs of presuppositions again organized as mutually exclusive alternatives.[3] These assumptions apply both to individuals who are likely to be representatives and those who are likely to be represented. Though it is possible for a theorist to believe that representatives are fundamentally different from those they represent, we will restrict ourselves to the more common case (Table 2).

Third, since theorists also have ideas about what kinds of actions tend to result because of the nature of man—that is, they have beliefs about how *HN* relates to likely behavior—we list five typical behavioral regularities (BR_1–BR_5).

Finally, fourth, there are the recommendations that theorists make about representative institutions, which is, of course, the variable we seek to explain. A recommendation (*R*) can be thought of as a hypothetical imperative addressed to constitution makers of the form: "If you want to achieve such-and-such a *D* and believe such-and-such *HN*s, then do *R*." Theorists seldom formulate their hypothetical imperatives explicitly; more often than not they simply assert, "Do *R*." They may even mask that logic (either deliberately or unintentionally) by emphasizing considerations that they hope will win support for *R* in whatever group they are addressing. Our framework helps uncover the logic that supports, not the psychological or sociological factors that may actually have led each theorist to, the particular *R* that he recommends.

1. Preferred Dispositions (D) of Representatives

The first component of this scheme, then, is the classification of the various preferred dispositions that theorists may have for representative action. Our contention is not that this list exhausts all the possible preferred dispositions theorists can have for a representative system, but it does, we think, take account of the most important ones. There are five dispositions in this set. They fall into two major groups, the first dealing with who or what should be represented and the second dealing with how representatives should represent their constituents.

The question of who or what should be represented is considered by all theorists. One dimension of this question deals with theorists' views of *the preferred time perspective of the representative's actions*. Since policies have short- and long-range consequences, theorists may differ about what the representative's proper time horizon should be. Some issues, for example, may force a choice between immediate benefits and delayed costs, including externalities that will be only realized in the distant future, perhaps by later generations. The designer of a representative system must therefore decide what role short- and long-range considerations should play, and which institutions will encourage the law-making perspective that the designer holds to be desirable.

The second dimension of this subset is the scope of representation, consisting of a continuum of possibilities that ranges from, at one end, representatives *who respond to the special concerns of particular regions, persons or interest groups* to, at the other end, *representatives who attempt to do what is best for the good of the community as a whole*, however defined. Different theorists will prefer, and seek to set up, representative systems that operate at different points on this continuum.

Apart from the question of who or what should be represented, there is the question of how representatives should represent their constituents. This subset consists of three dimensions. The first concerns *the choice between encouraging or discouraging representatives to link their actions with one another's.* This is particularly important in cases where there is little or no overlap in constituent preferences. The possibility of making bargains, trading off issues of different saliencies or forging compromises can be crucial to the function of government. A theorist's position on this dimension reflects whether he wants individual representatives to cooperate in a systematic and regularized fashion (such as in factions or a strong party system) or prefers that they act and think independently.

Another dimension in this subset deals with *how much consistency is desirable in a representative's actions over time.* On the one hand, almost all theorists believe it undesirable to have representatives who shift their positions with every whimsical change in their constituents' preferences; on the other hand, they believe it equally undesirable to have representatives who are unresponsive even to important changes. But theorists can differ widely about the rate at which representatives should adapt to changes in the environment—for instance, new electoral interests.

Lastly, there is *the dimension of reliability,* which refers to the correlation of a representative's promises and actions: when X says that he will do certain things in office, can he be trusted to implement these policies after his election? Whereas the previous dimension concerns the consistency of a representative's actions over time, this one looks at the consistency of words and actions. Although it is advantageous to constituents to have a reliable legislator, since this facilitates their evaluation of his record, at the same time a perfectly consistent legislator will be less able to cope with unforeseen events, or to build coalitions by skillful bargaining. Once again, different theorists will weigh these considerations differently, aiming at constitutional arrangements

that reflect their estimate of where the balance lies. The preferred dispositions are represented in Table 1.

2. *Presuppositions About Human Nature (HN)*

The institutions that theorists propose in order to implement their ideas about representation are related not only to their preferences regarding the dispositions they want representatives to have but also to fundamental premises about human nature. Theorists may derive their premises empirically or assume them a priori, but in either case, they form the rationale for the theorist's expectation that a given institution will produce a particular outcome. In this set of presuppositions, we distinguish two types. The first we call "structural" because they are beliefs about whether and how easily human nature can be changed; the second subset we call "behavioral," because they are beliefs about the nature of human preferences and decision making.

The most crucial structural dimension is concerned with the theorist's *beliefs about the malleability or intractability of human nature.* The assumption of intractability is most frequently associated with a pessimistic view of human nature: not only is human nature flawed but nothing can be done about it. Attempts to change individuals by legal, moral or educational means are disparaged. The intractability of man's evil state is even perceived by some theorists as an advantage, in that, since the individuals always act to protect their self-interests, institutions founded upon these interests have a solid base. By contrast, the assumption of malleability is usually associated with an optimistic view of human nature. If individuals are not born with the right social instincts, then these can be instilled by education or socialization. In fact, from this point of view, being "well represented" may be thought to require that representatives and the represented alike be raised from their self-interested perspectives to a higher public consciousness.

The theorist's position on this dimension governs the choice between taking human na-

Table 1. Dispositions set

	Dispositions	Range of the Continuum	
	D_1 Time perspective	Short (a)	Long (b)
What is represented	D_2 Scope	Parochial (a)	Common (b)
	D_3 Degree of cooperation	Independence (a)	Coordinated (b)
How to represent	D_4 Consistency over time	Changing action (a)	Consistency (b)
	D_5 Reliability of promises	Adaptability (a)	Reliability (b)

ture as a given and trying to change human nature. A theorist who believes that human nature is malleable will choose what we shall call "preference-altering mechanisms," and a theorist who believes that human nature is not malleable will choose in contrast "preference-accepting mechanisms." In the preference-altering case the theorist holds, for instance, that institutional norms shape the preferences of individuals, which in turn determine their actions. Hence he uses institutions to channel preferences in the desired direction. Good examples of this type of mechanism are the role of the Communist Party in the Soviet Union and the institutional norms that shape Congressional committee behavior in the United States. In the preference-accepting case, the theorist holds that the institutions do not shape human nature; human nature being fixed, he adjusts institutions to produce behaviors of the desired kinds. In a word, changes in the prevailing pattern of behavior are caused by manipulating the institutional context of decisions. This approach is exemplified by Madisonianism and, more generally, by economic approaches to institutional design.

While the intractability dimension is the primary structural assumption in most modern theoretical designs, a second dimension is needed in order to understand many early representation theories, namely, *whether secular or transcendental laws govern human behav-*

ior. If a theorist, e.g., Aquinas, believes there are transcendental laws, i.e., laws that have a supernatural source—or even if, like Machiavelli, he himself disbelieves in such laws but holds that men in general believe in them—he will take them into account in framing his proposals for representation. First, the theorist is likely to hold that the scope and substance of laws of the state are constrained by the condition that legislation must not violate transcendental principles. Second, he is likely to think that the behavior of representatives is not prescribed exclusively by institutional incentives.

Apart from these two structural presuppositions, there are other presuppositions that deal with the conditions of human knowledge and preferences. The most common of these is *Whether individuals are primarily self-regarding or other-regarding in orientation.* The pessimistic position holds that power, self-interest and greed are the only enduring human motives. Theorists who take this position—Hobbes and Madison, for instance, and in the modern period, Morgenthau—argue for a realist approach to institutions and against overly high expectations about human behavior. They recommend building institutions that take advantage of men's weaknesses (such as pitting self-interest against self-interest to achieve a stable equilibrium). In contrast, other theorists hold that man is basically good and that power, self-interest and greed are no more intrinsic or natural than the opposite qualities. If man is weak or bad, it is only because society has corrupted him. In his designs, the law giver can rely on altruism and/or a concern for the public good.

A second presupposition about preferences concerns individuals' varying *attitudes towards risk.* Theorists frequently differ over whether individuals inherently prefer stability to change, predictability to unpredictability, certainty to uncertainty. These alternatives can all be grouped under the rubric of differential attitudes towards risk. Theorists who believe that the public is inherently cautious about change, especially theorists whose own natural preference is for stability, are suspicious of reformers. Burke, for instance, admired what he thought was the Englishman's pragmatic conservatism, and believed that this explained why England was spared the disastrous experience of the French Revolution. Others, such as Jefferson or Mao Tse Tung, who also believed that man is innately conservative but who did not share Burke's preference for stability, designed measures that facilitated adaptive change, emphasizing, for instance, the need for bringing about a constant string of small revolutions. Not all, of course, believed that man is innately risk-averse: some like Hobbes saw man as a gambler who, unless deterred by the strong hand of the sovereign, would risk chaotic disequilibrium.

Finally, theorists also differ as to *whether or not individuals are capable of anticipating relevant future secondary effects of present actions (i.e., their real interests).* To assume that individuals can know their true interests is to assume clairvoyant expectations on the part of one or some of the political actors (e.g., the public, their representatives, or at the very least, the theorist himself). This is not simply a rationality of maximization, but one of preference formation (i.e., it is assumed individuals have the "right," or rational, preferences). The theorist of course need not believe that every actor in the political system is perfectly rational in this strong sense, but only that at least one actor is and that he will steer the rest of the population in the direction of their real in-

terests. The contrasting assumption is that individuals cannot know their real preferences, or, to put it another way, that the long-term consequences of complex actions cannot be known.

The set of presuppositions about human nature (*HN*) is represented in Table 2.

3. *The Set of Behavioral Regularities (BR)*

Given his assumptions about human nature (*HN*), every theorist will have expectations about how people are likely to behave unless institutional devices and/or specially learned dispositions influence them to behave otherwise. The total number of behavioral regularities in which political theorists and other people believe is obviously large. For illustrative purposes we list five such regularities, chosen both because they are typical and also because they correspond to the five dimensions of dispositions (*D*) discussed earlier. Our intention is to bring out an important point, viz., a theorist's recommendations regarding representative institutions are relative not only to his beliefs about human nature and to dispositions he hopes representatives will have, but also to his beliefs about how people, including representatives, are likely to act in the absence of institutions designed to cause them to act in a different manner.

(*BR₁*) *Time horizon.* The length of a person's time horizon is correlated with his belief about how well he can anticipate the future and with how risk averse he is. If people doubt their ability to predict the future and if they are risk-averse, they are likely to have short time horizons; if they are confident of their ability to predict the future and if they are risk-accepting, they are likely to have longer time horizons.

(*BR₂*) *Range of interest.* The range of a person's interests is correlated with his belief about how well he can anticipate the future and with the self-regarding/other-regarding orientation of his interests. People will have more parochial inter-

Table 2. Human nature presuppositions set

	Presuppositions	Range of the Continuum	
Structural presuppositions	HN_1 Malleability of human nature	Intractable (a)	Malleable (b)
	HN_2 Laws governing human nature	Secular (a)	Transcendental (b)
	HN_3 Self-interestedness of preferences	Self-regarding (a)	Other-regarding (b)
Conditions of human knowledge and preference	HN_4 Attitudes toward risk	Risk-averse (a)	Risk-acceptant (b)
	HN_5 Capacity to know real interests	Incapable (a)	Capable (b)

ests if they doubt their ability to predict the future and if their orientation is self-regarding; less parochial interests if they are confident of their ability to predict the future and if their orientation is other-regarding.

(BR_3) *Self-regardingness.* If people are self-regarding they tend to act more independently; if other-regarding they tend to act less independently.

(BR_4) *Consistency.* A person's attitude toward change is correlated with his belief about how well he can anticipate the future and with how risk-averse he is. People will be more resistant to changes in their actions if they doubt their ability to predict the future and if they are risk-averse; less resistant to change if they are confident of their ability to predict the future and if they are risk-accepting.

(BR_5) *Reliability.* A person is more likely to keep a promise if he believes he can predict the consequences of keeping it and if he is other-regarding; less likely to keep a promise if he is doubtful of his ability to predict the consequences of keeping it and if he is self-regarding.

4. Recommendations (R)

We turn now to the particular institutional designs (the specific sets of Rs) that different

theorists recommend. The design will depend on whether the theorist's dispositional preferences (D) are D_{1a} or D_{1b}, D_{2a} or D_{2b}, D_{3a} or D_{3b}, . . . , and on whether his beliefs about human nature are HN_{1a} or HN_{1b}, HN_{2a} or HN_{2b}, HN_{3a} or HN_{3b}, ... For instance, we said earlier that HN_1 dictates whether a theorist adopts the preference-altering or the preference-accepting strategy for changing behavior if he deems it undesirable and for encouraging it if he deems it desirable or at least innocuous. The first approach to altering a representative's time horizon (BR_1) would be to try to encourage norms or beliefs that were longer-range in perspective or less risk-averse: the second approach would increase the perceived risk of short-term maximizing behavior in order to encourage long-term maximizing behavior.

It is theoretically possible that a theorist might think that the preference-altering strategy is applicable to a certain subset of people's preferences and that a preference-accepting strategy is applicable to another subset (some preferences are malleable, others are not). But such a theorist might find that his use of a preference-altering strategy to change (say) malleable attitudes toward risk aversion would conflict with a preference-accepting strategy to produce (say) long-range maximizing behavior in people whose time horizons are not malleable. Thus a theorist who thought that different strategies are appropriate for different preferences would find himself involved in complications and refinements escaped by theorists who opt for one or the other of the two strategies. This being the case, in the history of political theory theorists of representation tend to fall into one camp or the other.

We said at the outset that our goal in this paper is to explain the recommendations that political theorists have made regarding representation. We have argued that a recommendation is explained when it is shown to be predictable from the other variables in the framework. This is, so far, only a claim. In the next section we hope to justify it.

III. Some Institutional Recommendations by Bentham and Rousseau

The explanatory power of this framework can be demonstrated by showing how it applies to two theorists—Bentham and Rousseau. Our choice of Bentham for this exercise will probably be thought natural, but Rousseau may occasion some surprise. When political philosophers, if not political scientists, think of Rousseau they think first of *The Social Contract* and only later, if at all, of "A Constitutional Project for Corsica" and "Considerations on the Government of Poland." It is true that Rousseau believed, and argued in *The Social Contract,* that direct democracy is the only kind of government in which the problem of consent can be solved. But he also recognized that direct democracy was impossible in the Europe of his day and that some form of representative government was therefore necessary. We think it useful, in demonstrating the value of our framework, to show the kinds of goals for representation that were adopted by a thinker whose moral theory was such as to cause him to prefer a nonrepresentative type of government.

The comparison of Bentham and Rousseau is useful from another perspective: Bentham exemplifies a preference-accepting approach to institutional reform while Rousseau represents a preference-altering approach. Bentham's approach is preference-accepting because he believed that nature was intractable (HN_{1a}). Attempts to educate men to act altruistically were not only doomed to failure, they were pernicious because they fostered hypocrisy and pretension. Bentham considered various challenges to the inevitability of self-preference and dismissed them. Religion, for instance, was a false consciousness that was encouraged by "hypocritical knaves" who "with the full consciousness of its absurdity" inculcate a doctrine of "sympathy" and perpetuated by "the miserable dupes" who refused to recognize its absurdity.[4]

In contrast, Rousseau believed human nature to be malleable; hence his approach is preference-altering. Indeed, because men internalized the belief and value systems of the institutions in which they lived, human nature was diverse for Rousseau as well as malleable—diverse because the basic drives were mediated and articulated by the internalized value system; malleable because, having been shaped by one set of institutions, they could be re-shaped by a different set.

Any theorist who proposed to rely exclusively on "mechanical devices"[5]—among which Rousseau would almost certainly have included any Benthamite system of external sanctions—would be defeated by what looked like an intractable human nature and by the power of such passions as patriotism and religious fervor, which often resisted any rational calculus of pleasures and pains. But a theorist who took account of the national character of the people for whom he is designing a representative system and who understood their history would find human nature malleable enough.

This is not to say that Bentham never proposed preference-altering suggestions or that Rousseau never proposed preference-accepting ones. Rather, the point is that on the whole they seemed to take divergent approaches to the problem of institutional reform. How this difference in approach affected specific proposals will now be illustrated by examining six institutional issues that were considered by both theorists. Of these six, Bentham and Rousseau disagreed sharply on the value of two (i.e., factitious honors and mechanisms for controlling the conduct of the legislators); partially agreed on the value of two others (i.e., monarchy and separation of powers) and agreed on the last two (i.e., the importance of public opinion and the frequency of elections). We will consider the following questions: (1) What was the basis for their positions? (2) If they disagreed, was it because of a difference in dispositions (*D*), beliefs about human nature (*HN*), or assumptions about behavioral regularities (*BR*)? (3) If they agreed, were their reasons similar? and in any case, (4) Are their reasons explained by the proposed framework?

1. Institutions About Whose Value They Disagreed

Given the fact that Bentham and Rousseau had fundamentally different approaches to institutional design, it is not surprising that they disagreed about certain specific institutions. One of these was the use of *factitious honors*. Bentham strongly opposed their use as a method of rewarding public service, because, unlike "natural dignities," factitious honors tended to be conferred by a third party (typically, a monarch), not by those who directly perceived the value of the act being rewarded. It was important to Bentham that rewards not be mediated by third parties: in his words, "affection, esteem and respect, which is the result of judgment which is unperverted by any delusion from source, is preferred to that respect which is the joint offspring of sinister interest, caprice, imposture and chance."[6] Under a system of factitious honors, individuals are likely to be accorded honor by accident of birth, or because they please the monarch, rather than by such utility-maximizing criteria as whether their actions foster aggregate utility.

Bentham also felt that these kinds of awards were a source of great waste,[7] and they unnecessarily aggravated inequality. He knew that inequality is an inevitable by-product of competition. But individuals who earn their inequality by the merit of their actions actually contribute to the general good: the benefit of that contribution exceeds the cost of reward. But when reward is conferred by a third party, there is no guarantee of benefit to the public—indeed, the opposite is more likely to occur.

The proper method of bestowing honor, therefore, is to keep the public informed with

the "utmost degree of clearness, correctness and completeness possible," regarding the actions of representatives and other officials so that good actions will be rewarded with natural dignity—i.e., dignity that comes directly from public esteem.

Rousseau, by comparison, supported the use of factitious honors because he believed that the particular pattern of a man's motives is shaped by the value system he has internalized. Bentham's notion of there being an incentive system in which "judgment is unperverted by any delusion from source" was itself a delusion, the product of Bentham's oversimplified view that men are always and only animated by pleasure and pain. *All* incentive systems, Bentham to the contrary, are mediated by third parties—that is, by the culture in which the individual lives. The only question is what sort of value system is in fact mediating that individual's incentive system, whether it is socially helpful or socially harmful. It is always possible, by altering the value system, to reorient a socially harmful incentive system in a socially beneficial direction.

Thus most Europeans lived in a society that valued money above all else, and unfortunately "of all the incentives known to me, money is at once the weakest and most useless for the purpose of driving the political mechanism toward its goal and the strongest and most reliable for the purpose of deflecting it from its course."[8] But this did not have to be the case. That "reserve of grand passions" which exists "in all hearts" can be redirected away from greed and toward honor, which is a socially useful motive. "I should like to have all ranks, offices, and honorific awards distinguished by external signs, so that no public figure would ever be allowed to go incognito, but would be followed by the marks of his rank and dignity; this would make people respect him at all times, and to dominate over opulence."[9]

A second proposal regarding which Bentham and Rousseau diverged was the need to monitor the behavior of legislators. Bentham stipulated careful day-to-day monitoring of the behavior of representatives, but he left them free to vote in accordance with their best judgment on all issues that came before them.

Rousseau, in contrast, believed that representatives should be bound to vote on all issues according to the detailed instructions they had received from the electorate, but he did not think that the day-to-day conduct of representatives required any monitoring.

Attendance was particularly crucial for Bentham because, though legislators who did not attend produced half the pernicious effect of bad bills passed in their absence, they were not held responsible unless the cause of their absence could be known. He therefore proposed that attendance be mandatory. The legislative chamber was to have only one entrance at which the legislator would be paid each day by the doorkeeper. The moments of arrival and of departure would be recorded in an "Entrance and Departure Book." Each day's attendance record would be printed in the newspaper the next day, and the monthly totals would also be reported. If a representative was ill, he would have to present a "sickness ticket," attested to by a physician, which would indicate the number of days missed and the nature of the illness. In the case of absence, for whatever reason, the legislator was encouraged to designate a substitute. The legislator and not his constituents should choose the substitute: otherwise he could blame the substitute's votes on his constituents. This was consistent with Bentham's arguments that the legislator was responsible for his own judgment and that he should not be allowed to duck the public's retrospective evaluation.

Not surprisingly, there is nothing in Rousseau that corresponds to Bentham's minute recommendations for monitoring the day-to-day behavior of representatives. The key here is the difference, to use Rousseau's own terminology, between thinking of the electorate as an aggregate and thinking of it as an association. Societies, as Bentham conceived them, are what Rousseau called aggregates. That is, each is a collection of molecular individuals. This being the case, in the Benthamite system it is essential that there be no statistical biases in the sample of legislators when votes on bills are taken. If the diverse interests of the aggregate which is the legislature systematically reflect the diverse interests of the aggregate which is the electorate, then the votes of the representatives will, with no more ado, reflect those interests, and the greatest possible good will thereby be achieved. Obviously, monitoring of voting is not required, though monitoring of attendance is.

Rousseau, in contrast, believed that what he called an association, that is, a society with a real community of interest, is possible and, what is more, that both the electorate itself and its representatives can know what that community of interests is. It follows that representatives are "not to express their own private opinions but to declare the will" of the electorate.[10] Before the start of every session of the legislature, each representative was to be provided with a set of written instructions, which "have been drawn up with great care," and at the end of each session the representative must give his constituents a full report of his actions during that session. Rousseau viewed this report as having "the utmost importance," for it prevented a representative's actions "from ever being anything but the real expression of the will" of the community he represented.[11]

What then can we say generally about the basis of their disagreements over honors and monitoring procedures? To begin with, their differences in these instances seem to be related more to different assumptions about human nature than to different preferred dispositions of representatives. The exception would be their disagreement over D_5, i.e., reliability. Bentham did not think reliability was important. He viewed representatives as professionals who were not bound to carry out their job in such and such a specific way but only to act in a manner that they judge best.[12] Hence, representatives were responsible only for giving the electorate good reasons for voting as they did.

Rousseau, however, believed that reliability was important, and felt that representatives should be bound to specific instructions. Rousseau's representative was not, like Bentham's, a professional whose duty was to use his own best judgment; his representative was a citizen whose duty was to reflect the will of his fellow citizens.

Apart from their disagreement about reliability, the chief reason for Bentham and Rousseau's divergence on these two proposals was Bentham's fundamental skepticism about any proposal that was not rooted in self-interest and Rousseau's skepticism about any institution that depended upon self-interest—in short, their disagreements about HN_1 and HN_3. Bentham's position here was, in Morgenthau's sense of the term, realistic. Individuals were driven by basic self-interested motives: "Nature has placed mankind under the governance of two sovereign masters, pain and pleasure."[13] The legislator had at his command "two instruments—punishment and reward—each of which, or both, as in his eyes occasion requires, he employs, in the performance of his work."[14]

Though Bentham acknowledged that there might be individuals who act against their own interests for the sake of some social good—a kind of false consciousness on their part—these cases are exceptional. Since the "self-regarding interest is predominant over all other interests put together,"[15] institutions should be built on the statistical tendency of the many to pursue their self-interest and not on the exceptional behavior of the few: "It is in what has place in the conduct on the part of the thousands, and not in what has place in the conduct of one in every thousand, that all rational and useful political arrangements will be grounded." Once this principle is recognized, he claimed, "all pretence to this species of purity will be regarded as would an assertion of chastity in the mouth of a prostitute at the very moment of solicitation."[16]

As for Rousseau, although there are occasional passages in which he sounds as "realistic" as Bentham—for instance, "the great springs of human conduct come down, on close examination, to two, pleasure and vanity; and . . . in the last analysis . . . everything comes down to practically pure vanity"—nevertheless it was a central thesis of his that human nature is basically good: Since "everything is good as it comes from the hands of the Maker,"[17] it follows that "man [too] is naturally good."[18]

To say that man is naturally good—that he is "born free"[19]—means that at birth his ca-

reer is open. In favorable environment he will develop into a virtuous adult and a good citizen: "a young man brought up in happy simplicity is drawn by the first movement of nature to the tender kindly passions"; he has a "compassionate heart"; he is "the most generous and most lovable of men."[20] Unfortunately, man is "everywhere in chains"[21]—that is, in most European countries children grow up in such an unfavorable environment that, become men, they "pervert and disfigure everything."[21]

Thus Bentham was skeptical of factitious honors because he was skeptical of anything other than self-interest as a motive, and he favored the constant monitoring of legislators because he did not trust representatives to act for the common good on their own. By comparison, Rousseau's belief in factitious honors was rooted in his faith in other-regarding motives and in his willingness to believe that legislators would act to further the common good without constant monitoring. Note, however, that though Rousseau's proposal that the citizens "bind the representatives to follow their instructions exactly"[22] is consistent with his goal that representatives should reflect the common interest of small communities, it is inconsistent with his belief that representatives can be, and should be, socialized to work for the common good. If small communities naturally foster civic-mindedness, an identity of interests between the representative and the represented would develop without instruction. Perhaps this anomaly betrays a suppressed but realistic suspicion about the limits of civic-minded motives.

Another presupposition involved in their different positions regarding these two institutions is whether the representative can know the real interests of the community or not (i.e., HN_5). This is implicit both in their disagreement over honors in the sense that honors could be an effective incentive only if people understood the higher interest they served and in their disagreement over monitoring in the sense that Bentham's representatives could only know the particular interests that elected them whereas Rousseau's representatives could know and be bound to the common good. Bentham denied that men have real interests which are other than, and better for them than, their perceived self-interests. Of course, he recognized that actions have secondary consequences: the "fecundity" of pain and pleasure was an important consideration for him, inasmuch as laws must be judged by their distant as well as proximate consequences; Bentham was aware of the need to discount for the bias of nearness. But it did not enter Bentham's head to try to liberate individuals from their self-interested perspective, nor did he think that anything could be in an individual's interest if it did not make him better off, or at least not worse off.

In contrast to Bentham, Rousseau held that there are "real," in distinction from merely "apparent," interests. Men's real interests are to live simply, in peace and amity with one's neighbors; to "seek satisfaction within oneself rather than in one's fortune"; to "perceive God everywhere in his works."[23] That is happiness. That being the case, Rousseau had to ask himself why most people pursue only apparent goods? His answer was, first, that the profit motive has made men "scheming, ardent, avid, ambitious, servile and knavish"—in a word, unhappy—and, second, that there was nothing in the contemporary educational system to counteract these tendencies, for whereas "justice and goodness are not merely abstract terms, moral entities created by the understanding, but real affections of the soul,"[24] the educational system unfortunately emphasizes only "book learning," that is, what is verbal and abstract.

The fact that Bentham held positions HN_{3a} and HN_{5a} made him skeptical of procedures that counted on other-regarding motives and the capacity of men to know their real interests. Rousseau's opposite opinions led him to different conclusions about these proposals.

2. Institutions About which Bentham and Rousseau Partly Agreed

Despite such differences it is nonetheless possible to find institutions on which Bentham and Rousseau agreed despite their different approaches to institutional design. The first set that we will examine are those in which they

partly disagreed. An example is their partial concurrence about *monarchy*. Whereas Bentham adamantly opposed this institution in any circumstances, Rousseau was opposed to monarchy but was willing to make adaptations to local customs and preferences. Bentham's reasons for opposing monarchy in any form or under any conditions were consistent with the basic premises of his theory of representation. The goal of the representative was to maximize the aggregate utility of the whole population. This requires that all preferences be equally weighted. But in a monarchy, since the preferences of the monarch weigh more heavily, the principle of the greatest happiness to the greatest number is necessarily violated. Far from pursuing measures that increased aggregate welfare, the monarch would inevitably look out for his own interests: "In pursuance of the self-preferences inherent in human nature, the end of his government will be the greatest possible happiness of his individual self."[25]

Further, since, as Bentham held, all individuals base their decisions on a calculation of self-interested costs and benefits, and since in a monarchy the citizens are not in a position to inflict costs on the monarch, the monarch in turn had less of an incentive to act benevolently towards the citizens: "The more extensively a man feels himself exposed to ill-treatment at the hands of others, the stronger is the inducement he has to bestow upon them good treatment . . . but the monarch is of all men the one who stands the least extensively exposed to ill-treatment at the hands of others."[26]

Rousseau, too, opposed monarchy. Because the interests of the monarch almost inevitably conflicted with the common interest of the citizens, the monarch would try to disrupt that general will if it existed or to prevent its formation if it had not yet come into being. Nevertheless, when Rousseau was invited to draft a constitution for Poland he recommended modification of the monarchy and the nobility, rather than abolition. He believed that changes could not only substantially reduce its danger to the state, but actually turn it into a socially useful institution.

Since Rousseau did "not believe that a state as large as Poland could possibly get along without" a king, the problem for the Poles was to limit the monarch's power to do harm. Election helped, he thought, but did not remove the danger of autocracy. Another way to weaken the power of the monarch was to "prescribe by constitutional law that the crown should never pass from father to son, and that every son of a Polish king should forever be excluded from the throne."[27] Still another was to let the king continue to appoint the great officers of state but to "restrict his choice to a small number of nominees presented" to him by the legislature, thus making it impossible for him to "fill these offices with his creatures."[28] Rousseau also urged the Poles to "minimize, as far as possible, the handling of money by the king."[29]

But in the long run, and in accordance with Rousseau's constant emphasis on the importance of an internalized belief system, he held it better to try to change the king's perception of his interests than to rely exclusively on constitutional sanctions to confine those interests. That is, Rousseau wanted to change the king's dispositions from D_{1a} to D_{1b} and from D_{2a} to D_{2b}. How could these changes be brought about? How, that is, could the king's perception of his personal interests be changed to coincide with the common interest? Since "only a base soul is insensible of posthumous reputation," the Poles should make use of the king's natural concern for history's judgment of him.[30] A special institution should therefore be established, to come into being immediately after a king's death, to evaluate his reign and to award him monuments and honor if he merited them—or to withhold them. It was important that this judgment be made during the interregnum, lest the new king use his position to influence, and mitigate, the assessment of his predecessor.

A second area of partial agreement was *bicameralism*. Once again, they both opposed the institution, but Rousseau favored compromise. Bentham was firmly opposed to bicameralism because he held that if one chamber properly embodied the will of the aggregate, a second

legislative body must be either opposed to that will or redundant. In states where there is a second house that is different in composition from the first house, it is usually a permanent aristocratic body, such as the House of Lords in England. Such houses act against the best interests of the whole population and in the interests of a privileged few. The argument that the members of the second house might have special intellectual aptitudes did not sway him: cleverness was pernicious when it opposed the will of the people.

On the other hand, if the composition of the second house was like that of the first, it would be redundant: unnecessary delays would be caused while the two legislatures passed things back and forth. If the first house was sufficiently numerous, Bentham thought, it would probably make the right decision since the "probability of right judgment will in every instance be in the exact ratio of the number of the majority to the minority."[31] Complicating the legislative process by introducing a second house would only make it easier for individuals intent on mischief to succeed.

Like Bentham, Rousseau believed that ideally there should be but one legislative body, but in many states an upper class already existed, represented by a senate which had large powers because its members were either hereditary nobles or else served for life. This was the case in Poland, and instead of recommending abolition of the Polish senate, Rousseau characteristically proposed a number of changes which he thought would reduce the senate's power and yet enable it to make a positive contribution to the state.

For instance, the right to appoint senators should be transferred from the king to the provincial assemblies. This would have two advantages: first, the king's power would be reduced; second, Poland would move further in the direction of federalism. Though in a nation as large and diverse as Poland it was unlikely that a communality of interest could be achieved for the whole nation, such a communality, Rousseau thought, might be possible in each of the "tiny states" which, federated together, compose the nation. It seems, then, that he advocated for the whole state something like a balance of powers, with each of the several powers representing one more or less common interest.

As a broad generalization, the basis of Bentham and Rousseau's agreement on these two proposals was their common belief that the interests of the whole community and not of a specific individual should be paramount (i.e., D_{2b}), whereas their disagreements were based on the value of consistency (i.e., D_{4b}). Bentham believed that the best policies were those that maximized the greatest happiness to the greatest number. This would arise if individuals freely maximized their own interests. Those who sought to promote their happiness without diminishing that of others would find themselves "capable of acting without obstruction," but when an individual's pursuit of his own happiness diminished the happiness of others he would "find obstruction thrown in his way."

Bentham and Rousseau both, in effect, enunciate a version of the Pareto principle: improvements would be made if some individual or group could be made better off without making anyone else worse off. Bentham believes there was no need for special measures to assure cooperation; it could occur on its own:

Thus, then, the principle of self-preference has for its regulator in the breast of each, the consciousness of the existence and power of the same principle in the breasts of all the rest: and thus it is that the whole mechanism is at all times kept in a state of perfect order, and at all times performs to admiration everything it was made for.[32]

Rousseau, for his part, agreed that cooperation would occur naturally in communities small enough for sympathetic feelings to develop among the citizens. But in larger societies it had to be deliberately cultivated—here he differed from Bentham—but not by the kinds of "mechanisms" that Bentham would have favored had he not believed the free market would itself produce cooperation. For Rousseau, cooperation would be achieved by cultivating national pride, national patriotism, a national religion, and a national, in contrast to a regional, educational system—not by external sanctions, but by knowing "how to direct opinion, and thus to govern the passions of men."[33]

Even though Bentham and Rousseau disagreed about how the common interest of society would be arrived at, they still recognized that the creation of a monarchy would promote a parochial interest—i.e., that of the monarch. Where they disagreed, however was over the value of consistency of actions, practices and institutions (i.e., D_4). Both believed that men were inherently risk-averse and preferred the status quo to change. However, Bentham had little concern for the continuity of tradition or convention. He believed that legislators should constantly search for ways to improve existing laws: "the most defective parts will continually tend towards amelioration upon the plan of the most perfect."[34]

By comparison, Rousseau thought that what Bentham viewed as a steady tendency "towards amelioration" was, in societies without a common interest, only the result of the representatives bargaining and jockeying for position, as the relative strength of factions changed over time. So, far from being a matter of congratulation, it was further evidence of the corruption of most modern societies. The situation was different, of course, where a true common interest exists. Then representatives would be responsive to changes in that common interest, but it was likely to change only slowly, especially if the community were based on agriculture, rather than on finance and manufacturing, and if most citizens were smallholders.

Rousseau was therefore willing to work with the imperfect institutions that a society may have grown accustomed to having, whereas Bentham was not. In part, this is because a preference-altering approach requires that people believe in the norms of a society, and frequent change undermines the credibility of those norms. A preference-accepting approach, such as that taken by Bentham, only requires that people be mindful of their self-interests: the form their self-interests take is of little concern. A preference-altering approach is more likely to favor evolutionary development, whereas, as Burke and others have observed, the preference-accepting approach favors more abrupt and revolutionary change.

3. Institutions That Both Theorists Agreed About

A third category of institutions are those that Bentham and Rousseau seem to agree about, although, as we shall see, their reasons are often very different. For instance, both were aware of the power of public opinion over the behavior of representatives and both proposed institutions to focus and direct public opinion. But because of their different beliefs about human nature, the institutions they recommend differ markedly. Bentham, being concerned about the need to check on the honesty and competence of public officials, proposed the establishment of what he called the Public Opinion Tribunal. The duties of this institution were several: it would provide evidence of and make judgments on matters of public interest, it would have the power to render or withhold offices and it could make recommendations for improvement. He proposed to admit all who wanted to be members to this tribunal, drawing an analogy with committees in the House of Commons for which there was a rule that all who came to the committee should have voices. At another point he compared the Tribunal's function with that of a jury which oversaw and judged the conduct of functionaries, bringing "the force of the popular or moral sanction to bear with greatest advantage upon the conduct of public functionaries in the several departments."[35]

It is surprising that Bentham, who was so careful to prevent biases in the sample of preferences in other decision-making bodies—such as his proposed Assembly or even the electorate itself—should not have had a similar concern about membership in his Tribunal. He did indeed express some concern lest aristocratic members have interests that diverged from those of the more democratic members, and warned that when the Tribunal delegated functions to smaller sections, it should carefully limit or exclude the aristocratic members. But the possibility of other sampling biases, e.g., interest groups, was ignored. This omission is important, for unlike the legislators, who were instructed to use the calculus of utility to derive the common good, members of the Public Opinion Tribunal were to decide on the basis of their own interest, and the opinion of the group was the sum of these interests. If, as seems likely, Bentham intended the Tribunal as a kind of running Gallup poll, he neglected the various sampling biases one would expect to find, given his assumptions about human nature (HN_{1a}, HN_{3a}). If individuals are utility maximizers and if there are costs to information, attendance would covary with interest, and the decisions of the Tribunal would reflect the intense interests of particular interest groups rather than the aggregate utility of the whole population.

The nearest equivalent in Rousseau's thought to Bentham's Public Opinion Tribunal was the special tribunal which, as we have seen, he thought should convene on the death of the Polish king to render a verdict on his reign. Since this tribunal was certainly not a running Gallup poll, and since it had a one-time-only function, the possibility that sampling biases might affect its verdict was of much less importance than in the case of Bentham's Public Opinion Tribunal. What was essential was that the king know ex ante that a tribunal would be convened; it was less important that the tribunal actually reflect public opinion accurately than that the king believe it would make "a just and rigorous judgment of his conduct."[36]

But in any case, Rousseau's lack of concern about the possibility of sampling biases occurring in the expression of public opinion reflects his view that in a society in which a truly common interest exists, sampling errors simply could not occur, whereas in a society which did not already have a common interest no amount of care in sampling would produce one. Thus whereas Bentham supported the Public Opinion Tribunal as a mechanism for discovering the public good, Rousseau saw his (rough) equivalent of it as part of the socialization process discussed earlier, a way of shaping the minds of officials. Thus differences in assumptions about human nature lay behind their differences about the function of public opinion.

Another institution about which Bentham and Rousseau agreed was the value of frequent elections. The electoral incentive was crucial to Bentham's scheme. The essence of creating a responsible legislature was to make the legislator dependent on his constituents but independent of various interest groups, and to instill in the legislator a sense of impermanence. Bentham therefore recommended annual elections. They would diminish the incentive to act corruptly since the "short-livedness of the power" would "diminish both to producers and thence to sellers the venal value" of office. Secondly, incompetent representatives could be got rid of without long delay.[37] Lastly, frequent elections would keep representatives on their toes.[38]

In addition to annual elections, Bentham proposed what he called an "all-comprehensive temporary nonrelocability system."[39] The idea was that no member of the current legislature would be permitted to run again unless the number of those who had served previously was two or three times the number of those currently in the legislature. This proposal would guarantee that the country would develop a large pool of experienced candidates.

To provide a place for those ineligible to run again, Bentham proposed the establishment of a "continuation committee," to provide the continuity lacking in a pure system of limited terms. Bentham recognized the importance of balancing the advantages of frequent turnover with those of stability. Since consideration of complex bills might extend over the life of several legislatures, work on them might be unnecessarily interrupted without the continuation committee, which would also help counteract the inexperience of new legislators.

As for Rousseau, though he allowed two-year terms for his legislature, instead of the one-year terms Bentham recommended, he agreed that "short-livedness" of the legislature was desirable. "England," Rousseau thought, "has lost her liberty for having neglected [to require] frequent re-elections." In England "a single parliament lasts so long that the court, which would go bankrupt buying it annually, finds it profitable to buy it for seven years, and does not fail to do so."[40]

Rousseau also recognized the desirability of something not unlike Bentham's "all-comprehensive temporary nonrelocability system," in that he did not allow legislators to succeed themselves indefinitely. He also provided a functional equivalent of the "continuation committee' in that there was to be a constant circulation of the elites between legislature and magistry.

It is curious that Bentham, who cared much less about consistency (i.e., D_4) than Rousseau, should have made such elaborate provision to ensure that there would be carryover from one legislative session to the next, and it is equally odd that Rousseau, who believed that small communities could develop a notion of the common good (D_2), should suggest short terms of office for public officials. Given his assumptions about human nature, it is somewhat surprising that he believed that term of office would have a significant effect on legislators' behavior. In a sense therefore, the two theorists agree on the value of short terms of office with some provision for carryover only because each strayed a bit from his assumptions and goals.

Their agreement about the role of public opinion and of elections was grounded upon their consensus that the responsiveness of legislators depended upon the threat of public disapproval. Both believed that legislators would be risk-averse and that the threat of losing their jobs was an important way of ensuring proper representation. Bentham, in particular, assumed that representatives would seek to make their positions secure; as he put it, they would try to minimize their dependence on public opinion. However, Bentham was keenly aware that in order to control public officials it was essential that they be insecure and that their dependence on the public be maximized: "if the possessor of the power is, at all events, to keep his hold of it so long as he lives, or even so long as he remains legally unconvicted of a specific misdeed, the difficulty of dealing with him may be unsurmountable." Accordingly, "those who establish government must begin with establishing insecurity: insecurity, viz. as against those in whose hands the means of security against others are reposed."[41]

However, though they concurred about elections and public opinion, it is clear that they envisioned these institutions as operating in very different fashions. Apart from differences in presuppositions about human nature that we have discussed already, another reason for this is that Bentham and Rousseau had in mind different time perspectives as appropriate for representatives. Bentham's legislator maximized short-term welfare whereas Rousseau's legislator was interested in a long-term common good. Since future considerations mattered for Bentham only so far as they could be probabilistically assessed and only so far as they affected the present generation, every utility maximizer would necessarily have a short time horizon. He would present pleasure to avoid greater future pain only if the probabilities of alternative consequences could be estimated. An individual's future entered into his calculations only insofar as his present pleasures and pains were affected by his thoughts about various possible future states. Similarly, future generations were to be taken into account by a present generation only insofar as the present generation's pleasures and pains were affected by its thought of future generations. Legislators in the present had no power over or responsibility for future constituents: "The power thus unlimited is that of the legislature for the time being."[42]

For Rousseau, time past and time future were "ingredient" (Whitehead's term) in time present. What was true of a man's personal life—that he identified in memory with the child he once was and also lived in anticipation with the older person he was going to be— applied to a society and to the present generation in its relation to past and future generations. Patriotism, for instance, was an emotion binding men to the past of their society and also, and equally, to its future.[43] In sum, the narrowly egoistic and time-bound calculations that Bentham approved as "rational," were condemned by Rousseau as products of "base

philosophy, petty self-interest and inept institutions."[44]

Thus, the Public Opinion Tribunal was for Bentham a means of guiding the daily decisions of his legislators. Since a job of the legislator was to reflect accurately the interests of the community so that these could be aggregated in an unbiased fashion, the Public Opinion Tribunal provided the legislator with up-to-date information on where various interests stood on the issues of the day. Rousseau, being less concerned with the short-run fluctuations of public interests, wanted the tribunal to serve as an incentive for the monarch to act in the best interests of the community. Indeed, it was the prospect of future judgment that would motivate the monarch to think of long-term interests.

IV. Conclusion

We have proposed a framework in this paper for analyzing proposals that theorists have made for implementing their ideas about representation. The value of this approach is fourfold. First, it provides a standard means of comparing the proposals that theorists make. Often, comparisons are difficult because theorists themselves neither use a common language nor refer to standard categories. Hence students tend to see their values, beliefs and proposals as being more idiosyncratic than they actually are. By developing general categories for goals of representation and for beliefs about human nature, we hope to provide a method for discovering the common choices made in institutional design.

The second value of this framework is that it points out how specific proposals are the joint product of a theorist's goals for representation, his beliefs about human nature, and his choice of one or the other of two possible strategies for dealing with people's preferences. Knowing only how the theorist would like representatives to behave is not sufficient information to understand why he proposed a particular rule or institution: two theorists with the same goals might take different positions on a proposal because their beliefs about human nature differ. Similarly, it is not sufficient to know a theorist's views about human nature or his views about preferences. Rather, all three kinds of information are necessary conditions.

Third, this framework helps us to see that theorists are not always consistent with their premises. Sometimes, their proposals betray doubts and uncertainties about their stated beliefs and values. At other times, the connection between a theorist's beliefs and proposals are logically inconsistent. This framework therefore gives us a way of criticizing the specific proposals of political theorists in a systematic and logical manner.

Finally, the framework not only facilitates comparisons. It makes it possible to choose with better confidence among the many different interpretations of a given theorist's view that historians of political theory have from time to time proposed. By providing historians of theory with a set of standard, and well-defined, categories for analysis, reliance on overall gestalt-like impressions is no longer necessary. Though we are certainly not so optimistic as to suppose that use of the framework will eliminate all disagreements among historians of political theory, we believe its use will at least narrow those disagreements by focussing attention on the points still in dispute. That in itself would be an advance.

Notes

1. Angus Campbell et al., *The American Voter* (New York: Wiley, 1960); and Richard Fenno, *Home Style* (Boston: Little, Brown, 1978).
2. W. T. Jones, *A History of Western Philosophy* (New York, 1969), vol. 3, p. 275.
3. The goals entered in the set of dispositions (*D*) and the beliefs about human nature entered in the Human Nature set (*HN*) are derived from earlier studies, by one of the present authors, of differences in "world view," or implicit presuppositions. These differences were in the first instance formulated to account for the many nonterminating disagreements in which metaphysicians and epistemologists are characteristically enmeshed ("Philosophical Disagreements and World Views," *Proceedings and Addresses of the American Philosophical Association* 43 (1970): 24–42). But subsequent empirical studies strongly suggest that these same differences in implicit presuppositions underlie many other kinds of theoretical disagreement (Cal-

ifornia Institute of Technology, Social Science Working Papers Nos. 354, 355, 357; Humanities Working Papers Nos. 61, 75, 83). In the present paper some of the beliefs have been rephrased in order to bring out their relevance to the question of representation, but it is important to see that they were not reformulated with any particular political theorists in mind. Accordingly, to the extent that there is a good fit between the framework and the views of specific political theorists, this is supporting evidence for the general thesis of the papers cited above that the same, or closely similar, presuppositions underlie many different kinds of theories and other cultural products.
4. *Constitutional Code,* in *The Works of Jeremy Bentham,* ed. John Bowring, 11 vols. (London: Simpkin, Marshall and Co., 1863), p. 35. All subsequent Bentham citations are from the Bowring edition; the abbreviated titles are as follows: *Promulgation of Laws* for *Essay on the Promulgation of Laws; Introduction to Principles* for *An Introduction to the Principles of Morals and Legislation;* and *Plan* for *Plan of Parliamentary Reform.*
5. J. J. Rousseau, "A Constitutional Project for Corsica," in Frederick Watkins, trans., *Rousseau: Political Writings* (New York: Nelson, 1953), p. 277.
6. *Constitutional Code,* p. 90.
7. Ibid., pp. 80–81.
8. J. J. Rousseau, "Considerations on the Government of Poland," in Watkins, *Rousseau: Political Writings,* p. 227.
9. Ibid., p. 229.
10. Ibid., p. 194.
11. Ibid., pp. 193–194.
12. *Constitutional Code,* p. 145.
13. *Introduction to Principles,* p. 1.
14. *Constitutional Code,* p. 35.
15. *Constitutional Code,* p. 5.
16. Ibid., p. 61.
17. *The Emile of J. J. Rousseau,* ed. and trans. William Boyd (New York: Teachers College Press, 1966), p. 11.
18. Ibid., p. 106; "Poland," p. 325.
19. J. J. Rousseau, *The Social Contract,* trans. G. D. H. Cole (New York: Dutton, 1930), p. 5.
20. *Emile,* p. 102.
21. Ibid., p. 11.
22. "Poland," p. 193.
23. J. J. Rousseau, *The Creed of a Priest of Savoy,* trans. Arthur H. Beattie (New York: Ungar, 1957), pp. 3, 20.
24. *Emile,* p. 105.
25. *Constitutional Code,* p. 128.
26. Ibid., p. 130.
27. "Poland," p. 210.
28. Ibid., p. 207.
29. Ibid., p. 208.
30. Ibid., pp. 264–265.
31. *Constitutional Code,* p. 115.
32. Ibid., p. 63.

33. "Poland," p. 175.
34. *Promulgation of Laws,* p. 161.
35. *Constitutional Code,* p. 42.
36. "Poland," p. 265.
37. *Plan,* p. 445.
38. Ibid., p. 542.

39. *Constitutional Code,* p. 172.
40. "Poland," p. 188.
41. *Constitutional Code,* p. 58.
42. Ibid., p. 160.
43. "Poland," pp. 164–165.
44. Ibid., p. 163.

Suggested Further Reading

Arblaster, Anthony. *Democracy*. 2nd ed. Buckingham: Open University Press, 1994.

Arrow, Kenneth. *Social Choice and Individual Values*. 2nd ed. New York: Wiley, 1963.

Barry, Brian. "Is Democracy Special?" In *Philosophy, Politics and Society*, 5th series, edited by P. Laslett and J. Fishkin. New Haven: Yale University Press, 1979.

———. *Sociologists, Economists and Democracy*. London: Collier-Macmillan, 1970.

Beitz, Charles R. *Political Equality: An Essay in Democratic Theory*. Princeton: Princeton University Press, 1989.

Benn, S. I., and R. S. Peters. *Principles of Political Thought*. Chicago: Free Press, 1959.

Bentham, Jeremy. *An Introduction to the Principles of Morals and Legislation*. New York: Methuen, 1982.

Birch, Anthony H. *The Concepts and Theories of Modern Democracy*. London: Routledge, 1993.

Braybrooke, David. *Three Tests for Democracy: Personal Rights, Human Welfare, Collective Preference*. New York: Random House, 1968.

Brennan, Geoffrey, and Loren E. Lomasky, eds. *Politics and Process: New Essays in Democratic Thought*. Cambridge: University Press, 1989.

Buchanan, James, and Gordon Tullock. *The Calculus of Consent*. Ann Arbor: University of Michigan Press, 1962.

Chapman, John W., and Ian Shapiro. *Nomos XXXV: Democratic Community*. New York: New York University Press, 1993.

Cohen, Joshua, and Joel Rogers. *On Democracy*. New York: Penguin, 1983.

Copp, David, Jean Hampton, and John E. Roemer, eds. *The Idea of Democracy*. Cambridge: Cambridge University Press, 1993.

Crozier, Brian. *The Minimum State: Beyond Party Politics*. London: Hamish Hamilton, 1979.

Dahl, Robert. *Democracy and Its Critics*. New Haven: Yale University Press, 1989.

———. *A Preface to Democratic Theory*. Chicago: University of Chicago Press, 1956.

Dahl, R. A. *Democracy, Liberty, and Equality*. Oslo: Norwegian University Press, 1986.

Dunn, John, ed. *Democracy: The Unfinished Journey, 508 B.C.–A.D. 1993*. New York: Oxford University Press, 1992.

Farrar, Cynthia. *The Origins of Democratic Thinking: The Invention of Politics in Classical Athens*. Cambridge: Cambridge University Press, 1988.

Fralin, Richard. *Rousseau and Representation*. New York: Columbia University Press, 1978.

Gilbert, Alan. *Democratic Individuality*. Cambridge: Cambridge University Press, 1990.

Gildin, Hilail. *Rousseau's Social Contract*. Chicago: University of Chicago Press, 1983.

Glassman, Ronald M. *Democracy and Equality: Theories and Programs for the Modern World*. New York: Praeger, 1989.

Hamilton, Alexander, John Jay, and James Madison. *The Federalist Papers.* New York: Modern Library, 1937.

Harrison, Ross. *Democracy.* London: Routledge, 1993.

Held, Virginia. *Models of Democracy.* Stanford, Calif: Stanford University Press, 1987.

Kariel, Henry, ed. *Frontiers of Democratic Theory.* New York: Random House, 1970.

Levin, Michael. *The Spectre of Democracy: The Rise of Modern Democracy as Seen by Its Critics.* London: Macmillan, 1992.

Lewin, Leif. *Self-Interest and Public Interest in Western Politics.* Oxford: Oxford University Press, 1991.

Lucas, J. R. *Democracy and Participation.* Baltimore, Md.: Penguin, 1976.

MacPherson, C. B. *Democratic Theory.* Oxford: Clarendon, 1973.

——. *The Real World of Democracy.* Oxford: Clarendon, 1966.

Masters, Roger D. *The Political Philosophy of Rousseau.* Princeton: Princeton University Press, 1968.

Nelson, William N. *On Justifying Democracy.* London: Routledge and Kegan Paul, 1980.

Olson, Mancur. *The Logic of Collective Action.* Cambridge, Mass.: Harvard University Press, 1971.

Pateman, Carole. *Participation and Democratic Theory.* Cambridge: Cambridge University Press, 1970.

Pennock, J. R. *Democratic Political Theory.* Princeton: Princeton University Press, 1979.

——. *Liberal Democracy.* New York: Rinehart, 1950.

Pennock, J. R., and J. W. Chapman, eds. *Nomos X: Representation.* New York: Atherton, 1968.

——. *Nomos XVI: Participation in Politics.* New York: Lieber-Atherton, 1978.

Phillips, Anne. *Democracy and Difference.* University Park, Pa.: Pennsylvania State University Press, 1993.

Pitkin, Hanna F. *The Concept of Representation.* Berkeley: University of California Press, 1967.

Pitkin, Hanna F., ed. *Representation.* New York: Atherton, 1969.

Plamenatz, John. *Democracy and Illusion: An Examination of Certain Aspects of Modern Democratic Theory.* London: Longman, 1973.

Rejai, M. *Democracy.* New York: Atherton, 1967.

Revel, J.-F. *Democracy Against Itself: The Future of the Democratic Impulse.* New York: Free Press, 1993.

Roberts, Jennifer Tolbert. *Athens on Trial: The Anti-Democratic Tradition in Western Thought.* Princeton: Princeton University Press, 1994.

Schumpeter, Joseph A. *Capitalism, Socialism, and Democracy.* 3rd ed. New York: Harper and Brothers, 1950.

Sen, A. K. *Collective Choice and Social Welfare.* San Francisco: Holden-Day, 1970.

Singer, Peter. *Democracy and Disobedience.* New York: Oxford University Press, 1973.

Spitz, Elaine. *Majority Rule.* Chatham, N.J.: Chatham House, 1983.

Sunstein, Cass R. "Preferences and Politics." *Philosophy and Public Affairs* 20 (1991): 3–34.

Thompson, Dennis F. *John Stuart Mill and Representative Government.* Princeton: Princeton University Press, 1976.

Walzer, Michael. "Philosophy and Democracy." In *What Should Political Theory Be Now?* edited by J. S. Nelson. Albany: SUNY Press, 1983.

Wollheim, Richard. "Democracy." *Journal of the History of Ideas* 19 (1958): 225–242.